JERUSALEM
THE ETERNAL CITY

JERUSALEM

THE ETERNAL CITY

DAVID B. GALBRAITH
D. KELLY OGDEN
ANDREW C. SKINNER

Deseret Book Company
Salt Lake City, Utah

Illustration on page 187 adapted and used by permission of Leen Ritmeyer, Ritmeyer Archaeological Design, Harrogate, North Yorkshire, England. Illustration on page 171 by James Christiansen, © The Church of Jesus Christ of Latter-day Saints. Used by permission.

Visit us at DeseretBook.com

First printing in hardbound 1996
First printing in paperbound 2008

Library of Congress Cataloging-in-Publication Data

Galbraith, David B.
    Jerusalem : the eternal city / David B. Galbraith, D. Kelly Ogden,
    Andrew C. Skinner.
        p.   cm.
    Includes bibliographical references and index.
    ISBN 978-1-57345-052-9 (hardbound)
    ISBN 978-1-59038-874-7 (paperbound)
    1. Jerusalem—History. 2. Jerusalem in Christianity. 3. Church
of Jesus Christ of Latter-day Saints—Doctrines. I. Ogden, D.
Kelly (Daniel Kelly), 1947– . II. Skinner, Andrew C., 1951– .
III. Title.
DS109.9.G35   1996
956.94'42—dc20   95-52277
                                                                            CIP

Printed in the United States of America
Worzalla Publishing Co., Stevens Point, WI

10   9   8   7   6   5   4   3   2   1

CONTENTS

Maps

PREFACE

This volume is a study of the holy city of Jerusalem from 2000 B.C. to A.D. 2000—from Melchizedek to the Millennium. Through the disciplines of theology, history, geography, anthropology, archaeology, linguistics, and political science, this book is a comprehensive analysis of Jerusalem's multifaceted influence on world history through forty centuries, its preeminence and centrality in the human drama. After a philosophical introduction to this most famous city on earth and a chapter describing the physical setting of the city, various periods of its history are examined: Jerusalem in the days of Melchizedek and Abraham, David, Solomon, the Divided Kingdoms, the Fall and the Return, Hellenistic Jerusalem, Jerusalem at the time of Jesus, Jerusalem in revolt, Aelia Capitolina, and Jerusalem in the days of Byzantines, Muslims, Crusaders, Ottomans, Arab Palestinians, and Israeli Jews. The politics of modern Jerusalem are explored throughout world wars, Arab-Israeli conflicts, United Nations intercessions, and mediations of the major powers.

Jerusalem, the Eternal City also focuses on the broad cultural diversity in Jerusalem today: its ethnic and religious groups, its expansive growth and modernization, its architecture, its factious government, and its political tensions.

A unique emphasis of the book is the role of Jerusalem as a Temple City, past and future. Also unique is a view of Latter-day Saint involvement in the City, especially the Brigham Young University Jerusalem Center for Near Eastern Studies. This study presupposes Latter-day Saint commitment to understand the role of Jerusalem while anticipating its ultimate destiny through a painful transition into the City of God, the City of Holiness.

This volume is written from a Latter-day Saint point of view, though other views are presented, analyzed, and discussed. Problems of transmission and translation have raised questions, even doubts, about the reliability of some ancient texts, yet in this work generally there is unequivocal credence given to holy scripture and to the words of modern prophets. We believe that God has spoken in times past, that he continues to speak in our day, and that he is involved in the affairs of humankind.

There is no intention in this work to make controversial or politically sensitive conclusions, except where the word of God clearly dictates our opinion. All historical and theological interpretations and opinions expressed herein are our own and those of others whom we quote. These interpretations and opinions do not necessarily represent the official position of The Church of Jesus Christ of Latter-day Saints or any other ecclesiastical or educational institution.

In this book certain spellings and usages are preferred over others. Following is a concise list of those preferences:

The word *Temple* is always capitalized when referring to a proper Sanctuary of God, as approved by God and his prophets (which occasionally requires a judgment on our part), but it is not capitalized when referring to pagan structures and shrines (except, of course, in quotations from other works). Similarly, the word *Church* is capitalized when identifying the Church of Jesus Christ, which he established; the apostate church, contrariwise, is rendered in lowercase.

The designation *Near East* is preferred over *Middle East*.

The name *Palestine* is reserved for that time in history when it was used to designate the former land of Canaan, or Israel, which time began in the second century after Christ, in the days of the Roman Emperor Hadrian, and has continued through the twentieth century. In the days of Jesus, the country was simply called Judaea. Following the King James Version rendering from the Greek, the name is spelled *Judaea* rather than *Judea;* so also *Hasmonaeans* instead of *Hasmoneans,* and so forth.

The years given in parentheses after rulers' names apply to their reigns, not the years they lived.

Islamic or Arabic terms are standardized as follows: *Muslim* (over *Moslem*), *Muhammad* (over *Mohammed*), *Qur'an* (over *Koran*); *Caliph* (a Muslim leader), *hajj* (the pilgrimage to Mecca), *al-Quds* (the name of

Jerusalem in Arabic, meaning "the Holy"), *Haram esh-Sharif* (what most Jews and Christians call the "Temple Mount"), and *al-Aqsa* (the sacred mosque on the Haram esh-Sharif).

B.C. (meaning "before Christ") and A.D. (*Anno Domini*, "the year of our Lord," meaning "after the birth of Christ") are preferred over the terms used by those who avoid the name of Christ: B.C.E. ("before the common era") and C.E. ("of the common era").

The abbreviation *ca.*, which comes from the Latin *circa* ("about"), indicates an approximate date.

We have quoted primarily from the King James Version of the Bible (KJV). Occasionally we have used other versions, as follows: New American Bible (NAB), New English Bible (NEB), New International Version (NIV), and Revised Standard Version (RSV).

"Bible Map" refers to one of the twenty-two full-color maps at the end of the Latter-day Saint edition of the King James Version of the Bible.

Such possibly unfamiliar terms as *hierocentrality, wadi, tel, ostraca, Levant, Shephelah,* and others are defined in the glossary.

We extend appreciation to certain individuals who have made such a comprehensive volume possible.

Our work has been improved by the kind and careful scrutiny of such experts as Professors Ellis T. Rasmussen, Daniel H. Ludlow, James A. Toronto, and Daniel C. Peterson, who read all or parts of the manuscript and offered valuable suggestions. We also express appreciation for the research assistance of Daniel Galbraith relating to the chapters on modern political developments.

Brett Holbrook helped research and organize our original materials. Jeffry S. Bird, cartographer at Brigham Young University, helped prepare the unique series of maps. Thomas S. Child produced two of the drawings. Most of the photography is the work of author D. Kelly Ogden, but some is used with permission of the Church Educational System and Daniel O. Noorlander Jr.

The paintings are presented here with the generous permission of artists Al Rounds and Kelly Hale.

The dedicated work of editor Suzanne Brady, designer Kent Ware, typographer Tonya-Rae Facemyer, and the entire production team at Deseret Book Company is also acknowledged and deeply appreciated.

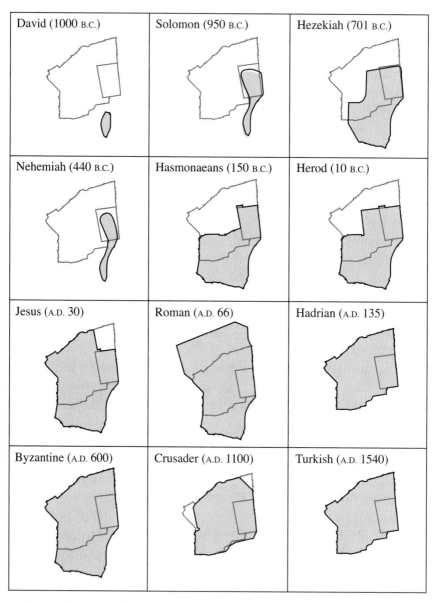

The size of Jerusalem through the ages. The larger gray outline in each illustration is that of today's Old City, which dates from the days of Hadrian in the second century after Christ; the smaller outline represents the Temple Mount

Chart of Four Thousand Years of Jerusalem's History

Date	Persons, Places, and Events	Reference
B.C.		
ca. 2000	*Shalem* or *Salem,* city of Melchizedek	Gen. 14:17–20; JST Gen. 14:25–40; Heb. 7:1–4
	Abraham and Isaac at Moriah	Gen. 22:1–18
1900–1800	*Rushalimum* or *Urusalimum* in Egyptian Execration Texts	
ca. 1400	*Urusalim* in El Amarna Tablets; Abdi-Heba; City of Amorites/Canaanites at time of Israelite conquest; King Adonizedek	Josh. 10:1–5
1200	City of Jebusites	Josh. 15:63; Judg. 1:21
1000	City of David; also called Zion	2 Sam. 5:7, 9; 2 Kgs. 19:31
960	City of Solomon; Temple established	1 Kgs. 1, 6–8
940	Pharaoh Shishak raids Jerusalem, Temple	1 Kgs. 14:25–26
920	City of Rehoboam; later expansion under Uzziah, Jotham, Hezekiah	1 Kgs. 14; 2 Kgs. 14, 15, 18
740	Prophet Isaiah	Isa. 6
721	Fall of Israel to Assyria	2 Kgs. 17:3–7
701	Threatened siege by Assyrians; Hezekiah's Tunnel; *Ursalimmu* or *Uruslimmu* in Sennacherib Inscription	2 Kgs. 18:13– 19:37
609	King Josiah killed by Pharaoh Necho	2 Kgs. 23:29–30
605, 598	Incursions of Babylonians	2 Kgs. 24
600	Prophets Jeremiah, Lehi	Jer. 1; 1 Ne. 1
586	Destruction of City and Temple by Nebuchadnezzar	2 Kgs. 25
538	Persians under Cyrus encourage return of exiles	Ezra 1:1–4
520–515	Second Temple built under Zerubbabel Haggai, Zechariah	Ezra 5:1–2; Haggai 1:1

1838	Edward Robinson's researches
1841	Orson Hyde in Jerusalem
1867	First archaeological excavations; C. Warren for Palestine Exploration Fund
1898	Visits of Kaiser Wilhelm II, Theodor Herzl
1917	Balfour Declaration; General Allenby; British Mandate
1947	UN vote to partition Palestine; Jerusalem, an "international zone"
1948	Creation of State of Israel; Jerusalem, a divided city
1967	Six-day War; Israel proclaims a united Jerusalem
1987	BYU's Jerusalem Center for Near Eastern Studies completed; outbreak of Palestinian Uprising (*Intifada*)
1991–	The peace process

1

INTRODUCTION

No other city has so shaped this earth's history and destiny as has Jerusalem. Many of the world's greatest empires, nations, and individuals have concerned themselves with Jerusalem. Egyptians, Hittites, Assyrians, Babylonians, Persians, Greeks, Romans, Byzantines, Muslims, Crusaders, Turks, British, Arabs, and Israelis have all paraded through the pages of Jerusalem's history. Pivotal personalities, many of whom indelibly influenced the chronicles of humanity, helped write the history of Jerusalem—people such as Abraham, David, Solomon, Isaiah, Lehi, Nephi, Jeremiah, Alexander the Great, Pompey, Cleopatra, Herod, Peter, Paul, Titus, Constantine, Muhammad, Richard the Lion-hearted, Maimonides, Saladin, Suleiman the Magnificent, and a host of others. The greatest person ever born in this world, Jesus Christ, brought about in Jerusalem the greatest events and the greatest contributions of all time: his atoning sacrifice and resurrection from the dead, the events that have immortalized the City and made the name Jerusalem forever holy.

Jerusalem was a small city in a small and insignificant land, yet we are reminded that "by small and simple things are great things brought to pass; . . . by very small means the Lord doth confound the wise and bringeth about the salvation of many souls" (Alma 37:6–7). Out of Jerusalem came the word of the Lord and a book that would affect the human story as no other book in the history of the world.[1]

An impressive array of buildings has been erected in the city of Jerusalem over the ages, buildings that represent an incalculable collective influence on the course of human history: palaces, synagogues, churches, shrines, monasteries, convents, mosques, madrasas, yeshivas, and other centers of government, learning, and worship. The most

Jerusalem (aerial view from the south)

influential of them all was the Temple of God, which stood for a thousand years on the eastern hill of Jerusalem, the "mountain of the Lord."

Many voices have sung the praises of Jerusalem. The rabbis, for example, wrote that there is no beauty like that of Jerusalem (Avot de-Rabbi Nathan 28, 85). Of the ten measures of beauty that came down to the world, Jerusalem received nine (Kiddushin 49b). Whoever has not seen Jerusalem in all its splendor has never seen a beautiful city in his life (Succah 51b).[2]

THE CENTRALITY OF JERUSALEM

In several ways Jerusalem has been a central place. It could be expected that a city at such a crossroads as the eastern Mediterranean lands[3]—the only region in the world where three continents come together—would naturally be a focal point of international concern, whether economic, political, or religious. Jerusalem, however, was never an economic or political superpower. Its physical position off the international trade route and paths of war would not allow that. Jerusalem's importance and influence has stemmed primarily from its religious relevance, from its designation as the place where God chose to put his

Name and his House. Even when the Name and the House were gone, Jerusalem forever afterwards served as a symbol of Deity's contact with earth.[4]

There have been and are now other holy cities in the ancient and modern worlds, but only Jerusalem plays a central role in three of the world's great religions: Judaism, Christianity, and Islam. To adherents of these religious beliefs, these ways of life, to the millions who have never even seen Jerusalem, the depth of feeling for the Holy City is revealed in the following expressions:

> If I forget thee, O Jerusalem, let my right hand forget her cunning. If I do not remember thee, let my tongue cleave to the roof of my mouth; if I prefer not Jerusalem above my chief joy. (Ps. 137:5–6)

> If Jerusalem did not exist, the Christians would have to invent it— indeed they have invented it, choking with emotion at the sight of sixteenth-century walls and tracing the Lord's footsteps through late medieval streets. It has always been an indispensable authentication for their faith and an abiding reminder of prophetic promises.[5]

> O Jerusalem, the choice of Allah of all his lands! In it are the chosen of his servants. From it the earth was stretched forth and from it shall it be rolled up like a scroll. The dew which descends upon Jerusalem is a remedy from every sickness because it is from the garden of Paradise.[6]

Strabo, a Greek geographer of the first century after Christ, discounted Jerusalem as inconsequential, describing it as a place that "would not be envied, one for which no one would fight."[7] That assessment has certainly not rung true to the war-cries of history; Jerusalem has always been a coveted, high-tension zone. K. J. Asali, a noted author on Jerusalem, wrote: "Jerusalem [is] loved and adored by hundreds of millions throughout the world and throughout the ages. Jerusalem lived through times of glory during which it was built and embellished on grand and impressive scales. Yet for the very reason of its unique place in the eyes of the faithful, Jerusalem was, in other times to suffer terribly. . . . But each time it was destroyed it was destined to rise again. The history of Jerusalem is a mixture of glories and catastrophes. In almost all cases, powerful religious feelings were present in the shaping of events."[8] Saul B. Cohen wrote: "No other city in the world has been subject to such intense competition for control as Jerusalem during its 4,000 years of recorded history."[9] Contrary to the opinion of Strabo, history concludes that few, if any, cities in the world have seen as much armed conflict and destruction as has Jerusalem. Isaiah's foreshadowing that "they all gather themselves together and come to thee" (Isa. 60:4) has certainly seen its negative as well as its positive fulfillment.

Thomas Idinopulos noted that "nothing sacralizes stones like blood, and Jerusalem is a city founded on sanctity, sacrifice, and blood. A lot of blood."[10] In fact, as Barbara Tuchman asserted in *Bible and Sword,* "more blood has been shed for Jerusalem than any other spot on earth."[11] "With Jerusalem's sanctification," wrote Norman Kotker, "has come bloodshed—the sacrifice of animals at the temple, the sacrifice of Christ, the endless sacrifice of its citizens striving to defend the holy city against the attacks of enemies. . . . Abraham sacrificed there, the victim to be his own son Isaac, until God saved the boy by sending a ram as a substitute. And then, it is said, God Himself performed a sacrifice at Jerusalem, to Himself, of Himself, the victim, His own son Jesus."[12]

RELIGIOUS CONQUEST CENTERED IN JERUSALEM

"Religion and war run side by side. Piety and blood, belief and battle have mingled here for more than three thousand years," Idinopulos observed. "Always in this city one group is up and another down, and those who are down are waiting, with grudging patience, to be up again. The spirit of conquest rules Jerusalem. . . . [It is] a city besieged, defended, conquered, damaged or destroyed, and rebuilt forty times in thirty centuries, always in the name of God."[13]

Often the conquest of Jerusalem served as a symbolic statement of the conquest of one religious faith over another. The religious subjugation of Jerusalem was considered the ostensible manifestation of the supremacy of one god or pantheon of gods or system of belief over another. For example, Roman paganism in the second century after Christ seemingly triumphed over Judaism and Christianity through the occupation and usurpation of Jerusalem; then paganism and Judaism were superseded in Jerusalem by Constantine's state religion, Christianity; Umar and the Umayyad caliphs cleared the site of the former Jewish Temple and erected a shrine in honor of Muhammad overshadowing the

Christian Basilica of the Resurrection.[14] Over the ages struggles for religious ascendancy involved various forms of paganism, Baalism, and Hellenism and various forms of Judaism, Christianity, and Islam. Religious faith has played a decisive role in the biography of Jerusalem.

RELIGIOUS TRADITIONS INTENSIFY JERUSALEM'S RENOWN

Religious traditions also added to the hierocentrality and preeminence of Jerusalem. Many people have prayed toward Jerusalem and toward the Temple.[15] Millions over the centuries have revered the City as the center of the earth, believing that the *omphalos,* or umbilical cord, connecting heaven and earth attached directly to the Foundation Stone of the Temple or to Golgotha or to the Holy Sepulchre.[16]

Earth was considered the center of the universe; the Holy Land was the center of the earth; Jerusalem was the center of the Holy Land; the Temple was the center of Jerusalem; the Holy of Holies was the center of the Temple; the Ark with its mercy seat of God was the center of the Holy of Holies; God, therefore, was at the center of centers.[17]

The rabbis taught that "Adam was created from the dust of the place where the sanctuary [the Temple in Jerusalem] was to rise for the atonement of all human sin."[18] Adam's grave is supposed by many to have been at the Temple Mount or at Golgotha.[19] The place of Abraham's sacrifice of Isaac (or of Ishmael, according to Muslims) was Mount Moriah, later the Temple Mount and still later the Haram esh-Sharif ("the Noble Sanctuary"). Jerusalem is seen by many as the site of the Final Battle, when the political entities representing the forces of good and the forces of evil will clash in a last confrontation to end this world.[20] According to all three faiths, Jerusalem will also be the scene of the Final Judgment at the Kidron Valley, which is also called the Valley of Jehoshaphat (the symbolic name meaning "Jehovah will judge").[21] Tradition has identified Jerusalem as the location of the great resurrection; those buried in the Holy City, especially on the Mount of Olives and the Temple Mount, will be first to resurrect (the reason for Jewish, Christian, and Muslim cemeteries there). Jerusalem, the navel of the earth and the light of the world, is destined to become the metropolis of all countries,[22] a capital for all the world.

For untold millions Jerusalem has been not an appendage to their life but the heart and soul of their existence. "Most cities look to the past,"

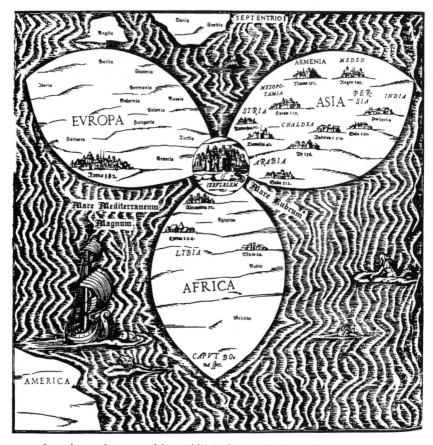

Jerusalem as the center of the world (woodcut map by Heinrich Buenting, 1580)

noted Idinopulos, "some recall ancient glory; [but] the people of Jerusalem drag the past forward into their homes and hearts, so that the past becomes a part of them, uniting them, justifying them in their grievances, instilling hope for the future. . . . Jerusalem is an eschatological city, always in the end-time, awaiting any moment the cataclysm that will inaugurate the New Age."[23]

FORTY CENTURIES OF WORLD-CHANGING HISTORY

A study of Jerusalem cannot focus only on the past but must examine the present and also look to the future. Jerusalem is never far from front and center of world news. Indeed, it appears destined to be the nexus of an insoluble, mainstream issue for the foreseeable future as part of the Arab-Israeli conflict. Even Jerusalem's prophetic, premillennial status indicates world-shaking events that must be reckoned with. It is essential to know the past to understand the present, and it is essential to know the past and present to appreciate the future.

The name *Jerusalem* has been immortalized because of the culminating events in the mortal life of Jesus Christ, the Son of God. For thousands of years God's faithful looked forward to those events, and for thousands of years the faithful have looked back on those events. But the name *Jerusalem* lives on because cities by that name will continue to influence the world through the great millennium of peace, and, in the end, the Celestial City of God will bear the name "heavenly Jerusalem" (Heb. 12:22). Abraham Joshua Heschel wrote: "The words have gone out of [Jerusalem] and have entered the pages of holy books. And yet Jerusalem has not given herself away. There is so much more in store. Jerusalem is never at the end of the road. She is the city where waiting for God was born, where the anticipation of everlasting peace came into being. Jerusalem is waiting for the prologue of redemption, for new beginning. What is the secret of Jerusalem? Her past is a prelude. Her power is in reviving."[24] The real Jerusalem more than once has died, but the ideal Jerusalem will never die—it has become in the mind and theology of God's people the Eternal City.

Modern scripture reveals that in the last days, the continents will reconverge, and Old Jerusalem and Zion, a New Jerusalem, will be on the same continent: "The land of Jerusalem and the land of Zion shall be turned back into their own place, and the earth shall be like as it was in the days before it was divided" (D&C 133:24). With Jerusalem's centrality and preeminence in history from 2000 B.C. onward, we wonder about the City and its Holy Place during the previous two thousand years, especially from Adam to the division of continents. Could Jerusalem have been, along with the site of the future New Jerusalem, already central during the earliest era when there was only one landmass? Could Jerusalem have been the center of the world, the *umbilicus mundi,* at the beginning as well as at the end?[25] Without further instruction from a divine Source, we cannot know. After examining the physical setting of the city, we are left to begin our study of Jerusalem already two millennia into its telestial existence, at the time of Melchizedek and Abraham.

NOTES

1. The Bible is the most widely read and influential book in history, with more distributed copies than any other book. It has been translated more times into more languages than any other book. Millions of individuals have been named after biblical people. Names of many cities and other places come from the Bible. Great musical and literary master-pieces and great works of art are based on biblical people and stories. Countless people have found hope, comfort, and guidance from the Bible during times of trouble and uncertainty.

2. *Encyclopedia Judaica*, 9:1556.

3. The term *Mediterranean* itself means, in Latin, the "center of the earth."

4. Though the physical structure was destroyed, the concept of the Temple and its spiri-tual influence could not be. The idea or meaning of the Temple transcended its ephemeral form. The Temple was not only "heaven on earth" but to faithful Saints was also the gate of heaven, or gateway to exaltation. There were functions of the Temple in which all aspirants to the Presence of God must participate and endowments and ordi-nances which they must receive. Without the physical structure, there was no sanctified place for receiving such endowments and ordinances (except temporarily on a moun-taintop or other such places), so the faithful have always awaited the restoration of the New Jerusalem and of the Temple. Observant Jews, for instance, for centuries have pleaded with God for the "rebuilding of Jerusalem, thy holy city" and for the Holy One to "soon rebuild his house; speedily, speedily soon, in our days, O Eternal, rebuild it, O Eternal, rebuild it, rebuild thine house in time." Passover Haggadah.

5. Nibley, *Mormonism and Early Christianity*, 335.

6. From the Hadith of Muhammad. According to orthodox Islam, the three holiest places in the world are, first, the Kaba in Mecca; second, the Mosque of Muhammad in Medina; and third, the Haram esh-Sharif (the Temple Mount itself, not just the Al-Aqsa Mosque) in Jerusalem. The holiness of Jerusalem is derived from Muhammad's Night Journey and Ascension to heaven (described in Sura 17 of the Qur'an), the official opin-ion of Muslim theologians being that Muhammad in reality walked the ground of Jerusalem. See *Encyclopedia Judaica*, 9:1575.

7. *Harper's Bible Dictionary*, 463.

8. Asali, *Jerusalem in History*, 9.

9. Cohen, *Jerusalem*, 11.

10. Idinopulos, *Jerusalem Blessed, Jerusalem Cursed*, 9.

11. Cited in Tal, *Whose Jerusalem?* 123.

12. Kotker, *Earthly Jerusalem*, 4–5.

13. Idinopulos, *Jerusalem Blessed, Jerusalem Cursed*, 3, 5, 13.

14. See details of these examples and more in Eckardt, *Jerusalem*, 13–31.

15. See 1 Kgs. 8:30, 38, 44, 48; Dan. 6:10. "When praying one is obligated to face Jerusalem and if he 'stands in Jerusalem he should turn his heart toward the Temple' (Ber. 30a)." *Encyclopedia Judaica*, 9:1555. Of prayer actually offered in the Holy City, Kotker wrote: "Whoever prays in Jerusalem, the Muslims believe, will be sure of having a line of descendants to pray there too, and each of their prayers will outweigh in merit a thou-sand prayers uttered elsewhere." *Earthly Jerusalem*, 6. Others believe that the prayers of all the faithful ascend to heaven via Jerusalem, the portal of the heavens.

16. "The idea of Jerusalem as a 'navel' is reflected in Jewish Midrashim: 'God created the world like an embryo. Just as the embryo begins at the navel and continues to grow from that point, so too the world. The Holy One, blessed be He, began the world from its navel. From there it was stretched hither and yon. Where is its navel? Jerusalem. And its [Jerusalem's] navel itself? The altar' (Jellinek, *Beth ha-Midrash*, V, 63). Clearly the above midrash employs the symbolism of the navel to indicate the centrality of Jerusalem and its altar within the cosmos. Still earlier, Jub. 8:19 (cf. Enoch 26:1) refers to Mount Zion [the Temple Mount] as 'the center of the navel of the earth.'" *Interpreter's Dictionary of the Bible*, 622. See also Ben-Arieh, "Jerusalem as a Religious City," 11; *Encyclopedia Judaica*, 9:1558–59. "The site of Zion was related to the navel of the earth. Solomon's temple is built on a rock which is the earth-center, the world mountain, the foundation stone of creation, the extremity of the umbilical cord which provides a link between heaven, earth, and the underworld." Terrien, "Omphalos Myth and Hebrew Religion," 317. See also Nibley, *Mormonism and Early Christianity*, 323; Kotker, *Earthly Jerusalem*, 6; *Anchor Bible Dictionary*, 3:748; Asali, *Jerusalem in History*, 33.

17. "The land of Israel lies in the center of the world; Jerusalem lies in the center of the land of Israel; the holy precinct lies in the center of Jerusalem; the Temple building lies in the center of the holy precinct; the ark of the covenant lies in the center of the Temple building; the Sacred Rock, however, lies before the ark of the covenant, for from it the world was founded." From Midrash Tanhuma, as cited from Jeremias in Finegan, *Archeology of the New Testament*, 272.

18. *Jewish Encyclopedia*, 1:177.

19. "The body of Adam [was] preserved in a chest until about 1800, when 'Melchizedek buried the body in Salem (formerly the name of Jerusalem), which might very well be the middle of the habitable world.'" *Encyclopedia of Freemasonry*, 15.

20. See Kotker, *Earthly Jerusalem*, 8.

21. Kotker, *Earthly Jerusalem*, 7; see also *Encyclopedia Judaica*, 9:1576.

22. Genesis Rabbah 59:5 and Rabbi Johanan in Exodus Rabbah 23:10, in *Encyclopedia Judaica*, 9:1559.

23. Idinopulos, *Jerusalem Blessed, Jerusalem Cursed*, 11, 16.

24. Heschel, *Israel*, 8.

25. Jewish tradition has Jerusalem's history going back to Adam. "By a universal tradition, we know that the Temple which David and Solomon built stood on the site of Araunah's threshing floor; and that is the place where Abraham had built an altar to sacrifice his son Isaac; and that is where Noah built an altar when he emerged from his ark; and that Cain and Abel offered sacrifices on the altar there, and that Adam offered a sacrifice there when he was created, and that indeed, it was from that spot that he was created. . . . and why do I say that the original sanctity of the Temple and Jerusalem applies forever? Because it stems from the Divine Presence, and the Divine Presence is never abrogated." Maimonides, in Tal, *Whose Jerusalem?* 17. Christian tradition also has Jerusalem's history going back to Adam. The Holy City is the place where history began and where it will end. See *Encyclopedia Judaica*, 9:1568.

2

The Geographical Setting of Jerusalem

Jerusalem is mentioned by name more than eight hundred and forty times in the Bible and appears, in addition, under more than seventy other titles (for example, Ariel, Zion, City of Righteousness, City of God, City of the Great King, the Holy City). For Jerusalem we have more scriptural detail than for any other city in the biblical world, including references to walls, gates, towers, waterworks, quarters, streets, gardens, fields, tombs, and buildings.

Once established by King David as his royal capital, Jerusalem maintained permanency at the same site, although throughout many centuries it has expanded and contracted to accommodate the political and economic priorities of its various rulers and inhabitants, thus assuring the city a certain fluidity of size and space. The city's prominence was secured by David's establishment of the site as his imperial capital, yet the location was apparently significant and considered holy a full thousand years before David.

Jerusalem is situated in the top of the Judaean Hills seventeen miles west of the northern end of the Dead Sea and thirty-six miles east of the Mediterranean Sea (see Bible Map 1). Its highest points reach 2,550 feet above sea level.

Jerusalem lies far from the international coastal highway and the Transjordanian highway. The major north-south and east-west crossroads in the hill country lie five miles to the northwest of Jerusalem; in fact, the city's position just off the main intersection has given it a certain protection. The Rift Valley fault escarpment, the wilderness to the east, and the steep and deep V-shaped valleys to the west increase

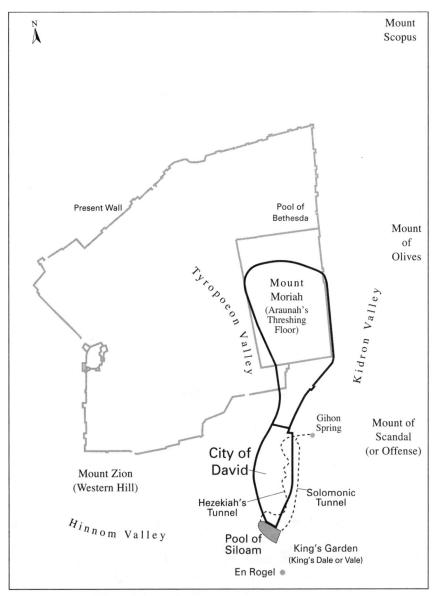

The geographical setting of Jerusalem

Jerusalem's naturally protected position. The Jerusalem hills form a saddle between the Bethel hills to the north, which are higher, and the Hebron hills to the south, which are higher still (some reach heights of more than 3,000 feet). There was relative seclusion or isolation—and, therefore, security—high in the hill country. Contrast the Philistines in their otherwise productive coastal lands who were gradually obliterated or assimilated, whereas more isolated Judah was able to perpetuate its identity. Approaching armies had to conquer the Jordan Valley or the coastal plains before attacking the chief population centers and the capital of Judah. A would-be attacker faced a climb upwards from *any* direction to reach the political eagle nesting in the top of the Judaean Hills.[1]

Geologically the hill country of Jerusalem is mostly hard limestone (dating to the Cenomanian period), with terra rosa soils breaking down from the stone. The natural vegetation of the region is forest; dense oak and terebinth once covered the hills.[2] The economy of the hills is "mountain agriculture," especially grapes, olives, and figs.

The usual prerequisites for settlement in the Holy Land in ancient times were water supply, arable land (that is, adequate soil for agricultural production to sustain the population), proximity to communication routes, and strategy for defensibility. Even the greatest and most important Old Testament cities, such as Jerusalem, Gezer, and Megiddo, covered barely fifteen to twenty acres. With the need for defensively strong walls, administrative centers were necessarily compact.

Jerusalem is an excellent example of a place originally settled despite its lack of the four usual prerequisites. Geographical disadvantages are immediately apparent. There is no easy access to the area; roads to Jerusalem have been relatively inconvenient and irregular. Soils are rather poor; there is little valuable agricultural land. Natural water resources are not plentiful. Though the Gihon Spring is the single richest water source in the hill country of Judah, it was the only natural source of water for ancient Jerusalem.

The former Jebusite enclave was selected by David as his capital, not so much for geographical advantage as for an astute political motive. He knew that Israel's topography did not lend itself to political unity and that a rift already existed between northern and southern tribes during the reign of Saul. To unite the tribes into one kingdom from the onset, he purposely chose the neutral site immediately on the border between north and south, much like the United States capital of Washington in the District of Columbia, which does not belong to any of the fifty states. The City of David was technically in the tribal inheritance of Benjamin, but that tribe had not succeeded in capturing it from the Jebusites.

Jerusalem became one of the great political capitals of the world, originally because of the inspired decision of one man: David. Jerusalem has also become one of the great spiritual centers of the world because of the wise decision of Solomon to continue his father's plan and construct the glorious Temple on the sacred parcel of ground known as Mount Moriah. For the first time in the nation's history, under King David its religious and political capitals were the same: Jerusalem was a holy city as well as a royal city.

Though today's beautiful city of Jerusalem, with its broad municipal territory and more than half a million inhabitants, appears stunning to almost every visitor, the Holy City looked anything but inviting to Elder Orson Hyde in 1841. The land was denuded. Arabs eked out a primitive existence with their flocks on the bare hills. Some time later, in conversation with Brigham Young and other apostles, Elder Hyde remarked: "The country around the city of Jerusalem is a desert and almost desolation. The land is in such a depleted condition that I could see nothing desirable in the location of the city of Jerusalem."[3]

It is clear that the site of Jerusalem was not chosen as a royal or a holy city because of its geographical endowments. As we will see by examining its history throughout antiquity, other factors led to Jerusalem's becoming the world's most famous city.

TOPOGRAPHY

The Mount of Olives

Immediately east of the ancient city is the Mount of Olives (see Bible Map 17). There are three sections of the Mount of Olives range. The northernmost is called Mount Scopus, where Babylonian and Roman armies camped to "overlook" (Greek, *scopus*) the city. The middle section, which is simply called the Mount of Olives, is the main part of the range and directly east of the Temple Mount. The southernmost is called the Mount of Scandal or the Mount of Offense, the site of Solomon's wives' shrines to idol gods. More than seventy thousand graves have been cut into the soft (Senonian) chalky limestone of the Mount of Olives. The ridge, which includes Mount Moriah, the Ophel, and the City of David, is semihard (Turonian) limestone. The land

Mount of Olives, showing the Orson Hyde Memorial Park

westward consists predominantly of hard (Cenomanian) limestone. The type of stone has influenced the location of habitation over the centuries. Only in our day, with the use of dynamite to excavate for building projects, has the city been able to move westward into areas of harder stone.

The Kidron Valley

Lying between the Mount of Olives and the Temple Mount, the Kidron Valley was always the eastern boundary of ancient Jerusalem. It was deeper in antiquity.[4]

Mount Moriah, Ophel, the City of David

Moriah was the site of Abraham's near-sacrifice of his son Isaac. Araunah's threshing floor, Solomon's Temple, and the Second Temple (Zerubbabel's and Herod's) all occupied the same spot. Today there are more than one hundred structures on the mount, including mosques, arcades, religious schools, prayer platforms, porticos, fountains, and a museum. "Mount Ophel" and the "City of David" are names often used interchangeably for the original, eastern hill of Jerusalem, the former city of the Jebusites. Some, however, make a case for Ophel (the Hebrew term meaning "hill" or "mound," the biblical equivalent of acropolis or citadel) being the area between the Temple Mount (Arabic, *Haram esh-Sharif*, "the Noble Sanctuary") and the City of David, the recently excavated area just south of the southern wall of the Temple Mount.

Psalm 125:2 says, "As the mountains are round about Jerusalem, so the Lord is round about his people." When one stands in the City of David (and only there), one can see that Jerusalem is literally surrounded by mountains. The Temple Mount itself is a mountain or hill; it had to be ascended on all sides. The City of David was surrounded by deep, protective valleys (Arabic, *wadis*) on three sides (east, south, and west) but needed strongly fortified walls on the exposed northern side.

The Valley

Flavius Josephus, the Jewish historian writing around A.D. 70–80, called this valley the Tyropoeon ("Cheesemakers") Valley. It runs from the vicinity of the Northern (Damascus) Gate southward just west of the Temple Mount and west of the City of David. It was a pronounced valley in antiquity, but Herod filled it in somewhat to expand the city westward in the first century before Christ, and Hadrian filled it in further during the second century after Christ.[5] Today a valley is still discernible on the ground and even more so from the air.

The Western Hill, or the Upper City

The Western Hill is today's Mount Zion. Originally the term *Zion*, which occurs one hundred fifty times in the Bible, applied to the City of David and later to the Temple Mount. Today it refers to the Western Hill. Josephus mistakenly identified the Western Hill as the biblical "Stronghold of Zion," or the original City of David (thus the traditional "David's Tomb" on that hill).[6] Although the Western Hill might at first seem the logical hill for earliest settlement—being broader and higher and more defensible—the Eastern Hill was first settled because of the one prolific water source, the Gihon Spring.

The Hinnom Valley

Called in Hebrew *Gei ben-Hinnom* and in Greek *Gehenna* ("hell"), the Hinnom Valley was the border between the tribes of Benjamin and

Jerusalem under snow at the Lion's Gate of the Old City

Judah, in the period of the Judges, as delineated in Joshua 15:8 and 18:16. Sacrifices, even child sacrifices, were made in this valley in biblical times, probably at its eastern end, and rubbish of the city was burned there, giving rise to the concept of hell as a place of continual burnings. Note, for example, the phrase in the Sermon on the Mount: "Whosoever shall say, Thou fool, shall be in danger of hell fire (Matt. 5:22)." In Hebrew "hell fire," *esh gei Hinnom,* means literally fire of the Hinnom Valley. Jesus used the expression at least ten times.

OLD JERUSALEM'S WALLS

Today's Old City features two and a half miles of city walls. The shape of the city is more or less that of Hadrian's Roman Colony, Aelia Capitolina, which was built over the Jerusalem destroyed in the Second Revolt (A.D. 132–135).[7] The north wall is the longest and the east wall the shortest. There are eight gates. The walls were highest and most magnificent in the time of Herod the Great. The southern wall had a height of a modern fifteen-story building. The walls were about three to five yards thick, built of enormous ashlar blocks weighing up to one hundred fifty tons each. One stone discovered along the Western Wall of the Temple Mount is purported to weigh four hundred tons. Mark 13:1 reports the disciples saying, "Master, see what manner of stones and what buildings are here!"

WATER SOURCES

Springs

The Gihon Spring is the main reason for the initial settlement of the original hill of Jerusalem; it is the richest of the springs along the Judaean ridge. It is a typical syphon-karst spring, whose waters intermittently "gush forth" (the meaning of the Hebrew name *giha*).[8] A gush may last forty minutes, with a break of about six to eight hours. Total discharge averaged more than a thousand cubic meters, about 264,200 gallons per day. The water was used for drinking and horticulture.[9] The spring was situated at the foot of the Eastern Hill (the City of David), at the western edge of the Kidron Valley. Ancient Jerusalemites, especially before the construction of Hezekiah's Tunnel, normally exited their city through the Water Gate (cf. Neh. 3:26; 8:1), hiked down to the spring, drew water, and then hiked back up into the city.

Wells

En Rogel, situated at the southern end of the Kidron Valley in the King's Dale, or King's Garden, was apparently a spring in early times. Later, when the water table lowered, it was used as a well. James Barclay reported on 26 October 1852 that one thousand donkeys hauled water-skins from En Rogel to the Old City. On 12 September 1853 he reported two thousand donkeys carried four thousand waterskins to Jerusalem every day, totaling more than 25,000 gallons.[10]

Cisterns

W. F. Albright postulated that the collection of rainwater in cisterns waterproofed with mortar was an Israelite invention. Many small and several large cisterns are known from ancient times. In 1860 Jerusalem had 992 cisterns; in 1948, about 1,050 cisterns containing a million cubic meters, or some 264 million gallons, of water. There are 37 cisterns under the Temple Mount courtyards capable of holding sixteen thousand cubic meters, or about 10 million gallons, of water; 25 of the cisterns are still in use.[11]

Pools

In the Second Temple period Jerusalem had at least ten big pools for water storage (for example, Siloam and Bethesda). The natural disadvantages of open pools, of course, are heavy evaporation, silting, and exposure to pollutants.

Aqueducts

The City of David used two other water conduits, or tunnels, in addition to the Jebusite water system: the Siloam, or Solomonic, Tunnel from the tenth century and Hezekiah's Tunnel from the late eighth century before Christ. Jerusalem in the Second Temple period also had remarkable stone-pipe water channels from the Hebron hills (which are higher than Jerusalem) to the Temple Mount, a distance of twenty-five to thirty miles with water flowing at a one percent gradient.

Despite the meager natural water resources for a large population at ancient Jerusalem, the ingenuity of the inhabitants in preserving their winter rainfall and channeling in water from other locations provided them with adequate supplies. We have no record of citizens of Jerusalem succumbing to thirst in any of its sieges or surrendering because of lack of water. Modern Jerusalem, besides using ground water, is supplied with water from the Rosh HaAyin Spring east of Tel Aviv and also from the Sea of Galilee. The water is transported by the National Water Carrier, using a combination of surface canals and underground pipes, which was completed in 1964.

DEMOGRAPHY

The original Israelite Jerusalem, the City of David, was about twelve to fifteen acres in size and had a population of 2,000 to 3,000 people. Solomon's Jerusalem was about thirty-two acres and had 4,000 to 5,000 inhabitants. Later in the First Temple period, during the reign of King Hezekiah, Jerusalem could have expanded to one hundred twenty-five acres with a population of more than 20,000. In the early Roman period Jerusalem boasted between 100,000 and 200,000 inhabitants.[12] It was the largest walled city in the country and one of the largest in the Near East. Population in the mid 1990s is well over half a million (roughly 450,000 Jews and 150,000 Arabs, as well as others.) Greater Jerusalem is expected to have a population of 900,000 by the turn of the millennium.[13]

CLIMATE

The geographical position of Jerusalem between the Mediterranean Sea and the desert has greatly affected its history. The region's climate is best defined as the outcome of the struggle between those two powerful influences. It is a healthful climate, similar to that of southern California. North latitude of thirty-two degrees corresponds to that of the San Diego area.

Jerusalem has two seasons: the hot, dry season and the cold, wet season. July and August are the hottest months of the year; January and February, the coldest. Some relief may be found in the hill country during the hot summer season. During morning hours, often the most unpleasant time of day, the sun beats down on the earth, heating the land. The hot air over the land rises and draws in cooler air from the Mediterranean, creating late afternoon and evening breezes. In late evening the temperature equalizes, the land cools, and the breezes cease. Sometimes hot air over the Mediterranean, already equalized with hot air over the land, sponsors no cooling breezes.

Between the two seasons are transitional periods with very unpredictable weather. Sometimes during these transitional periods, generally in April and May and again in September and October, there occurs a wind called *khamsin* (Arabic) or *sharav* (Hebrew). The official term is *sirocco* (variant spelling *scirocco,* an Italian word deriving from Arabic *sharq,* which means "east"). A Near East sirocco, similar to the Santa Ana in California, is caused by atmospheric depressions moving along the Libyan desert track, which bring strong, dry winds with high temperatures and dust storms. The same depressions cause hot, dry air from the Arabian desert to move north and west across the Holy Land. The translation in the New American Bible of the book of Sirach (Ecclesiasticus) 43:22–23 vividly expresses the devastating effects of khamsin conditions and the relief of subsequent moisture:

> When the mountain growth is scorched with heat [khamsin],
>> and the flowering plains as though by flames,
> The dripping clouds restore them all,
>> and the scattered dew enriches the parched land.

The prophet Hosea lamented of sinful Samaria (RSV Hos. 13:15):

> Though he may flourish as the reed plant,
>> the east wind, the wind of the Lord, shall come,
>> rising from the wilderness;
> and his fountain shall dry up,
>> his spring shall be parched.

Ezekiel, using the familiar image of Israel as a vine, recorded the following allegory (RSV Ezek. 17:9–10):

> Can such a vine flourish?
> Will not its roots be broken off
>> and its fruit be stripped,
> and all its fresh sprouting leaves wither,
> until it is uprooted and carried away
> with little effort and few hands?
> If it is transplanted, can it flourish?
> Will it not be utterly shrivelled,
> as though by the touch of the east wind,
>> on the bed where it ought to sprout?

Read Ezekiel's words a second time with the exile of the Jews to Babylon in mind.

Jesus used this same meteorological phenomenon in his own teaching:

> When you see cloud[s] banking up in the west, you say at once, "It is going to rain," and rain it does. And when the wind is from the south, you say, "There will be a heat-wave" [RSV, "scorching heat"], and there is. (NEB Luke 12:54–55)

Moisture is provided in the land of Jerusalem by rain in winter and dew in summer. A real curse would be the deprivation of both, such as David's curse on the Gilboa mountain range following the death of Saul and Jonathan there: "Ye mountains of Gilboa, let there be no dew, neither let there be rain, upon you" (2 Sam. 1:21). Elijah also cursed the land: "As the Lord God of Israel liveth . . . there shall not be dew nor rain these years, but according to my word" (1 Kgs. 17:1).

Dew is of vital importance for agriculture during the five- to six-month period with no rain. Great humidity during the dry season results in dew at night. (In Hosea 14:5 the Lord says: "I will be as the dew unto Israel." See also Gen. 27:28; Deut. 33:28; Zech. 8:12.)

The average relative humidity in Tel Aviv is 70 percent, in Eilat 20 percent, and in Jerusalem 50 percent—the ideal.

Temperatures in Jerusalem average 47° F in January, the coldest month, and 75° F in August, the hottest month. In the hill country temperatures over 100° F are considered very hot and are unusual. The lowest temperature recorded in Jerusalem in the past one hundred years was 19.4° F (-7° C).

Jerusalem averages two to three days of snowfall a year. During the winter of 1992 Jerusalem experienced its heaviest snowfalls in a century. Early in January a snowstorm blanketed the city with eighteen inches, and by February the whole country was declared a natural disaster area. A meteorological report on February 15 declared the winter of 1992 the wettest since records began to be kept in 1904.[14]

Jerusalem sits at the southern edge of the European storm-belt systems, which means that in some years the land may be untouched by rain. The following description of the promised land, given by the Lord himself, shows how trust in God and obedience to him is critical for anyone living in that "testing ground":

> But the land, whither ye go to possess it, is a land of hills and valleys, and drinketh water of the rain of heaven:
> A land which the Lord thy God careth for: the eyes of the Lord thy God are always upon it, from the beginning of the year even unto the end of the year.
> And it shall come to pass, if ye shall hearken diligently unto my commandments . . .
> That I will give you the rain of your land in his due season [January-February, mostly], the first rain [October-November] and the latter rain [April-May], that thou mayest gather in thy corn [grains], and thy wine [grapes], and thine oil [olives]. (Deut. 11:11–14)

Then God warns his people not to turn aside to serve false gods lest they suffer his consequent indignation and punishment:

And then the Lord's wrath be kindled against you, and he shut up the heaven, that there be no rain, and that the land yield not her fruit; and lest ye perish quickly from off the good land which the Lord giveth you." (Deut. 11:17)

According to the Lord's own explanation, if his people turned aside and polluted their land inheritance by sin, the Lord, instead of pouring out the vital rains, would pour out his anger and indignation on them by shutting up the heavens. The resulting formula would be: No rain equals no crops equals the people perish. Whenever there is an account in the Bible of a famine in the land,[15] it generally means no rain fell that year. Thus God could prove his people even by rainfall. Man is helpless in this testing ground without the rains; he is dependent upon God. And just as God warned, now and then, when the people stray far enough, he is bound to shut up the heavens that there be no rain: "The heavens over your head shall be brass, and the earth under you shall be iron" (RSV Deut. 28:23). Following are two vivid examples:

> "I gave you cleanness of teeth in all your cities,
>   and lack of bread in all your places,
> yet you did not return to me,"
>   says the Lord.
>
> "And I also withheld the rain from you
>   when there were yet three months to the harvest . . .
> yet you did not return to me,"
>   says the Lord. (RSV Amos 4:6–8)
>
> "You have played the harlot with many lovers;
>   and would you return to me?"
>   says the Lord.
>
> Lift up your eyes to the bare heights, and see!
>   Where have you not been lain with?
> By the waysides you have sat awaiting lovers
>   like an Arab in the wilderness.
> You have polluted the land
>   with your vile harlotry.
> Therefore the showers have been withheld,
>   and the spring rain has not come. (RSV Jer. 3:1–3)

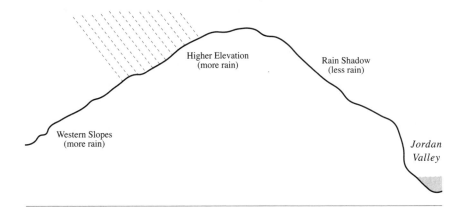

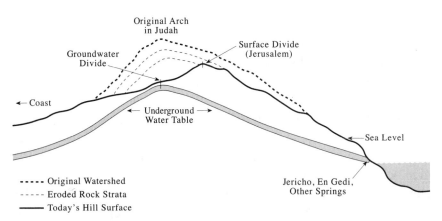

Rainfall and watershed of the Jerusalem area

Consider also the prophetic future when two witnesses in the Holy City will be empowered "to shut heaven, that it rain not" for a period of three and a half years (Rev. 11:6).

As a general rule, farther north or west means more rain; farther south or east means less. More rain falls on western slopes and higher hills, and the result is more vegetation there. Less rain falls on eastern slopes and valleys, creating a rain shadow or topographical desert, such as the Judaean wilderness and the Jordan Valley immediately east of Jerusalem.

A phenomenon that surprises most travelers to the Holy Land is the series of copious freshwater springs along the west side of the Jordan Valley at Jericho, En Feshka, and En Gedi. The water appears to be coming out of the dry, desolate wilderness. Indeed, the water *is* coming out from the wilderness—from *under* the wilderness.

After the Judaean Hills were originally pushed up, centuries of erosion of the high western slopes ensued, leaving the surface water divide and the underground water divide in quite different places. The surface watershed runs along the ridge just west of Mount Zion, where Montefiore's windmill and the King David Hotel are located. The underground watershed is at Zova, about ten kilometers (just over six miles) west of Jerusalem.[16] Therefore, the water which drains off the surface west of the Jerusalem ridge runs in the wadis to the Mediterranean, but whatever seeps into the ground (remember there is a lot of rain high on the western slopes) flows into the underground aquifers and eastward to the Jordan Valley. The Rift Valley fault cut the aquifers, which produced the springs. The springs are the reason for the well-watered plains there.

Jerusalem actually has about the same annual average rainfall as London: twenty-two to twenty-five inches.[17] In Jerusalem, however, the rain falls over a period of about fifty days, whereas in London it falls over a period of about three hundred days.[18] Jerusalem often receives more annual rainfall than does Athens, Vienna, or Paris.

In summary, the geographical setting of Jerusalem—its topography, elevation, water supply, soils, communication links, defensibility, climate, and rainfall—has influenced its history. The stage itself and the physical props have had a pivotal effect on the players and on every act of the enduring drama played out over the ages in Jerusalem.

NOTES

1. From the Galilee, the Jordan Valley, the Coastal Plains, or anywhere else in the country, it is a journey *up* to Jerusalem. The writers of the Bible commonly used the phrase "up to Jerusalem." To the Jews, Jerusalem was the high point of temporal and spiritual life. See Ogden, *Where Jesus Walked*, 5–6.

2. Various reasons are suggested for the eventual destruction of forests in the land, from the Romans crucifying thousands of people (Josephus wrote that the Romans cut down numerous trees in Galilee and Judaea to construct siege walls during the war of A.D. 66–70) to the tax laws of the Ottoman Empire, which required payment according to how many trees were on a property. To reduce their taxes, people cut down their trees, thus causing erosion and other problems.

3. The Church of Jesus Christ of Latter-day Saints, Journal History Manuscript, 19 June 1859.

4. See Smith, *Jerusalem*, 31–43.

5. See Yadin, *Jerusalem Revealed*, 13; Simons, *Jerusalem in the Old Testament*, 19–20.

6. Avigad, *Discovering Jerusalem*, 26–27.

7. Mare, *Archaeology of the Jerusalem Area*, 19, 33.

8. Gill, "How They Met," 22, 25, 27.

9. Yadin, *Jerusalem Revealed*, 75.

10. Har-El, *This Is Jerusalem*, 271.

11. Har-El, *This Is Jerusalem*, 159–61; Simons, *Jerusalem in the Old Testament*, 350–51; Bahat, *Illustrated Atlas of Jerusalem*, 48.

12. Ben-Dov, *Shadow of the Temple*, 75.

13. Rubenstein, *Jerusalem Post*, 21 July 1982.

14. For more information on snow in Jerusalem, see Ogden, *Where Jesus Walked*, 63.

15. For example, Abraham to Egypt because of famine in Canaan (Gen. 12:10); famine while Isaac lived in the Negev and Philistia (Gen. 26:1); Jacob's family to Egypt because of famine (Gen. 41:54 to 42:5); Elimelech and family to Moab because of famine in Judah (Ruth 1:1); three-year famine in David's time (2 Sam. 21:1); three-and-one-half-year famine by Elijah's word (1 Kgs. 17:1); and seven-year famine in Elisha's day (2 Kgs. 8:1).

16. See Amiran et al., *Atlas of Israel*.

17. Baly and Tushingham, *Atlas of the Biblical World*, 25. See also Baly, *Geography of the Bible*, 48; Smith, *Jerusalem*, 1:77. Arden-Close claims that Jerusalem's annual average is nearer twenty-five inches. "Rainfall of Palestine," 123.

18. Orni and Efrat, *Geography of Israel*, 147.

3

MELCHIZEDEK AND ABRAHAM AT SALEM, CA. 2000 B.C.

From the Hebrew Bible (the Old Testament) and other historical documents we know only a little about Jerusalem before the fourteenth century before Christ—the approximate time of Israelite penetration into the land. Some scholars claim that the earliest occurrence of a city called *Salim* may be in commercial documents from Ebla in Syria about 2400 B.C.[1] The name *Rushalimum* or *Urusalimum* occurs in Egyptian Execration Texts (incantations against Egypt's enemies) between 1900 and 1800 B.C.[2] Half a millennium later the El Amarna Letters (diplomatic correspondence between local city-states and the ruling power in Egypt at the time, Amenhotep IV or Akhenaton)[3] mention the *land* of Jerusalem as a non-Israelite entity and, in fact, name the king, Abdi-Heba. Six of the El Amarna Letters were sent by Abdi-Heba from his city called *Urusalim*. Another half-millennium later the city is attested in an inscription from Sennacherib as *Ursalimmu* or *Uruslimmu*.[4] A Nabataean inscription shows the Aramaic form *Ursalem;* a Mandaic document preserves the form *Urashalem;* a Syriac, *Urishlem;* and an Arabic, *Ursalimu*.[5] For two thousand years, then, the texts, whether in Egyptian, Akkadian, or West Semitic languages, consistently present Jerusalem under the name meaning "City of Shalem," or "City of Peace or Perfection."[6] The city was known by the various linguistic adaptations of the name *Jerusalem* long before the Israelite incursion and settlement of the land.

There is an apparent connection between the name-title *Shalem* and *Salem,* where Melchizedek, a prince of peace, reigned as king in a city called "Peace." The toponym *Salem* seems to be a short form of the later Jerusalem.[7]

Archaeological evidence from this period, which is usually identified as the Early Bronze Age (third millennium B.C.), consists of pottery, even painted ware, found in the earliest levels of excavation in the southeastern spur of Jerusalem. Remains of the eastern city wall and tower fortification at the city gate, all from the later Middle Bronze Age—the period of the Patriarchs—have also been uncovered in excavations.[8]

Besides the meager archaeological remains from these early periods, the Bible provides scant details about persons and events of the time. Following is what we are told about an encounter between Melchizedek and Abraham, for example:

> And the king of Sodom went out to meet [Abram] . . . at the valley of Shaveh, which is the king's dale.
> And Melchizedek king of Salem brought forth bread and wine: and he was the priest of the most high God.
> And he blessed him, and said, Blessed be Abram of the most high God, possessor of heaven and earth:
> And blessed be the most high God, which hath delivered thine enemies into thy hand. And he [Abram] gave him [Melchizedek] tithes of all. (Gen. 14:17–20)

> For this Melchisedec, king of Salem, priest of the most high God, who met Abraham returning from the slaughter of the kings, and blessed him;
> To whom also Abraham gave a tenth part of all; first being by interpretation King of righteousness [i.e., the name *Melchizedek*], and after that also King of Salem, which is, King of peace. . . .
> *Now consider how great this man was,* unto whom even the patriarch Abraham gave the tenth of the spoils. (Heb. 7:1–4; emphasis added)

Modern revelation gives us essential instruction about the roles of Melchizedek in ancient Salem. Read, in particular, Genesis 14:25–40 in the Joseph Smith Translation; Alma 13:1–19; Doctrine and Covenants 84:6–26; 107:1–4.

LEARNING ABOUT MELCHIZEDEK AND ABRAHAM
FROM FIRSTHAND EXPERIENCE

In October 1983 about twenty students with the Brigham Young University Jerusalem Study Abroad program and their instructor began a three-day journey in the footsteps of Abraham and Isaac from

Beersheba to Mount Moriah in Jerusalem (see Bible Map 1). That first morning as we rode the bus to Beersheba to begin the fifty-three-mile walk, we asked ourselves, "Why did the Lord send Abraham (who was well over a hundred years old by this time) more than fifty miles away, and uphill? Why not send him to one of the nearby hills in the Negev? What was so special about Mount Moriah to the Lord or to Abraham?"

We thought it seemed likely that Moriah might have already been a significantly sacred spot in the days of Abraham. Maybe Melchizedek had a holy Temple or sanctuary at Salem there before, and perhaps Abraham knew something about the great expiatory drama that would unfold there in the meridian of time. The prophet Jacob in the Book of Mormon taught that Abraham's poignant trial, the offering up of his son Isaac, was a "similitude of God and His Only Begotten Son" (Jacob 4:5; see also Moses 5:7; D&C 138:12–13). Abraham and Isaac not only experienced a similar ordeal, with similar deep and agonizing feelings, but accomplished it at the same place—at Moriah, in Salem/Jerusalem—where the Father would later sacrifice his Beloved Son.

The first verse of Genesis 22 has God "tempting" Abraham. The Hebrew verb is *nissah,* which means "to test, try, or prove." What was the test? "Take now thy son, thine only son Isaac, whom thou lovest, and get thee into the land of Moriah; and offer him there for a burnt offering upon one of the mountains which I will tell thee of" (Gen. 22:2). Abraham himself had nearly been sacrificed earlier in his life to the idolatrous gods in his Chaldean homeland. He himself had been laid out on a sacrificial altar, with the cold blade raised to shed his blood, when the angel of the Lord appeared to rescue him (see Abr. 1:7–16). Abraham knew how repulsive human sacrifice was and how foreign such a practice is to the true worship of our Heavenly Father. But Abraham also knew that one of God's expressed purposes for his children during mortality is to "prove them herewith, to see if they will do *all things* whatsoever the Lord their God shall command them" (Abr. 3:25; emphasis added).

Abraham was called on to sacrifice, to give up, the best he had, just as our Heavenly Father would give the best he had. Genesis 22 does not give many details of time or place; the message is most important. But there is one poignant detail: "thine *only son* Isaac, *whom thou lovest.*" God himself knew the magnitude of the trial. Paul wrote that "by faith

Abraham, when he was tried, offered up Isaac: and he that had received the promises offered up his *only begotten son*" (Heb. 11:17; emphasis added).

PREVIOUS EVENTS IN THE LAND OF MORIAH

Abraham's instruction to go to the "land of Moriah" for the offering of his son is the first biblical reference to a place called Moriah. Numerous and long-standing Jewish and Christian traditions, as well as the historian Josephus, all support the thesis that Moriah is the same place as Jerusalem's Temple Mount.[9] The biblical record itself indicates that "Solomon began to build the house of the Lord at Jerusalem in mount Moriah, where the Lord appeared unto David" (2 Chron. 3:1).

Partly because of the sanctity of the place, David purchased the rock on Moriah *to make an altar to the Lord* (see 2 Sam. 24:18–25), and he instructed Solomon to build the holiest edifice in ancient Israel at that spot. But what about Abraham, a millennium earlier? Did he make the long strenuous trek to that same hill to enact one of the most stirring and emotional scenes in all of human history because there was something sacred about that place already?

We do know that Abraham had met with Melchizedek[10] sometime before "at the valley of Shaveh, which is the king's dale [identified in Bible times and today as the confluence of the Kidron, Tyropoeon, and Hinnom valleys on the southeast of the City of David—i.e., Old Testament Jerusalem]" (Gen. 14:17).[11]

We know, too, that Melchizedek ruled over his people at Salem, later called Jerusalem.[12] An ancient Israelite psalmist used the names interchangeably in synonymous parallelism, "In Salem also is his tabernacle, and his dwelling place in Zion" (Ps. 76:2). Melchizedek was a type of the Savior: both are called "King of Righteousness" (the meaning of the name *Malki-zedek* or *Melchizedek*), and both are referred to as "Prince of Peace" (JST Gen. 14:33; Isa. 9:6). Melchizedek grew up as a prince and then reigned as king in Salem, reigning under or after his father (see Alma 13:18). Jesus too was of royal lineage and if the country had not been under Roman subjugation at the time, Jesus might have been king in Jerusalem; as it was, he was accepted by the righteous as their true King. Melchizedek converted his wicked people to righteousness and established such a great degree of peace and righteousness that they "obtained heaven"; they were translated to join the City of Enoch (JST Gen. 14:34);[13] Jesus provided the way for all humankind to obtain heaven and be exalted. And we suppose, therefore, that Melchizedek and the Savior both accomplished their mortal missions at the same place.

Melchizedek was both king and God's high priest ("Melchizedek was such a great high priest"; D&C 107:2). The holy priesthood of God was thus exercised in Jerusalem a thousand years before David established the priestly orders and Solomon built the Temple. Melchizedek was also keeper of the "storehouse of God" at Salem (JST Gen. 14:37). Abraham paid tithes to that storehouse. (Anciently, Israel's Temple also served as the storehouse and treasury of the kingdom.) How could a great high priest function in his priesthood without a tabernacle or Temple? Or how could a people establish such righteousness as to be transferred from this telestial world without first having the blessings of a Temple, where holy ordinances are performed?[14]

The Prophet Joseph Smith taught that the main object of gathering the people of God in any age of the world is "to build unto the Lord a house whereby He could reveal unto His people the ordinances of His house and the glories of His kingdom, and teach people the way of salvation; for there are certain ordinances and principles that, when they are taught and practiced, must be done in a place or house built for that purpose."[15]

It is possible that a Temple or sanctuary existed on Moriah during Abraham's early life. Josephus wrote that "[Melchizedek] the Righteous King, for such he really was; on which account he was [there] the first priest of God, and first built a temple, [there,] and called the city Jerusalem, which was formerly called Salem."[16] During the time Melchizedek was the Lord's presiding authority on the earth ("there were many before him, and also there were many afterwards, but none were greater"; Alma 13:19), he and Abraham lived not far from each other in Canaan. Abraham early in his life had wanted to be "a prince of peace" (Abr. 1:2) as was Melchizedek.

Abraham received the priesthood from Melchizedek (see D&C 84:14), though we do not know when or where.[17] Abraham tells us: "I sought for the blessings of the fathers, and the right whereunto I should be ordained to administer the same; having been myself a follower of *righteousness* [possibly a title, denoting God, and his Son, who is called "Son of Righteousness"; see 2 Ne. 26:9; Ether 9:22; recall that *Malki-zedek* means "King of *Righteousness*"], desiring also to be one who possessed great knowledge, and to be a greater follower of *righteousness,* and to possess a greater knowledge, and to be a father of many nations, a *prince of peace,* and desiring to receive instructions, and to keep the commandments of God, I became a rightful heir, a *High Priest,* holding the right belonging to the fathers. It was conferred upon me from the fathers" (Abr. 1:2–3), by which we understand (with the help of D&C 84:14) that Melchizedek bestowed on him the priesthood either in the land of the Chaldeans or in the land of Salem. When Abraham "sought for [his] appointment unto the Priesthood" (Abr. 1:4), he either traveled to Canaan or else Melchizedek traveled to Mesopotamia.[18]

We may conclude that for Abraham, Moriah was already a place with holy associations when he took Isaac there to be bound and offered up. Past, present, and future continually come together at this sacred space. To be sure, the mount was to be a place of centuries of sacrifices in anticipation of the Great Sacrifice that would be accomplished there in the future.

As with Bethel ("house of God") and Gethsemane ("oil press") and other toponyms that have particular meaning for the historical events that occurred at those places, so the name of Abraham's mount is significant. *Moriah* is composed of two words: *mor,* which comes from the verb *ra'ah,* meaning "to see" (and having also a host of other meanings, including "to provide"), and *-iah,* or *-jah,* which is a contraction of the Divine Name *YHWH* (Jehovah). The name of the place, *Moriah,* could have something to do with where the Lord himself would be seen or provided.

ABRAHAM AND ISAAC: THREE DAYS TO MORIAH

Three days was a lot of time for Abraham to think about what was going to happen. On day two they passed through the area where a future town would be called *El Khalil* or *Hebron,* meaning "the friend," referring to Abraham, "the Friend of God" (James 2:23). Then "on the third day" (cf. Luke 24:46) Abraham "lifted up his eyes [as one would do who is walking along], and saw the place afar off" (Gen. 22:4). The area of the Mount of Olives and Mount Moriah can be seen from the south on the Road of the Patriarchs, about ten miles away.

Abraham laid the wood upon Isaac to carry to the place of sacrifice; Jesus also carried the wood, the cross, to the place of his death (cf. John 19:17). Isaac then asked the heartrending question, "My father: . . . Behold the fire and the wood: but where is the lamb for a burnt offering?" (Gen. 22:7). Abraham prophetically responded, "My son, God will provide himself a lamb for a burnt offering" (v. 8). The Hebrew text is *Elohim* (God) *jir'eh* (again the verb *ra'ah*, "to see or provide"). That is, God the Father will provide a lamb for a burnt offering. "Burnt offering" in the Hebrew is *olah* (from the verb *la'alot*, "to go up"); literally, it means "that which goes up to heaven from the altar." The offering had to be a perfect male, or *zakhar tammim*. A male lamb without blemish was offered by individuals and the nation as a symbol of atonement for sins. According to Leviticus 1:11, when a lamb was slain on the great altar of the Temple, it was slain on the north side of the altar. Golgotha, the place of Jesus' crucifixion, was on the north side of the ridge of Moriah.[19]

When they came to the designated place, Abraham built an altar, laid the wood on it, and bound Isaac; Jesus, too, was bound on wood on his altar of sacrifice. Isaac himself was willing to carry out the sacrifice, as later the Savior was willing to accomplish his Sacrifice. It was probably late in the afternoon when Abraham and Isaac arrived at Moriah and finished constructing their altar; Temple procedure later stipulated that passover lambs be slain later in the afternoon.

When Abraham had passed his test and the angel of the Lord was sent to stop the sacrifice of the son, a ram (not a lamb, as promised in Gen. 22:8) was substituted, and "Abraham called the name of that place Jehovah-jireh: as it is said to this day, In the mount of the Lord it shall be seen" (v. 14). In Genesis 22:8, Elohim (the Father) had promised to provide a lamb for sacrifice; in verse 14 Jehovah (the Son) will appear: Jehovah will be seen or provided. This phrase in Hebrew is *b'har YHWH jera'eh*, and should read in English: "In the mount [many manuscripts read *bahar hazeh*, "in *this* mount," meaning Moriah] the Lord shall be seen, or, the Lord shall be provided."[20] All of this clearly signifies that Abraham knew something of the meaning of his similitude sacrifice. He had uttered prophetically—not unintentionally or accidentally—that our Heavenly Father would provide a lamb as a sacrifice or atonement for sin, and he knew that the Son would be that sacrifice, to be made at that very place. Said Jesus, "Your father Abraham rejoiced to see my day: and he saw it, and was glad" (John 8:56).

THE SIGNIFICANCE OF MOUNT MORIAH IN SALEM

It seems the mount of Moriah was already a spiritually important location to Abraham, and the similitude sacrifice he was commanded to make was to be carried out on the very mountain where Jesus would suffer in the meridian of time. Moriah is *the* mount of sacrifice. There have been altars on it from the days of Melchizedek, Abraham, David, and Jesus. All sacrifices offered from Moriah were supposed to be a type of the Great Sacrifice.

If a Temple and altar and holy place of offering existed on Moriah two thousand years before Christ and during the meridian of time, then what about A.D. 2000—our own day? Knowing how history, prophecy, and divine symbolism always come full circle (God's course is "one eternal round"), we cannot help believing that there will once again be a holy Temple at that place.[21]

As the Prophet Joseph Smith taught, the object of gathering in any age is to build a Temple. Where father Abraham unwaveringly offered his beloved son, and where Father in Heaven offered his beloved Son, at that same mountain the Lord will again be seen, when "the Lord, whom ye seek, shall suddenly come to his temple" (Mal. 3:1).

NOTES

1. *Harper's Bible Dictionary,* 465; Mare, *Archaeology of the Jerusalem Area,* 20, 35.

2. The Execration Texts are documents from the period of Egypt's Middle Kingdom that augment our knowledge of important people and settled places in Canaan during the biblical period of the Patriarchs. Execrations or imprecations were written on pottery vessels or figures and then smashed and buried, symbolizing the destruction of enemies. Such places as Jerusalem, Ashkelon, Shechem, and Beth-shan are mentioned by name as enemies of Egypt.

3. Amenhotep IV (Greek, *Amenophis;* also *Ikhnaton*) instigated a profound religious revolution, which shook the foundations of the Egyptian New Kingdom, ca. 1400 B.C. Whereas Amon had reigned supreme among the gods of Karnak at Thebes, now Amenhotep abandoned the temple and the gods and the tens of thousands of priests and the capital city in favor of worshipping one god, the sun disk, Aton. Amenhotep

changed his name to Akhenaton and changed his capital to Akhetaton, known today as Tel el Amarna, which lies on the Nile halfway between Thebes and Memphis. At his new capital, Akhenaton was preoccupied with his monotheism and with love poetry written to his beautiful wife, Nefertiti. Possibly more is written about Akhenaton than about any other pharaoh in all of Egypt's illustrious history, in part because of his dramatic abandonment of Thebes and Amon, to be sure, but also because of his artistic revolution, portraying himself and his family in statuary with grotesque features: long, emaciated face, pot belly, fat thighs, etc. Another reason for the attention given Akhenaton is the discovery in 1887 of three hundred seventy-seven letters at El Amarna. About half are letters of complaint and appeals for military help from kings in Canaan to Amenhotep III and Akhenaton about local problems with people called *khabiru* (or *apiru*) who were causing political commotion in Canaan. The letters were written in cuneiform script on clay tablets in the Akkadian language (thus showing not only Egyptian but also Mesopotamian influence in Canaan in the early second millennium before Christ). Akhenaton seems to have been too busy with his religious movement to respond to the letters; they apparently went unanswered onto the shelves of an archive in El Amarna. Archaeologist Yigael Yadin claimed that the El Amarna archive constitutes the most important source of information about the Holy Land before Joshua. The letters mention numerous city-states and their rulers by name, including Damascus, Acco, Megiddo, Shechem, Gezer, Ashkelon, Gaza, Lachish, Hebron, and Jerusalem. For details of the contents of the letters, see Pritchard, *Ancient Near Eastern Texts*, 483–90; Thomas, *Documents from Old Testament Times*, 38–45; Smith, *Jerusalem*, 2:10–14.

4. *New Encyclopedia of Archaeological Excavations*, 698; Mare, *Archaeology of the Jerusalem Area*, 20.

5. Clay, "Amorite Name Jerusalem," 28–32. Compare Smith, *Jerusalem*, 1:250–65.

6. Assyriologists have long interpreted the first element of the name, *Ur* or *Uru*, as "city." More recently scholars have abandoned that translation in favor of "foundation," from the Hebrew root *yarah*, "to found." *Shalem* has customarily been assumed to be the name of some otherwise unknown local god, Shalem. It is most unlikely that Melchizedek, the king of righteousness and priest of the Most High God (whom the Latter-day Saints understand to be Jehovah, God and Creator of the world), would perpetuate the name of a pagan god as the name of his holy city. For reasons increasingly apparent in the text, the present writers hold to the interpretation "City of Peace." See also Bible Dictionary, s.v. "Salem," and Josephus, *Antiquities* 7.3.2. On *Salem* as meaning "peace" or "perfection," see *Encyclopedia Judaica*, 9:1559. The etymology of *Jerusalem* and the same conclusion about the improbability of reference to a pagan deity are discussed in DeYoung, *Jerusalem in the New Testament*, 5–12. Indeed, *Shalem* may actually refer to Jehovah, who is a God of peace. It is one of the supreme ironies of history that the City of Peace has probably seen more armed conflict, bloodshed, conquests, and internecine strife than any other city on earth. See Werblowsky, "Jerusalem: Holy City of Three Religions," 437.

7. Simons, *Geographical and Topographical Texts of the Old Testament*, 216. See also Yadin, *Jerusalem Revealed*, 1; Mare, *Archaeology of the Jerusalem Area*, 20. Compare Isa. 33:7b, in which the correct reading for "peace" is probably *Shalem*. Simons, *Geographical and Topographical Texts of the Old Testament*, 440.

8. Avigad, *Discovering Jerusalem*, 23; Bahat, *Illustrated Atlas of Jerusalem*, 22.

9. Ginzberg cites several traditions to this effect. See Ginzberg, *Legends of the Jews*, 5:253. See also Josephus, *Antiquities* 1.13.2; 7.13.4. Eckardt writes: "For Jews and Muslims the Temple Mount is identified with Mount Moriah on which Abraham prepared to

sacrifice his son Isaac (or Ishmael in Muslim tradition) in obedience to God's command." *Jerusalem*, 23. Rabbis Sherman and Zlotowitz write in *Yechezkel*, 674: "As explained by *Rambam* (*Beis HaBechirah* Ch. 2) the altar's location is of vital significance: The location of the altar is pinpointed with extreme precision and it may never be moved to another place . . . [for] we have a universally recognized tradition that the place upon which David and Solomon built the altar . . . is the exact place upon which Abraham built the altar and bound Isaac upon it." See also Yadin, *Jerusalem Revealed*, 6; Levine, *Jerusalem Cathedra*, 2:12; Ben-Dov, *Shadow of the Temple*, 33.

10. Many rabbis over the centuries identified Melchizedek with Shem, son of Noah. See Delcor, "Melchizedek," 115–35; *Jewish Encyclopedia*, 8:450; *Anchor Bible Dictionary*, 4:686; 5:1195.

Other references equate Melchizedek with Shem, with Shem possibly being his name and Melchizedek his title. The Book of Jasher 16:11 notes that "Adonizedek, king of Jerusalem, the same was Shem, went out with his men to meet Abram and his people with bread and wine, and they remained together in the Valley of Melech [Hebrew, "the King's Valley"]." John Taylor wrote in "Ancient Ruins," *Times and Seasons* 5 (15 December 1844): 746: "And with the superior knowledge of men like Noah, Shem (who was Melchizedek) and Abraham, the father of the faithful, three contemporaries, holding the keys of the highest order of the priesthood. . . ." Joseph F. Smith made a list of the great and mighty ones whom he envisioned assembled in a vast congregation of the righteous in the spirit world; included were Adam, Eve, Abel, Seth, "Noah, who gave warning of the flood; Shem, the great high priest; Abraham, the father of the faithful," as well as others (D&C 138:41). We note that Melchizedek, without question one of the greatest of the "mighty ones," is not mentioned, and Shem is identified as "the great high priest," which is a title highly reminiscent of Melchizedek's. Some have questioned the identification of Melchizedek with Shem, however, because of Doctrine and Covenants 84:14, which indicates that Melchizedek received the priesthood "through the lineage of his fathers, even till Noah." The suggested plurality of generations between Melchizedek and Noah seems to preclude Melchizedek's being Noah's son. Others point out that if the reference to Melchizedek's fathers pertains to the fathers from Adam to Noah—in reverse direction of the customary reading—the identification of Melchizedek with Shem is still possible. (Cf. Abr. 1:3.) Nevertheless, the verses surrounding Doctrine and Covenants 84:14 clearly suggest lineage going back in time.

11. See *Anchor Bible Dictionary*, 5:1168.

12. The identity of Salem, Melchizedek's city, with Jerusalem is presupposed in many rabbinic sources cited by Ginzberg (*Legends of the Jews*, 226), Theophilus, Clemens, and Jerome. Baring-Gould recorded a Jewish legend to this effect: "Melchizedek, priest of God, King of Canaan, built a city on a mountain called Sion, and named it Salem. . . . Salem, of which he was king, is that celebrated Jerusalem." *Legends of the Patriarchs and Prophets*, 205, 207. "They afterward called Salem Jerusalem," wrote Josephus in *Antiquities* 1.10.2; see also Josephus, *Wars* 6.10.1. Salem is identified with Jerusalem in the Genesis Apocryphon of the Dead Sea Scrolls. See Vermes, *Scripture and Tradition in Judaism*. The Targumim pointedly say, "Melchizedek [was] king of Jerusalem." Baring-Gould, *Legends of the Patriarchs and Prophets*, 205; *Anchor Bible Dictionary*, 5:905; Emerton, "Riddle of Genesis XIV," 412–13; DeYoung, *Jerusalem in the New Testament*, 9–11.

13. For some generations the posterity of Abraham or their messengers were sent to Mesopotamia for wives. They didn't go to Salem because Melchizedek and his people were no longer there; they had been taken up to the City of Enoch. "And men having

this faith, coming up unto this order of God, were translated and taken up into heaven.
. . . And his people wrought righteousness, and obtained heaven, and sought for the city
of Enoch which God had before taken, separating it from the earth, having reserved it
unto the latter days, or the end of the world" (JST Gen. 14:32, 34). Alma 13:12 notes that
"there were many, exceedingly great many, who were made pure and entered into the
rest of the Lord their God." See also *Anchor Bible Dictionary*, 4:686.

14. See Alma 13:16. "We may assume that Melchizedek, as a holder of the Melchizedek
Priesthood and builder of a temple, received his temple blessings—as one might also
infer from reading Abraham 1:2–4." Derrick, *Temples in the Last Days*, 26. "Elder John A.
Widtsoe believed that 'all people of all ages have had temples in one form or another.'
There is ample evidence, he was convinced, that from the days of Adam 'there was the
equivalent of temples,' that in patriarchal times 'temple worship was in operation,' and
that even after the Flood, 'in sacred places, the ordinances of the temple were given to
those entitled to receive them.'" Cowan, *Temples to Dot the Earth*, 1. Sidney B. Sperry
wrote of Abraham's tithes: "Such income would be used in part for erecting houses of
worship and for building or maintaining a temple 'which my people are always commanded to build unto my holy name' [D&C 124:39]. . . . Abraham was acquainted with
the sacred endowment and hence a temple or its equivalent in which they would be
administered." Sperry, "Ancient Temples," 814.

15. Smith, *Teachings of the Prophet Joseph Smith*, 308.

16. Josephus, *Wars* 6.10.1. Or, as Josephus wrote in *Antiquities* 1.10.2: "They afterward
called Salem *Jerusalem*."

17. "Abraham says to Melchizedek, I believe all that thou hast taught me *concerning the
priesthood and the coming of the Son of Man*; so Melchizedek ordained Abraham and
sent him away. Abraham rejoiced, saying, Now I have a priesthood." Smith, *Teachings of
the Prophet Joseph Smith*, 322–23; emphasis added.

18. The usual legends surround Melchizedek's instructing Abraham in the laws of the
priesthood and blessing, consecrating, and clothing him with heavenly power. See
Ginzberg, *Legends of the Jews*, 1:233, 274; Baring-Gould, *Legends of the Patriarchs and
Prophets*, 189.

19. In rabbinic sources where mention is made of the site of the altar, the word *gulgoleth*
(meaning "skull") is used, which appears again in *Golgotha*, the place of the crucifixion
of Jesus. See Ginzberg, *Legends of the Jews*, 5:126–27. Edward Robinson, the first great
biblical geographer, and others since, have concurred that the Crucifixion could have
occurred outside the northern gate of the city, at the north end of Moriah. *Biblical
Researches in Palestine*, 2:80. See also Edersheim, *Life and Times of Jesus the Messiah*,
134, in which he observes that the lamb was bound on the north of the altar, as Isaac
was bound on the north side of the altar. In Spiegel, *Last Trial*, 74, the following is noted:
"When Gentile or Jew, man or woman, male or female slave, recite this verse, 'Safonah
[*northward*] before the Lord,' the Holy One, blessed be He, recalls the Akedah (the binding) of Isaac ben Abraham." Temple sacrifices were divided into two types: those of
greater and those of lesser sanctity. Those of greater sanctity, such as an *olah* (a burnt
offering), had to be *slaughtered north of the Altar*. See Reznick, *Holy Temple Revisited*,
93, 95; emphasis added. "Outside of the tripartite temple building itself, the most sacred
area of the temple precinct was north of the sacrificial altar. Lesser sacrifices may be
slaughtered in any part of the court, but the sacrifices of a higher sanctity must be
offered on the north side." Parry, *Temples of the Ancient World*, 427. See also Talmud,
Menahot 3a and Zevahim 55a. Smith, in his two-volume *Jerusalem*, documents the
topographical and geological connection between the Temple Mount and its northern

end, now outside the Old City walls (1:33ff). See also Simons, *Jerusalem in the Old Testament*, 25.

20. When Abraham called the name of the place *Adonai-jireh*, he meant that "he will find the appropriate ransom—as if to say, This is the place destined for salvation and here the Lord in His graciousness will make Himself available." Spiegel, *Last Trial*, 68.

21. When examining the cycle of history, it may also be asked if it is a mere coincidence that in the place where this world's history began—the Garden of Eden, in what today is called Missouri, USA—this world's history will also conclude, when the Lord appears at his great Temple in the New Jerusalem.

4

Jerusalem at the Time of David, ca. 1000–960 b.c.

Between the time of Abraham and the time of David, many peoples occupied the land of Jerusalem. During the early centuries of the second millennium before Christ, while Akkadians flourished in the east, *Amurru* ("westerners") flourished in the western regions of the Near East. The Bible calls them *Amorites*. During the Middle Bronze Age, Amorite dynasties were firmly entrenched throughout the Levant (eastern Mediterranean coastal lands). Early Amorites mentioned in the Bible are Og, king of Bashan, and Sihon, king of the Amorites at Heshbon. Joshua and the Israelite armies conquered these kings and controlled their former domain in Transjordan during the early stages of the Israelite advance on Canaan.

From 1600 to 1350 b.c. Hittites and Hurrians from the Anatolian Plateau and Northern Mesopotamia controlled much of the Levant (see Bible Map 2). Their influence in Canaan was met with seeming indifference during the reign of Egypt's Akhenaton, but a later pharaoh of the New Kingdom, Ramses II, confronted the Hittite ruler, Hattusilis, in the Battle of Kadesh on the Orontes River. Their encounter resulted in the first known peace treaty in history, by which the Near East was divided between two major powers.

CANAANITES AND NEIGHBORS

No one power has ever conquered, occupied, and controlled all of the Near East. The topography of the region lends itself to fragmentation. With mountainous deserts and sand deserts, high hills and low hills, river valleys and rift valleys, mountain plains and coastal plains, the lands of the Near East are dissected to the point that enclaves of various peoples could live side by side for centuries. From the biblical Book of Judges we learn that Hittites, Hivites, Horites, Girgashites, Perizzites, Jebusites, Philistines, Arameans, Sidonians, Israelites, Kenites, Amorites, Amalekites, Midianites, Egyptians, Moabites, Ammonites, Edomites, and Ishmaelites all occupied or attacked parts of the land of Canaan. Indeed, the Book of Judges is the historical report of invasions of Israel's neighbors into Israelite-occupied lands.

In a geographical sense all the peoples who lived in Canaan are called "Canaanites" (see Bible Maps 4–6). Some inhabitants of Canaan were relatives of Israel, such as Ammonites, Moabites, Edomites, Midianites, and Ishmaelites. Other neighbors, such as Sidonians, Arameans, Hittites, and Amalekites, were not directly related to Israel, but throughout this period their histories were intertwined, and there were frequent military confrontations and political imbroglios. Hittites, for example, were originally from the Anatolian Plateau and were ever-present in the early history of the Hebrew/Israelite people in Canaan. Abraham bargained with Ephron the Hittite for a burial place for his family (see Gen. 23). David enlisted some loyal Hittites for his personal bodyguards. Uriah, whom David arranged to have killed so he could marry his wife, was a Hittite (apparently a Hittite converted to the true God, because his name means literally "Jehovah is my Light"). Sidonians were sometimes friends with King David of Israel but otherwise antagonists. Arameans, or Syrians, with their main capital at Damascus, frequently warred with Israel and were generally the implacable, land-hungry enemy.

At the end of the Late Bronze Age, about 1200 B.C., massive migrations and displacements of peoples throughout the eastern Mediterranean world involved ethnic groups called "Sea Peoples." At the beginning of the Iron Age, these Sea Peoples, apparently originating from the Aegean region of Greece and Asia Minor, had already caused havoc with the Hittite kingdom to the north and had shaken the foundations of the Egyptian kingdom to the south. Ramses III had barely managed to repulse them from the border of Egypt. Among these Sea Peoples were raiders the Egyptians called "Peleset," known in the Bible as "Philistines." They fell back along the coast of Canaan and settled it, thus setting the stage for friction and conflict with their Israelite neighbors who had recently occupied parts of the hill country.

JERUSALEM AS ENEMY TO ISRAEL

At the time of the conquest of Canaan by the armies of Israel, the king of Jerusalem, Adoni-zedek (literally, "Lord of righteousness," a name conspicuously similar to the earlier Malki-zedek), resisted the advancement of Israel's armed forces into the central hills of Canaan and led a coalition of Amorite kings from prominent southern city-states against the Israelites. The first specific biblical reference to the name *Jerusalem* occurs in Joshua 10:1–4, which is part of the conquest narrative.

Ezekiel 16:3 says of Jerusalem: "Thy birth and thy nativity is of the land of Canaan; thy father was an Amorite, and thy mother an Hittite." This statement suggests that Jerusalem, before the conquest and settlement by Israelites, was a city of the various Canaanite peoples and specifically of the Amorites and Hittites.

One group of these Canaanites, called Jebusites, sometime after Israel's incursion into the land, moved onto the ridge just south of Mount Moriah, the later Temple Mount, and occupied the site during the twelfth and eleventh centuries before Christ. "As for the Jebusites the inhabitants of Jerusalem," observed the historian writing Joshua 15:63, "the children of Judah could not drive them out: but the Jebusites dwell with the children of Judah at Jerusalem unto this day." A later chronicler wrote that Judah did subjugate Jerusalem: "Now the children of Judah had fought against Jerusalem, and had taken it, and smitten it with the edge of the sword, and set the city on fire" (Judg. 1:8), but a few verses later it is recorded that "the children of Benjamin did not drive out the Jebusites that inhabited Jerusalem; but the Jebusites dwell with the children of Benjamin in Jerusalem unto this day" (Judg. 1:21).

The site of Jerusalem was technically in the territory allotted to the tribe of Benjamin, not Judah, as specified in Joshua 18. Apparently neither the Judahites nor the Benjaminites took the city on their border from the Jebusites; the people of Judah may possibly have taken the outskirts of the city or parts of "the land of Jerusalem," but it is clear that the city was not taken at that time. Jebusites occupied the site for most of two centuries until Jerusalem was taken by King David (see 1 Chron. 11:4; Josh. 15:8; Judg. 19:10; Bible Map 6).

"Jebus" is likely an ethnic name, not necessarily the city name. Joshua 18:16 and 28 call the city "Jebusi," meaning the city inhabited by Jebusites. The El Amarna texts clearly identify the city as "Jerusalem," thus casting doubt on the assumption by some that the pre-Davidic city was named Jebus.

A section of the wall of the Jebusite city (twenty-seven feet wide) has been excavated on the lower eastern slope of the hill. The city-site was small, only about ten and a half acres. A water system in this early period was a diagonal, stepped tunnel one hundred twenty-eight feet (thirty-nine meters) long from inside the city to outside the city, underground, where vessels could be lowered down a vertical shaft some forty feet (more than twelve meters) deep[1] to a horizontal feeder tunnel sixty-six feet (twenty meters) long into which water was channeled from the city spring later called Gihon. This water system continued in use for more than a thousand years through Old and New Testament periods. Significant diversions and additions to this original system were made in the days of Solomon and Hezekiah.

REASONS FOR DAVID'S SELECTING JERUSALEM AS HIS CAPITAL

After the death of Saul, the first king of united Israel, David went up to Hebron and was anointed king over Judah. Following the death of Saul's son, Ish-bosheth, "all Israel" went to Hebron to anoint David king over the whole land (2 Sam. 5:1–3). Recognizing the political need for a neutral capital, neither in the middle of the southern tribe of Judah nor in the north, he decided to remove the Jebusite enclave living in what the Bible calls "the strong hold of Zion," the first mention of that place-name in the Bible. The word *Zion* may derive from the Hebrew root *tsayan*, meaning "perfection," which is also a meaning of the former city name Salem or Shalem, "city of perfection." This Zion-Salem connection becomes more understandable when it is remembered that much earlier the city of Enoch had also been called Zion (see Moses 7:18–19) and that Melchizedek's community had later "sought for the city of Enoch" and "obtained heaven" (see JST Gen. 14:32–34).[2]

David's move from Hebron to Jerusalem is probably the single

City of David (aerial)

most important event—geographically—in the Bible. David selected the site of Jerusalem not only for water and for political convenience between northern and southern tribes but also because it was a sacred place. As we have said, a king of righteousness *(Malki-zedek)* ruled and served as a political and religious leader there one thousand years before him. David appointed Zadok (a name preserving the sacred and royal appellation *Zedek*) as head of the priesthood, and the family of Zadok perpetuated the priestly role for most of another thousand years. David also named his son who would build the holy House of God, Solomon (Hebrew, *Shlomo,* from the root word meaning "peace"), which name preserves that of the original city of Melchizedek, Salem.

TAKING THE CITY FROM THE JEBUSITES

We have in 2 Samuel 5:6–9 (also 1 Chron. 11:4–8) a brief account of how the fortress or citadel (Hebrew, *metsuda*) of Jebusi was taken:

> And the king and his men went to Jerusalem unto the Jebusites, the inhabitants of the land: which spake unto David, saying, Except thou take

away the blind and the lame, thou shalt not come in hither: thinking,
David cannot come in hither.

Nevertheless David took the strong hold of Zion: the same is the city
of David.

And David said on that day, Whosoever getteth up to the gutter, and
smiteth the Jebusites, and the lame and the blind, that are hated of David's
soul, he shall be chief and captain. Wherefore they said, The blind and the
lame shall not come into the house.

So David dwelt in the fort, and called it the city of David.

The word translated "gutter" in the King James Version of 2 Samuel
5:8 is *tsinnor* in Hebrew. In other translations it is rendered "water channel" or "water shaft" (Revised Standard Version; New International
Version). According to this signification, David's general was able to get
up into the Jebusite city through their water system, through the same
tunnel and up the same shaft discovered by Charles Warren in 1867 and
cleared out by Yigal Shiloh in 1980.[3] Some historians and archaeologists
have objected to this definition of *tsinnor,* accepting instead other possible meanings, such as a trident which could be useful in combat and in
scaling operations, or a utensil or instrument of magic of some sort (to
counter the Jebusites' use of magic in setting their blind and lame on the
walls for a taunt), or a musical instrument like a shofar—suggesting that
the Jebusite city may have fallen with the aid of shofars, as was the case at
Jericho.[4] Others have claimed that such a water system could only have
been constructed after the time of David. There are similarities between
the Warren's Shaft system and later underground water systems at other
locations such as Gibeon and the ones constructed at Hazor and
Megiddo during the time of Ahab (ca. 870 B.C.). Nevertheless, differences
between those systems and ancient Jerusalem's system suggest that it was
of unique design and earlier construction. A most notable difference is
that the Jerusalem system did not bring a tunnel all the way down to
water level. Although underground water systems are thought to have
been mainly an Israelite invention of later centuries, it is possible, even
probable, that the unique system at Jerusalem was initiated earlier by the
Jebusites.[5]

Benjamin Mazar, one of the greatest of modern Israel's archaeologists, went so far as to argue that the interpretation of *tsinnor* as a water
shaft "must be abandoned in view of the physical impossibility of such a

feat,"[6] and Yigal Shiloh, the head of the City of David excavation team, supported Mazar's conclusion, or at least regarded the ascent up the Jebusite shaft as improbable when, as part of his expedition in the late 1970s and early 1980s, he called in professional mountain climbers with sophisticated alpine equipment to scale the vertical shaft and they accomplished the task only with some difficulty. Their assessment of "impossible" or "improbable" is contradicted by the fact that the British adventurer Captain Charles Warren accomplished the ascent in 1867, and a member of the Parker expedition (1909–11) also made the ascent,[7] as did another young man who studied in Jerusalem in the early 1990s and who, with no previous experience and with no equipment (but with a dash of youthful bravado) one day ascended the same Jebusite shaft, as David's general must have done. The young man's conclusion, from first-hand experience: difficult but definitely possible.

With the growing realization that Warren's Shaft incorporates several geological and technological features that are natural and certainly pre-Davidic, scholars are now reassessing former conclusions and are more inclined to favor the identification of the *tsinnor* with the Jebusite shaft. Indeed, the recent, definitive examination of ancient Jerusalem's water systems (by the geologist of the City of David excavation team), and the recent, thorough study of the term *tsinnor* in its biblical context (by a Hebrew University biblicist), conclude that David's conquest of the Jebusite stronghold was undoubtedly via the natural karstic shaft of the water system in use at that time.[8]

MAKING A ROYAL CITY AND A HOLY CITY

For many years the Philistines had been pleased with the apparent friction and rivalry between the northern tribes of Israel and the tribe of Judah. Saul's Benjamin-based monarchy had somewhat moderated that divisiveness, but during David's fugitive years the Philistines sought every opportunity to drive the wedge between the north and the south of Israel, wanting to take advantage of the rivalry between Saul and David for their own political purposes.

While Ish-bosheth reigned for two years from Transjordan and David reigned from Hebron, the Philistines must have appreciated the disunity and instability of the separate states. Once David was crowned king over all Israel, however, the Philistines lost no time in mobilizing their military forces to stop him. The unity created under a leader as dynamic as David threatened Philistine dominion. The Israelites under David did in fact repulse the subsequent attacks of the Philistines and severely reduce their influence in the land. David declared the former Jebusite center as his new administrative capital, and Jerusalem became the seat of the Davidic dynasty—"one of the longest-surviving royal houses in world history, lasting for over four hundred years."[9]

Twenty years before the establishment of Jerusalem as David's capital, the Ark of the Covenant had been returned following havoc wrought in Philistine territory. It had been sent to the town of Beth-shemesh, and the residents of the town had in turn sent it up into the hills to Kiriath-jearim (see Bible Map 6). David went down to Kiriath-jearim and took the Ark up to Jerusalem with great pageantry, music, and dancing (see 2 Sam. 6). He later felt guilty for living in a house of cedar while the Ark was housed within curtains, and he offered to build a Temple to the Lord. Despite David's willingness, the prophet Nathan received word from the Lord that the king's hands were too full of blood from a lifetime of wars; his son should erect the Temple. With the sacred Ark now in the capital city and the plans being laid for a future Temple, David preserved Jerusalem as a spiritual center, a Holy City. Jerusalem would be not only the "city of David" (2 Sam. 5:7) but the "city of God" (Ps. 46:4).

Another step in elevating Jerusalem's spiritual status was David's acquisition of Araunah's threshing floor as an altar-place for offering sacrifices to God, at the site of the future House of God (see 2 Sam. 24:18–25; 1 Chron. 21:18–26).[10] It was understandably located outside the city, in a place where afternoon winds could pick up and carry off the chaff (the empty hulls of the grain) without interfering with the property rights of other citizens. David insisted on paying the previous owner the full price for the property. At Araunah's importuning the king to accept it as a gift, David remonstrated by declaring with profound conviction, "I will surely buy it of thee at a price: neither will I offer burnt offerings unto the Lord my God of that which doth cost me nothing" (2 Sam. 24:24). A thousand years before David, father Abraham and his son had paid a heavy price at that place; a thousand years after David another Father and Son would pay the heaviest price of all at the same place.

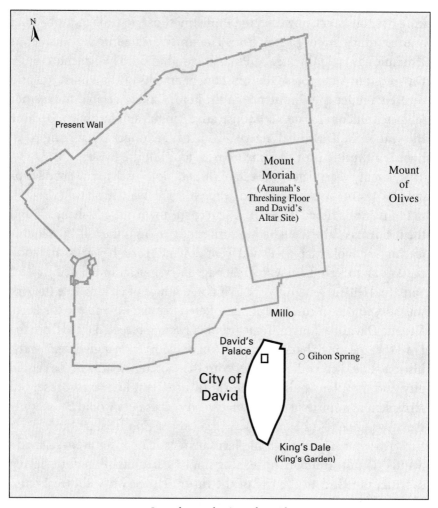

Jerusalem at the time of David

BUILDING A CITY AND AN EMPIRE

King David set about strengthening his new capital by fortifying the Canaanite walls and building up the "Millo." The root word of the Hebrew *Millo* suggests an earth fill, terrace, or elevation as part of the defense bastion (2 Sam. 5:9, fn. *b;* see also 1 Chron. 11:8). The term, which virtually all Bible translators prefer to leave in the original and merely transliterate from the Hebrew, refers to some kind of fortification, possibly Jebusite in origin, that was successively repaired by David,

Solomon, and Hezekiah. In 1 Kings 9:15 is the following historical note: "This is the reason of the levy which king Solomon raised; for to build the house of the Lord, and his own house, and Millo, and the wall of Jerusalem, and Hazor, and Megiddo, and Gezer." Other passages highlight the strategic importance of the Millo. For example, "Pharaoh's daughter came up out of the city of David unto her house which Solomon had built for her: then did he build Millo" (1 Kgs. 9:24); "Solomon built Millo, and repaired the breaches of the city of David his father" (1 Kgs. 11:27); "also he [Hezekiah] strengthened himself, and built up all the wall that was broken, and raised it up to the towers, and another wall without, and repaired Millo in the city of David" (2 Chron. 32:5). The Millo seems to have been located at the shallow saddle between David's citadel on the south and the Temple Mount on the north[11] and may have helped fortify the city at its weakest point, at the north end of the city. The term *Millo* was apparently replaced by the word *Ophel* in later usage.[12]

David's political genius is reflected in the fact that he and his own mercenaries actually conquered the Jebusite stronghold, so it was literally the city of *David,* not having been the conquest of any other Israelites.

David took advantage of the services of various non-Israelites. The architects and builders of his palace were Lebanese/Phoenicians, not Israelites or Judahites; his bodyguards were mostly Hittites and Philistines; and at least some Jebusites remained in his city (or more likely settled parts outside the City of David, such as the Western Hill), and were assigned certain administrative functions in his new government.[13]

"And Hiram king of Tyre sent messengers to David, and cedar trees, and carpenters, and masons: and they built David an house" (2 Sam. 5:11). This is David's royal palace, his "house of cedar" (2 Sam. 7:2), which most researchers assume was built at the northern crest of the City of David on a ten-story-high solid stone terrace possibly dating from the fourteenth to the twelfth century before Christ; in other words, David built his palace over the former administrative buildings of the Canaanite and Jebusite city.[14] David also built a "house of the mighty," possibly to house his bodyguards (Neh. 3:16).

The royal palace was the scene of the most tragic event in David's life. "It came to pass, after the year was expired, at the time when kings go forth to battle [that is, the summer months; during winter months few wars are fought in the Near East], that David sent Joab, and his servants with him, and all Israel; and they destroyed the children of Ammon, and besieged Rabbah. But David tarried still at Jerusalem" (2 Sam. 11:1). While his army was fighting fifty miles away at Rabbah, the capital of the Ammonites (same as today's Amman, Jordan), David took a stroll one evening looking out over his city from the palace, saw a woman washing herself, watched long enough to notice she was beautiful, inquired about her, and called her to his palace. David gave orders for Bathsheba's husband, one of his "mighty men," to be killed in battle so David could conceal his adultery with marriage.

Because of his great sins, David was punished with terrible family and national problems and hostilities. Said Nathan, the prophet, "Now therefore the sword shall never depart from thine house. . . . Behold, I will raise up evil against thee out of thine own house" (2 Sam. 12:10–11).

Absalom, a son of David, had a beautiful sister, Tamar, and his half-brother Amnon (David's son by a different wife) fell in love with her. Amnon was so enamored of her that he became sick and devised a way of getting her into his room alone so that he could rape her. Absalom hated Amnon because of what Amnon had done to Tamar, and he plotted for two years just how to kill him. Finally Absalom arranged for all the king's sons to attend a sheepshearers' party and on that occasion had Amnon slain. In fear of his father, King David, Absalom fled for several years. Then, upon being reconciled to his father, he returned to live in Hebron. There he conspired against the king, stirring up rebellion and eventually leading a force of men against the capital itself. David, preferring to avoid bloodshed, fled, head covered and barefoot and weeping, up over the Mount of Olives and through the wilderness to Transjordan (see 2 Samuel 13–15). Possibly during this time Absalom "reared up for himself a pillar, which is in the king's dale" (2 Sam. 18:18). A monument that stands in the Kidron Valley today, by tradition called "Absalom's Pillar," actually dates to a much later (Graeco-Roman) period. Absalom's pillar would have been erected farther south where the "king's dale" or "king's garden" was. Absalom and his rebel troops pursued David's men across the Jordan and engaged them in battle in the land of Gilead, in "the wood of Ephraim." Absalom was killed, and David returned to

Jerusalem, mourning over the personal, family, and national catastrophes that had befallen him.

Another son of David, Adonijah, later claimed the kingdom when the time of his father's death approached. To ensure the peaceful continuity of his dynasty, David had his son Solomon, the second son of Bathsheba, anointed as his successor by the priest Zadok at the Gihon Spring. Solomon at the Gihon, and Adonijah at the other spring called En Rogel—each one claimed the throne at a water source, the most important place in any Near Eastern city.

SUMMARY OF KING DAVID'S ACCOMPLISHMENTS

David's forty-year reign saw him conquer much new territory, creating for the first time in Israelite history an empire, which extended from the Sinai Peninsula to the Euphrates River. As history testifies, a strong Israelite kingdom was possible only if Israel was spiritually strong, living according to the commandments of God and thus receiving his protection. At the time of David, the surrounding kingdoms and empires were feeble or involved in their own internal problems, and the resulting power vacuum allowed the Israelites strength, prosperity, and even expansion. David subdued the non-Israelite cities in Canaan, especially in the Jezreel Valley and other strategic points along the International Highway, such as Megiddo and Beth-shan; he also subdued the surrounding lands of the Arameans, Ammonites, Moabites, Edomites, Amalekites, and Philistines (see Bible Map 7). The only neighboring nation that was not subdued or required to pay tribute was Lebanon, or Phoenicia. Both David and Solomon maintained peaceful relations with Hiram, king of Tyre. Hiram supplied David with building materials for his palace, and he supplied materials and workers to Solomon for the great Temple. Their navies also trained together and supported each other. David more or less ruled the lands and the Phoenicians ruled the seas to their mutual commercial advantage.

David tried to create additional stability in foreign relations by making allies of former enemies through numerous political marriages—bringing the daughters of other royal families into his own citadel at Jerusalem. From there David controlled all military positions in Israel, all national and local government administrators, the state and tribal tax and revenue collectors, scribes, and other officials. David ruled as absolute monarch. Along with consolidating all political power under one head in Jerusalem, as we have noted, David also established the center of religious worship in Jerusalem by setting up the Ark, designating the focus of sacrificial ceremonies at the top of Moriah, and gathering materials and assigning personnel to build the House of God.

Upon his death, in contrast to the usual practice of burial outside the city walls, David was buried inside his city, at what came to be known as the "sepulchres of the kings," the royal cemetery for the Davidic dynasty. "So David slept with his fathers, and was buried in the city of David" (1 Kgs. 2:10; cf. Neh. 3:16). For nearly three hundred years kings from David through Hezekiah were buried in the royal tombs.[15]

NOTES

1. Gill and Shiloh concluded that the vertical shaft is a natural karstic sinkhole. See *Anchor Bible Dictionary*, 2:61; see also Gill, "How They Met," 20–38, 64.

2. Ogden and Chadwick, *Holy Land*, 203. See also Smith, *Jerusalem*, 1:258.

3. See Shiloh, "Jerusalem's Water Supply During Siege," 24–39. See also *Encyclopedia Judaica*, 9:1381.

4. Sukenik, "Account of David's Capture of Jerusalem," 12–16; Gill, "How They Met," 30, 34–35; Bahat, *Illustrated Atlas of Jerusalem*, 24; Levine, *Jerusalem Cathedra*, 2:9.

5. Ogden and Chadwick, *Holy Land*, 211; Gill, "How They Met," 20–38, 64.

6. Mazar, *Mountain of the Lord*, 168.

7. Paul and Dever, *Biblical Archaeology*, 129.

8. Gill, "How They Met," 20–33, 64; Kleven, "Up the Waterspout," 34–35; see also Shanks, "Sprucing Up for Jerusalem's 3,000th Anniversary," 59–61.

9. Mazar, *Archaeology of the Land of the Bible*, 369. As biblical theology and prophecy clarify, the Davidic dynasty is actually eternal—in the sense that the "son of David," the Messiah, would occupy the throne of David forever (see 2 Sam. 7:16; Ps. 89:29, 36–37). Of archaeological interest is the discovery in 1993 of an inscription possibly referring to the "House of David." The inscription, from the ninth century before Christ, was found at the site of biblical Dan in northern Israel and is claimed to be the first known occurrence of the name "David" outside the Bible and thus the only extrabiblical reference to the dynasty of Israel's greatest king. See Biran, "'David' Found at Dan," 26–39; for refutation of the claim, see Davies, "'House of David' Built on Sand," 54–55. A burial cave in Givat HaMivtar in north Jerusalem discovered in 1971 features an inscription that possibly reads "of the House of David"; see further, with photo, *New Encyclopedia of Archaeological Excavations*, 2:755. See also possible mention of "House of David" in the Mesha Stela, or Moabite Stone, in Lemaire, "'House of David' Restored in Moabite Inscription," 30–37.

10. According to Franken, *Araunah* is a Hurrian word that also occurs in Hittite and refers to a ruler. Franken, "Jerusalem in the Bronze Age 3000–1000 B.C.," 34. Avi-Yonah proposed that Araunah, or Ornan, the owner of the threshing-floor, was probably the last king of Jebusite Jerusalem. See *Encyclopedia Judaica*, 9:1381; see also 2 Sam. 24:23; Levine, *Jerusalem Cathedra*, 2:10.

11. See *New Encyclopedia of Archaeological Excavations*, 2:704.

12. Mazar, *Mountain of the Lord*, 173; see also Rasmussen, *Zondervan NIV Atlas of the Bible*, 193; Ben-Dov, *In the Shadow of the Temple*, 33.

13. *Encyclopedia Judaica*, 9:1381; Payne, *Kingdoms of the Lord*, 43; Smith, *Jerusalem*, 2:37, 42–43.

14. Bahat, *Illustrated Atlas of Jerusalem*, 27; Mazar, *Archaeology of the Land of the Bible*, 374; *Anchor Bible Dictionary*, s.v. "City of David," 2:56.

15. According to the books of Kings and Chronicles, the following were buried in the City of David: David (1 Kgs. 2:10); Solomon (1 Kgs. 11:43; 2 Chron. 9:31); Rehoboam (1 Kgs. 14:31; 2 Chron. 12:16); Abijah (1 Kgs. 15:8; 2 Chron. 14:1); Asa (1 Kgs. 15:24; 2 Chron. 16:14); Jehoshaphat (1 Kgs. 22:50; 2 Chron. 21:1); Joram/Jehoram (2 Kgs. 8:24; 2 Chron. 21:20); Ahaziah (2 Kgs. 9:28; 2 Chron. 22:9); Joash (2 Kgs. 12:21; 2 Chron. 24:25); Amaziah (2 Kgs. 14:20; 2 Chron. 25:28); Uzziah/Azariah (2 Kgs. 15:7; 2 Chron. 26:23); Jotham (2 Kgs. 15:38; 2 Chron. 27:9); Ahaz (2 Kgs. 16:20; 2 Chron. 28:27); Hezekiah (2 Chron. 32:33). In the early 1900s R. Weill discovered in his excavations at the southern end of the City of David two long, horizontal, rock-cut shafts that he tentatively identified as the sepulchres of the kings. There is no conclusive chronological data to verify this identification, but neither has any better alternate site been proposed. See Shanks, "Tombs of Silwan," 38–51.

5

Jerusalem at the Time of Solomon, 960–921 B.C.

Solomon is not mentioned in extrabiblical texts; we must therefore reconstruct his history almost exclusively from the Bible. He was the second son of David and Bathsheba and was given at birth the name *Jedidiah,* meaning "beloved of Jehovah" (it includes a form of the Hebrew name *David,* meaning "beloved"; see 2 Sam. 12:24–25). He was later, and for all time, known by his throne name Solomon (Hebrew, *Shlomo*), which derives from the same root as *shalom,* meaning "peace." Solomon was catapulted to kingship at a young age with the help of some ambitious engineering on the part of his mother. He was anointed with the horn of oil from the tabernacle while David still lived to establish a peaceful transition to something previously unknown in Israelite history—a royal dynasty. Solomon was supported in his accession to the throne by Nathan the prophet, Zadok the priest, and Benaiah the leader of the royal bodyguard (see 1 Kgs. 1:38–39). At his coronation Solomon rode the king's mule, a type of the Messiah's entry into Jerusalem a millennium later (see Zech. 9:9; JST Matt. 21:2–5).

For a brief time Jerusalem was the capital of an empire. Solomon inherited the empire of his father, King David, with relations and influence from Mesopotamia to Egypt, though the actual domain was within the traditional limits of Israelite occupation, "from Dan to Beersheba" (Judg. 20:1; 1 Sam. 3:20; see Bible Map 7). During the early decades of the first millennium before Christ, Israel was dominant in international trade, controlling the two major trade routes: the Coastal Highway (Via Maris) and the inland King's Highway. Israel collected tolls and promoted commercial relations with many countries. Solomon built a fleet of ships and conducted maritime operations from his Red Sea port of Ezion-geber (otherwise called Eloth or Elath). His partners in world trade were his adventurous friends, the Phoenicians. Solomon imported horses and chariots from Cilicia in southeast Anatolia (today's Turkey) and from Egypt, gold from Ophir in East Africa, cedar and fir (cypress) wood from Lebanon, and such other goods as almug trees (sandalwood), precious stones, ivory, apes, and peacocks (1 Kgs. 5:8–10; 9:26–28; 10:11, 22). "The king made silver to be in Jerusalem as stones, and cedars made he to be as the sycomore trees that are in the vale, for abundance" (1 Kgs. 10:27). Store cities and chariot cities were created in strategic parts of the nation: "Solomon had four thousand stalls for horses and chariots, and twelve thousand horsemen; whom he bestowed in the chariot cities, and with the king at Jerusalem" (2 Chron. 9:25).

The wisdom of Solomon is legendary. Much of the book of Proverbs is attributed to him, and the biblical text indicates that he wrote three thousand proverbs and a thousand five psalms (1 Kgs. 4:32). The proverbs of Solomon are human observations and divinely inspired teachings that present universal and timeless principles for righteous living. There is no doubt that in Solomon's early years, God blessed him with great spiritual understanding. "Solomon's wisdom excelled the wisdom of all the children of the east country, and all the wisdom of Egypt. For he was wiser than all men" (1 Kgs. 4:30–31). Best known are the stories of his astute judgment regarding the parentage of a baby and the visit of the queen of Sheba to investigate the intellectual prowess and fame of Israel's king. Sheba is likely the land of Saba, or modern-day Yemen in southwestern Arabia. "The queen of the south . . . came from the uttermost parts of the earth to hear the wisdom of Solomon" (Matt. 12:42). Her reaction to Solomon's wisdom and his building projects and other accomplishments is summarized by the biblical writer:

> When the queen of Sheba had seen all Solomon's wisdom, and the house [palace] that he had built,
> And the meat of his table, and the sitting of his servants, and the attendance of his ministers, and their apparel, and his cupbearers, and his ascent by which he went up unto the house of the Lord. . . .
> And she said to the king, It was a true report that I heard in mine own land of thy acts and of thy wisdom.
> Howbeit I believed not the words, until I came, and mine eyes had seen

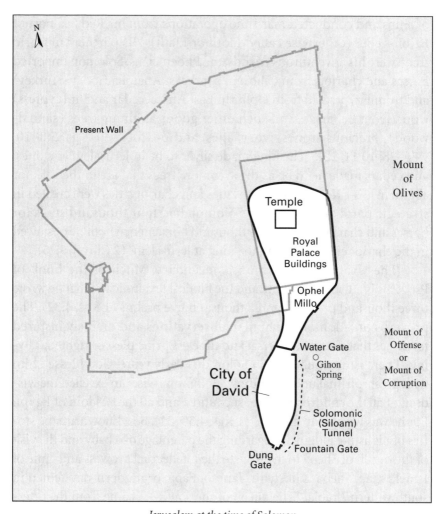

Jerusalem at the time of Solomon

it: and, behold, the half was not told me: thy wisdom and prosperity exceedeth the fame which I heard. (1 Kgs. 10:4–7)

The queen apparently had visited Jerusalem and seen "Solomon in all his glory" (Matt. 6:29).[1]

SOLOMON'S BUILDING PROJECTS

Solomon fortified important military positions in the north and along the International Highway through the Jezreel Valley and the coastal plain at Hazor, Megiddo, and Gezer (Solomonic gates have been discovered by archaeologists at the entrance to each of those cities). He reinforced Lower Beth-horon at the entrance to the most strategic route from the coast up into the hills around Jerusalem (see 1 Kgs. 9:15–17; Bible Map 8).[2]

In addition to these strongholds and emplacements for the national defense, Solomon carried out an extensive building campaign at Jerusalem. In fact, except for Herod the Great, no individual in the long history of Jerusalem has had a greater effect on its physical character than Solomon. He intentionally strengthened Jerusalem's position as the spiritual, political, and economic center of Israel. He constructed the Temple over a period of seven years. Immediately south of the House of the Lord, for thirteen years he built the complex of the house of the king, including the "house of the forest of Lebanon." This largest of all the palatial buildings was a hypostyle hall with forty-five cedarwood columns. He also built the porch, or hall of pillars; the throne hall of judgment, the main ceremonial hall furnished with a great ivory throne with gold overlay and surrounded by lions; and a house for Pharaoh's daughter, his principal wife. All of these structures were made of costly hewn stones and cedarwood (see 1 Kgs. 7:1–11) and were probably in the large area south of the summit of Moriah where the Temple stood, where the Muslim fountain known as El Kas and the Al-Aqsa Mosque presently stand and beyond them southward to meet the old wall and fortifications of the City of David. Nothing is left today of any of Solomon's buildings in Jerusalem; the site was totally reworked by King Herod.

Solomon repaired the Millo and built the wall of Jerusalem. Some researchers believe that he enclosed at least part of the Western Hill, which was the only direction in which the city could expand.[3] He also extended the usefulness of the Gihon Spring with an aqueduct carrying water into the Kidron Valley and to a collection pool at the southern end of the city; this aqueduct is usually called the Siloam (or Shiloah) Channel.[4] The name *Siloam* derives from the Hebrew verb *shalah*, which means "to send" (cf. John 9:7). Its course runs below the city wall on the lower, eastern slope of the City of David. It is partly a stone-covered canal and partly a tunnel carved through the stone of the hill slope. At intervals were placed floodgates to allow water to flow into the valley for irrigation.[5]

GOVERNMENT AND TAXATION

Solomon levied heavy taxes on his foreign territories and on his own people to finance his fortifications and building projects (see 1 Kgs. 9:15). He appointed officers over twelve administrative districts outside Judah to oversee collection of his taxes (see Bible Map 8). Each district was required to provide supplies for the royal court one month each year.[6] The daily ration was 330 bushels of fine flour; 660 bushels of meal; ten fat oxen and one hundred sheep, as well as gazelles, roebucks, harts, fowl, barley, straw, and so forth. Some have estimated that supply would have been sufficient for thirty-five thousand people—wives, officials, servants, soldiers, and others, even outside Jerusalem, for Jerusalem itself did not have that many people in those days. Furthermore, the annual payment to Hiram of Tyre for Solomon's building projects amounted to 220,000 bushels of wheat and 180,000 gallons of olive oil. These demands on the agricultural economy of his nation would have been incredibly high.[7]

Solomon set up his twelve administrative districts to differ from the old tribal boundaries in order to weaken former loyalties and strengthen allegiance to his central government in Jerusalem. Judah's exemption from imposts and taxes must have been a source of irritation and resentment to the rest of Israel. During the very next generation the northern tribes rebelled against the unfair economic policies and conspicuous favoritism of the king. Solomon's name does mean "peace," but the scriptural record hints that all was not peaceful during his reign.

Besides the excessive taxation, Solomon raised a *corvee,* or a conscription, of tens of thousands of Israelite men. Sufficient slaves were not available, and the king did not want to deplete the national treasury, so he required male citizens to devote part of their time to cut cedars in Lebanon, float them by rafts to Jerusalem's port at Jaffa, haul them up by wagon to the capital, and build the Temple, the palace complex, and other projects.

MARRIAGES AND SUBSEQUENT APOSTASY

As part of his foreign policy, and probably accompanying some peace treaties, Solomon contracted marriages to the daughters of many royal families. The decision to ally himself politically and familially with Egypt's pharaoh was unwise: "The Lord was not pleased with Solomon, for he made affinity with Pharaoh, king of Egypt, and took Pharaoh's daughter to wife,[8] and brought her into the house of David" (JST 1 Kgs. 3:1). The biblical historian recorded:

> King Solomon loved many strange [foreign] women, together with the daughter of Pharaoh, women of the Moabites, Ammonites, Edomites, Zidonians, and Hittites;
>
> Of the nations concerning which the Lord said unto the children of Israel, Ye shall not go in to them, neither shall they come in unto you: for surely they will turn away your heart after their gods: Solomon clave unto these in love.
>
> And he had seven hundred wives, princesses, and three hundred concubines: and his wives turned away his heart. (1 Kgs. 11:1–3)

The warning voice had been raised centuries before by Moses:

> When the Lord thy God shall bring thee into the land whither thou goest to possess it, and hath cast out many nations before thee, the Hittites, and the Girgashites, and the Amorites, and the Canaanites, and the Perizzites, and the Hivites, and the Jebusites . . . ;
>
> And when the Lord thy God shall deliver them before thee; thou shalt smite them, and utterly destroy them; thou shalt make no covenant with them, nor shew mercy unto them:
>
> Neither shalt thou make marriages with them; thy daughter thou shalt not give unto his son, nor his daughter shalt thou take unto thy son.
>
> For they will turn away thy son from following me, that they may serve other gods: so will the anger of the Lord be kindled against you and destroy thee suddenly. (Deut. 7:1–4)

The Lord knew that the Israelites would eventually clamor for a king "like as all the nations," and he gave an itemized list of what the future king should and should not do:

> When thou art come unto the land which the Lord thy God giveth thee, and shalt possess it, and shalt dwell therein, and shalt say, I will set a king over me, like as all the nations that are about me; . . .

But he shall not multiply horses to himself, . . .

Neither shall he multiply wives to himself, that his heart turn not away: neither shall he greatly multiply to himself silver and gold.

And it shall be, when he sitteth upon the throne of his kingdom, that he shall write him a copy of this law in a book . . .

. . . and he shall read therein all the days of his life. (Deut. 17:14–19; emphasis added.)

God knew Solomon, and He knew the children of Israel; the warning voice, in poignant foreshadowing, had been raised by the Lord to the king and to his people:

If ye shall at all turn from following me, ye or your children, and will not keep my commandments and my statutes which I have set before you, but go and serve other gods, and worship them:

Then will I cut off Israel out of the land which I have given them; and this house, which I have hallowed for my name, will I cast out of my sight; and Israel shall be a proverb and a byword among all people:

And at this house . . . every one that passeth by it shall be astonished, and shall hiss; and they shall say, Why hath the Lord done thus unto this land, and to this house?

And they shall answer, Because they forsook the Lord their God. (1 Kgs. 9:6–9)

Solomon's numerous marriages to foreign women—thereby creating a harem next to the holiest place in the kingdom—led to moral and religious excesses,[9] even to the construction of pagan shrines on the hill east of the City of David:

Then did Solomon build an high place for Chemosh, the abomination of Moab, in the hill that is before Jerusalem, and for Molech, the abomination of the children of Ammon. And likewise did he for all his strange wives, which burnt incense and sacrificed unto their gods. And the Lord was angry with Solomon, because his heart was turned from the Lord God of Israel, which had appeared unto him twice. (1 Kgs. 11:7–9).

How Solomon could erect the glorious Temple and dedicate it to the exclusive worship of Jehovah but then countenance and even contribute to the fabrication of shrines to idol gods seems impossible to understand. But it leads us to wonder about the wisdom of Solomon. Because of the king's apostate indulgences, the hilltop east of Jerusalem came to be known as the Mount of Offense (or Scandal) or "the mount of corruption" (2 Kgs. 23:13). King David drove out the Canaanites and their gods; King Solomon brought them back in.

Solomon is a most enigmatic figure. He was at once a wise and spiritually minded king, priest, almost a prophet, and yet he was a ruler of questionable wisdom. He purged his opponents (both early and late in his rule), he and his court lived luxuriously, even profligately, at the expense of his subjects, he craved political security through nuptial alliances, and—most serious of all—he went a-whoring after other gods. Despite the magnificence of his capital and the majesty and renown of his kingdom, and though Solomon was a legend in his own day, his name and the historical reports of his reign suggesting peace, yet all was not well in Solomon's kingdom.

One thing, however, definitely was well, a happy result of the mixture of Solomon's early spiritual and temporal effort. The House of the Lord, the Temple of God, that Solomon built shone for four centuries from the high point of Zion, a symbol to which all Israel could look for light and to which, even through tumultuous days of political intrigue and religious abandon, Israel's God could come and reveal his will to his prophets.

A HOUSE OF THE LORD

Other sanctuaries and holy places were apparently approved by the Lord and in use during the Israelite period,[10] but the Temple at Jerusalem was to be the spiritual focal point and center of worship for God's people. The statement of the Samaritan woman at Jacob's Well centuries later is instructive: "Ye say, that in Jerusalem is the place where men ought to worship" (John 4:20). In his reply, Jesus noted that "salvation is of the Jews" (v. 22). The Hebrew word meaning "salvation" is *yeshua*, which is the same as the English name *Jesus*. Certainly Jesus, who is the salvation of all people, did come of the Jews. But the context suggests that "Jerusalem [was] the place where men ought to worship" because the Temple was located there; that is where worshippers could sacrifice to God and participate in sacred ordinances and learn of him. The Prophet Joseph Smith explained that the main object of gathering the people of God in any age of the world was "to build unto the Lord a house whereby He could reveal unto His people the ordinances of His house and the

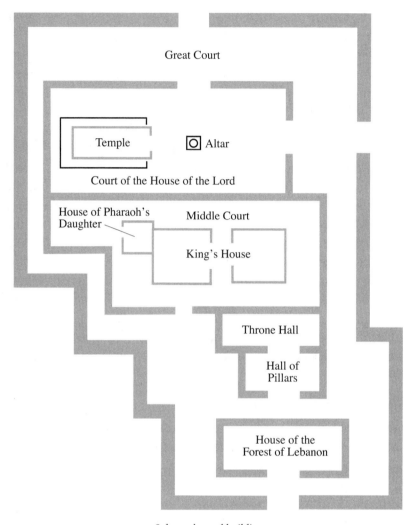

Solomon's royal buildings

glories of His kingdom, and teach the people *the way of salvation;* for there are certain ordinances and principles that, when they are taught and practiced, must be done in a place or house built for that purpose."[11]

As we have seen, the northern end of the eastern hill of Jerusalem, the mount called Moriah, was already a sacred site a thousand years before Solomon, and when the Israelites finally entered the land promised to their fathers, it was again the place where God chose to "put his name" (Deut. 12:5; 1 Kgs. 11:36; 14:21; 2 Kgs. 21:7). Jerusalem would become not "the holy city" (Neh. 11:1; Isa. 48:2; 52:1) but, as the Hebrew words *Ir Hakodesh* are translated literally, "the city of holiness."[12] Jerusalem became the city of the sanctuary—the Temple—earning the distinctively holy title of "Temple City."

LOCATION AND DESCRIPTION OF THE TEMPLE[13]

"The location of the Temple Mount in Jerusalem, and thus of the place where the three successive temples were built in biblical antiquity, has never been in doubt," wrote Carol Myers in the prestigious *Anchor Bible Dictionary*. "The site is that of the Muslim shrine known as the Dome of the Rock (Qubbet es-Sakhra). . . . This spot is presumed to be very close to the site of the three ancient temples, if not above the actual place where the innermost sanctum (holy of holies) of the temples once stood."[14]

Solomon's Temple was built on Mount Moriah at the site of Abraham's and David's altars.[15] "Then Solomon began to build the house of the Lord at Jerusalem in mount Moriah, where the Lord appeared unto David his father, in the place that David had prepared in the thresh-ingfloor of Ornan [Araunah] the Jebusite" (2 Chron. 3:1). George Adam Smith explained that the rock mass (es-Sakhra) under the Dome of the Rock must have been part of the great altar of sacrifice in front (to the east) of Solomon's Temple:

> Here, it is generally agreed, lay the site which he chose for the Temple, the threshing-floor of Araunah on which David had erected an altar. For here in the time of the Maccabees we find the Second Temple, and there can be no doubt that this occupied the site of Solomon's, nor that the Mosque of Omar [a misnomer for the Dome of the Rock] with its imme-diate platform occupies much the same site to-day: the Mount Sion of several Old Testament writers, the 'Mount Moriah' of the Chronicler. Round es-Sakhra, which is the summit of this part of the East Hill, the rock has been frequently levelled and scarped, but the present contours ascertained by the Ordnance Survey are sufficient evidence that there was upon it ample room for Araunah's threshing-floor. . . . Moreover, the Rock es-Sakhra, now under the dome of the Mosque of Omar, is venerated by Mohammedans as second only to the shrine of Mecca. From the tenacity with which such sites in the East preserve their character, we may infer

Model of Solomon's Temple

that in ancient times also the Rock was holy; and Professor Stade points out that . . . it is probable that the appearance of the angel to David by the threshing-floor, *between earth and heaven,* was believed to have taken place on this very summit. Moreover, the Rock itself bears proofs of having been used as an altar. A channel penetrates from the surface to a little cave below, whence a conduit descends through the body of the Hill; obviously designed to carry off either the blood or the refuse of sacrifices. Similar arrangements are seen on other Semitic altars. From all these data the conclusion is reasonable that the Rock, es-Sakhra, represents the Altar of Burnt-offering. . . . Solomon, at least at first, simply used the bare Rock es-Sakhra for his sacrifices. . . . The Rock es-Sakhra became the national altar, the court around it the national auditorium.[16]

Also in the court to the east of the Temple proper were ten mobile basins ("lavers" or wash-basins), five on each side. They were decorated with floral and faunal motifs and used for ritual cleansing of offerings. First Kings 7 gives details of other appurtenances of the Temple, such as basins, pots, bowls, shovels, snuffers, tongs, censers, and spoons. The

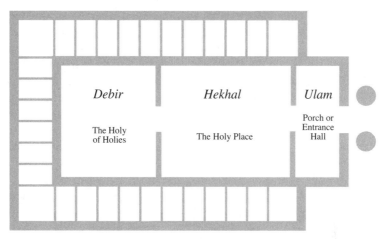

Diagram of Solomon's Temple

"molten sea," a huge bronze basin at least fifteen feet in diameter, was supported by twelve large bulls or oxen, representing the twelve tribes of Israel, each three facing one of the four cardinal points of the compass.[17] The bronze basin or font has been calculated to have a possible capacity of sixteen thousand gallons. Temples of other religions customarily had such basins for the storage of water for ceremonial ablutions. No record of baptisms or ritual immersions in this basin has been found, though we recall that the Book of Moses and the Joseph Smith Translation of the Bible mention baptism from Adam's time to that of Enoch. Joseph Smith's translation of Genesis 17 records that proper baptism had ceased among the apostate peoples at Abraham's time, and no further mention of it is made. Christians in general, and Latter-day Saints in particular, have wondered about the likelihood of baptism in Solomon's Temple. Various forms of washing of the outward body to symbolize inner, spiritual cleansing were common. The tractate of the Mishnah, which gives specifications for the ceremonies of Yom Kippur (Day of Atonement), indicates that the priest officiating in the slaughter of the sacrificial animal was repeatedly "baptized" (the Hebrew word used means "immersed") and clean garments were placed upon him after each immersion, before each successive step in offering the sacrifice. Doctrine and Covenants 124:36–39 allows for baptism of living persons in the ancient Temple. Elder Bruce R. McConkie explained:

It must be remembered that all direct and plain references to baptism have been deleted from the Old Testament (1 Ne. 13) and that the word *baptize* is of Greek origin. Some equivalent word, such as *wash,* would have been used by the Hebrew peoples. In describing the molten sea the Old Testament record says, *"The sea was for the priests to wash in."* (2 Chron. 4:2–6.) This is tantamount to saying that the priests performed baptisms in it.

In this temple building dispensation the Brethren have been led by the spirit of inspiration to pattern the baptismal fonts placed in temples after the one in Solomon's Temple.[18]

The Temple itself, usually called the *Hekhal* (otherwise meaning "palace," "large building") and *Bet YHWH* or *Bet Elohim* ("the House of Jehovah" or "the House of God"), was built with the Lord's specifications but also using Phoenician artisans, especially Hiram of Tyre and his expert and experienced craftsmen, carpenters, and masons (see 1 Kgs. 5, 7). It was double the size of the former Tabernacle in all its dimensions but still not large, only sixty cubits long by twenty wide by thirty high (using the standard eighteen inches to the cubit, 90 feet long by 30 wide by 45 high; compare the Salt Lake Temple, which measures 186 by 118 by 210 feet).

The Temple faced east and was a tripartite structure, built in three stages leading to the inner sanctuary: the porch or entrance hall (*ulam*), the Sanctuary or Holy Place (*hekhal*), and the Holy of Holies or Most Holy Place (*debir*). At the east entrance stood two ornately decorated thirty-seven-foot-high bronze columns, apparently symbolic in nature[19] but nonfunctional, named *Jachin* and *Boaz,* "He [God] shall establish" and "In him [God] is strength." Above and to the sides of the two holy rooms were three stories of side chambers with approximately thirty rooms on each level. These rooms were utilitarian in nature, storing clothing and other items for Temple service. Inside the Holy Place were ten lampstands (*menorot*), five on the north side and five on the south side, which gave light to the room. Other appurtenances included the Table of Shewbread (pronounced *Showbread*), the bread of the Presence, which was eaten by the priests, and the altar of incense. Inside the Holy of Holies, a room cube in shape and completely panelled with cedar and cypress wood covered with gold, with no stone visible (see 1 Kgs. 6:18), sat one object only: the sacred Ark of the Covenant, which had been regarded by Israel for centuries, along with the tablets of the Law (by now the only item in the Ark; see 1 Kgs. 8:9), as their most holy symbol. The Ark with its Mercy Seat was covered with solid gold and sat beneath two large olivewood cherubim, also overlaid with gold, each measuring fifteen feet high and with a fifteen-foot wingspan (see 1 Kgs. 6).[20]

When the Temple construction was completed, the appointed priests and Levites brought the Ark and the old Tabernacle[21] and all its vessels (see 1 Kgs. 8:4) to the sacred precincts with solemn pageantry, and King Solomon proceeded with tens of thousands of sacrifices and dedication services and a week-long feast and celebration.

Solomon's Dedicatory Prayer, on which many dedicatory prayers have since been patterned, is recorded in 1 Kings 8:22–53. The king knelt down before the great altar, and acting as king and priest (recall Melchizedek as king and priest), with hands spread up to heaven, he pled with the Lord to hear the prayers and forgive the obedient who "pray toward this place" (vs. 30, 35, 42, 44, 48). He expressed supplication for the Lord's eyes to always be on his House, the place where he chose to put his Name. Solomon entreated the Lord that if famine came, or pestilence, or plague, or enemies, and the people repented, that He would forgive and help them. The Dedicatory Prayer included also a foreshadowing of Israel's apostasy and exile and return again to their land of promise (vv. 33–34, 46–49).

At the dedication of the Temple fire came down from heaven to consume the sacrifices (see 2 Chron. 7:1) and the holy cloud filled the house of the Lord (see 1 Kgs. 8:10–11); the glory of the Lord was again manifest at Jerusalem. "The Lord appeared to Solomon the second time . . . [and] said unto him, I have heard thy prayer and thy supplication, that thou hast made before me: I have hallowed this house, which thou hast built, to put my name there for ever; and mine eyes and mine heart shall be there perpetually" (1 Kgs. 9:2–3). The word of the Lord in Kirtland, Ohio, in the nineteenth century after Christ is reminiscent of the similar occasion in the tenth century before Christ:

> For behold, I have accepted this house, and my name shall be here; and I will manifest myself to my people in mercy in this house.
>
> Yea, I will appear unto my servants, and speak unto them with mine own voice, if my people will keep my commandments, and do not pollute this holy house.

Yea the hearts of thousands and tens of thousands shall greatly rejoice in consequence of the blessings which shall be poured out....

And the fame of this house shall spread to foreign lands; and this is the beginning of the blessing which shall be poured out upon the heads of my people. (D&C 110:7–10)

ORDINANCE WORK IN SOLOMON'S TEMPLE

Neither ancient texts nor modern revelations give us much detail about what kinds of ordinances were performed in the first Israelite Temple in Jerusalem (which is understandable; such sacred ordinance work is not published to the world[22]). One of our few explanations is recorded in D&C 124:37–39.

How shall your washings be acceptable unto me, except ye perform them in a house which you have built to my name?

For, for this cause I commanded Moses that he should build a tabernacle, that they should bear it with them in the wilderness, and to build a house in the land of promise, that those ordinances might be revealed which had been hid from before the world was.

Therefore, verily I say unto you, that your anointings, and your washings, and your baptisms for the dead, and your solemn assemblies, and your memorials for your sacrifices by the sons of Levi, and for your oracles in your most holy places wherein you receive conversations, and your statutes and judgments, for the beginning of the revelations and foundation of Zion, and for the glory, honor, and endowment of all her municipals, are ordained by the ordinance of my holy house, which my people are always commanded to build unto my holy name.

Washings and anointings had been performed from the early days of Israel, in the Tabernacle in Sinai (see Ex. 29:4, 7; 40:12–13), and must have continued in the Temple at Jerusalem. Baptisms for the dead would not have been performed in Old Testament-period Temples, of course, because ordinance work for the dead was initiated by the Savior in the Spirit World following his crucifixion.[23] Solemn assemblies were called in the ancient sanctuaries (see Lev. 23:36; Deut. 16:8; 2 Chron. 7:9), and we have hundreds of verses describing sacrifices executed by the sons of Levi. Was there an ancient parallel to "oracles in your most holy places wherein you receive conversations"? Was there a type of endowment available to righteous Israelites? Were there equivalent statutes and judgments for the "foundation of Zion" in first millennium B.C. Jerusalem? Moses had received the oracles and the Torah (Hebrew, "instruction") from the Lord, and Moses set up the ceremonies and ordinances for the Tabernacle of the Congregation, at least some of which may have been carried on in the Temple at Jerusalem. Modern Temples focus on the Creation of the earth, the creation of man and woman, and the Fall and Redemption. Could the ancient House of the Lord, for example, have included conversations and recitations of the material in the first chapters of Genesis, which are preserved for us in dignified brevity?[24] Certainly the Gospel was taught from the beginning (see Moses 5:58–59), and the law of sacrifice was practiced (see Moses 5:5–8). The Saints of God have always been taught to live chaste lives, and the faithful have always longed to live the law of consecration, which Melchizedek and his people had done in Salem.

Most ordinances of the Temple require the use of the Melchizedek Priesthood, and this higher priesthood had been withdrawn from Israel (see JST Ex. 34:1 and D&C 84:23–25). The prophets of God through the Old Testament period held the Melchizedek Priesthood,[25] but the Israelites in general lived without it. "This greater priesthood administereth the gospel and holdeth the key of the mysteries of the kingdom, even the key of the knowledge of God" (D&C 84:19). "The power and authority of the higher, or Melchizedek Priesthood, is to hold the keys of all the spiritual blessings of the church—to have the privilege of receiving the mysteries of the kingdom of heaven" (D&C 107:18–19). Ancient Israel must therefore have been limited in what they received in the holy place.[26] For what they did receive, by way of spiritual growth in worship and learning, they rejoiced and praised the Lord.

REJOICING IN THE HOUSE OF THE LORD

The book of Psalms was compiled over several centuries, beginning in the days of David and Solomon. The Hebrew title is *Tehillin*, meaning "praises." Many of the psalms are praises; all are songs. This is ancient Israel's hymnbook. It is the Old Testament book most quoted in the New Testament. Jesus referred to the Psalms more often than any other Old Testament book. The Psalms were mostly written, as far as we know, in the Holy City of Jerusalem. Therefore, some of the world's greatest literature, some of the most exalted outpourings of praise and sensitive expressions of devotion came out of the Temple City of the God of Israel.

Following are excerpts from the Psalms which preserve the feelings of kings and priests and saints about the dwelling-place of God on earth, the House of the Lord. (Incidentally, any statement about the House of the Lord in David's lifetime, before Solomon built the Temple on Moriah, refers either to the Tabernacle which was still standing at Gibeon [see 2 Chron. 1:3] or to the tent where the Ark was housed in the City of David [2 Chron. 1:4.]) The Psalms were meant to be sung, or at least to be recited aloud. As a conclusion to our study of Jerusalem in the days of Solomon, read the following verses from the Psalms—out loud—in a quiet place, and with a spirit of reverent praise:

> In Judah is God known: his name is great in Israel.
> In Salem also is his tabernacle, and his dwelling place in Zion. (Ps. 76:1–2)

> Who shall ascend into the hill of the Lord? or who shall stand in his holy place?
> He that hath clean hands, and a pure heart; who hath not lifted up his soul unto vanity, nor sworn deceitfully. (Ps. 24:3–4)

> I will wash mine hands in innocency: so will I compass thine altar, O Lord:
> That I may publish with the voice of thanksgiving, and tell of all thy wondrous works.
> Lord, I have loved the habitation of thy house, and the place where thine honour dwelleth. (Ps. 26:6–8)

> One thing have I desired of the Lord, that will I seek after; that I may dwell in the house of the Lord all the days of my life, to behold the beauty of the Lord, and to enquire in his temple. (Ps. 27:4)

> We took sweet counsel together, and walked unto the house of God in company. (Ps. 55:14)

> O God, thou art my God; early will I seek thee: my soul thirsteth for thee, my flesh longeth for thee in a dry and thirsty land, where no water is;
> To see thy power and thy glory, so as I have seen thee in the sanctuary.
> Because thy lovingkindness is better than life, my lips shall praise thee.

Thus will I bless thee while I live: I will lift up my hands in thy name. (Ps. 63:1–4)

Blessed is the man whom thou choosest, and causest to approach unto thee, that he may dwell in thy courts: we shall be satisfied with the goodness of thy house, even of thy holy temple. (Ps. 65:4)

My soul longeth, yea, even fainteth for the courts of the Lord: my heart and my flesh crieth out for the living God.
For a day in thy courts is better than a thousand [elsewhere].
I had rather be a doorkeeper in the house of my God, than to dwell in the tents of wickedness. (Ps. 84:2, 10)

Psalms 120 through 134 are called "Songs of Degrees" or "Songs of Ascent," and they were apparently sung while ascending the Temple steps to the Holy Place. There are fifteen of them, the same as the number of steps leading to the inner court, at least in the Second Temple. Psalm 122 expresses deep-felt praise and gratitude for the Holy City of Jerusalem and for the House of the Lord.

I was glad when they said unto me, Let us go into the house of the Lord.
Our feet shall stand within thy gates, O Jerusalem.
Jerusalem is builded as a city that is compact together:
Whither the tribes go up, the tribes of the Lord, unto the testimony of Israel, to give thanks unto the name of the Lord.
For there are set thrones of judgment, the thrones of the house of David.
Pray for the peace of Jerusalem: they shall prosper that love thee.
Peace be within thy walls, and prosperity within thy palaces.
For my brethren and companions' sakes, I will now say, Peace be within thee.
Because of the house of the Lord our God I will seek thy good.

Notes

1. The writer of 1 Kings 10 remarks that "Solomon gave unto the queen of Sheba all her desire, whatsoever she asked" (v. 13)—even a son, according to some traditions. Ethiopians claim that the land of Sheba is really their ancient land of Ethiopia and that for centuries their rulers have been direct descendants of a child born of the Queen of Sheba and Solomon. It was written in the 1955 constitution of Ethiopia that the royal line "descends without interruption from the dynasty of Menelik I, son of the Queen of

Ethiopia, the queen of Sheba, and King Solomon of Jerusalem." It should be noted, however, that there is no positive evidence to support such a tradition.

2. See also Aharoni and Avi-Yonah, *Macmillan Bible Atlas,* Map 112.

3. See Paton, *Jerusalem in Bible Times,* 89–101. Compare Aharoni and Avi-Yonah, *Macmillan Bible Atlas,* Map 114.

4. Gill, "How They Met," 22–23.

5. The Siloam Channel is mentioned three times in the writings of Isaiah. The first is a poetic allusion to the "waters of Shiloah that go softly" (Isa. 8:6). The other two, found in Isaiah 7:3 and 36:2, are geographic references to "the conduit of the upper pool in the highway of the fuller's field" (see also 2 Kgs. 18:17). The "conduit" is the old Siloam Channel; the "upper pool" refers to the Gihon Spring and its small collection pool, from which the Siloam Channel drew; and the "highway of the fuller's field" refers to the Kidron Valley. Ogden and Chadwick, *Holy Land,* 212.

6. In 1 Kings 4:7–19 is a list of the twelve districts with their procurement officers. One of the twelve officials, the one over Mount Ephraim, was named Ben-Hur, and two others were the king's sons-in-law.

7. Rasmussen and Ogden, *Old Testament,* 333.

8. This princess may have been the daughter of Pharaoh Siamun (or Tiamun) of the twenty-first dynasty, who reigned at Tanis in Egypt's Delta.

9. Read from the Book of Mormon on the excesses involved: Jacob 1:15 and 2:23–24; cf. also D&C 132:1, 38. Some wives of David and Solomon were given to them by the Lord through the prophet Nathan, but Doctrine and Covenants 132:38 clearly suggests that some were *not* given to them by the Lord. The plurality of wives per se was not the issue and was not abominable; rather, it was the kings' abuse of the law that was abominable. See Deut. 7:1–4.

10. For example, Gideon's shrine in the eastern Jezreel Valley (Judg. 6:24–26); Solomon's high place at Gibeon (1 Kgs. 3:2–5); and Elijah's altar on Mount Carmel (1 Kgs. 18:30; cf. Judg. 19:18). The only Israelite temple ever found in archaeological excavations was uncovered at Arad in the Negev. This temple has a strikingly similar layout to and was contemporary with Solomon's Temple in Jerusalem. See Aharoni, "Arad," 18–27; *New Encyclopedia of Archaeological Excavations,* 1:83.

11. Smith, *Teachings of the Prophet Joseph Smith,* 308; emphasis added.

12. Many centuries before David and Solomon, the great general and prophet Enoch had "built a city that was called the City of Holiness, even Zion," two of the same names later used by these kings. See Moses 7:18–19.

13. Josephus describes Solomon's Temple in *Antiquities* 8.3.

14. *Anchor Bible Dictionary,* 6:354, s.v. "Jerusalem Temple." See also *New Encyclopedia of Archaeological Excavations,* 2:736. It has long been assumed that the ancient Israelite Temples were located where the Dome of the Rock has stood for thirteen centuries, although there is at present no way to verify the assumption archaeologically. Professor Asher Kaufmann concluded from his years of research that the two Temples actually stood about one hundred meters north of the site of the Dome of the Rock. See Kaufmann, "Where the Ancient Temple of Jerusalem Stood," 40–59. Dr. Leen Ritmeyer, on the other hand, has convincingly argued that the traditional location must still be regarded as the site of the Temples. See Ritmeyer, "Locating the Original Temple Mount," 24–45, 64–65; *New Encyclopedia of Archaeological Excavations,* 2:743.

15. Ben-Dov, *Shadow of the Temple*, 33; Simons, *Jerusalem in the Old Testament*, 382–83. See also Chap. 3, n. 9.

16. Smith, *Jerusalem*, 2:58–59, 60, 64, 67. Smith notes the dimensions of es-Sakhra as 17.7 by 15.5 meters and 1.25 to 2 meters above ground level, or, according to another researcher he cites, about fifty-eight feet by fifty-one, and from four to six feet high—all of which dimensions, Smith concludes, are too great for it to have stood in the Holy of Holies (61, fn. 1). Eminent professor/archaeologists G. Ernest Wright and Floyd Vivian Filson concurred that the Rock was the spot for the altar of burnt offering; see *Westminster Historical Atlas to the Bible*, 105; see also Kenyon, *Jerusalem*, 58; Yadin, *Jerusalem Revealed*, 13; Amiran et al., *Urban Geography*, 16; Avi-Yonah, *Sefer Yerushalayim*, 187; Reznik, *Holy Temple Revisited*, 113, 158; Mare, *Archaeology of the Jerusalem Area*, 22; Finegan, *Archeology of the New Testament*, 192, 196.

17. Mazar, *Archaeology of the Land of the Bible*, 377; Kenyon, *Jerusalem*.

18. McConkie, *Mormon Doctrine*, 104.

19. In Madsen, *Temple in Antiquity*, 135–50. Some have wondered if the highly decorated pillars perpetuate the familiar tree of life motif.

20. An interesting comment on the elaborate adornment of Solomon's Temple is recorded in Nephi's description of his own Temple, the first Nephite Temple: "I, Nephi, did build a temple; and I did construct it after the manner of the temple of Solomon save it were not built of so many precious things; for they were not to be found upon the land, wherefore, it could not be built like unto Solomon's temple. But the manner of the construction was like unto the temple of Solomon; and the workmanship thereof was exceedingly fine" (2 Ne. 5:16).

21. According to Sotah 9a in the Talmud, the Tabernacle was dismantled and placed under Solomon's Temple. See *Talmud of Babylonia*, trans. Neusner, 72–74.

22. "The detailed history of the performance of the saving ordinances of the gospel as practised in ancient times was never recorded in any detail, because such ordinances are sacred and not for the world." Smith, "Was Temple Work Done in the Days of the Old Prophets?" 794. Joseph Smith's journal entry for 4 May 1842 records that he was "instructing them in the principles and order of the Priesthood, attending to washings, anointings, endowments, . . . [and] setting forth the order pertaining to the Ancient of Days [Adam], and all those plans and principles by which any one is enabled to secure the fullness of those blessings which have been prepared for the Church of the First Born, and come up and abide in the presence of the Eloheim in the eternal worlds. *In this council was instituted the ancient order of things for the first time in these last days." History of the Church*, 5:2; emphasis added.

23. See D&C 138. "Before the resurrection of our Lord, ordinance work for the dead could not be carried out either in the temples in Palestine or on [the American] continent. . . . Following the Savior's resurrection, ordinance work for the dead must have been carried on in sacred structures erected in the Mediterranean world." Sperry, "Ancient Temples," 827.

24. Hugh Nibley states: "The rites of the Temple are always a repetition of those that marked its founding in the beginning of the world. . . . After a life-time of study Lord Raglan assures us that when we study all the rituals of the world we come up with the discovery that the pristine and original ritual of them all, from which all others take their rise, was the *dramatization of the creation of the world*. And Mowinckel sums up the common cult pattern of all the earliest civilizations: 'It is the creation of the World that is being

repeated.'" In Madsen, *Temple in Antiquity,* 25–26; emphasis added. See also Parry, *Temples of the Ancient World,* 118–25.

25. "All the prophets had the Melchizedek Priesthood and were ordained by God himself." Smith, *Teachings of the Prophet Joseph Smith,* 181.

26. "As long as prophets . . . were around, a full endowment could be given the righteous; otherwise a limited endowment within the Aaronic Priesthood would probably be administered." Sperry, "Ancient Temples," 826.

6

JERUSALEM IN THE DAYS OF THE DIVIDED KINGDOM, 921–721 B.C.

When the northern tribes of Israel learned that Rehoboam intended to increase the oppressive taxation and conscripted labor of his father, Solomon,[1] they declared themselves independent from the Judah-based monarchy.[2] Things might have proceeded differently had the Israelites understood the wisdom in a principle later taught by Jesus: "Every kingdom divided against itself is brought to desolation; and every city or house divided against itself shall not stand" (Matt. 12:25). Notwithstanding the justifications for partitioning the kingdom, the division of Israel was clearly effected under the direction of the Lord himself; Israel's God has always been directly involved in the destiny of his people: "Behold, I will rend the kingdom out of the hand of Solomon, and will give ten tribes to thee[Jeroboam]: (But he shall have one tribe for my servant David's sake, and for Jerusalem's sake, the city which I have chosen out of all the tribes of Israel:) But I will take the kingdom out of his son's hand, and will give it unto thee, even ten tribes" (1 Kgs. 11:31–32, 35).

The northern tribes called on Jeroboam, one of Solomon's former officers in charge of the royal services in the tribes of Joseph (Ephraim and Manasseh), to lead them. Jeroboam had been promised kingship over ten of the Israelite tribes by a prophet from Shiloh (see 1 Kgs. 11:28–40), and because Solomon had sought to kill him, he had fled to Egypt and remained there under the protection of Shishak, king of Egypt, until Solomon died.

The northern tribes declared independence at Shechem. Jeroboam built his capital there, along with a Transjordanian center at Penuel (see

Bible Map 9). He soon rearranged the religious priorities of the kingdom as well. While in Egypt, Jeroboam had seen the apis bull used in Egyptians' cultic practices, and he attempted to secure the loyalty of his Israelite subjects by instituting this perversion of the true religion. To divert religious traffic from Jerusalem, the rival capital, he built shrines at Dan and Bethel, on the northern and southern frontiers of his new kingdom of Israel. His imitation of true religion included "two calves of gold" and a non-Levitical priesthood and sacrifices and holy days (see 1 Kgs. 12:26–33). These aberrations were known for centuries thereafter in the writings of historians and prophets as "the sin of Jeroboam."

Our present biblical text (1 Kgs. 12:20) indicates that only the tribe of Judah followed the house of David, but the Septuagint, the Greek Old Testament, includes Benjamin in the southern kingdom (see footnote *b* to 1 Kgs. 12:20; cf. 2 Chron. 11:12; 15:9). The tribe of Simeon had also been assimilated into Judah by this time (see Bible Map 9), and Levites and others from the various northern tribes had fled the apostate corruptions in the north, seeking spiritual refuge in Jerusalem. "The priests and the Levites that were in all Israel resorted to [Rehoboam]. . . . For the Levites left their suburbs and their possession, and came to Judah and Jerusalem: for Jeroboam and his sons had cast them off from executing the priest's office unto the Lord. . . . And after them out of all the tribes of Israel such as set their hearts to seek the Lord God of Israel came to Jerusalem" (2 Chron. 11:13–16). That may explain why Lehi and his relatives from the tribes of Joseph were later living at Jerusalem (see also 1 Chron. 9:3; 2 Chron. 15:9–10).

The southern kingdom of Judah, however, was not without its own apostate practices. "They also built them high places, and images, and groves, on every high hill, and under every green tree. And there were also sodomites in the land: and they did according to all the abominations of the nations which the Lord cast out before the children of Israel" (1 Kgs. 14:23–24). The Israelites' abandonment and provocation of Jehovah had immediate and dire consequences for both kingdoms.

INVASION OF PHARAOH SHISHAK

Not long after the division of the Israelite kingdom in the later part of the tenth century before Christ, the Libyan-Egyptian pharaoh

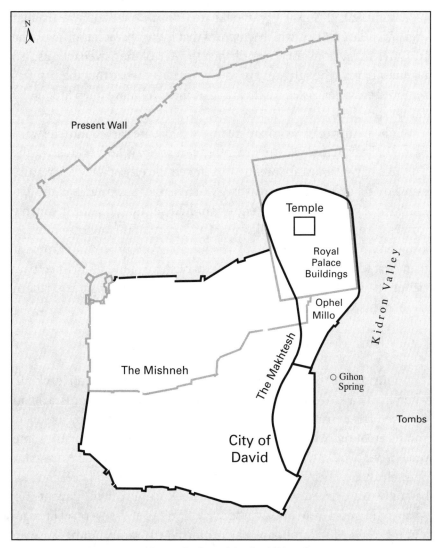

Jerusalem in the days of the divided kingdom

Shishak[3] invaded Canaan with twelve hundred chariots, sixty thousand cavalry, and "innumerable" foot soldiers. "In the fifth year of king Rehoboam Shishak king of Egypt came up against Jerusalem, because they had transgressed against the Lord . . . and took away the treasures of the house of the Lord, and the treasures of the king's house; he took all: he carried away also the shields of gold which Solomon had made"

(2 Chron. 12:2, 9). Shishak's campaign in Canaan is the basis for the film *Raiders of the Lost Ark,* which supposes that if the pharaoh took away the treasures of the house of the Lord, then the Ark of the Covenant was also taken to Egypt (though there is no historical evidence that the Ark was removed from Jerusalem at this time; it may well have been hidden by Temple officials).

The names of cities conquered by Shishak are carved into the walls of the Karnak Temple in Upper Egypt.[4] Jerusalem is not included in the lists. Shishak's armies apparently threatened the city at its outskirts and were bought off by Temple treasure, which further impoverished the formerly prosperous capital. Rehoboam had set up a line of defensive fortresses on the west, south, and east to protect the heartland of his kingdom (see 2 Chron. 11:5–12). His fortifications proved ineffective at their first test. Rehoboam refused to establish any kind of fortified barrier on the north because of his hope of someday restoring the northern tribes to his kingdom.[5]

OVERVIEW OF THE PERIOD

During the two hundred years between Solomon and Hezekiah, when the two kingdoms coexisted, the northern kingdom of Israel had nineteen rulers from nine dynasties, eight of which began by violence, and seven of those by assassination. Judah had twelve rulers in the same period, only one of whom came to the throne by violence—the daughter of Ahab and Jezebel. Judah survived 130 years longer than Israel and still had only twenty rulers, one more than Israel, and all but the daughter of Ahab and Jezebel from one dynasty. David was promised a royal lineage, and he received it. Jeroboam was promised the same, but because he turned away from the Lord and did not repent, the promise was not fulfilled.

During those two centuries, Jerusalem lost its standing as the capital and the center of religious worship of all of Israel. When the northern kingdom ultimately fell to the Assyrians, however, Jerusalem once again became the unrivalled political and religious center of the Israelites. Following are the twelve rulers in Jerusalem during this two-hundred-year period:[6]

Names	Years Ruled	Comments
Rehoboam	921–915 B.C.	
Abijah, or Abijam	915–913	
Asa	913–873	
Jehoshaphat	873–849	
Jehoram, or Joram	849–842	Married Athaliah, daughter of Ahab and Jezebel; introduced religious perversion
Ahaziah	842	
Athaliah	842–837	The only female ruler in Israel or Judah and the only one not of the royal Davidic dynasty
Jehoash, or Joash	837–800	
Amaziah	800–783	
Uzziah, or Azariah	783–742	
Jotham	742–735	
Ahaz	735–715	

THE STRUGGLE TO CONTROL THE BENJAMIN PLATEAU

For two hundred years the political histories of Israel and Judah were inextricably linked and filled with frequent hostilities—especially in the border land of Benjamin just north of Jerusalem: "And there was war between Rehoboam and Jeroboam all the days of his life" (1 Kgs. 15:6). "And there were wars between Rehoboam and Jeroboam continually" (2 Chron. 12:15). Those disputes persisted for generations. One border feud involving Abijah of Jerusalem is described in 2 Chronicles 13:1–8, 13–20; another one, a generation later, involving Asa of Judah and Baasha of Israel, is recounted in 1 Kings 15:16–22. "And there was war between Asa and Baasha king of Israel all their days" (v. 16). Baasha attacked Judah's northern border and built up Ramah, just five miles north of Jerusalem, to control traffic between the two kingdoms. "Then Asa took all the silver and the gold that were left in the treasures of the house of the Lord, and the treasures of the king's house, and delivered them into the hand of . . . Ben-hadad . . . king of Syria, that dwelt at Damascus" (v. 18), with the request for Syria to attack Israel and thereby alleviate pressure on Judah's northern border. The Syrian king was glad to comply with Asa's handsomely paid plea and invaded northeastern

Israel. Asa seized Baasha's building stones at Ramah and built up Geba and Mizpah to secure his own position on the border. (The locations of all that action may be seen just north of Jerusalem on Bible Map 9).[7]

Both the northern and the southern kingdoms viewed control of the border region immediately north of Jerusalem as vital to their own interests. Surrounding peoples, such as the Syrians (Hebrew, *Arameans*) of Damascus, the Ammonites, the Moabites, and the Philistines, took advantage of this internal dissension and broke away, reestablishing their own independence and reducing the Israelite kingdoms' prominence internationally.

ELIJAH THE PROPHET, HOLDER OF PRIESTHOOD KEYS

Shechem and Tirzah had been capitals of the northern kingdom of Israel, but Samaria was established as its capital and rival to Jerusalem during the reign of Omri in the first half of the ninth century before Christ. "Ahab the son of Omri did evil in the sight of the Lord above all that were before him. And it came to pass, as if it had been a light thing for him to walk in the sins of Jeroboam the son of Nebat, that he took to wife Jezebel the daughter of Ethbaal king of the Zidonians, and went and served Baal, and worshipped him. And he reared up an altar for Baal in the house of Baal, which he had built in Samaria. And Ahab made a grove [an *asherah*, a fertility goddess]; and Ahab did more to provoke the Lord God of Israel to anger than all the kings of Israel that were before him" (1 Kgs. 16:30–33). During the reign of one of the most infamous figures ever in Israel came one of the greatest, one sent of God to decry the depravity of Israel's king.

Some scholars and historians claim that after Moses, Elijah was the greatest man in Israel's religious life. And some regard him as the most popular personality in Hebrew history. Although there are no extant writings from Elijah himself, historians have preserved his story in 1 Kings 17 through 2 Kings 2. Elijah's first recorded use of the sealing power was to shut up the heavens, causing a dearth of rain for three and a half years. His purpose in stopping the rains was the same as that expressed by Nephi, son of Helaman, in the Book of Mormon: "O Lord, do not suffer that this people shall be destroyed by the sword; but . . . rather let there be a famine in the land, to stir them up in remembrance of the Lord their God, and perhaps they will repent and turn unto thee" (Hel. 11:4; compare Amos 4:6–11).

The severe famine that resulted caused Elijah himself to flee to the brook Cherith to find drinking water. That brook has traditionally been identified with Wadi Kelt, which is east of Jerusalem and flows down to Jericho.

A most dramatic event in Elijah's prophetic career was his encounter with Jezebel's priests and prophets of Baal on Mount Carmel. That site, between Phoenicia and Israel, was the geographic meeting point between Phoenicia's Baal and Israel's Jehovah. The contest on Mount Carmel was to see whose deity could bring rain and fertility back to the land after the three and one-half years of drought brought on by Elijah's sealing the heavens. Baal was supposed to be a storm god, a fertility god. But the true God Jehovah sent the rain. His mighty control of the elements was evidenced by the ensuing fierce winds and pounding rain (see 1 Kgs. 18:41–46).

After Elijah supervised the execution of hundreds of Jezebel's priests and prophets, the queen sought to kill Elijah. He fled south for more than a hundred miles to Beersheba and continued on to Horeb (Mount Sinai). The discouraged prophet needed encouragement. At Mount Sinai the Lord told Elijah he had work to do, to get a companion, and be assured that many other righteous souls had not embraced the worship of Baal. Elijah was not alone. It is noteworthy that Elijah did not flee to Jerusalem, to the House of the Lord. Perhaps, for a righteous prophet in the northern kingdom of Israel, Jerusalem no longer had religious significance.[8] Elijah was the last prophet in Old Testament times to hold the keys of the sealing powers of the priesthood.[9] Because Melchizedek Priesthood holders were generally not functioning in the Temple at Jerusalem, perhaps Elijah fled to an earlier holy place, to Mount Sinai, where the God of Israel had made his last known appearance to a prophet.[10]

ATHALIAH, THE EVIL QUEEN OF JERUSALEM

Jehoshaphat's son Jehoram married the daughter of Ahab and Jezebel,[11] probably as a political marriage to help improve the relationship between Samaria and Jerusalem. Having lived all her life under the influence of Baalism, "that wicked woman" Athaliah (as she is called in 2 Chron. 24:7) introduced the worship of Baal to the holy city of Jerusalem.

That both Israelite kingdoms adopted some of the Canaanite religious practices is evidenced by Israel's prophets frequently condemning the "groves" (the *asheroth,* or fertility goddesses) and the *baalim.* What the prophets denounced says something specific about the ills of their society. God's prophets reproved the Ammonites for worshipping Moloch, the Moabites for sacrificing infants to the fire-belching Chemosh, and the Philistines for trusting in their grain or fish god, Dagan, but they also rebuked their own Israelite nations for whoring after the gods of the Canaanites. Fertility was a dominant motif in Canaanite art. Figurines and statuettes, found in great numbers even in Jerusalem and near the sacred Temple Mount, often have greatly exaggerated sexual features. There were elements of remarkable crudity in ritual prostitution. Canaanite temples included rooms where young women sacrificed their virginity to strangers as a sacrifice to the goddess of fertility. Israelites had been warned of the perversions they would encounter in the land of Canaan, and they were constantly admonished to avoid any contact with such profane abuses (see Ex. 34:11–17; Judg. 2:3, 11–13; 3:7).[12]

Besides promoting Baalism, Athaliah tried to destroy the Davidic dynasty by killing all male descendants of David, but a counterrevolution by the priests eliminated the queen and reinstalled the Davidic line in the person of the young prince Joash (or Jehoash), whom they had hidden in the Temple and the priestly precincts for the six years of the queen's rule (see 2 Kgs. 11:2–3). Once the queen was executed near the royal palace and the priests and shrines of Baal were destroyed, the Temple priests, the king, and the people joined in a solemn covenant to worship and obey Jehovah (see 2 Kgs. 11:17–18). Joash later carried out extensive repairs to the Temple.[13] King Joash continued loyal to the Lord as long as the faithful priest Jehoiada lived, but after the priest's death, the king rapidly apostatized and refused to repent. He even had Jehoiada's son, Zechariah, murdered in the court of the Temple. He later met the same fate at the hands of his own servants in his palace bedroom (see 2 Chron. 24:20–25).

THE RISE OF ASSYRIA

Some of the most dramatic and long-remembered events in the history of ancient Israel resulted from their contacts with Assyria. The name Assyria derives from the name of its oldest capital city, Asshur, which is situated along the Tigris River south of Nineveh and Calah (see Bible Maps 2 and 10). The heartland of the Assyrian kingdom lay in northern Mesopotamia (in modern Iraq). Its chief cities were built along the Upper Tigris and at the foot of the Zagros Mountains, which separate it from the Iranian Plateau to the east.

Assyria developed into a flourishing state and empire during the later part of the second millennium before Christ. Its prosperity and independence fluctuated periodically with the success or failure of military exploits against its western neighbors, Mitanni and Aram. By 1100 B.C. Tiglath-pileser I had crossed the Euphrates twenty-eight times in attempting to control the Arameans (Syrians), who frequently attacked Assyria. A period of Assyrian decline followed.

In 911 B.C. Adad-nirari II reorganized the political structure of the kingdom, and the Neo-Assyrian empire began. With the renewed expansion, Assyria became directly involved with people and places mentioned in the Bible. Ashurnasirpal II conducted wars of plunder and conquest; and in the year 859 B.C. his son, Shalmaneser III, pushed Assyrian imperialism westward. In 853 an alliance of Levantine states— including Cilicians, Phoenicians, Arameans, Ammonites, Arabians, Egyptians, and Israelites—met the Assyrians at Qarqar on the Orontes River, and blocked the Assyrian advance.[14]

ISRAEL VERSUS SYRIA

Assyria and *Syria,* though seemingly related terms, are two totally different entities and names. *Assyria* is Greek for the Hebrew word *Asshur. Syria* is Greek for the Hebrew *Aram.* Both *Syria* and *Aram* are used in the Bible. Several Aramean states lay northeast of Israel, including Aram-Zobah, Aram-Beth-Rehob, Aram-Maacah, and Aram-Naharaim (Greek, *Mesopotamia*), but the most often mentioned state is Aram-Damascus—that is, Aram, or Syria, with its capital at Damascus (see Bible Map 7). Ben-hadad, meaning "son of [the storm-god] Hadad," was the name-title of several kings in Damascus during the centuries of the divided kingdoms of Israel.

Having dealt with the more ominous threat of Assyria at Qarqar, Israel's king, Ahab, convinced Jehoshaphat, king of Judah, to join him in trying to regain from the Syrians the town of Ramoth in Gilead, formerly held by the Israelites. The battle with Ben-hadad of Damascus resulted in the death of Ahab—as prophesied by Elijah.

When Ahab, the northern kingdom's most powerful king, was killed in battle, Moab broke away from the political and tributary impositions of Israel. Second Kings 3 describes a coalition formed among Israel, Judah, and Edom to end the rebellion. Nevertheless, Moab succeeded in throwing off the yoke of Israel and reconquering what they considered their homeland. "In those days the Lord began to cut Israel short: and Hazael smote them in all the coasts of Israel; from Jordan eastward, all the land of Gilead, the Gadites, and the Reubenites, and the Manassites, from Aroer, which is by the river Arnon, even Gilead and Bashan" (2 Kgs. 10:32–33).

"Then Hazael king of Syria went up, and fought against Gath, and took it: and Hazael set his face to go up to Jerusalem. And Jehoash king of Judah took all the hallowed things that . . . his fathers, kings of Judah, had dedicated, and his own hallowed things, and all the gold that was found in the treasures of the house of the Lord, and in the king's house, and sent it to Hazael king of Syria: and he went away from Jerusalem" (2 Kgs. 12:17–18).

PROSPERITY UNDER UZZIAH

Damascus was later captured by Assyria, which allowed Israel, under Jeroboam II, and Judah, under Uzziah, their greatest expansion in the history of the divided kingdoms. Uzziah had already conquered Edom, rebuilt Elath on the Red Sea, and subjugated much of Philistia. Then, while Assyria and their northern and western antagonists were involved in their own local conflicts and internal revolts, Israel and Judah united to win back all of Transjordan and expand to the size of the former Davidic kingdom.[15] In Judah, Uzziah strengthened his army, built new fortifications, prepared new siege engines and weaponry for the

walls of Jerusalem, and fostered extensive projects of agriculture, viti-
culture, and husbandry (see 2 Chron. 26:6–15).[16]

Sometime during this period, Jerusalem expanded northwest to
include about 150 more acres, making it much larger than any other
Judahite town of the time—Lachish, for instance, the second largest city
of Judah, was only twenty acres in size. Two new commercial and residential districts are now mentioned in the histories: the *Makhtesh* (the
"hollow"), in the Central or Tyropoeon Valley, and the *Mishneh* (literally,
the "second"; the new Second Quarter of the city), which encompassed
the entire Western Hill.[17] Later in his long reign, Uzziah contracted lep-
rosy and lived in a separate house; it appears that he reigned during his
final years with his son Jotham as co-regent (see 2 Kgs. 15:1–7).[18]

The many years of military victories and territorial expansion
resulted in prosperity, pride, and a false sense of security. Prophets
appeared to condemn the moral and spiritual failings of the Israelites.
The warning voices of Amos, Isaiah, Micah, and Hosea were heard in the
lands of Israel and Judah. They pronounced with emphatic clarity that
Assyria was the greatest political threat to Israelite existence (see Isa.
7:17; 8:4, 7; Hos. 8:9; cf. Amos 5:27).[19]

ASSYRIAN EXPANSION WESTWARD

The great expansionist Tiglath-pileser III, the "father of the
Assyrian Empire," reigned from 745 to 727 B.C. He began the systematic,
permanent absorption of foreign territories as provinces of Assyria by
deporting people from one part of the empire to another.

Assyrians were infamous for their barbarous conquests and treatment of captured enemies. They forced captives to parade through the
streets of Nineveh with the severed heads of other captives around their
necks. The Assyrians were masters of torture, cutting off noses and ears
and yanking out tongues of live enemies. They flayed prisoners—
skinned them while they were still alive. The reliefs commemorating the
siege at Lachish show Judahites impaled outside the walls of that city of
Judah. No wonder Jonah had no interest in serving a mission to the capital city of Nineveh![20] When the Lord called him to go northeast to his
mission field, he fled in the opposite direction.

THE POLITICAL BACKGROUND OF ISAIAH 7:1–9 AND 8:4

Around 735 B.C. Rezin, king of Syria, and Pekah, king of Israel, tried to form a new coalition of Levantine states to stand against Assyria—their only chance, they thought, for national survival. When Judah refused to join them, Syria and Israel planned to invade Jerusalem and replace the Davidic king Ahaz with someone who would support them (see 2 Kgs. 16:5).[21]

The great prophet Isaiah called a meeting with Ahaz[22] at the Gihon Spring to warn him not to fear the "two tails of these smoking fire-brands" (Isa. 7:4) and to refuse to join their losing effort. Furthermore, Isaiah warned him against forming any kind of alliance with Assyria, who was an infinitely greater threat. Against Isaiah's advice, Ahaz turned to Assyria for help. He took treasures out of the House of the Lord and out of the king's house and sent them to Tiglath-pileser with a request that the Assyrian king rid him of his adversaries to the north.[23] Tiglath-pileser was more than pleased to accommodate Ahaz, of course. He sub-jugated Philistia in 734 B.C., the northern and eastern lands of Israel in 733, and Damascus in 732, deporting their peoples to other parts of the Assyrian Empire. The Bible records:

> In the days of Pekah king of Israel came Tiglath-pileser king of Assyria, and took Ijon, and Abel-beth-maachah, and Janoah, and Kedesh, and Hazor, and Gilead, and Galilee, all the land of Naphtali, and carried them captive to Assyria. (2 Kgs. 15:29)
>
> So Ahaz sent messengers to Tiglath-pileser king of Assyria, saying, I am thy servant and thy son: come up, and save me out of the hand of the king of Syria, and out of the hand of the king of Israel, which rise up against me.
>
> And Ahaz took the silver and gold that was found in the house of the Lord, and in the treasures of the king's house, and sent it for a present to the king of Assyria.
>
> And the king of Assyria hearkened unto him: for the king of Assyria went up against Damascus, and took it, and carried the people of it cap-tive . . . and slew Rezin. (2 Kgs. 16:7–9)

THE FALL OF ISRAEL

Hoshea, the last king of Israel (a vassal king), decided to ally him-self with Egypt to throw off the Assyrian yoke (see 2 Kgs. 17:4). Assyria's response was rapid and terminal. Shalmaneser V (724–722 B.C.) besieged Samaria, the capital city of the northern kingdom of Israel, for three years. "In the ninth year of Hoshea the king of Assyria took Samaria, and carried Israel away into Assyria, and placed them in Halah and in Habor by the river of Gozan, and in the cities of the Medes" (2 Kgs. 17:6). The phrase "and carried Israel away into Assyria" seems to refer to the king of Assyria mentioned, but such is not the case. Shalmaneser besieged Samaria from 724 to 722 B.C. and in September of 722 he finally captured the city. He apparently died in December of the same year. Sargon II (721–705 B.C.) succeeded Shalmaneser on the throne of Assyria, and he is the one responsible for carrying away the northern Israelites—the lost (ten) tribes—and making Samaria a province of Assyria. He boasted full credit for the conquest and deportation of the Israelites in one of his annalistic inscriptions: "I besieged and conquered Samaria, [and] led away as booty 27,290 inhabitants of it."[24]

The historian of 2 Kings sadly began Israel's epitaph: "For so it was, that the children of Israel had sinned against the Lord . . ." (17:7).

Sargon followed Tiglath-pileser's policy of deporting conquered peoples, doing as his predecessor had done to the Transjordanian and northern Israelites ten years earlier. But he took it a step further. He initiated a policy of "transpopulation," that is, deporting one people and then importing people from other conquered lands to take their place. Sargon brought to Samaria foreigners from Babylon and Cuthah in southern Mesopotamia and from Hamath, north of Damascus (see Bible Map 10). The eventual intermarriage of these foreigners with the Israelites who remained in the land produced the people who came to be known as "Samaritans."

The kingdom of Judah submitted to Assyria and was spared destruction, becoming instead a vassal kingdom of the empire.

ISAIAH, SEER OF JERUSALEM'S HISTORY
AND PROPHET OF HER DESTINY

Whether interpreting Jerusalem's past, decrying her present, or revealing her future, the most imposing figure during the days of the divided kingdoms was Isaiah the prophet. That prophet-statesman had unquestionably the greatest effect on Jerusalem's history of all the prophets from David to Christ. Later, during the reign of Hezekiah, he even rallied the city from the verge of destruction by the sheer strength of his solitary faith. Despite the outward prosperity and security of the kingdom of Judah during the early years of his life, Isaiah knew that the time was fast approaching when no kingdom of the Levant would, for ages to come, exercise political importance or influence; the empires of the east (Assyrian, Babylonian, and Persian) and the west (Hellenistic, Roman, and Byzantine) would in turn dominate the Mediterranean world for more than a thousand years.

At his call to the prophetic office, Isaiah saw the Lord.[25] Isaiah was an eyewitness. His vision dispels the sectarian notion of a God without body, parts, and passions; the Lord was sitting on a throne and his train (the skirts of his robe), symbolic of his glory, filled the Temple. The new prophet was instructed to likewise fill the streets of Jerusalem with the voice of warning, to identify the sins of the people and command repentance in the name of the Lord. He lamented the depths of their fallen condition: "How is the faithful city become an harlot! it was full of judgment; righteousness lodged in it; but now murderers" (Isa. 1:21). In the first five chapters of his writings Isaiah itemizes the dark list of sins: rebellion, apostasy, oppression of the poor and innocent, corruption of court and legal processes, thievery, bribery, idolatry, sorcery and wizardry, materialism, pride, haughtiness, collapse of social order, juvenile gangs, delinquency, lawlessness, violence, insolence against elders, immorality, drunkenness, and riotous living.[26] He even compared the city to Sodom![27]

There were particularly inexcusable problems in the religious establishment. Isaiah denounced the ceremonies and ordinances of the Temple and its officiators. They portrayed some semblance of religiosity but were at the same time hypocritical; they had a form of godliness, but their hearts were far from the Lord. Isaiah cried, "Hear the word of the Lord, ye rulers of Sodom; give ear unto the law of our God, ye people of Gomorrah. To what purpose is the multitude of your sacrifices unto me? saith the Lord: I am full of the burnt offerings of rams, and the fat of fed beasts; and I delight not in the blood of bullocks, or of lambs, or of he goats. When ye come to appear before me [literally, "When you come to *see my face*," that is, "When you come to my Temple"], who hath required this at your hand, to tread my courts? [We might say, 'Why have you come here—just to improve statistics?'] Bring no more vain oblations; incense is an abomination unto me; . . . it is iniquity, even the solemn meeting. Your new moons and your appointed feasts my soul hateth: they are a trouble unto me; I am weary to bear them. And when ye spread forth your hands, I will hide mine eyes from you: yea, when you make many prayers, I will not hear: your hands are full of blood [of sacrifices, but also of murders]" (1:10–15).

On another occasion Isaiah condemned those who "swear by the name of the Lord, and make mention of the God of Israel, but not in truth, nor in righteousness. For they call themselves of the holy city" but do not trust in their God (48:1–2).

According to Isaiah all the ills in Jerusalem's society would result in a host of ills in the once-great city: "The daughter of Zion[28] is left as a cottage in a vineyard, . . . as a besieged city" (1:8); "Jerusalem is ruined, and Judah is fallen" (3:8); "I will lay it waste" (5:6); "as the fire devoureth the stubble, and the flame consumeth the chaff, so their root shall be as rottenness, and their blossom shall go up as dust: because they have cast away the law of the Lord of hosts, and despised the word of the Holy One of Israel. Therefore is the anger of the Lord kindled against his people, and he hath stretched forth his hand against them" (5:24–25). Isaiah pointedly identified the executor of God's judgments on his people: "The Lord shall bring upon thee . . . days that have not come, from the day that Ephraim departed from Judah [from the division of Solomon's kingdom]; even the king of Assyria. . . . And many among [you] shall stumble, and fall, and be broken, and be snared, and be taken" (7:17; 8:15).

The God whose Temple was in Jerusalem was the God of all peoples, and he used other nations to accomplish his purposes with his covenant people. Assyria was the "rod of mine anger, and the staff in their hand is mine indignation. I will send him against an hypocritical nation, and against the people of my wrath" (Isa. 10:5–6). "Nebuchadrezzar the king of Babylon, my servant" was later brought up against the people of Jerusalem and did "utterly destroy them, and make them an astonishment, and an hissing, and perpetual desolations" (Jer. 25:9; cf. 27:6). And still later, the Lord said of Cyrus, as Isaiah wrote, "He is my shepherd [in the next verse he is called 'his anointed'], and shall perform all my pleasure: even saying to Jerusalem, Thou shalt be built; and to the temple, Thy foundation shall be laid" (Isa. 44:28).

As far as Jerusalem's immediate future was concerned, Isaiah prophesied that if the people did not believe and hearken to the Lord's words, they would not be established permanently in the land (see Isa. 7:9). Isaiah proclaimed that the people who walked in darkness would see a great light (see Isa. 9:2). After the severe, dark blow of foreign foes, a Light would come, a Child would be born, a Son would be given. Though the tribes of Israel were carried off and lost to Israelite history, the tribe of Judah would not be completely destroyed. A remnant must return to their homeland, for the Messiah was to come through Judah and be born in the land of Jerusalem.

Following the prophetic pattern, Isaiah prophesied of doom but also of hope.[29] As did other prophets of Israel, Isaiah pronounced strong warnings of doom, desolation, and destruction, but he also announced that after the discipline of exile would come reinstatement, restoration, and redemption. Isaiah's prophecies of the ultimate destiny of "my holy mountain Jerusalem" (66:20) are the glorious outpourings of faith in a brighter day. Jerusalem would someday rise to its exalted status as the Holy City of God:

> It shall come to pass in the last days, that the mountain of the Lord's house shall be established in the top of the mountains, and shall be exalted above the hills; and all nations shall flow unto it.
> And many people shall go and say, Come ye, and let us go up to the mountain of the Lord, to the house of the God of Jacob; and he will teach us of his ways, and we will walk in his paths: for out of Zion shall go forth the law, and the word of the Lord from Jerusalem. (2:2–3)

> In that day shall the branch of the Lord be beautiful and glorious, and the fruit of the earth shall be excellent and comely for them that are escaped of Israel.
> And it shall come to pass, that he that is left in Zion, and he that remaineth in Jerusalem, shall be called holy, even every one that is written among the living in Jerusalem:
> When the Lord shall have washed away the filth of the daughters of Zion, and shall have purged the blood of Jerusalem from the midst thereof . . .
> And the Lord will create upon every dwelling place of mount Zion, and

upon her assemblies, a cloud and smoke by day, and the shining of a flaming fire by night. (4:2–5)

And it shall come to pass in that day, that the great trumpet shall be blown, and they shall come which were ready to perish in the land of Assyria, and the outcasts in the land of Egypt, and shall worship the Lord in the holy mount at Jerusalem. (27:13)

For the people shall dwell in Zion at Jerusalem: thou shalt weep no more: he will be very gracious unto thee at the voice of thy cry; when he shall hear it, he will answer thee. (30:19)

Speak ye comfortably to Jerusalem, and cry unto her, that her warfare is accomplished, that her iniquity is pardoned: for she hath received of the Lord's hand double for all her sins....

O Zion, that bringest good tidings, get thee up into the high mountain; O Jerusalem, that bringest good tidings, lift up thy voice with strength; lift it up, be not afraid; say unto the cities of Judah, Behold your God! (40:2, 9)

Awake, awake; put on thy strength, O Zion; put on thy beautiful garments, O Jerusalem, the holy city: for henceforth there shall no more come into thee the uncircumcised and the unclean.

How beautiful upon the mountains are the feet of him that bringeth good tidings, that publisheth peace; . . . that publisheth salvation; that saith unto Zion, Thy God reigneth!

Thy watchmen shall lift up the voice; with the voice together shall they sing: for they shall see eye to eye, when the Lord shall bring again Zion.

Break forth into joy, sing together, ye waste places of Jerusalem: for the Lord hath comforted his people, he hath redeemed Jerusalem. (52:1, 7–9)

Arise, shine; for thy light is come, and the glory of the Lord is risen upon thee.

And the sons of strangers shall build up thy walls, and their kings shall minister unto thee: for in my wrath I smote thee, but in my favour have I had mercy on thee.

Therefore thy gates shall be open continually; they shall not be shut day nor night; that men may bring unto thee the [wealth] of the Gentiles, and that their kings may be brought.

The sons also of them that afflicted thee shall come bending unto thee; and all they that despised thee shall bow themselves down at the soles of thy feet; and they shall call thee, The city of the Lord, The Zion of the Holy One of Israel.

Whereas thou hast been forsaken and hated, so that no man went through thee, I will make thee an eternal excellency, a joy of many generations.

Thy people also shall be all righteous: they shall inherit the land for ever, the branch of my planting, the work of my hands, that I may be glorified. (60:1, 10–11, 14–15, 21)

But be ye glad and rejoice for ever in that which I create: for, behold, I create Jerusalem a rejoicing, and her people a joy.

And I will rejoice in Jerusalem, and joy in my people: and the voice of weeping shall be no more heard in her, nor the voice of crying. (65:18–19)

Rejoice ye with Jerusalem, and be glad with her, all ye that love her . . . ye shall be comforted in Jerusalem. (66:10, 13)

NOTES

1. Pressure from his young counselors and Rehoboam's own pride seem to have caused his stinging response to northern Israelites' complaints: "Now whereas my father did lade you with a heavy yoke, I will add to your yoke: my father hath chastised you with whips, but I will chastise you with scorpions" (1 Kgs. 12:11).

2. The division of Israel must have pleased the Egyptian government, as the pharaoh was planning some imperialistic moves of his own.

3. Sheshonk I in extrabiblical texts, founder of Egypt's Twenty-second Dynasty.

4. For details of Shishak's route of conquest and archaeological evidences of his invasion, see Mazar, *Archaeology of the Land of the Bible,* 397–98. A fragment of a monumental stela apparently erected by Shishak and bearing his name was discovered in excavations at Megiddo.

5. Cf. Aharoni and Avi-Yonah, *Macmillan Bible Atlas,* Maps 119–20.

6. Dates of the kings' reigns given here are based on the work of W. F. Albright. See also the chart in Jackson, *1 Kings to Malachi,* 487, which is based on Bright's *A History of Israel;* contemporary kings of Israel may be seen there and in the chronology chart of the LDS Bible Dictionary, 637–38. Be aware that other scholars' lists include wide-ranging dates, differing by as much as fifty years. For example, our list has Rehoboam beginning his reign late in the tenth century before Christ, around 921, which allows for only six years in his reign, and 1 Kings 14:21 specifically states that he reigned seventeen years in Jerusalem. Virtually all attempts at producing accurate chronological tables this early in Israelite history reflect serious difficulties and differences.

7. See Aharoni and Avi-Yonah, *Macmillan Bible Atlas,* Map 123.

8. Smith, *Jerusalem,* 2:96.

9. Smith, *Teachings of the Prophet Joseph Smith,* 172.

10. Elijah went to Sinai to seek the Lord's face, to approach and talk with the Holy One of Israel. His predecessor and mentor in the prophetic office, Moses, had there talked with God face to face (see Ex. 33:11; Deut. 34:10; Moses 1:2). At the end of his mortal mission Elijah journeyed to the place where Moses was taken up without tasting death;

Moses and Elijah were translated at the same place—just east of the Jordan River, opposite Jericho (see Deut. 34; 2 Kgs. 2). They appeared together on the Mount of Transfiguration to bestow the keys of the kingdom and sealing power (see Matt. 17) and again in 1836 at the Mountain of the Lord's House in Kirtland, Ohio, for the same purpose (see D&C 110).

11. There is some question about whether Athaliah was the daughter of Ahab and Jezebel or Ahab's sister or half-sister. For additional information, see Jackson, *1 Kings to Malachi,* 34.

12. For more on Baalism, see Ogden and Chadwick, *Holy Land,* 76–78; Rasmussen and Ogden, *Old Testament,* 2:69.

13. Stonemasons, carpenters, and others were paid with money collected in contribution boxes in the Temple, after the money had been carefully audited. See 2 Kgs. 12:4–16.

14. See Aharoni and Avi-Yonah, *Macmillan Bible Atlas,* Map 127; Beitzel, *Moody Atlas of Bible Lands,* 132.

15. The mention of "Uzziah king of Judah" and "Jeroboam the son of Joash king of Israel" in the prophecy of Amos clearly places that prophet in the middle of the eighth century before Christ. His preaching is also dated as beginning "two years before the earthquake." Though seismic disturbances are anything but rare in the land of Amos, this very earthquake, the only one explicitly mentioned in the Bible, was apparently so severe that it was used for some time to date historical events. It was of such unusual intensity and inflicted such devastation that the memory of it survived for more than two and a half centuries. In Zechariah 14:5, this earthquake in the days of Uzziah served as a pattern of extremely intense and destructive earthquakes: "And ye shall flee as you fled from the earthquake in the days of Uzziah, king of Judah." The earthquake in the days of Uzziah caused damage over a wide area; evidence of it has been discovered in archaeological excavations from one end of the country to the other, particularly at Hazor in the north, Deir-Alla in the Rift Valley, and Beersheba in the south. Yadin dates the earthquake to approximately 760 B.C.; *Hazor,* 113, 181. Ben-Dov also notes evidence of this earthquake in excavations at Jerusalem's Temple Mount; see *In the Shadow of the Temple,* 55.

16. See Aharoni and Avi-Yonah, *Macmillan Bible Atlas,* Map 142.

17. Avigad, *Discovering Jerusalem,* 24; Ben-Dov, *In the Shadow of the Temple,* 34–35; Mazar, *Archaeology of the Land of the Bible,* 417–24; Emerton, *Congress Volume,* 2; *New Encyclopedia of Archaeological Excavations,* 2:705–8. Compare Broshi, "Expansion of Jerusalem in the Reigns of Hezekiah and Manasseh," who explains that the great expansion occurred because of the influx of immigrants from the north after the fall of Israel in 721 B.C.; Mazar draws the same conclusion. See Levine, *Jerusalem Cathedra,* 2:18.

18. Compare the Chronicler's account of the king's transgression in the Temple by attempting to usurp priesthood power (see 2 Chron. 26:16–21). An item of archaeological interest relates to the death of Uzziah: a tomb plaque dating from the Second Temple period has been found in the ancient cemetery on the Mount of Olives. The stone plaque bears an Aramaic inscription explaining that the bones of King Uzziah had been transferred from their original burial place to a new plot on the Mount of Olives. See 2 Chron. 26:23; Amiran, *Urban Geography,* 14; Bahat, *Illustrated Atlas of Jerusalem,* 50; see also photograph of the inscription in Thompson, *Bible and Archaeology,* 336.

19. Amos counseled that God will do nothing concerning his people without first revealing his will to his prophets (see Amos 3:7; cf. 2 Ne. 25:9: "Never hath any of them been destroyed save it were foretold them by the prophets of the Lord"). Amos' central

message was to "look to God and live"; Amos 5:4. The names *Isaiah* and *Hosea* are forms of the Hebrew word meaning "Jehovah saves," "salvation" or "deliverance." As is the case with other prophets, Hosea's name has something to do with his message. In Hosea 12:10 the Lord tells us that he has spoken by the prophets, and multiplied visions, and "*used similitudes,* by the ministry of the prophets" (emphasis added). Just as the great Abrahamic test was in similitude of God and his Only Begotten Son (see Jacob 4:5), so Hosea's life may have been a similitude—a living drama, of the Lord's relationship with his bride to whom he was married—his covenant people. As Abraham would have some understanding of the Father's sacrifice of his Son, so Hosea would have some understanding of the Lord's merciful caring for his unfaithful people.

20. The brutality of the Assyrians is graphically documented in Bleibtreu, "Grisly Assyrian Record of Torture and Death."

21. See Aharoni and Avi-Yonah, *Macmillan Bible Atlas,* Map 144.

22. King Ahaz by this time had reinstituted the worship of Baal in Jerusalem. He was worshipping at all the high places and was even carrying out child-sacrifice rituals in the Hinnom Valley. He also set up a replica of a heathen altar he had seen in Damascus and ordered changes in the sacred vessels and procedures in the House of the Lord (see 2 Kgs. 16).

23. This pillaging of the treasures of the Temple and the royal treasures of the king's palace is beginning to sound like a routine ultimate recourse; over these two centuries, Rehoboam gave treasures from the temple to Shishak (see 1 Kgs. 14:26); Asa, to Ben-hadad (see 1 Kgs. 15:18); Jehoash (Joash) of Judah, to Hazael (see 2 Kgs. 12:18); and Ahaz, to Tiglath-pileser (see 2 Kgs. 16:8). Another episode was the incursion of Jehoash of Israel into Jerusalem (see 2 Kgs. 14:13–14), where, as it is written, the king of Israel broke down part of the wall of Jerusalem and carried away the treasures of the House of the Lord and the king's house to Samaria—the only time on record that *Israel* ever plundered the Temple. The Temple was the repository of the wealth of the kingdom; "from the analogy of other ancient temples, they also comprised the Temple funds, and deposits by private persons. The sanctuaries of those days were banks. . . . The Temple was growing in material wealth. Its treasures were accumulating, and when these were taken from it to meet some national emergency, they seem to have been quickly restored. To other Temples, kings repaid their forced loans by gifts of lands or new treasure, and that this happened also in the case of the Judaean Temple appears from the fact that there were always funds in it when they were required." Smith, *Jerusalem,* 2:109, 111.

24. Pritchard, *Ancient Near Eastern Texts,* 284ff; in Hayes and Miller, *Israelite and Judaean History,* 433. Archaeological evidence of the destruction of Samaria by the Assyrian army is presented in Kenyon, *Royal Cities of the Old Testament,* 129–34. Second Kings 17:6 says that Sargon placed them in Halah (unknown), in Habor by the river of Gozan, and in the cities of the Medes. Bible Map 10 shows Gozan, west of Nineveh in Upper Mesopotamia. A river flows right by Gozan. In the regular and small editions of the Bible that river is not named for lack of space, but in the large-print edition it is; it is called the Habor. The word *by* in verse 6 is italicized. Italicized words in the King James Bible are not there in the original Hebrew text; they have been supplied to give the passage more sense in English. Sometimes italicized words have been incorrectly supplied, however, as is the case here. The phrase should actually read that Sargon deported them and placed them along the Habor, the river of Gozan, and in the cities of the Medes (the northern part of modern-day Iran). Thus the initial locations of the "Lost Tribes" are known.

25. This is probably the experience Nephi referred to in 2 Ne. 11:2.

26. An example of the vanity of Jerusalem's leadership is later given in Isaiah 22:15–19. Shebna was some kind of "secretary of state," and he had apparently misused city funds by carving out for himself an elaborate sepulchre in Jerusalem's necropolis. In recent decades the "Royal Steward's Inscription" was found in the hillside east of the City of David, and it appears to be an inscription referring to this very man—the only contemporary individual condemned specifically in the book of Isaiah. Verse 18 records that although he had carved out a sepulchre in Jerusalem, he would be buried elsewhere. For more information on the plan of the tomb and photo, see Shanks, "Tombs of Silwan," 47–49; see also Stern, *New Encyclopedia of Archaeological Excavations,* 2:712–13; Yadin, *Jerusalem Revealed,* 64.

27. Not only did the Lord condemn the male leaders of Jerusalem but he also rebuked the "daughters of Zion." The pride and haughtiness that goad men in their vain ambitions are manifested often in women through their outward adornment and apparel. The women of Isaiah's day were concerned about their physical appearance, and they were devoted to drawing attention to it. The Lord's first epithet was "haughty"; he went on to detail their offensive behavior (Isa. 3:16–24). The following is from archaeologist Gabriel Barkay's 1986 report of his excavations along the west side of Jerusalem's Hinnom Valley. He describes findings from the richest tomb opened, which gives tangible documentation of what Isaiah wrote regarding Jerusalem's fine society women: "The abundant jewelry found in the tomb provides the first material evidence to support the frequent allusion in the Bible to the wealth of Jerusalem during the First Temple period. Isaiah had mocked the ostentation of Jerusalem's society ladies when he wrote: 'On that day the Lord will take away the finery of their anklets, the head bands and their crescents; the pendants, the bracelets and the scarfs; the headdresses, the armlets, the sashes, the perfume boxes and the amulets; the rings and the nose jewels.' The tomb produced six gold items and 95 silver items as well as jewelry made of rare stones, glass and faience—many of them of great beauty including earrings, rings, beads and pendants. This is the first time that a representative selection of jewelry worn by the women of Jerusalem at the end of the First Temple period forms part of an archaeological assemblage." (Rabinovich, "Word for Word," 11.) Of all the treasures discovered by Barkay, the one receiving the most publicity is two solid silver amulets which contain the priestly benediction, almost identical in wording to Numbers 6:24–26: "The Lord bless thee, and keep thee: The Lord make his face shine upon thee, and be gracious unto thee: The Lord lift up his countenance upon thee, and give thee peace." The name of God was etched three times onto the tiny amulets—the earliest mention of the name of God, the Tetragrammaton (*YHWH*), ever found in Jerusalem. This represents the first time in one hundred fifty years of excavations in Jerusalem that the Hebrew form of the name of God has been discovered. (See also Barkay, "Divine Name Found in Jerusalem," 14–15; Mazar, *Archaeology of the Land of the Bible,* 524; *New Encyclopedia of Archaeological Excavations,* 2:715; Geva, *Ancient Jerusalem Revealed,* 99–106.)

28. Several times Isaiah identifies Jerusalem as the "daughter of Zion." Zion was a name of the former City of Holiness—the city of Melchizedek; now her offspring or successor is called the *daughter* of Zion. Cities were often labelled as a feminine entity.

29. For examples of this pattern from other Old Testament writings, see Jackson, *1 Kings to Malachi,* 59–60.

7

EVENTS LEADING TO THE FALL OF JERUSALEM IN 586 B.C.

Judah was desperate for a king who "did that which was right in the sight of the Lord" (2 Chron. 29:2). That need was fulfilled in Hezekiah, who reigned from 715 to 687 B.C. He kept the commandments and trusted in the Lord to a greater degree than had any other king during Jerusalem's three centuries as a political and spiritual capital. He ordered the Temple to be cleansed, appointed proper courses of priests and Levites, commanded that Israelites from Dan to Beersheba join in a grand Passover celebration once again, and decreed that they pay their tithes (see 2 Chron. 29–31). Hezekiah removed the high places and altars, broke down the images, and cut down the groves. He destroyed the bronze serpent that Moses had made in Sinai because the Judahites had been burning incense to it, thus perverting a symbol of the Messiah (see 2 Kgs. 18:4; 2 Chron. 31:1). Hezekiah also made plans to reunite all the tribes of the north and south, thus reasserting the claim of the house of David to rule over all the lands of Israel.[1] "And in every work that he began in the service of the house of God, and in the law, and in the commandments, to seek his God, he did it with all his heart, and prospered. And the Lord was with him; and he prospered whithersoever he went forth: and he rebelled against the king of Assyria, and served him not" (2 Chron. 31:21; 2 Kgs. 18:7).

A glance at Bible Map 10, which shows the extent of the mighty Assyrian Empire and the tiny tributary kingdom of Judah, is sufficient to convince anyone of the daring of Hezekiah in rebelling against Assyria. The map does not tell the whole story, however. With the death of Sargon in 705 B.C., cities up and down the coasts of Phoenicia and Canaan revolted against Assyria. Babylon also had a new and ambitious king. Egypt was ready to oppose Assyrian penetration. Hezekiah knew the time was right to break away from the Assyrian overlords, but he also realized that it was only a matter of time until the brutal armies of the empire would return to crush the rebellion.

HEZEKIAH'S PREPARATIONS FOR WAR

Hezekiah began refortifying the city walls to prepare Jerusalem for the retaliatory invasion. A two-hundred-foot (sixty-five-meter) section of Hezekiah's wall has been uncovered in recent years in today's Jewish Quarter of the Old City.[2] The "broad wall," as it is called in Nehemiah 3:8 and 12:38, is twenty-five feet wide (seven meters), testimony of the serious fortification works of Jerusalem's king. As archaeologists cleared away the debris of centuries, they exposed to view houses that were destroyed along the course of Hezekiah's protective wall, just as Isaiah noted: "Ye have seen also the breaches of the city of David, that they are many: and ye gathered together the waters of the lower pool. And ye have numbered the houses of Jerusalem, and the houses have ye broken down to fortify the wall" (Isa. 22:9–10).

Hezekiah cut an underground tunnel to ensure a constant supply of water from the Gihon Spring into the city. Second Chronicles 32:30 says, "This same Hezekiah also stopped the upper watercourse of Gihon, and brought it straight down to the west side of the city of David." This refers to Hezekiah's famous water tunnel, which still exists today, twenty-seven hundred years later. An inscription discovered in 1880, twenty feet inside the south end of the tunnel, tells the story of how the two teams of workmen, one from each end, chiseled 1,748 feet (nearly one-third of a mile) through solid limestone and how they met in the middle. It is the longest biblical Hebrew inscription ever found in the Holy Land and the only monumental commemorative Hebrew text ever discovered on the west side of the Jordan.[3]

With fortifications in place, Hezekiah and Judah awaited the Assyrian onslaught.[4]

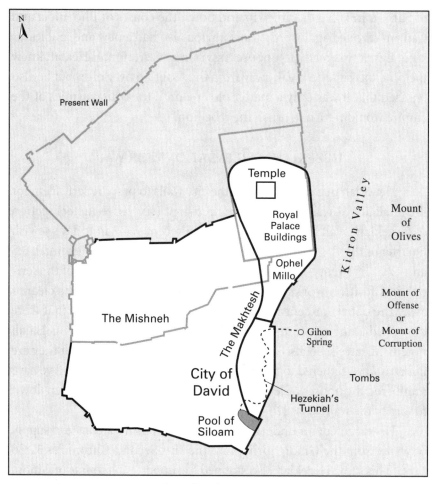

Jerusalem about 586 B.C.

SENNACHERIB, KING OF ASSYRIA, 705–681 B.C.

"Now in the fourteenth year of king Hezekiah did Sennacherib king of Assyria come up against all the fenced cities of Judah, and took them. And Hezekiah king of Judah sent to the king of Assyria to Lachish, saying, I have offended; return from me: that which thou puttest on me will I bear. And the king of Assyria appointed unto Hezekiah king of Judah three hundred talents of silver and thirty talents of gold" (2 Kgs. 18:13–14).

Another archaeological discovery that helps corroborate the Bible is King Sennacherib's record of the invasion called the Sennacherib Prism.[5] It confirms that Hezekiah did try to buy off the Assyrians, but the tribute imposed was eight hundred talents of silver and thirty of gold. According to 2 Kings 18:15–16, Hezekiah gathered together all the silver and gold in the Temple and in the king's house, even stripping off gold from Temple doors and pillars.

A contingent of Assyrian officials was sent to Jerusalem from Lachish, where Sennacherib was besieging Judah's strongest fortified position in the Shephelah, the region of low hills southwest of Jerusalem.[6] Of all the conquered cities and fortifications, Sennacherib must have been particularly proud of his siege of Lachish. When he returned to Nineveh he had his artisans carve thirteen panels at his palace—a magnificent battle panorama—depicting details of the siege of Lachish. It shows the battering rams used to penetrate the strong and heavily guarded walls of Lachish. The panorama also shows the fighting gear and apparel of Assyrians and Judahites and the barbaric methods the Assyrians used to kill their captives. These palace wall-reliefs were excavated in the mid 1800s in Nineveh and are now in the British Museum.[7] Excavations at Lachish reveal intense destruction in its thick layers of ash—Sennacherib's "calling card" at Lachish.[8]

Sennacherib sent officers to Jerusalem to harass and threaten King Hezekiah and his people. The Assyrians "stood by the conduit of the upper pool, which is in the highway of the fuller's field"—in other words, across from the Gihon Spring—and taunted the citizens of Jerusalem in their own Hebrew language, warning them not to trust in Hezekiah or in the God of Israel or in the bruised reed of Egypt:

> Let not Hezekiah deceive you: for he shall not be able to deliver you out of [the king of Assyria's] hand:
> Neither let Hezekiah make you trust in the Lord, saying, The Lord will surely deliver us, and this city shall not be delivered into the hand of the king of Assyria....
> Hath any of the gods of the nations delivered at all his land out of the hand of the king of Assyria? ...
> Who are they among all the gods of the countries, that have delivered their country out of mine hand, that the Lord should deliver Jerusalem out of mine hand? (2 Kgs. 18:29–30, 33, 35)

Sennacherib planned to remove systematically all opposition at

Jerusalem's western approaches in the Shephelah and then advance on the political eagle nesting in the top of the hills. After heavy losses in the Shephelah, Jerusalem had no hope of standing up to Sennacherib's war machine.

King Hezekiah took a written message from Sennacherib up to the House of the Lord, and there, in the holy sanctuary, he spread the threatening letter before the Lord and prayed fervently (see 2 Kgs. 19:14-15; Isa. 37:14-15). In that very hour the voice of a lone man speaking for God was heard in the city, and word was sent to King Hezekiah, assuring him and his subjects that the place God had chosen to put His Name was still in His hands. The Assyrian blasphemers, Isaiah prophesied, would find only death and destruction *for themselves* if they came to Jerusalem:

> Thus saith the Lord, Be not afraid of the words which thou hast heard, with which the servants of the king of Assyria have blasphemed me.
>
> Behold, I will send a blast upon him, and he shall hear a rumour, and shall return to his own land; and I will cause him to fall by the sword in his own land. . . .
>
> Therefore thus saith the Lord concerning the king of Assyria, He shall not come into this city, nor shoot an arrow [here], nor come before it with shield, nor cast a bank against it.
>
> By the way that he came, by the same shall he return, and shall not come into this city, saith the Lord. (2 Kgs. 19:6-7, 32-33)

MIRACULOUS DELIVERANCE OF JERUSALEM

In 701 B.C. Sennacherib was poised to strike Jerusalem with full military might to reduce the rebels to humiliating submission. The following account of his view of the campaign is excerpted from the Sennacherib Prism:

> As to Hezekiah, the Jew, he did not submit to my yoke. I laid siege to forty-six of his strong cities, walled forts and to the countless small villages in their vicinity, and conquered [them] by means of well-stamped [earth-]ramps, and battering-rams brought [thus] near [to the walls] [combined with] the attack by foot soldiers, [using] mines, breeches as well as sapper work. I drove out [of them] 200,150 people, young and old, male and female, horses, mules, donkeys, camels, big and small cattle beyond counting, and considered [them] booty. Himself I made a

prisoner in Jerusalem, his royal residence, like a bird in a cage. I surrounded him with earthwork in order to molest those who were leaving his city's gate.[9]

Sennacherib's final statement is a boast that is historically untrue, as we learn from the biblical account. Isaiah had prophesied that the king would "not come into this city, nor shoot an arrow [here], nor come before it with shield, nor cast a bank [a siege ramp] against it" (2 Kgs. 19:32).

Following is what actually did happen to Sennacherib and his hosts:

> It came to pass that night, that the angel of the Lord went out, and smote in the camp of the Assyrians an hundred fourscore and five thousand: and when they arose early in the morning [those who were still alive], behold, they were all dead corpses.
>
> So Sennacherib king of Assyria departed, and went and returned, and dwelt at Nineveh.
>
> And it came to pass, as he was worshipping in the house of Nisroch his god, that . . . his sons smote him with the sword. (2 Kgs. 19:35–37)

The Greek historian Herodotus, in the fifth century before Christ, suggested in his writings that mice caused the Assyrians to withdraw as some kind of plague swept through their camp.[10] That Sennacherib did return and dwell at Nineveh is confirmed in Assyrian annals, and that his sons later murdered him (twenty years later, in 681 B.C.) is also confirmed in Assyrian documents. Thus were the prophecies of Isaiah fulfilled.[11]

The confrontation between Hezekiah and Sennacherib and the miraculous deliverance of Jerusalem made an indelible impression on the citizens of Judah. The episode has received further fame in a more modern day through the splendid poetry of Lord Byron in *The Destruction of Sennacherib* (1815).[12]

> The Assyrian came down like the wolf on the fold,
> And his cohorts were gleaming in purple and gold,
> And the sheen of their spears was like stars on the sea,
> When the blue wave rolls nightly on deep Galilee.
>
> Like the leaves of the forest when summer is green,
> That host with their banners at sunset were seen:

Like the leaves of the forest when autumn hath blown,
That host on the morrow lay withered and strown.

For the Angel of Death spread his wings on the blast,
And breathed in the face of the foe as he pass'd
And the eyes of the sleepers wax'd deadly and chill,
And their hearts but once heaved, and forever grew still!

And there lay the steed with his nostril all wide,
But through it there roll'd not the breath of his pride;
And the foam of his gasping lay white on the turf,
And cold as the spray of the rock-beating surf.

And there lay the rider distorted and pale,
With the dew on his brow, and the rust on his mail:
And the tents were all silent, the banners alone,
The lances unlifted, the trumpet unblown.

And the widows of Ashur are loud in their wail,
And the idols are broke in the temple of Baal;
And the might of the Gentile, unsmote by the sword,
Hath melted like snow in the glance of the Lord!

When Hezekiah was found to be deathly ill, he learned that the Lord intervenes not only in national crises but also in personal crises. The Lord granted good king Hezekiah another fifteen years to live (see 2 Kgs. 20; Isa. 39).

Another episode during this period should not go unmentioned. Hezekiah openly showed the treasures of the kingdom to a Babylonian delegation, which had undoubtedly come to Jerusalem with ulterior motives. Isaiah responded to Hezekiah's political naivete with a prophecy that the nation's treasures and some of the king's descendants would be carried away into Babylon, a prophecy that stood as a warning to Jerusalemites for the next century (see 2 Kgs. 20:12–18; Isa. 39).

During the reigns of the Assyrian kings Esarhaddon (681–669 B.C.) and his successor, Ashurbanipal, the empire was at its height, extending from Persia to Egypt. Esarhaddon destroyed the once-renowned Egyptian city of Memphis. And to the last strong Assyrian king, Ashurbanipal (669–627 B.C.), is attributed the dubious honor of having sacked one of the greatest cities of the ancient world, Thebes in Upper Egypt, in 663 B.C.[13]

Because of rivalry between the rulers of Assyria and Babylon, the Assyrian Empire rapidly deteriorated. Ashur, Nineveh, Calah, and Dur-Sharrukin all fell to the Neo-Babylonian Empire between 615 and 612 B.C.

Ironically, good King Hezekiah's son Manasseh (687–642) and his grandson Amon (642–640) were two of the worst kings Judah had ever seen. Manasseh, who reigned longest of all Judah's kings, introduced shockingly sacrilegious and profane practices into the Holy City: he set up altars to Baal and an *asherah* (a fertility-cult goddess) for worship in the court of the Temple of Jehovah. Manasseh led the people in worshipping the "host of heaven," sacrificing children, engaging in Satanic spiritualism, and murdering innocent citizens who refused to participate in such perversions. By God's own judgment Manasseh was characterized as worse than all the peoples who had been removed from the land so the Israelites could inherit it (see 2 Kgs. 21:3–11).[14] Manasseh's son, Amon, followed in his father's footsteps, continuing the spiritual havoc in Jerusalem. Note the prophetic pronouncement of what those evils would bring upon Jerusalem: "Thus saith the Lord God of Israel, Behold, I am bringing such evil upon Jerusalem and Judah, that whosoever heareth of it, both his ears shall tingle . . . and I will wipe Jerusalem as a man wipeth a dish, wiping it, and turning it upside down" (2 Kgs. 21:12–13).

REFORMS OF KING JOSIAH

In the later part of the seventh century before Christ, the Assyrian Empire weakened rapidly because of internal agitation and pressures in its widespread conquered lands. With Assyrian disintegration Judah was able to expand—its last period of greatness—under King Josiah (640–609 B.C.). Josiah extended Jerusalem's control to former Israelite territories that had been for most of a century provinces of greater Assyria. He also instituted some rigorous religious reforms, as his great-grandfather, Hezekiah, had done (2 Kgs. 22:4–20). He made repairs in the Temple, during which a copy of the book of the Law was found. No direct record identifies the book, but many of the king's reforms parallel Deuteronomy 16:2; 18:10–11; 23:2–4, 7, 17–18, 21, 24; 31:11. The king and the priests read in the book of the Law the terrible curses that would follow such spiritual rebellion and apostasy as had persisted during the previous two generations. They knew that the Lord was angry with the nation of Judah. They asked a prophetess, a woman named Huldah (a contemporary of Jeremiah and Lehi), whether the curses would be forthcoming. Huldah's response was specific and foreboding:

> Thus saith the Lord, Behold, I will bring evil upon this place, and upon the inhabitants thereof, even all the words of the book which the king of Judah hath read:
> Because they have forsaken me, and have burned incense unto other gods, that they might provoke me to anger with all the works of their hands; therefore my wrath shall be kindled against this place, and shall not be quenched.
> But to the king of Judah . . . shall ye say to him, Thus saith the Lord God of Israel, As touching the words which thou hast heard;
> Because thine heart was tender, and thou hast humbled thyself before the Lord, when thou heardest what I spake against this place, and against the inhabitants thereof, that they should become a desolation and a curse, and hast rent thy clothes, and wept before me; I also have heard thee, saith the Lord.
> Behold therefore, I will gather thee unto thy fathers, and thou shalt be gathered into thy grave in peace; and thine eyes shall not see all the evil which I will bring upon this place. (2 Kgs. 22:16–20)

Josiah called a solemn assembly with priesthood leaders, prophets, and all the inhabitants of Jerusalem listening as he read the book of the covenant that had been found in the Temple. The king and all the people covenanted to keep the Lord's commandments. The king and priests burned all Baalistic objects in the Kidron Valley. The statue of the fertility goddess that had been in the House of the Lord was ground to powder. Josiah ousted all idolatrous priests and destroyed all shrines from Geba to Beersheba, the borders of Judah at that time (see Bible Map 9). He ordered the destruction of all "the high places that were before Jerusalem, which were on the right hand of the mount of corruption, which Solomon the king of Israel had built for Ashtoreth" and other idol gods. The king also ordered wreckers to break down and burn the altar and high place that were still at Bethel from the days of Jeroboam (see 2 Kgs. 23:1–15).

Josiah's enlightened reign ended with his early death at Megiddo, where he had gone to stop the Egyptian advance under Pharaoh Nechoh, who was marching towards the Euphrates River to help the last Assyrian king against Babylon. Josiah apparently wanted to keep Egypt, Assyria's loyal ally to the end, from acquiring any control over Canaan. Because Nechoh was detained by Josiah at Megiddo, his efforts to assist Assyria were seriously impaired, and Assyria was defeated by the powerful new Babylonian ruler, Nebuchadnezzar, in 609 B.C. Falling back to his Egyptian homeland, Nechoh imposed Egyptian authority over Judah, from 609 to 605 B.C., before the Babylonian invasions of Judah. Josiah's death marked the beginning of the end for the kingdom of Judah.

The history of the Holy Land is essentially an account of the struggles between Mesopotamia and Egypt to control the land-bridge of the Near East. The contest between Babylon and Egypt at the end of the seventh century before Christ is a classic illustration of this historical axiom. During this struggle Judah was eventually annihilated. By the year 604 B.C. the entire Levant was the domain of Nebuchadnezzar of Babylon: "And the king of Egypt came not again any more out of his land: for the king of Babylon had taken from the river of Egypt unto the river Euphrates all that pertained to the king of Egypt" (2 Kgs. 24:7).

THE BABYLONIAN EMPIRE

The southern part of Mesopotamia was known in antiquity as Babylon or Chaldea. Its chief cities were Babylon (Hebrew, *Babel*, literally, "gate of God"), Ur, Erech (Uruk), and Nippur (see Bible Map 11). The city of Babylon was itself one of the wonders of the ancient world, with its ziggurat and many miles of hanging (terraced) gardens. Babylon was the imperial capital of the Babylonians and was later the imperial capital of the Persians and of Alexander of Macedonia.

The Babylonian Empire was mighty, but it was short-lived. Compared to its predecessor, Assyria, and its successor, Persia, each of which endured for more than two centuries, the new Babylonian Empire rose to greatness, left its heavy mark on ancient Near Eastern history, especially Jewish history, and then was swept into oblivion—all within seventy years. Babylon's strength and evil grandeur became proverbial in later scripture as a symbol of the wicked. She is called the apostate, the whore of all the earth, the mother of harlots (a foil to Zion, who represents the righteous).[15] Doctrine and Covenants 133:14 records the Lord's warning to the Latter-day Saints: "Go ye out from among the nations, even from Babylon, from the midst of wickedness, which is spiritual Babylon." And in our modern hymns we still sing of Babylon as the representative of darkness in the earth: "O Babylon, O Babylon, we bid thee farewell" and "Babylon the great is falling; God shall all her towers o'erthrow."[16]

THE VOICE OF WARNING: JEREMIAH, LEHI, AND OTHERS

Jeremiah had begun his ministry in Jerusalem more than twenty years before the conquests of Nebuchadnezzar of Babylon.[17] He was unpopular and was considered treasonous by some factions in the capital because he advocated acquiescence[18]—surrender to the Babylonians, submit to exile, and make the most of a new but temporary home: build houses, plant gardens, marry, rear families, even pray for the peace of Babylon! (see Jer. 29:4–7)—all to preserve a remnant that would return to Jerusalem just a few decades later, as prophesied.[19]

On one occasion Jeremiah stood in the court of the Temple warning that the Lord was going to make his House like Shiloh, and the city of Jerusalem desolate without an inhabitant (see Jer. 26:9).[20] "All the people were gathered against Jeremiah in the house of the Lord," intending to kill him (just as when Jesus later prophesied the destruction of the next Temple at the same place; the people tried to kill Jesus; see Matt. 24:1–2; John 8:20, 37–59). Certain elders of the people reminded the crowd to be careful what they did with Jeremiah—other prophets had also spoken in the name of the Lord and prophesied the destruction of Jerusalem; for example, Micah of Moresheth-gath in the days of Hezekiah, and a contemporary of Jeremiah, one Urijah of Kiriath-jearim (see Jer. 26:17–20).

Yet another prophet was in the city at the time, teaching the same things. Lehi warned of the impending destruction of Jerusalem, and he testified of the people's wickedness and of the coming of a Messiah. "When the Jews heard these things they were angry . . . and they also sought his life" (1 Ne. 1:20).[21]

The Book of Mormon says, "There came many prophets, prophesying unto the people that they must repent, or the great city Jerusalem

Lehi and family leaving Jerusalem (painting by Kelly Hale)

must be destroyed" (1 Ne. 1:4). Amos taught that God would do nothing without first revealing it to his prophets (see Amos 3:7). The Lord always gives plenty of warning. The Book of Mormon's "many prophets" is true: Jeremiah, Lehi, Huldah, Zephaniah, Habakkuk, Daniel, Ezekiel, and Urijah were all contemporaries.

Lehi's sons Laman and Lemuel did not believe that Jerusalem could be destroyed (see 1 Ne. 2:13). There was no historical precedent for such a bold prophecy: Jerusalem had never been destroyed in all of Israelite history, and in fact, Jerusalem may have been regarded by some as inviolable; for example, at the time of Sennacherib's siege it had been miraculously preserved.[22] The prophets, on the other hand, knew that the City's inviolability was based on her spirituality. Judah's God had been patient and long-suffering and had given ample warning and sufficient time to repent. Even after Lehi fled Jerusalem to escape its imminent destruction, fourteen years transpired before Nebuchadnezzar's armies leveled the City and the Temple.

NEBUCHADNEZZAR, KING OF BABYLON

Emerging as victor at the Battle of Carchemish on the Euphrates, Nebuchadnezzar II (Nabu-kudurri-usur; 605–562 B.C.) solidified his dominions in the Levant. Josiah's son, Jehoahaz, had been made king in Jerusalem after his father's death in 609 B.C., but Pharaoh Nechoh had taken him away to Egypt and put his brother Eliakim on the throne. Eliakim's name was changed to Jehoiakim.

Nebuchadnezzar pursued the Assyrian policy of population deportation. There were three major deportations: in 605, 597, and 586 B.C. One might suppose that by the third invasion of Babylon's armies, somebody would have been believing the prophets.

In 605–604 B.C. the Babylonian warrior-king exiled some Jews from Jerusalem, including Daniel and his three friends. Jehoiakim reigned for eleven years, until 598–597 B.C., after which Nebuchadnezzar carried him away to Babylon or had him killed. Jehoiakim's son Jehoiachin was allowed to rule as a vassal or puppet king of the Babylonians. His reign lasted only three months, as Nebuchadnezzar summoned him to Babylon along with "ten thousand captives, and all the craftsmen and smiths" (2 Kgs. 24:14), including Ezekiel.[23] He also carried away the

Temple treasures (2 Kgs. 24:13). Jehoiachin's uncle Mattaniah began to reign, and Mattaniah's name was changed to Zedekiah. The first page of the Book of Mormon dates to the commencement of Zedekiah's reign.[24] Lehi and his family fled Jerusalem by way of the wilderness, possibly taking the old desert road southeast to En Gedi and then turning south for another 150 miles to the Red Sea and beyond.[25]

Zedekiah reigned for eleven years in Jerusalem; in his ninth year the Babylonian armies returned to conduct the two-year siege that culminated in the utter destruction of the city.[26] Zedekiah was the last of the royal Davidic dynasty to reign in ancient Jerusalem.

> And it came to pass in the ninth year of his reign, in the tenth month, in the tenth day of the month, that Nebuchadnezzar king of Babylon came, he, and all his host, against Jerusalem, and pitched against it; and they built forts against it round about.
> And the city was besieged unto the eleventh year of king Zedekiah.
> And on the ninth day of the fourth month the famine prevailed in the city, and there was no bread for the people of the land.
> And the city was broken up, and all the men of war fled by night by the way of the gate between two walls, which is by the king's garden: (now the Chaldees were against the city round about:) and the king went the way toward the plain.
> And the army of the Chaldees pursued after the king, and overtook him in the plains of Jericho: and all his army were scattered from him.
> So they took the king, and brought him up to the king of Babylon to Riblah; and they gave judgment upon him.
> And they slew the sons of Zedekiah before his eyes, and put out the eyes of Zedekiah, and bound him with fetters of brass, and carried him to Babylon. (2 Kgs. 25:1–7)[27]

We know from Jeremiah 34:7 that two fortified positions were the last to hold out against the armies of Babylon: "When the king of Babylon's army fought against Jerusalem, and against all the cities of Judah that were left, against Lachish, and against Azekah: for these defenced cities remained of the cities of Judah."

Archaeological discoveries corroborate the biblical record of the Babylonian sieges and the destruction of Jerusalem. Three specific discoveries will be mentioned here.

The Chronicle of Nebuchadnezzar II is a cuneiform inscription that mentions the siege of "the city of Judah" (Jerusalem) in 598–597 B.C., the displacement of Jehoiachin as king of Judah, and the appointment of Zedekiah to the throne (see 2 Kgs. 24:10–18).[28]

The Lachish Ostraca were found by J. L. Starkey in the gateway guardroom at Tel ed-Duweir (biblical Lachish) in 1935. They are letters or drafts of letters communicating information between military commanders in Lachish and Jerusalem during the Judeo-Babylonian war before the fall of Jerusalem—written, therefore, about 588 B.C.[29] Lachish Letter 4 paints the same woeful picture as Jeremiah. One sentence from the letter reads: "And let [my lord] know that we are watching [over] the signals of Lachish, according to all the indications which my lord hath given, for we cannot see [the signals of] Azekah"[30]—meaning that Azekah had fallen to the enemy. Only Lachish was left; then the Babylonians marched on Jerusalem.[31]

The Babylonian armies camped on the hills overlooking Jerusalem. One principal camp was on the northern end of the Mount of Olives, also called Mount Scopus (which now includes the site of Brigham Young University's Jerusalem Center for Near Eastern Studies). By surrounding the city, the Babylonians blocked efforts to resupply its citizens. The situation became extremely desperate when food storage was used up and starvation set in (see Jer. 37:21; 52:6; 2 Kgs. 25:3). The besieging armies systematically broke down the walls of Jerusalem, and Nebuchadnezzar's captain eventually "burnt the house of the Lord, and the king's house, and all the houses of Jerusalem, and every great man's house burnt he with fire" (2 Kgs. 25:9; see also Jer. 52:13). Babylon thus earned undying opprobrium for having razed the nearly four-centuries-old Temple of God and leaving it in ruins.[32]

Excavations in the City of David and in today's Jewish Quarter attest to the destruction in the 587–586 B.C. siege of Jerusalem: many arrowheads, a destroyed four-room house, a burnt room, and clay *bullae* (letter seals or stamps)[33] baked hard by a great conflagration that swept over the whole city. The bullae were found in what has come to be known as "the bullae house," which the excavator Yigal Shiloh speculated may have been an official administrative archive.[34] Inscribed on the bullae were fifty-one different names of scribes, court officials, and ministers, a high percentage of them with the theophoric suffix *-yahu* (Jehovah). Most of the names are known from the Bible and other inscriptions. One such name is Gemariah, son of Shaphan, likely the same man mentioned in Jeremiah 36, a sort of secretary of state in the court of Jehoiakim, king of Judah from 609 to 598 B.C.[35] Another seal mentions the scribe and friend of the prophet Jeremiah, Berechiah, son of Neriah. Berechiah is the long form of Baruch. This same Baruch ben Neriah served as scribe for Jeremiah and recorded his teachings, including predictions of the downfall of Judah and Jerusalem (see Jer. 36:10–25).[36]

As late as 1962 the most widely used textbook on biblical archaeology lamented that "from Jerusalem no archaeological evidence of the Babylonian destruction has been recovered."[37] The excavations of Kathleen Kenyon and Yigal Shiloh make such a statement no longer true. There is now considerable physical evidence[38] of the fulfillment of Lehi's and Jeremiah's prophecies of the destruction of Jerusalem.[39] Numerous houses were destroyed in the Babylonian siege of the city. In or near one such four-room house, two Aramaic ostraca were found with the inscribed name *Ahiel,* possibly the owner of the house.[40] Other inscriptions found in excavations in the City of David are of interest in light of the Book of Mormon. Professor Shiloh reported finding three different sherds of local pottery inscribed with South Arabian names in the South Arabian script of ca. 600 B.C. According to Shiloh, "The discovery of such objects, in the Jerusalem of the eve of its destruction, is of particular importance in connection with the cultural ties between Judah and the Red Sea and South Arabia in this period."[41] Such finds support the authenticity of the story of Lehi's trek, for he, too, seems to have been acquainted with travel routes between Judah and the Red Sea, and South Arabia is the area to which he led his family, probably following the "Frankincense Trail" along the western edge of the Arabian peninsula.[42]

Though Babylonians did carry out mass deportations, they did not follow the Assyrians' policy of transpopulation. Jews were forced away from their land, but nobody was brought in to settle it. The few remaining Jews, mostly poor, eked out a bare existence and paid tribute to their conquerors. The administrative center of the Babylonians was about seven miles north of Jerusalem, at Mizpah. Details of the political intrigue that ensued at Mizpah, the murder of the Babylonian governor, the release of Jeremiah from prison, the flight of many Jews to Egypt, and their forcing Jeremiah to accompany them are all recorded in Jeremiah 39 to 44.

THE GREAT EXILE

Both Israelite kingdoms had been destroyed and their people banished from the land of promise. The great Jehovah had desired from the days of Abraham and of Moses that his people would seek the Lord and live, keep his statutes, stay long upon the land, and make Jerusalem the City of Righteousness. "And the Lord God of their fathers sent to them by his messengers, rising up betimes, and sending; because he had compassion on his people, and on his dwelling place: but they mocked the messengers of God, and despised his words, and misused his prophets, until the wrath of the Lord arose against his people, till there was no remedy" (2 Chron. 36:15–16; see also 1 Ne. 1).

The feelings of the exiles as they languished in the heart of Babylon are captured in Psalm 137:

> By the rivers of Babylon, there we sat down, yea, we wept, when we remembered Zion.
> We hanged our harps upon the willows in the midst thereof.
> For there they that carried us away captive required of us a song; and they that wasted us required of us mirth, saying, Sing us one of the songs of Zion.
> How shall we sing the Lord's song in a strange land?
> If I forget thee, O Jerusalem, let my right hand forget her cunning.
> If I do not remember thee, let my tongue cleave to the roof of my mouth; if I prefer not Jerusalem above my chief joy.[43]

Another Israelite psalmist described his people as a vine that the Lord planted in the vineyard of Israel, which flourished and expanded for a time and was then uprooted. The psalmist added a plea to the Lord of the vineyard to visit his vine and have mercy on it:

> Thou hast brought a vine out of Egypt: thou hast cast out the heathen, and planted it.
> Thou preparedst room before it, and didst cause it to take deep root, and it filled the land.
> The hills were covered with the shadow of it, and the boughs thereof were like the goodly cedars.
> She sent out her boughs unto the sea [Mediterranean], and her branches unto the river [the Jordan].
> Why hast thou then broken down her hedges, so that all they which pass by the way do pluck her?

The boar out of the wood doth waste it, and the wild beast of the field doth devour it.

Return, we beseech thee, O God of hosts: look down from heaven, and behold, and visit this vine;

And the vineyard which thy right hand hath planted, and the branch that thou madest strong for thyself. (Ps. 80:8–15)

Unlike her predecessor—Melchizedek's Salem, which was taken up—Jerusalem was broken down and lay in ruins. Nevertheless, the Eternal City, with a divine foundation and with a divine destiny, was not to be left permanently in oblivion. A remnant would always return.

Notes

1. Mazar, *Mountain of the Lord,* 54.

2. Archaeologist Nahman Avigad unearthed the massive wall, which he believed encompassed the entire plateau of the Western Hill (see *Anchor Bible Dictionary,* 3:755) and which is estimated to have stood more than twenty-five feet high. "Avigad reasoned that only a king could have ordered the building of so major a structure, and the fact that new housing had to be destroyed in the process indicates that the wall was erected during a crisis." Rosovsky, "Thousand Years of History in Jerusalem's Jewish Quarter," 26. Additional information and photos of the wall may be seen in Avigad, *Discovering Jerusalem,* 37, 46–49; *New Encyclopedia of Archaeological Excavations,* 2:706; Bahat, *Illustrated Atlas of Jerusalem,* 29; *Anchor Bible Dictionary,* 3:756.

3. Simons, *Jerusalem in the Old Testament,* 185. Read the biblical references to this amazing engineering feat of Hezekiah in 2 Kgs. 20:20 and 2 Chron. 32:2–4, 30. The inscription in the tunnel reads as follows in English translation: "This is the story of the boring through: while [the tunnelers swung] the pickax each towards his fellow, and while three cubits [yet remained] to be cut through, [there was heard] the voice of a man calling to his fellow, for there was a split [or fissure] in the rock on the right hand and on [the left]. And on the day of the boring through, the tunnelers struck through, each in the direction of his fellows, pickax against pickax. And the water started to flow from the spring to the pool for twelve hundred cubits; a hundred cubits was the height of the rock above the head of the tunnelers." (Cf. translation in Kenyon, *Jerusalem,* 70; Pritchard, *Ancient Near Eastern Texts,* 321; Thomas, *Documents from Old Testament Times,* 210.) The Prophet Isaiah wrote: "You collected the waters of the lower pool. . . . You made a reservoir between the two walls for the water of the old pool" (RSV Isa. 22:9, 11), indicating that Hezekiah had created a new pool for collecting the Gihon Spring water that flowed through his newly carved tunnel—and all within the newly built city walls. See Paton, *Jerusalem in Bible Times,* 105–6. Amiran said that Hezekiah's Tunnel is "properly considered to be the largest of the known ancient hydro-technical projects in [Israel]." Yadin, *Jerusalem Revealed,* 77. It has been estimated that the time it took to dig the tunnel, with workers laboring around the clock, twenty-four hours a day, was approximately seven to eight months. A photo of the inscription and more information on the tunnel may be found in Gill, "How They Met," 20–38, 64; *New Encyclopedia of*

Archaeological Excavations, 2:710–11; Ogden and Chadwick, *Holy Land,* 213–14. The original inscription is now in the Archaeological Museum in Istanbul, Turkey.

4. See Aharoni and Avi-Yonah, *Macmillan Bible Atlas,* Map 152.

5. Three original copies of the inscribed cylinder made in ancient Assyria have been found: one is in the British Museum in London, another in the Oriental Institute in Chicago, and the third in the Israel Museum in Jerusalem. See Harker, *Digging Up the Bible Lands,* 41–44; Thompson, *Bible and Archaeology,* 150–51; Thomas, *Documents from Old Testament Times,* 64–70 (all references include photographs).

6. See Bible Map 9, C6; see also Aharoni and Avi-Yonah, *Macmillan Bible Atlas,* Map 154.

7. See Mazar, *Archaeology of the Land of the Bible,* 427–35; Pritchard, *Ancient Near East in Pictures,* 371–74.

8. Archaeologists working there have claimed that there is no other archaeological site in the Holy Land whose remains illustrate so accurately the records of the Old Testament. A detailed account of Sennacherib's siege of Lachish, with photographs and superb drawings, is contained in *Conquest of Lachish by Sennacherib,* a large volume by the head of the Lachish Expedition, Professor David Ussishkin.

9. Pritchard, *Ancient Near Eastern Texts,* 288; cf. Thomas, *Documents from Old Testament Times,* 64–69.

10. Herodotus, *History* 2.141.

11. Scholars are often reluctant to attribute anything "miraculous" to the intervention of God himself. For example, Kathleen Kenyon, excavator of Jerusalem, explains that Jerusalem "was saved by a mixture of active defensive measures and diplomacy." *Royal Cities of the Old Testament,* 134. Mazar notes that "the Assyrian siege of Jerusalem was terminated abruptly (probably due to internal problems in Assyria), an event which was seen by the Judeans as a miraculous deliverance." *Archaeology of the Land of the Bible,* 405.

12. *Norton Anthology of Poetry,* 588–89.

13. Ashurbanipal is also famous for his impressive library at Nineveh, the single most important source of Akkadian literature. He seems to have been one of the few literate kings of the ancient Near East—he could read his own texts. More than twenty-five thousand documents have been recovered, including the creation story called *Enuma Elish* and the *Gilgamesh Epic,* which preserves the tradition of the biblical Flood.

14. Also 2 Chron. 33:2–9. The verses that follow, 2 Chron. 33:11–13, suggest that Assyrian officers bound Manasseh and hauled him off with hooks and chains to Babylon. His suffering brought him to humility and repentance, and he was restored to his throne in Jerusalem. This account is not confirmed by the parallel and subsequent accounts in the biblical books of Kings or by the prophets or by tradition.

15. See 1 Pet. 5:13; Rev. 14:8; 17:5; and D&C 1:16; 35:11; 64:24; 86:3.

16. *Hymns,* nos. 319, 7.

17. Jeremiah was a Levite from Anathoth (see Josh. 21:18), one of the Levitical cities, which lay about one hour's walk over the Mount of Olives northeast of Jerusalem (still called in Arabic *Anata*). He is mentioned in the Book of Mormon, and Laban, an elder of the Jews, must have been acquainted with him (see 1 Ne. 5:13; 7:14; Helaman 8:20). The first year of Nebuchadnezzar was 605 B.C. Jeremiah began his ministry about 627 B.C., and he continued prophesying right to the day Nebuchadnezzar entered Jerusalem in 587 B.C.—a total of forty years (see Jer. 25:3). People may have begun to wonder about

Jeremiah's prophecies when five years passed, then ten, then twenty. They could have become a little complacent, especially with false prophets predicting opposite and more comfortable prophecies. ("The prophets prophesy falsely, and the priests bear rule by their means; and my people love to have it so"; Jer. 5: 31.) Lamentations of Jeremiah are the prophet's eyewitness feelings over the destruction of Jerusalem. They are worth reading—aloud—for the depth of feeling in the loss of the City and Temple. The title of the book in the Greek Septuagint is *Threnoi,* and in the Latin Vulgate is called *Threni,* both meaning "tears." The Septuagint prefaces Lamentations with these lines: "And it came to pass after Israel had been taken away into captivity and Jerusalem had been laid waste that Jeremiah sat weeping and lamented this lamentation over Jerusalem and said . . ."

18. Some people think prophets have no business involving themselves in politics. If so, they've never read the Old Testament. Elijah and Elisha were very involved in the politics of their day. Isaiah, Amos, Jeremiah, Daniel, and others, too, were also very involved in the politics of their day. The Lord is not limited in his sphere of influence.

19. Jeremiah, like Isaiah and other prophets, followed the pattern of doom-hope. He foresaw doom-desolation-destruction, but he also foresaw a glorious time of reinstatement-restoration-redemption. Biblical scholars and archaeologists have also recognized this pattern in the prophets' writings. See, for example, Levine, *Jerusalem Cathedra,* 2:23. Specific references in Jeremiah to the Jews' return to Jerusalem ("the Jews" is used here in a national sense, meaning Israelites then living in the southern kingdom of Judah), and their prosperity in it are found in 3:17–18; 16:14–15; 23:3; 24:6–7; 30:3; 31:17; 32:37–38, 42; 33:15–16. Lehi similarly prophesied of hope in the future; see, for example, 1 Ne. 10:3.

20. Read and compare Jeremiah 7, another scathing speech by the prophet in the court of the Temple. He condemned the people's false sense of security because of the Temple, and he cataloged the abominations for which they would be punished. The Lord's House would be destroyed, just as the holy sanctuary at Shiloh had been destroyed (see v. 12).

21. On the flight of Lehi's colony from Jerusalem and the two return trips to the city for records and companions—for ancestry and prophecy and posterity—see Jackson, *1 Nephi to Alma 29,* 17–33.

22. "Some remarkable deliverance must be assumed . . . [which] served to strengthen belief in the inviolability of Zion until it became, in later years, a fixed national dogma. . . . The inviolability of Temple, city, and nation [became] in the popular mind . . . an indisputable dogma." Bright, *History of Israel,* 288, 332.

23. Ezekiel envisioned the Shekhinah (the Divine Presence or Glory of God) departing from the Temple, leaving it vulnerable for destruction (see Ezek. 10:18–19; 11:23).

24. Placing the date of the inauguration of Zedekiah's reign at 597 B.C., as most chronologies do, seems to be a discrepancy with the Book of Mormon account, which specifically identifies the first year of his reign as six hundred years before Christ (cf. 1 Ne. 1:4; 5:10–13; 10:4; 19:8; headnote to 3 Ne.; 3 Ne. 1:1). There is a similar discrepancy of three or four years when we date the death of Herod the Great at 4 B.C., after his attempt to kill the infant Jesus by his infamous extermination order. It is a problem of calendaring.

25. During military clearing operations for a new road in the southeastern Shephelah in 1961 at a site called Khirbet Beit-Lei, an undisturbed cave, now called the "Jerusalem Cave," was broken into and discovered to contain some hastily carved figures and words. Some have wondered—because the figure of a man appears to have arms extended

toward heaven and an inscription speaks of the God of Judah in Jerusalem, because the graffiti are so hastily scrawled on the cave walls, and because there is even the semblance of a ship—if perhaps this could have been the work of the prophet Lehi and company fleeing Jerusalem on their way to the Red Sea in the year 600 B.C. Some rather elaborate "evidences" have been devised to support claims about this "Lehi Cave." We do know, however, that—

(1) There is no evidence that the cave incisions date to 600 B.C. Some scholars suggest that the cave's temporary tenants could have been refugees from the Babylonians during the war atmosphere of the late seventh century before Christ, but others have proposed that the refugees were fleeing the Assyrians a century earlier.

(2) There is no evidence that Lehi or anyone else heading toward the Red Sea would have traveled southwest instead of southeast. Indeed, the Book of Mormon specifies that they abandoned their home in the land of Jerusalem and fled into the wilderness—in a southeastern route. See 1 Ne. 2:2, 4.

(3) There is no evidence that Lehi and his group knew anything about the future prospect of building a ship; that was yet eight years away.

For more information about the moribund controversies over this cave and its graffiti, see Berrett, "The So-called Lehi Cave."

The cave walls have been transferred to the Israel National Museum mainly because the graffiti represent the earliest known appearance of the name *Jerusalem* in archaic Hebrew. The inscription reads: "I am Jehovah thy God; I will protect the cities of Judah and will redeem Jerusalem." See Mazar, *Mountain of the Lord,* 60.

26. Jerusalem fell to Babylon in the summer of 587 or the summer of 586 B.C., depending on whose calendaring system is used. See the discussion of the chronology problem in Hayes and Miller, *Israelite and Judaean History,* 474–75. The year 586 seems to be the most accepted date. See Horn, "When Was the Babylonian Destruction of Jerusalem?" 63.

27. In Jeremiah 39:6 we have another record of Zedekiah's sons being killed. From Helaman 8:21 we learn that one son, Mulek, escaped, and helped lead a colony of Jews to the other side of the world.

28. Thomas, *Documents from Old Testament Times,* 80–81; see also Avi-Yonah, *Our Living Bible,* 156; Mazar, *Mountain of the Lord,* 59.

29. Eighteen letters were discovered, all written with carbon ink on potsherds. They constitute one of the greatest archaeological evidences of the Old Testament ever discovered. Torczyner, who wrote the definitive commentary on the subject, noted: "In these letters we have the most valuable discovery yet made in the biblical archaeology of Palestine and the most intimate corroboration of the Bible to this day." *Lachish I: Lachish Letters,* 18. See also Nibley, "The Lachish Letters," 48–54; Kenyon, *Royal Cities of the Old Testament,* 146–47; Thompson, *Bible and Archaeology,* 158 (photo).

30. Pritchard, *Ancient Near Eastern Texts,* 322; Thomas, *Documents from Old Testament Times,* 216; Aharoni and Avi-Yonah, *Macmillan Bible Atlas,* Map 162; Hayes and Miller, *Israelite and Judaean History,* 473–74.

31. Note the setting for all this action on Bible Map 9; Azekah is near Socoh. See also Aharoni and Avi-Yonah, *Macmillan Bible Atlas,* Map 162.

32. The biblical account (see 2 Kgs. 25:13–17; 2 Chron. 36:18) lists the objects taken from the Temple by the Babylonians. The sacred Ark of the Covenant is not mentioned; it

may have been carried away in some previous depredation of the Temple treasures, or it may have been—during the previous occasions and again on this occasion—hidden up and preserved. In any case, the Ark is now lost to our knowledge. Josephus described the plundering of the Temple as follows: "Now it was that the king of Babylon sent Nebuzaradan, the general of his army, to Jerusalem, to pillage the temple; who had it also in command to burn it and the royal palace, and to lay the city even with the ground, and to transplant the people into Babylon. Accordingly, he came to Jerusalem, in the eleventh year of king Zedekiah, pillaged the temple, and carried out the vessels of God, both gold and silver, and particularly that large laver which Solomon dedicated, as also the pillars of brass, and their chapiters, with the golden tables and the candlesticks: and when he had carried these off, he set fire to the temple . . . he also burnt the palace, and overthrew the city." *Antiquities* 10.8.5.

33. In the ancient Near East seals were used much as we use a signature to indicate ownership and to authenticate documents. Egyptian private seals were most often in the shape of scarabs, and Mesopotamian seals were cylinders. They were made of semiprecious stones, limestone, bone, glass, or metals. Most contained a name and an artistic design. Some seals were used to seal rolled-up papyrus documents. Such written documents were tied with a string, and then a small wet glob of clay was applied to the tie and impressed with a seal. These clay seal impressions are called *bullae* (singular, *bulla*). The importance of sealing a document is reflected in the account of a business transaction involving the prophet Jeremiah (see Jer. 32:9-14).

34. *Anchor Bible Dictionary,* 3:755.

35. "If our identification is correct, the personage whose name appears on the bulla from the City of David was one of the scribes active at the royal court in Jerusalem. His father was a scribe at the court of Josiah in his 18th year (622 B.C.E.). Eighteen years later . . . Gemariah son of Shaphan, and his son Micaiah, are also mentioned. The location of Gemariah's chamber, in 'the upper court at the entry of the new gate' of the Temple (Jeremiah 36:10), where Baruch the scribe read Jeremiah's scroll, certainly testifies to the importance of this personage." Shiloh, "Group of Hebrew Bullae," 34. See also *New Encyclopedia of Archaeological Excavations,* 2:708; *Anchor Bible Dictionary,* 2:59.

36. Avigad, "Baruch the Scribe and Jerahmeel the King's Son," 52–56; Schneider, "Six Biblical Signatures," 26–33. See also Geva, *Ancient Jerusalem Revealed,* 55–61.

37. Wright, *Biblical Archaeology,* 182.

38. Shiloh writes: "The Babylonians' destruction of Jerusalem in 586 B.C.E. is well documented in the biblical sources (2 Kgs. 25:8-10; 2 Chr. 36:18-19), which describe the destruction, burning, and collapse of houses and walls. The archaeological evidence for this phase in Jerusalem's history, which rounds out the historical account, can be counted among the most dramatic at any biblical site." In *New Encyclopedia of Archaeological Excavations,* 2:709; see also *Anchor Bible Dictionary,* 2:59.

39. Specific prophecies concerning the destruction of Jerusalem are as follows:

Lehi. 1 Ne. 1:4, 13, 18; 2:13; 3:17; 7:13; 10:3; 2 Ne. 1:4.

Jeremiah. Jer. 1:14-15; 9:11; 13:13-14; 19:7-9; 21:9-10; 34:2; Helaman 8:20-21. (Cf. Ezek. 4:1-3; 5:5-12; 11:1-10; 14:21; 15:6-8.)

40. *New Encyclopedia of Archaeological Excavations,* 2:708.

41. Shiloh, *Qedem 19, City of David I,* 19. See also Shanks, "Yigal Shiloh," 22.

42. Ogden and Chadwick, *Holy Land,* 207.

43. The exiles' feelings are hauntingly paralleled by the medieval Jewish poet Yehuda Halevi, who lived in Spain, in the famous couplet expressing his longing for the national homeland, "My heart is in the east, but I at the farthest west." Many displaced Jews of the Babylonian Captivity must have experienced similar heart-wrenching yearning for their homeland.

8

THE RETURN TO JERUSALEM, 539–333 B.C.

For more than half a century, the City of Jerusalem and the Temple of God lay in ruins. But the great exile in Babylon, as Jeremiah prophesied, was to endure only a generation or two: "For thus saith the Lord, That after seventy years be accomplished at Babylon I will visit you, and perform my good word toward you, in causing you to return to this place" (Jer. 29:10; cf. Dan. 9:2). By the time the exiles returned to Jerusalem and rebuilt and dedicated a second Temple (515 B.C.), exactly seventy years had passed away. "To fulfil the word of the Lord by the mouth of Jeremiah, until the land had enjoyed her sabbaths: for as long as she lay desolate she kept sabbath, to fulfil threescore and ten years" (2 Chron. 36:21). The Lord had said through Moses that if Israel desecrated the Sabbath Day and became rebellious and disobedient, "I will scatter you among the heathen, and will draw out a sword after you: and your land shall be desolate, and your cities waste. Then shall the land enjoy her sabbaths, as long as it lieth desolate, and ye be in your enemies' land; even then shall the land rest, and enjoy her sabbaths" (Lev. 26:33–34).

THE PERSIAN EMPIRE

Nebuchadnezzar's successor, Nabonidus (555–539 B.C.), promoted the worship of his own idol god, which affronted priests of the Babylonian gods Marduk and Bel in the empire's capital. Nabonidus spent ten years away from Babylon at the Arabian town of Teima, in a mystic retreat, leaving his son Belshazzar to reign in his stead at Babylon.

Then the priests of Marduk led the citizens in a revolt. Cyrus the Persian walked into the city in a bloodless conquest (see Dan. 5:1–30).

Cyrus II (538–529 B.C.) had united the Persians and the Medes to form the greatest empire ever known to that point in the history of the ancient Near East (see Bible Map 12). The two kingdoms, Media in the north and Persia in the south, together occupied the million square miles of the Iranian plateau. The core of the Persian homeland extended from the Tigris Valley on the west, the Persian Gulf on the south, the Indus Valley on the east, and the Armenian mountains and Caspian Sea on the north. The dominions of the Persian Empire—also called the Achaemenid Empire because it was ruled by the dynasty of an eponymous king named Achaemenes—eventually extended from the Indus Valley in the east to Ethiopia in the southwest and Macedonia in the northwest (see Esth. 1:1).

The Persian Empire was among the first to issue gold coinage. It operated a postal system and constructed a network of highways.[1] Capitals or chief cities of the empire were Ecbatana (*Achmetha* in Ezra 6:2), Pasargadae, Persepolis, and Susa. This last city was the capital of the region called Elam. Called *Shushan* in the Bible, Susa was the setting for some of the greatest concluding historical and religious accounts in the Old Testament.[2]

Unlike their predecessors, the early Persian rulers were beneficent and humane, allowing local autonomy and freedom of religion. Cyrus himself was possibly a Zoroastrian but apparently a religious eclectic, adopting the gods of various conquered peoples and collectively worshipping them all. Isaiah foretold the rise of the Persian Empire under Cyrus two centuries before the dramatic events actually occurred, and he called Cyrus the Lord's anointed, a type of the Messiah, foreordained to sponsor the great Return of the Jews. "[The Lord] saith of Cyrus, He is my shepherd, and shall perform all my pleasure: even saying to Jerusalem, Thou shalt be built; and to the temple, Thy foundation shall be laid" (Isa. 44:28; see also Isa. 45:1).

CYRUS THE GREAT

Cyrus established 127 *satrapies* (provinces or states; see Esth. 1:1) throughout the empire, and his chief prince or president was Daniel, the

Hebrew prophet.³ One of the provinces, the land of Judah, was called by the imperial government *Yehud,* being part of the Persian satrapy "Beyond the River" (Hebrew, *Avar Nahara,* meaning the region west of the Euphrates).⁴ Few events in all of ancient Near Eastern history can parallel in importance the events that Cyrus set in motion:

> Now in the first year of Cyrus king of Persia, that the word of the Lord spoken by the mouth of Jeremiah might be accomplished, the Lord stirred up the spirit of Cyrus king of Persia, that he made a proclamation throughout all his kingdom, and put it also in writing, saying,
>
> Thus saith Cyrus king of Persia, All the kingdoms of the earth hath the Lord God of heaven given me; and he hath charged me to build him an house in Jerusalem, which is in Judah. Who is there among you of all his people? The Lord his God be with him, and let him go up. (2 Chron. 36:22–23; Ezra 1:1–3; see also Dan. 1:21; 6:28; 10:1)

Cyrus encouraged the Jews to return to their homeland⁵ and rebuild their capital and Temple, as prophesied. He even placed some of the wealth of the empire in their hands to accomplish those tasks. Perhaps Daniel had some influence on that decision. The Jewish historian Josephus wrote in the first century after Christ how Cyrus was influenced by the prophecies of Isaiah:

> [The Lord] stirred up the mind of Cyrus, and made him write this throughout all Asia:—"Thus saith Cyrus the King:—Since God Almighty hath appointed me to be king of the habitable earth, I believe that he is that God which the nation of the Israelites worship; for indeed he foretold my name by the prophets, and that I should build him a house at Jerusalem, in the country of Judea." This was known to Cyrus by his reading the book which Isaiah left behind him of his prophecies [Did Daniel show the king those prophecies?]; for this prophet said that God had spoken thus to him in a secret vision:—"My will is, that Cyrus, whom I have appointed to be king over many and great nations, send back my people to their own land, and build my temple." This was foretold by Isaiah one hundred and forty years before the temple was demolished. Accordingly, when Cyrus read this, and admired the divine power, an earnest desire and ambition seized upon him to fulfil what was so written; so he called for the most eminent Jews that were in Babylon, and said to them, that he gave them leave to go back to their own country, and to rebuild their city Jerusalem, and the temple of God, for that he would be their assistant.⁶

BUILDING A SECOND TEMPLE IN JERUSALEM

The first six chapters of Ezra record history of the century before Ezra (the sixth century before Christ) and include a list of the people in the first exodus from Babylon back to the land of Jerusalem. One migration of Jews numbered nearly fifty thousand (see Ezra 2:64–65).[7] The first generation returned under the direction of Sheshbazzar, Jehoiachin's son and newly appointed governor of Yehud. "And all they that were about them [meaning those who declined to make the trip themselves?] strengthened their hands with vessels of silver, with gold, with goods, and with beasts, and with precious things, beside all that was willingly offered" (Ezra 1:6). In addition, the Persian government returned the sacred vessels that had been taken by the Babylonians out of the Jerusalem Temple: "Also Cyrus the king brought forth the vessels of the house of the Lord, which Nebuchadnezzar had brought forth out of Jerusalem, and had put them in the house of his gods; even those did Cyrus king of Persia bring forth by the hand of [his] treasurer, and numbered them unto Sheshbazzar, the prince of Judah" (Ezra 1:7–8).[8]

The next generation of Jews returned under Zerubbabel ben Shealtiel, grandson of Jehoiachin and nephew of Sheshbazzar.[9] Zerubbabel was a descendant of King David, the last of the royal lineage in the Old Testament period, and was an ancestor of Jesus Christ (see Matt. 1:12). Another leader of this wave of returnees was the Levitical high priest Jeshua (or Joshua) ben Jozadak (see Ezra 2:2; 3:2; 5:2).

The principal concern of the exiles returning in the sixth century before Christ was the Temple. Upon arriving in Jerusalem they immediately rebuilt the Temple altar and resumed morning and evening sacrifices (see Ezra 3:1–5). They also kept the Feast of Tabernacles.[10] They employed Phoenicians to import cedar from Lebanon and engaged masons and carpenters to begin rebuilding the Temple. The workers laid the stone foundation, and the congregation of Israel sang and shouted for joy, though many of the older generation also wept aloud as they stood among the ruins and recalled the glorious structure that had previously graced the Temple Hill of Jerusalem. We reflect again on the statement by the Prophet Joseph Smith that the main object of gathering the people of God in any age of the world was "to build unto the Lord a house whereby He could reveal unto His people the ordinances of His house and the glories of His kingdom, and teach the people the way of salvation."[11]

The newly returned Jews set about restoring regular worship in the Temple but quickly learned, as the Saints have learned in all ages of the world, that when a House of the Lord is to be erected, serious opposition is often mounted to obstruct the effort. In this case, the Samaritans became the adversaries. Those mixed remnants of northern Israel[12] had appropriated the land of Jerusalem since the dispersion of Judah—claiming it, because they considered themselves "the remnant of Israel," as their own. When they sought to help the former exiles and requested permission to participate with the Jews in reconstructing the Temple in Jerusalem, they were rebuffed. They then sought revenge and antagonized the Jews in their struggle to reestablish themselves once again in their homeland.

Samaritans later built their own rival holy place on Mount Gerizim,[13] but they now had no intention of allowing the Jews to reconstruct their Temple in Jerusalem. They hired legal counsel to frustrate, obstruct, and delay the Jews' efforts (see Ezra 4:4–5). A letter drafted by the Samaritan leaders was sent to the Persian capital advising the government that the Jews had arrived in Yehud and were building up "the rebellious and the bad city" of Jerusalem (Ezra 4:12). The Samaritans warned the imperial court that if the former exiles were permitted to reestablish themselves in Jerusalem, the Jews would not "pay toll, tribute, and custom" and thus "endamage the revenue of the kings." Challenge was also given to search the archives and "know that this city is a rebellious city, and hurtful unto kings and provinces, and that they have moved sedition within the same of old time: for which cause was this city destroyed" (vv. 13–15). A search was made, and it showed that Jerusalem did indeed have a history of insurrection, rebellion, and sedition. All work on the Temple was ordered to stop.

Soon thereafter the Jewish leaders sent their own letter to the Persian capital at Babylon, requesting that another search be made to discover that authorization to rebuild the Temple at Jerusalem had been decreed years before by the great Cyrus. Upon finding the decree in the royal palace at Achmetha in the province of the Medes, King Darius[14] reissued the proclamation to the governor "beyond the river" and all his administrative staff: "Let the work of this house of God alone; let the governor of the Jews and the elders of the Jews build this house of God in his place" (Ezra 6:7). Moreover, the Persian monarch ordered that the king's goods out of the Yehudan provincial treasuries should be given forthwith to the Jews, "that they be not hindered," and Darius added the encouraging threat: "Also I have made a decree, that whosoever shall alter this word, let timber be pulled down from his house, and being set up, let him be hanged thereon; and let his house be made a dunghill for this" (Ezra 6:8, 11).

THE TEMPLE OF ZERUBBABEL

After a decade and a half of opposition and antagonism by Samaritans and other enemies, work on the Temple resumed in 520 B.C. Zerubbabel, the governor of Judah, supervised the reconstruction along with Jeshua the priest, and the prophets Haggai and Zechariah encouraged the laborers.

> In the second year of Darius the king, in the sixth month, in the first day of the month, came the word of the Lord by Haggai the prophet unto Zerubbabel the son of Shealtiel, governor of Judah, and to Joshua the son of Josedech, the high priest. (Haggai 1:1)
> Then the prophets, Haggai the prophet, and Zechariah the son of Iddo, prophesied unto the Jews that were in Judah and Jerusalem in the name of the God of Israel, even unto them.
> Then rose up Zerubbabel the son of Shealtiel, and Jeshua the son of Jozadak, and began to build the house of God which is at Jerusalem: and with them were the prophets of God helping them. (Ezra 5:1–2)

Zerubbabel followed Melchizedek and Solomon in establishing a Sanctuary or Temple for at least the third time on the Temple Mount in Jerusalem. At the same time, the prophet Zechariah prophesied yet another and greater Temple there in the distant future (see Zech. 6:12–15; 14:20). The prophet Ezekiel also envisioned the future Temple, or at least an ideal Temple. In the twenty-fifth year of the Babylonian captivity Ezekiel envisioned and wrote a detailed description of that distant Temple. In the King James Version of the Bible, immediately following Ezekiel's vision of the battle of Armageddon and a major earthquake in the latter days, is a four-chapter account of the future House of the Lord.[15]

The Temple of Zerubbabel was completed and dedicated in the sixth year of the reign of Darius, in March of 515 B.C. The dedicatory services were held with much rejoicing and many sacrifices and were followed by celebration of the Feast of Passover (see Ezra 6:15–19). This Temple, called the Second Temple, stood for five hundred years. Half a millennium after its initial construction, the Temple was not merely renovated but completely reconstructed by Herod. Yet Herod's Temple was still known as the Second Temple.[16]

In structure and appurtenances this new Temple was not as grand and impressive as the First Temple, though it was basically the same size and architectural style. Those who remembered the previous Temple wept and lamented the inferiority of the restored Sanctuary, which no longer contained the Ark of the Covenant or the Urim and Thummim. Nevertheless, even without the protection of walls and fortifications, and with only a small population, Jerusalem once again became a Temple City.

Enjoying considerable governmental autonomy, the Jews of Jerusalem enjoyed some peace and prosperity during the ensuing decades. From the dedication of the Temple in 515 B.C. until the arrival in 445 B.C. of Nehemiah, another governor for Yehud, seventy years transpired. We know very little about Jerusalem during those seventy years.

EZRA THE PRIEST AND NEHEMIAH THE GOVERNOR

During the rule of Artaxerxes I (reigned 465–424 B.C.) both Ezra and Nehemiah received appointments from the Persian government to carry out religious and political tasks in Yehud. The prophet Malachi also ministered during this period.

Additional migrations of Jews back to their homeland were initiated through the efforts of Ezra in particular.[17] Ezra, a righteous priest and scribe, was appointed in 458 B.C. to organize a group of Jewish exiles to return to the land of their fathers (see Ezra 7:1–11). Numerous Jews joined the perilous caravans to help restore dignity to their former land and society. Ezra set religious affairs in order and initiated rigorous reforms in Jerusalem and Judah.

Though tens of thousands returned to their homeland, many wealthy and influential Jews remained in Babylon, or Persia, and Jewish communities and academies flourished there for centuries—accumulating, among other things, the voluminous legacy of the Babylonian Talmud, with its seemingly endless treatment of rabbinic legal and religious polemics and formulations. Because so many Jews remained in the land of their exile, fire-signals were sent from Jerusalem's Mount of Olives via the highest peaks all the way to the Babylonian Jewish communities to signal the commencement of the holy days.

Nehemiah, a royal cupbearer (one who tested the king's food and drink—a trusted official!) and minister in the Persian court (see Neh. 1:11; 2:1), received an appointment more than a decade after Ezra (in 445 B.C.) to serve as the next governor of Judah, the same position that Zerubbabel had occupied during the previous century. Nehemiah held that position for twelve years (see Neh. 5:14). Although history shows that "it is the nature and disposition of almost all men, as soon as they get a little authority, as they suppose, they will immediately begin to exercise unrighteous dominion" (D&C 121:39), during Nehemiah's twelve-year administration (445–433 B.C.), he refused to overstep his prerogatives as ruler or to be a burden to the people by taxing them for his own sustenance; he labored with his people, a sign of noble humility.[18] Nehemiah, whose name means "Jehovah is comfort," is characterized as sensitive, spiritual, and humble (Neh. 1:4–11).[19]

NEHEMIAH'S NIGHTTIME INSPECTION OF THE WALLS

The principal concern of those returning from exile in the fifth century before Christ was the city walls. A report had come to Nehemiah in the palace at Shushan that "the remnant that are left of the captivity there in the province [of Yehud] are in great affliction and reproach: the wall of Jerusalem also is broken down, and the gates thereof are burned with fire" (Neh. 1:3). For nearly a century and a half Jerusalem's walls lay broken down; Nehemiah sought opportunity to travel there and help provide security for those who resided in the Holy City.[20] Three days after Nehemiah's arrival, his mission still a secret, he made a nighttime reconnaissance of the walls to determine the work that was needed. Nehemiah 2:11–16 gives us the most detailed description in all the Old Testament of the walls, towers, and gates of Jerusalem. These verses explain the features and fortifications in more or less topographical sequence. They

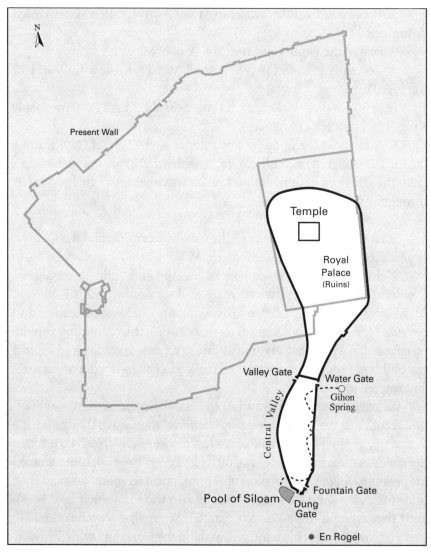

Jerusalem at the time of the return

show Jerusalem as a small city, much reduced from its extent during the First Temple period. Besides what is reported of the Temple, we have virtually no literary or archaeological evidence of other structures in the City in Nehemiah's day. In his nocturnal inspection the new governor apparently rode his donkey and walked along the following course:[21]

1. Exited the Valley Gate, at the northwest corner of the City of David.

2. Proceeded southward along the Central Valley (later called Tyropoeon).

3. Passed the Dung Gate, near the Pool of Siloam.

4. Continued around to the "Dragon Well" (probably En Rogel, or Job's Well).

5. Proceeded to the Fountain Gate, near the King's Pool (probably King Hezekiah's Pool of Siloam).

6. Attempted the upper eastern slopes of the City of David, along the former wall, but found them impassable (there was so much rubble from the Babylonian destruction that he was unable to ride his donkey through it[22]).

7. Continued north up the Kidron Valley.

8. At the northeast corner of the City of David, turned west.

9. Reentered the City through the Valley Gate.

Nehemiah called for the Jews to "rise up and build"; he assigned families to reconstruct various gates and sections of walls (see Neh. 2:17–18; 3).[23] Because of their inspiring and organized leader, and because "the people had a mind to work" (4:6), the rebuilding rapidly progressed, despite hostility and animosity. Enemies conspired against the building program, and some of the Jews criticized, offered excuses, and wanted to give up.

Samaritan, Ammonite, and Arab opposition mounted. One antagonist scoffed at the wall-builders by claiming "that which they build, if a fox go up, he shall even break down their stone wall" (Neh. 4:3). When the enemies threatened to fight against Jerusalem, Nehemiah encouraged his people to follow certain measures of practical religion: "we made our prayer unto our God, and set a watch against them day and night" (4:9), and "they which builded on the wall, and they that bare burdens . . . every one with one of his hands wrought in the work, and with the other hand held a weapon" (4:17). Adversaries tried to get rid of Nehemiah by calling him to negotiations in another part of the land (an assassination plot; see 6:2), by false accusations (or "blackmail"; see 6:6–7), and by intimidation (see 6:10). Nehemiah's magnanimous replies are recorded in Nehemiah 6:3, 8, and 11, showing him to be a wise and spiritual man. Mainly because of their leader's determination, the people finished the important wall around Jerusalem in just fifty-two days. Even their enemies were forced to admit God's hand was in its completion (see 6:16).

The walls of the southeast hill were reconstructed in the same general course and position as the previous walls, except for the walls on the eastern slope, which were not rebuilt. Nehemiah's wall was built near the crest of the five-centuries-old City of David, and for the next three centuries there was little, if any, settlement on the western hill. It remained in ruins, uninhabited.[24] Small segments of Nehemiah's walls have been exposed in several recent excavations.[25]

Nehemiah arranged for 10 percent of the population of Yehud to move to Jerusalem to defend it: "And the rulers of the people dwelt at Jerusalem: the rest of the people also cast lots, to bring one of ten to dwell in Jerusalem the holy city, and nine parts to dwell in other cities. And the people blessed all the men, that willingly offered themselves to dwell at Jerusalem" (Neh. 11:1–2).

ANOTHER KIND OF WALL AROUND JERUSALEM

Having fortified the City with a wall of stone, another kind of wall was needed. The old Solomonic proverb advised, "He that hath no rule over his own spirit is like a city that is broken down, and without walls" (Prov. 25:28). Under the governmental and ecclesiastical jurisdiction of Nehemiah and Ezra, the Law was read in the hearing of the people, religious and moral reforms were carried out, and the great Abrahamic covenant was renewed among the people (see Neh. 8–10). Those who were sealed in this covenant made three promises: not to marry out of the covenant, not to buy and sell or work on the Sabbath, and to pay all tithes and offerings and perform Temple service (10:30–39). Following a visit to the Persian capital, Nehemiah returned with his appointment as *Tirshatha,* or governor, renewed only to find some of the people and even some priests already violating their covenants. He learned that one of his old enemies had been impiously invited to dwell in the sacred Temple area, that the Levites' portion of the sacrificial offerings had not been given them, that the Sabbath was being desecrated, and that marriages were being made outside the covenant. Nehemiah boldly expelled the intruder, immediately rectified the injustice to the Levites, testified against the Sabbath-breakers and contended with them, commanded that the gates be shut during the Sabbath, and warned those who lodged outside the gates on the Sabbath of the consequences if they continued the practice (see Neh. 13:6–22).

The prophet Malachi ministered during these same decades and called for the Lord's people to repent of various sins and apostate practices of the time, especially marriage out of the covenant and divorce.

Very little literary or archaeological evidence has been discovered relating to Jerusalem for the one hundred fifty years after Ezra, Nehemiah, and Malachi. The Talmud declares that with the death of the prophets Haggai, Zechariah, and Malachi, the Holy Spirit departed from Israel,[26] but the remnant of Israel did not vanish—their ethnic and institutional identity has persisted and indeed has never been totally lost. Through the succeeding centuries after the great Exile, more Jews lived away from their homeland than lived in it. Numerous colonies of Jews flourished in Mesopotamia, in Asia Minor, in Egypt,[27] and in other lands. Wherever Jews lived, they perpetuated their Jewishness.

ANOTHER VISION OF JERUSALEM'S FUTURE

Ancient prophets and Saints were often reaching beyond their own time for something brighter and more enduring. A thousand years before Christ, the Israelite psalmists yearned for the House of the Lord and for the Messiah who would come to his holy House. During the trouble and darkness of Assyrian hegemony, Isaiah the prophet foresaw the great light of the Messiah, and he saw beyond that to the last days, when the mountain of the Lord's House would be established in the top of the mountains and all nations would flow unto it, and Jerusalem would be beautiful and glorious and quiet and peaceful—a praise and a rejoicing in all the earth. In the concluding period of the Old Covenant came the prophet Zechariah, whose name *Zachar Yah* means "Remember the Lord." He writes that in a later day the Lord would again choose Jerusalem and his House would be built therein:

> Jerusalem shall be inhabited as towns without walls . . .
> For I, saith the Lord, will be unto her a wall of fire round about, and will be the glory in the midst of her. (2:4–5)

> Sing and rejoice, O daughter of Zion: for, lo, I come, and I will dwell in the midst of thee, saith the Lord.

And many nations shall be joined to the Lord in that day, and shall be my people: and I will dwell in the midst of thee, . . .

And the Lord shall inherit Judah his portion in the holy land, and shall choose Jerusalem again. (2:10–12)

Thus speaketh the Lord of hosts, saying, Behold the man whose name is The BRANCH; and he shall grow up out of his place, and he shall build the temple of the Lord:

Even he shall build the temple of the Lord; and he shall bear the glory, and shall sit and rule upon his throne; and he shall be a priest upon his throne. . . .

And they that are far off shall come and build in the temple of the Lord, and ye shall know that the Lord of hosts hath sent me unto you. And this shall come to pass, if ye will diligently obey the voice of the Lord your God. (6:12–15)

And it shall come to pass in that day, that I will seek to destroy all the nations that come against Jerusalem.

And I will pour upon the house of David, and upon the inhabitants of Jerusalem, the spirit of grace and of supplications: and they shall look upon me whom they have pierced, and they shall mourn . . . and shall be in bitterness. . . .

And one shall say unto him, What are these wounds in thine hands? Then he shall answer, Those with which I was wounded in the house of my friends. (12:9–10; 13:6)

Judah also shall fight at Jerusalem; and the wealth of all the heathen round about shall be gathered together, gold, and silver, and apparel, in great abundance.

For I will gather all nations against Jerusalem to battle; and the city shall be taken, and the houses rifled, and the women ravished; and half of the city shall go forth into captivity, and the residue of the people shall not be cut off from the city.

Then shall the Lord go forth, and fight against those nations, as when he fought in the day of battle.

And his feet shall stand in that day upon the mount of Olives, which is before Jerusalem on the east, and the mount of Olives shall cleave in the midst thereof toward the east and toward the west, and there shall be a very great valley; and half of the mountain shall remove toward the north, and half of it toward the south.

And ye shall flee . . . like as ye fled from before the earthquake in the days of Uzziah king of Judah: and the Lord my God shall come, and all the saints with thee.

And it shall be in that day, that living waters shall go out from Jerusalem; half of them toward the former sea [the Dead Sea], and half of them toward the hinder sea [the Mediterranean]: in summer and in winter shall it be.

And the Lord shall be king over all the earth: in that day shall there be one Lord . . .

. . . and there shall be no more utter destruction; but Jerusalem shall be safely inhabited.

And it shall come to pass, that every one that is left of all the nations which came against Jerusalem shall even go up from year to year to worship the King, the Lord of hosts. . . .

In that day shall there be upon the bells of the horses, HOLINESS UNTO THE LORD; and the pots in the Lord's house shall be like the bowls before the altar.

Yea, every pot in Jerusalem and in Judah shall be holiness unto the Lord of hosts. (14:14, 2–5, 8–9, 11, 16, 20–21)

NOTES

1. The fifteen-hundred-mile Persian Royal Road from Susa to Sardis in Asia Minor is shown in the large-print Bible, Map 12.

2. See Dan. 8:2; Esth. 1:2; Neh. 1:1.

3. Daniel was taken from Jerusalem to Babylon as a young man in 605 B.C. and continued as a government official and a prophet through two empires until about 515 B.C. He served as a chief prince and president of the great Persian Empire, having served in similar positions in the Babylonian Empire: "It pleased Darius to set over the kingdom an hundred and twenty princes, which should be over the whole kingdom; and over these three presidents; of whom Daniel was first: that the princes might give accounts unto them, and the king should have no damage [the Aramaic word means "not be bothered"]. Then this Daniel was preferred [the Aramaic means "distinguished himself"] above the presidents and princes, because an excellent spirit was in him; and the king thought to set him over the whole realm" (Dan. 6:1–3). The book of Daniel divides evenly into two parts: chapters 1–6 contain stories of Daniel and his friends, and chapters 7–12 contain Daniel's eschatological visions and revelations (those relating to the "end of times"). One story Daniel tells is of continuing his lifelong habit of prayer to the God of Israel in defiance of a treacherous royal decree and subsequently being accused and cast into a den of lions (see Dan. 6). Because the episode is set in the reign of Darius, Daniel must have been an old man already in his eighties and quite unwilling to compromise his religious principles in the face of any peril to his life.

4. See Aharoni, *Land of the Bible,* 357; cf. Ezra 4:10; 8:36; Neh. 2:7, 9.

5. The *Cyrus Cylinder,* dating to 536 B.C., is a baked clay cylinder or barrel with cuneiform inscription confirming the biblical account that Cyrus permitted captives to return to their respective countries and rebuild their temples. The Cylinder, now in the British Museum, is more than nine inches long and is written in the Babylonian language. The scriptural echoes of Cyrus' proclamation are found in Ezra 1:1–4 (in Hebrew) and in

Ezra 6:1–5 (in Aramaic, the official or archival account of the decree given in the *lingua franca* of the time). See Pritchard, *Ancient Near Eastern Texts,* 316; Thomas, *Documents from Old Testament Times,* 92–94; Shanks, *Ancient Israel,* 165–66; Lundquist, "Life in Ancient Biblical Lands," 43, including photograph.

6. Josephus, *Antiquities* 11.1.1–2.

7. See also Aharoni and Avi-Yonah, *Macmillan Bible Atlas,* Map 169. "Related to the general category of [exiles who were] temple ministrants is a group of individuals who claimed to be priesthood holders and thus eligible to participate in temple rites but whose genealogy could not be certified (Ezra 2:59–63). This group is discussed here in the genealogical register because of the danger they posed in possibly contaminating the temple and desecrating its prescribed rites. We are reminded that the Lord's kingdom is one of order and that all things associated with God's temples are to be done with exactness and propriety. Thus uncertified priests of Zerubbabel's day were forbidden to partake of 'the most holy things' (Ezra 2:63)—special portions of food reserved for the male descendants of Aaron (Lev. 2:3; 7:31–33). It seems their exclusion was not intended to be permanent but only until a divine decision could be received through the use of Urim and Thummim." Jackson, *1 Kings to Malachi,* 341; see also D&C 85:11–12 for a modern application of this same policy.

8. The following verses give an accounting of the thousands of sacred vessels returned to Jerusalem; see also Ezra 6:3–5.

9. Some consider these two men—Zerubbabel and Sheshbazzar—to be the same person. *Sheshbazzar* may simply be the Persian version of the Babylonian *Zerubbabel.* The latter name means "Offspring of Babylon." Jackson, *1 Kings to Malachi,* 338–40; Shanks, *Ancient Israel,* 152; Klein and Klein, *Temple beyond Time,* 73.

10. All through the Second Temple period Jews observed three annual pilgrimage festivals in Jerusalem and at the Temple: *Pesach,* or Passover, commemorating the miraculous deliverance of Israel from Egypt; *Shavuot,* or Pentecost, celebrating receipt of the Law in Sinai; and *Succot,* or Tabernacles, remembering the booths or tabernacles in which their ancestors lived during the Sinai Desert wanderings. These pilgrimages demonstrate the centrality of Jerusalem in Israelite life through these six centuries.

11. Smith, *Teachings of the Prophet Joseph Smith,* 308.

12. Assyrian kings had initiated transpopulation as a method of subjugating conquered peoples. In the eighth century before Christ they deported northern Israelites and imported people from other conquered lands to take their place. Sargon sent to Samaria foreigners from southern Mesopotamia and from north of Damascus. The eventual intermarriage of these foreigners with the Israelites who remained in the land produced what came to be known as Samaritans. Southern Israelites always regarded the Samaritans as genealogical half-breeds and antagonists. The Samaritan woman later said to Jesus, "The Jews have no dealings with the Samaritans" (John 4:9).

13. Avi-Yonah wrote: "An unfortunate result of the energetic enforcement of the full rigor of the Law was the deepening schism between the Jews and the Samaritans. One of the sons of Jehoiada, the son of Eliashib, had married the daughter of Sanballat the Horonite; when Nehemiah drove him out of Jerusalem, he went over to Samaria and helped to establish the rival worship on Mount Gerizim which has continued to this day. With the building of the temple on Mount Gerizim somewhat later the two communities were completely and irrevocably sundered." *Our Living Bible,* 167; see also Shanks, *Ancient Israel,* 174. Recall the Samaritan woman saying to Jesus, "Our fathers

worshipped in this mountain [meaning Gerizim]; and ye say, that in Jerusalem is the place where men ought to worship" (John 4:20).

14. Following the reign of Cyrus' son, Cambyses II (529–521 B.C.), Darius I took control of the empire. Also called Hystaspes and Darius the Great, he reigned from 521 to 486 B.C.

15. Ezekiel's Temple followed closely the plan of Solomon's Temple; see Ezekiel 40–43; Talmage, *House of the Lord*, 37–38. Rabbis N. Sherman and M. Zlotowitz wrote the following: "The ultimate goal of history is . . . sanctification; Israel's acquisition of homeland and construction of Temple are milestones along the way, not the end of the journey. Therefore, the nation could be stripped of these precious treasures temporarily, but not be deterred from its pursuit of the one overriding goal. This concept of transience of Israel's bond to land, city, and Temple is an indispensable basis of the unsparing and unflinching predictions of exile and destruction which form such a major part of [Ezekiel's] prophetic activity. . . . History will have run its course; lessons will have been learned from centuries of exile . . . and the bond to land, city, and Temple will be seen to be permanent after all." *Yechezkel*, p. 668.

16. Simons, *Jerusalem in the Old Testament*, 382; *Anchor Bible Dictionary*, 6:362–63, s.v. "Jerusalem Temple."

17. See Aharoni and Avi-Yonah, *Macmillan Bible Atlas*, Map 169.

18. Compare King Benjamin three centuries later in Book of Mormon lands. See Mosiah 2:14.

19. All through this period of history is repeated evidence that Jews gained influence and authority in high places because they humbly sought the Lord's guidance. See Ezra 7:10, 27; 8:21; Esth. 4:16; Dan. 2:16–19, 20–23; 6:10; 9:3–4.

20. Julian Morgenstern did an exhaustive study of the cause of Nehemiah's grief in hearing the report of Jerusalem's pathetic condition. His admittedly startling conclusion was that Jerusalem had experienced yet another siege and destruction after the Babylonian conquest of 586 B.C. After more than seventy pages of analyses of passages from Lamentations, Ezekiel, Obadiah, Malachi, Psalms, (Deutero- or Trito-) Isaiah, Joel, and Nehemiah (many of which have been detached from their actual historical and prophetic contexts), Morgenstern concluded that a second destruction and depopulation of Jerusalem, a devastation even more extreme and catastrophic than that of 587–586 B.C., had occurred one hundred years later, in 486–485 B.C., at the accession of Xerxes to the Persian throne, when a coalition of Edomites, Moabites, Ammonites, Philistines, Tyrians, Sidonians, and Persians overran Yehud, massacred and enslaved the Jews, burned the Second Temple, destroyed the walls of Jerusalem, and left the city in ruins. Such was the cause of Nehemiah's grief over the report he received in "Shushan the palace." All of this speculation was developed by Morgenstern, "Jerusalem 485 B.C.," 101–79.

21. See Aharoni and Avi-Yonah, *Macmillan Bible Atlas*, Map 170; Bahat, *Illustrated Atlas of Jerusalem*, 34; Meyers, *Ezra-Nehemiah*, 112–19.

22. Kenyon, *Jerusalem*, 108; Williamson, "Nehemiah's Walls Revisited," 81–88.

23. The various gates and towers are described and speculative locations identified in Paton, *Jerusalem in Bible Times*, 117–27.

24. *New Encyclopedia of Archaeological Excavations*, 2:709; Avigad, *Discovering Jerusalem*, 62; *Anchor Bible Dictionary*, 3:757, s.v. "Jerusalem." Compare Ben-Dov, *Shadow of the Temple*, 60, in which he argues that Nehemiah restored the walls of both eastern and western hills.

25. *New Encyclopedia of Archaeological Excavations,* 2:709; Kenyon, *Jerusalem,* 111. Sections now identifiable are the Broad Wall (Neh. 3:8, 12:38), the Valley Gate, the Dung Gate, the Fountain Gate, the Siloam Pool Wall, the Water Gate, and "the stairs that go down from the city of David" (Neh. 3:15)—found in R. Weill's excavations in 1923–24; see *Anchor Bible Dictionary,* s.v. "Stairs of the City of David," 6:183. See also Bahat, *Illustrated Atlas of Jerusalem,* 34. Official "Yehud" seal impressions on jar handles have also been found from this period.

26. *Malachi,* 254.

27. One group of refugees from the first dispersion fled to Egypt and during ensuing centuries established themselves as influential people in the economic and political life of Hellenistic and Roman Egypt. One military colony erected a Jewish temple to Jehovah on Elephantine Island (Yeb) at the first cataract of the Nile, at modern Aswan. See Shanks, *Ancient Israel,* 162–64; Thomas, *Documents from Old Testament Times,* 266–68; Porten, *Archives from Elephantine.*

9

HELLENISTIC JERUSALEM, 332–63 B.C.

Though we know something about the restoration of Jerusalem under Ezra and Nehemiah, the rest of the city's Persian phase is largely shrouded in darkness. The many jar handles inscribed with the words *Jerusalem* or, simply, *the city*, attest to the capital's importance as a religious and administrative center in the province of *Yehud* (Aramaic, "Judah") in the Persian Empire.[1]

In 332 B.C. the darkness lifts as sources recount Jerusalem's peaceful submission to Alexander the Great, inaugurating Jerusalem's Hellenistic period. The principal account of Alexander's visit to the Jewish capital comes from the later Jewish historian Josephus (A.D. 37–100). He describes how the great conqueror went up quickly to Jerusalem to secure his victory in Gaza. Upon his approach, however, he was greeted in a manner different from all other nations. The Jewish high priest, Jaddua, had been warned in a dream to adorn the city, throw open its gates, and make it ready to receive the conqueror. He had Jerusalem's inhabitants dress in white and form a reception line. With everything in place, he went forth with courage to meet the Macedonian warrior.[2]

Josephus tells us that Alexander was saluted and honored by all the Jews of Jerusalem with a single voice of acclamation. He was ushered into the city and led to the Temple. There, we are told, he offered sacrifice to Israel's God according to the precise instructions given him by the high priest.[3] After being shown a passage in the book of Daniel that declared that one of the Greeks would overthrow the Persians[4] and supposing that person to be none other than himself, Alexander then granted the citizens of Jerusalem "all they desired," even promising to allow all other

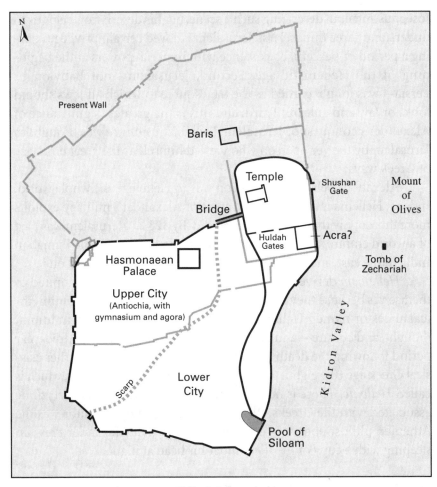

Hellenistic Jerusalem

Jews in Babylon and Media to enjoy their own unique laws and customs.[5] Alexander's wise policy of toleration fostered good will between subjects and ruler.

From what is known about the sanctity of the holy precinct and the postexilic regulations to keep both the priesthood and the religion of Jehovah pure and uncontaminated, Alexander's sacrifice at the Temple may sound implausible at first. Nonetheless, Talmudic sources also repeat the tradition, though they ascribe it to the time of the high priest Simon the Just, who lived years after Jaddua. We cannot know with certainty

Josephus' intent in describing such a scene, but his description helps us to understand three things. First, Jerusalem enjoyed certain privileges during a period of peaceful coexistence with imperial powers at the beginning of the Hellenistic age. Second, Jerusalem—not Babylon or Persia—was long regarded as the true source to which all Jews should look for law and culture. Third, and this is the greatest significance of Alexander's conquest of Jerusalem, Hellenistic culture was brought to Jerusalem by the very person who viewed himself as the great emissary of Greek ways.

Alexander believed his mission was to Hellenize the whole world. Indeed, Hellenism conquered the areas of Alexander's military exploits more thoroughly than his armies ever did. By 323 B.C. Jerusalem was part of a world empire stretching from Gibraltar in the west to the Punjab in India in the east, and Hellenism was the culture superimposed on it.

Hellenism derives from *Hellenes,* the term the Greeks applied to themselves because they believed they were descendants of a semimythical ancestor named Hellen. *Hellenistic* means Greeklike—in idiom, thought, and culture—and is used to distinguish the two-hundred-year period following the death of Alexander the Great from the earlier classical Greek age (the eighth to the fourth centuries before Christ), which is called *Hellenic.* There is no question that Alexander loved *everything* associated with the Greeks. When he was a little boy, his tutor was the Athenian philosopher Aristotle, and it is said that Alexander grew up sleeping with a copy of the *Iliad* under his head at night.

JERUSALEM UNDER THE PTOLEMIES

After the death of Alexander (323 B.C.), his empire was carved up among three of his generals and their successors, who are known by the family names of the generals. The Ptolemies took Egypt, the Seleucids took Syria and Mesopotamia, and the Antigonids took Macedonia. There was much rivalry among the three groups of rulers. Jerusalem suffered through a series of wars for the ownership of Judaea. The city first came under the domination of Ptolemy I, king of Egypt from 323 to 285 B.C. He deported part of Jerusalem's population because, in a key battle, the Jews refused to fight on the Sabbath day.[6] But after 301 B.C., Ptolemaic rule stabilized with improved relations between Judaea and Egypt.[7] The

Jews enjoyed prosperity and broad autonomy in domestic affairs. Jerusalem remained the administrative and religious center and basked in the relative calm of Ptolemaic overlordship for more than twenty-five years, at least on the surface.

At the head of the city's administration was the Aaronic high priest aided by the Men of the Great Assembly—a group of powerful teachers also identified with the *Soferim* (Hebrew, "scribes") of the late Persian period. The high priest was not just the religious head of Jerusalem but was also its chief political and administrative leader. The Temple continued to be the center of the religious and social life of Jerusalem. Because of it, many priests lived in the city and formed an important part of a very powerful aristocracy.[8]

Hellenism spread in Jerusalem and Judaea as it did everywhere else. The richer and more aristocratic Jews—those in closest contact with Ptolemaic Egyptian authorities—tended to embrace Hellenistic culture. But the stricter religionists staunchly resisted it. Hellenism intrigued many wealthy and educated Jerusalemites because of its emphasis on human reason, science, art and architecture, physical beauty, aesthetics, nature, the glorification of the human body, and the observable world. To others, however, Hellenism polluted the truth of God's will as communicated by Jehovah through revelation. These feelings against Hellenism simmered below the surface.

The favorable conditions enjoyed by the Judaean community under the Ptolemies started to decline about 275 B.C., when the Greek Seleucids from Syria attempted to conquer parts of the Holy Land, thus inaugurating the so-called Syrian Wars. For the next seventy-five years, strategically important Judaea was the tramping ground of all the opposing armies coming from Egypt to the south and Syria to the north. One effect of the turmoil was the decline and final disappearance of the *Soferim* as a body, and the concomitant steady disintegration of a unified religious life in Jerusalem and Judaea.[9]

JERUSALEM UNDER THE SELEUCIDS

In 223 B.C. the young and ambitious Antiochus III (223–187 B.C.) ascended the Seleucid throne in Syria and set his sights on all of the land southwest of him. In 201 B.C. his forces conquered Gaza but retreated in the face of an advancing Ptolemaic army led by Scopas, who reached the gates of Jerusalem and occupied the city, for many of the Jews favored Antiochus III. Scopas proceeded to Panias near Dan (later called Caesarea Philippi), where Antiochus lay in wait for him. In one of the watershed battles of ancient history, the Ptolemies were soundly defeated at the battle of Panias in 198 B.C., and Antiochus III (later called "the Great") went back to Jerusalem as the power broker of the Near East (see Dan. 11:13–16).[10]

Citizens of the capital city received him willingly, resupplied his army, and even fought alongside him when he attacked the garrison left in Jerusalem by Scopas. In return, Antiochus III, the first Syrian ruler of Judaea, was well disposed toward the Jews and granted them many favors. He gave them wine, oil, frankincense, wheat, flour, salt, and ritually clean cattle for sacrifices at the Temple. He endowed the priests and Levites with materials for Temple maintenance and gave the Jews a large measure of freedom and autonomy, permitting them to live according to their unique laws and customs, as Alexander had done.[11]

At this time, Jerusalem was still confined to an area within the boundaries of the City of David and the Temple Mount, as it had been in the days of Nehemiah. It is difficult to date with exactness the beginning of the city's expansion to the Western Hill, but it probably started at the beginning of the second century before Christ, after Antiochus' victory. This expansion was an important milestone in the history of Jerusalem's development. Undoubtedly population pressure within the City of David was a major reason for this expansion.[12]

The Jews of Jerusalem were not slow to take advantage of their situation under Antiochus III. One pressing need of the time was to revive in some form what the *Soferim* had provided. A governing Council of Elders, called in Greek the *Gerousia* ("assembly"), was established to attend to the general administrative, political, judicial, and social affairs of the community. This governing body, later known as the Sanhedrin, was headquartered in Jerusalem. At its head stood pairs of teachers (Hebrew, *zuggoth*), one of whom was the *nasi* (Hebrew, "prince" or "president") and the other the *av beth din* (Hebrew, "father of the court"). Some scholars have seen in the establishment of this dual system an attempt to separate strictly religious law from civil law.[13]

Antiochus exempted the *Gerousia*, the priests, and the Temple scribes from paying head and salt taxes. The other citizens of Jerusalem enjoyed the same privilege for three years. The Syrian ruler also ordered political prisoners released and forbade ritually impure meat to be imported into Jerusalem. For several years Jerusalem and Judaea remained relatively stable under Seleucid rule.[14]

But as time passed, the situation deteriorated. The Jews had coalesced into groups according to their disposition towards Hellenism and thus in their attitude toward the Seleucids, who championed Hellenistic culture. Since 198 B.C. the pace of Hellenization had been picking up, and that brought two worldviews into direct conflict. The battleground was Jerusalem. Among the members of the pro-Hellenistic party were aristocratic Jews, the Zadokim, or high priestly families (later called the Sadducees), who were excited by Greek culture and who favored the status quo. The anti-Hellenists formed a group called the Hasidim or Hasideans (Hebrew for "pious ones," though no relation to the modern Hasidic Jews). The ancient Hasidim were the predecessors of the Pharisees; they were orthodox religionists and meticulous supporters of God's laws as revealed in the Torah (see 1 Macc. 2: 42–43).[15]

In addition, some men in Jerusalem were ready to offer money to the Seleucids in return for positions of power. One such was Simon of the house of Tobias. In the reign of Seleucus IV (187–175 B.C.), successor to Antiochus III, Simon encouraged the king's chief minister in Jerusalem to seize the sacred Temple treasury and blame it on the current high priest, Onias III of the house of Onias. The feud between the rival houses came to a head in the reign of Antiochus IV (175–163 B.C.) who succeeded his brother, Seleucus IV, as king of Syria.[16]

Hellenizers in Jerusalem (the aristocratic pro-Seleucid Jews) viewed the accession of Antiochus IV as the opportunity they had been waiting for. During an absence from the country, the legitimate high priest, Onias III, whose loyalties were pro-Ptolemaic, was replaced by his pro-Seleucid brother, Jason, with the help of the Hellenizers, who bribed the Syrian king to enforce the change (see 2 Macc. 4:7–10). Antiochus IV then supported Jason and the Hellenizers in rebuilding Jerusalem along Hellenistic lines—transforming it into a new Greek *polis* named Antiochia, whose citizens called themselves Antiochenes (Antioch being the capital of Syria). This reform project required a wider geographical expanse, which was available on the Western Hill of Jerusalem. Thus, the

Hellenistic style of building—with its ambience of wealth—became dominant in that sector.[17] Most importantly, a Greek-style gymnasium was constructed in the Holy City, and Jews were encouraged to dress after the Greek fashion. An intertestamental text (part of the Apocrypha) entitled 1 Maccabees describes the situation:

> In those days lawless men came forth from Israel, and misled many, saying, "Let us go and make a covenant with the Gentiles round about us, for since we separated from them many evils have come upon us." This proposal pleased them, and some of the people eagerly went to the king. He authorized them to observe the ordinances of the Gentiles. So they built a gymnasium in Jerusalem, according to Gentile custom, and removed the marks of circumcision, and abandoned the holy covenant. They joined with the Gentiles and sold themselves to do evil. (1 Macc. 1:11–15)[18]

The challenge to Judaism was not so much that of a rival religion as that of a rival culture. "It was the challenge of secularism,"[19] the classic confrontation between revelation and reason, the meeting of two disparate worldviews, the meeting of Jerusalem and Athens, as it were, head on. The religion of the Jews was yet to be attacked directly, but for all intents and purposes the Torah as Jerusalem's constitution had been effectively abrogated. And the important factor in spreading this rival culture was undoubtedly the gymnasiums, which sprang up not only in Jerusalem but throughout the Greek world. According to one scholar: "They expressed fundamental tendencies of the Greek mind, . . . its delight in the [human] body."[20]

The gymnasium changed the whole spiritual and social atmosphere of Jerusalem. It was a place where athletes exercised naked (as the etymology of the word *gymnasium* indicates),[21] and because of this, certain Jews—in their zeal to conform to Hellenism—sought to remove the marks of circumcision, the great symbol for the Jews of the Abrahamic covenant, just as the author of 1 Maccabees indicates. The gymnasium began to rival the Temple as the center of cultural activity and religious-like devotion. The gymnasium was under the patronage of the Greek gods Hermes (Mercury) and Hercules, and its Jewish patrons seem to have wanted to imitate those gods more than their own Jehovah. According to 2 Maccabees 4:12–15, the gymnasium was erected "under the citadel," and "There was such an extreme of Hellenization and increase in the adoption of foreign ways because of the surpassing wickedness of Jason, who was ungodly and no high priest, that the priests were no longer intent upon their service at the altar. Despising the sanctuary and neglecting the sacrifices, they hastened to take part in the unlawful proceedings in the wrestling arena after the call to the discus, disdaining the honors prized by their fathers and putting the highest value upon Greek forms of prestige."

Orthodox Jews, especially the Hasidim, or Pious Ones, were outraged at the spread of this virulent and aggressive Hellenism. After all, the appointment of the high priest was God's prerogative, independent of the approval of a Gentile ruler. And even though the new high priest, Jason, was a member of the legitimate high priestly family, he also represented the Tobiads and was the leader of Hellenistic reform. Things went from bad to worse when Menelaus ousted Jason from office, with the help of the Tobiad family, by offering the Syrian king yet a larger bribe than his predecessor had given (see 2 Macc. 4:23–26).

The followers of Menelaus were so openly supportive of the Greek way of life that they set themselves against the Hasidim. Menelaus' brother Lysimachus even used the Temple treasury as his own. The split widened until fighting broke out in Jerusalem between the pro-Hellenist and the pro-Torah parties.

About this time, encouraged by a rumor that Antiochus IV had died in a campaign against the Ptolemies (170–169 B.C.), the former high priest, Jason, hurried back to Jerusalem and drove out Menelaus (see 2 Macc. 5:5–10). The conflict that followed was not simply a matter of Jew versus Syrian, or even Jew versus Jew, but also urbanite versus suburbanite. Opposed to the large pro-Hellenistic party in Jerusalem were the great majority of Jews in the countryside, who had aligned with the Pious Ones. Thus, as one scholar remarked, "During a considerable part of the second century B.C. 'Jerusalem versus Judaea' correctly describes Jewish internal affairs."[22] It was the sophisticated city folk against the ignorant and superstitious country bumpkins.

The rumor of the death of Antiochus proved false, and the revolt brought the Syrian leader's wrath down upon the Jewish people. On his way back from Egypt, Antiochus took Jerusalem by storm, drove out Jason, restored Menelaus to office, and occupied the Acra—a fortress built by his predecessor, Antiochus III, close to and higher than the Temple so that all happenings within the sacred precinct could be observed.[23] Antiochus IV then let loose his soldiers upon the orthodox populace, who were massacred in a great slaughter (see 2 Macc. 5:11–14). The Temple was desecrated and the sacred vessels plundered (see 1 Macc. 1:20–28).

When it became obvious to Antiochus that he had the support of the Hellenizers in Jerusalem but that his policy of Hellenization was violently opposed by most of the Jewish people, he determined to wipe out the Jewish religion altogether. In 168 B.C. Antiochus IV set about to destroy every distinctive feature of the Jewish faith. Sacrifices were forbidden. Sabbath and feast days were no longer to be observed. The rite of circumcision was abolished. Books of the Torah were desecrated or destroyed. Jews were forced to eat swine flesh and perform sacrifices at idolatrous altars set up throughout the land. Disobedience to any aspect of his decree was punishable by death.

Antiochus IV desecrated the Temple by erecting an altar to the Greek god Zeus—perhaps cast in the image of Antiochus himself—on the altar of burnt offering within the Temple court (see 1 Macc. 1:41–61). Antiochus had claimed that Zeus had manifested himself to him, and thus he referred to himself as Epiphanes, Greek for "God manifest" (2 Macc. 4:7). His enemies, however, now applied the epithet and pun, Epimanes, Greek for "madman."[24] His conversion of the Jerusalem sanctuary into "the temple of Olympian Zeus" (2 Macc. 6:2) has been seen by some as fulfillment of Daniel's prophecy of the establishment of the "abomination of desolation" (Dan. 11:31; 12:11); however, Latter-day Saint scripture clarifies the matter.[25]

Many chose to die rather than be defiled by the Syrian sacrilege or forced to profane the covenant (see 1 Macc. 1:62–63). Many fled Jerusalem and crowded into villages where they were pursued by royal agents intent on erasing the Jewish faith. Second Maccabees 6–7 and 4 Maccabees contain stories of the valiant martyrs. Meanwhile, a Seleucid garrison remained in the Holy City, supported by the Hellenizers.

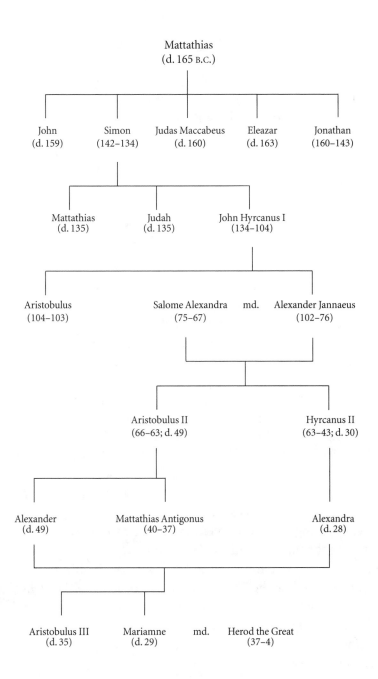

Mattathias
(d. 165 B.C.)

John
(d. 159)

Simon
(142–134)

Judas Maccabeus
(d. 160)

Eleazar
(d. 163)

Jonathan
(160–143)

Mattathias
(d. 135)

Judah
(d. 135)

John Hyrcanus I
(134–104)

Aristobulus
(104–103)

Salome Alexandra   md.   Alexander Jannaeus
(75–67)   (102–76)

Aristobulus II
(66–63; d. 49)

Hyrcanus II
(63–43; d. 30)

Alexander
(d. 49)

Mattathias Antigonus
(40–37)

Alexandra
(d. 28)

Aristobulus III
(d. 35)

Mariamne   md.   Herod the Great
(d. 29)   (37–4)

The Hasmonaean (or Maccabaean) Dynasty

JERUSALEM UNDER THE HASMONAEANS

Open revolt against Syrian depredations began in Modi'in, a village about twenty miles northwest of Jerusalem, where a priest named Mattathias, of the house of Hasmon (the Hasmonaeans) lived with his five sons (see 1 Macc. 2:1–6).[26] When a Syrian official came to Modi'in to enforce heathen sacrifice, Mattathias slew both a traitorous Jew who offered the sacrifice and the Syrian official. He and his sons fled into the mountains, where they were joined by many zealous Jews, including the Hasidim (see 1 Macc. 2:23–43). They organized an army, "struck down [the] sinners," and "rescued the law out of the hands of the Gentiles and kings, and they never let the sinner gain the upper hand" (1 Macc. 2:44–48).

After the death of Mattathias the struggle was carried on by three of his sons in turn, Judas (166–160 B.C.) surnamed Maccabeus ("the Hammerer"), Jonathan (160–143 B.C.), and Simon (142–134 B.C.). Success followed success in their guerrilla campaigns against Syrian forces. After Judas' fourth victory near Beth-Zur, south of Jerusalem, the freedom-fighters were able to occupy the Temple Mount.[27] On the 25th of Kislev (December), 165 B.C., on the very day on which it had been desecrated three years before (see 1 Macc. 4:54), the Temple at Jerusalem was cleansed and rededicated under the leadership of Judas, and true worship was restored (see 1 Macc. 4:36–59; 2 Macc. 10:1–7). This event has been commemorated ever since as the Festival of Hanukkah (Hebrew, "dedication"), sometimes known as the Festival of Lights. (John 10:22 refers to it as the Feast of Dedication.)

The fighting continued, and despite all the victories of Judas in various places throughout Judaea, Jerusalem remained divided. Mount Zion, that is, the Temple Mount, lay in the hands of the rebel Hasmonaeans, while the Acra continued to be held by the Hellenizers. Finally, in 162 B.C., Syria made generous terms with the Jews, guaranteeing them full religious liberty (see 1 Macc. 6:58–60; 2 Macc. 13:23–26). Just before this treaty Antiochus IV died, overcome with grief at the news of his military losses (see 1 Macc. 6:5–17).

Judas, not content with religious freedom only but seeking full political independence as well, continued to fight on against the Syrians. He was killed in 160 B.C. (see 1 Macc. 9:18). Jonathan succeeded his brother as leader of the movement for Jewish independence. The Syrians tried to win his friendship by appointing him high priest and governor of the Jews in 152 B.C.[28] He was allowed to occupy the whole of Jerusalem, except for the Acra, which was still held by the king's garrison. Growing suspicious of his power, the Syrian general Tryphon assassinated Jonathan in 143 B.C. (see 1 Macc. 12:48; 13:23). But Jonathan's appointment had established a new dynasty of high priests who later became priest-kings.

Simon succeeded his brother Jonathan and set about consolidating his position, finally expelling the Syrian garrison and cleansing the Acra of its pagan occupants.[29] In 142 B.C. he won immunity from taxes from the Syrian king, Demetrius II (148–145 B.C.), and the Jews proclaimed their independence (see 1 Macc. 10:28–29; 13:41). In 141 B.C. a bronze decree was set up in the Temple precinct celebrating Jerusalem's deliverance and conferring on Simon the office of high priest as a hereditary right. "And the Jews and their priests decided that Simon should be their leader and high priest forever, until a trustworthy prophet should arise, . . . So Simon accepted and agreed to be high priest, to be commander and ethnarch of the Jews and priests, and to be protector of them all" (1 Macc. 14:41, 47).

The high priesthood of the Aaronic order was now made hereditary in the Hasmonaean line, and an independent Jewish state emerged in which the civil head and military leader were at the same time the high priest. This union continued throughout the Hasmonaean dynasty. Simon himself was treacherously slain in 134 B.C. by his son-in-law, Ptolemy. His own son, John Hyrcanus I (134–104 B.C.) succeeded him to the high priesthood (see 1 Macc. 16:13–17).

Early in the reign of John Hyrcanus, Jerusalem was besieged by the Syrian king, Antiochus Sidetes VII, but this ended in a treaty. Jerusalem then became the splendid capital of an independent Hasmonaean kingdom. From 129 B.C. until 63 B.C., almost sixty years, no enemy menaced the city or breached its walls. Under Hyrcanus, Jerusalem's influence was extended. He seized Idumea in the south, forcing its inhabitants to be circumcised; in the north he succeeded in destroying the rival temple on Mount Gerizim. The Temple at Jerusalem was restored to its central position as the cultural and religious center of Israel as well as the capital for people who had just come under the sway of Judaism owing to

Hyrcanus' conquests. Jews in the Diaspora, as well as proselytes to Judaism and sympathizers with her principles, contributed to the wealth of Jerusalem by paying a half-shekel tax.[30]

The city of Jerusalem reached a peak of glory during later Hasmonaean and Herodian times. A great Hasmonaean palace was built in the western portion of Jerusalem—the Upper City, formerly the Greek quarter, in an area overlooking the Temple Mount.[31] In addition, the Temple towers were strengthened, and a bridge was built across the Tyropoeon Valley to connect the Upper City with the Temple Mount. The remnants of this bridge are now called Wilson's Arch in honor of an early archaeologist of Jerusalem. The Citadel in the Upper City (today also called David's Tower, near Jaffa Gate) was strengthened by adding towers. The prosperity of Hasmonaean Jerusalem, with its well-stocked markets and accessible water supplies, is portrayed in a pseudepigraphical work called the "Letter of Aristeas." To this period also belong some of the great tomb-monuments found in the Kidron Valley, including the Tomb of the Sons of Hezir (a priestly family), the so-called Tomb of Zechariah, and Absalom's Pillar.

The greatest building project of the Hasmonaean period[32] was a new city wall built in the middle of the second century before Christ by Jonathan, brother of Judas: "And Jonathan dwelt in Jerusalem and began to rebuild and restore the city. He directed those who were doing the work to build the walls and encircle Mount Zion [the Western Hill] with squared stones, for better fortification; and they did so" (1 Macc. 10: 10–11).

Simon finished the project begun by his brother. Two things are apparent from archaeological investigation: the new wall incorporated remains of the wall of the First Temple period, and the Hasmonaean wall was built in stages, as indicated by 1 Maccabees 4:60; 10:10–11; 12: 36–37; and 13:52.[33] The Hasmonaeans understood how much the walls aided in the protection of the city (see 1 Macc. 4:60); remnants of it are still visible to the discerning traveler in Jerusalem.

JERUSALEM AND THE JEWISH SECTS

Beginning at the time of the Temple rededication (165 B.C.), the Hasidim, or part of them, withdrew their support from the Maccabees, or Hasmonaeans. First, the purposes of the Hasidim had been largely religious rather than political. Second, they had seen an important aim fulfilled with the liberation of the holy sanctuary which would enable proper worship to recommence. Third, in 162 B.C. the Syrian king, Demetrius I, appointed Alcimus to the high priesthood. He was recognized by the Hasidim as a true high priest of the Aaronic lineage. The naivete of this support was clearly manifest when Alcimus' Syrian allies turned on the Hasidim and massacred sixty of them in one day.

Though this action undoubtedly left the group deeply suspicious of political rulers and their religious appointees, the Pious Ones did not die out. By the time of John Hyrcanus I (134–104 B.C.), they seem to have evolved as a separate and powerful religious party known to history as the Pharisees (from the Hebrew *parushim*, "separated ones" or "separatists"). They existed in distinct opposition to the other main religious party, the Sadducees, who trace their spiritual and ideological ancestry to the Zadokim, the priestly aristocracy, and elements of pro-Hellenism in Jerusalem.

Though the Pharisees existed in the time of Jonathan (160–143 B.C.), according to Josephus,[34] he states in another place that they first appeared in conflict with Hyrcanus I.[35] Nonetheless, they exercised great influence over Judaism for the next several centuries and determined the future shape and course of the religion.

The Pharisees opposed the Hasmonaeans because they grew increasingly worldly and irreligious, even favoring Greek ways. When one of the Pharisees demanded that Hyrcanus relinquish the office of high priest, the Hasmonaean ruler threw his support behind the Sadducees. The Hasmonaeans increasingly spoke of themselves as kings and viewed themselves as Judaism's elite. The Pharisees were drawn largely from the middle class and were viewed, ideologically, as the great "democratizers" of the religion.[36] Hyrcanus assumed the royal office and his successor, Aristobulus I (103 B.C.), was the first to officially take the title of king.

Matters between the Hasmonaeans and the Pharisees in Jerusalem came to a head during the reign of Alexander Jannaeus (102–76 B.C.). He married the widow of his brother, though it was illegal for the high priest to do so. He revealed his attachment to Greek ways and flaunted the use of the title "king" in both Greek and Hebrew letters on coins. He disregarded the sanctity of Jewish ritual—on one occasion during the Feast of Tabernacles, he poured out the water libation onto the ground instead of onto the altar. In a fit of uncontrolled rage he slew many Jews within the Temple court when they pelted him with citrons (fruit used in worship during the Feast of Tabernacles) on account of his sacrilege. Finally, he promoted a civil war in Jerusalem that lasted six years and claimed some eight hundred lives.

Jannaeus' wife, Salome Alexandra (75–67 B.C.), ruled after him and restored peace to the Holy City and its environs. But in the meantime the Pharisees had become very powerful. Alexandra appointed her son, Hyrcanus II, to be high priest. Hyrcanus was favorably disposed toward the Pharisees, and by his influence they grew even stronger. With increased civil and religious power in their hands, the Pharisees imposed their own views on all of Judaism from the capital city. In particular, they made life difficult for their Sadducean rivals, who turned to Alexandra's younger son, Aristobulus.

After the death of his mother, Hyrcanus was forced to give up his office when his brother defeated him in battle near Jericho. Aristobulus (66–63 B.C.) became king and high priest in 66 B.C., but his reign was cut short three years later when he was taken captive by Pompey's armies. The story of the Hasmonaeans draws to a close when Hyrcanus II was reconfirmed in the high priesthood and appointed ethnarch of Judaea by the mighty hand of Rome, which forever changed the course of Jerusalem's history as well as that of the entire Near East.

Not all of the Hasidim identified themselves with the Pharisees, however. During the second century before Christ, a group strictly devoted to Jehovah, in the spirit of what they believed to be "true hasidism," elected to withdraw from Jerusalem and go into the wilderness of Judaea, near the northwest shore of the Dead Sea at a settlement called Qumran, under the tutelage of one whom they called "the Teacher of Righteousness." This leader formed his followers into a well-organized religious community that vowed to adhere to a new covenant dedicated to obeying the Law of God (expounded in both old and new scripture) until the dawning of the messianic age. They instituted a strict lifestyle, prescribed special rules for admission to their semimonastic society, including communal property, and administered oaths, covenants, and ceremonial washings.[37]

The Qumran Covenantors spent much time copying sacred and important manuscripts on parchment scrolls (animal skins stitched together), using ink made of powdered charcoal. Their collection includes biblical texts (every book of the Old Testament except Esther), targums (Aramaic translations of biblical books), apocryphal and pseudepigraphical compositions, commentaries, prayers, songs, liturgical curses, and rule-books (the Manual of Discipline being a well-known example).[38] The library of ancient Qumran, discovered between 1947 and 1955 in caves near the ruins of the community, as well as other archaeological and literary data, make identification of this Dead Sea group as a branch of the Essenes virtually certain. The Essenes were a sect of pious Jews living throughout Judaea and were described by the historians Josephus, Philo, and Pliny.[39] The modern scholar who would posit a different identity for the Qumran sectarians "places himself in an astonishing position."[40]

What is not so certain is the exact history of the Qumran community or the names of those who bore the titles and epithets presented in the documents of the Covenantors' library. Nonetheless, the general picture that emerges from the sect's Damascus Rule, Habakkuk Commentary, and Nahum Commentary sheds important light on the Jerusalem of this era. The birth of the Qumran community is said to have occurred in the "age of wrath"—a time when wicked priests and leaders dominated Jerusalem and the Temple. Though these Jewish rulers did not reign without experiencing God's chastisement at the hands of the "Chief of the Kings of Greece,"[41] the Qumran Covenantors felt it necessary to leave the defiled environment of Jerusalem. They nevertheless continued to look upon the city itself with reverence and waited for the day of cleansing. As one of their documents testifies, "Jerusalem is the camp of holiness, and is the place which He has chosen from among all the tribes of Israel. For Jerusalem is the capital of the camps of Israel."[42]

According to the Qumran Covenantors, a person called the Wicked Priest was opposed to the Teacher of Righteousness, whom God sent to guide the faithful. The Wicked Priest was, for a time, "called by the name of truth"—that is, he apparently met with the sect's approval before he became Israel's ruler and was then corrupted by wealth and power. Subsequently, he defiled Jerusalem and the Temple. He also sinned against the Teacher of Righteousness and his disciples, who finally went into exile in the "land of Damascus." The Wicked Priest and his associates are described as erring in matters of ritual cleanliness, justice, chastity, the dates of festivals, and Temple worship. He "vilified and outraged the elect of God, plotted to destroy the poor," and stole other people's property. His successors, "the last Priests of Jerusalem," are also charged with amassing great wealth and plundering the people.[43]

The longest of the Dead Sea Scrolls is a document called the Temple Scroll. It measures some thirty feet in length, dates to around the second century before Christ, and was written in ancient Hebrew in biblical style. Presented as the words of God to Moses, it supplies laws dealing with issues important to the Qumran sect.[44] Much of the thinking done at Qumran, as revealed in the Temple Scroll, was about what a true Temple should be. Of particular interest in the scroll is the description of a future Temple to be built in Jerusalem, along with details concerning the attendant Temple rituals and standards of behavior, all of which were to replace the defiled edifice and corrupt practices which then existed in the Holy City.[45] The Qumran community was destroyed in the First Jewish Revolt (A.D. 66–70), before any of the anticipated restoration could occur.

Such were the conditions in Jerusalem during the early history of the Qumran sect. Though attempts to identify the actual characters who bore the names used in the documents remain tenuous, the most likely candidate for the role of the Wicked Priest seems to be Simon, younger brother of Judas Maccabeus and Jonathan. It was to Simon and his house that the high priesthood was given forever, "until a faithful prophet arise" (1 Macc. 14: 30–39). This seems a tacit admission of the illegitimacy of the transference of the high priesthood from the Zadokite dynasty, appointed by David, to the Hasmonaean dynasty.[46]

Jerusalem of the Hellenistic age was a city of tremendous contrasts and controversy in a time replete with heroes and villains well documented in nonbiblical texts. The city witnessed magnificent building, prosperity, expansion, and progress but also great degradation and calamity. It witnessed the last free and independent Jewish state for two thousand years. Jews still look back on the period between 129 and 63 B.C. as an idyllic time—a resurgence of the old Davidic kingdom.

But such independence and material progress came at a very great price. Apostasy took its toll—a theme mentioned many times by the authors of the Maccabean books. "And very great wrath came upon

Israel" (1 Macc. 1:64; compare 2 Macc. 6: 12–16). This is the period some viewed as being the fulfillment of the Talmudic declaration that with the deaths of the prophets Haggai, Zechariah, and Malachi, the Holy Spirit departed from Israel.[47] Ultimately, this period laid the foundation for the atmosphere at the time of the Messiah's birth, described by President J. Reuben Clark Jr. as witnessing "some of the most terrible passions that were loose in the world at that time."[48]

NOTES

1. Avi-Yonah, *Jerusalem*, 20.

2. Josephus, *Antiquities of the Jews* 11.8.4–5.

3. Josephus, *Antiquities of the Jews* 11.8.4–5.

4. Perhaps these included Dan. 8:3–8, 20–22; 11:3.

5. Josephus, *Antiquities* 11.8.4–5.

6. Avi-Yonah, *Jerusalem*, 20.

7. In 301 B.C. Ptolemy triumphed over Antigonus at the Battle of Ipsus. See Aharoni and Avi-Yonah, *Macmillan Bible Atlas*, Map 176.

8. Epstein, *Judaism*, 86. See also Avi-Yonah, *Jerusalem*, 20.

9. Epstein, *Judaism*, 89.

10. Aharoni and Avi-Yonah, *Macmillan Bible Atlas*, Maps 178, 180.

11. Aharoni and Avi-Yonah, *Macmillan Bible Atlas*, Map 180.

12. Bahat, *Illustrated Atlas of Jerusalem*, 37–38.

13. Epstein, *Judaism*, 89–90.

14. Aharoni and Avi-Yonah, *Macmillan Bible Atlas*, Map 180.

15. Russell, *Between the Testaments*, 27, 50.

16. Russell, *Between the Testaments*, 26–27.

17. Bahat, *Illustrated Atlas of Jerusalem*, 38.

18. The Revised Standard Version (RSV) of the Apocrypha has been used throughout for quotations from 1 and 2 Maccabees.

19. Russell, *Between the Testaments*, 19.

20. Edwin Bevan, *Jerusalem Under the High Priests*, 35, as cited in Russell, *Between the Testaments*, 19.

21. The Greek root *gymnos* means "naked." Hence, a *gymnasion* is a place where one trained naked.

22. Russell, *Between the Testaments*, 27.

23. *Acra* is a Greek word meaning "high place" or "fortress." The exact location of the Acra is unknown, but Josephus indicates that it stood in a place between the Lower City (the hill of the City of David) and the Temple Mount (Josephus, *Wars of the Jews* 5.4.1). See

Bahat, *Illustrated Atlas of Jerusalem,* 38–40. For a different proposal for the location of the Acra, as well as an excellent summary of its history in the Hasmonaean period, see Aharoni and Avi-Yonah, *Macmillan Bible Atlas,* Map 204. The annotation reads, in part: "A hillock at the eastern end of this new Hellenistic city, protected by a small valley to the west, served as its fortress. In the Maccabean period it was called Acra—not to be confused with the old Acra, the citadel (Baris) of the days of Nehemiah, which was situated north of the Temple Mount."

24. See the annotation to 2 Macc. 4:7 in the Oxford Annotated Bible with Apocrypha (RSV), New York: Oxford University Press, 1973.

25. See, for example, Perrin, *New Testament,* 320. Compare with JS–M 1:12, 31–32, and the LDS Bible Dictionary, which describes the "Abomination of Desolation" as occurring when the Romans besieged Jerusalem in A.D. 70 and again in the Last Days.

26. The Hasmonaeans were so called because they traced their lineage to a traditional ancestor named Hashmonia, or Asamoneus, father of Mattathias, according to Josephus, *Wars* 1.1.3.

27. Aharoni and Avi-Yonah, *Macmillan Bible Atlas,* Map 188.

28. This was not entirely satisfactory to the conservative elements of the people because such an appointment was still an illegal seizure of power. In addition, Jonathan, though a priest, was not a Zadokite.

29. Aharoni and Avi-Yonah, *Macmillan Bible Atlas,* Map 204.

30. Avi-Yonah, *Jerusalem,* 25.

31. See Bahat, *Illustrated Atlas of Jerusalem,* 38.

32. Bahat, *Illustrated Atlas of Jerusalem,* 37.

33. For a more complete discussion, see Bahat, *Illustrated Atlas of Jerusalem,* 37–38; Aharoni and Avi-Yonah, *Macmillan Bible Atlas,* Map 204.

34. Josephus, *Antiquities* 13.5.9.

35. Josephus, *Antiquities* 13.10.5–7.

36. Russell, *Between the Testaments,* 50.

37. Vermes, *Dead Sea Scrolls,* 87–115; 142–46. This work contains an excellent summary of the history of the sect and uses many quotations from the primary sources themselves.

38. Vermes, *Dead Sea Scrolls,* 46–86.

39. See Josephus, *Wars* 2.8.2–13 and *Antiquities* 18.1.5. Compare with Philo, *Hypothetica* 11.1–18; *Every Good Man Is Free* 12–13; and Pliny, *Natural History* 5.15.73.

40. Shanks, *Understanding the Dead Sea Scrolls,* 25.

41. Vermes, *Dead Sea Scrolls,* 142–46.

42. Qimron and Strugnell, "For This You Waited 35 Years," 59.

43. Qimron and Strugnell, "For This You Waited 35 Years," 59.

44. The best overall summary to date is Yadin, *Temple Scroll.*

45. Klein and Klein, *Temple beyond Time,* 107–8.

46. Shanks, *Understanding the Dead Sea Scrolls,* 31.

47. Soncino, *Malachi,* 254.

48. Clark, *Behold the Lamb of God,* 18.

10

JERUSALEM AT THE TIME OF JESUS

Centuries after the Roman Republic was established, and after the wars with Gaul, the Punic Wars with Carthage (Hannibal), the Macedonian Wars, and other civil wars and revolution, the great *Pax Romana* ensued, an age of relative peace and toleration. Pompey, Crassus, Julius Caesar, Cleopatra, Brutus, and Mark Antony had passed across the stage of history.

The Roman Empire extended from Britain to Mesopotamia to Egypt, with a population of perhaps one hundred million people. The Roman army at the time of Augustus (27 B.C.–A.D. 14) consisted of approximately twenty-eight legions, a legion being about 1,500 men. A *legion* was composed of *cohorts* of 480 men and *centuries* of 80 men.

In 63 B.C. Pompey marched his Roman armies down the Jordan Valley and up to Jerusalem, entered the Holy of Holies of the Temple, and proclaimed Jerusalem subject to the authority of Rome.

HEROD THE GREAT (37–4 B.C.)

In 40 B.C., having stood by the Romans during an invasion of Parthians from the east, Herod was received with honors in Rome. Octavian and Mark Antony persuaded the Senate to appoint Herod king of the Jews. Because the whole of Judaea was in rival hands and most of the populace hostile to Herod, he had to fight for his kingdom. He managed to overcome all obstacles, however, and established himself by 37 B.C. as the undisputed ruler of Judaea, Peraea, and Galilee.

Few in history have been led by their jealousies and suspicions to murder more family members and others than did Herod, and yet there has been no greater builder in the history of the Holy Land than Herod.[1]

He built the city of Caesarea Maritima ("on the sea") with its theater, amphitheater, stadium (Greek, *hippodrome*), marketplace, palaces, underground sewage system, aqueduct, and its incredibly engineered and technologically advanced port facility. He also built the cities of Samaria (Sebaste), Antipatris, and Phasaelis; he constructed the fortresses of Machaerus, Alexandrion, Cypros, Hyrcania, Herodium, and Masada; he erected a white marble temple to Augustus in Caesarea Paneion (NT, Caesarea Philippi) and an impressive shrine over the Cave of Machpelah, the burial place of the patriarchs and their wives in Hebron.[2]

Of all Herod's building enterprises there were none greater than in the capital, Jerusalem.[3] He rebuilt the former Hasmonaean fortress and named it the Antonia Fortress in honor of his Roman friend, Mark Antony. He constructed his royal palace and towers,[4] a theater, an amphitheater, a stadium,[5] and monumental gates and staircases to the Temple Mount.[6] His grandest edifice was the Temple in Jerusalem.[7]

THE ROMAN GOVERNMENT OF JUDAEA

Before Herod the Great died, he prepared four different wills distributing inheritances to the sons of his ten wives. His final will stipulated, subject to the emperor's concurrence, that his eighteen-year-old son Archelaus become king in his stead and that two autonomous principalities (tetrarchies) be assigned to Archelaus' younger brother Antipas[8] (Galilee and Peraea) and to his half-brother Philip (the newly acquired northeastern territories, today's Golan and beyond). Archelaus was to have the title of king but no jurisdiction over his brothers.[9]

The Jewish people, on the other hand, wanted to reinstate the sacerdotal government of the Hasmonaean period and abolish the monarchy. They sent a deputation of fifty persons to Augustus in Rome. When Augustus gave audience to it, eight thousand Jews of the Roman capital escorted the deputation to the temple of Apollo to endorse resumption of priestly rule in their homeland. The emperor disregarded the Jews' petition and honored Herod's will.

Archelaus, who was half Idumaean and half Samaritan (hardly a popular combination with the Jews), was such a brutal tyrant that after ten years Rome banished him to Vienna in Gaul, and in A.D. 6 his principality of Judaea and Samaria came under direct Roman administration. To be governor, a man was chosen from the knights, the equestrian order (not from the Senate, as were most provincial governors), and was appointed by the emperor himself, to whom he was directly responsible. He bore the title of *praefect*.[10] For the most part, the governors of the new province lacked ability and experience, which was unfortunate because Jewish issues were complex and volatile. Violence often erupted.

The seat of government was Herod's port city of Caesarea. The praefect was commander-in-chief of five cohorts of infantry and a cavalry wing, and a Roman commandant served in Jerusalem with a garrison stationed at the Antonia Fortress overlooking the Temple Mount.[11]

Provincial status involved the oath of loyalty to the emperor, permanent military occupation, taxation by Roman officials, and Roman supervision of public order. At the establishment of Judaea as a province, Quirinius, the legate of Syria, conducted a census (see Luke 2:1–2; Acts 5:37). This action reminded the people that they would be paying taxes to the new agents of an old brand of bitter servitude. It was believed that taxation would undoubtedly increase.

The Council of Elders and its successor, the Sanhedrin, ruled as a Jewish law court in matters of faith, manners, and law in which Roman interests were not directly affected. The Council possessed no powers of capital jurisdiction (without confirmation of the imperial magistrate), except against a pagan who trespassed into the inner courts of the Temple beyond the permitted Court of the Gentiles.[12] The Council consisted of members of the Sadducean aristocracy and more moderate Pharisees and scribes.

Jewish religious practices were usually respected by Roman authorities. Jews were exempt from military service, and their privilege of the Sabbath was safeguarded. Jews throughout the empire were allowed to collect and send to Jerusalem the Temple tribute. Jewish prohibition of statues or images in Jerusalem was generally honored. Romans avoided images of the emperor on coins circulated in Judaea, and standards with effigies of the emperor were left in Caesarea when soldiers went up to Jerusalem. Romans (all non-Jews) knew that setting foot in the Temple interior was forbidden under penalty of death, and a warning was inscribed at the inner court in Latin and Greek.[13]

Roman governors at first kept charge of the sacred high priestly vestments in the Antonia Fortress, but this was considered interference by the Romans in Jewish ritual matters. It was bad enough when Herod had kept them, but the Roman control was in flagrant violation of Jewish law, which prohibited the robes being taken outside the Temple.[14] This issue was for some years a provocation to Jewish religious leaders.

The First Praefects[15]

The governors of Roman Judaea under Augustus Caesar were Coponius (A.D. 7–8), Marcus Ambivious (A.D. 9–12), and Annius Rufus (A.D. 12–15). The next Roman emperor, Tiberius, appointed Valerius Gratus, who served a comparatively long term (A.D. 15–26). Gratus appointed Joseph Caiaphas to the priestly hierarchy, and this Caiaphas, who was son-in-law of Annas, the previous high priest (see John 18:13), cooperated with Annas in laying down religious policy. Caiaphas remained in office through the long rule first of Gratus and then of Pontius Pilate (A.D. 18–36) and was involved in the trial of Jesus.[16]

The Administration of Pontius Pilate

The relationship between Romans and Jews deteriorated during Pilate's rule.[17] His was described by Philo as a harsh and corrupt regime.[18] Pilate was widely disliked, was influenced by bribery, and angered the Jews by his extortions and frequent executions without trial. Pilate was supported during the first part of his administration (until A.D. 31) by Sejanus, commander of the praetorian guard and chief spokesman in Rome for an anti-Jewish policy. Upon Sejanus' fall and for the last five years of his rule, Pilate was forced to be more sensitive to his subjects.

Several incidents helped destroy the legitimacy of Pilate's administration in the eyes of his Jewish subjects. The first serious clash occurred when Pilate took a cohort's ensigns bearing the emperor's image into Jerusalem and set them up under cover of darkness, contrary to custom and the policy of his predecessors.[19] Pilate refused to yield, so his infuriated Jewish subjects marched to Caesarea to insist the ensigns be withdrawn. Pilate surrounded the crowd with his men and threatened to cut them all down, but the Jews stood their ground. When he realized they were so dedicated to their belief as to be willing to die for it, he ordered the offense removed.

Another uproar followed Pilate's use of sacred Temple money

known as *Corbanas* to build an aqueduct to Jerusalem.[20] Pilate may have thought he was acting within Jewish custom, because water channels were among those items for which the Temple treasure might be expended. The Jews, however, had another point of view. *Corban* is the Hebrew word for sacrifice, and some deemed it altogether improper to use funds from this part of the treasury for anything but the purchase of sacrificial animals. Pilate refused to acquiesce, because he was sure of the emperor's backing for the project. This time, during the Jews' public protestation, he disguised his soldiers in Jewish garb and ordered them to attack the crowds with clubs.

Pilate displayed conspicuous disregard for Jewish custom once again when he minted coins with superscriptions showing pagan symbols—something all his predecessors had scrupulously avoided. Even Pilate's harsh successors never dared mint such coins.

During the second half of Pilate's rule, he set up in Herod's palace in Jerusalem some gold shields that had been dedicated to Tiberius. The shields contained references to pagan deities. A cross-section of all Jewish society, including four of Herod's sons, united in protesting this desecration of the Holy City as a straightforward affront to the Jewish religion. Finally, the Jews sent a letter to Tiberius himself, whereupon the emperor ordered the shields removed to Caesarea, where they were placed in the temple of Augustus.

The incident that probably led to Pilate's dismissal was his brutal suppression of a disturbance among the Samaritans, some of whom had followed a would-be messiah to the top of Mount Gerizim, where he promised to show them holy vessels that Moses had allegedly hidden on the mountaintop. Pilate's heavily armed infantry and cavalry blocked the ascent and massacred the Samaritans. The Samaritan council complained to the governor of Syria, and Pilate was removed from office and sent to Rome to answer charges, thus ending ten years of civil disturbance under the most notorious of the Roman praefects of Judaea.

A temporary governor named Marcellus was appointed for Judaea by the governor of Syria. Marcellus adopted several measures to appease the Jews and calm the country. He abolished Gentile supervision of the high priestly vestments and eliminated certain taxes.

Caligula's Attempted Desecration of the Temple

The first two years of Caligula's emperorship (A.D. 37–38) saw continued clemency toward the Jews, but then Judaeo-Roman relations changed sharply with Caligula's attempts to establish a cult of his own divinity. To the Jews, it was shades of Antiochus IV Epiphanes once again. Caligula viewed his own divinity with fanatical belief. Emperor worship was decreed binding on all Romans and Roman subjects as the very expression of loyalty to the imperial state.

The Jews explained to Caligula that their law proscribed sacrificing *to* him, but they could gladly make offerings *for* him. Caligula retorted, "What is the good of that? You have not sacrificed *to* me." He unabashedly pointed out that failing to observe his divinity showed the Jews to be not so much criminals as lunatics.[21]

A stone altar constructed by non-Jews in a coastal town to offer sacrifices to the emperor (thus violating the ancient Jewish ban on idolatry in the territory of Judaea) was smashed by Jews. The report of this incident infuriated the emperor, and he vowed he would teach the Jews a lesson: he would forcibly install his cult in Jerusalem itself by erecting a colossal statue of Zeus in the likeness of Caligula in the holy Sanctuary proper.[22] The whole project was to be carried out by Publius Petronius, legate of Syria (A.D. 39). "Petronius now earned a place of honor in Jewish history by risking grave personal danger in attempting to prevent a desecration of the Temple."[23] Petronius stalled. He commissioned the great statue from artisans at Sidon, but they could take their time. He knew—and it was no secret to Caligula either—that a massive revolt of the Jews could follow, maybe even touching off determined assistance by the Jews of Babylon. Judaean Jewry threatened mass martyrdom. Petronius wrote the emperor and urged him to revoke the order to avoid all-out war.

Meanwhile, Agrippa I, grandson of Herod the Great, arrived in Rome. Upon hearing of Caligula's determination to force the issue, he suffered a nervous breakdown or stroke. After recovering somewhat, he listed all his persuasive arguments against such a move in a long, carefully worded appeal to his friend the emperor. Agrippa was in fact risking his own life to avert a Judaeo-Roman clash. His arguments were impressive enough that Caligula canceled his order to have the idol placed in the Temple. There is evidence, however, that Caligula intended to have the statue manufactured in Italy and then surprise the Jews during a visit to the east by placing it in the Temple himself. That was avoided by the emperor's assassination on 24 January, A.D. 41.

Agrippa was in Rome at the time of Caligula's assassination. His intermediary role in preparing the senators for the idea of Claudius as emperor prevented a great deal of potential bloodshed. Agrippa's successful negotiations between senate, praetorian guard, and Claudius himself were rewarded by the new emperor when he was made ruler over the whole of Samaria, Judaea, and Idumaea. Provincial status and Roman praefects were discontinued, and Agrippa ruled a kingdom about equal in size to his grandfather Herod's at its height. Agrippa was elevated to the rank of consul and confirmed by a treaty of alliance in the Forum and by Claudius appearing with him in the Senate.[24]

The restoration of the monarchy after thirty-five years of Roman rule was viewed with gratification and pride by most Jews, especially by those the New Testament calls *Herodians,* who favored the rule of the Herods over Roman governors. Herod Agrippa ruled confidently from Caesarea on the coast. He won the devotion of many of his subjects by such gestures as dedicating a solid gold chain (a gift from Caligula) to the Temple and paying for the expenses of the Nazarite sacrifices from his own purse.

Pharisees and scribes regarded his reign as a golden age. Christians, however, were subjected to some harsh repressions during his short reign. At a Passover celebration Agrippa arrested and executed James the son of Zebedee, one of the First Presidency of the Church, and imprisoned Peter, the chief apostle and president of the Church (see Acts 12:1–19).

Roman suspicions about Agrippa arose when he constructed a new wall (the Third Wall) to enclose and fortify Jerusalem at the north, the weakest point in the city's defenses.[25] The governor of Syria understandably inquired against whom the fortifications were designed. Syria's governor reported to the emperor. Agrippa responded by celebrating Roman victories in Britain with a series of victory games at Caesarea in honor of the emperor. On the second day of the celebrations, while he was presiding over the events in a solid silver robe, he suddenly fell ill and died (at age fifty-four). Christians believed his death was caused by his being struck down by an angel of God and eaten by worms (see Acts 12:23).

The Procurators

Agrippa I had announced that his son would succeed him as Agrippa II, but the suddenness of his death raised questions about whether a young man just turned seventeen could handle the challenge of such a kingdom. Rome remembered what disasters followed when a similarly young son of Herod the Great ruled Judaea. Claudius agreed that Judaea should revert to direct Roman provincial rule. The new procuratorial government lasted twenty-two years (A.D. 44–66), from the death of Agrippa I until the First Revolt.

The first procurator, Cuspius Fadus (A.D. 44–46), encountered frequent political and religious insurrection. Fadus was succeeded by Tiberius Julius Alexander, who served as procurator from A.D. 46 to 48. His chief problem while ruling Judaea was a famine:

> And in those days came prophets from Jerusalem unto Antioch.
> And there stood up one of them named Agabus, and signified by the Spirit that there should be great dearth throughout all the world: which came to pass in the days of Claudius Caesar.
> Then the disciples, every man according to his ability, determined to send relief unto the brethren which dwelt in Judaea:
> Which also they did, and sent it to the elders by the hands of Barnabas and Saul. (Acts 11:27–30)

Relief also came from a Parthian country in the east called Adiabene, whose royal house had been converted to Judaism. The mother of the country's King Izates, Helena, made a pilgrimage to Jerusalem to take grain from Alexandria and figs from Cyprus to relieve the grateful Jews. Jerusalem became the family's favorite place of residence. After a twenty-four-year reign, Izates died, and his mother returned to Adiabene. Shortly thereafter she, too, died, and her remains were sent to Jerusalem and buried in what today is misleadingly called the "Tombs of the Kings" in East Jerusalem.[26]

The administration of the third procurator, Ventidius Cumanus (A.D. 48–52), was characterized by continuous clashes between Jews and Romans. About this time Claudius felt that some responsibility could now be given to Agrippa II, so at the age of twenty-two he was given the kingdom of Chalcis. In A.D. 50, Agrippa II inherited the rights to supervise the Temple and its treasury and to appoint high priests—hence he often went to Jerusalem.

Cumanus was disgraced and exiled, and Antonius Felix was appointed procurator in A.D. 52. Felix's second wife was the sister of Agrippa II. In A.D. 53, Agrippa II was granted a larger kingdom, including all of northern Transjordan, which he ruled from his capital at Caesarea Philippi. Felix ruled Judaea from Caesarea Maritima on the coast (see Bible Map 14).

During the administration of Felix, the Sicarii, a guerrilla group opposed to Roman rule, caused much violence in Jerusalem. Also, an Egyptian Jew professing to be the Messiah gathered four thousand followers onto the Mount of Olives, from which point he promised to bring down the walls of Jerusalem—as Joshua had brought down Jericho's walls—before their very eyes and deliver the Roman garrison into their hands. Then he would reign as king. Felix's soldiers killed many of the crowd, but the "prophet" escaped.[27]

Felix also had to deal with Paul. Rescued from a lynching party of Jews at the Temple by the Roman garrison commander, Claudius Lysias, Paul was protected by his Roman citizenship from being flogged and was instead escorted by four hundred infantrymen and seventy cavalrymen to Caesarea. In Jerusalem Paul had had his famous encounter with Ananias, whom he had called a "whited wall" (Acts 23:3). Three times within twenty-four hours Paul used Roman troops to save his life. Felix deferred judgment, and the apostle remained under house arrest in Caesarea for two years (see Acts 24:27). He later spoke with Agrippa II, who was paying his brother-in-law Felix a visit. A Roman citizen was protected, probably by a law of Augustus, from arrest and trial or summary punishment by Roman officials outside Italy and was therefore entitled to appeal to Caesar for protection from a provincial governor's measures, so Paul eventually sailed to Rome to appeal to Nero (see Acts 25:12).

Felix left Judaea about A.D. 60 and was replaced by Porcius Festus (60–62), who found the country in turmoil because of extremist organizations. Festus died in office in A.D. 62, and before his successor, Albinus, arrived, the Sanhedrin carried out some executions without first obtaining procuratorial authorization. James the brother of Jesus, a leader of Jerusalem's Christian community, was one of those taken before the Council and then stoned to death.[28]

During Albinus' rule, Nero denied the Jews' demand for citizenship, a decision that led to war. Gessius Florus (A.D. 64–66) was the last procurator of Judaea before the First Revolt, and his administration hastened the rebellion.

The year of Florus' appointment, a young man of twenty-six named Josephus went to Rome as a member of a deputation to secure the release of Jewish priests sent there by Felix. Josephus became a friend to a Jewish actor at the court of Nero. The actor introduced him to the empress, who arranged for the success of his mission and sent him home laden with gifts. Josephus was an aristocratic Jew and a Pharisee, but he returned to Judaea convinced that friendship with the Romans was the only course for Jewish well-being.

Agrippa II ruled through part of the Emperor Domitian's reign (A.D. 81–96). When Agrippa II died sometime after A.D. 93, the Herodian dynasty ended, and his territories were absorbed into the Roman empire.

Summary of Imperial and Local Rulers

Caesar	Praefect
Augustus, 27 B.C.–A.D. 14	Coponius, A.D. 7–8
	Marcus Ambivious, A.D. 9–12
	Annius Rufus, A.D. 12–15
Tiberius, A.D. 14–37	Valerius Gratus, A.D. 15–26
	Pontius Pilate, A.D. 26–36
	Marcellus, A.D. 36–37
Caligula, A.D. 37–41	Herod Agrippa I, A.D. 41–44
	Procurator
Claudius, A.D. 41–54	Cuspius Fadus, A.D. 44–46
	Tiberius Julius Alexander, A.D. 46–48
	Ventidius Cumanus, A.D. 48–52
	Antonius Felix, A.D. 52–60
Nero A.D. 54–68	Porcius Festus, A.D. 60–62
	Albinus, A.D. 62–64
	Gessius Florus, A.D. 64–66

JERUSALEM IN THE NEW TESTAMENT

The two greatest events in the history of the world took place in Jerusalem: the atoning sacrifice and the resurrection of Jesus Christ. "Jerusalem [was] the city of the great King" (Matt. 5:35). His dwelling-place or meeting-place was there. There he manifested himself to his servants, the prophets. For a thousand years he was worshipped in Jerusalem. His people "looked for redemption in Jerusalem" (Luke 2:38). From Melchizedek to Malachi, the Messiah was anticipated and announced, always looking forward to the meridian of time:

> When the time was come that he should be received up, [Jesus] set his face to go to Jerusalem. (Luke 9:51)

> It cannot be that a prophet perish out of Jerusalem. (Luke 13:33)

> Behold, we go up to Jerusalem, and all things that are written by the prophets concerning the Son of man shall be accomplished. (Luke 18:31)

> From that time forth began Jesus to show unto his disciples, how that he must go unto Jerusalem, and suffer many things of the elders and chief priests and scribes, and be killed, and be raised again the third day. (Matt. 16:21)

There seems to be constant intentional juxtaposition of Jerusalem and the rest of Judaea in the New Testament. Jerusalem was the capital, the chief and Holy City, and merited preferential status or at least singular mention alongside any other place.[29] Thus, "there went out unto him all the land of Judaea, and they of Jerusalem" (Mark 1:5), "a great multitude of people out of all Judaea and Jerusalem" (Luke 6:17). "Ye shall be witnesses unto me both in Jerusalem, and in all Judaea" (Acts 1:8).

Jerusalem was synonymous with leadership. The headquarters of the early Christian Church were centered in the place where centuries earlier God had chosen to place his name, where the Holy Temple had epitomized Judaic life for a millennium. Like that of some of the old prophets, Jesus' most important work was performed and his life was given in Jerusalem. And though nearly all the members of the original Quorum of the Twelve Apostles were originally from Galilee, it was clear to them that the center place of Zion, from which the law and the word must go forth, was Jerusalem. "Ye shall be witnesses unto me," Jesus told

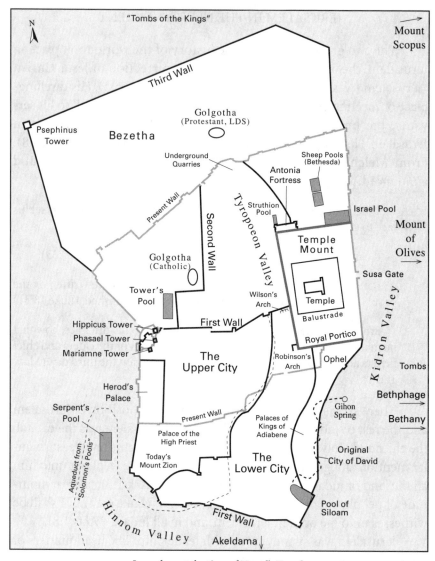

Jerusalem at the time of Herod's Temple

them, "both in Jerusalem, and in all Judaea, and in Samaria, and unto the uttermost part of the earth" (Acts 1:8). Jerusalem would become the capital of a far-reaching spiritual empire.

Jesus wept over the City as he recalled her past and prophesied her future. Although Herod's Jerusalem must have appeared to any would-be attacker as a high-walled, formidable fortress, Jesus prophesied of war that would destroy Jerusalem not long after he left the earth. Among other things, he warned, "let them which are in Judaea flee to the mountains; and let them which are in the midst of it depart out" (Luke 21:21). At first it may seem puzzling to speak of inhabitants of Judaea fleeing to the mountains when most already lived in the tops of the mountains, but the other side of the parallelism helps: "let them which are in the midst of it depart out." Jesus may have been suggesting that Judaeans flee eastward through the wilderness, the usual course of flight, and find safety in the mountain refuges on the edge of the wilderness where David had hidden from the armies of Saul a thousand years earlier.

Jesus left no doubt concerning the immediate future of Jerusalem. His were vivid prophetic pronouncements about the next generations:

> Jesus turning unto them said, Daughters of Jerusalem, weep not for me, but weep for yourselves, and for your children. (Luke 23:28)

> When ye shall see Jerusalem compassed with armies, then know that the desolation thereof is nigh. . . . And they shall fall by the edge of the sword, and shall be led away captive into all nations: and Jerusalem shall be trodden down of the Gentiles. (Luke 21:20, 24)

What was it all for? Why would Jesus and Jerusalem both suffer indignities and anguish and death? Their end was but a beginning. Both Jesus and Jerusalem would be resurrected and live again. Both had to be buried and brought forth anew.

The Mount of Olives

The two-mile-long Mount of Olives range lies east of the most ancient parts of Jerusalem. Its distance from the city is given in the New Testament: "The mount called Olivet . . . is from Jerusalem a sabbath day's journey" (Acts 1:12)—that is, about three thousand feet.

The Mount of Olives may be divided into three sections. The northernmost section was called by Josephus and is still called today Mount Scopus (Greek, *scopos*, "lookout point"), where Babylonian and Roman armies camped and watched the city they were besieging. The Hebrew name of Mount Scopus is *Har HaTsofim*, meaning the "mount of watchmen." The whole of the Mount of Olives is certainly a

Graves on the Mount of Olives (the stones on the graves have been placed there by mourners)

watchtower over Jerusalem, a guardian especially of the holy Temple Mount below.

The middle and southern sections, east and southeast of the Temple Mount, are today called the Mount of Olives, although the southernmost section, directly east of the ancient City of David, was in Old Testament times also known as the Mount of Scandal, the Mount of Offense, or the "mount of corruption" (2 Kgs. 23:13) because of the shrines Solomon allowed to be erected there for his wives' idol gods (see 1 Kgs. 11:7–8).

The midsouthern portion of the Mount of Olives is one of the oldest continuously used cemeteries in the world. Already by Jesus' day thousands of tombs had been cut in the soft, chalky Senonian limestone, which is more easily cut than the harder Turonian and Cenomanian limestones to the west. Hundreds of Old Testament period tombs have now been investigated by archaeologists, and many hundreds of ossuaries (small stone boxes for reburial of bones) have been uncovered from the New Testament period.[30] Presently more than seventy thousand graves are visible on the Mount of Olives. Jewish traditions have encouraged the pious to be buried on the Mount of Olives in order to be part of the first resurrection when the Messiah comes. Indeed, according to Christian scripture, some disciples have already risen from that cemetery: "The graves were opened; and many bodies of the saints which slept arose, and came out of the graves after his resurrection, and went into the holy city, and appeared unto many" (Matt. 27:52–53).

The Mount of Olives is mentioned in the Gospels in connection with places where Jesus taught and prayed: "And as he sat upon the mount of Olives over against the temple, Peter and James and John and Andrew asked him privately, . . . Tell us, when shall these things be? and what shall be the sign of thy coming, and of the end of the world?" (Mark 13:3; Matt. 24:3). "And he came out, and went, as he was wont, to the mount of Olives; and his disciples also followed him" (Luke 22:39). "Jesus ofttimes resorted thither with his disciples" (John 18:2).

Jesus began his triumphal entry into the city from the east, beginning on the eastern side of the Mount of Olives: "And when he was come nigh, even now at the descent of the mount of Olives, the whole multitude of the disciples began to rejoice and praise God with a loud voice for all the mighty works that they had seen" (Luke 19:37).

The Mount of Olives is where Jesus descended below all (the Atonement) and where he ascended above all (the Ascension). With his mortal work finished, Jesus departed into heaven from the eastern mountain of Jerusalem (see Luke 24:50). His return in the end of time will be to the same Mount: "And when he had spoken these things, while they beheld, he was taken up; and a cloud received him out of their sight. And while they looked stedfastly toward heaven as he went up, behold, two men stood by them in white apparel; which also said, Ye men of Galilee, why stand ye gazing up into heaven? this same Jesus, which is taken up from you into heaven, shall so come in like manner as ye have seen him go into heaven" (Acts 1:9–11; see also v. 12; cf. D&C 45:48–54).

The Eastern Limits of Jerusalem

When Jesus went to Jerusalem,[31] he usually stayed in Bethany, which "was nigh unto Jerusalem, about fifteen furlongs off" (John 11:18) on the eastern side of the Mount of Olives range. The fifteen furlongs, or *stadia,* is approximately two miles. Bethany is likely the same as Ananiah of the Old Testament (see Neh. 11:32), though the names have different meanings (*Ananiah* signifies "Jehovah covers"—as a cloud does—and

Bethany allegedly means "house of dates"). Today, the name of the town is *el-Azariyeh,* preserving the name of its famous former citizen, Lazarus. Jesus often lodged with his friend Lazarus and his two sisters, Mary and Martha (see John 11:1). On other occasions he stayed with "Simon the leper," that is, a man named Simon who had been a leper but was healed (see Matt. 26:6). The traditional tomb of Lazarus that visitors see today may actually be the tomb from which Jesus' friend was raised.

"They drew nigh unto Jerusalem, and were come to Bethphage" (Matt. 21:1). Two of the three passages referring to Bethphage mention it side by side with Bethany—the two towns were near each other on the eastern slope of the Mount of Olives. Bethphage means "house of figs," and many fig trees grow in the vicinity. Rabbinic literature cites Bethphage as the eastern limit of the city of Jerusalem.[32]

Jesus' first coming to Jerusalem as King was from the east, as his Second Coming is prophesied to be. At Passover time, a time of celebrating independence, of triumph over oppressors, and of Messianic expectation, Jesus accepted the acclamation of King and triumphantly proceeded into the city (see Matt. 21). He likely entered the Temple Mount where today's Golden Gate is located and then turned into the Temple, instead of going into the Antonia Fortress to take on the Romans. That made all the difference—it showed that the Messiah was a spiritual, not a political, deliverer.

Pools of Water in Jerusalem

Jerusalem enjoyed highly developed water resources during the late Second Temple period.[33] Wells, springs, cisterns, aqueducts, and pools served the need for water of one of the greatest walled cities in the Near East. Moving water—groundwater and water transported via aqueduct—was the best water, because open pools have the disadvantages of heavy evaporation, silting, and exposure to sewage and other pollutants. Notwithstanding the disadvantages, Jerusalem had at least ten large pools in this period. Two are mentioned in the New Testament: the Pool of Siloam and the Pool of Bethesda.[34]

Jesus one day sent a man blind from birth to the Pool of Siloam. He answered the man's plea for sight by making a clay paste, applying it to his eyes, and instructing him to go to the pool and wash it off. The blind man obeyed and was healed (see John 9:1–11).

The Pool of Siloam stands at the end of the ancient City's unique hydrotechnical project: Hezekiah's Tunnel. We recall that in the year 701 B.C., King Hezekiah, encouraged by the prophet Isaiah, prepared for the attack of the Assyrian king Sennacherib's forces by repairing the city walls and carving out of solid limestone an underground water channel nearly eighteen hundred feet long to camouflage the Gihon Spring, the city's main water source, and carry its waters inside the city for safe access. By Jesus' day, the pools at the south end had provided water storage for seven centuries.

The double pool called the Pool of Bethesda (or Bethzatha, possibly Aramaic, "House of Mercy") was situated just north of the Temple Mount gate called in Greek *probatike* (pertaining to sheep), the gate through which sheep are supposed to have been brought into the Temple for sacrifice.[35] "Now there is at Jerusalem by the sheep market a pool, which is called in the Hebrew tongue Bethesda, having five porches" (John 5:2). Five porticoes, or porches, surrounded the twin pools: four around the sides and one between them. Certain medicinal or curative properties were ascribed to the pool. A superstitious tradition had an angel coming down and "troubling" the waters—probably the result of a siphon-karst spring flowing into the pool, causing bubbling at the surface. At this pool Jesus met a man who had been lame or paralyzed for thirty-eight years. On the Sabbath Day he raised him up, completely healed (see John 5:1–16).

Hinnom, the Valley of Hell

In the Old Testament the Hebrew word *sheol* is translated *grave, hell,* and occasionally *pit.* The scriptural context clearly requires its association with the situation of the dead who have departed the earth. It does not mean the future place of punishment, which is our usual definition of *hell.* A Greek term often translated in the New Testament as *hell* is *hades,* a word with pagan origins. But *hades* carries the same meaning as the Hebrew *sheol:* the place where the dead temporarily reside, awaiting resurrection. The hell to which people are cast down or cast out, the place of punishment by ever-burning fire, is represented by the Greek word *Gehenna,* a Greek transliteration of the Hebrew *Gei Hinnom,* the Valley of Hinnom (or the full name, the Valley of the Son of Hinnom).

The Hinnom Valley was the designated border between the tribes of Judah and Benjamin (see Josh. 15:8; 18:16). The valley lay to the southwest just outside of the original Zion, the City of David. It lies below what is today called Mount Zion. Centuries before the Roman period, the Hinnom Valley was used for burning incense (see 2 Chron. 28:3) and for burning children as sacrifice to idol gods (see 2 Kgs. 23:10; 2 Chron. 33:6; Jer. 7:31). Prophets warned of fiery judgments upon all involved in such horrendous practices.

The Hinnom Valley was also named Tophet, possibly deriving from an Aramaic term meaning "place of fire" (see Isa. 30:33). The burning came to symbolize in the New Testament the devouring fire of judgment, giving rise to the concept of hell as a place of continual burnings and eternal punishment. The book of Revelation describes hell as a lake of fire and brimstone. There are twelve occurrences in the New Testament of *Gehenna*, translated *hell* or *hell fire*. The most famous is Jesus' teaching in the Sermon on the Mount: "I say unto you, That whosoever is angry with his brother without a cause shall be in danger of the judgment: and whosoever shall say to his brother, Raca [Hebrew and Aramaic, *reyk,* 'empty, vain, worthless'], shall be in danger of the council [Greek, *Sanhedrin*]: but whosoever shall say, Thou fool, shall be in danger of hell fire [Hebrew, *esh Gei Hinnom,* literally, 'fire of the Hinnom Valley,' or Greek, *Gehenna*]" (Matt. 5:22).

Another burial place has been associated since at least the first century before Christ with the southern slopes of the Hinnom Valley: "And it was known unto all the dwellers at Jerusalem; insomuch as that field is called in their proper tongue, Aceldama, that is to say, The field of blood" (Acts 1:19). According to Acts 1:18, Judas Iscariot (Hebrew, *ish Kerioth,* "man from Kerioth," a Judaean village) purchased with his betrayal money a field that was to be the scene of his suicide. Matthew 27:5-7, on the other hand, preserves the account of Judas casting down the coins in the Temple and going out and hanging himself, whereupon the chief priests bought with the money "the potter's field, to bury strangers in. Wherefore that field was called, The field of blood" (Matt. 27:6-8). Greek *Akeldama* is transliterated from the Aramaic *khakel dema* ("field of blood"). According to the New Testament record, then, the renaming of this burial ground in or near Jerusalem had its origins in the betrayal of Jesus and the death of Judas Iscariot.[36]

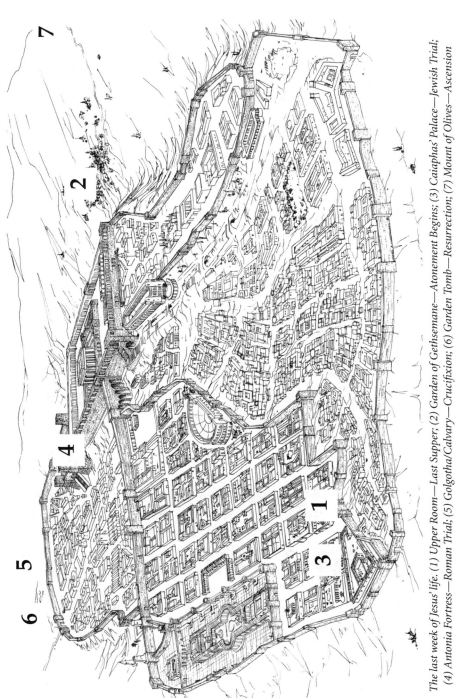

The last week of Jesus' life. (1) Upper Room—Last Supper; (2) Garden of Gethsemane—Atonement Begins; (3) Caiaphas' Palace—Jewish Trial; (4) Antonia Fortress—Roman Trial; (5) Golgotha/Calvary—Crucifixion; (6) Garden Tomb—Resurrection; (7) Mount of Olives—Ascension

The Upper Room

The most important events of the last week of Jesus' life[37] began in "a large upper room furnished and prepared" (Mark 14:15). The longest and strongest traditions indicate that the house containing the Upper Room was on the hill today called Mount Zion (the Western Hill).[38] That room was where Jesus celebrated the Passover meal with his apostles, where he instituted the sacrament of the Lord's Supper (see Matt. 26:26–29; Luke 22:15–20), where he gave special meaning to the washing of feet (see John 13:2–17), and where he revealed who would betray him (see Matt. 26:20–25; John 13:18–30).

In finding the guest chamber, Jesus instructed Peter and John to follow a man bearing a pitcher of water from the Gihon Spring, or the Pool of Siloam. Because women usually carried the water, some suppose that this man may have been part of the semimonastic Essene community known to have resided in that part of the Upper City. The apostles proceeded as Jesus had directed and made final preparations for celebrating the Passover—according to John, a day earlier than the community at large, because by sundown on Friday evening Jesus, as the Passover Lamb, would have been sacrificed (at the same time as the Passover lamb on the Temple altar[39]) and would be in the tomb (see John 13:1; 18:28; 19:14).

The Upper Room was a furnished room (Greek, *estromenon;* specifically refers to a feast or festival setting). The room likely included a *triclinium,* a U-shaped, low-lying table around which persons reclined with their feet toward the outside. If this Upper Room is the same chamber where the resurrected Jesus appeared to many disciples (Luke 24:36–49) or where the apostles and a hundred others were met to fill the vacancy in the Quorum of the Twelve Apostles (Acts 1:13–26), then it may have been the home of John Mark's mother, which served as a meeting place for the followers of Jesus after the Resurrection (Acts 12:12).

When Jesus and the eleven apostles had concluded their early observance of the Passover—the last legitimate Passover in history—and after he had given his farewell instructions about unity, love, and the Holy Spirit to his closest associates, "he went forth with his disciples over the brook Cedron, where was a garden, into the which he entered" (John 18:1). The Kidron (New Testament, *Cedron*) is a wadi that begins about a

Olive trees in the Garden of Gethsemane

mile north of the Temple Mount and turns southward to run between the Mount of Olives and the Temple Mount, continuing past the former City of David, where it joins its tributaries, the Tyropoeon and Hinnom, and then continues southeastward for twenty miles through the Judaean Desert to the Dead Sea.

The Garden of Gethsemane

On the slope of the Mount of Olives was a garden area to which Jesus liked to retire for meditation and prayer. "Jesus ofttimes resorted thither with his disciples" (John 18:2; see also Mark 14:32). The Garden was named *Gat Shemen,* which in Hebrew means "oil press." Just as the juice of the grape or olive is pressed and crushed by the heavy stone in the press, so the heavy burden of the sins of the world that Jesus carried would press the blood out of the body of this Anointed One. In Gethsemane, among the olive trees[40] that were themselves symbolic of the people of Israel, was accomplished, along with its consummation at Golgotha, the most selfless suffering in the history of humankind.

Rather than the small area now enclosed by the walls surrounding the Franciscan property that includes the Basilica of the Agony, the

Garden of Gethsemane must have extended a considerable distance up the slope of the Mount of Olives. Upon entering the garden, Jesus left eight of his apostles to watch and pray, and he continued up the slope with Peter, James, and John. He then left those three to watch and pray while he hiked "a stone's cast" (Matt. 26:36–39; Luke 22:41) beyond them.

After Jesus' agony in Gethsemane, a multitude consisting of chief priests, elders, and soldiers arrived to seek his arrest. At their head was Judas, who kissed Jesus profusely (according to the emphatic form of the Greek verb used in Mark 14:45), greatly confusing the emotions of the moment with a false display of affection. When the mob's intention was known, Peter stepped forward, swinging his sword, and cut off the ear of the high priest's servant (see John 18:10). What was Peter doing with a sword? In the darkness of the night, a sword offered some security at Passover time when many tens of thousands of people flocked to Jerusalem, more than could be housed inside the walls. Crowds of pilgrims camped as close outside the city as possible. When the arresting party arrived with "lanterns and torches and weapons" (John 18:3), some disciples ventured, "Shall we smite with the sword?" (Luke 22:49), possibly intending to defend themselves or still expecting Jesus to assume the popular role of the Messiah as the one who would overthrow his adversaries and establish a glorious new Jewish kingdom (cf. Luke 24:21; Acts 1:6).

The Palace of the High Priest Caiaphas

Quirinius, the legate of Syria who had conducted a census at the establishment of Judaea as a province, also established Ananus (*Hanan,* or *Annas* in the New Testament) as the high priest in Jerusalem. He and his influential family, including Joseph Caiaphas, his son-in-law (see John 18:13), virtually monopolized that office for the succeeding thirty-five years. The high priests were drawn from the narrow Sadducean circle and were regarded by Roman governors as their intermediaries with their Jewish subjects.

The Palace of Caiaphas was situated either on the summit of today's Mount Zion, just outside the Zion Gate in the Armenian cemetery, or down the slope a hundred yards on what are now the grounds of St. Peter in Gallicantu (Latin, "cockcrow"). At the latter site, excavations uncovered a complete set of Jewish weights and measures, possibly indicating judicial purposes. Also found was a large lintel inscribed with the

Possible site of Caiaphas' Palace (St. Peter in Gallicantu)

Hebrew word *corban* (offering), suggesting that the residents served in priestly functions.

At the palace some of the Sanhedrin convened illegally for the trial of Jesus. Jewish law forbade a court to sit at night and on or before the preparation day for the high Holy Day. In the porch, or colonnaded courtyard, of this palace (see Matt. 26:71), Peter denied knowing Jesus as he warmed himself at a fire during the early morning hours (see Luke 22:55–62; John 18:15–18).

Pilate's Hall of Judgment

Jesus' trial before the Roman governor Pontius Pilate took place on what John called "the Pavement, but in the Hebrew, Gabbatha" (John 19:13). The Hebrew (or Aramaic) *Gabbatha* is equivalent to the Greek *lithostroton,* meaning the stone courtyard of the hall of judgment: "Then led they Jesus . . . unto the hall of judgment: and it was early; and they themselves went not into the judgment hall, lest they should be defiled; but that they might eat the passover" (John 18:28; see also 18:33; 19:9; Acts 23:35).

The hall of judgment was also called in the New Testament the

Praetorium (Mark 15:16), a Latin term for the palace with its hearing room to which the Roman governor came to transact public business. In the same room was Pilate's judgment seat (Greek, *bema*), a raised platform resembling a throne on which the governor sat in judgment. "When Pilate therefore heard that saying, he brought Jesus forth, and sat down in the judgment seat" (John 19:13).

Tradition and modern scholarship have identified two main possibilities for the place where Jesus was accused before Pilate: the Antonia Fortress and Herod's Palace.

The Antonia Fortress was the massive governmental and military headquarters at the northwestern corner of the Temple Mount. Originally constructed by the Hasmonaeans and known as the Bira (Greek, *Baris*), it was reconstructed and fortified by Herod the Great and named after Mark Antony.[41] "It is quite possible to argue that Pilate's seat of judgement was in the Antonia, as is persuasively done by Pere Vincent," wrote Dame Kathleen Kenyon, excavator of Jerusalem.[42] A substantial contingent of soldiers was stationed at the Antonia, the biggest fortress in Jerusalem, to keep watch over the Temple Mount—the soldiers' main reason for being in Jerusalem.[43] Years later, Roman soldiers and then Temple guards took the Apostle Paul down to the Sanhedrin at their meeting place in the Temple and returned with him back up into the Fortress, also called "the castle" (Acts 21:34, 37; 22:24; 23:10).

Some ancient sources and modern scholars propose, on the other hand, that the official residence of Roman governors who came up from Caesarea was at Herod's Palace, on the west side of the city,[44] so Jesus' encounter with Pilate must have occurred there. Without additional evidence, it is impossible to conclusively determine which of the two sites might be the location of Jesus' presentation before Pilate.

The accusation brought against Jesus before some of the Sanhedrin was blasphemy—claiming to be God or insulting or violating the sanctity of God, the greatest crime in Jewish law. Romans cared little about the God of the Jews; they themselves had numerous gods whom they cursed at will. There was, however, an accusation that was serious enough to cause the governor to arise very early in the morning to hear—sedition against the Roman government. In fact, the chief reason Pilate had come up to Jerusalem from his usual residence in Caesarea on the coast was to keep his Roman eyes on the Temple Mount, the traditional focus of would-be insurrection and any initiatives to independence, during the Passover. Pilate had already dealt viciously with several messianic revolutionary movements. Some Jewish leaders, though anxious to see this popular preacher Jesus disposed of, were interested in passing the responsibility for his death to the Romans, so they shifted the charge from blasphemy to treason to bring about a Roman sentence of death (see Luke 23:1–2).

Though Jews would usually not resent active hostility against the Romans, in this case they pressed the charge that Jesus was conspiring to become king of the Jews and was, therefore, a threat to Caesar (as well as to the comfortable position of the Sadducees and high priests who held their positions by the good graces of the Romans). Jesus' Jewish accusers even went so far as to accuse Pilate of being no friend to Caesar if he dismissed the charges against Jesus (see John 19:12). Pilate tried several means to placate the Jews. First he proposed the release of one notable prisoner for the festival: Barabbas or Jesus (see Matt. 27:15–18; John 18:39–40). Barabbas was a revolutionist who may have appropriated a messianic title: his name means "son of the father"; Jesus, on the other hand, claimed to actually be the "Son of the Father." The Jews chose to have Barabbas released. Then Pilate scourged Jesus—flogging him with a leather whip containing jagged pieces of stone, metal, or bone—in the hope of satisfying the accusers (see Luke 23:16; John 19:1–5).

With no reliable witnesses and on the testimony of the accused alone, despite Pilate's inclination to acquit Jesus because of lack of evidence (see Luke 23:4, 15, 22; John 18:38; 19:4, 6), and despite Pilate's own suspicion of the accusers' motives (see Matt. 27:18), Jesus was ordered to be crucified, the usual method of execution for a noncitizen.[45] Tradition claims that Peter later was also crucified; in contrast, Paul, a Roman citizen, was beheaded.

Golgotha/Calvary, the Place of Execution or Burial

The King James Version of Luke identifies the place of Jesus' execution as Calvary, whereas the other three Gospel writers call the place Golgotha: "He bearing his cross went forth into a place called the place of a skull, which is called in the Hebrew Golgotha" (John 19:17; see also Matt. 27:33; Mark 15:22).

All four writers associated the execution site with a skull. Hebrew *gulgoleth* and Aramaic *gulgutha* both mean "skull." Luke's *Calvary* is actually the Latin translation of the Greek *kranion*, which means "skull." Luke 23:33 reads in the Greek: "When they were come to the place, which is called *kranion*, there they crucified him."

To what does "skull" refer? The site could have had the physical appearance of a skull, or the name could have derived from the place's long-standing use for executions. It probably involves its being a place of burial. John 19:17 in the Joseph Smith Translation indicates that Jesus was taken "into a place called the *place of a burial;* which is called in the Hebrew Golgotha" (emphasis added).

The Tomb of Jesus

As with other sites of the events of the last days of Jesus' mortal life, there are two major possibilities for the location of his crucifixion, burial, and resurrection. According to scripture and Jewish customs, the site must have certain characteristics:

1. It must be outside the city walls, "nigh to the city" (John 19:20).

2. It must be near a main thoroughfare (see Matt. 27:39; Mark 15:29; John 19:20).

3. It must be a place of execution (see Mark 15:27; Luke 23:33).

4. There must be a garden nearby (John 19:41; 20:15).

5. The garden must contain at least one tomb (the tomb was near the place of crucifixion—John 19:41–42).

6. The rock tomb must be newly cut (Matt. 27:60; Luke 23:53; John 19:41).

7. It may have an anteroom (a mourning chamber) and several places for burial; in any case, it must be large enough to walk into (Mark 16:5; Luke 24:3; John 20:8).

8. It must have a large, heavy stone to seal the entrance, with a groove or trough for the stone to roll in (Matt. 27:60; Mark 15:46; 16:4; Luke 24:2).

9. The tomb entrance must be small, so that one has to stoop to look inside; a person looking in from the outside could see the place where the body was laid (Luke 24:12; John 20:5, 11–12).

10. The tomb must have someplace where linen burial clothes could lie and where a "young man" could sit (Mark 16:5), or where two angels

The Garden Tomb

could sit, one at the head and one at the foot of where Jesus' body had lain (John 20:12).

Let us consider these criteria as we examine the two options for the site of Jesus' crucifixion, burial, and resurrection.

Site one. The Church of the Holy Sepulchre has long been the traditional site of these venerated events. In the fourth century A.D., Constantine's mother, Helena, made a pilgrimage to the Holy Land and identified the spot, which had a pagan temple built over it. Recent excavations show that this site, though now within the walls of the Old City of Jerusalem, was outside the walls in Jesus' day. Its location just outside the western city wall could have provided a busy thoroughfare for travelers. There is no evidence that it was a place of execution or that there was a garden nearby. A stone quarry existed at the Holy Sepulchre site in the first century after Christ. Roman period tombs have been discovered in the bedrock below the church. They are *kokhim,* typical sepulchres from that period, rock-cut burial niches with enough space for a single body. There may have been room for someone to walk into the entry chamber of the tomb. There is no evidence that large stones could be rolled to seal the entrance or that there was a bench or shelf on which a body could be placed or on which someone could sit inside the sepulchre. Two angels could in no fashion situate themselves inside a *kokh*.[46]

Site two. The other possible site is the Garden Tomb, just outside (north) of the Damascus Gate of today's Old City. This tomb, discovered only last century, is now a place of pilgrimage for many thousands of Christians. This site was outside the walls of the city in Jesus' day alongside a main thoroughfare. It appears to have been a place of execution; today's Damascus Gate was called "St. Stephen's Gate" during the first millennium after Christ, suggesting that Stephen was killed in this area.[47] St. Stephen's Church (St. Etienne), from the fifth century after Christ, is immediately north of this site. One of ancient Jerusalem's biggest cisterns and a wine-press identify the grounds as possibly having been a garden at that time.

Many tombs have been discovered in the vicinity, most of them dating to the seventh and eighth centuries before Christ. The Garden Tomb itself appears to be part of a complex of Judaean tombs from those centuries; most of the complex lies north of the Garden Tomb in what is now the property of the Ecole Biblique, the French School of Archaeology. These tombs, unlike the later *kokhim*, are chambers with side rooms branching off in several directions. Each chamber contained, usually, three benches on which bodies were placed. Underneath one of the benches in each room was a respository for bones, suggesting reuse of the tombs over many generations.

A "new tomb" could also mean a newly remodeled tomb not yet used in the newly cut form. The Garden Tomb is nearly identical in style to the older tombs but has some features of later styles. There is no repository for bones, no evidence that it was used many times. It does have more than one room and is large enough to walk into. There is no stone at its entrance, but the trough for rolling one into place is clearly visible. The original entrance was short enough to require stooping to enter. And there was a bench or shelf (before Byzantines or others later carved out a sarcophagus) on which burial clothes could have lain and on which angels could have sat, on the right side as one enters the tomb (see Mark 16:5).

Some have objected to the Garden Tomb as the burial place of Jesus because its structure appears to be of the style used seven or eight centuries earlier. There are tombs from the early Roman period, however,

Khirbet Midras—tomb with a rolling stone, dating from the time of Jesus

that combine both old Judaean and Roman-period styles. At Khirbet Midras in the Shephelah, for example, is a tomb complex dating to the first century before Christ that has the older chambers containing benches but also features the later *kokhim*, or niches, and sarcophagi and ossuaries. Even the St. Etienne tomb complex, of which the Garden Tomb seems to be a part, has a chamber with sarcophagi quite distinct from the other chambers. While investigating ornate tombs in the Hinnom Valley, Leen Ritmeyer noted that some of the tombs that originated in the First Temple period were adapted and reused in the Second Temple period (early Roman period). "One of [the] side chambers with First Temple-period burial benches leads into an elaborate system of five tomb chambers with *kokhim*. In this way, too, the First Temple-period tomb was re-used and extended in the Second Temple period."[48]

Of the two possible sites, the enduring reverence of tradition favors the Holy Sepulchre site, but the Garden Tomb more completely matches the scriptural description. There is presently no way to know if one of these two sites or yet another site was used for Jesus' burial. Regardless of investigations and evidences and surmises and conclusions, it is not wise to affix faith to a particular site. Belief is beyond physical territory.

To the Christian the most important message is, "He is risen; he is not here" (Mark 16:6).

Theological Rationale for Jesus' Burial Site

A more theological or philosophical reasoning may be advanced for looking to the north for the place where Jesus' sacrifice occurred. We recall that two millennia before Christ, Abraham made the long, strenuous trek from Beersheba to Mount Moriah, later known as the Temple Mount (2 Chron. 3:1). He knew how repulsive and foreign human sacrifice is to the true worship of God, yet the command had been given to sacrifice his son. The test was perfectly designed for Abraham, who with Sarah had waited so many years for the covenant son, whom he loved. Now the Lord called on him to sacrifice, to give up, that beloved son. Paul wrote that "by faith Abraham, when he was tried, offered up Isaac: and he that had received the promises offered up his only begotten son" (Heb. 11:17). Abraham's offering of his son Isaac was a similitude of God's offering his Only Begotten Son. And both may have been accomplished at the same location. By following the hill of Moriah northward to just outside the Second Wall of the city, we see a prominence where the Garden Tomb and other nearby tombs are situated, which was apparently a site of execution and burial in antiquity.[49]

When Abraham and Isaac approached Moriah, Isaac reminded his father that they had the wood for the sacrifice but asked where the sacrifice was. Abraham prophetically responded, "My son, God [*Elohim* in the Hebrew text] will provide himself a lamb" (Gen. 22:7–8). When Abraham's test was consummated, and the angel of the Lord stopped the sacrifice of the son, a ram (not a lamb) was substituted. But two thousand years later, possibly on the northern extension of this same mountain, God did provide a lamb—the Lamb of God was sacrificed. We recall that a lamb slain on the great altar of the Temple was slain on the north side of the altar (see Lev. 1:11).

Abraham knew something of the meaning of his similitude-sacrifice. He had uttered prophetically—not unintentionally or accidentally—that God would provide a lamb as a sacrifice, and he knew that the Son would be that sacrifice, to be made at that very place—the reason for the long trek to Moriah instead of using some hill in the Negev. Jesus said in the Temple itself, "Your father Abraham rejoiced to see my day: and he saw it, and was glad" (John 8:56).

Thus, the Passover Lamb was slain at Passover time on the north of the Altar of Moriah as an atonement for sin, the symbolic and typical purpose of all the lambs slain on the Temple altar over the centuries—those sacrifices all prefigured that greatest Sacrifice.[50]

The Temple at the Time of Jesus[51]

No single place in all the world was holier to Jews and to Christians at the time of Jesus than Jerusalem's Temple Mount. It was known as *Har Habayit*, the "Mountain of the House [of God]," and no mountain on earth has such a unique history. To this most sacred parcel of ground the God of all creation could come to converse with his servants, the prophets and priests. "The Temple was the approach of a Nation to their God," wrote George Adam Smith.[52] And Jesus said, "In this place is one greater than the temple" (Matt. 12:6). There is evidence in word and in deed that Jesus considered the Temple to be the legitimate sanctuary of the true God. At one point he called it "my Father's house" (John 2:16); later he called it "my house" (Matt. 21:13).

Jesus' life from beginning to end was bound up with the Temple. An angel of the Lord appeared to Zacharias in the Holy Place, announcing the birth of the prophet who would prepare the way for the Messiah (see Luke 1:5–22). When Mary had fulfilled the forty-day ritual of purification after giving birth, Jesus was taken to the Temple in Jerusalem for the ceremonial redemption of the firstborn, at which the old Temple worker Simeon looked upon the promised Messiah in the flesh (see Luke 2:22–32). At age twelve, he was found "in the temple, sitting in the midst of the doctors, and they were hearing him, and asking him questions" (JST Luke 2:46).[53]

Near the commencement of his ministry, "Jesus was taken up into the holy city, and the Spirit setteth him on the pinnacle of the temple" (JST Matt. 4:5), where Satan tempted him. Of the whole length of the Temple Mount retaining walls, the southeast corner is the highest point—two hundred eleven feet, or sixty-four meters. But the distance from the top of Herod's Portico to the bottom of the Kidron Valley was more than four hundred feet. That is the traditional "pinnacle of the temple" to which it is believed Jesus was brought because it is the highest man-made height ever achieved anciently in the Holy Land. The point of Satan's temptation was to entice Jesus into misusing his divine power by throwing himself off the dizzying height and counting on angels to rescue him from the fall (see Matt. 4:6).[54]

Some researchers, on the other hand, consider the southwestern corner of the Mount to be a more logical location for the temptation of Jesus. That corner has a much better angle for looking out over the city, and a specially carved platform stone was discovered in the toppled ruins below, the stone indicating by a Hebrew inscription where one of the priests would blow the shofar, or ram's horn trumpet, to signal the advent and the departure of the Sabbath and other holy days.[55]

The Gospels frequently note Jesus' activity in the Temple courts and in the Temple itself when he was in Jerusalem during his three-year ministry:

> The blind and the lame came to him in the temple; and he healed them. (Matt. 21:14)

> Now about the midst of the feast Jesus went up into the temple, and taught. (John 7:14)

> And early in the morning he came again into the temple, and all the people came unto him; and he sat down, and taught them. (John 8:2)

> And he taught daily in the temple. (Luke 19:47)

> And all the people came early in the morning to him in the temple, for to hear him. (Luke 21:38)

> I spake openly to the world; I ever taught in the synagogue, and in the temple, whither the Jews always resort; and in secret have I said nothing. (John 18:20)

Jesus routinely adapted his teaching to objects or conditions from his immediate environment, often referring to something appropriate to the place where he taught. On one occasion in the Jerusalem Temple he made figurative use of the Temple. Hebrew literati for ages had metaphorically compared the human body to a temple. "Jesus answered and said unto them, Destroy this temple, and in three days I will raise it up. Then said the Jews, Forty and six years was this temple in building, and wilt thou rear it up in three days? But he spake of the temple of his body" (John 2:19–21).[56]

According to the testimony of John, this was said near the beginning of Jesus' ministry, which would make this declaration the first recorded foreshadowing of Jesus' death and resurrection. Evidently the Jews understood his figurative language, that he referred not to Herod's Temple but to his own body, which he claimed power to raise up again after its death. At his hearing before the chief priests, one of the false witnesses testified, "This fellow said, I am able to destroy the temple of God, and to build it in three days" (Matt. 26:61). At the cross, "they that passed by reviled him, wagging their heads, and saying, Thou that destroyest the temple, and buildest it in three days, save thyself" (Matt. 27:39–40). Nevertheless, through all of this, the Jewish leaders understood Jesus' figure of speech. The following report is preserved of a conversation soon after Jesus' death: "Now the next day, that followed the day of the preparation, the chief priests and Pharisees came together unto Pilate, saying, Sir, we remember that that deceiver said, while he was yet alive, *After three days I will rise again.* Command therefore that the sepulchre be made sure until the third day" (Matt. 27:62–64; emphasis added).

Jesus further prophesied that not one stone of the Temple would be left standing on another (see Mark 13:1–2; Luke 21:6). The magnificent Temple, the House of the Lord, to which many Jerusalemites must have looked with a confident sense of inviolability, would be leveled to the ground and the Temple Mount plowed! Isaiah had once assured the Lord's people that as birds protectively hovered over their young, so the Lord of hosts would defend and preserve Jerusalem (see Isa. 31:4–5). But with no allegiance and devotion to their God, the leaders of the Jews and many of their followers had abandoned the Hope of Israel. Without faith and faithfulness, the Lord's hand would not be stretched out to protect them or the Holy Temple. The Lord's hand, like his word, could be a sharp two-edged sword, providing either protection or destruction. In this case, the Temple would be destroyed—as foreseen by Daniel, the prophet: "[Then] shall Messiah be cut off . . . and the people of the prince [Latin, *princeps,* as the Roman general Titus] that shall come *shall destroy the city and the sanctuary*" (Dan. 9:26, emphasis added).

The largest and grandest of the Temples in Jerusalem would also be the shortest lived.[57]

The Temple at the time of Herod (painting by Al Rounds)

The Temple of Herod

The Temple of Herod was constructed beginning in 20 B.C. with the help of ten thousand workmen. One of Herod's main purposes was to provide greater space for the hundreds of thousands of worshippers who came to the Temple during the pilgrimage festivals and high holy days. One thousand priests who had trained as masons and carpenters helped to build the holiest parts,[58] and a thousand wagons transported materials. The Temple proper was under construction for a year and a half, and the courtyards and porticoes for eight years (though embellishment of the outer courts actually continued for more than eighty years). It was said that whoever had not seen the Temple of Herod had never seen a beautiful building in his life.[59] No other temple complex in the Graeco-Roman world compared with it in expansiveness and magnificence. According to Josephus, the polished white marble exterior of the Temple was covered with so much gold that when the sun shone on it, those who looked upon it could be blinded.[60] Although the architectural glories of Herod's Temple far surpassed those of Solomon's Temple, Herod's Temple had little of its predecessor's spiritual atmosphere. The Ark of the Covenant, the mercy seat, the cherubim, the Urim and Thummim

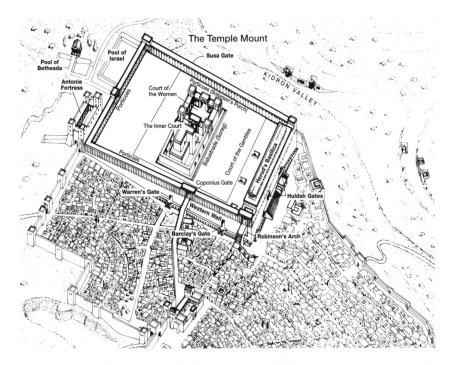

The Temple Mount

Pool of Israel

Pool of Bethesda

Susa Gate

Antonia Fortress

Court of the Women

Porticoes

Porticoes (Solomon's Porch)

KIDRON VALLEY

The Inner Court

Balustrade (Soreg)

Court of the Gentiles

Herod's Basilica

Porticoes

Coponius Gate

Warren's Gate

Huldah Gates

Western Wall

Barclay's Gate

Robinson's Arch

providing revelatory contact with God, and other holy objects were lacking. And yet it was a place of revelation, as seen in the story of Zacharias (Luke 1), and Jesus acknowledged it as the Father's and his own House.

Herod nearly doubled the size of the Temple Mount from what it was during the period of the First Temple, making it in Jesus' day approximately forty acres in area (compare with the ten-acre area of Temple Square in Salt Lake City). He had to extend the platform of the mount to the north, to the west, and to the south. He built a massive retaining wall, trapezoidal in final shape, around the entire Temple Mount. That retaining wall alone was the longest, highest, and most impressive around any shrine in the ancient world, and the artificial esplanade, or enclosure, inside is the largest of its kind in antiquity.[61] Below floor level to the north and west was earth-fill, but to the south Herod supported the floor with vaults—twelve rows of arched colonnades with a total of eighty-eight pillars. The area under the floor of the southeast portion of the Temple courtyard, therefore, was hollow. This space is now occupied by a large, columned chamber erroneously called Solomon's Stables. Because it was constructed by Herod, the place did not exist in Solomon's day, though it was later used by the Crusaders for stabling horses.

The Temple Mount was a huge space measuring more than 157,000 square yards (144,000 square meters).[62] The Forum in Rome was only half that size, the Acropolis in Athens one-fifth that size, and the largest temple complex in the world—Karnak, in Upper Egypt, which was two thousand years in the building—is only a third bigger. Above ground on all sides of the Mount were extraordinary colonnaded *porticoes*, or *porches* (also called *cloisters*, that is, covered walkways with colonnades opening to the inside). Each portico had a double row of Corinthian columns, each column a monolith (cut from one block of stone), and the columns rose to more than thirty-seven feet high. According to Josephus, Herod extended the Mount northward, westward, and southward and erected porticoes inside these newly positioned walls, but he built up the eastern portico in the same position as on the previous Temple Mount. This eastern portico was called Solomon's Porch (see 1 Kgs. 6:3; Acts 3:11). There Jesus, having come to the Passover at age twelve, conversed with the learned rabbis; there he later walked and taught at the Feast of Dedication (Hanukkah) and testified that he was God's Son; and there the Jews tried to stone him (see John 10:22–39). Also Peter and John, after performing a miracle at the gate of the Temple, drew a large crowd in Solomon's Porch and preached and called for repentance following the denying and killing of the Holy One. They were arrested by Temple police and Sanhedrin officials (see Acts 3:1–4:3).

The southern portico, grander than the others, is often called Herod's Basilica. The word *basilica* (from the Greek *basileus*, "king," and therefore designating a royal portico) meant a public hall that was rectangular in shape and had colonnaded aisles. A similar ground plan was later adopted for early Christian churches. The Royal Basilica, or Portico, contained 162 Corinthian columns. At its foot were ramps leading onto the Temple courtyard from the south.

The eastern gate of the Temple Mount was called the Susa Gate, because it faced eastward toward Susa (*Shushan* in the Bible), the Persian capital where the biblical stories of Daniel, Esther, Nehemiah, and others in part unfolded (see Dan. 8:2; Esth. 1:2; Neh. 1:1). When this gate was originally built in the early Second Temple period, the memory of Shushan was fresh in the minds of the remnant that returned from

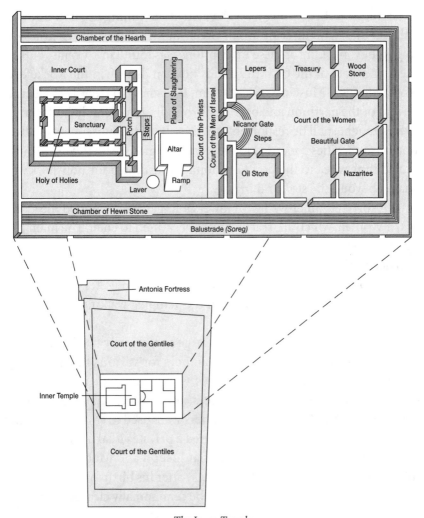

The Inner Temple

Babylon. This gate was said to have been lower than the other gates so that the priests gathered across the bridge on the Mount of Olives for the sacrifice of the red heifer[63] might still look directly into the Temple.

The Courts of the Temple

The outer court was called the Court of the Gentiles, from which Jesus cast out the money changers. Non-Jews were allowed to enter this far onto the Temple Mount.[64] Surrounding the Temple proper was a balustrade (Hebrew, *soreg*), an elevated stone railing about four and a half feet high with inscriptions in Greek and Latin warning Gentiles not to pass beyond. One of these inscriptions was found in 1935 just outside the Lion's Gate of the Old City and is now on display in the Rockefeller Archaeological Museum in Jerusalem. It reads: "No Gentile shall enter inward of the partition and barrier surrounding the Temple, and whosoever is caught shall be responsible to himself for his subsequent death."[65] Roman authorities conceded to the Jewish religious leaders control of the sacred inner area to the point of capital punishment for non-Jews who passed beyond the stone railing.

A fortified inner wall with towers and gates surrounded the Court of the Women, which all Israelites were permitted to enter. The main gate into the Court of the Women was called the Beautiful Gate because of its rich decoration. At this gate Peter and John, on their way to Temple worship, stopped to hear the petition of a lame man. Peter dramatically healed the man, who joined them in the Temple, "walking, and leaping, and praising God" (Acts 3:1–11).

The Court of the Women was a large space nearly two hundred feet square. In the four corners were chambers for various functions. The eastern chambers served the Nazarites, where those who had made special vows could prepare their sacrifices, and another chamber was used for storing wood. The western chambers were used to store olive oil and for purification of lepers, which required a private ritual bath. It was perhaps to this Court of the Women that Joseph and Mary brought the infant Jesus five to six weeks (forty days) after his birth for him as a firstborn to be redeemed and for Mary to be ceremonially cleansed (see Luke 2:22–23).

This whole court was surrounded by porticoes. Against the walls inside the porticoes, the place called the Treasury, were trumpet-shaped boxes for charitable contributions, where the widow cast in her mites (see Mark 12:41–44) and where Jesus taught during the Feast of Tabernacles (see John 8:20). In this court stood giant lampstands (*menorot*), seventy-five feet in height, giving light to the Temple Mount and to much of the City.[66] There Jesus proclaimed himself the Light of the world. There he bore witness of his own divinity, dealt mercifully with the woman taken in adultery, announced his Messiahship, and bore testimony that he was the God of Abraham. Jews tried to stone him again (see John 7–8).

Fifteen curved steps and then the Gate of Nicanor led into the innermost court. (Nicanor was a wealthy Jew from Alexandria who had donated the ornate doors of the gate.) Only priests and other authorized Temple officiators and participants would enter this court. To the sides of its porticoes were the Chamber of the Hearth, where priests on duty spent their nights, and the Chamber of Hewn Stone, where the Sanhedrin met. In the latter chamber, before the council, Stephen was transfigured (see Acts 6:12–15) and Paul later testified (see Acts 22:30–23:10).

On the north side of this court, which was actually a double court—first the Court of the Men of Israel, then the Court of the Priests—was the Place of Slaughtering. On the south side was the giant brass wash basin, or laver, supported on the backs of twelve lions.[67] Millions of gallons of water were brought in from "Solomon's Pools," south of Bethlehem, and stored in a connected series of rock-cut reservoirs, or cisterns.

Near the Laver the great horned Altar of Sacrifice or burnt offering stood, measuring forty-eight feet square and fifteen feet high. Some think that the huge rock mass inside the Dome of the Rock—which now measures approximately forty by fifty by seven feet high—once formed the base of the Altar of Sacrifice.[68] It is clear from scripture that King David purchased the rock to build an altar to the Lord (see 2 Sam. 24:18–25). The altar consisted of whitewashed unhewn stone, and it had a ramp leading up to it from the south that was forty-eight feet long and twenty-four feet wide. The altar either stood off-center in the court or was low enough in the center of the court so that the priest sacrificing the red heifer on the Mount of Olives could see straight into the giant entryway of the Holy Sanctuary, which stood sixty-six feet high and thirty-three feet wide.

The Sanctuary, or Holy Place, was made of marble. Two columns in front were named Jachin and Boaz (meaning "He will establish" and "In him is strength"), after the names of the entry columns of Solomon's Temple. The Temple proper was more than one hundred fifty feet high[69] (today's Dome of the Rock reaches a height of just over one hundred feet) and was surrounded on top by golden spikes to discourage birds from landing on and tarnishing the stone.

Inside the Holy Place was the veil leading to the most sacred chamber, the Holy of Holies. That same veil was torn from top to bottom at the death of Jesus (see Matt. 27:51). Whereas only the high priest once a year could enter the symbolic presence of God, now Jesus, through his death, rent that partition, signifying the accessibility of God's presence to all people (see Heb. 9:11–14; 10:19–22 for Paul's explanation of the symbolism). The rending of the Temple veil may also denote the rending of the Judaism of the Mosaic dispensation.

Overall, the Temple area consisted of a series of rising platforms. From the Court of the Gentiles one ascended stairs to the Court of the Women; from there, one ascended fifteen curved stairs (possibly singing fifteen Psalms of Ascent; see Ps. 120–34) to the Court of the Men of Israel and the Court of the Priests; and a final ascent was required to enter the Holy Place itself. Thus the phrase "Jesus went up into the temple" (John 7:14) is quite literal. The three courtyards surrounding the holiest place where the Divine Presence could be manifest may appropriately be compared to three degrees of glory and three settings for instruction in modern Temples: telestial, terrestrial, and celestial. It is not enough to progress into the third courtyard or heaven; it is incumbent upon each worshipper, now that the Great High Priest has made it possible for all, to actually enter into the highest degree of that realm, to symbolically enter into the Presence of God and be exalted.

We recall again the message of one of the Psalms of Ascent: "I was glad when they said unto me, Let us go into the house of the Lord. Our feet shall stand within thy gates, O Jerusalem. . . . Whither the tribes go up, the tribes of the Lord, unto the testimony of Israel, to give thanks unto the name of the Lord. . . . Pray for the peace of Jerusalem: they shall prosper that love thee. . . . Because of the house of the Lord our God I will seek thy good" (Ps. 122).

NOTES

1. Herod's building energies carried him all over the Mediterranean world. He erected a gymnasium in Ptolemais and one in Tripoli, a marketplace and temples in Tyre and Berytus, a theater in Sidon, and a gymnasium and theater in Damascus. He erected

buildings in Athens, Sparta, Nicopolis, and other Greek cities. He gave gifts to Pergamum, Samos, Cilicia, Pamphylia, and Lycia. He rebuilt the Temple of Apollo on the island of Rhodes, and he repaved the main street of Syrian Antioch with marble along the entire length of the city and adorned it with a double colonnade. He was a generous contributor to the Olympic games and was given the permanent title of Chairman of the Games. See also in Josephus, *Antiquities* 16.5.1–3 and *Wars* 1.21.11–12; *Anchor Bible Dictionary*, 3:166, s.v. "Herod the Great"; Pritchard, *Harper Atlas of the Bible*, 158–59; Avigad, *Discovering Jerusalem*, 82.

2. Many of these building projects are beautifully illustrated in Connolly, *Living in the Time of Jesus.*

3. See Aharoni and Avi-Yonah, *Macmillan Bible Atlas*, Map 221.

4. The king's palace was built in 23 B.C. on the western side at the highest spot in the city. Three towers were erected to secure his palace, which had a wall on all sides to protect not only the city in general on the west but also the palace from his own subjects on the east. On the north end of the palace complex were military barracks and a camp for his guards; the rest of the palace consisted of banquet halls, guest apartments, baths, and so on—some of which were adorned with lovely mosaics and frescoes. Landscaping included groves of trees, aqueducts, pools, water-spouting statues, and fountains. The largest of Herod's towers at the north end of his palace was named after his brother Phasael (148 ft./45 m.)—some of this tower remains today in the Citadel at Jaffa Gate; another tower to the east was named in honor of a friend, Hippicus (132 ft./40 m.); and a third tower was named after his beloved wife Mariamne, whom he executed because he suspected her of involvement in some treachery (90 ft./27 m.). The towers had elaborate residential quarters in the upper sections, and the Hippicus tower held a deep water reservoir above its base. Outside the palace to the east was the *agora* (Greek, "marketplace"; Latin, *forum*), a colonnaded shopping mall with an open plaza in the middle. The area east and south of Herod's palace was known as the Upper City, in contrast to the Lower City on the eastern hill, the ancient City of David. The Upper City boasted a wealthier Jewish housing district with Hellenistic town-planning: well laid-out streets and houses built around courtyards with gardens and cisterns.

5. For details of other monuments and structures in Herodian Jerusalem, see Ogden, *Illustrated Guide*, 32–33.

6. On the west side of the Temple Mount a bridge built by the Hasmonaeans connected the Mount with the Upper City (the Western Hill); it is now named after its nineteenth-century discoverer Charles Wilson, thus, Wilson's Arch. A monumental staircase projected from the southwest corner of the Temple Mount. The beginnings of the staircase is now called Robinson's Arch, after the nineteenth-century American scholar and explorer Edward Robinson, who stood at then-ground level and examined, measured, and postulated over the purpose of the arched bridge. Though once it was considered another bridge spanning the valley to the Upper City, it is now known through excavation that the bridge was in fact an arched stairway, the largest known anywhere in the classical world, conducting pedestrians into the twelve-meter-wide street of the Central (Tyropoeon) Valley. See Mazar, "Herodian Jerusalem," 230–37; Ben-Dov, *Shadow of the Temple,* 120–33; *New Encyclopedia of Archaeological Excavations*, 2:740–41; Ben-Dov, *Ophel Archaeological Garden;* a painting of the staircase may be seen in Connolly, *Living in the Time of Jesus,* 4–5. The main entrance and exit to the Temple Mount were the two sets of gates, called the Huldah Gates, leading in and out of the Temple Mount from the south. Through the one on the right a person would enter to perform the holy work in the Temple, after having gone through ritual washings or cleansings accomplished in

small pools or fonts (*mikvehs*) outside the retaining walls of the sacred enclosure. Through the gate on the left a person would exit following the Temple work or service. Now partly visible after recent archaeological restoration is a beautiful stone staircase leading up to the wall. The elaborate stairway was originally two hundred ten feet wide. There are thirty steps, alternating steps and landings—conducive to a slow, reverent ascent or descent. From here rabbis sometimes taught the people. Jesus could have taught on this stairway also, at one point in his scathing condemnation of hypocrites even gesturing eastward over the Kidron toward the city's necropolis and comparing hypocrites to whited sepulchres, radiant and impressive on the outside but on the inside full of dead men's bones and corruption (see Matt. 23:27–31). On the Huldah Gates and the monumental stairway, see Yadin, *Jerusalem Revealed*, 25–30; *New Encyclopedia of Archaeological Excavations*, 2:739.

7. According to Broshi, finances for Herod's extensive building projects came from heavy taxes and duties, agriculture, exports, transit trade, and donations to the Jerusalem Temple (half-shekel dues, etc.). "Role of the Temple in the Herodian Economy," 31–37.

8. Herod Antipas reigned longer than any other ruler in the Second Temple Period: forty-three years. He is the Herodian administrator most often mentioned in the New Testament. Jesus referred to him as "that fox" (Luke 13:32). Antipas beheaded John the Baptist.

9. See Aharoni and Avi-Yonah, *Macmillan Bible Atlas*, Map 222; Bible Map 14; Bible Dictionary, 701, s.v. "Herod."

10. See Bible Dictionary, 644–45, s.v. "Chronology—New Testament."

11. "Clearly the fortress was strategically located to accomplish Herod's purpose of dominating the temple through a garrison which could readily allay any disturbance that might arise in the temple precincts." *Anchor Bible Dictionary*, 1:274, s.v. "Antonia, Tower of." "A Roman garrison was permanently stationed in the city, based in the Antonia Fortress, which controlled the Temple area." *New Encyclopedia of Archaeological Excavations*, 2:719.

12. Compare Talmud, Sanhedrin I, 18a, and Shabbat 15a.

13. Josephus, *Antiquities* 15.11.5 and *Wars* 5.5.2; 6.2.4.

14. Talmud, B. Yoma 69a.

15. During the reigns of Augustus and Tiberius, the governors of Judaea were equestrians with the title *praefectus*. Later, probably beginning in the reign of Claudius, the title *procurator* was used. See *Anchor Bible Dictionary*, 5:473–74, s.v. "Procurator"; Finegan, *Archeology of the New Testament*, 139.

16. In 1990 archaeologists discovered a burial cave in the Peace Forest in south Jerusalem that contained several ossuaries, or burial boxes. One of the ossuaries has two inscriptions bearing the name *Caiaphas;* it is generally agreed that this refers to the same high priest involved in securing the death penalty for Jesus. See *New Encyclopedia of Archaeological Excavations*, 2:756; see also Greenhut, "Burial Cave of the Caiaphas Family," 29–44, 76.

17. An inscription mentioning Pontius Pilate was found in 1961 in the stage area of the Roman theater at Caesarea. The inscription refers to some edifice named in honor of the Emperor Tiberius and indicates that Pontius Pilatus was *praefectus Iudaeae*. See *Anchor Bible Dictionary*, 5:473, s.v. "Procurator"; Finegan, *Archeology of the New Testament*, 138–39.

18. Philo, *Embassy to Gaius,* 301.

19. Josephus, *Antiquities* 18.3.1.

20. The aqueduct carries water from Arub Springs near Hebron to the Temple Mount in Jerusalem through an open canal and several tunnels for forty-two miles (sixty-eight km., though only thirteen miles, or twenty-one kilometers direct). Josephus, *Antiquities* 18.3.2 and *Wars* 2.9.4. See also *Encyclopedia Judaica,* 9:1540; Yadin, *Jerusalem Revealed,* 79–80.

21. Philo, *Embassy to Gaius,* 353–67.

22. Philo, *Embassy to Gaius,* 199–206. See also Josephus, *Antiquities* 18.8; *Wars* 2.10; Tacitus, *Histories* 5.9.2.

23. Avi-Yonah, *Herodian Period,* 137.

24. Josephus, *Antiquities* 19.4–5; *Wars* 2.11.

25. This is apparently the Third Wall Josephus refers to in *Wars* 5.4.2. The wall runs north from the northeast corner of the Temple Mount and then west; it was begun by Agrippa (A.D. 41–44) and finished by Jewish zealots during the First Revolt, just before the Romans destroyed it. The northeastern gate traditionally called St. Stephen's Gate, now called the Lion's Gate, was part of this work of Agrippa about a decade after the Crucifixion; the gate was not there yet when Stephen, a short time after the Crucifixion, was stoned to death (see Acts 7:58–59). An older tradition suggests Stephen's martyr-dom took place outside the northern gate of the city—today's Damascus Gate—where there was an execution place and where Jesus had also been martyred. For more on the Third Wall, see *New Encyclopedia of Archaeological Excavations,* 2:744–45.

26. Josephus, *Antiquities* 20.2 and 4.3; Bahat, *Illustrated Atlas of Jerusalem,* 53; Yadin, *Jerusalem Revealed,* 18–19.

27. Josephus, *Antiquities* 20.8.6; *Wars* 2.8.5; Acts 21:38.

28. Josephus, *Antiquities* 20.9.1.

29. During this period Jerusalem covered approximately three hundred acres and had one to two hundred thousand residents. See Edersheim, *Life and Times of Jesus,* 115; Ben-Dov, *Shadow of the Temple,* 75. Jerusalem was the largest walled city in the Holy Land and one of the largest in the entire Near East. The importance of Jerusalem is demon-strated in the writings of Philo, an Alexandrian philosopher contemporary with Jesus, who issued a veiled threat to Caligula (who wanted to set up his own statue in Jerusalem). Philo wrote that the holy city of Jerusalem was "the mother city not of one country Judaea but of most of the others in virtue of the colonies sent out at diverse times to the neighbouring lands Egypt, Phoenicia, the part of Syria called the Hollow [Coele-Syria: that is, the Beq'a] and . . . Pamphylia, Cilicia, most of Asia [Minor] up to Bithynia and the corners of Pontus, similarly also into Europe, Thessaly, Boeotia, Macedonia, Aetolia, Attica, Argos, Corinth and most of the best parts of Peloponnese. And not only are the mainlands full of Jewish colonies but also the most highly esteemed of the islands Euboea, Cyprus, Crete. I say nothing of the countries beyond the Euphrates. . . . So that if my own home city is granted a share of your goodwill the benefit extends not to one city but to myriads of the others situated in every region of the inhabited world." Philo, *Embassy to Gaius,* 281–83.

Jerusalem was an international city, and Jerusalemites could expect to see travelers from all parts of the Roman world. One of the most comprehensive lists of place names in the Bible recites the origin of those attending the Shavuot Festival, the day of Pentecost, shortly after Jesus' departure into heaven: Luke reported "Jews, devout men, out of every nation under heaven . . . Parthians, and Medes, and Elamites, and the dwellers in Mesopotamia, and in Judaea, and Cappadocia, in Pontus, and Asia, Phrygia, and Pamphylia, in Egypt, and in the parts of Libya about Cyrene, and strangers of Rome, Jews and proselytes, Cretes and Arabians" (Acts 2:5, 9–11).

30. Of interest to students of the New Testament are inscriptions found on ossuaries at Dominus Flevit, the place where Jesus is traditionally believed to have looked out over Jerusalem and wept. The inscriptions include the names Yeshua (Jesus), Mary, Martha, Salome, Sapphira, Jonah, Simeon, Zechariah, John, Joseph, and others. See *New Encyclopedia of Archaeological Excavations,* 2:753; Finegan, *Archeology of the New Testament,* 370. For further information on early Roman-period burial practices and on such famous burial monuments as King Herod's Family Tomb, the Uzziah Tomb inscription, Absalom's Pillar, Tomb of Zechariah, the tomb of the priestly family of Hezir, Tomb of the Kings, Sanhedrin Tombs, and others from the first century before Christ to the first century after, see Bahat, *Illustrated Atlas of Jerusalem,* 50–55; *New Encyclopedia of Archaeological Excavations,* 2:714–15, 747–56; Ogden and Chadwick, *Holy Land,* 328–31; Connolly, *Living in the Time of Jesus,* 60–61; Finegan, *Archeology of the New Testament,* 292–318.

31. The Gospels record seven visits Jesus made to Jerusalem:

1. At forty days (see Luke 2:22–39), likely in the Court of the Women with Simeon and Anna; 2. At age twelve (see Luke 2:41–50), teaching in the Temple (Court of the Men of Israel?); 3. Overthrowing money changers (see John 2:13–22) in the Court of the Gentiles; 4. Healing the paralyzed man (see John 5) at the Pool of Bethesda; 5. Teaching at the Feast of Tabernacles (see John 7:1–10:21) "in the treasury" (John 8:20) and healing a blind man and sending him to the Pool of Siloam (see John 9:1–7); 6. Teaching at the Feast of Dedication (see John 10:22–42) in Solomon's Porch; 7. Week of the Atoning Sacrifice, the Triumphal Entry through the eastern gate of the Temple Mount. See Aharoni and Avi-Yonah, *Macmillan Bible Atlas,* Maps 234, 235.

32. See Danby, *Mishnah,* 500, n. 11. See also Finegan, *Archeology of the New Testament,* 163.

33. For descriptions of Jerusalem's waterworks during this period, see Yadin, *Jerusalem Revealed,* 79–84; Bahat, *Illustrated Atlas of Jerusalem,* 48–50; *New Encyclopedia of Archaeological Excavations,* 2:746–47.

34. The other eight were the Pool of Israel, the Pool of St. Mary, the Struthion Pools, the Leger Pool, the Pool of Amygdalon (Hezekiah's Pool), the Serpent's Pool (or Sultan's Pool), the Mamilla Pool, and Solomon's Pools (with water conducted via aqueducts to Jerusalem). For details, see Ogden and Chadwick, *Holy Land,* 321–26.

35. "The lower of the two pools was probably used for washing sheep, which were then sold for sacrifices at the nearby Temple." *Encyclopedia Judaica,* 9:1539; see also Bahat, *Illustrated Atlas of Jerusalem,* 57; Ogden and Chadwick, *Holy Land,* 322.

36. According to recent investigation along the southern shoulder of the Hinnom Valley— traditionally called Akeldama—these tombs are far too elaborate to be burial places for the poor and strangers. They are more likely the burial places of the high priest Annas and his family and of other prominent citizens of Jerusalem. See Ritmeyer and Ritmeyer, "Akeldama—Potter's Field or High Priest's Tomb?" 22–35.

37. Just as there were seven major visits of Jesus to Jerusalem, so were there seven major events in Jesus' final days: 1. The Last Supper in an upper room, apparently on what today is called Mount Zion; 2. Atonement for sin in the Garden of Gethsemane, on the Mount of Olives; 3. The "trial" before Jewish leaders at Caiaphas' Palace, on today's

Mount Zion; 4. The "trial" before the Roman governor in the Praetorium in the Antonia Fortress or Herod's Palace; 5. Execution on Golgotha/Calvary, just outside the city wall; 6. Burial and resurrection from the tomb in a garden near Golgotha; 7. Ascension into heaven after the forty-day ministry, from the Mount of Olives. See also Aharoni and Avi-Yonah, *Macmillan Bible Atlas,* Map 236.

38. The word *Zion,* in biblical terms, originally referred to the Eastern Hill of ancient Jerusalem, the City of David. The name then shifted to the Temple Mount. Since the Second Temple period, and since Josephus so labeled it in his writings, people have called the Western Hill "Mount Zion" because they supposed that this hill was the original City of David. Thus we have David's Tower at Jaffa Gate and David's Tomb on the Western Hill. See Pixner, "Church of the Apostles Found on Mt. Zion," 16–35, 60; Ogden and Chadwick, *Holy Land,* 331–35.

39. *Harper Atlas of the Bible,* 166.

40. Concerning Gethsemane's ancient olive trees: "Carbon-14 tests on roots from the trees show that they are 2300 years old. Such dating is notoriously flexible, but the antiquity of the trees is also supported by Prof. Shimon Lavi, director of the Orchard Department of the Volcani Institute, who estimates that they are between 1600 and 1800 years old, but quite possibly more." "Gethsemane's Ancient Trees," 50; Bahat, *Illustrated Atlas of Jerusalem,* 56.

41. See *New Encyclopedia of Archaeological Excavations,* 2:742–43; Ogden and Chadwick, *Holy Land,* 336–38.

42. Kenyon, *Digging Up Jerusalem,* 226. Under today's Sisters of Zion Convent may be seen some large Roman flagstones from the time of Hadrian's Aelia Capitolina, nearly a century after Jesus but probably similar to what must have existed nearby in Herod's former fortress.

43. Avi-Yonah (Aharoni and Avi-Yonah, *Macmillan Bible Atlas,* Map 236 and text) argues that Pilate's *praetorium* was set up in the Antonia. See also Josephus, *Wars* 5.5.8: "There always lay in this tower a Roman legion . . . in order to watch the people, that they might not there attempt to make any [insurrection]. . . . The tower of Antonia [was] a guard to the temple."

44. Philo, *Embassy to Gaius,* 299; *Harper Atlas of the Bible,* 166–67; Yadin, *Jerusalem Revealed,* 55, 87; *Anchor Bible Dictionary,* 5:447–49, s. v. "Praetorium." Finegan presents the case for yet a third candidate for the Praetorium—the old Hasmonaean Palace—but in the end he, too, sides with Herod's Palace as the most likely possibility. See *Archeology of the New Testament,* 249–53.

45. Many thousands of crucifixions were carried out by Romans in the first century after Christ. Many of those crucifixions used metal spikes or nails. In 1968 the bones of a crucified man were found in a tomb on Givat HaMivtar, a housing area in north Jerusalem. The large iron nail, which was normally pulled out following the crucifixion and reused, had imbedded in a knot, so the man's leg bones were cut off and buried with the large nail still in position through the bones of both feet. See illustrations in Connolly, *Living in the Time of Jesus,* 51; see also *New Encyclopedia of Archaeological Excavations,* 2:754.

46. Nor, for that matter, could angels have sat, one at the head and one at the foot, inside an *arcosolium,* a bench or shelf carved along a chamber wall that featured a shallow arch for a ceiling. See *New Encyclopedia of Archaeological Excavations,* 2:749.

47. For more on St. Stephen's Gate, see note 25 above.

48. Ritmeyer and Ritmeyer, "Akeldama—Potter's Field or High Priest's Tomb?" 34.

49. For references to sacrifices on the north side of the altar and the topographical and geological connection between the Temple Mount and its northern end, the place of execution and burial, see Smith, *Jerusalem,* 1:33ff. See also Simons, *Jerusalem in the Old Testament,* 25.

50. "The ongoing cycle of sacrificial offerings and especially the annual sin offering were epitomized and fulfilled, once and for all, by the sacrifice of Jesus' life. Jesus' entry into the eternal Temple on behalf of humanity ruled out forever the need for further sacrifices at either an earthly or a heavenly temple (see Heb 8:10). The crucifixion of Jesus in association with the Passover meant an understanding of his death in terms of the slaughter of the Paschal lamb and, by extension, in terms of the full sacrificial component of the Temple." *Anchor Bible Dictionary,* 6:367.

51. Sources for particulars about the Temple Mount during the late Second Temple period include Josephus, *Antiquities* 15.11 and *Wars* 5.4, and the tractate of the *Mishnah* called *Middoth* ("Measurements"). See also Bahat, *Illustrated Atlas of Jerusalem,* 42–43; Yadin, *Jerusalem Revealed,* 14–20. For visual illustrations and reconstructions, see Ogden, *Illustrated Guide; A Model of Herod's Temple* (slide set), circulated internationally by Ritmeyer Archaeological Design, York, England; Connolly, *Living in the Time of Jesus.*

52. Smith, *Jerusalem,* 2:522.

53. We wonder, as we did with Solomon's Temple, what ordinance work would have been performed in Herod's Temple. The only clarifying scriptural passage on this subject is D&C 124:38–39. Elders Joseph Fielding Smith and Bruce R. McConkie supposed that Peter, James, and John received their endowment on the Mount of Transfiguration. See Smith, *Doctrines of Salvation,* 2:165; McConkie, *Doctrinal New Testament Commentary,* 1:400. Such sacred ordinances would not have been available in the Temple in Jerusalem because it was operating without the Melchizedek Priesthood—although it may be instructive to compare Luke 24:49 with D&C 95:8–9. Baptisms for the dead at least could be performed after the Savior's preparation for such work in the spirit world (see D&C 138) and after his resurrection. Truman Madsen wrote: "There is some evidence, in addition to the statement in 1 Corinthians 15:29, that proxy baptism for the dead was practiced among and by early Christians. Indeed, in the iconography, in the typology, and in the baptismal instruction of the early church fathers one may discern at least two different sorts of initiation: one through water baptism, and the other through certain initiatory oblations and anointings and baptism for the dead. That men and women are privileged to 'go through' each and all of the patterns and ordinances for and in behalf of their deceased families and others is unusual in contemporary religious practice. But, again, the proxy and representational ideas are not at the periphery of early Jewish and Christian practice; they are at the core." Madsen, *Temple in Antiquity,* 12. See also Adams, "Iconography of Early Christian Initiation"; Nibley, "Baptism for the Dead in Ancient Times"; Foschini, "Those Who Are Baptized for the Dead," 328–44.

54. See Finegan, *Archeology of the New Testament,* 203–4.

55. The inscription reads: *"Leveit hatekiya lehakh . . ."* (to the place of trumpeting to [announce?] . . .). See illustration in Bahat, *Illustrated Atlas of Jerusalem,* 44; Yadin, *Jerusalem Revealed,* 27; *New Encyclopedia of Archaeological Excavations,* 2:740.

56. Some Jews saw in Jesus' remark an irreverent slight of their holy Temple. Later, Stephen and Paul were denounced for their seeming disrespect for the Temple. False witnesses accused Stephen: "This man ceaseth not to speak blasphemous words against this holy place" (Acts 6:13). Stephen was killed. Paul was censured for allegedly taking a Gentile

into the sacred precincts of the Temple (Acts 21:26–32); enraged Jews sought to kill him, too.

57. See *Anchor Bible Dictionary,* 6:365. Jesus' prophecy was fulfilled literally—not one stone was left standing atop another of the Temple itself; what is left standing to this day is the retaining wall around the hill of the Temple.

58. Herod was aware of the Jews' distrust of him and their sensitivities regarding their holiest place. Before he began the actual reconstruction of the Temple itself, he had all the stone and other materials cut and prepared and in place. Then the demolition of the old Temple and rebuilding of the new proceeded. See Josephus, *Antiquities* 15.11.2. We note that the use of priests as masons gave rise over the ages to masonry—temple workers who were also builders.

59. Talmud, Succah 51b, and Baba Bathra 3b, 4a.

60. Josephus, *Wars* 5.5.6.

61. Ben-Dov, *Shadow of the Temple,* 78. See also Bahat, *Illustrated Atlas of Jerusalem,* 42–43; *Anchor Bible Dictionary,* 6:365; Broshi, "Role of the Temple in the Herodian Economy," 31–37. Of the Western Wall of Herod's Temple Mount, popularly called the Wailing Wall, only a middle portion is visible today. Fourteen courses (fifty-two feet) of beautifully carved stones with Herod's characteristic marginal dressing are now underground. The top portion of the Western Wall is also not to be seen today, having been destroyed by the Romans, though the Ottoman Turkish ruler Suleiman in the early 1500s restored the upper courses of stone along with the ramparts. Suleiman's work is quite inferior to the work of Herod's engineers more than fifteen hundred years earlier. The original retaining wall was some thirty yards above the paved road (as high as a modern ten-story building) and the towers were thirty-five yards high. The prodigious undertaking of bringing into position all of Herod's massive building stones is evidenced by the finding of one stone measuring more than fourteen yards long, three yards high, four yards thick, and weighing about four hundred tons. See Ben-Dov, *Shadow of the Temple,* 88; Bahat claims that the largest of these stones could weigh 570 tons. See Geva, *Ancient Jerusalem Revealed,* 181; Bahat, "Jerusalem Down Under," 39. At the southeast corner of the Temple Mount, about one hundred feet (thirty-two meters) north of the corner, is a "seam." An obvious difference in the cut of the stone is visible. To the north, stones were left rough on the exterior and to the south, very smooth. North of the seam is pre-Herodian work; the extension south is definitely Herod's addition to the platform of the Temple Mount. See *New Encyclopedia of Archaeological Excavations,* 2:743.

62. Avi-Yonah, *Herodian Period,* 215; Yadin, *Jerusalem Revealed,* 14; *New Encyclopedia of Archaeological Excavations,* 2:737; Ben-Dov, *Shadow of the Temple,* 77.

63. On the sacrifice of the red heifer, whose ashes, mixed with water, were used to represent purification from sin and were symbolic of the Savior's atoning sacrifice, see Num. 19:1–10 and the Mishnaic tractate *Parah.* See also Heb. 9:11–16; McConkie, *Mortal Messiah,* 1:136, 152.

64. Similarly, non-Latter-day Saints and Church members without temple recommends are allowed onto Temple Square in Salt Lake City to within a certain proximity of the Temple.

65. See Bahat, *Illustrated Atlas of Jerusalem,* 44. Another warning inscription was discovered earlier, in 1870. See *New Encyclopedia of Archaeological Excavations,* 2:744; see also photo in Connolly, *Living in the Time of Jesus,* 36. Josephus mentions the partition wall with warning inscriptions in *Antiquities* 15.11.5 and *Wars* 5.5.2.

66. Succah 5:2–3.

67. Edersheim, *Temple*, 55.

68. *Anchor Bible Dictionary*, 6:354, s.v. "Jerusalem Temple"; *New Encyclopedia of Archaeological Excavations*, 2:736; Kaufmann, "Where the Ancient Temple of Jerusalem Stood," 40–59; Ritmeyer, "Locating the Original Temple Mount," 24–45, 64–65; *New Encyclopedia of Archaeological Excavations*, 2:743.

69. *Encyclopedia Judaica*, 9:1398.

11

JERUSALEM IN REVOLT, A.D. 66–70

The Essenes of Qumran represented one kind of pious response to the problems in Jerusalem during the two centuries before the meridian of time. The Qumran sectarians regarded the problems as severe, though largely internal in origin, and stemming from apostasy. But other difficulties emerged with Roman domination from 63 B.C. onward. In response to the economic oppression and political tyranny imposed upon Jerusalem and Judaea, a group of men arose who would not withdraw from society and sequester themselves away until the advent of a great messianic age brought an end to their misery. Rather, they fought openly against the political and military enemies of an independent Israel. Traditionally this sect, called Zealots, has been viewed as a group of ardent patriots who combined an intense love of their country with a devotion to Torah and who were ready to fight and die for both.[1] Unfortunately, the movement also gathered to it those whose motives were less pure.

Josephus traces the origins of the Zealot sect to a man from the northern region of the Holy Land, the Galilee, an area which was known as a hotbed of Jewish revolt. After the death of Herod the Great in 4 B.C. tumults broke out against the Romans near Sepphoris in Galilee.[2] They were led by Judas, son of Hezekiah, from the northern city of Gamala.[3] The rebellion was put down with bloodshed by Herod's son and successor in Judaea, Archelaus (4 B.C.–A.D.6). But ten years later Judas reemerged as "Judas the Galilean." In A.D. 6 the Romans decided to make Judaea and related territories into a province. They appointed Coponius as procurator and ordered a census of people and property. Josephus states that the new sect was established at that point, when Judas the Galilean incited the people to revolt.[4]

We learn from Josephus that Judas the Galilean was not alone in his encouragement of his fellow countrymen to oppose direct Roman rule. A Pharisee named Sadduc joined Judas in leading the revolt and founding the sect:

> For Judas and Sadduc, who excited a fourth philosophic sect among us, and had a great many followers therein, filled our civil government with tumults at present, and laid the foundation of our future miseries, by this system of philosophy, which we were before unacquainted withal; . . . the infection which spread thence among the younger sort, who were zealous for it, brought the public to destruction.[5]

Josephus refers to the new sect as Judaism's "fourth philosophy" to distinguish it from the other three—the Pharisees, Sadducees, and Essenes.[6] Significantly, he indicates that the movement was responsible in some fundamental way for the later downfall of the Jewish state.

Apart from the three years in which Herod's grandson Agrippa I (A.D. 41–44) ruled as king in Judaea, the country was governed by a succession of Roman praefects and procurators from A.D. 6 to 66. Jewish discontent increased during this period until it found its most dangerous expression in the activities of the Zealots, who regarded the rule of the Romans as intolerable. In the beginning the Zealots were essentially zealous for God, believing themselves to be "agents of his wrath against the idolatrous ways of the heathen."[7] Judas the Galilean taught his followers that "Heaven would be their zealous help to no lesser end than the furthering of their enterprize until it succeeded."[8] But the sect did not remain unified. Several groups emerged in Judaea under the guise of freedom fighters, but they were little different from common thieves, brigands, and robbers. In the end, by the time Roman military might had destroyed Jerusalem and its Temple, the Zealot sect had deteriorated into competing factions, each pursuing its own ends.

Most Jews probably regarded the Roman governors as idolaters, as indeed, they were. They were also, for the most part, both brutal and greedy, seeking to amass quick wealth and not above misusing their considerable powers for selfish purposes. They shuttled between their official headquarters in Caesarea on the coast and Jerusalem in the Judaean mountains because their constant presence in the Holy City would have antagonized the Jews there.

Against the backdrop of growing unrest in Judaea, Jerusalem remained relatively stable and free from revolutionary uprisings during the period from 4 B.C. to about A.D. 55. There were probably several reasons. First, the memory of failed revolts to the north in 4 B.C. and A.D. 6 likely discouraged revolutionary activity. Second, the founding rulers of the Roman Empire, Augustus (27 B.C.–A.D. 14) and Tiberius (A.D. 14–37), were perceived as being favorably disposed toward the Jews and thus promoters of an underlying toleration. Third, when Roman officials did act offensively, the Jews of Jerusalem pursued nonrevolutionary ways to deal with the matter.[9]

Fourth, even though tensions were mounting, Jerusalem remained relatively quiet on account of the influence of strong high priests, most of whom, until A.D. 44, came from the family of Annas.[10] Beginning in A.D. 6 the high priest again became the political head of state. Appointed by the Roman governor,[11] the high priest was chosen from a small elite of Jerusalem families among whom the high priestly office was hereditary. These families were the nucleus of the governing aristocracy in Israel. The high priest in this period supervised and officiated at Temple rituals and as head of the Sanhedrin was responsible to the Romans for administration of Jewish affairs.[12]

Fifth, Jerusalem remained free of bloody revolution for half a century because the Pharisees generally did not support it—Sadduc, the associate of Judas the Galilean, notwithstanding. It will be remembered that the Pharisees were separatists—they saw themselves and Israel as a people set apart for obedience to the Lord. They advocated putting the whole of life under the control of the Law, urging all Jews to carry out the purity regulations originally prescribed in the Torah only for priests functioning in the Temple. The Pharisees viewed all of Israel as a "kingdom of priests" (Ex. 19:6). Most of the time, they were concerned with matters of state only when religious practices were affected. As long as they and all other Jews were free to pursue the Law of God, it made little difference to them what government was in power.

Sixth, and finally, there seems to have been a general desire among Jews of Jerusalem to accommodate themselves to "equitable" Roman officers in their provincial arrangement.[13] Influenced by the Pharisees, some may actually have welcomed direct Roman rule after A.D. 6, with the idea that it would bring the Jews greater autonomy than they had had under the Herodian vassal kings.[14]

PRELUDE TO WAR

The progressive deterioration of the relationship between the Jews and the Romans after A.D. 48 is shown in the writings of Josephus. He gives a brief notice from the procuratorship of Tiberius Alexander (A.D. 46–48) about the family of Judas the Galilean: "The sons of Judas of Galilee were now slain; I mean of that Judas who caused the people to revolt, when Cyrenius came to take an account of the estates of the Jews, as we have shewn in a foregoing book. The names of those sons were James and Simon, whom Alexander commanded to be crucified."[15]

We know nothing of the activities of Judas' sons before this incident. James and Simon may have been quite young in A.D. 6. or they may have just been emerging at the time of Tiberius Alexander to initiate renewed resistance to Rome. Their executions occurred a few years before revolutionary activity really picked up. In his narrative of the later period, Josephus implies that a dynasty of family leaders dedicated to the ideals of revolution had developed between A.D. 6 and 66. Menahem, who took over the siege of the palace in Jerusalem at the opening of the great revolt in A.D. 66, was a son of Judas.[16] Eleazar, son of Jairus, who fled to Masada, was also a descendant of Judas.[17] Therefore, though Josephus tells us nothing specific about the Zealots or their activities for the six decades after the revolt of A.D. 6, certainly they did not cease to exist. Jesus had one of their number among his associates in the Quorum of the Twelve Apostles (Simon, called Zelotes; see Luke 6:15). At any rate, James and Simon were crucified apparently without any immediate effect upon the peace of Judaea.

But peace did not last long. Events during the procuratorship of Cumanus (A.D. 48–52) led to armed clashes between Jews and Romans, and, tragically, between Jews and Jews. The first incident occurred in Jerusalem at the Feast of Passover when one of the Roman soldiers standing on the roof of the Temple portico bared his private parts and gestured obscenely to the multitude. The Jews worshipping below were deeply incensed at this blasphemous affront to God. The crowd demanded that Cumanus punish the soldier, when some "seditious persons" threw stones at the troops. Cumanus, fearing a riot, responded by calling up reinforcements. The troops did not attack, but many Jews were crushed in the ensuing panic and flight from the Temple precinct.[18]

National mourning over these deaths had hardly ceased when a group of seditious Jews plundered the caravan of a Roman imperial official on the road to Jerusalem near Beth-Horon in Judaea. During the course of punishing nearby villages assumed to have been involved in the attack, a copy of the Torah was torn and burned by a Roman soldier. Outraged Jews from all over the country rushed to Cumanus to demand punishment of the soldier. Eventually the procurator, probably in fear of an all-out rebellion, had the offending soldier beheaded.[19] This was the last act of passive resistance against Rome recounted in the narratives of Josephus.[20]

With Jewish frustration intensifying, the atmosphere throughout the villages in the Holy Land became volatile. Some Galilean Jews on their way to Jerusalem for the Feast of Tabernacles were attacked by Samaritans at a village called Gema, and one of the Jews was killed. The Galilean leaders went to Cumanus, asking that he punish the murderers at once. But the procurator, busy with other matters, neglected their petitions. When masses of Jews at the feast in Jerusalem heard of the murder, being tired of Roman inaction and insensitivity, they marched out of the city to Samaria where they burned several villages and killed the inhabitants. Roman retribution was swift. Cumanus took his troops, armed the Samaritans, and killed some members of the pillaging intruders while taking others prisoner. The rulers of Jerusalem, Josephus says, begged for the rest of the multitude to disperse so that the Romans would not retaliate in the Holy City as well.[21]

Complete disaster was averted that time as the Jews complied and returned home. But Josephus indicates that from that time forth active insurrection against the Romans became widespread: "The Jews complied with these persuasions of theirs, and dispersed themselves; but still there were a great number who betook themselves to robbing, in hopes of impunity; and rapines and insurrections of the bolder sort happened over the whole country."[22] "And after this time all Judea was overrun with robberies [or, infested with bands of brigands]."[23]

This disorder in the countryside went from bad to worse during the tenure of the next procurator, Felix (A.D. 52–60). He was ill-prepared for his governmental post; corruption of both his public and his private life as well as ineffectiveness plagued his administration and made him offensive to the Jews.[24] An example of this corruption is found in Acts 24:24–27, which recounts Felix's attempt to extort a bribe from Paul, who was under house arrest at Caesarea. During the time of Felix a new group began to disrupt life in Judaea and Jerusalem. Called Sicarii, they got their name from their use of a dagger (Latin, *sica*) for assassinations, and they initiated many acts of general plunder as well as opposing Jewish cooperation with the Romans.[25] Though the Sicarii hated the Roman leaders, they did not refrain from following their example in accepting bribes, plundering, murdering to get gain, and the like.

The last three procurators—Festus (A.D. 60–62), Albinus (A.D. 62–64), and Florus (A.D. 64–66)—worsened the already chaotic situation and reflected the corruption of the Roman emperor himself, Nero (A.D. 54–68). Albinus stole public and private funds, accepted bribes to release brigands, and emptied the prisons of all but the worst criminals.[26] Revolutionary activity in the Judaean countryside was widespread. The utter absence of authority in the land and the offensive actions of the Romans outraged the ordinary Jewish citizen and gave incentive to robbers and Sicarii to wreak havoc at will.[27]

DISSENSION IN JERUSALEM

The unrest and disorder in the countryside of Judaea, which began late in the procuratorship of Cumanus (A.D. 48–52) ultimately became manifest in Jerusalem as well. During the time of Felix (A.D. 52–60), a series of assassinations by the newly emerged Sicarii created an atmosphere of distrust and fear in the city:

> When the country was purged of these, there sprang up another sort of robbers in Jerusalem, which were called Sicarii, who slew men in the daytime, and in the midst of the city; this they did chiefly at the festivals, when they mingled themselves among the multitude, and concealed daggers under their garments, with which they stabbed those that were their enemies; and when any fell down dead, the murderers became a part of those that had indignation against them; by which means they appeared persons of such reputation, that they could by no means be discovered. The first man who was slain by them was Jonathan the high priest, after

whose death many were slain every day, while the fear men were in of being so served was more afflicting than the calamity itself; and while everybody expected death every hour, as men do in war, so men were obliged to look before them, and to take notice of their enemies at a great distance.[28]

The Sicarii did not inflict their tyranny and terror only on Roman sympathizers, nor were they bent on eliminating only those Jews who cooperated with Rome, such as Jonathan the high priest. Rather, the Sicarii and other bands of robbers also had economic and personal motives. Josephus portrays "the general Jewish populace as moderate, peace-loving Jews who were at the mercy of the revolutionaries, unwilling victims of their tyranny, their greed and their factional conflicts."[29] Terrorism was used with impunity by the revolutionaries. Their activity bears a striking resemblance to the work of secret combinations described in the Book of Mormon. A prime example is in Helaman 2:8, which describes the intentions of Kishkumen and his band of insurrectionists, who were eventually led by the notorious Gadianton: "It was his object to murder, and also that it was the object of all those who belonged to his band to murder, and to rob, and to gain power, (and this was their secret plan, and their combination)."

Nephi, son of Helaman, describes the plans and principles by which secret combinations have operated in all ages of history (see 3 Ne. 6:28–30). He notes that their members covenant with one another in secret. They combine against the righteous, the innocent, and the unwitting. They seek to deliver the guilty from the grasp of justice. They set at defiance the laws of their own country. And they destroy their governors. Nephi's teachings parallel those of his father, whose observations about his own times round out our picture of the way in which secret combinations hasten the dissolution of civilized societies:

> They did unite with those bands of robbers, and did enter into their covenants and their oaths, that they would protect and preserve one another in whatsoever difficult circumstances they should be placed, that they should not suffer for their murders, and their plunderings, and their stealings.
>
> And it came to pass that they did have their signs, yea, their secret signs, and their secret words; and this that they might distinguish a brother who had entered into the covenant, that whatsoever wickedness

his brother should do he should not be injured by his brother, nor by those who did belong to his band, who had taken this covenant.

And thus they might murder, and plunder, and steal, and commit whoredoms and all manner of wickedness, contrary to the laws of their country and also the laws of their God. (Hel. 6:21–23)

All of the destructive elements in Nephite society can also be observed in the social environment of Jerusalem just before its fall in the first century A.D. In the late fifties, a conflict arose among the priests and the leaders of Jerusalem. The exact cause of the conflict is not clearly specified, but the two groups first hurled insults at each other and then stones. Josephus writes: "And there was nobody to reprove them; but these disorders were after a licentious manner in the city, as if it had no government over it."[30]

This lawlessness played into the hands of the Sicarii during the rule of the procurator Albinus (A.D. 62–64), who came to Jerusalem during a festival time to restore peace in the land by "destroying many of the *sicarii.*" The Sicarii entered Jerusalem by night just before the festival to kidnap the secretary to the Temple governor. The secretary was used as a hostage to gain the release of ten Sicarii imprisoned by the Romans. The high priest Ananias, who also was the father of the Temple governor, negotiated with Albinus for the release of the Sicarii prisoners. But, Josephus says, "This was the beginning of greater calamities; for the robbers perpetually contrived to catch some of Ananias's servants; and when they had taken them alive, they would not let them go till they thereby recovered some of their own *sicarii;* and as they were again become no small number, they grew bold, and were a great affliction to the whole country."[31]

Impetus to revolt against Roman authority, and even authority in general, was now running high both in Jerusalem and in the rest of the country. Many feared war. Yet the people did not suppress the revolutionaries. Much of the unrest was directed against the upper-class Jews, who had preserved for themselves such lucrative positions as tax collector, often by bribing Roman officials. There was oppression in Jerusalem by the aristocracy. Landowners exploited their workers to meet tax obligations to the Romans. Small farmers were threatened with the expropriation of their land if they were unable to pay tribute. Nero's decision in

A.D. 60 to deny the Jews of Caesarea equal rights with the Syrian population increased tensions throughout the land. Josephus records that this decision caused Jewish hatred to smolder "till a war was kindled."[32] Another scholar writes, "The hostility and fear created throughout the nation by this situation contributed greatly to the atmosphere in Jerusalem where a clash between Jews and Roman troops opened the war."[33]

THE FIRST JEWISH WAR

The actions of the procurator Gessius Florus (A.D. 64–66), who returned to the policy of ruling with a strong hand, provided the final impulse to bloody revolution. A violent clash between Jews and Greeks at Caesarea resulted in the imprisonment by Florus of a delegation sent to him to seek justice for the Jews of that port city. When word of the tumult reached Jerusalem, the citizens there regarded the matter as serious but "restrain[ed] their passion" until Florus "blew up the war into a flame."[34]

In the summer of A.D. 66, the procurator confiscated seventeen talents from the Temple treasury, claiming the people were in arrears in tribute to Caesar. This pretext so shocked the people that they broke into a riot, whereupon Florus marched against Jerusalem with an armed force and allowed a cohort to plunder that part of the city called the Upper Market Place. The inhabitants of Jerusalem had been prepared to submit to Florus, but his troops behaved so badly ("no method of plunder was omitted") and the activity of revolutionaries so intensified that moderation was swept aside. The people cut off Roman communications and erected fortifications between the Antonia Fortress and the Temple. Fearing for his safety, Florus departed from Jerusalem, leaving a cohort to reinforce his garrison. Thousands of Jewish citizens of Jerusalem had been slain, including "many of the quiet people" (innocent victims).[35]

King Agrippa II tried to persuade the citizens of Jerusalem to submit to Rome. Josephus relates that when Agrippa's speech was concluded, the people cried out that they were taking up arms not against the Romans but against Florus, because of all he had done to them. The people agreed to rectify their own acts of war by collecting the tribute they had refused to pay and by repairing the porticoes between the

Temple and the Antonia Fortress that had been torn down in their battle with Florus. But when Agrippa tried to persuade the citizens of Jerusalem to submit to Florus until a new procurator arrived, the Jews heaped abuse upon the king and banished him from the city.[36] Thus, the main motive for the opening battle of the First Jewish War seems to have been Jerusalem's outrage over the abuses of Florus and his attempted control of the Temple and the state.

With Jerusalem's population in rebellion and control of the city in the hands of the chief priests, the Temple officiators became caught up in the revolt. Led by the Temple governor, Eleazar, son of Ananias the high priest, and supported by the revolutionary leaders of the people, these lower priests stopped the twice-daily sacrifices offered on behalf of the Roman Empire and the emperor—an action tantamount to a declaration of war. They also refused to accept any offerings or sacrifices from Gentiles.[37] These actions broke the treaty with Rome and put Israel officially outside the empire.[38]

Control of the city thus slipped from the hands of the chief priests and leading Pharisees when they were unable to dissuade the lower priests from this "strange innovation" that would provoke war with Rome. Civil war broke out. Eleazar and his followers occupied the Temple and the Lower City; the chief priests, who sent to Florus and Agrippa for military support, occupied the Upper City. The factions battled for control of Jerusalem and the state, as Josephus tells us:

> So they made use of stones and slings perpetually against one another, and threw darts continually on both sides! and sometimes it happened that they made excursions by troops, and fought it out hand to hand, while the seditious were superior in boldness, but the king's soldiers in skill. These last strove chiefly to gain the temple, and to drive those out of it who profaned it; as did the seditious, with Eleazar (besides what they had already) labour[ing] to gain the upper city. Thus were their perpetual slaughters on both sides for seven days' time; but neither side would yield up the parts they had seized upon.[39]

During this time Eleazar held a Temple festival and excluded his opponents. The Sicarii joined the followers of Eleazar in their cause. The Sicarii besieged the chief priests in the Upper City and burned the house of the high priest, Ananias, and other buildings, including archives, so that the insurrectionists, particularly the Sicarri, could "dissolve their obligations for paying debts." Then Menahem, son of Judas the Galilean, arrived in Jerusalem with his own armed brigands after he had secured Masada with its stores of arms.[40] He took over leadership of the revolt from Eleazar and successfully besieged Herod's Palace in the Upper City. The three royal towers—Hippicus, Phasael, and Mariamne—fell to Menahem's band. One by one the strongholds of Jerusalem were captured, and by August the entire city was in the hands of the rebel Jews. The high priest, Ananias, was captured in an aqueduct and executed.[41]

Menahem's control of the rebellion was ended when Eleazar's partisans rejected Menahem's messianic claims to absolute authority. They tortured and killed him and forced his followers, including the Sicarii, to flee to Masada. Among those who fled was another Eleazar, son of Jarius and kinsman of Menahem, who became the leader of the group at Masada. The Sicarii and Menahem had enabled the insurgents to succeed against traditional Jewish authority and Roman loyalists. But Eleazar, the Temple governor, resumed leadership of the revolt. The Roman garrison in the city, which had taken refuge in the Antonia towers, requested a safe exit from Jerusalem in return for their surrender. Once the Romans laid down their arms, Eleazar's party attacked and killed them. Only the Roman commander, Metilius, was spared because he promised to become a Jew and be circumcised.[42] Josephus tells us ironically that this event took place on the Sabbath, "on which day the Jews have a respite from their works on account of divine worship."[43]

It is not clear who was in charge of Jerusalem between the massacre of the Romans in August of A.D. 66 and the arrival of Cestius Gallus, governor of Syria, in October. It is clear, however, that the rebellion begun in Jerusalem spread to Caesarea, Scythopolis, and finally to Tyre. Hearing of the outbreak of war at Jerusalem, Gallus entered Judaea with the Twelfth Legion Fulminata ("the Thundering One"), advancing by way of the coast through Beth-Horon until he arrived at the capital city. Gallus penetrated Jerusalem but faltered before the walls of the Temple. Eleazar's party led the fight against him. During the battles, the leaders of the revolt killed Gallus' envoys because they feared that a promise of amnesty in return for surrender would be accepted by the people. The revolutionaries also thwarted a plot by some leading citizens of Jerusalem to open the gates to the Syrian governor to prevent further tragedy. Gallus unexpectedly abandoned his siege of Jerusalem as winter was setting in and retreated by way of the Beth-Horon pass. There his troops suffered disastrous losses at the hands of a band of rebels led by Simon bar Giora.[44] Great damage was done and valuable weapons and stores were seized, which the Jewish victors brought back to Jerusalem while singing songs of triumph.[45]

So unexpected and sensational was this victory that most Jews leaned toward the rebels, who put Jerusalem under a provisional war government with a former high priest at its head. The high priesthood thus resumed its traditional political leadership of the Jewish people. Jerusalem minted its own silver coins, collected taxes when it could, and divided the country into seven military districts, each with its own commander. The most famous appointment was made for the most important district—Galilee—which bore the brunt of the early Roman offensive. Its commander was a young priest, Joseph, son of Mattathias, who lacked any military experience. Later, he wrote histories under the romanized name of Josephus.[46]

Shaken by the success of the Jewish revolt, Nero sent Rome's best military commander, Vespasian, with three hand-picked legions to crush the insurrection at all costs. Massive and bloody actions followed in A.D. 67 and 68. In the north, Josephus spent most of his time suppressing factions of revolutionaries. Finally, his army dispersed almost without fighting, and he took refuge in the fortress of Jotapata, where he was besieged. Forty-seven days later he defected to the Romans.[47] The more radical elements of the revolt in Galilee were led by John, son of Levi, and had their headquarters at a town called Gischala. They opposed Josephus and his moderate methods but could do little to prevent their entire region from falling into the hands of Vespasian's son, the Roman general Titus. John, however, did manage to save himself and some of his followers by escaping to Jerusalem.[48]

In the south, the revolutionaries at Masada—the Sicarii, as Josephus labeled them—did nothing to stop the Roman advance. But they did conduct raids against other Jews, which was apparently their main activity. One tragic foray was directed against the village of En-gedi on Passover eve, which illustrates the bitterness of the factionalism. The Sicarii held out at Masada for the entire war and did not come to the aid of any of their fellow Jews during the final siege of Jerusalem.[49] It is apparent that to Josephus the Sicarii on Masada and the Zealots at the Temple were two separate factions of the revolutionary movement, and neither was held in high regard.[50]

In the winter of A.D. 67–68, a group of revolutionaries led by yet another Eleazar (son of Simon) seized the Temple and formed a new government by choosing a new high priest by lot. Josephus specifically cites Eleazar, son of Simon, as the one who caused the Zealots to break with the people and withdraw into the sacred precincts.[51] He was the most influential man of the party because of his ability to conceive and carry out important measures.[52]

The Zealot party in Jerusalem included priests and lay revolutionaries who had been responsible a year earlier for instigating the war.[53] Eleazar, son of Simon, had been the chief revolutionary leader during the siege of Cestius Gallus, and after the Jewish victory he controlled the money and the spoils gained from it.[54] The lofty ideals upon which the Zealot sect had been founded were now subjugated to less noble values. Eventually Eleazar and his group began to suspect that the provisional government was moderating its prosecution of the war. When the head of the provisional government threatened to influence the people to suppress terrorism in the city of Jerusalem, Eleazar persuaded the various revolutionary factions to come together and take their stand in the Temple, choose a new high priest, and make use of the weapons seized earlier from the retreat of Cestius Gallus.[55]

The reemergence of the Zealots was not without grave difficulties for the city of Jerusalem. After the people had established their own high priestly government, they besieged the Temple, where the Zealots were located.[56] The Zealots, expecting the provisional government to betray the city into the hands of the Romans, sent for radical Jews from Idumaea to come to their aid. This strategy was suggested by John of Gischala, who had pretended to support the provisional government but now sided with the Zealots in the Temple, at least temporarily.[57] An army of Idumaeans promptly appeared at the gate of the city but was prevented from entering by the chief priests. Some Zealots managed to escape their Temple holdout and let them in during a night rainstorm. The Zealots, freed from their confinement in the Temple, controlled all of Jerusalem by the next morning.[58]

Thousands of Jerusalemites were killed and the city looted by the fury of the Zealots and Idumaeans. The leader of the provisional government and his immediate subordinate were executed while many of the citizens of the city were being slaughtered. The youth of the nobility were also killed, tortured, or imprisoned. Eminent citizens were brought before a newly summoned Sanhedrin on charges of treason and sometimes executed without due process.[59] It is little wonder that Josephus accused the Zealots of bringing about the dissolution of laws and society in Jerusalem and Judaea.[60]

THE SIEGE OF JERUSALEM, A.D. 70

By the spring of A.D. 69, Vespasian had completely isolated Jerusalem. By the summer the Jews held only four fortified locations—Jerusalem, Herodium, Masada, and Machaerus on the opposite shore of the Dead Sea. In July Roman troops at Alexandria and Caesarea proclaimed Vespasian emperor of Rome after three men had succeeded one another to the imperial office within one year's time. In the spring of 70, Vespasian ascended the throne in Rome and ordered his eldest son, Titus, to continue the campaign in Judaea. Titus led the massive force of the Fifth, Tenth, Twelfth, and Fifteenth legions.[61]

With the approach of the Romans, the wrenching conflicts between the Zealots and the people of Jerusalem finally ceased as the insurrectionists realized they were facing total destruction at the hands of their common enemy, Rome. Command of the forces in Jerusalem was divided between Simon bar Giora and John of Gischala. Their combined armies did not exceed twenty-five thousand, in contrast to the eighty thousand Roman troops.[62]

The Romans set up a main camp northwest of the city (the area known today as the Russian Compound) and a secondary one on the Mount of Olives. Titus planned to attack from the north, the city's vulnerable side, which lacked protection by hills and valleys. Titus established his headquarters on Mount Scopus, the northern end of the Mount of Olives range. The soldiers breached the northern sections of the third and second walls by the end of May, and the main camp of the Romans was then moved inside the city. Titus ordered a siege wall constructed around the city to starve out its defenders—a tactic that was particularly effective because many supplies had been destroyed in the previous months of fighting. In July the Antonia Fortress, at the north-west corner of the Temple platform and under the command of John of Gischala, was taken and razed. But the defenders built a new wall and continued to hold the Temple courtyard and the Temple proper.[63]

By August 6, the daily Temple sacrifices were halted because of a shortage of both priests and animals. From outside the walls, Josephus shouted appeals to the Jewish defenders to surrender and thus save the Temple. But the Zealots fought on, standing on the roofed porticoes around the Temple courtyard to hurl missiles of all kinds—stones, arrows, and firebrands—down upon the Roman soldiers. On August 15, Titus ordered the wooden roofs and porches around the Temple to be burned. The Romans then moved into the outer courtyard, the Court of the Gentiles, as the defenders fought on from the inner courts, the Court of the Women, the Court of the Men of Israel, and then the Sanctuary itself. Flaming brands were tossed into the Temple itself through an open window, and the House of God was burned on the ninth of Ab (August 28).[64]

> As the Temple burned, frenzy gripped both attackers and defenders. Roman shock troops burst through, and Titus was able to dash into the Temple just long enough for a brief look; then heat forced him out. His soldiers continued burning whatever could be kindled, and killing all they could reach, whether combatants, women, or children. Many Jews flung themselves into the fire and perished with their Temple. Others, hiding in corners, were burned to death as Roman torches set new fires.[65]

On August 30, Roman forces captured the Lower City. But the Upper City, on the Western Hill overlooking the Temple Mount, held out stubbornly. It took the Romans one month to overpower the last strong-hold of Jewish resistance. With full fury, the soldiers set the houses on fire and slaughtered the inhabitants.

> Pouring into the alleys, sword in hand, [the soldiers] massacred indis-criminately all whom they met, and burnt the houses with all who had taken refuge within. Often in the course of their raids, on entering the houses for loot, they would find whole families dead and the rooms filled with victims of the famine. . . . Running everyone through who fell in their way, they choked the alleys with corpses and deluged the whole city with blood, insomuch that many of the fires were extinguished by the gory

stream. Towards the evening they ceased slaughtering, but when night fell the fire gained the mastery.[66]

The Upper City had been a residential district inhabited by royalty, aristocracy, and well-to-do Jews living in beautiful homes. In the Upper City archaeologists and historians have found people's dwellings complete with ritual baths, mosaic tile floors, and frescoes. It is today called the Herodian Quarter, to identify the strata dating from between 37 B.C. and A.D. 70. Excavations there have uncovered some of the most dramatic evidence ever found of the Roman destruction. The Burnt House and the Herodian Mansion are, perhaps, the most striking reminders of the horror and anguish experienced by the inhabitants during the months of August and September, A.D. 70. Almost everything discovered in the Herodian Quarter clearly reflects destruction by fire and recalls the images presented by Josephus. Among the items found in the Burnt House, so-called because of the discernible burn layer dating to 70, were the skeletal remains of a human arm in the burnt kitchen, hand spread out grasping at a step, and a spear in a corner of another room—ample witness to brutality played out there.[67]

By the decree of Titus, the people of Jerusalem were taken captive and its buildings leveled:

> Now the number of those that were carried captive during this whole war was collected to be ninety-seven thousand; as was the number of those that perished during the whole siege, eleven hundred thousand, the greater part of whom were indeed of the same nation [with the citizens of Jerusalem,] but not belonging to the city itself.[68]

> Caesar [Titus] gave orders that they should now demolish the entire city and temple, but should leave as many of the towers standing as were of the greatest eminency; that is, Phasaelus, and Hippicus, and Mariamne, and so much of the wall as enclosed the city on the west side. . . . but for all the rest of the wall it was so thoroughly laid even with the ground by those that dug it up to the foundation, that there was left nothing to make those that came thither believe it had ever been inhabited.[69]

Titus left the city and traveled in a roundabout route back to Rome, pausing for victory festivals in which Jewish captives had to fight each other in gladiatorial games or face wild animals. Arriving home in A.D. 71, he, his father, Vespasian, and his brother Domitian, all rode in a great triumphal procession. Carried ahead of Titus were the now-famous trophies from the Temple: the *menorah* or seven-branched candelabrum, a great ritual table, and a Torah scroll. The leaders of the revolt were paraded with nooses around their necks. Simon bar Giora was executed next to the Forum, and John of Gischala was imprisoned for life. Jewish captives were sold in the slave markets of the empire. Roman coins were struck to memorialize the outcome of the great Jewish revolt against Rome. They depicted a woman with bound hands and bowed head sitting at the foot of a palm tree. Below her read the words in Latin, "Judea vanquished; Judea captive"![70]

Back in Judaea the Jews tried to comprehend the magnitude of the disaster that had changed their capital city, their religion, and their lives forever. The only parts of the Temple precinct that remained relatively intact were the four massive retaining walls that supported the Temple platform. Among the gigantic ashlars, or sections, of the western wall— called in Hebrew the *Kotel Ma'aravi*—one has become famous. For nineteen centuries Jewish pilgrims have mourned there the loss of the Temple; their laments uttered at a certain section of the western retaining wall led to its being called by a name Jews neither used nor approved of: "The Wailing Wall."

The destruction of the Temple on the ninth of Ab became an annual occasion for great mourning in Judaism. "Grief greater than words could express afflicted the faithful as they recalled what had been the fate of their Temple and its defenders. Some rabbis were said to have suffered permanent facial wounds, so furrowed were their cheeks by tears shed for the Temple. . . . A sorrow that seemed to grow with passing generations became part of the memorial of the vanished Temple."[71]

CONCLUSION

Can anyone doubt that wickedness destroyed Jerusalem—more specifically, the wickedness born of conspiracy, brigandage, assassinations, and clandestine abductions? Such was the wickedness that destroyed other civilizations, just as a Book of Mormon prophet had warned: "Whatsoever nation shall uphold such secret combinations, to get power and gain, until they shall spread over the nation, behold, they shall be destroyed" (Ether 8:22). This was the kind of wickedness that Josephus described firsthand. He writes of the revolutionaries:

> All sorts of misfortunes also sprang from these men, and the nation was infected with this doctrine to an incredible degree; one violent war came upon us after another, and we lost our friends, who used to alleviate our pain; there were also very great robberies and murders of our principal men. This was done in pretence indeed for the public welfare, but in reality for the hopes of gain to themselves; whence arose seditions, and from them murders of men, which sometimes fell on those of their own people, (by the madness of these men towards one another, while their desire was that none of the adverse party might be left,) and sometimes on their enemies . . . nay the sedition at last increased so high, that the very temple of God was burnt down by their enemy's fire.[72]

The first century after Christ was not the only time in Jerusalem's history when the evils associated with secret combinations contributed to the fall of the Holy City. Jeremiah and Ezekiel cite conspiracy, robbery, and oppression as causes for the destruction of 586 B.C. (see Jer. 11:9; Ezek. 22:25, 29–31). But behind the wickedness of the Zealots, Sicarii, and secret combinations of the First Jewish Revolt was an even greater evil to be reckoned with. Reflecting on the disaster of A.D. 70 takes us immediately back to the prophecies Jesus made forty years earlier of the destruction of Jerusalem and its Temple and of the death and scattering of its people. In a chilling prophecy of near-future events, Jesus said to those mourners who followed him to Golgotha only hours before his own death:

> Daughters of Jerusalem, weep not for me, but weep for yourselves, and for your children.
>
> For, behold, the days are coming, in the which they shall say, Blessed are the barren, and the wombs that never bare, and the paps which never gave suck.
>
> Then shall they begin to say to the mountains, Fall on us; and to the hills, Cover us. (Luke 23:28–30)

Truly this prediction was fulfilled in the devastation of Jerusalem in the year A.D. 70, described by the Savior in his Olivet discourse as the "abomination of desolation" (JS–M 1:12). On that occasion, also during the last week of his mortal ministry, he had warned his disciples that in the coming days there would be "great tribulation on the Jews, and upon the inhabitants of Jerusalem, such as was not before sent upon Israel" (JS–M 1:18).

Why did all the prophecies, scriptural predictions, forestalled chastisements, and careful warnings of past ages converge in force during the years from A.D. 66 to 70 in Jerusalem? Why was all the robbery, murder, and work of secret combinations unleashed with such fury so quickly?

The reason Jerusalem and her inhabitants were destroyed is that they had rejected their true king. The ultimate act of Israel's disloyalty was manifest in the dismissal of Jesus' claims to be the long-foretold Messiah, the Lord of Life, the great Jehovah of the Old Testament, who came to earth in fulfillment of millennia-old prophecies, only to be crucified ignominiously between two thieves.

The events of A.D. 70 should not have been surprising to the inhabitants of the Holy City. Toward the end of his ministry Jesus had said, "Except ye repent, ye shall all likewise perish" (Luke 13:5). And then he gave the parable of the fig tree as a graphic illustration: "And if it bear fruit, well: and if not, then after that thou shalt cut it down" (Luke 13:9). Not only did contemporary Jewish teachings describe Israel as a fig tree but rabbinical teachings affirmed that "all the prophets prophesied only concerning the days of the Messiah."[73] And yet, after the Crucifixion, after so many witnesses, Jerusalem's leaders sank deeper into the mire of hatred for Jesus, though they knew the truth, as the book of Acts confirms (see Acts 4:1–30; 5:17–33). The words of Elder Bruce R. McConkie are poignant:

> And now the ax was laid at the root of the rotted tree. Jerusalem was to pay the price. Daniel had foretold this hour when desolation, born of abomination and wickedness, would sweep the city. . . . Moses had said the siege would be so severe women would eat their own children. (Deut. 28.) Jesus specified the destruction would come in the days of the disciples.
>
> And come it did, in vengeance, without restraint. Hunger exceeded human endurance; blood flowed in the streets; destruction made desolate the temple; 1,100,000 Jews were slaughtered; Jerusalem was ploughed as a field; and a remnant of a once mighty nation scattered to the ends of the earth. The Jewish nation died, impaled on Roman spears, at the hands of Gentile overlords.
>
> But what of the saints who dwelt in Jerusalem in that gloomy day?

They heeded Jesus' warning and fled in haste. Guided by revelation, as true saints always are, they fled to Pella in Perea and were spared.[74]

Josephus was a remarkable eyewitness to the great calamity of the first century after Christ. He felt that he had been raised up by God to recount the episodes of Jerusalem's tragedy, that he would betray "the commands of God if he died before they were delivered."[75] He seems to have identified with Israel's ancient prophets who predicted Jerusalem's downfall on account of disobedience. He also believed that the tragedy itself evolved out of the establishment of the Zealot sect, that the high ideals of the founding members of the movement in A.D. 6 had become hollow rhetoric by 70. In fact, the bands of robbers, assassins, and other brigands that finally brought about the desolation of the Holy City were a natural consequence of the root cause of the desolation of A.D. 70—rejection of the Messiah. But this returns us to Josephus' point: It was God who sentenced the Temple to the flames; its destruction could not have been stopped though Titus himself endeavored to quench the flames.[76]

Notes

1. Epstein, *Judaism,* 105.

2. Josephus, *Wars* 2.4.1; *Antiquities* 17.10.5.

3. Gamala was technically in the district of Gaulanitis, but it was popularly identified with Galilee. See Rhoads, *Israel in Revolution,* 48.

4. Josephus, *Wars* 2.8.1.

5. Josephus, *Antiquities* 18.1.1.

6. Josephus, *Antiquities* 18.1.1, 6.

7. Russell, *Between the Testaments,* 38.

8. This translation of Josephus, *Antiquities* 18.1.1 is found in Rhoads, *Israel in Revolution,* 49.

9. A good example is the clash caused by Pilate's arrival as praefect in A.D. 26. It will be remembered that he brought into Jerusalem, under cover of night, Roman troops carrying army standards bearing Roman images. This action violated Jewish law against graven images. The ensuing popular march to Caesarea and protest before Pilate won the removal of the offensive standards from Jerusalem without armed revolt. See Kraeling, "Episode of the Roman Standard," 263–89.

10. Annas was high priest in the days of Jesus' youth and a man of tremendous influence, even though he had been deposed by the Romans in A.D. 15. His son-in-law was

Caiaphas, the high priest before whom Jesus was arraigned at the time of the Crucifixion. But so powerful was Annas that Jesus was taken first to him (see John 18:13). Annas' five sons also served in turn as high priest.

11. Josephus, *Antiquities* 18.2.1.

12. Rhoads, *Israel in Revolution*, 28–29.

13. Josephus, *Wars* 2.6.2.

14. Josephus, *Wars* 2.6.1; *Antiquities* 17.11.1. See also Rhoads, *Israel in Revolution*, 51.

15. Josephus, *Antiquities* 20.5.2.

16. Josephus, *Wars* 2.17.8.

17. Josephus, *Wars* 7.8.1.

18. Josephus, *Wars* 2.12.2; *Antiquities* 20.5.3.

19. Josephus, *Wars* 2.12.2; *Antiquities* 20.5.4.

20. Rhoads, *Israel in Revolution*, 71.

21. Josephus, *Wars* 2.12.5.

22. Josephus, *Wars* 2.12.5.

23. Josephus, *Antiquities* 20.6.1. The bracketed words are an alternate translation of the passage.

24. See Tacitus, *Histories*, 5.9.

25. Josephus uses the term *sicarii* in narratives of the period before A.D. 66 more to describe a method of resistance than a formal sect. After A.D. 66 he uses the word *Sicarii* to refer to the specific group that ends up on Masada. Rhoads, *Israel in Revolution*, 56: "The group led by Judas' descendants who are designated during the war period as 'Sicarii' were probably among the revolutionaries of the fifties and sixties, but Josephus' functional use of *sicarii* and 'brigands' in his narrative of the prewar period does not reveal the connection explicitly."

26. Rhoads, *Israel in Revolution*, 73.

27. Rhoads, *Israel in Revolution*, 73–74.

28. Josephus, *Wars* 2.13.3.

29. Rhoads, *Israel in Revolution*, 12. See also the many passages that support this assessment in Josephus, including *Wars* Preface, 4; 4.7.1; 4.9.10; 5.1.5; 5.6.1; 5.6.2; 5.10.4.

30. Josephus, *Antiquities* 20.8.8.

31. Josephus, *Antiquities* 20.9.3.

32. Josephus, *Antiquities* 20.8.9.

33. Rhoads, *Israel in Revolution*, 93.

34. Josephus, *Wars* 2.14.5–6.

35. Josephus, *Wars* 2.14.4–9.

36. Josephus, *Wars* 2.17.1.

37. Josephus, *Wars* 2.17.2.

38. Rhoads, *Israel in Revolution*, 99.

39. Josephus, *Wars* 2.17.5.

40. Masada was a mountain fortress hideaway near the western shore of the Dead Sea. It had belonged to Herod the Great and was then used by the Romans as an outpost until Menahem and his followers stormed it in A.D. 66.

41. Josephus, *Wars* 2.17.6–9.

42. Josephus, *Wars* 2.17.9–10.

43. Josephus, *Wars* 2.17.10.

44. Josephus, *Wars* 2.19.2.

45. Josephus, *Wars* 2.19.3–9. See also the excellent summary in Aharoni and Avi-Yonah, *Macmillan Bible Atlas,* Map 251.

46. Josephus, *Wars* 2.20.4. Also Aharoni and Avi-Yonah, *Macmillan Bible Atlas,* Map 251. Eleazar, son of the high priest Ananias, was assigned to Idumea in the south.

47.   Aharoni and Avi-Yonah, *Macmillan Bible Atlas,* Map 252, is an excellent summary.

48. The antagonism between Josephus and John was extreme. Josephus had a reputation as a moderate; John of Gischala was a radical and an instigator. Josephus sent letters to those towns where John had followers, threatening to destroy their houses and property if they did not transfer their allegiance to him. Three thousand deserted John, leaving him only fifteen hundred men. John remained in Gischala for fear of Josephus. See Josephus *Wars* 2.21.8. Gischala was the last city to be taken in the Galilean campaign. John's escape and night flight are described by Josephus in *Wars* 4.2.4–5.

49. Their numbers were composed largely of followers of Menahem, son of Judas the Galilean. See the very negative assessment of Rhoads, *Israel in Revolution,* 117–18.

50. Rhoads, *Israel in Revolution,* 105–6.

51. Josephus, *Wars* 5.1.2.

52. Josephus, *Wars* 4.4.1.

53. Rhoads, *Israel in Revolution,* 103.

54. Josephus, *Wars* 2.20.3.

55. Rhoads, *Israel in Revolution,* 105.

56. Josephus, *Wars* 4.3.11–13.

57. Josephus, *Wars* 4.3.13–4.4.2.

58. Josephus, *Wars* 4.4.6–4.5.1.

59. Josephus, *Wars* 4.5.3–4.

60. Josephus, *Wars* 4.3.14.

61. Aharoni and Avi-Yonah, *Macmillan Bible Atlas,* Maps 255, 256.

62. Aharoni and Avi-Yonah, *Macmillan Bible Atlas,* Maps 255, 256.

63. Many sources contain excellent summaries of the siege. See especially Aharoni and Avi-Yonah, *Macmillan Bible Atlas,* Map 256; Klein and Klein, *Temple beyond Time,* 111–15; Kenyon, *Digging Up Jerusalem,* 249–55. For specific points see Josephus, *Wars* 5; 6.

64. Aharoni and Avi-Yonah, *Macmillan Bible Atlas,* Map 256.

65. Klein and Klein, *Temple beyond Time,* 112. For Josephus' description of events, see *Wars* 6.4.6–7.

66. This quotation is excerpted from a translation of Josephus, *Wars* 6.8–10 in Avigad, *Discovering Jerusalem,* 137.

67. Avigad, *Discovering Jerusalem,* 137; see also 120–39 for a discussion of the Burnt House.

68. Josephus, *Wars* 6.9.3.

69. Josephus, *Wars* 8.1.1.

70. Klein and Klein, *Temple beyond Time,* 115.

71. Klein and Klein, *Temple beyond Time,* 115.

72. Josephus, *Antiquities* 18.1.1.

73. Tractate Sanhedrin, cited in *Thy People Shall Be My People,* 75.

74. McConkie, *Doctrinal New Testament Commentary,* 1:644–45. "Mothers snatched food from their children's mouths and one mother roasted her own son to survive. The time foreseen by Jesus when she who had no child or babe at the breast would bless herself, or when one might call upon mountains to fall and bring merciful release, was at hand. Women of Jerusalem were bitterly weeping for themselves [see Josephus, *Wars* 6.3.4]." Peterson and Tate, *Pearl of Great Price,* 190.

75. Josephus, *Wars* 3.8.5.

76. Josephus, *Wars* 6.4.5.

12

JERUSALEM AS AELIA CAPITOLINA, A.D. 71–324

Selfishness, secret combinations, and, above all, the rejection of Jesus and his message brought about the First Jewish Revolt and sealed the fate of Jerusalem. Elder Marion G. Romney explained: "All of this destruction and the dispersion of the Jews would have been avoided had the people accepted the gospel of Jesus Christ and had their hearts changed by it."[1]

The period after the revolt is one of the most complex in Jewish history.[2] Though Jerusalem remained in ruins for some sixty-one years after the devastation of A.D. 70, it was not unpopulated. Some of its former inhabitants returned and tried to rebuild their lives. Jews and some members of the early Christian community who had fled during the siege to Pella, in Jordan, resettled around the camp of the Roman Tenth Legion on the site of what had been Herod's Palace on the Western Hill of Jerusalem.[3] Today this area is in the Armenian Quarter of the Old City. The legion, which had helped conquer the city, was now given the task of guarding over it. Excavations in the area have uncovered clay pipes, roof tiles, and bricks, usually bearing the stamp of the legion's initials "Leg.X.F" (Legio X Fretensis) and its emblem, a wild boar or such maritime symbols as ships, dolphins, or the sea god Neptune.[4]

Some authorities maintain that a large Jewish population remained in Jerusalem after A.D. 70 and continued to worship at the Temple site.[5] There was no Temple, however, no altar, no sacrifice, and no tangible symbol of the Lord's presence. Later sources report that the Jews had as many as seven synagogues in the area, implying that the population rose considerably between A.D. 71 and 130.[6] But archaeological excavations during the last three decades of the twentieth century show that caves and hovels provided much of the living space. That hardly compares to the magnificence of Jerusalem before A.D. 70. It does, however, provide significant witness to the fulfillment of prophetic utterance. Elder Erastus Snow observed:

> It has become a matter of history that Jerusalem [became] heaps of ruins. . . . It is a matter of history that the very site of that wonderful Temple was ploughed as a field, and its destruction was rendered so complete that every foundation stone was [razed]; and that there might be no vestige of it left, around which the Jews might cling, the Roman Emperor caused that it should be ploughed up as a field, thus literally fulfilling the words of the Prophet [Micah] and the words of the Savior. This woe and destruction was predicted and overtook that people, and they were eventually scattered, because of their wickedness, and because of the corruption of their princes, judges and rulers.[7]

Immediately after Jerusalem was destroyed, imperial attention was riveted briefly on Masada, Herod's former fortress-hideaway, where the followers of Menahem, son of Judas the Galilean, had escaped during the First Revolt. Because this band of Zealots took no further part in the war against Rome and posed no real military threat, the empire was in no hurry to move against them. Sometime after the fall of Jerusalem in A.D. 70, Lucilius Bassus was appointed legate in Judaea, and he spent his energies conquering two of Herod's other fortresses, Herodium and Machaerus. Probably in the winter of 73, Bassus' successor, Flavius Silva, marched to the western base of Masada, on top of which the Zealot camp stood. There he began his siege.[8]

To reach the wall on the summit of Masada, 150 yards above his camp, Silva built a huge ramp for an iron-covered siege tower that was equipped with ballistae on top and a battering ram below. The Zealots had time to prepare their defenses and even enjoyed a moment of hope when torches thrown against one of their walls flamed back against the tower. But their jubilation was short-lived when the wind changed and the wall began to burn.

Confident that the battle was all but over, the Romans withdrew for the night. This lull gave Eleazar, the leader of the Zealots on Masada, a chance to make a long speech in which he exhorted his fellows not to receive their punishment at the hands of the Romans but rather from

God himself as they determined their own fate. His followers resolved to kill themselves, even though such an action went against Jewish law. Each father killed his immediate family, and then ten men were selected by lot to execute those who remained; one, again chosen by lot, then slew the other nine and finally stabbed himself. Josephus records that 960 perished that night. It was Passover, A.D. 74. When the Roman troops burst into the fortress the next morning, an awful silence greeted them. Two women and five children who had survived the carnage by hiding in a cistern recounted to the troops all that had happened. Although Josephus was not at Masada, he had access to the official reports from the field and may even have consulted Flavius Silva, who was in Rome in A.D. 81 when Josephus wrote his account.[9]

Surprisingly, Roman dealings with the Jews in Judaea after the First Revolt were restrained and measured. There was no attempt to reduce the size of the province or to change its name. That happened later, after the Bar Kokhba, or Second Jewish Revolt, in A.D. 135, when Judaea became Syria-Palestina. Between A.D. 71 and 130, Roman authorities corrected certain abuses in the system of administration that had contributed to the unrest before A.D. 66. Recognizing that the earlier praefects and procurators were drawn from the equestrian class and had shown little talent for dealing with the local inhabitants, Rome now determined that the governors of Judaea would come from the senatorial class. Along with this official was appointed a procurator in charge of finances—a move undertaken to ensure that the procurator did not use his office to increase his personal wealth. A new tax (the *fiscus Judaicus*) was imposed on all Jews in place of the annual contribution they had formerly given to their Temple. This tax added insult to injury because this money was donated to the temple of Jupiter Capitolinus in Rome. Other than this tax, however, no collective punishment was meted out to the Jews.[10]

Another important development after A.D. 70 was the widening of the breach between Judaism and Christianity. The destruction of the Temple ended once and for all any possibility for the early Jewish Christians to remain an integral part of the Jewish community.[11] It reassured some Christians about the correctness and eventual triumph of their cause. Some saw the fall of Jerusalem and the Temple as just retribution for the crucifixion of Jesus. They believed the Christian church was the branch of Israel that God now favored: a new system had replaced the old. With the fall of Jerusalem, Christians cast their lot with the world that lay outside Judaism, the Holy City, and the Temple.

Even before A.D. 70, Christianity had cut many of its Jewish ties, as its missionaries turned more toward Gentile towns and less toward Jerusalem. Yet wrenching apostasy, predicted by both Jesus and his apostles, began to afflict and finally to devastate the Church. After 70, Jerusalem was no longer the exclusive capital of the Christian faith; ironically, as its center of affairs gravitated increasingly toward Rome, Christianity became increasingly persecuted by the Roman Empire. By then the Christian faith was no longer the receptacle of pure doctrine as taught by Christ. Apostles and prophets had died or were killed, and "grievous wolves" entered the church, "not sparing the flock"; self-appointed leaders arose, "speaking perverse things, to draw away disciples after them" (Acts 20:29–30).

HADRIAN, A.D. 117–138

In A.D. 117, almost half a century after Jerusalem was destroyed, Hadrian ascended the imperial throne in Rome. Roman historians generally portrayed him as a somewhat benevolent ruler who benefited his country. At first, the Jews entertained rather high hopes for the new emperor. He was hailed by an Alexandrian Jew as a second Cyrus—the tolerant Persian monarch who had permitted the reconstruction of Jerusalem and the Temple nearly seven centuries earlier.[12]

To the Jews, the circumstances of A.D. 70 and the years immediately following bore a striking resemblance to the catastrophe of 586 B.C. when the First Temple was destroyed. The Jews had returned then to Jerusalem after not quite fifty years and restored the Temple, ultimately to a condition of splendor under Herod. That memory was both comforting and encouraging. If Cyrus had been moved upon to rebuild Jerusalem and the Temple, could not Hadrian do likewise? In fact, there is a strong Jewish tradition that Hadrian actually authorized such a move; that is, he ordered the removal of the Emperor Trajan's statue from the Temple site and the rebuilding of the Temple itself. But tradition adds that when Samaritan opposition arose, the emperor broke his promise and forbade the revival of the Temple.[13] From the Jewish perspective, Hadrian then acted even more unsympathetically towards the Jews than had any other emperor. And the Jews responded with hatred.

Discord was almost inevitable, given Hadrian's belief that his empire was composed of regions proud to be unified under the great commonwealth of Rome. Not only that, Hadrian was an enthusiastic Hellenist who was convinced that every province must be fully integrated into the Greek culture that formed the backbone of his Graeco-Roman civilization. Dissent or separatism was out of the question. To the Jews this was all too reminiscent of the Hellenization undertaken by Antiochus IV Epiphanes—who, not incidentally, was immortalized by Hadrian himself when the emperor completed a temple dedicated to Antiochus at Athens in A.D. 128.[14]

The situation became very grave when Hadrian banned the practice of circumcision. The Jews regarded the ban as a deliberate repression of them and their religion. In fact, the prohibition was at first intended as an extension of the long-standing Roman ban of bodily mutilation. But Hadrian also meant the ban to eradicate the separateness that he regarded as his sworn duty to overcome throughout the empire.

In A.D. 130 Hadrian visited Jerusalem and determined to rebuild it as a Roman city. He planned to construct on the Temple Mount a temple to the Roman god Jupiter and restore the ravaged city to glory as an eastern center of the commonwealth. In addition, Jerusalem was henceforth to be called Aelia Capitolina after Hadrian himself, who belonged to the family Aelii (his full name was Publius Aelius Hadrianus) and also after Jupiter Capitolinus, patron deity of the rebuilt city. But Hadrian's plan was doomed from the start: "Throughout its history, Jerusalem has known many periods of florescence, but only when it was a spiritual center for the country's inhabitants."[15]

According to the Roman historian Dio Cassius in his early third-century work *History of Rome,* news of Hadrian's intention to found a new colony on top of Jerusalem—thus ending all hope of reconstructing the Temple—rekindled the flames of full-fledged revolution against Rome.[16] Antagonism had been smoldering for a long time, and Hadrian's decrees banning circumcision and announcing plans for Aelia Capitolina precipitated the outbreak of new hostilities. Eusebius, fourth-century bishop of Caesarea, suggests that the Second Revolt was not simply a sudden eruption of Jewish nationalism and religious fervor but rather

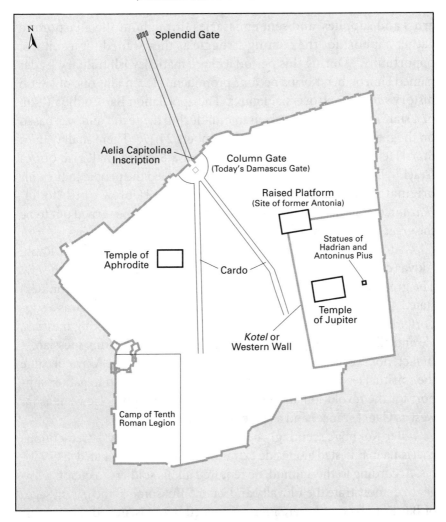

Jerusalem as Aelia Capitolina, A.D. 71–324

the culmination of several decades of unrest following the destruction of the Temple in A.D. 70.[17]

THE BAR KOKHBA REVOLT

Only sparse and fragmentary data exist on this next war against Rome. Dio Cassius tells us that while Hadrian was in Judaea and Egypt (A.D. 130–131), the Jews planned their tactics, accumulated stores of arms and supplies, and sent emissaries throughout the Diaspora to gather support for the coming struggle as they waited for a suitable opportunity.[18] During this period a charismatic Jewish military leader named Simeon ben Kosiba became prominent. He remains one of Jewish history's most controversial figures. The appellation Bar Kokhba ("son of a star") was apparently given to him during the revolt and was based on the messianic interpretation of Numbers 24:17: "There shall come a Star [Hebrew, kokhab] out of Jacob, and a Sceptre shall rise out of Israel."[19] Disillusionment in the wake of defeat led the people to turn his original name, ben Kosiba, into a pun on the Hebrew word "to lie" (kazab), that is, Bar Koziba ("son of a liar"). To them he turned out to be the great false messiah.[20]

Among those who hailed Bar Kokhba as the Messiah was Rabbi Akiva (ca. A.D. 50–135), the foremost Jewish scholar and sage of the era. The great medieval Jewish scholar Moses ben Maimon (Maimonides) stated, "Rabbi Akiva, the greatest of the sages of the Mishnah, was a supporter of King Ben Koziva, saying of him that he was the king messiah. He and all the contemporary sages regarded him as the king messiah."[21] In fact, not every sage regarded him as the Messiah. But Akiva became the spiritual leader of the revolt; he even traveled abroad to gather support for the revolution among the Jews of the Diaspora. He went as far west as Gaul (France) and as far east as Babylonia.

Bar Kokhba's seemingly contradictory personality—tremendous charisma manifested alongside extreme harshness—fascinated later rabbis. According to the Talmud, he required all his soldiers to cut off a finger to demonstrate their loyalty and valor.[22] But some of the Jewish sages of Bar Kokhba's time were more disgusted than fascinated. They wondered how long he would continue to turn all Israel into maimed men. His reliance on his own powers rather than on help from heaven caused great conflict between him and some of the rabbis, who regarded his attitude as the epitome of haughtiness.[23] Bundles of letters and related documents found in the Judaean desert not far from the Dead Sea Scroll community at Qumran depict Bar Kokhba as a stern military commander who sought to rule Judaea with authoritarian power. These Judaean sources, especially letters to subordinates, reveal a leader who insisted on his views and ruled both the people and his officers with an iron fist.[24]

When Hadrian left the region in late A.D. 131 or early 132, the Jews seized their opportunity and openly rebelled, first near Modi'in.[25] They seized small towns and fortified them with walls and underground tunnels. Rather than fight pitched battles, the rebels inflicted heavy losses on the Romans with guerrilla maneuvers. Caught off guard, the Roman governor, Tinius Rufus, ordered the evacuation of Jerusalem. The Tenth Legion abandoned its encampment in the city and headed for Caesarea. Under Bar Kokhba's leadership, the rebels established a provincial government in their former capital city, made plans to rebuild the Temple, and in the interim resumed ritual sacrifices at a temporary altar on the Temple site. A new calendar was proclaimed, and new coins were struck. One side of such a coin reads, "Shimon [Bar Kokhba] prince [Hebrew, *nasi*] of Israel," and on the reverse side, "Year one of the redemption of Israel."[26] In the minds of the rebels an independent Jewish state had once again been reestablished with Bar Kokhba as "King-Messiah" or redeemer—a notion also confirmed in the Judaean desert documents. Rabbi Akiva explicitly linked the title *nasi* with the idea of "King-Messiah."[27]

In point of fact, an important contrast between the First Jewish Revolt in A.D. 70 and the situation in A.D. 132 was that the Jews of the Second Revolt were united under a single commander-in-chief. Bar Kokhba saw his government as the only legal rule in the Holy Land, and those who opposed him, Christians of Jewish ancestry, for example, who did not believe Bar Kokhba to be the Messiah, were persecuted.[28]

Dio Cassius states that the insurrectionists of 132 were well prepared, and the uprising spread until all of Judaea was in revolt. The Jews throughout the world supported the uprising, as did many non-Jews, and it was "as though the whole world raged."[29] The Gentiles who supported the Jewish revolutionaries came mainly from the oppressed classes of the local inhabitants. Apparently even some Samaritans joined the Bar Kokhba rebels. Isolated evidence shows that the revolt spread north to Beth-Shean and the Galilee,[30] but the main conflict took place in Judaea, the Shephelah, the mountain region, and finally in the Judaean desert.

Absolutely critical to those waging the Bar Kokhba rebellion, symbolically as well as strategically, was Jerusalem. It represented every Jew's yearning for freedom and was the political rallying point for the rebels. In fact, one Judaean desert document is dated "the third year of the freedom of Jerusalem." This source also tells us that Jerusalem was still in the hands of Bar Kokhba and his followers in the third year of the revolt (A.D. 134).

Hadrian sent for reinforcements under the command of one of his ablest generals, Sextus Julius Severus, governor of Britain. Because of the great number of insurrectionists and the intensity of their fury, Severus refrained from engaging in open battles, preferring instead to surround the Jews in their fortress towns and blockade them so that they ran out of supplies. One of his armies dared to advance rashly against rebel forces and was completely wiped out—a tragic but valuable lesson to the Romans.[31]

Pressure put on the Bar Kokhba revolutionaries was intense. The emperor himself joined Severus in Judaea. Besides the Sixth and the Tenth legions already stationed there, components of other legions were brought in from Syria, Arabia, Egypt, the Danube region of Europe, and elsewhere. Roman armies surrounded Jerusalem on every side. The city was inadequately fortified to withstand another Roman siege, and the rebels abandoned it near the end of the third year of the revolt. In the spring of 135, Bar Kokhba and his army took refuge in the fortress of Bethar, in the Judaean hills southwest of Jerusalem, where the final siege began.[32]

Situated on a hill overlooking a deep canyon, Bethar seemed a stronghold for the rebels, but it lacked a secure water supply. By the end of the summer of 135, the Romans breached the rebels' wall. The surviving defenders were slaughtered, and Bar Kokhba himself was slain.[33]

When word reached the remnants of Bar Kokhba's army that total defeat was imminent, they fled to caves in the Judaean desert near the Dead Sea. There, in places now called the "Cave of the Pool," "Cave of Letters," and "Cave of Horror," the last participants in the Bar Kokhba or Second Jewish Revolt met their deaths. Remains of Roman military camps found above the caves show that the Romans could not directly assault the fugitives, so they waited for hunger and thirst to do their work.[34]

The Romans destroyed 985 villages and killed more than a million people—not including those who died of disease and hunger. Roman losses too were extremely heavy; in fact, when Hadrian informed the Senate of his eventual victory in Judaea, he did not begin his speech with the usual formula, "I and my army are well."[35] His army was not well at all; it was decimated.

The Jewish population of Judaea was largely exterminated or exiled after the fall of Bethar. Massacres, the sale of Jews into slavery, and the uprooting of people from the soil were all part of the Roman program. The failure of Bar Kokhba brought to a brutal end Jewish self-government, along with all of the material attributes of nationhood.[36] A free and independent Jewish state would not be seen again for more than eighteen hundred years.

Maimonides believed that Bar Kokhba's messianic pretenses were nothing less than unmitigated wickedness and the source of tremendous misery.[37] Eusebius states that Bar Kokhba regarded himself as the savior who had come down to the Jews like a star from heaven. But, says the church historian, he was really a bloodthirsty bandit who used the strength of his name to get what he wanted.[38] It is significant and arresting that the true Savior prophesied of false messiahs who would arise after great tribulation overtook the Jews and the inhabitants of Jerusalem:

> For then, in those days, shall be great tribulation on the Jews, and upon the inhabitants of Jerusalem, such as was not before sent upon Israel, of God. . . .
>
> All things which have befallen them are only the beginning of the sorrows which shall come upon them. . . .
>
> Behold, these things I have spoken unto you concerning the Jews; and again, after the tribulation of those days which shall come upon Jerusalem, if any man shall say unto you, Lo, here is Christ, or there, believe him not;
>
> For in those days there shall also arise false Christs, and false prophets, and shall show great signs and wonders, insomuch, that, if possible, they shall deceive the very elect, who are the elect according to the covenant. (JS–M 1:18–22)

If one ascribes the destructions of A.D. 70 (Jerusalem, the Temple, and 1.1 million people) to be the fulfillment of the Savior's prophetic view of Jerusalem's unprecedented tribulations ("tribulation . . . upon the inhabitants of Jerusalem, such as was not before sent upon Israel"), then Bar Kokhba becomes an uncontestable fulfillment of Christ's prophetic vision of the rise of false Christs or messiahs. Note that the Savior says "*again, after* the tribulation of those days which shall come upon Jerusalem . . . there shall also arise false Christs, and false prophets, and shall show great signs and wonders" (emphasis added). Bar Kokhba came *after* the First Revolt to bring *again* another revolt and more misery. For a time he and his followers did amazing things—they established a government run by the posterity of the Abrahamic covenant (that is, the Jews), achieved astounding victories over Roman might, and stirred a sense of final redemption as indicated by inscriptions on their coins. But Bar Kokhba was a false messiah, and he deceived no less a figure than the great Rabbi Akiva—one of Israel's elect, in their view. Bar Kokhba's claims to messiahship proved the decisive break between Judaism and Christianity, because Christians, who already knew who the true Messiah was, refused to follow another.

It is inspiring to realize that the destiny of Jerusalem was foretold by many, including the very Son of God. It is sobering to contemplate the as yet unfulfilled part of his prophecy:

> And again, this Gospel of the Kingdom shall be preached in all the world, . . . and then shall the end come, or the destruction of the wicked;
> And again shall the abomination of desolation, spoken of by Daniel the prophet [concerning the destruction of Jerusalem], be fulfilled (JS–M 1: 31–32).

AELIA CAPITOLINA

After they suppressed the Bar Kokhba Revolt, the Romans erected the pagan center of Aelia Capitolina on the site of the city. No Jews remained in Jerusalem after the revolt because Hadrian banned them from even entering the city upon penalty of death. A yearly exception was made on the ninth of Av, the anniversary of the destruction of the Temple, when Jews were allowed to come and weep by the *Kotel,* or western wall.[39] This ban remained in effect for at least a century, at which time (A.D. 235) the empire began to experience difficulties of its own.

Part of the reason for constructing Aelia Capitolina was to build up several cities to reinforce the eastern flank of the empire against invaders. Roads were laid in Judaea to connect Aelia Capitolina with Caesarea (Maratima), Legio (Megiddo), and other cities. The main entrance to

Jerusalem all during this later Roman period was by way of the road that led through the northern gate—one of four main gates in the city wall at the cardinal points of the compass. Those gates were in the approximate location of today's Damascus Gate to the north, Jaffa Gate to the west, Lion's Gate to the east, and Zion Gate to the south.[40]

The location of the wall around Aelia Capitolina is much debated and is inferred from the city wall depicted on a Byzantine mosaic map from Jordan known as the Madaba Map. Excavations under the present-day Damascus Gate, beginning in 1938, have revealed the splendid Roman triple-arched gate from which began the main road to Caesarea, the capital of the country at that time. Above the eastern entrance was an inscription reading: "The colony of Aelia Capitolina, [the inscription] was placed here by decree of the decurions [members of the city council]."[41] Large sections of the gate and its attendant tower were constructed with dressed stones apparently taken from Herodian structures demolished during the devastation of 70. Though a city council is mentioned in this inscription, it is still not clear how Aelia Capitolina was administered.

The city gates served as entrances to the paved streets of Aelia Capitolina. The two main thoroughfares were called the *Cardo* (Latin, "heart"). These two streets originated at a spacious square inside the northern gate where, according to the Madaba Map, a large column stood with a statue of the emperor. The large paving stones of the main streets still bear the typical Roman serrations carved into the slabs to help prevent passersby from slipping on their polished surfaces.[42]

Another important feature of Jerusalem under imperial rule was its four monumental triumphal arches. Perhaps the most conspicuous was erected north of today's Damascus Gate, near the area of the Second Temple-period Third Wall. It bore at least two inscriptions from the reigns of Hadrian (117–138) and Antoninus Pius (138–161). It is believed to have been built by Hadrian to commemorate his victory over Bar Kokhba and was later embellished by Antoninus. The best known of the Roman arches is the Ecce Homo Arch, called thus because Christian tradition holds that it was there that Pontius Pilate brought Jesus before the masses and proclaimed "Behold the man!" (Latin, *Ecce Homo*). Nevertheless, this arch is generally considered by historians to have been built by Hadrian, owing to its three entrances, which resemble the other three-entrance arches constructed in Jerusalem during Hadrian's rule.[43]

The paucity of literary sources for this period is frustrating, but some important data about Aelia Capitolina come from the large number of coins minted during this time. Soon after 135, a series of coins carried the inscription *Colonia Aelia Capitolina condita* ("the colony of Aelia Capitolina has been founded"). They also showed the image of the emperor plowing a furrow along the course of the new city walls about to be built. This was a fitting representation for the Jews because it was the material fulfillment of one of Micah's visions: "Thus saith the Lord of hosts; Zion shall be plowed like a field, and Jerusalem shall become heaps, and the mountain of the house as the high places of a forest" (Jer. 26:18).[44]

Coins also depict the religious practices carried out in the city. The main activity centered on the cult worship of the three Capitoline gods whose images appear on coins of the period. From Hadrian's time, coins portray the temple he erected. Jupiter is shown sitting inside, facing the goddess Minerva, and the goddess Juno stands behind him. Jupiter and the two goddesses were the patron deities of the city and were called the Capitoline Trinity. Other sources confirm the existence of a temple to the Capitoline gods on the Temple Mount. The third-century historian Dio Cassius describes its establishment, as does the seventh-century *Chronicon Pascale* (Easter Chronicle). According to an early Christian pilgrim, the Bordeaux Traveler, the pagan temple was situated on the Temple Mount, and when Jews visited the site on the ninth of Av every year, they did so in its shadow.[45]

Politically, Aelia Capitolina was a quiet little provincial city. The great events were imperial visits, such as the one by Septimius Severus in 201, which was commemorated by an inscription discovered near the Western Wall.[46] A coin struck in 176 memorializes a visit from Marcus Aurelius and his son, the future emperor Commodus. In 289 the Emperor Diocletian transferred the Tenth Legion from Aelia Capitolina to Elath (modern Eilat), after a sojourn in Jerusalem of almost two hundred years. That occurrence signaled the approaching end of the city's Roman period, for the Tenth Legion had destroyed Jerusalem, watched over it, destroyed it again, and finally maintained it.

Jerusalem's Roman period, ending in 324, was a watershed era in the history of the Eternal City. Jewish hopes were raised only to be brutally dashed. The Jews paid a heavy price for their first rebellion and a heavier price still for their second. Everything they treasured about Jerusalem was gone, even the opportunity to be inhabitants of the once glorious capital. All the horrifying prophecies of destruction were fulfilled completely. Hugh Nibley reminds us that the world-renowned Temple site even became the city dump during Jerusalem's Byzantine period.[47]

The Roman period of Jerusalem's history changed the city religiously, politically, culturally, and architecturally. Even its name was changed. Moreover, Hadrian changed the name of the country in which Jerusalem was from Judaea to Palestine, calling it after the Philistines as a further embarrassment to the Jews. There is little doubt that the layout of Aelia Capitolina, established by the Romans, set the physical character of Jerusalem up to the present day. It might be argued, however, that God still oversaw its religious character.

NOTES

1. Romney, in Conference Report, 76–77.

2. Shanks, *Christianity and Rabbinic Judaism,* 125.

3. Avigad, *Discovering Jerusalem,* 205.

4. See Bahat, *Illustrated Atlas of Jerusalem,* 58.

5. Clarke, "Worship in the Jerusalem Temple," 269–80; see also Aharoni and Avi-Yonah, *Macmillan Bible Atlas,* Map 258.

6. Avi-Yonah, *Jerusalem,* 38.

7. Erastus Snow, in *Journal of Discourses,* 16:202.

8. All of our information comes from Josephus, *Wars* 7. For the exploits of Lucilius Bassus, see *Wars* 7.6.1. For the siege of Masada, see *Wars* 7.8.1–7.9.2. An excellent, readable summary is found in Murphy-O'Connor, *Holy Land,* 344–45.

9. Murphy-O'Connor, *Holy Land,* 344–45.

10. Shanks, *Christianity and Rabbinic Judaism,* 127–28.

11. Shanks, *Christianity and Rabbinic Judaism,* 128–29.

12. Grant, *Jews in the Roman World,* 244.

13. For the source of the tradition see Genesis Rabba, lxxviii,1. It ends with a curse upon Hadrian: "Rot his bones!"

14. Grant, *Jews in the Roman World,* 244–45.

15. Ben-Dov, *Shadow of the Temple,* 189–90.

16. Dio Cassius, *History of Rome,* 69.12.

17. Eusebius, *History of the Church,* 6.4. See Shanks, *Christianity and Rabbinic Judaism,* 144–46.

18. Aharoni and Avi-Yonah, *Macmillan Bible Atlas,* Map 259; *Encyclopedia Judaica,* 4:231, s.v. "Bar Kokhba." Both summarize Dio Cassius, *History of Rome,* 69.

19. The terms *bar* (Aramaic) and *ben* (Hebrew) are used interchangeably during the period. Both mean "son of."

20. Eban, *Heritage,* 99; *Encyclopedia Judaica,* 4:229–30, s.v. "Bar Kokhba"; see also Eusebius, *History of the Church,* 6.4.

21. Maimonides, Mishneh Torah (Yad Hazakah), Melakhim, 11:3, in *Encyclopedia Judaica,* 4:231, s.v. "Bar Kokhba." See also Eban, *Heritage,* 99; Aharoni and Avi-Yonah, *Macmillan Bible Atlas,* Map 259.

22. Jerusalem Talmud, Tan'anit 4:8; Lamentations Rabbah 2:2.

23. Jerusalem Talmud, Tan'anit 4:8; Lamentations Rabbah 2:2. ; see also *Encyclopedia Judaica,* 4:231, s.v. "Bar Kokhba."

24. *Encyclopedia Judaica,* 4:231, s.v. "Bar Kokhba."

25. *Encyclopedia Judaica,* 4:231, s.v. "Bar Kokhba."

26. Eban, *Heritage,* 99.

27. Maimonides, Mishneh Torah (Yad Hazakah), Melakhim, 11:3. See also *Encyclopedia Judaica,* 4:230–31, s.v. "Bar Kokhba."

28. Aharoni and Avi-Yonah, *Macmillan Bible Atlas,* Map 259.

29. *Encyclopedia Judaica,* 4:233, s.v. "Bar Kokhba."

30. The evidence consists of a tomb inscription and third-century Talmudic references (see, for example, Bava Kamma 80a). See also Aharoni and Avi-Yonah, *Macmillan Bible Atlas,* Map 259.

31. Aharoni and Avi-Yonah, *Macmillan Bible Atlas,* Map 259.

32. Aharoni and Avi-Yonah, *Macmillan Bible Atlas,* Maps 259, 260.

33. Aharoni and Avi-Yonah, *Macmillan Bible Atlas,* Maps 260, 261.

34. Aharoni and Avi-Yonah, *Macmillan Bible Atlas,* Map 262.

35. *Encyclopedia Judaica,* 4:233, s.v. "Bar Kokhba."

36. Epstein, *Judaism,* 118.

37. *Encyclopedia Judaica,* 4:231, s.v. "Bar Kokhba."

38. Eusebius, *History of the Church,* 6.4.

39. Epstein, *Judaism,* 118.

40. Bahat, *Illustrated Atlas of Jerusalem,* 61.

41. Bahat, *Illustrated Atlas of Jerusalem,* 62.

42. Bahat, *Illustrated Atlas of Jerusalem,* 59, 61, 63.

43. Bahat, *Illustrated Atlas of Jerusalem,* 64–65.

44. Bahat, *Illustrated Atlas of Jerusalem,* 60.

45. Bahat, *Illustrated Atlas of Jerusalem,* 65–67.

46. Avi-Yonah, *Jerusalem,* 40–41.

47. Nibley, *Mormonism and Early Christianity,* 405.

13

Jerusalem and the Rabbis, A.D. 70–500

Before the disaster of A.D. 70, much of the direct political and religious power over Jewish life was vested in a council of the most important Jewish leaders in Jerusalem, the Great Sanhedrin of Israel. Their Greek and Roman overlords granted this body considerable self-government, up to but just short of capital punishment. As the highest native court in both civil and ecclesiastical matters, and operating under the authority of the high priest, the Great Sanhedrin created and enforced the laws governing the Jewish people.

For many decades, the Pharisees exercised the dominant influence in the Sanhedrin, though there were Sadducean elements.[1] For a time the governing body was led by pairs of Pharisaic teachers called *zuggoth* (Hebrew, "pairs"), one of whom was the *nasi* (Hebrew, "president") and the other the *ab beth din* (Hebrew, "chief of the court").[2] The Pharisees also predominated among the scribes and rabbis. (Before A.D. 70 the term *rabbi*—Hebrew, literally "my great one" or "my master"—was a title of respect given to the great teachers and leaders of Judaism by their disciples.)

Far more important than the influence and power they wielded before A.D. 70 is the fate of the twenty-four parties and sects of Judaism[3] at the time. The only group to survive the national cataclysm was the Pharisees. When the Temple was destroyed and the last vestiges of Jewish autonomy disappeared from Jerusalem, so did all the splinter groups of the religion except the Pharisees. In practical terms, this means that every form of Judaism today ultimately derives from the Pharisees. In *The Earthly Jerusalem,* Norman Kotker offered this analysis:

The temple priests had lost their function; they and their descendants, many named Aaronson or Cohen, which means priest, became merely a caste with minor ritual obligations undistinguished otherwise from the mass of Jews. Their aristocratic allies, the Sadducees, had lost the basis of their power. There was no longer any Jewish political administration for them to control. Whatever national life remained now centered on the Pharisees, who devoted themselves to preserving the only precious thing the Jews had left, the law which they endlessly studied, memorized, and interpreted. By keeping them a people apart, the law in turn was to preserve the Jews.[4]

FROM JERUSALEM TO JABNEH

In the wake of the great devastation, a reorganization of Jewish life and government developed gradually at Jabneh, or Jamnia, between Jerusalem and the coast, near Rehovot in modern Israel. Jabneh thus became the new center of religious learning. A leader in the work of reconstruction was the preeminent Pharisaic scholar, Rabbi Jochanan ben Zakkai. Seeing that the city was doomed to destruction before the end of the First Jewish Revolt, he had left Jerusalem and gone to Jabneh to establish a cultural center for the Jewish people.[5]

The story of his escape from Jerusalem is recounted in rabbinic literature. He was carried out of the city in a coffin by his disciples, and once outside the gates, went to the camp of the Roman general (and future emperor) Vespasian to request that the Jewish sages of Jochanan's generation be saved—which was to say, the town of Jabneh with its teachers and masters of the Torah. He was given permission to go, though probably not to reestablish a supreme institution for the nation. Jabneh had been the site of a small *bet din* (law court), as well as the seat of the sages of the family of Bene Bathyra. "Thus," the modern Jewish scholar Isidore Epstein notes, "for the first time was Jerusalem and its Temple given up by men representing those elements in the Jewish people who, with all their patriotism and attachment to the Holy Land, did not want spiritual progress to be subjected to geographical limitations."[6]

Though ben Zakkai had foreseen the destruction of Jerusalem, when word reached him that the Temple had been destroyed, he reacted with profound grief: "Rabban Johanan sat and watched in the direction of the wall of Jerusalem to learn what was happening there, even as Eli sat upon his seat by the wayside watching [1 Sam. 4:13]. When R. Johanan b. Zakkai saw that the Temple was destroyed and the *heikal* [the Sanctuary] burnt, he stood and rent his garments, took off his *tefillin* [phylacteries], and sat weeping, as did his pupils with him."[7]

Jochanan spent much time consoling the righteous among his followers, who lamented the ruin of the Temple.[8] But more than that, he worked tirelessly to reconstruct the leadership of the Jewish nation by building up the *bet din* at Jabneh. The Jews still had the Torah, and that became the center of Jewish life, their anchor and basis for decision making in place of the Temple and priestly rule.

Ben Zakkai was succeeded as president of the *bet din* and patriarch of Judaea by Gamaliel II, the grandson of Paul's teacher (see Acts 5:34; 22:3) and the great-great-grandson of Hillel, the most famous and profound of the rabbinic authorities. (Hillel was one of the *zuggoth* in charge of the Sanhedrin.) During Gamaliel II's lifetime at Jabneh, the *bet din* was reconstructed as the Great Sanhedrin and entrusted with the functions of education, legislation, adjudication, and government.[9] It was at once both an academy and a legislative body. This reconstituted Sanhedrin lost no time in propounding a wide range of religious, civil, and criminal laws—as far as Roman rulers allowed. Measures were adopted to deal with rules that had centered on the Temple and priesthood but were now thrown into chaos. The liturgy was recast and adapted to include petitions for the swift restoration of the Temple and the rebuilding of Jerusalem.

The Sanhedrin soon established itself as the central religious authority in Judaism, with jurisdiction over Jewish life recognized by Jews as far distant as Persia and Media. One of the most important ways the Jabneh Sanhedrin exercised authority over world Jewry was by taking over the prerogative, hitherto reserved for the Jerusalem Sanhedrin, of deciding the liturgical calendar, communicating to distant Jewish communities the day of the new moon (new month) and, thus, the times for celebrating ensuing feasts and fasts. This Sanhedrin also became the Jewish nation's accredited representative to the Roman authorities.

Educationally, the most important task in which the Sanhedrin and its sages were engaged was the teaching and transmission of the oral

Torah. The rabbis believed that God had revealed two Torahs to Moses on Mount Sinai. The first, or written, Torah became known as the five books of Moses in the Old Testament, also called the Pentateuch or the Law. The second was the oral Torah, which was handed down orally from one rabbinic master to another.[10] Preserving and teaching the oral Torah was carried out through two methods that had been practiced in academies and schools in Palestine and Babylonia long before the destruction of the Temple. One method was called *Midrash,* and the other was called *Mishnah.*

Midrash is derived from the Hebrew root *darash,* meaning "to teach, to inquire," and involved the explication and interpretation of the biblical text by discussion—that is, by asking questions about a specific biblical verse or set of verses. When this method of exposition yielded a point of law or a legal teaching, it was categorized as *Halakhah,* from the Hebrew verb *halakh,* "to walk." It showed the way a person should walk, what path one ought to follow to please God, by making clear how the law could be obeyed in every detail. D. S. Russell has said that halakhic Midrash "was an exegesis of biblical laws out of which could be formed authoritative regulations for the life of the people. It is this Halakah which forms the oral tradition or unwritten Torah of Judaism."[11]

When the midrashic method yielded anything that was not Halakhah, or Jewish law, the exposition was categorized as Aggadah, from the Hebrew root *nagad,* "to tell, to recount, to narrate." This narrative part of rabbinic literature developed and expounded biblical stories rather than biblical law. Aggadah is composed, then, of illustrations, legend, folklore, and exhortation as well as true stories. Though it was and is highly valued in Judaism, it did not have the binding authority of Halakhah.

Though Jesus was sometimes critical of oral tradition or the "tradition of the elders" (see, for example, Matt. 15:2–3), he also recognized the value of the Midrash and the midrashic method. He said that scribes—they were the practitioners of the midrashic method in his day—who became disciples of the true master, or "great one," were like a householder who brought forth out of his treasure things both old and new (see Matt. 13:52). Jesus himself used midrash to teach the truths of the gospel. For example, much of the Gospel of John is halakhah, or explication of the old laws He had given: the meaning of the serpent raised up in the wilderness (John 3); the bread of life (John 6); and the woman taken in adultery (John 8). The danger, of course, was that without the Spirit, midrashic expositors could and did look beyond the mark (see Jacob 4:14) and set aside the very laws they were embellishing.

In addition to the midrashic method of perpetuating the oral law, after the fall of the Temple another method of teaching the oral Torah became prominent. Instead of elaborating one verse of scripture at a time, the Jabneh sages, under the direction of Jochanan ben Zakkai, began to arrange the *Halakhot* (plural of *Halakhah),* or individual laws, of Judaism in order according to subject rather than according to the biblical text. This method was known as *Mishnah,* from the Hebrew root *shanah,* "repetition," and the sum of the repetition was thus known as the Mishnah. The Mishnah has been described, again by D. S. Russell, as the "systematic (topical) classification of the discussions and decisions of Rabbis . . . as to the right interpretation and expansion of the Torah."[12] The Mishnah, like the Midrash, also contains Halakhah and Aggadah, but Halakhah predominates overwhelmingly in the Mishnah.

Rabbi Jochanan ben Zakkai led out in practicing the mishnaic method, and a later teacher named Rabbi Akiva (d. 135) clarified and elaborated the arrangement of the Halakhot, or laws, as they continued to be passed down orally. Akiva's pupil, Rabbi Meir, further refined, organized, and expanded the body of mishnaic exposition. This process of organization and refinement reached its peak in the work of Rabbi Yehudah ha-Nasi ("Judah the Prince"), the greatest of the mishnaic sages. Rabbi Judah made a final critical review of mishnaic exposition, and sometime between 217 and 230 the edited body of mishnaic oral law was codified in writing as the Mishnah of Judah the Prince. This quickly became the standard version of the Mishnah. Next to the Bible itself, the Mishnah remains the foundation of Jewish life and literature.

Between A.D. 200 and 500, the rabbis and sages continued to discuss the Mishnah, providing valuable commentary on it, as they studied at the rabbinic academies in Palestine and Babylonia, another center of Jewish civilization. Both sets of commentary, Palestinian and Babylonian, became known as Gemarah (Hebrew, "completion"), and when each was put with the Mishnah of Rabbi Judah, the two collections were known as the Jerusalem Talmud and the Babylonian Talmud. The latter became the standard text of the Talmud because of its greater detail and thoroughness; however, the Jerusalem Talmud, though considered inferior, is a valuable historical resource because it preserves facts and cultural details that otherwise would have been lost.

Both Talmuds contain much information about Jerusalem and rabbinic attitudes toward it because the Jabneh sages, as well as later rabbis and commentators at academies elsewhere, had to deal with both the adaptation of old Temple and priesthood laws to a new way of life without the Temple, as well as hopes and plans for rebuilding a third Temple in a reconstructed Jerusalem. "The obsession of the Jewish sages with being prepared for a rebuilt Temple meant the preservation of a wealth of information about the last of the Jerusalem Temples as well as about the general way of life in Jerusalem before it fell to Rome."[13] Thus, the importance of the great Jewish sages and rabbis exiled from Jerusalem after its destruction lies in their spending so much time talking about the nature of the city as it existed before its destruction. They recreated a new Jerusalem in their minds and passed it down from generation to generation. That idealized concept of Jerusalem perpetuated by the rabbis became such a powerful image that the idea took on a life of its own. Some of the characteristics they ascribed to Jerusalem before A.D. 70 may have been nothing more than idealized notions of the city which they projected back into history.

JERUSALEM IN RABBINIC LITERATURE

The halakhic statements of the rabbis after A.D. 70 declare that Jerusalem was treated differently in Jewish law from all other cities because of its special holiness. No one tribe of Israel was allowed to claim ownership of the city because it was the city of the patriarchs as well as the home of the heavenly king, a place set apart for all the covenant people.[14] Thus, the rabbis said it had been forbidden by Halakhah to rent houses to pilgrims in Jerusalem before its destruction, so visitors were to be given lodgings free of charge. According to Rabbi Eleazar ben Simon, it had been forbidden even to rent beds. It was said that at festival times, residents of the city sometimes vacated their homes to accommodate travelers. As the Mishnah said: "No one ever said 'The place is too confined for me to lodge in Jerusalem.'"[15] During the Second Temple period no foreigner was allowed to live within Jerusalem's walls.[16]

Because of Jerusalem's special sanctity, the rabbis said that a series of halakhot had been observed before A.D. 70 to remove from the Holy City anything that would increase ritual impurity. The rabbis declared, for example, that no trash heaps were allowed inside the city walls, because they produced insects. Burials were allowed only outside the city walls; the prohibition against leaving a corpse in Jerusalem overnight was strictly enforced.[17]

Even after its destruction, or perhaps especially after, Jerusalem retained its holiness, and special halakhot to perpetuate this sanctity continued to be promulgated. When praying, one was obligated to face Jerusalem; if one stood in Jerusalem, he should turn his heart toward the Temple. Entrance to the Temple Mount itself was forbidden because of the perpetual state of ritual impurity engulfing all people since the Temple's destruction. In other words, the Temple Mount itself encompassed sacred space. The obligation of making pilgrimage to Jerusalem remained in force, but the obligation of mourning for Jerusalem's destruction was added. Besides the national fast days and the established days of mourning, one was forbidden to eat meat or drink wine on any day when one viewed firsthand the ruins of the destroyed city and Temple.[18] Abstaining from such luxuries and pleasures engendered a greater awareness of and sense of sorrow over the destruction of Jerusalem and the Temple.

In fact, the rabbis went further and reasoned that it was impossible to mourn such an event too much; one should mourn the destruction of Jerusalem every day of one's life and in every place. Accordingly, Halakhah prescribed remembrances of Jerusalem's sorrows to be kept by Jews even in the seemingly simple or mundane activities of life that might be associated in any way with renewal or pleasure. A man might whitewash his house, but he should leave a small area unfinished in remembrance of Jerusalem. A man might prepare a full-course meal, but he should leave out an item of the menu in remembrance of Jerusalem. A woman might put on all her jewelry except one or two pieces in remembrance of Jerusalem.[19]

Under the influence of these types of halakhot, certain customs have developed in Judaism that dictate that even in moments of supreme joy, one should remember the destruction of the Temple and the calamities that have befallen the Jewish people ever since. One such custom, carried out by most Jews as though it possessed the same weight as Halakhah, is the breaking of a glass at the end of the wedding ceremony.[20]

Rabbinic statements about Jerusalem found in Aggadah are plentiful and may be categorized as those dealing with the historic city, those discussing the extrahistorical city, and those describing millennial Jerusalem. According to the rabbis, there has never been nor will be any place like Jerusalem either in time or in eternity, and there is no beauty like Jerusalem's. Of the ten measures of beauty that came into the world at creation, Jerusalem took nine.[21] The rabbis said that a man who had not seen Jerusalem in all its splendor had never seen a beautiful city.[22]

According to an aggadic midrash on Psalms, the history of Jerusalem began at the time of creation. "At the beginning of the creation of the world the Holy One, blessed be He, made as it were a tabernacle in Jerusalem in which He prayed: May My children do My will that I shall not destroy My house and My sanctuary."[23] But God's wish was not to be, as the sages taught. In fact, the rabbis after A.D. 70 spent so much time discussing why Jerusalem and the Temple had fallen because they hoped to speed the Temple's reconstruction by correcting whatever problems had brought it about. They wanted to enjoy God's approbation once more.

Rabbi Jochanan ben Zakkai ascribed the Temple's destruction to Israel's general failure to do the will of God. We have seen the increase of the social evils that plagued Jewish society before the destruction of A.D. 70. Ben Zakkai himself refers to the increase in the number of murderers as well as in the number of adulterers living in Jerusalem.[24] But even though ben Zakkai recognized that the chief responsibility for Jerusalem's destruction lay with the city's citizens themselves, those who performed the destruction were not absolved of responsibility. According to Rabbi Jochanan, with the Temple's passing, the atonement for sins (a concept integrally tied to the performances carried out in the Holy Sanctuary) was denied not to Israel but rather to those Gentiles who had destroyed the Temple.[25] Thus, Gentile accountability could not and should not be dismissed.

Some rabbis, who also believed in Israel's culpability, were quite specific in their analysis of Jerusalem's calamity. They blamed the city's fall on the desecration of the Sabbath or on the neglect of study and the contempt demonstrated by Jerusalem's society for men of learning. One rabbi, who supported this idea, said that Jerusalem was destroyed because schoolboys played truant. Others said it had fallen because the Jews of the city obeyed the letter of the law rather than its spirit; their dealings with their fellow human beings were not merciful enough.[26] Jochanan ben Torta maintained that "in the Second Temple period we know that they studied the Torah, were strictly observant of the *mitzvot* (Hebrew, "commandments") and of the tithes, and every kind of good manners was found among them, but they loved money and hated one another without cause."[27]

Whatever the many explanations offered, Latter-day Saints cannot help but feel that the rabbis did not get to the root cause of Jerusalem's devastation and the Temple's destruction. A modern apostle has written: "Why . . . did the Great Jehovah permit his holy house to be desecrated by the Gentiles and made by them into a dung hill? Why were the chosen people scourged and slain and scattered and made a hiss and a byword in all nations? The answer is clear and certain. It was because they crucified their King. It was because they rejected the God of their fathers."[28]

Jerusalem fell because its inhabitants rejected the greatest rabbi or master of them all—Jesus Christ. Nevertheless, one is not unsympathetic to the anguish felt by the sages. It is a sympathy born of deep appreciation for the Jewish people—for the righteous inhabitants of Jerusalem in every age—and a profound feeling that Jerusalem is indeed holy and was at one time filled with magnificence and splendor, a circumstance yet again to be realized.

Of particular interest to Latter-day Saints are the many hopeful and forward-looking statements by the sages about the Jerusalem of the future, the ideal Jerusalem to be rebuilt by God himself, with the masses of exiled Israel gathered safely home. Samuel ben Nahmani said that "Jerusalem will not be rebuilt until the exiles are gathered in, and if anyone tells you that the exiles have gathered together but Jerusalem is not rebuilt, do not believe it."[29] The rabbis insisted that in the coming age not only would God rebuild Jerusalem with fire (an interesting irony considering how it was destroyed) but he would extend its boundaries. Rabbi Jochanan taught that Jerusalem would be extended on all sides, even to the extent that the city "will reach to the gates of Damascus"[30] (an idea unattractive to modern Syrians, one would think).

According to the rabbis, the millennial Jerusalem will be an idyllic place to live. Rabbi Simeon ben Lakish said: "The Holy One blessed be He will in days to come add to Jerusalem more than a thousand gardens and a thousand towers."[31] A midrashic aggadah on Exodus teaches that the Holy One will bring forth living waters from Jerusalem and with those waters will heal everyone who is sick. The borders of Jerusalem in time to come will be full of precious stones and pearls, and Israel will take their jewels from those borders. At that time the Holy One will build Jerusalem out of sapphires, "and these stones will shine like the sun, and the nations will come and look upon the glory of Israel."[32]

In rabbinic literature, the earthly Jerusalem of the future is connected with a heavenly city of Jerusalem. The sages constantly referred to the earthly Jerusalem as the center of the world and the *tabbur ha-aretz* ("the navel of the earth"). A midrashic statement on Ezekiel says that just as the navel of a human is set in the middle of the body, so Eretz Israel is the navel of the world, Jerusalem the center of Eretz Israel, the Temple the center of Jerusalem, and the *heikal* the center of the Temple— even the foundation from which the world was started. The umbilical cord that stretches from the heavenly Jerusalem connects with the earth at the city of Jerusalem, specifically at the Temple. Thus, the heavenly Jerusalem is located directly opposite the earthly Jerusalem, and each is intimately connected with the other.[33]

The sages of the Talmud naturally stressed the affinity between the earthly and the heavenly Jerusalem and that future time when the earthly Jerusalem would be restored to splendor to match its counterpart, the heavenly Jerusalem. The earthly Jerusalem would then be a place as hospitable to God as its heavenly counterpart. Said Rabbi Jochanan: "The Holy One blessed be He declared, 'I shall not enter the heavenly Jerusalem until I can enter the earthly Jerusalem.'"[34]

Unlike medieval Christians, who repudiated belief in a restoration of the earthly Jerusalem and emphasized instead the descent of a heavenly Jerusalem and a heavenly Temple coming down to the earth at the end of the world,[35] Latter-day Saints are in accord with the image promulgated by the Talmudic sages of a gathered portion of Israel established in and around a restored earthly Jerusalem. Thousands of years ago a prophet in the western hemisphere spoke of a restored earthly

Jerusalem, separate and apart from a heavenly Jerusalem descending to the earth:

> And that it [the American continent] was the place of the New Jerusalem, which should come down out of heaven, and the holy sanctuary of the Lord. . . .
>
> And he spake also concerning the house of Israel, and the Jerusalem from whence Lehi should come—after it should be destroyed it should be built up again, a holy city unto the Lord; wherefore, it could not be a new Jerusalem for it had been in a time of old; but it should be built up again, and become a holy city of the Lord; and it should be built unto the house of Israel. (Ether 13:3–5)

Latter-day Saints have an abiding interest in the restoration of Old Jerusalem for at least two reasons. First, they are part of the house of Israel and will reverence two Jerusalems during the coming millennial reign of God. The restored Old Jerusalem in the Holy Land will become an abode of the Lord, along with the New Jerusalem on the American continent. Second, according to modern prophetic utterance, the restoration of Old Jerusalem must precede the Second Coming of Christ. Joseph Smith said: "Judah must return, Jerusalem must be rebuilt, and the temple, and water come out from under the temple, and the waters of the Dead Sea be healed. It will take some time to rebuild the walls of the city and the temple, etc.; and all this must be done before the Son of Man will make His appearance."[36]

So important was the idea of a restored Jerusalem to the rabbis, beginning with those at Jabneh, that their yearnings for a fulfillment of all the positive prophetic promises concerning Jerusalem became part of their liturgy. The mention of Jerusalem became obligatory in all the statutory prayers of the Jewish people. The most important of these is the *Amidah,* or eighteen benedictions, which formed a central part of the synagogue worship service and which are still recited daily by pious Jews as they stand facing Jerusalem. Some of the specific petitions of the *Amidah* originated during the Temple service and were probably incorporated into the structure of the eighteen benedictions sometime soon after 70. Others were created anew by the rabbis.[37] The most powerful is the fourteenth benediction, which is devoted entirely to Jerusalem. It petitions God: "Return in mercy to thy city Jerusalem and dwell in it as

thou hast promised; rebuild it soon, in our days, as an everlasting structure, and speedily establish in it the throne of David. Blessed art thou, O
Lord, Builder of Jerusalem."[38]

Latter-day Saints, like the rabbis, wait for the day when such things
are completely realized. More like Christians of the early Middle Ages
and less like the rabbinic sages of the Talmudic period, however, Latter-
day Saints also believe in and look forward to the descent of the heavenly
Jerusalem, along with its Temple. This heavenly Jerusalem is the proto-
type for the earthly city, rather than, as the rabbis believed, the earthly
Jerusalem being the pattern for the heavenly Jerusalem.[39] An American
prophet said: "It [the American continent] was the place of the New
Jerusalem, which should come down out of heaven, and the holy sanctuary of the Lord. Behold, Ether saw the days of Christ, and he spake
concerning a New Jerusalem upon this land. . . . And that a New
Jerusalem should be built up upon this land, unto the remnant of the
seed of Joseph, for which things there has been a type" (Ether 13:3–6).

When the petitions of the sages and all the words of the prophets
are fulfilled, it will be a glorious day indeed for Jerusalem and her admir-
ers.

NOTES

1. When John Hyrcanus, at first a supporter of the Pharisees, reconstituted the Sanhedrin,
   he packed it with Pharisaic members and ruled the country by means of the great council. But when the Pharisees objected to his combining the high priesthood with temporal power, Hyrcanus became irritated and went over to the Sadducees.

2. Epstein, *Judaism*, 89.

3. Jerusalem Talmud, Sanhedrin 10:5, gives the number of sects and parties as twenty-four.

4. Kotker, *Earthly Jerusalem*, 120.

5. Kotker, *Earthly Jerusalem*, 112.

6. Cited in Kotker, *Earthly Jerusalem*, 112–13.

7. Avot de-Rabbi Nathan (2d ed.), 7.21, in *Encyclopedia Judaica*, 10:152, s.v. "Johanan Ben
   Zakkai." The terms *heikal* and *tefillin* are Hebrew for, respectively, "inner sanctuary of
   the Temple," and "phylacteries," small leather boxes containing verses of scripture worn
   on the forehead and left arm during Jewish worship services.

8. *Encyclopedia Judaica*, 10:153, s.v. "Johanan Ben Zakkai."

9. Eban, *Heritage*, 100.

10. See the explanation in one of the most famous rabbinic works entitled Ethics of the

Fathers (Pirke Avot) 1:1. A good source for this work is Birnbaum, *Daily Prayer Book,* 477–78.

11. Russell, *Between the Testaments,* 67.

12. Russell, *Between the Testaments,* 68.

13. *Anchor Bible Dictionary,* 6:367.

14. Babylonian Talmud, Bava Kamma 82b, Arakhin 32b. See also *Encyclopedia Judaica,* 9:1553–55, s.v. "Jerusalem."

15. Babylonian Talmud, Yoma 21a; Pirke Avot 5:5.

16. Tosefta Nega'im 6:2.

17. Bava Kamma 82b.

18. Babylonian Talmud, Berakhot 30a; Tosefta Nedarim 1:4. See *Encyclopedia Judaica,* 9:1553, s.v. "Jerusalem."

19. Babylonian Talmud, Bava Batra 60b, in *Encyclopedia Judaica,* 9:1555–56, s.v. "Jerusalem."

20. Jacobs, *Book of Jewish Practice,* 43.

21. Babylonian Talmud, Kiddushin 49b.

22. Babylonian Talmud, Sukkah 51b.

23. Midrash Tehillin (Psalms) 76:3, in *Encyclopedia Judaica,* 9:1557, s.v. "Jerusalem."

24. *Encyclopedia Judaica,* 10:152, s.v. "Johanan Ben Zakkai."

25. *Encyclopedia Judaica,* 10:152, s.v. "Johanan Ben Zakkai."

26. See the excellent, brief summary of many rabbinic passages in Kotker, *Earthly Jerusalem,* 119–20.

27. Jerusalem Talmud, Yoma 1:1; *Babylonian Talmud,* Yoma 9b, in *Encyclopedia Judaica,* 9:1557, s.v. "Jerusalem."

28. McConkie, *Millennial Messiah,* 298.

29. Tanhuma No'ah 11, in *Encyclopedia Judaica,* 9:1559, s.v. "Jerusalem."

30. *Encyclopedia Judaica,* 9:1559, s.v. "Jerusalem."

31. Babylonian Talmud, Bava Batra 75b.

32. See the midrashic collection entitled *Exodus Rabba* 15:21.

33. *Encyclopedia Judaica,* 9:1558–59, s.v. "Jerusalem."

34. Babylonian Talmud, Ta'anit 5a, in *Encyclopedia Judaica,* 9:1560, s.v. "Jerusalem."

35. *Encyclopedia Judaica,* 9:1560, s.v. "Jerusalem."

36. Smith, *Teachings of the Prophet Joseph Smith,* 286.

37. Kotker, *Earthly Jerusalem,* 120.

38. Birnbaum, *Daily Prayer Book,* 90.

39. That the rabbis believed the heavenly Jerusalem to be modeled or fashioned after the earthly Jerusalem seems to be in little doubt. "The heavenly Jerusalem 'was fashioned out of great love for the earthly Jerusalem.'" See the rabbinic collection Tanhuma, Pekudei, 1, in *Encyclopedia Judaica,* 9:1560, s.v. "Jerusalem."

14

Byzantine Jerusalem, A.D. 324–638

For more than two centuries after the destruction of the Temple, Jerusalem was governed by pagan rulers who attached no extraordinary religious significance to the Holy City. But in the fourth century after Christ all of that changed. By 311 Constantine the Great (311–337) had emerged as coruler of the vast Roman Empire. His influence on Christianity was felt beginning in 313 when he issued his Edict of Milan, granting Christianity favored status among the religions of the empire. In 324 Constantine became master of the entire empire and thus all of Palestine as well. He chose to reside in the eastern part of his empire and built a new capital he named Constantinople after himself. The new city was built on the site of a former Greek outpost known as Byzantium on the Bosphorus Strait, a thousand miles east of Rome. The Roman Empire continued, but it acquired a decidedly Greek flavor with the name Byzantine. These events were not inconsequential for Jerusalem. Churchmen and Christian governors began to make new plans for the Holy City.

At the Council of Nicaea, convened by Emperor Constantine in 325, Makarios, bishop of Jerusalem, reported on the status of Christian holy sites in the city. He immediately obtained permission to remove the Roman Temple of Aphrodite (Venus) from the site that tradition maintained was that of the Holy Sepulchre. He also encouraged the emperor's mother, Helena, to visit the Christian holy places,[1] which she did in 326, at the age of seventy-nine. At the same time, new discoveries were made, traditions about the locations of certain events were firmly linked to specific geographical locations, and new traditions were promoted. In short, Jerusalem was transformed, in both status and appearance, and the Byzantine period of the city's history began.

The Byzantine phase of Jerusalem's history shaped Christianity's understanding of the city's history and spiritual significance. Christianity began then to view Jerusalem itself as a shrine of preeminent holiness, marking the spiritual center of the cosmos.[2] Ironically, "Christian Jerusalem" really began in the Byzantine period rather than at the time of Christ. Jerusalem of the fourth through the seventh centuries was seen as the New Jerusalem of prophecy—and Christians believed it was to be their exclusive possession.[3] In their worldview, Jerusalem was a Jewish city or a pagan city before the Byzantine period. Nevertheless, Robert Wilken notes:

> As the generations passed and Palestine became a Christian country— indeed, the Christian country par excellence—a slow turning took place in Christian attitudes toward the land. What transpired in Jerusalem and Judea has no parallel elsewhere in Christian memory or experience. No other city, not even Rome, has the same place in Christian affection and imagination. What happened to Christians during the fourth to seventh centuries has parallels to the experiences of the Israelites centuries earlier. Christians began to think of Jerusalem as their city, indeed as *the* Christian city, and Palestine as a place set apart.[4]

CONSTANTINE'S AND HELENA'S JERUSALEM

After the Council of Nicaea, Constantine became more than just a political leader. He began to be accepted as a divinely appointed director of both spiritual and secular life. Contemporary writers referred to him as a thirteenth apostle, which laid the foundation for the practice of *Caesaropapism* in the Byzantine Empire (in which the ruler is both caesar and pope, head of state and head of the church). The emperor appointed clergymen and defined dogma, settled theological disputes, and used the wealth of the state to serve the church (and vice versa). Once Jerusalem came firmly under the control of Constantine, the city's Christianization accelerated. No longer Aelia Capitolina, Jerusalem had become an important capital of Christian faith. Greatly influenced by his mother's Christian conviction and her visit to Palestine, the emperor began to build and endow splendid Christian churches in Constantinople, Rome, Asia Minor, and Jerusalem. He also consecrated sites in

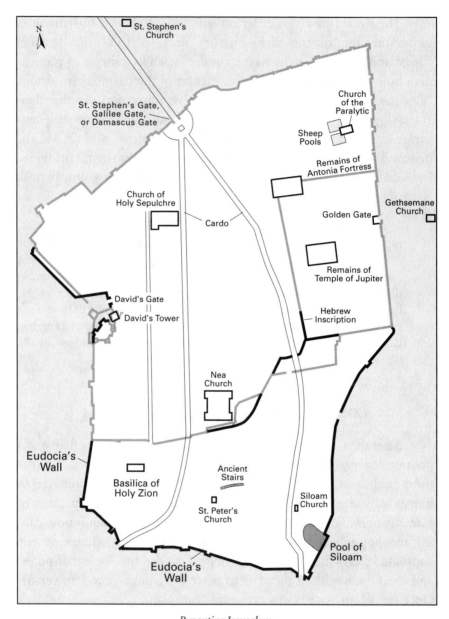

Byzantine Jerusalem

Palestine associated with Christ's birth, life, death, burial, resurrection, and ascension.[5]

Constantine ordered the Church of the Holy Sepulchre to be built in place of the demolished Temple of Aphrodite. This structure was one of the first major changes in the landscape of Byzantine Jerusalem. The builders of the church used some of the remains of the pagan temple, which are still visible today.[6] The significance of the spot on which the church was built, at least for Roman Catholic and Greek Orthodox Christians, lies in their belief that the church was constructed over both the Rock of Crucifixion (Golgotha) and the very tomb where Jesus was laid to rest on the third day before his resurrection. An eyewitness to the building excavations, Eusebius, the fourth-century historian and bishop of Caesarea, records: "At once the work was carried out, and, as layer after layer of the subsoil came into our view, the venerable and most holy memorial of the Savior's resurrection, beyond all our hopes, came into view."[7] According to a tradition dating from 351, Helena found fragments of the actual cross of crucifixion in a cave or cistern adjacent to the Rock of Crucifixion during her tour of Jerusalem in 326. Unfortunately, the late provenance of the tradition makes it problematic.

The site where the Church of the Holy Sepulchre was built was at that time called the "Martyrium," and so the church was called by that name as well.[8] Eusebius left us a fairly detailed description of the edifice. It consisted of four main sections: the atrium, an internal courtyard entered via the Cardo, or main street, of Jerusalem; the basilica, or large prayer hall, entered through one of three entrances from the atrium; the Triforum, or "Holy Garden," a large colonnaded courtyard housing what was believed to be the Rock of Golgotha (by then cut down to a large cube); and the rotunda, a large circular structure covered by a golden dome in Byzantine style, under which the supposed tomb of Jesus lay and which was the focal point of the entire structure.[9] The question of whether the Church of the Holy Sepulchre preserves the site of Jesus' crucifixion continues to be debated, and there are compelling reasons to look elsewhere for it.

The facade of the church in Byzantine times faced east and pointed out to the Cardo (the main entrance today is on the south side). The design of the building was deliberate. Worshippers moved through the four sections of the building, from the atrium to the rotunda, in similitude of the stages of the Savior's passion and thus, by extension, through gradations of sanctity. The church was planned and built by the architects Zenobius and Eusthatius of Constantinople[10] and was consecrated on 14 September 335, though the rotunda was probably not finished until sometime after 340. This event was also the occasion of a church council at Jerusalem. One scholar noted: "This council took place ten years after the first Ecumenical Council at Nicaea, the scene of a major controversy regarding the divine and human aspects of Jesus Christ and which led to the split in the Christian world. As a consequence of the Jerusalem Council, the Christian world was reunified and the holiness of Jerusalem was considered to have increased by virtue of the fact that it induced a spirit of peace among all Christians."[11]

Other churches in Palestine were constructed during Constantine's lifetime. But according to Eusebius, the emperor's building program was really directed by his mother, Helena.[12] She was interested in all the traditional sites that were venerated for their association with Christ's ministry. In particular she focused her attention on three caves linked to the "key mysteries of the faith." These included the birth cave in Bethlehem, the rock-cut tomb near Golgotha, and the cave on the Mount of Olives associated with the Ascension.[13] Helena ordered churches to be built over these caves. As we have already noted, the Church of the Holy Sepulchre was built over the traditional site of Golgotha. The first church in Bethlehem, an octagonal chapel situated directly above the cave of the Nativity, was dedicated by Helena on 31 May 339. According to the apocryphal work The Acts of John, a cave on the Mount of Olives was the place where Jesus taught his disciples during his forty-day postresurrection ministry. By 333, Helena had apparently directed the construction of a church over this cave, for a new basilica was seen that year by an early European Christian pilgrim to the Holy Land, a person early medieval documents call the Bordeaux Pilgrim. This church in Byzantine times was called "Eleona" (from Greek *elaion,* meaning "of olives"). It was destroyed in 614 by the Persians. Nevertheless, "the memory of Jesus' teaching remained, but there was a significant shift in its content. It tended to become the place where he taught the disciples the Our Father [the 'Lord's Prayer']." Today, the Church of the Pater Noster (Latin for "Our Father") occupies the ground.[14]

In addition to his impressive building program, Constantine encouraged pilgrimages to the Holy Land. Constantine recognized that Christians wanted to, in the words of Origen, "trace the footsteps of Jesus."[15] And pilgrims did travel to Jerusalem from many different countries, espousing different doctrinal views: Ethiopians, Armenians, Copts, Syrians, and, above all, Greek Orthodox, who became the dominant Christian power in the city. [16] An inscription in the Armenian chapel of the Church of the Holy Sepulchre displaying the words "O Lord we have come," together with a crude picture of a boat, indicates that the traveler to Jerusalem had come some distance. [17]

These pilgrimages stimulated the development of Jerusalem in all areas. Next to the south end of the Temple Mount, Byzantine Christians built baths and houses, which were later buried beneath three vast structures of the Islamic Umayyads in the eighth century. The picture presented by archaeological investigation is one of relative opulence.[18] The travels of the Bordeaux Pilgrim to Jerusalem in 333 are the first and best-known example of the pilgrimages that occurred,[19] and his observations are an important source of information about Jerusalem during the time of Constantine. He describes several features of the city and its environs, especially the new basilicas at Bethlehem, Mamre, and the Mount of Olives. He also discloses contemporary beliefs about where events of Christ's life took place. He mentions the Temple Mount, including its subterranean structures and water systems; the pinnacle of the Temple, where the Lord was tempted; the House of Caiaphas; the Praetorium in the Tyropoeon Valley, where Jesus was arraigned before Pilate, and the column where Christ was scourged; and the Church of the Holy Sepulchre, which was still under construction.[20]

The example of the Bordeaux Pilgrim also shows that Christians continued to visit the site of the Temple, but they did not build any significant structure there. Nothing was stated concretely in Byzantine times about the rationale for such a practice, but the tenth-century historian Eutychius (940) provided the reason for this unspoken policy. He makes it clear that Christians considered the words of Jesus, recorded in Matthew 23:38 and 24:2, to be a curse pronounced upon the Temple area: "Behold, your house is left unto you desolate," and "There shall not be left here one stone upon another, that shall not be thrown down." Christians believed he meant nothing other than the Temple. Thus, concludes Eutychius, "On this account the Christians left it [the Temple Mount] desolate, and built no church upon it."[21] Apparently Helena, Constantine, and others were in harmony with this belief.

Many of the holy sites visited today by tourists in Jerusalem, and venerated worldwide by Catholic and Orthodox Christians, owe their memorialization to Constantine and Helena. By the end of the emperor's life, Jerusalem had assumed a predominantly Christian character. The Roman prohibition against Jews entering the city was again strictly enforced (with the exception of the annual visit to the Temple Mount on the ninth of Av), and Jerusalem steadily grew in importance as a Christian center.[22] As laudable as the achievements of Constantine might seem, it still must be remembered that he did not always help Christianity, for he influenced and altered its doctrines. With Constantine, for the first time, the church came under the direction of a political head of state, one who did not even officially accept the faith until the end of his life; and it took a nineteenth-century restoration of divine truths to set aright the course of Christ's original institution. Perhaps, then, it is legitimate to ask, If the doctrines, tenets, and truths of the Christian faith were changed by the Emperor Constantine, how sure can we be of the geographical sites he and Helena chose to immortalize?

JERUSALEM IN THE LATER FOURTH CENTURY

During the reign of Emperor Julian (361–363), later called the Apostate, there was a short-lived halt to the practice of Christianity in Jerusalem. Though a nephew of Constantine and raised in his uncle's household, Julian considered paganism the authentic religion and attempted to reinstitute it throughout the empire. In addition, he not only favored Judaism but even revoked the ban on Jews in the Holy City and ordered the reconstruction of their Temple in 363. This was in part a deliberate affront to Christians, who viewed the destroyed Temple as fulfillment of Christ's words, as well as validation of the triumph of their cause.[23] On the southern section of the western retaining wall of the Temple Mount, recent excavations show a carving made by an excited Jewish pilgrim to the city during that time, an altered version of the Hebrew text of Isaiah 66:14: "And when you see this [the restored Temple?], your heart shall rejoice and their [the Bible reads "your"] bones shall flourish like an herb."[24]

The noted Latter-day Saint historian and biographer Andrew Jenson saw in the reign of Emperor Julian an illustration of the inability of humans to interfere with the designs of God. Writing in 1895, Jenson described how the apostles of Jesus asked their master for a sign of his Second Coming and the end of the world. Jesus replied that Jerusalem would "be trodden down of the Gentiles, until the times of the Gentiles be fulfilled" (Luke 21:24). Even Julian the Apostate could not alter this prophecy. In Jenson's words, the Emperor was

> a man who hated the Christian as he hated his bitterest enemy. His greatest desire was to show to the world that Christ was not a prophet, that he was not the Savior of mankind, that his words were no greater, and no more importance need be attached to them than to the words of any other man. In looking over the declarations of the Savior, he saw this prediction: "Jerusalem shall be trodden down of the Gentiles, until the times of the Gentiles shall be fulfilled;" and this man, who had at his command the combined wealth of the then civilized world, who had at his command armies which had conquered almost the whole civilized world, issued an edict, promulgated a decree, in which he granted to the Jews the privilege of returning to Jerusalem, building up their city and reconstructing their temple. . . . When the decree was issued by Julian, the Jews went in great multitudes. They carried their treasure with them. They labored cheerfully, believing that the time had come when the words of the prophets would be fulfilled, that the blessings which had been promised to their fathers would be verified. Julian was not content with this. He said: "In order that I may make this thing sure, in order that I may demonstrate that my word is greater than the words of Jesus of Nazareth, I will go up myself." And he went, with his treasures, with his army, and his whole efforts were directed to the accomplishment of this work which he had set out to do. But the times of the Gentiles had not yet come in. Jerusalem was yet to be trodden under foot until that time should arrive, and that temple was destined not then to be built. It was utterly impossible for him to accomplish that work.[25]

Before much of anything could be done to rebuild the Temple, a fire broke out among the stores of materials, apparently the result of an earthquake.[26] Subsequently, Julian's death in Persia on 16 June 363 while he was campaigning against the Persians in Mesopotamia and the ascendance of a fervently Christian emperor, Jovian, put an end to the Temple restoration project.

During the reigns of Jovian and his successors, several important Catholic bishops held the holy see in Jerusalem. The first was the great preacher and theologian Cyril. During his tenure as bishop (350–386)

Christian pilgrims from Britain, Gaul, Ethiopia, India, Persia, and Italy flocked to Jerusalem.[27] These pilgrims perpetuated all kinds of traditions about where certain events had taken place, and, as a result, commemorative buildings were built. Some of the preserved sites may have been quite accurate, as with the earliest church built at Bethany to identify the place where Lazarus was raised from the dead. That church was destroyed by an earthquake after 390.[28]

Monks who had practiced their ascetic ways in other parts of the Roman Empire, in Armenia or Cappadocia, for example, also left their native lands to live in the deserts nearest Jerusalem. Some of these monks saw themselves in the symbolic mold of Abraham, to whom God said "Go . . . to the land that I will show you" (Gen. 12:1; translation from the Hebrew). They called themselves inhabitants of "this holy land," meaning the land surrounding Jerusalem.[29]

The arrival of these practitioners of Christianity reflected the increasing tendency of the church to bestow upon the city of Jerusalem and the land around it "the laurels that rightfully belonged to the Temple."[30] Though the land certainly was holy, this transfer of sanctity to sites and buildings within Jerusalem reveals, in the words of Hugh Nibley, "Christian envy of the Temple."[31] That is one reason why the cultural atmosphere of Byzantine Jerusalem developed the way it did. In every ancient culture, temples represented the meeting place of heaven and earth. The destruction of the Temple in Jerusalem left a gaping hole in the life of the Christian movement after the first century, especially its theology. Thus, "many Christian writers have expressed the conviction that the church possesses no adequate substitute for the Temple."[32] After the first century, Christianity seems always to have been looking for a surrogate to replace the rituals as well as the physical structure of the Temple.

FIFTH-CENTURY JERUSALEM

Cyril's successor was Bishop John II (386–417). During his episcopate several aristocratic and wealthy families left Rome and settled in Jerusalem, lured by the presence of the holy places. They were led by the famous scholar Hieronymous Sophronius, or St. Jerome (340–420). Among them were two notable women, Melania and Poemenia, whose piety and largesse made the Mount of Olives a gathering place for religious men and women. They endowed and built churches and monasteries in or around Jerusalem, including the Church of the Ascension (378) and the Church of Gethsemane (390).[33]

Melania, perhaps the most famous female aristocrat-turned-ascetic, had renounced her husband and children to pursue a monastic life in the East. Such was the pull of the land of Christ's nativity. Like Poemenia she first traveled to Egypt but eventually settled in Jerusalem. There she and her friend Rufinus founded a monastery and hospice on the Mount of Olives. These institutions attracted other well-connected pilgrims who knew they would not only be welcome coworkers in the kingdom but also live at a Christian crossroads where they could hear the latest ecclesiastical gossip.[34] Not to be outdone by Melania and Rufinus, Jerome and a female companion named Paula founded a monastery in Bethlehem near Helena's Church of the Nativity. This establishment fostered tension with the other monastery on the Mount of Olives, a circumstance hardly in harmony with Christ's teachings.[35]

During the early fifth century the prestige of Jerusalem increased significantly within the church. One new structure of the period that accorded greater status to the city was the Basilica of Holy Zion, erected in 390 by Bishop John. Built on the site where the Church of the Apostles had stood since 347, and possessing especially large and impressive dimensions, the Basilica of Holy Zion was called the "Mother of all Churches." For a time, it housed the remains of St. Stephen, the early Christian martyr.[36]

As a result of Jerusalem's increasing prestige in the Christian world, Juvenal, who was appointed bishop of Jerusalem in 428, assumed the authority and standing of patriarch in the church hierarchy, though he was not authorized by church leaders to do so. He put forward his claims at the Council of Ephesus, but they were rejected. Then, in 451, owing to his leadership and maneuvering, he was officially appointed to that office, and Jerusalem was elevated to the status of Patriarchate of the Orthodox Church—meaning that it was officially regarded as one of five centers of church leadership along with Rome, Antioch, Alexandria, and Constantinople. As patriarch, Juvenal gained authority over all the churches of Palestine and Arabia.[37]

EUDOKIA'S JERUSALEM

In 438, the wife of Emperor Theodosius II, Empress Eudokia, visited Jerusalem for the first time. She became enamored of the city, and when in 444 she had a falling out with her family (in particular the Emperor's sister, Pulcheria) she was exiled to Jerusalem, where she lived until her death in 460. She ruled Palestine on account of her rank.[38] More than any other individual except Helena, Eudokia changed the face of Jerusalem in the Byzantine period.

Under Eudokia, Jews were again allowed to live legally in Jerusalem. She spent lavish sums to build churches and restore other city structures. She built the episcopal palace on the northwest side of the Church of the Holy Sepulchre. She funded a new church built on the site of the house of Caiaphas, the high priest, another at the traditional site of Pentecost (where the Holy Spirit visited the apostles, as described in Acts 2), and a church overhanging the Pool of Siloam dedicated to the Virgin Mary. Her last act was building a basilica outside the north gate of Jerusalem (today's Damascus Gate), called St. Stephen's. The edifice was completed in 460, and the martyr's remains and relics were transferred there from the basilica on Mount Zion. Eudokia was also buried there.[39]

Eudokia's name is especially associated with the construction of a southern wall around Jerusalem, which enclosed the City of David, the Tyropoeon Valley, and the Western Hill, which was called Mount Zion. (This wall was excavated in 1896.) Eudokia viewed her participation in the construction of the wall as fulfillment of Psalms 51:18: "Do good in thy good pleasure unto Zion: build thou the walls of Jerusalem." The Greek word for good pleasure is *eudokia*.[40]

Toward the end of Eudokia's life in Jerusalem, she became embroiled in a theological dispute that divided Christianity. The Monophysite Controversy—a wrenching conflict over the nature of Christ's person—gained Eudokia's support. The Monophysites claimed that Christ contained within his person a single, wholly divine nature. At the other end of the theological spectrum were the Nestorians, theologians who saw Christ as two distinct persons, human and divine. Centered in Alexandria, the Monophysites won supporters in Armenia, Egypt, and Syria, and caused the formation of separate churches that persist today. The Egyptian Monophysites called themselves Copts, and the Syrian Monophysites became the Jacobites. A Monophysite monk named Theodosius was appointed bishop of Jerusalem, and Juvenal returned as patriarch only with the help of a Byzantine army.[41]

In 451 a majority of orthodox bishops convened the Council of Chalcedon and declared Monophysites as well as Nestorians to be heretics. The orthodox position was a compromise: Christ was both perfect God and perfect man. His two natures, though different, were inseparably combined in the single person of Jesus Christ. Eudokia looked at the confusion in the church, sought advice from a holy man named Simeon Stylites (who lived on top of a pillar near Antioch), and finally was reconciled with the orthodox position.[42]

Though Eudokia was by far the most important and influential person of fifth-century Jerusalem, another fascinating personality was active in the Holy City during the later years of the century. Known as Peter the Iberian, he is noteworthy not only because he founded a monastery near David's Tower (at today's Jaffa Gate) but also because his biography gives much information about the physical appearance of Jerusalem, including the many churches built during the fourth and fifth centuries. We find in his biography first-time references to churches erected on the ruins of the Praetorium (where the "trial" of Jesus took place) and a church built on the dam that divided the two Sheep's Pools.[43]

SIXTH-CENTURY JERUSALEM

Jerusalem reached its peak during the Byzantine period under the Emperor Justinian, who ruled from 527 to 565. Justinian is known for his monumental building projects throughout the empire, and in this regard there is reason to believe that he saw himself in the mold of the great Israelite kings. His greatest architectural triumph was the Church of the Hagia Sophia (Church of the Holy Wisdom) in Constantinople, one of the largest Christian churches in the world. At its dedication, Justinian is reported to have exclaimed: "Glory to God who has judged me worthy of accomplishing such a work as this. O Solomon, I have outdone thee!"[44] Justinian was encouraged in his projects by his brilliant and beautiful wife, the former prostitute Theodora.

Little wonder, then, that Jerusalem at the time of Justinian was truly a city of churches. A pilgrim named Theodosius, who traveled from the

Byzantine capital to Jerusalem, counted twenty-four churches on the Mount of Olives alone. In 529 a Samaritan revolt devastated parts of Jerusalem. Justinian rebuilt the destroyed churches and added a magnificent basilica, the Nea ("new one"), within the Holy City. Consecrated in 543, the Nea Church was one of the most splendid in the empire. Its official name was "The New Church of St. Mary, Mother of God." It was destroyed by the Muslims in the eighth or ninth century.[45]

The Nea Church was discovered in excavations of the Jewish Quarter of the Old City after 1967. Most of the church was in the southern sector of the Jewish Quarter and a small part outside the present-day southern wall of the Old City. Before archaeological investigation was possible, it was known from the writings of Procopius, a biographer and historian who lived during Justinian's time, that the Nea was actually a complex of buildings covering a large area. In addition to the church there was a monastery, hostel, hospital, and library.[46]

This stage of the city's development is also shown in another valuable source, the Madaba Map, a sixth-century creation discovered in a church in the town of Madaba, east of the Jordan River. This mosaic map depicts the land of Palestine, its towns and cities, with Jerusalem represented in a scale of approximately 1:1600.[47] It furnishes us with many significant details of the Holy City. Justinian's two most impressive projects completed in Jerusalem are portrayed in the map: the Nea and the Cardo. Inside the north gate (today's Damascus Gate) is shown a semicircular plaza with a column in its center (still commemorated in the Arabic name of the north gate—*Bab al-'Amud*, "Gate of the Column"). Extending southward from the plaza are the two colonnaded streets forming the Cardo. The western branch of the Cardo passed the Church of the Holy Sepulchre and continued on to Zion Gate by way of the Nea Church. The other branch of the Cardo passed a public bath and ended at an inner city gate. The Temple Mount at this time was a wasteland, with only a few scattered buildings.[48]

EARLY SEVENTH-CENTURY JERUSALEM

The end of Jerusalem's Byzantine period began with the conquest of the city by the Persians in 614 and was finished with the Muslim conquest of 638. Various groups of Persians had been attacking Roman interests since 41 B.C., but in A.D. 224 warriors known as the Sassanians conquered the Parthians and created a powerful new Sassanid Persian Empire. Border disputes between Rome and the Persians became commonplace until the year 611, when they reached a climax. Led by King Chosroes II (590–628), the Persian forces carried out an invasion that destroyed three centuries of Christian building in the Holy Land. The reputation of Jerusalem played an important role in this invasion.[49]

The Holy City by that time had become famous for its numerous treasures and accumulated wealth from contributions made by pilgrims and Byzantine officials throughout the empire. Thus, conquering Jerusalem became an important objective for the Persians, who wished to enrich their royal treasury. A post-Byzantine source proposes that another motive of Rome's eastern antagonists was their desire to overthrow Christian sovereignty and prove the inferior status of Christianity. Whatever the motive or combination of motives, the conquest of Jerusalem began in 614 without any bloodshed. Some of the inhabitants of the city opened the gates to the Persian commander, Shahr Baraz, who left only a garrison to control the city. After a brief period of quiet, the Jerusalemites revolted against the garrison, wiping them out. Shahr Baraz returned and laid siege to Jerusalem for twenty-one days. As the Persian forces mounted their assaults, the Patriarch Zacharias, who saw in the attacks punishment from God for the immorality prevalent in the city, advised surrender. The people refused to listen to him, and the army of Shahr Baraz finally entered Jerusalem, at once bathing its streets with the blood of those who could not fight back—old men, women, and children. Churches were destroyed, and crucifixes trodden under foot. Some thirty-three thousand inhabitants were slaughtered.[50]

Tradition-laden accounts of these events claim that the Jews opened the city gates and then participated with the Persians in the slaughter of Christians at the Mamilla Pool. Such traditions indicate the hatred that existed between Jew and Christian at that time. Many Christians who were not killed were sold into slavery, and prisoners who were thought likely to be useful to the Persians were carried away captive to Ctesiphon, the Persian capital. Among them was the Patriarch Zacharias, who went carrying the relic of the "true" or Holy Cross found by Helena and kept in the Church of the Holy Sepulchre.[51]

One hardly needs to be reminded of the tremendous irony of these events compared with those of A.D. 70. This time it was the Christians who were massacred and enslaved and their sacred symbols plundered. This time it was the beloved and holy Jerusalem of the Christians that was left devastated and ruined, once again "trodden down of the Gentiles," a shadow of its former glory—and Christians wept over it. A poem written by Sophronius, later patriarch of Jerusalem, lamented the fall of the city in 614:

> Holy City of God
> Home of the most valiant saints
> Great Jerusalem
> What kind of lament should I offer you?
> Children of the blessed Christians
> Come to mourn high crested Jerusalem
> In the face of such tragedy
> The flow of my tears is too brief
> The dirge of my heart
> Too measured before such suffering.[52]

The sack of Jerusalem caused theologians to confront an arresting and uncomfortable question, one that made honest Christian thinkers down through the centuries ponder their traditional attitudes toward the Jews and their own relationship to them: If expulsion from Jerusalem was proof of divine rejection of the Jews, did the principle not hold true for their Christian successors?[53]

The Persians ruled Jerusalem for only fifteen years. The Byzantine Emperor Heraclius (610–641) set out in 622 to drive the invaders from his empire. Following a series of victories, he signed a peace treaty with the Persian king, stipulating that the Persians withdraw from the territories of the Byzantine Empire and the Holy Cross be returned to the Christians in Jerusalem. The emperor arrived in the Holy City by way of the Golden Gate at the head of a triumphal procession, carrying the Cross over the Temple platform and back to the Church of the Holy Sepulchre on 21 March 631. The remains of the Cross did not stay in Jerusalem, however, but were sent to Constantinople by Heraclius in 633. In the meantime, the monk Modestus restored some of Jerusalem's destroyed churches, including the Church of the Holy Sepulchre.[54]

Though the Christians could claim technically that they did not stay beaten, their Holy City was only a shadow of its former self. Hardly any Christian monument surviving the Persian siege failed to show the cracks and scars of the devastation. Likewise, both Byzantines and Persians were so exhausted that the whole of Palestine fell to the Arab advance, despite desperate battles by the Christians. Moreover, the fate of Jerusalem in the seventh century caused theologians to rethink their beliefs about Byzantine Jerusalem. Perhaps it was not the New Jerusalem of prophecy. Indeed, they forged an eschatology that centered on a heavenly Jerusalem. And for a time the ancient promise to Abraham that his descendants—whom the Christians believed they were—would possess the land of Canaan was divorced from the fate of the earthly city of Jerusalem. Yet the idea of a holy people tangibly possessing the Holy Land—especially the Holy City—in this life and on this earth did not disappear forever. It reappeared four hundred years later in Christian Europe.[55]

Notes

1. Avi-Yonah, *Jerusalem*, 43.

2. Nibley, *Mormonism and Early Christianity*, 323.

3. Of course this is not scriptural. The promise given to Abraham was that his posterity (no qualifier) would inherit the land *when* they hearkened to the voice of the Lord. Nibley has written: "From Origen's time to the present, churchmen of all sects have been one in insisting that the New Jerusalem is for Christians only, since the Jewish city can never rise again. In the absence of scriptural support for this claim various stock arguments are used." *Mormonism and Early Christianity*, 325.

4. Wilken, *Land Called Holy*, xiv.

5. Bahat, *Illustrated Atlas of Jerusalem*, 70. For the churches built by Constantine, as well as his life as it relates to the rise of Christianity, see Jones, *Constantine and the Conversion of Europe*, 88, 153–54, 176–78, 192.

6. Bahat, *Illustrated Atlas of Jerusalem*, 70.

7. Eusebius, *Life of Constantine*, 3.28, as quoted in Murphy-O'Connor, *Holy Land*, 50.

8. Asali, *Jerusalem in History*, 94.

9. See the excellent diagram and description in Bahat, *Illustrated Atlas of Jerusalem*, 71.

10. Avi-Yonah, *Jerusalem*, 43.

11. Bahat, *Illustrated Atlas of Jerusalem*, 70.

12. Eusebius, *Life of Constantine*, 3.41.

13. See the excellent summary in Murphy-O'Connor, *Holy Land*, 128–29.

14. Murphy-O'Connor, *Holy Land*, 128–29. See also Wilken, *Land Called Holy*, 109.

15. Wilken, *Land Called Holy,* 108.

16. Ben-Arieh and Sapir, *A Collection of Papers,* 13–14.

17. Bahat, *Illustrated Atlas of Jerusalem,* 70. See also Hunt, *Holy Land Pilgrimage.*

18. See the detailed information on Byzantine residential quarters recovered by archaeologists in Ben-Dov, *Shadow of the Temple,* 243–59.

19. According to historians, there is no firsthand account of an actual Christian pilgrim's journey to Jerusalem until that of the Latin-speaking traveler of Bordeaux, who arrived four years before Constantine's death. See Wilken, *Land Called Holy,* 109.

20. See Wilken, *Land Called Holy,* 109–10; Bahat, *Illustrated Atlas of Jerusalem,* 70.

21. In Finegan, *Archeology of the New Testament,* 199.

22. Asali, *Jerusalem in History,* 94–95.

23. Mark 13:2 reads: "And Jesus answering said unto him, Seest thou these great buildings? there shall not be left one stone upon another, that shall not be thrown down."

24. Ben-Dov, *Ophel Archaeological Garden,* 13. Ben-Dov attaches eschatological significance to this inscription in light of Julian's reforms: "From the fourth century onward, we found, chapter 66 of Isaiah was interpreted as a reference to the End of Days, the resurrection of the dead, and the national resurrection of the Jewish people with the reconstruction of the Temple. What could be a more promising realization of that vision than the Julian era, a time when it seemed that the interpretation of the verses from Isaiah were actually coming true before one's eyes? . . . In the Bible the wording reads: 'And when ye see this, your heart shall rejoice, and your bones shall flourish like an herb,' while the version on the wall reads 'their bones.' The explanation seems quite logical: 'And when ye see this' refers to the people who will behold the inscription, whereas 'their bones' are those of the dead about to be resurrected." Ben-Dov, *Shadow of the Temple,* 219.

25. Jenson, *Collected Discourses,* vol. 5, 20 Jan. 1895. Though we cannot embrace all of Jenson's statements without critical examination of his historical understanding, his interpretive comments are valuable in light of scripture. His main point is that fulfillment of Jerusalem's prophetic future as decreed by God cannot be altered by human effort, no matter how mighty humans may think they are.

26. Bahat, *Illustrated Atlas of Jerusalem,* 70.

27. Wilken, *Land Called Holy,* 101–25.

28. Murphy-O'Connor, *Holy Land,* 137.

29. Wilken, *Land Called Holy,* xiv–xv.

30. Nibley, *When the Lights Went Out,* 55.

31. Nibley, *When the Lights Went Out,* 55.

32. Nibley, *When the Lights Went Out,* 56.

33. Bahat, *Illustrated Atlas of Jerusalem,* 70.

34. Wilken, *Land Called Holy,* 152–53.

35. Hunt, *Holy Land Pilgrimage,* 174. Numerous scriptures tell us to shun contention. When disciples complained to Jesus about others performing similar tasks, for example, he taught that feelings of rivalry are not appropriate and that sincere and authorized fellow laborers are not rivals in the kingdom.

36. Bahat, *Illustrated Atlas of Jerusalem,* 71.

37. Asali, *Jerusalem in History,* 98. See also Bahat, *Illustrated Atlas of Jerusalem,* 71, though his dates are in error.

38. Asali, *Jerusalem in History,* 98.

39. Asali, *Jerusalem in History,* 98.

40. Asali, *Jerusalem in History,* 98. See also Avi-Yonah, *Jerusalem,* 45.

41. Goldschmidt, *Concise History of the Middle East,* 20.

42. Asali, *Jerusalem in History,* 99.

43. Bahat, *Illustrated Atlas of Jerusalem,* 73–74.

44. Hollister, *Medieval Europe,* 36.

45. Avi-Yonah, *Jerusalem,* 45; Bahat, *Illustrated Atlas of Jerusalem,* 74–75. Ben-Dov, *Shadow of the Temple,* 233–41. An especially good discussion of the Nea Church is in Avigad, *Discovering Jerusalem,* 229–35.

46. Bahat, *Illustrated Atlas of Jerusalem,* 75.

47. Bahat, *Carta's Historical Atlas of Jerusalem,* 36.

48. Avigad, *Discovering Jerusalem,* 211–29.

49. Avigad, *Discovering Jerusalem,* 211–29; see also Asali, *Jerusalem in History,* 100–101; Bahat, *Illustrated Atlas of Jerusalem,* 78–79.

50. Bahat, *Illustrated Atlas of Jerusalem,* 78–79.

51. Bahat, *Illustrated Atlas of Jerusalem,* 78–79; see also Avi-Yonah, *Jerusalem,* 47.

52. Wilken, *Land Called Holy,* 227–28.

53. Nibley, *Mormonism and Early Christianity,* 325.

54. Murphy-O'Connor, *Holy Land,* 50.

55. Wilken, *Land Called Holy,* 245–46.

15

ISLAMIC JERUSALEM, A.D. 638–1099

Islam's association with Jerusalem did not begin until the seventh century because the religion itself did not appear until Muhammad's revolutionary concepts swept across the Arabian peninsula after A.D. 610. In the late sixth century Arabia was far removed from the centers of political power and culture. Its inhabitants belonged to numerous competing tribes led by warrior chieftains called *sheikhs*. Raids on other tribes were common; life was dominated by a warrior ethos. Wealth was derived from the trade routes through the land that transported goods from as far away as India to the east and Ethiopia to the west. It was along one of these routes, the ancient Frankincense Trail, that some scholars believe Lehi and his family traveled with their caravan when they left Jerusalem.[1]

The city of Mecca in particular flourished as a cosmopolitan center in Arabia. Merchants from many places mingled with the indigenous Arab population drawn to Mecca for two reasons. One was the increasing economic opportunities developing there, and the other was religious pilgrimage. Many tribes came annually to Mecca to worship at a shrine called the *Ka'bah* (Arabic, "cube"), a cube-shaped structure of Meccan granite. Embedded in the eastern corner of the building was a black stone that was a cult object for many Arabs before the seventh century after Christ. The Black Stone is of pre-Islamic origin, possibly a meteor fragment. Islamic teaching ascribes it to God, who gave it to Adam to help him obtain forgiveness of sins.

At that time the Arabians were polytheists, though not very pious ones. Above the multitude of *jinn* ("genies") and subordinate gods was the high god, Allah—remote and unapproachable. But in the early seventh century the forces of change were suddenly unleashed as a new prophet, Muhammad, appeared in Mecca. He galvanized the Arab world and propelled it to the forefront of world events. When Muhammad was about forty (A.D. 610), he suddenly proclaimed that the one true God, Allah, had spoken to him through the angel Gabriel and named him as His sole and last prophet or messenger. Allah's actual words given through Muhammad were preserved as the Qur'an.

Islam, like Mormonism, believes that God spoke again from the heavens. But unlike Mormons, Muslims believe that Muhammad was the last of the prophets. Latter-day Saint leaders have nevertheless been generally positive in their remarks about Muhammad. Parley P. Pratt, though not believing that Muhammad was a prophet in the fullest sense of the word, enthusiastically praised him and his religion.[2] In 1855 George A. Smith spoke of Muhammad's direct descent from Ishmael, son of Abraham, through one of the noble families of Arabia—the Quraysh. And even though Muhammad's preaching brought him tremendous persecution, he continued preaching a higher way of life: "There was nothing in his religion to license iniquity or corruption; he preached the moral doctrines which the Savior taught; viz., to do as they would be done by; and not to do violence to any man, nor to render evil for evil; and to worship one God."[3]

For Latter-day Saints, the single most important statement in modern times about Muhammad was issued by the First Presidency on 15 February 1978. It reads, in part: "The great religious leaders of the world such as Mohammed, Confucius, and the Reformers, as well as philosophers including Socrates, Plato, and others, received a portion of God's light. Moral truths were given to them by God to enlighten whole nations and to bring a higher level of understanding to individuals."[4]

Without doubt Muhammad was a messenger bearing some of God's teachings. He presented "a revelation" of magnitude to the warring, impious, polytheistic tribes of the Arabian peninsula. It revolutionized their way of life. But to ascribe to Muhammad the same kind of prophetic office and powers as Joseph Smith possessed goes too far. One LDS scholar on Islam has written that there is "clear reason to believe that, if the text of the Qur'an as we now have it actually goes back to Muhammad, which is likely, he was mistaken on certain issues too central to the Gospel as it has been revealed to the Latter-day Saints for us to be able to endorse or accept him as a prophet in the fullest sense."[5]

Muhammad taught that those who believe in Allah and submit, or surrender, to his will (*Islam* means "submission") are assured of happiness and a reward in heaven. Duties required of each follower or "surrenderer" (*Muslim* means "one who surrenders") are the five basic pillars of Islam: prayer, alms-giving, fasting, pilgrimage to Mecca, and confession of the faith ("there is no God but Allah and Muhammad is his prophet"). At first Muhammad's preaching gained only a few converts, but by 630 his following became strong enough to recapture Mecca, from whence he had been forced to flee eight years earlier. After this feat many Arab tribes began to join the prophet. Together they turned their attention to other tribes and persuaded them to join the true community of Allah. By the time Muhammad died in 632, a new "nation" had been forged, ready to burst out of the confines of Arabia and convert the world to the will of Allah and the word of Muhammad. This mission they undertook with great speed and intensity.

MUHAMMAD AND JERUSALEM

Between 632 and 656, under the banner of their new religion, Arab Muslims completed a series of military conquests that affected most of the civilized world. They destroyed the recently revived Persian Empire; engulfed the prized Byzantine provinces of Syria, Palestine, Egypt and North Africa; and made forays into India. By 700 Muslim naval forces virtually controlled the Mediterranean Sea. In 711 a Muslim army crossed from North Africa to Spain, overran the Visigoths, set up their own kingdom, and became known as the Moors. In 717 Arab forces were knocking on the gates of Constantinople, and though they were defeated in 718 by Leo II, they still had their sights set on Europe. By 732, however, the Muslim drive had greatly weakened. In one of the watershed battles of European history, Muslim forces were defeated at Tours in Gaul (modern France) by the Frankish leader Charles Martel exactly one century after the death of Muhammad.

Early Muslim conquerors had aimed to bring the holy city of Jerusalem under their control. Jerusalem is mentioned several times in the Qur'an. According to Sura 2:142–143 the earliest Qibla (the direction Muslims face as they pray five times daily) was the sacred city of Jerusalem. This practice followed the example of the Jews. Muhammad

The Dome of the Rock

first prayed facing toward Jerusalem. His deference to Jewish practice symbolized Islam's allegiance to the continuity of Allah's revelation, given first to Abraham's posterity through Old Testament prophets. But when the followers of Allah were driven from Mecca to Medina, the Ka'bah at Mecca was established as the Qibla. According to the Qur'an, Abraham and Ishmael had raised the foundations of the Ka'bah. A factor in this change seems to have been the Jews' rejection of Muhammad and his teachings, even though they were based on biblical precedent. According to Islamic scholars the change took place about sixteen and a half months after the Hijrah, the emigration of Muhammad and his followers from Mecca to Medina in A.D. 622, or A.H. (*anno Hegirae*) 1—that is, year 1 of the Muslim calendar.[6]

According to Sura 17:1, the sacred nature of Jerusalem was absolutely confirmed to Muhammad, and thus to all Muslims, by the prophet's Night Journey. In that account Jerusalem is referred to as *al Masjid al Aqsa* ("Farthest Mosque"), the site of Solomon's Temple, at or near which now stands the Dome of the Rock Mosque. It is the "Farthest" because it was the place of worship farthest west that was known to the Arabs in the time of Muhammad. It was to that site that the angel Gabriel took Muhammad at night and from which both ascended together into the heavens. The passage reads: "In the name of Allah, Most Gracious, Most Merciful. Glory to [Allah] Who did take His Servant For a Journey by night From the Sacred Mosque To the Farthest Mosque Whose precincts We did Bless,—in order that We Might show him some Of Our Signs: for He Is the One Who heareth And seeth [all things]."[7]

The "Sacred Mosque" is the Ka'bah at Mecca. Thus, for Muslims, Jerusalem acquired special sanctity, in addition to the other holy places of their religion, because the prophet entered heaven from there after having started out first from Mecca. Jerusalem became the third holiest site in all of Islam, next to Mecca and Medina. Since then Jerusalem has been regarded with reverence. At some point during the Islamic period it came to be called simply al-Quds, "the Holy."

Muhammad's followers regarded the Night Journey as a literal event. The official position of Muslim theologians is that Muhammad made this journey while awake and actually traversed the ground. The Hadith literature (sayings attributed to Muhammad that, with the Qur'an, form the basis of Islamic law) gives details of the Journey that help explain its meaning. The prophet was first transported to the seat of Allah's earliest revelations in Jerusalem and taken through the seven heavens in successive stages, ultimately reaching the Divine Throne. Muslim theologians theorize that such an experience, real for Muhammad, may also symbolize for the rest of humankind the journey of the human soul in its religious growth throughout life.

The prophet's Night Journey to Heaven (Miraj) had a powerful effect on his followers. Some embellished the story and others transmitted only the barest facts. Still, the story of the Miraj influenced other cultures. Tradition states that when the "Servant" (Muhammad) was sleeping near the Ka'bah, the angel Gabriel took him to a winged creature (al-Buraq) and they went to the "Farthest Mosque." From there they arose through the heavens, where they encountered the powers of good and evil. On reaching their destination they saw Abraham, Moses, and Jesus. Muhammad prayed in front of the prophets as their leader, which is to say that he was recognized as foremost among them. Miguel Asin, professor of Arabic at the University of Madrid, argues that the story greatly influenced the medieval literature of Christian Europe, especially Dante's Divine Comedy.[8] Ironically, that fourteenth-century Christian poet placed Muhammad in one of the lowest circles of Hell because he was a sower of scandal and schism. Such an assessment is neither accurate nor fair.

One scholar has synthesized the embellished versions of the story of Muhammad's Night Journey. According to them, the Night Journey began as Muhammad lay asleep in his bed in Mecca. Allah's summons impelled the prophet to accompany the "Archangel" Gabriel on the back of a horselike creature named al-Buraq ("Lightning"). The creature had the face of a woman and the tail of a peacock. Alighting at the Western ("Wailing") Wall of the Jewish Temple, Gabriel fastened al-Buraq to a ring in a gate that afterward became known to Muslims as the Gate of the Prophet. The ancient prophets were said to have tethered their mounts there also. (It is said the Western Wall itself is still called 'al-Buraq' by some Arabs.) This gate, located immediately south of today's Western Wall, has been closed for centuries. It is sometimes called Barclay's Gate after the American missionary who discovered it in the nineteenth century.[9]

Muhammad then went to the Holy Rock; as he started to climb to Paradise via a ladder of light, the Rock tried to follow him, but Muhammad commanded it to stay and put his hand upon it to force it down. The Rock, however, remained suspended in air, forever marked by the pressure of Muhammad's fingers, and the ground beneath it became a cave. Finally in the presence of Allah, Muhammad received instructions for his followers. The prophet afterwards descended to earth by the same ladder upon which he had ascended through the seven heavens and stood again upon the sacred Rock in Jerusalem. He returned to Mecca the way he had come—riding al-Buraq—and reached his bed before the night was over.[10]

The story of Muhammad's journey certainly has parallels in intertestamental Jewish literature. Midrashic works popular in Muhammad's time—*The Book of Jubilees, The Book of Enoch,* and *Toledot Moshe,* which is extant in an Arabic version—describe Moses' journey to heaven and his visits to paradise and hell. But Muhammad's experience alone elevated the holiness of Jerusalem in the eyes of more people at one time than any single teaching of Judaism or Christianity.

CONQUEST OF JERUSALEM

By far the most significant effects of Muhammad's Night Journey were destined to be felt in Jerusalem itself. The city and its inhabitants were brought under the control of intensely religious military warriors, and significant numbers of Jews again became an integral part of the Holy City. Curiously, however, Muslim conquerors, who spread their new faith across the face of the Near East, did not move against Jerusalem at their first opportunity. Their objectives in Palestine beginning in 634 included trade routes and other areas of urban habitation. But by Christmas Eve, 634, the Greek church patriarch Sophronius complained in a sermon that it was impossible to leave Jerusalem to go to Bethlehem because of the unrestrained Arab divisions garrisoned in the country. Several days later, 6 January 635, in his sermon on the Festival of Epiphany, the patriarch associated the Muslim advance in the Holy Land with Daniel's prophecy of the "abomination of desolation": "Why is there no end to the bloodshed? Why are churches being destroyed and the cross desecrated? The Saracens, 'abomination of desolation' foretold by the Prophet [Daniel 12:11], are passing through lands forbidden to them, plundering cities and destroying fields, burning villages and razing holy monasteries . . . and priding themselves that they will finally conquer the whole world."[11]

Sophronius had a right to be nervous. In July 634, Byzantine imperial troops had been defeated at Adjnadain, southwest of Jerusalem. The brother of Emperor Heraclius had been killed and the Byzantine general forced to take shelter in Jerusalem. There was no serious siege against Jerusalem until four years later, however; Islamic troops simply menaced the countryside. Perhaps Jerusalem's impressive fortifications encouraged the invaders to consolidate their positions all around the city before attacking it. Nevertheless, in those four years the city suffered greatly from lack of food and other supplies.[12] In some ways that may have made conquest a welcome alternative.

The various accounts of the Islamic conquest of Jerusalem differ considerably. According to the earliest and most reliable sources, Patriarch Sophronius became sole authority in the city after another defeat of the Byzantine army in 636. He negotiated a surrender after an Arab force sealed off Jerusalem. The city was simply handed over to

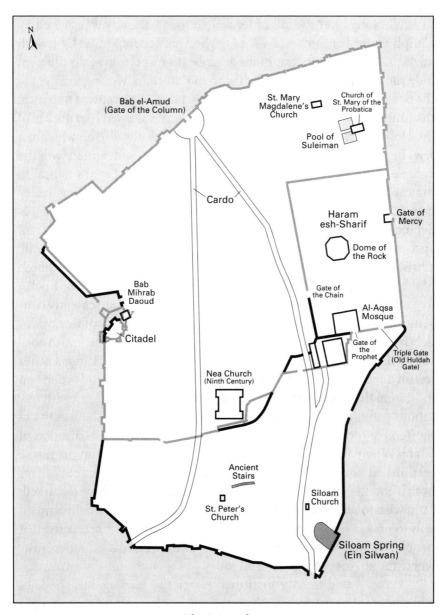

Islamic Jerusalem

Khalid ibn Thabit al-Fahmi, the leader of a not particularly outstanding unit, on the explicit condition that Jerusalem, including its people, churches, and buildings, be safe as long as the poll tax (*jizya*) was paid.[13]

Not long after the fall of Jerusalem (638), the city was visited by Caliph Umar (or Omar, 634–644), who was accompanied by Jewish advisers. Contradictory traditions describe his inspection of the different holy sites. The Christian Arabic historian Eutychius, writing in Egypt at the beginning of the tenth century, said that the caliph refused to pray at the Church of the Holy Sepulchre, so Sophronius showed him the site of the Holy Rock, or Foundation Stone (*even ha-shetiyyah*), on which the Jews believed the world was founded and which was identified with the Temple's Holy of Holies. One tradition indicates that Umar's refusal to pray at the Holy Sepulchre was rooted in his concern for setting a dangerous precedent. Had he prayed there, he said, the Church of the Holy Sepulchre would have been turned into a mosque by his followers and successors. Some Muslim writers, on the other hand, say that the Christians attempted to deceive the caliph by taking him to the Church of the Holy Sepulchre when he specifically asked about the Holy Rock.

Whatever the conflicts among the sources might be, scholarly consensus indicates that Umar cleared the Temple Mount of decay and debris and established there a place for Muslim worship. The Jewish convert to Islam, Kab al-Ahbar, was involved in this work. Umar's other Jewish advisers were entrusted with keeping the area in good order,[14] an indication that the caliph treated Jews with tolerance. Though Jewish traditions definitely influenced early Islamic attitudes about the sanctity of the Temple Mount and its surroundings, Umar opposed Judaization of Islam. When al-Ahbar suggested that the place of Muslim prayer be established north of the Foundation Stone, so worshippers could face both it and the Ka'bah when they prayed, Umar is said to have remarked: "You wish to resemble Judaism, but we Muslims have been commanded only to pray in the direction of the Ka'ba."[15] He subsequently ordered that the place of prayer be established south of the Foundation Stone, near where the al-Aqsa Mosque stands today.

Umar is said to have instituted restrictive laws against the Jews while he was in Jerusalem.[16] Nevertheless, not long after he conquered the Holy City, the body of supreme Jewish authority in Palestine, the *Gaonim* (Hebrew, "excellencies") was moved from Tiberias to Jerusalem and remained there until the eleventh century.

The Arab conquest also brought a permanent Jewish population to Jerusalem after an absence of five hundred years. A document written in

Judeo-Arabic found in the Genizah, or storage room, of the Ibn Ezra Synagogue in Cairo reveals that the Jews asked Umar for permission to settle two hundred families in Jerusalem. Because Sophronius strongly opposed the action, Umar fixed the number at seventy families. The Jews were assigned the quarter of the city southwest of the Temple Mount, where they lived from that time on during the Islamic period. They could pray in the vicinity of the Temple area, and a late source, Rabbi Abraham ben Hiyya (twelfth century), mentions that the Jews were even allowed to build a synagogue and school in that area.[17]

Though much welcomed by the Jewish people, this return was unable to assuage completely the anguish some felt as they saw the Holy City under the control of alien elements. Something of this sentiment can be seen in the words of the Jewish poet Amitai ben Sephatia, writing from his home in southern Italy about 900:

> I mention God and groan
> As I see every city built on its mound
> And the city of God utterly downtrodden.[18]

Nevertheless, the Jews benefited more than other non-Muslims living in Jerusalem. The Arab conquest of the Holy City was not at all beneficent to the Greek Christians. In fact, it dealt them a severe blow. Sophronius died 11 March 638, just a short time after the city was handed over to the conquerors, and no new patriarch was appointed until 706. The Arab conquest of Jerusalem transformed the ruling minority of Greek church officials into an unprotected minority, little remembered by church leadership outside Palestine for two generations. Still, Jerusalem retained a Christian hue for many years, and though many Arabs went to live in Jerusalem, most of the inhabitants were probably Christian. The city and its outlying monasteries became an important source from which Christian ideas entered Islam. The Muslim religious literature of the post-Islamic conquest reflects the importance of Jerusalem in the information network of the Near East at the time. Such phrases as "I asked the monk at the gate of Jerusalem" and "I heard from a Christian priest in the Jerusalem hills" are found in Muslim writings that discuss ideas with a Christian connection.[19]

Shortly after the conquest, Jerusalem was inhabited by important persons from among Muhammad's associates in Medina. Other Arabs also traveled great distances to live in the Holy City. Members of the Yemenite contingent of Islam's military force settled in Jerusalem.[20] Some Arabs who were unable to live in the city desired to spend time there so as to be blessed by its sanctity. Yet, on the whole, Jerusalem seems not to have attracted large numbers of long-term residents from among the Muslims. Many sayings are attributed to Muhammad about the importance of living in Jerusalem, including statements in which Allah promised material blessings to those who stayed in the city. Why go to such lengths to attract stable settlers if Muslims were already flocking to the Holy City to reside there?

One thing for which Jerusalem did not need to advertise was the poor. Umm ad-Darda, wife of the *qadi* (Muslim judge) of Damascus, spent half a year in the Syrian capital and half a year in Jerusalem, where she would "sit amongst the poor," attempting to help them where she could.[21] A special area of the city seems to have been set aside for the poor. "Apparently begging and giving charity were so interwoven with the holy city that even the conquerors did not consider dwelling in Jerusalem without the poor. Reliable sources characteristically attribute Caliph 'Uthman, whose reign commenced eight years after the conquest, with setting aside the Shiloah (Silwan) village gardens for the city's poor."[22]

UMAYYAD RULE

The prophet Muhammad made no provision for a successor to guide Islam. For thirty years after his death, from 632 to 661, his close associates picked one from among themselves to serve as caliph, to interpret and apply Allah's will as revealed by the prophet. Once Muhammad's personal associates died, struggles for leadership began. Muhammad's son-in-law Ali (656–661) became the fourth caliph. He claimed authority on the basis of kinship, which claim resulted in his assassination. In 661 the Emir of Syria, a man in his fifties named Muawiyya (661–680), was proclaimed caliph at Jerusalem. Three years before, in Jerusalem, he had outmaneuvered his rivals by signing a peace pact with the conqueror of Egypt, Amir ibn al-As. Then, in 661, Muawiyya, the man who had once been called the "Caesar of the Arabs" by Caliph Umar himself, saved the caliphate from anarchy and established the Umayyad dynasty, which held power until 750. During this time the center of the Muslim world was Damascus in Syria and Jerusalem in Palestine.[23]

Muawiyya regarded more than just the Foundation Stone on the Temple Mount as sacred or holy. He is known to have prayed at the tomb of Mary, the mother of Jesus, at the time of his coronation in 661. The Qur'an hails Jesus as a true prophet, but Muslim theology rejects as false all of Christ's teachings about himself as the Son of God. To imagine God as having any partners of any kind to share his nature or his activities is the great crime of *shirk,* or polytheism.

Muawiyya is credited with the construction of a Muslim house of prayer on the Temple Mount, probably on the place where the al-Aqsa Mosque was later built. The Frankish bishop Arkulf, who visited Jerusalem in 670, described it as a square-shaped building, put together in rough fashion with boards and bars. But it was claimed that the structure could hold three thousand persons. Professor Shlomo Goitein is of the opinion that Caliph Muawiyya planned the building of the Dome of the Rock and may have begun its construction, which Caliph Abd al-Malik (685–705) completed in 691 (A.H. 72).[24]

A desire to compete with the splendor of the Christian edifices in Jerusalem and the awakening of an aesthetic sense are considered the reasons behind the construction of the magnificent structure that still stands on the site where Solomon's Temple is believed to have stood.[25] Called in Arabic the *Qubbat al-Sakhra* ("Dome of the Rock") and sometimes but erroneously called the Mosque of Omar, the splendid cupola seemed to both Jews and Christians to be a metamorphosis of Solomon's Temple. For this reason, during the Crusades, Christians turned the Dome of the Rock into a church. Even today it is the best-known image of Jerusalem itself.

With the Qubbat al-Sakhra completed, Caliph Abd al-Malik sought to divert pilgrims from Mecca to Jerusalem because his rival in the struggle for the caliphate, Abdallah ibn al-Zubayr, had fortified himself in Mecca. Muslims did gather in Jerusalem to celebrate the Hajj; after all, it was the third holiest city of Islam, and if political or economic circumstances prohibited them from going to Mecca, Jerusalem was the next best thing. Nevertheless, the purpose of building the Dome of the Rock was not to rival the Ka'bah but rather to compete with the magnificent churches of Jerusalem, Lod, and the towns of Syria. An Arabic geographer has said that the Qubbat al-Sakhra should be seen as a counterpart to the Church of the Holy Sepulchre in shape and sanctity.[26] Many churches in Europe were later constructed on the model of the Qubbat.

Caretakers of the Qubbat al-Sakhra were accorded special status in Islam and exempted from paying the poll tax. The Jews considered this appointment to be a great honor, one which they enjoyed until after 750, the beginning of the Abbasid period.[27]

Caliph Abd al-Malik is also associated with other building projects in Jerusalem. Under his watchful eye, the city walls were repaired and gates set up. He also built in Jerusalem a government palace, which has been excavated within the last three decades and may be seen by tourists in the Ophel archaeological garden, south of the Haram esh-Sharif.

The first of al-Malik's sons and successors, Caliph al-Walid (705–715), erected the Al-Aqsa Mosque, which, over the course of time, has undergone many changes.[28]

All this activity attracted money to Jerusalem, as did the special religious status that was accorded the city on account of the construction of the Dome of the Rock over the very spot from which Muhammad made his Night Journey. Later but erroneous traditions associate the holy rock with the place where Abraham offered Ishmael as a sacrifice.[29] Muslims indeed believe that Ishmael was the son involved in Abraham's sacrifice rather than Isaac, but the site of the event in early Islamic theology is in Arabia. Nevertheless, numerous offerings were sent to Jerusalem, and pilgrims as well as tourists paid visits to the holy places, all of which contributed to the city's economic well-being and added to its reputation. The abundance of spices and incense scattered inside the Dome of the Rock were said to have been so thick that visitors gave off a pleasant smell for a long time after their visit to the shrine.[30]

Other accounts of Jerusalem in the late seventh and early eighth centuries comment on the city's pleasant streets, its well-organized drainage systems, and its prosperous lifestyle. Though some of the accounts are probably exaggerations, perhaps motivated by religious and emotional attachments of the travelers to the Holy City, on the whole, early Islamic Jerusalem seems to have given the impression of strength. The descriptions of Arabic geographers and other writers mention the strong city walls, which had eight gates and a moat on some sides. Arabic authors dwell on the al-Aqsa and the Dome of the Rock mosques.

Despite the religious significance of Jerusalem for the Umayyad dynasty, it never achieved the status of a capital city. Muslim Jerusalem was dealt a blow when Caliph Sulayman (or Suleiman), Abd al-Malik's second son and successor, founded the town of Ramla and made it the capital of Palestine in 716 instead of Jerusalem. The Holy City became a spiritual center with no political significance, but in the process its economy was also gravely affected. Trade routes did not reach it, and without a provincial administration or a strong military garrison, craftsmen had little work. Later complaints about the poverty of existence in Jerusalem—"food is scarce and provisions are limited"—were the result of conditions that developed in this period.[31] Al-Mutahhar bin Tahir noted that Jerusalem after 716 had become one of the provincial cities of Ramla, even though it had once been the royal city of David and Solomon.[32]

In 746 the Muslims of Palestine revolted against Caliph Marwan II, and the inhabitants of Jerusalem suffered greatly. Four years later the Umayyad dynasty ended, and a new chapter in the history of the Holy City was inaugurated.

ABBASID RULE

The Abbasid dynasty transferred the capital of the Islamic empire from Damascus to Baghdad, moving the center of activity even farther from Jerusalem. This action brought about slow but progressive decay in the Holy City. The first Abbasid caliphs continued to visit Jerusalem (al-Mansur in 758 and 771 and al-Mahdi in 780), but later rulers did not show any interest in the city. During the caliphate of al-Mansur (754–775), the Dome of the Rock was vandalized; gold and silver were removed from its doors to mint coins.[33]

Under the Abbasids Jerusalem remained predominantly non-Muslim, but the religious tolerance the citizens had enjoyed did not continue. High taxes were imposed on Jews and Christians. Jews were strictly prohibited from entering the Haram esh-Sharif, or the Temple Mount. A tenth-century source describes Jews praying at the gates of the holy precinct, and one from the eleventh century indicates that the

Mount of Olives became an important prayer site for Jewish pilgrims to the Holy City. When oppression by their Muslim rulers became unbearable, the Christians requested the help of Charlemagne in 797. The great Christian emperor called upon the Abbasid Caliph Harun al-Rashid (786–809) to alleviate the suffering of the Christians in the Holy City. As a token of their gratitude, the Christians sent the emperor the keys to the Church of the Holy Sepulchre, which were presented to him by the pope during an investment ceremony in Rome.[34]

Because cordial relations existed between emperor and caliph, Charlemagne succeeded in having several buildings erected in Jerusalem to accommodate Europeans visiting the city. These included a monastery, a convent, a marketplace, and a hospice for pilgrims. The emperor purchased gardens in the Kidron Valley and funded the construction of the Haceldama Monastery in the Hinnom Valley. These buildings were all destroyed in 1009 by the zealous Fatimid Caliph al-Hakim but were rebuilt a short time later when new Europeans, Italian merchants, settled in the city. They were demolished again when the Seljuk Turks invaded in 1071.[35]

The situation in Jerusalem deteriorated after the reign of Charlemagne (d. 814). A plague of locusts struck Palestine and caused a famine in Jerusalem; numerous Muslims left the city. In 841, the villagers around Jerusalem revolted against Muslim authorities. Led by Tamim Abu Harb, who billed himself as a messiah, the rebels eventually sacked the churches, mosques, and residences of Jerusalem. It took officials a year and a half to put down the revolt. The remoteness of Palestine from the center of government in Baghdad fostered the neglect of Jerusalem as it weakened Abbasid control over the entire country.[36]

FATIMID OPPRESSION

Toward the middle of the tenth century the power of the Abbasids declined generally, and extremist Muslim ideologies spread throughout the Islamic world. Attacks on non-Muslims and their holy sites increased. In 935 the eastern section of the Church of the Holy Sepulchre was turned into the Mosque of Umar, on the grounds that this was the site where Umar had prayed upon entering Jerusalem. In 938 Muslims attacked the Christians in the Holy City as they celebrated Palm Sunday, and they burned and looted the Church of the Holy Sepulchre. In 966 riots broke out against the Christians in the city, and Muslims, this time joined by Jews, killed the patriarch of Jerusalem and burned his body when he refused to make his usual payment to the Muslim governor of Jerusalem at the time of Pentecost.[37]

In 969, Palestine was overrun by the army of Caliph al-Muizz, whom tradition claims to be a descendant of Fatima, daughter of Muhammad. He established a state in North Africa, conquered Egypt as well as Palestine, and founded the Fatimid dynasty, which ruled until 1099, with a hiatus from 1071 to 1098. At first it seemed the Fatimids would bring stability to Jerusalem, which had been in decline for many years. Two Jewish converts to Islam held senior positions in the administration, one as chief vizier of the kingdom and the other as tax collector for Syria. Second, Karaite Jews began to migrate from Egypt to Jerusalem, and their numbers in the tenth century became as great as those of the rabbinical population of the city. (The Karaites believed only the biblical text and opposed such rabbinic teachings and traditions as the Talmud.) Jerusalem was again becoming a modest center of Jewish learning. But both Palestine and Jerusalem were plunged into turmoil when Bedouin tribes revolted and inflicted great misery once again upon the non-Muslim inhabitants of the Holy City.[38]

The attacks on non-Muslims reached their climax during the rule of Caliph al-Hakim (1006–1021). Islamic historians generally regard him as a madman. In 1009 he ordered all Jewish and Christian houses of prayer demolished. He forced non-Muslims to wear degrading badges (the head of a calf, for instance, reminiscent of the golden calf of biblical fame) and to convert to Islam or leave the country. A year before his death, al-Hakim changed his mind and permitted Jews and Christians to return to their religion and to rebuild their destroyed houses of prayer.[39] Both groups were in dire conditions and neither found it easy to rebuild.

From the middle of the eleventh century on, Jerusalem began to supersede Ramla as Palestine's main city for at least two reasons. First, serious earthquakes in 1033 and 1068 caused more damage to Ramla than to Jerusalem. Thousands of buildings were destroyed and tens of thousands of people died. In 1034 the Fatimid Caliph Taker Ali set about repairing the city walls, which gave Jerusalem an air of security. He demolished churches in the vicinity of the ruined walls and used their building stones to restore the walls. Second, and this is the ultimate curiosity of the eleventh century, despite the many difficulties and depredations experienced by the city's people and places, Jerusalem became a religious attraction in the Near East, especially to people from western Europe. Tourism in the Near East reached immense proportions in the peak year of 1065. One contingent alone consisted of twelve thousand pilgrims from southern Germany and Holland.[40]

Despite the oppression suffered by the Christians from the Abbasid period on, they maintained considerable property in and around Jerusalem. Monks lived their communal life undisturbed in the valleys surrounding Jerusalem. Only with the conquest of the Holy City by the Seljuk Turks were the monks driven out of the Kidron and Hinnom valleys.[41]

In 1071 the Seljuk Turks swept out of their homelands in south-central Asia and overran the Near East with massive military conquests. Once again Jerusalem was a prime target, and it became the brunt of large-scale destruction: "And they burned everything and cast out all."[42] The Seljuks, who were Sunni Muslims, banned all prayers recited in Jerusalem in honor of the Shiite Fatimid caliphs and reintroduced prayers for the welfare of the Abbasid caliphs, whom they regarded as the true caliphs because the Abbasids were Sunnis as well.

In 1076 a revolt against the Seljuks failed, and the Turkish commander who recaptured Jerusalem exacted a terrible price from the rebels. Not even those who fled to the al-Aqsa Mosque were spared. Such brutality did little good in the end, for the Fatimids retook Jerusalem in 1098. But their rule in turn lasted only a short while; the city was soon exposed to the fury of Christian soldiers from Europe when the First Crusade reached Jerusalem in 1099.

JERUSALEM IN MUSLIM THOUGHT

A Jewish midrash attributes seventy names to Jerusalem. The Arabs mentioned at least seventeen of their own ("a multiplicity of names is a sign of greatness"[43]), but only three of these had any practical importance. It appears that the Holy City was first called Ilia (the Arabic form of the Roman *Aelia*), which the Arabs took over from the Christians. But that quickly gave way to the city's official and principal name throughout the whole of the Islamic period, Bayt al-Maqdis, which is an abbreviation of Madinat Bayt al-Maqdis ("The City of the Holy Structure or Temple," meaning the Temple of Solomon). Today's Arabic name, al-Haram ("the sacred"), is simply another way of referring to the Bayt al-Maqdis.[44] The third name, al-Quds ("the Holy") is related etymologically to *maqdis* but is not found among early Arabic writers. Al-Maqdisi, writing around 985, uses it occasionally; and fellow Jerusalemite al-Mutahhar ibn Tahir (c. 966) mentions it once. The Persian traveler Nasir Khosraw, who visited Jerusalem in 1047, notes that the local people called the city al-Quds.[45] It is clear that for more than four centuries of the early Islamic period, Muslims, Jews, and even Christians perpetuated the central idea behind Jerusalem's founding, the essential and enduring characteristic of Jerusalem's long and varied history: holiness.

Orthodox Islam teaches that there are three shrines in the world to which special holiness is attached: the Ka'bah in Mecca, the Mosque of Muhammad in Medina, and the Dome of the Rock in Jerusalem, which is also the site of Solomon's Temple. Like Jews and some Christians, Muslims think of Jerusalem as the hub of the universe. Muslim tradition relates that the Holy Rock (*al-sakhra*), protected by the Dome of the Rock, is located exactly beneath Allah's throne in heaven and directly above a cave, the "well of spirits," where all the souls of the dead congregate twice weekly. Because of the rock's holiness, angels visited it two thousand times before the creation of the first man. It was there that Noah's ark came to rest, from which place civilization began again. Muslim scientists found corroboration for this view in their calculations that the Haram esh-Sharif is located in the center of the fourth climatic zone, the region best suited to develop civilized life.[46]

Despite the many changes Jerusalem experienced during the Islamic period, the city retained its special holiness among Muslims, who added layers of traditional belief about the sanctity of the Holy City to their religion. Many Islamic Hadiths speak of the great value of prayer uttered in Jerusalem.

Jerusalem also has a special place in Muslim mysticism. Mystics believed that living in Jerusalem purified the soul. For that reason, as had Christian ascetics before them, many Muslim mystics went to Jerusalem to be close to its holiness.

Muslim belief closely connects Jerusalem with the day of judgment. According to the faith, at the end of days, the angel of death, Israfil, will blow the ram's horn three times while standing on the Holy Rock. All the dead will congregate on the Mount of Olives. All humankind will cross a long bridge suspended from the Mount of Olives to the Haram esh-Sharif, which will be narrower than a hair, sharper than a sword, and darker than night. Along the bridge will be seven arches, and at each arch every person will be asked to account for his actions. The Scales of Judgment will be placed on the arches surrounding the Dome of the Rock. The righteous will be rewarded with sweet water from the rivers of paradise underneath the Holy Rock.[47] This is a concept for which Latter-day Saints have great affinity—this concept of a Jerusalem of renewal and reconciliation. It represents, as it were, a new Jerusalem.

Little wonder, then, that affection for Jerusalem grew among Muslims during its temporary occupation by the Crusaders. It was a powerful motivation for Muslims to regain the Holy Rock in the Holy City.

Notes

1. Combining a knowledge of scripture, history, and geography, Lynn and Hope Hilton retraced what they believe to be the probable route of Lehi's family. Situated along the western Arabian coastline between the Red Sea and the western mountains of the Arabian peninsula, this coastal plain was the ancient route of the Frankincense Trail. Today it is called Tihama by its residents. The Frankincense Trail leaves the seacoast at one point, turns east, following a pathway up one of the wadis, over the crest of the mountains, through sand and gravel desert, and joins other trails at the caravan city of Abha, now a regional capital in Saudi Arabia. See Hilton and Hilton, *In Search of Lehi's Trail*, 63, 95–96, 105.

2. Parley P. Pratt, in *Journal of Discourses*, 3:40.

3. George A. Smith, in *Journal of Discourses*, 3:31.

4. Palmer, *Expanding Church*, frontispiece.

5. Peterson, *Abraham Divided*, 121.

6. See the commentary in *Holy Qur'an*, 56.

7. *Holy Qur'an*, 774.

8. *Holy Qur'an*, 772.

9. Klein and Klein, *Temple beyond Time*, 127.

10. Klein and Klein, *Temple beyond Time*, 129.

11. Levine, *Jerusalem Cathedra*, 2:170.

12. Levine, *Jerusalem Cathedra*, 2:171.

13. Avi-Yonah, *Jerusalem*, 48.

14. Avi-Yonah, *Jerusalem*, 48–49.

15. Levine, *Jerusalem Cathedra*, 2:172.

16. Klein and Klein, *Temple beyond Time*, 134.

17. Avi-Yonah, *Jerusalem*, 50.

18. Levine, *Jerusalem Cathedra*, 2:169.

19. Ad-Din, *Great Familiarization*, 1.256.

20. Levine, *Jerusalem Cathedra*, 2:175.

21. Levine, *Jerusalem Cathedra*, 2:175.

22. Levine, *Jerusalem Cathedra*, 2:175.

23. Fisher and Ochsenwald, *Middle East*, 42–47; Goldschmidt, *Concise History of the Middle East*, 56.

24. Levine, *Jerusalem Cathedra*, 2:176.

25. Levine, *Jerusalem Cathedra*, 2:176.

26. Avi-Yonah, *Jerusalem*, 51.

27. Avi-Yonah, *Jerusalem*, 51.

28. Bahat, *Illustrated Atlas of Jerusalem*, 83–84; see also Levine, *Jerusalem Cathedra*, 2:178.

29. See Goldschmidt, *Concise History of the Middle East*, 48.

30. Levine, *Jerusalem Cathedra*, 2:177.

31. Levine, *Jerusalem Cathedra*, 2:180.

32. Levine, *Jerusalem Cathedra*, 2:180.

33. Bahat, *Illustrated Atlas of Jerusalem*, 86.

34. Klein, *Temple beyond Time*, 141–142.

35. Bahat, *Illustrated Atlas of Jerusalem*, 86.

36. Levine, *Jerusalem Cathedra*, 2:182–84.

37. Bahat, *Illustrated Atlas of Jerusalem*, 86–87.

38. Levine, *Jerusalem Cathedra*, 2:184–85.

39. Levine, *Jerusalem Cathedra*, 2:184–85.

40. Levine, *Jerusalem Cathedra*, 2:185.

41. Bahat, *Illustrated Atlas of Jerusalem*, 88–89.

42. Bahat, *Illustrated Atlas of Jerusalem*, 89.

43. Levine, *Jerusalem Cathedra*, 2:186.

44. Levine, *Jerusalem Cathedra*, 2:186–87.

45. Levine, *Jerusalem Cathedra*, 2:186–87.

46. Avi-Yonah, *Jerusalem*, 321.

47. Avi-Yonah, *Jerusalem*, 323.

16

CRUSADER JERUSALEM, 1099–1187

In 1095 the Byzantine Christian emperor, Alexius I Comnenus (1081–1118), appealed to the Roman Catholic Church for help against the advance of the Seljuk Turks. Conceiving the idea of an armed pilgrimage of Christian warriors to the east, one of the most powerful medieval popes, Urban II (1088–1099), discussed it with important ecclesiastical leaders and then made public his decision. In a stirring speech at Clermont in France before a large audience, the pope called upon the Christian knightly class to put aside their petty quarrels, join forces under papal leadership, and march eastward to free the Holy Land from the control of the Muslims. Calling for a holy war to save Christianity in the east he urged: "Come forward to the defence of Christ, O ye who have carried on feuds, come to the war against the infidels. O ye who have been thieves, become soldiers. Fight a just war . . . Set forth, then, upon the way to the holy Sepulcher; wrest that land from the evil race, and keep it for yourself. That land which floweth with milk and honey—Jerusalem."[1] The pope's speech was interrupted with shouts of support; such an undertaking was seen as the will of God—*Dieu lo vult!* ("God wills it").

At the heart of the crusading ideology was the concept of the sanctity of Jerusalem and the need to keep it free from sacrilegious usurpers. Ironically, Christianity had accepted the Jewish and Muslim view that the Holy City was at the center of the world and the starting point of creation. Jerusalem was seen as the one spot on earth where the devout could be physically closer to God. Over time, the church came to recognize pilgrimage as a way of gaining absolution for sins.[2] It was believed that the rigors of pilgrimage to the Holy Land were not only acceptable penance for past sins but also a way to secure indulgences against future sins. Consequently, the jails of Europe were emptied, and criminals found themselves on the top decks of ships heading for Palestine alongside priests, peasants, titled lords, and fine ladies.[3]

Thus, the Crusades were founded on three principles: the sanctity of Jerusalem, the necessity of fighting the enemies of Christ, and the personal efficacy of pilgrimage to the Holy City. The word *crusade* itself derives from the Latin *crux,* meaning "cross." Under the banner of the cross, the Crusaders set out to reconquer the sacred sites associated with Christ's life.

GRIEVANCES

To eleventh-century European Christians the list of grievances against the infidel Muslims was long indeed. Muslims had already made inroads into Europe four hundred years earlier, overrunning Spain in the eighth century. And though Christians had won back most of the northern territories in the ninth century, Muslim power revived in the late tenth century under al-Mansur the Victorious. He captured Barcelona and sacked Leon, the capital of the leading Christian kingdom.[4] But the Christians fought back after the death of al-Mansur in 1002. The great city of Toledo was retaken in 1085, and in 1089 Pope Urban II proclaimed that those who assisted in rebuilding certain towns would enjoy the same reward as pilgrims to Jerusalem. The Muslims, however, were reinforced by Berber tribesmen from North Africa and important cities were lost again.[5]

In Italy, Muslims had sacked Rome itself in 846, and their robber castles existed throughout the land into the eleventh century. The western Mediterranean was dominated by Muslim pirates until the Byzantines reopened sea lanes to traders and pilgrims in the tenth century.

But the most unconscionable acts against Christianity had been perpetrated in the Holy Land itself. Inhabitants of Palestine endured ups and downs at the hands of various Muslim rulers since the seventh century, though in the main tranquillity and tolerance prevailed. Between 1004 and 1014, however, the mad Fatimid Caliph al-Hakim persecuted Christians with a vengeance. He ordered the destruction of churches, including the Church of the Holy Sepulchre, and forced everybody to convert to Islam. In 1021 he disappeared, perhaps murdered by his sister; his chief adviser, Darazi, fled to Lebanon, where he founded a sect named after himself, the Druze.[6] Members of the sect believed that in due course al-Hakim would return, a prospect that made the most tolerant of Christians nervous.

Al-Hakim's havoc in Jerusalem made a deep impression on the west. At the end of the eleventh century, almost eighty years after Hakim's abuses had been moderated, the monks of the Moissac Abbey, in southern France, forged an encyclical (papal decree), purportedly sent out by Pope Sergius IV (1004–1012) to the faithful, calling for an army to be launched against Hakim. The document is important because it exemplifies the kind of crusading rhetoric that had been generated in Europe by the time of the First Crusade. That the Church of the Holy Sepulchre had by that time already been restored was immaterial.

> Let all Christians know that news has come from the east to the seat of the apostles that the church of the Holy Sepulchre has been destroyed from roof to foundations at the impious hands of the pagans. This destruction has plunged the entire church and the city of Rome into deep grief and distress. The whole world is in mourning, and the people tremble, breathing deep sighs. Never should our eyes be blessed with sleep, or our heart with joy, if we ever read in the prophets, in the Psalms or in the fathers that the Redeemer's tomb would be destroyed. Therefore, let this Christian intention be known: that we, personally, if it pleases the Lord, desire to set out from these shores with any Romans, Italians or Tuscans who wish to come with us. With the Lord's help we intend to kill all these enemies and to restore the Redeemer's Holy Sepulchre. Nor, my sons, are you to fear the sea's turbulence, nor dread the fury of war, for God has promised that whoever loses the present life for the sake of Christ will gain another life which he will never lose. For this is not a battle for an earthly kingdom, but for the eternal Lord.[7]

To European Christians, however, the persecutions of al-Hakim were not the worst problems to beset Christianity. In the tenth century, Turkestan was ruled by a Persian dynasty who converted their subjects to Islam. Turks poured into western Asia to take positions under Muslim rulers. Among them was a group of princes who called themselves Seljuks, after a common semimythical ancestor. These raiders overtook Armenia and Anatolia and were soon menacing the Byzantine Empire.

A tremendous showdown occurred in 1071 between Byzantine and Seljuk forces near a town called Manzikert, now in present-day Turkey. This battle was another watershed in history and the worst disaster to befall the eastern empire to that point. With the Byzantine army no longer a deterrent and the Fatimids in disarray, a Seljuk Turkish Muslim chieftain named Atsiz ibn Abaq invaded Palestine and captured Jerusalem. This conquest nearly halted pilgrim traffic to the Holy City and tipped the scales in favor of a crusade against the infidels who were causing trouble for travelers to Jerusalem.

Another impetus to pilgrimage was the veneration of relics. Pilgrims could see for themselves the precious objects of their faith—the crown of thorns, a hair from the head of John the Baptist, the mantle of the prophet Elijah. Astute pilgrims might even be able to purchase something to display back in their own dreary villages, which, in turn, could inspire others to make their own journeys. One recognized authority on the Crusades relates that when a woman of a certain French town "brought back from her travels the thumb of Saint John the Baptist, her friends were all inspired to journey out to see his body at Samaria and his head at Damascus."[8]

The success of the pilgrimages depended on two conditions: first, that life in Jerusalem be orderly enough for defenseless travelers to move about and worship in safety; and second, that the way to Jerusalem be kept open and inexpensive. The former necessitated peace and good government in the Muslim world; the latter, the prosperity and beneficence of Byzantium. By the middle of the eleventh century, however, pilgrims found neither. They were dramatically hampered in their quest to visit the most holy sites. In 1056 Muslims forbade westerners to enter the Church of the Holy Sepulchre and ejected some three hundred of them from Jerusalem. By the 1080s pilgrim traffic from the west was almost at a standstill.[9]

In his chronicle written soon after 1077, Lambert, a monk from an abbey in western Europe, described the ordeals suffered by a band of German pilgrims in Syria and Palestine. They had ill-advisedly revealed their wealth and importance to the inhabitants of the territories through which they passed as they made their way to the Holy City. The barbarians who poured out from their towns and fields to see such famous men were driven by a great desire for plunder. So, when the pilgrims were just a short distance from Rama, on Good Friday, around the third hour of the day, marauding Arabs attacked them. Many of the Christians, relying on their religion for assistance and salvation, had trusted in God's protection rather than in weapons when they set out for foreign parts. Among the many casualties was William, archbishop of Trier, whose arm was almost paralyzed by wounds. He was left naked and half-dead.[10]

Other warnings, like the one recorded in the biography of Bishop Altmann of Passau, also began to circulate in the west:

> On this pilgrimage a memorable event happened which I include as an example, so that those who obstinately oppose the counsels of the wise might take it as a dreadful warning. One of the pilgrims was a noble abbess, physically imposing and spiritually minded. Against all the best advice she resigned the care of the sisters committed to her and undertook this pilgrimage which was fraught with danger. She was captured by pagans and, in the sight of all, raped by a band of licentious men until she died. This event was a scandal to all Christian people. Brought low by incidents like this and other humiliations in the name of Christ, the pilgrims won high regard everywhere, by men and by angels, because they chose to enter the kingdom of God suffering many tribulations.[11]

Count Robert I of Flanders managed to make his way to Jerusalem in 1086 with the help of an armed escort. He paused on the way back to spend a season fighting for the Byzantine emperor. But the few humbler pilgrims who succeeded in overcoming the obstacles to their pilgrimage returned home weary and poor with doleful stories to tell.[12]

Given the graveness of the situation, it seems only natural that churchmen and laypersons alike should have decided that it was high time to recover the holy places and sacred objects from the infidels. Arming themselves with swords and metal helmets, the faithful went in successive waves for two hundred years to retrieve the Holy City wherein lay the tomb of Christ. Never before or since was the tomb fought over so savagely. From the end of the eleventh century through the end of the thirteenth, the cross of faith was transformed into a sword of destruction, cutting a swath of blood from the cathedral towns of western Europe to the very heart of Jerusalem, which, for much of the crusading era, was the ostensible object of the contests.

Socially as well as doctrinally, from the Roman Catholic point of view, the eleventh century was a perfect time for the Crusades. Centuries before, St. Augustine (354–430) had held that wars might legitimately be waged if called for by the command of God. The society that emerged in Europe after the invasions that brought hundreds of thousands of Germanic warriors under the umbrella of Christianity glorified the military hero. As doctrine mixed with the warrior mentality, war seemed not only permissible but desirable.

But warfare was becoming too much the preoccupation of medieval man, and the Roman church took steps to curb this development. Pope Leo IV in the mid ninth century declared that anyone dying in battle for the church would win a heavenly reward—but not in a war for personal gain. A few years later, Pope Nicholas I held that men under the sentence of the church for their sins (excommunication or interdiction) could bear arms only against the infidel. Unfortunately, most of the fighting at the time was between Christians who viewed each other as the infidel; monarchs fought against monarchs, lords against lords, dukes against neighboring dukes. When in 1038 the archbishop of Bourges ordered every Christian male over the age of fifteen to declare himself the enemy of anyone who broke the peace and, if need be, take up arms against the discordant, the archbishop's command was too fully obeyed. Castles of "recalcitrant nobles" were destroyed, and a village was burned. A more workable attempt to limit warfare was the proclamation of the Truce of God, which prohibited fighting on the Sabbath, major feast days of the church, and later on all Saturdays as well. But there was so much pent-up energy among the knightly class in Europe that the truce was often broken. The Crusades—holy wars for God and church—came at just the right time for relief from the warrior ethos run amok in western Europe and for maximum popular support.[13]

THE FIRST CRUSADE

From December 1095 until July 1096 Pope Urban toured France, preaching the Pope's Crusade. He also sent a letter to the people of Flanders, which represents the message he preached throughout Europe:

> Bishop Urban, servant of the servants of God, to all the faithful waiting in Flanders, both rulers and subjects: greetings, grace and apostolic blessing. We know you have already heard from the testimony of many that the frenzy of the barbarians has devastated the churches of God in

the east, and has even—shame to say—seized into slavery the holy city of Christ, Jerusalem. Grieving in pious contemplation of this disaster, we visited France and strongly urged the princes and people of that land to work for the liberation of the Eastern Church. At the council of Auvergne, we enjoined on them this undertaking for the remission of all their sins, and appointed our dear son Adhemar, bishop of Le Puy, as leader of the journey on our behalf, so that whoever should set out on such a journey should obey his orders as if they were our own.[14]

The remission of all of one's sins was a powerful inducement to join the cause. The pope further promised that all temporal property belonging to the participants would be kept safe and intact under the protection of the Holy Roman Church until the warrior returned home.[15] Though the pope decreed that God required pious intentions, the promise of protected worldly belongings, plus the hint that one might be able to gain additional wealth, even if only a little, could not be put completely from the minds of the potential defenders of the faith.

Each member of the expedition was to wear the sign of the cross as a symbol of his dedication to the glorious endeavor being undertaken. Anyone who adopted the sign of the cross was obligated to go all the way to Jerusalem. If he turned back too soon or failed to set out at all, he would suffer excommunication. The armed pilgrimage was not to be a war of mere conquest; it was for God's glory. Responding to the call, thousands sewed onto their clothing small red crosses and prepared for the sacred journey. Thus, the Crusades "represented a fusion of three characteristic impulses of medieval man: sanctity, pugnacity, and greed," or, put more alliteratively, God, glory, and gold, and not necessarily in that order.[16]

Before the great armies of western Europe came together and set out officially on the First Crusade, small groups of zealous peasants and artisans converged spontaneously and marched as an undisciplined horde through the Rhine and Danube valleys in the spring of 1096, headed for Jerusalem. In their minds the earthly Jerusalem was confused with the idea of the heavenly Jerusalem. Joshua Prawer writes that these peasants "would ask on approaching each new city if they had finally reached 'Heavenly Jerusalem.'"[17] The leader of the Peasants' Crusade was Peter the Hermit, so-called because of a hermit's cape he wore while riding a donkey. Foreboding in appearance and magnetic in his preaching,

Peter threatened violence against Jewish communities in his path, hoping to extort financial support for his crusade. This technique was also used by no less a person than the saintly Godfrey de Bouillon, duke of Lower Lorraine, who led one of the pope's armies and who later became the first ruler of the Kingdom of Jerusalem.[18]

Tragically, many of the Crusaders, both Peter's and the pope's, did more than merely threaten the Jews. As the crusading hordes of Christian soldiers swarmed across the European continent, thousands of Jews were massacred, their synagogues torched, and countless homes destroyed in the once-flourishing Jewish communities of the important cities of Worms, Mainz, Cologne, Metz, and Prague. Only in the town of Speyer, whose bishop was able to avert a disaster, were the horrifying scenes of forced baptism, murder, and pillage not carried out. The massacres did not reflect an official policy of the church. Nevertheless, the atrocities were not mindless attacks by an uninformed rabble.[19]

For many Crusaders it seemed preposterous to set out on such a long journey to kill God's enemies while the worst enemies, those who were responsible for putting Christ in his grave, were dwelling in the midst of the Christian world.[20] If the church assured salvation to all who took up the cross and destroyed the Muslim enemies of God, would not the same hold true for a war against the greatest of the infidels—the Jews?

Some five thousand Jews lost their lives during the First Crusade. Neither the church nor the secular princes offered any formidable resistance to the Crusaders to protect the Jews.[21] Both were caught off guard; neither could control the mobs who were all too ready to commit genocide as they charged their victims with deicide. Joshua Prawer has viewed the destruction of the Jews during this time as the beginning of a thousand years of Christian anti-Semitism: "This was the 'Doom of 1096,' as it is called in Jewish sources (*Gzeroth Tatnu*), an event never to be forgotten . . . perpetrated by those . . . who went to liberate the sepulchre of a God of love and peace universal."[22]

Peter the Hermit's rabble was followed by other, even less reputable, bands of warriors who could not wait to reach Jerusalem before they began their work of killing "the infidel." The German chronicler Albert of Aachen, writing after 1100, gives us the essence of many massacres as he writes specifically about a petty lord named Emich of Leisingen:

I do not know if it was because of a judgement of God or because of some delusion in their minds, but the pilgrims rose in a spirit of cruelty against the Jews, who were scattered throughout many cities in the Rhineland. They inflicted a most cruel slaughter on them, especially in the kingdom of Lorraine, claiming that this was the beginning of their journey and the killings would be of service against the enemies of Christianity. . . . Count Emich was the enemy of all the Jews—may his bones be crushed to pieces in millstones of iron. He was known as a man who had no mercy on the old, or on young women, who took no pity on babies or sucklings or the sick, who pulverized God's people like the dust in threshing, who slew their young men with the sword and cut open their pregnant women.[23]

Albert's use of the phrase "judgement of God" is interesting to Latter-day Saints because we share the same feelings of abhorrence about Crusader actions that come to all thoughtful students of the period. Without doubt, greed and thoughtless hatred were powerful motives in bringing about the untold misery of innocent Jews. Though nothing can condone or excuse such cruelty, the events described during the Crusades were foreseen by prophets of old, particularly by one who was himself a citizen of Judah, namely Nephi.[24] We note especially his reference to the crucifixion and resurrection of the Savior and the subsequent destruction of Jerusalem in A.D. 70: "And behold it shall come to pass that after the Messiah hath risen from the dead, and hath manifested himself unto his people, unto as many as will believe on his name, behold, Jerusalem shall be destroyed again . . . Wherefore, the Jews shall be scattered among all nations" (2 Ne. 25:14–15). Elsewhere Nephi tersely summarizes events that would beset the Jewish people after their dispersion: they would be scourged by other nations; they would wander and perish and "become a hiss and a by-word, and be hated among all nations" (1 Ne. 19:13–14).

Even Moses, the great lawgiver, clearly foretold the devastating conditions that would come upon his people should they reject their God: "Thou shalt become an astonishment, a proverb, and a by-word, among all nations. . . . And among these nations shalt thou find no ease, neither shall the sole of thy foot have rest: but the Lord shall give thee there a trembling heart, and failing of eyes, and sorrow of mind: and thy life shall hang in doubt before thee; and thou shalt fear day and night, and shalt have none assurance of thy life" (Deut. 28:37, 65–66). The Lord himself said: "I have caused my people who are of the house of Israel to be smitten, and to be afflicted, and to be slain, and to be cast out from among them, and to become hated by them, and to become a hiss and a by-word among them" (3 Ne. 16:9).[25]

Surely these prophecies saw partial fulfillment during the period of the Crusades. As the Jewish historian Abram Leon Sachar reminds us, during the two hundred years of the Crusades, "the Jew was stoned and pelted, spat upon and cursed, compelled to slink through the by-ways and side streets, in darkness and in shame. He was . . . a fugitive and a vagabond."[26] To use Nephi's vocabulary, he was indeed a hiss and a by-word.

Just as no amount of discussion can dismiss the prophecies about Jewish hardship and suffering, no amount of doctrinal double-talk or supersessionist theology can excuse the murder of, oppression of, and lack of gratitude for the Jewish branch of Israel's family. Nephi also testified of this truth:

> But thus saith the Lord God: O fools, they shall have a Bible; and it shall proceed forth from the Jews, mine ancient covenant people. And what thank they the Jews for the Bible which they receive from them? Yea, what do the Gentiles mean? Do they remember the travails, and the labors, and the pains of the Jews, and their diligence unto me, in bringing forth salvation unto the Gentiles?
>
> O ye Gentiles, have ye remembered the Jews, mine ancient covenant people? Nay; but ye have cursed them, and have hated them, and have not sought to recover them. But behold, I will return all these things upon your own heads; for I the Lord have not forgotten my people. (2 Ne. 29:4–5)

If we condemn the Jews, we do so at our own peril. Only those who are familiar with the history of the Jewish people, who are sensitive to their tragedies and triumphs, their travails and temptations, their rejection of the true Messiah and eventual return to him, their close connection to Jerusalem and the prophetic destiny of both people and place, can appreciate the special spot they hold in the Lord's heart.

With the restoration of the Church of Jesus Christ in 1830, a new message of hope and comfort was directed toward the Jews. It issued forth from those servants charged by the Lord in this last dispensation with laying the foundations for the gathering of Israel. In March 1840, just before he was officially called by the Prophet Joseph Smith to go to the Holy Land and dedicate it for the return of Abraham's posterity, Elder Orson Hyde received a vision of his future labors. The Spirit of the Lord laid before his eyes the great cities of the world, in which many of the children of Abraham were residing, and the Spirit directed the apostle in the following manner: "Speak ye comfortably to Jerusalem, and cry unto her, that her warfare is accomplished—that her iniquity is pardoned, for she hath received of the Lord's hand doubly for all her sins. Let your warning voice be heard among the Gentiles as you pass; and call upon them in my name for aid and assistance."[27]

The Jews are the Lord's people. All the prophecies about them in the Lord's written word will come to pass. Some of the horrors foretold by Nephi and others found fulfillment during the Crusades. But we also are assured that just as the Jews were scattered, smitten, and scourged, so will they be gathered in great mercy by their God, whom they did not know. In the meantime, however, they have had to bear terrible indignities at the hands of vile Gentiles who knew neither God nor restraint.

Ironically, the peasant Crusaders received a lethal dose of their own medicine. Very few of them reached Constantinople, and fewer still helped liberate Jerusalem. Most of the peasant Crusaders met their end at the hands of Hungarian warriors who retaliated against them for plundering the countryside. A contemporary historian, Cosmos of Prague, regarded their extinction as God's just wrath and retribution for the horrible massacre of the Jewish people.[28]

JERUSALEM FALLS TO THE CRUSADERS

Pope Urban II and Emperor Alexius had agreed that the Crusader armies should assemble at Constantinople and there join with Byzantine forces to reconquer the Holy Land. During the first half of 1096 four major armies of knights, foot soldiers, and hangers-on began to move eastward by various routes until they converged on Constantinople in the fall and winter. The leaders of the armies had no common plan of action. Although Urban II had designated a distinguished bishop to direct the crusading effort, the nobles were unwilling to accept direction. At times the armies looked very little different from mobs.

By the spring of 1097 as many as one hundred thousand Franks marched from France to assemble in the Byzantine capital. From there they moved to Antioch, in Syria, where they beat back the Muslims in June 1098 and found, as we are told, the lance that had pierced the body of Christ. This relic became a rallying point for the Christian soldiers, spurring them on to greater ferociousness in the cause of Christ.[29] One group left the main body of Crusaders to establish control over Edessa in Armenia, which became a Crusader state.

It took the Franks a year to advance from Antioch to Jerusalem as they marched southward, down the coast of Palestine, avoiding military engagements with the Muslims and saving their strength for the Holy City. By the middle of June 1099 the Christian warriors had reached the northern outskirts of the city. They camped on a hill named Nebi Samwil (Arabic, "Prophet Samuel") and wept tears of joy as they contemplated the city they had traveled so far to liberate. Jerusalem at that time was defended by a garrison of Egyptian Fatimid soldiers, who had driven the Seljuk Turks out of the city only a year before. All Greek Christians along with the Patriarch Simon had been expelled from the city by the Muslims. The Jews, who numbered a few hundred, had been allowed to stay and fight alongside the Muslims.[30]

After five weeks of combat, twelve hundred mounted knights and twelve thousand foot soldiers finally pushed through the northeastern wall of Jerusalem (at Herod's Gate, approximately opposite today's Rockefeller Museum), the city's perpetual weak point. Titus had attacked from that direction in A.D. 70, as did Yitzhak Rabin almost nineteen hundred years later, when he led a company of Israeli paratroopers to reclaim Jerusalem in the 1967 Six-Day War. Just as Jerusalem fell to the Israelis in 1967, so did the city fall to the Crusaders on 15 July 1099, and the invaders soon planted a large cross at the point of entry, in the area of today's Muslim Quarter.[31] At the same time Godfrey de Bouillon was leading his troops from Flanders and northern France over the northeastern wall, a Provençal force led by Raymond of St. Gilles surmounted the wall adjoining Mount Zion, and Normans from Sicily, headed by Tancred, entered Jerusalem from the northwest in the vicinity of a tower that came to bear his name.[32]

Thousands of Crusaders stormed into Jerusalem's streets and unleashed a horrible revenge upon the enemies of Christ. Their

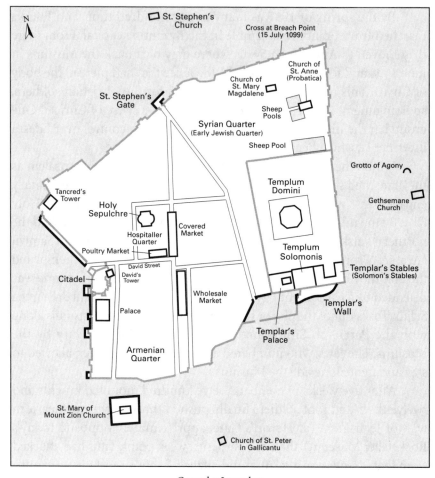

Crusader Jerusalem

philosophy was simple enough: "Kill them and let God sort them out!" Every Muslim in sight was killed; women and children were massacred. The streets were filled with blood, and blood flowed downhill into the Kidron Valley. Jews who were not immediately executed fled to their synagogue, which was set afire and its terrified inhabitants burned alive. Christian clergymen themselves were repulsed by the slaughter. Roman church bishop and historian William of Tyre recorded the scenes of carnage:

> It was impossible to look upon the vast numbers of slain without horror; everywhere lay fragments of human bodies, and the very ground was covered with the blood of the slain. It was not alone the spectacle of the

headless bodies and mutilated limbs strewn in all directions that roused horror in all who looked upon them. Still more dreadful it was to gaze upon the victors themselves, dripping with blood from head to foot, an ominous sight which brought terror to all who met them.[33]

When there was no enemy left to kill and nothing left to loot, Jerusalem fell silent. In a great display of piety, lords, bishops, knights, and peasants walked in solemn procession to the tomb of Christ, and there each in turn knelt to offer prayers to the God who had guided them and given them victory. At last the tomb of the Lord was in western Christian hands, and the holiest city in the world was freed from the wretched infidel.

The pious, courageous, but not very bright Godfrey de Bouillon became the first ruler of the kingdom of Jerusalem; he received the title Defender of the Holy Sepulchre. Godfrey refused to accept a crown and the title of monarch in the city where Christ alone was king.[34] He was also appointed patriarch of Jerusalem and given jurisdiction over the northwest section of Jerusalem (the Patriarch Quarter), though he had originally demanded sole religious authority over the entire city. This quarter had formerly belonged to Greek Orthodox Christians but passed to the Latin (Roman) church because the Greek patriarch, Simon, and his Greek bishops had moved to Cyprus.[35]

Godfrey ruled for only one year and was succeeded by his younger brother, Baldwin de Boulogne, a shrewd and cunning warrior. He had no qualms about taking the title of king of Jerusalem and inaugurated a period of expansion which, by the mid twelfth century, saw the borders of the Latin Kingdom of Jerusalem begin to rival those of David's ancient monarchy. The boundaries of the medieval kingdom stretched, roughly, from the Mediterranean in the west to the Transjordan in the east, and from Lebanon in the north to Elath (modern Eilat) in the south.

THE CULTURE OF CRUSADER JERUSALEM

Crusader rule in Jerusalem was difficult as well as harsh at the beginning. Surviving Muslims and Jews were forbidden to resettle in the city for several years after the conquest. Most of the Franks returned home after the tomb of Jesus was taken, leaving Jerusalem a lonely place.

Special inducements were offered to attract more Latin Christians. Rulers resorted to such measures as tax and customs exemptions as well as redistribution of property. In 1115 King Baldwin decided to allow back into the city Greeks, Syrians, and other native Eastern Christians from Transjordan. They began to inhabit the northeastern (formerly Jewish) quarter of Jerusalem, an area which came to be known as the Syrian Quarter until sometime in the early Ottoman period.[36]

The Syrian Christians provided the badly needed manpower to revitalize Jerusalem's economy, which was based on crafts manufacturing involving wood, leather, and metal. As these craftsmen began working in concert with Italian merchants, who imported raw materials and took away finished products, Jerusalem became the center of a trading monopoly in the Near East. The city's population grew to about twenty thousand full-time residents. Coincidentally, Orson Hyde tells us that this was the population in Jerusalem when he visited it in 1841.[37]

As the years passed, the Franks grew more tolerant of the Eastern Christians, although the latter felt that their European benefactors treated them with a haughtiness reminiscent of the former Muslim governors of Jerusalem. In fact, the Franks were looked upon as ignorant, coarse, domineering, abusive, and fanatically pious by several sects of Christianity. Coptic Christians from Egypt were said to have ended their annual pilgrimage to Jerusalem because of the rudeness and hostility shown them by the Franks.[38]

Two groups in Crusader Jerusalem were especially feared and disliked: the Knights Hospitaller and the Knights Templar. They were religious orders of military-minded monks who took vows of poverty, chastity, and obedience and combined this regimen with the skills of knightly warriors. They were indispensable to King Baldwin II and his successors, who always needed men for recurring skirmishes with the Muslims. Though originating with the Benedictine Order, both Hospitallers and Templars functioned as independent organizations in the Holy Land and were held in the highest regard by the pope, who saw them as Christianity's permanent foothold in Palestine.[39]

The largest of the orders was the Hospitallers, whose members settled in an area still called the Muristan (Persian, "hospital") Quarter. They did not get along well with the Latin patriarch and were happy to live in the sector of the city that had been appropriated from the

patriarch by Pope Paschal II in 1113. An example of the volatile relations
between the Hospitallers and the patriarch occurred when members of
the order felt slighted over a new liturgical arrangement in worship and
stormed the Church of the Holy Sepulchre with drawn swords, chasing
the priests until the knights calmed down.[40]

The Order of the Knights Templar, founded in Palestine in 1118,
settled on the Temple Mount when King Baldwin I vacated his headquarters in the al-Aqsa Mosque in favor of the order. He moved to the
Citadel, and the Templars renovated the mosque, calling it *Templum
Solomonis* ("Solomon's Temple"), from which they derived their full
name, The Order of the Poor Knights of the Messiah and of the Temple
of Solomon. At the time they took over the al-Aqsa Mosque, they
renamed the Dome of the Rock the *Templum Domini* ("Temple of the
Lord"). The Templars did not change the structure of the building but
did add a metal grill around the Sacred Rock (*es-Sakhra*). As Hugh
Nibley reminds us, the Templars' actions bespeak apostate Christianity's
obsession with regaining the Temple, its holiness and its ordinances, as
a critical pillar of the faith. They knew something terribly important had
been lost when the Temples of old were destroyed, but they were not
quite sure how to get it back.[41]

Northwest of the Templum Domini, the Templars built an elaborate
baptistry, known today as the Dome of Ascension. An administrative
center was constructed west of the Templum Solomonis, which today
serves partly as a women's mosque and partly as a museum of Islamic
art. The Templars also turned the subterranean vaults of the Temple platform into stables, which still retain the designation "Solomon's Stables."

The most important function of both orders through the twelfth
century was to protect pilgrims traveling to Jerusalem. Once pilgrims
had safely docked at Jaffa, knights of the orders would escort them overland to Jerusalem, a task made difficult by Egyptian, Turkish, and
Bedouin bandits on the roads. The crusading orders were not to be tri-
fled with, however, especially by inferior forces. Grateful pilgrims
remembered the service rendered on their behalf, and their gratitude
became a source of great wealth for the orders. Wealthier pilgrims often
bestowed gifts of money or property in their wills.[42]

The permanent inhabitants of Jerusalem during the years of the
Crusader kingdom were mostly Europeans. The Franks predominated,

and French was the official language of the kingdom. Germans established their own branch of the Hospitallers, called the Knights Teutonic, between the Temple Mount and Zion's Gate; Hungarians concentrated around their own hospice not far from today's New Gate; Spaniards had their own street near Damascus Gate; and speakers of Provençal established themselves near Zion's Gate.

The streets of Jerusalem itself had survived from Roman times. The Cardo, the main thoroughfare running from north to south (Damascus Gate to Zion Gate), bisected the main east-west artery ("St. Stephen's Gate" to Jaffa Gate), which divided the city into four quarters, each of which had taken on a different ethnic and architectural character over the centuries. Something of this diversity remained through the Crusader period.[43]

Another important element of Crusader Jerusalem was its marketplaces. Toward the southern end of the city were several markets that supplied citizens with necessities and pilgrims with souvenirs or keepsakes. The most important markets were the Vegetable Market, which was also called the Spice Market; the Vaulted Market, which had stalls of dry goods; and the Poultry Market, where one could purchase eggs, cheese, and other milk products.[44] Near these three was a market area of eating establishments frequented by pilgrims visiting Jerusalem—the medieval equivalent of the food court in American shopping malls. As one writer notes, Jerusalem has never been a city known for its cuisine. The dishes at this medieval dining market were apparently so badly prepared that it became known as the Rue de Malquisin—"Street of the Evil Cooking."[45]

Building was a principal activity of the Crusaders.[46] Shrines and churches were constructed or restored after centuries of neglect. The new churches were generally erected in places where Byzantine buildings had once stood and which were connected to events in the lives of Christ, his family, and his disciples. The most beautiful of all the Crusader churches in Jerusalem is that of St. Anne, named for the mother of the Virgin Mary. It was built in a delicate, ornate style and still offers some of the best acoustics of any building ever constructed in the Near East.

The Crusades were a time of great spiritual revival for Christianity in general. Deep-felt outpourings of religious devotion are evidenced by impressive hymns that originated in the twelfth and thirteenth centuries.

These include "Beautiful Savior"; "Jesus, the Very Thought of Thee" (attributed to Bernard of Clairvaux, ca. 1091–1153); and "All Creatures of Our God and King," by St. Francis of Assisi (1181–1226), who founded the Franciscan Order (ca. 1210), which eventually gained ownership of most of the important holy sites in Jerusalem. A man of great piety, St. Francis accompanied a group of Crusaders to Egypt in 1219, hoping to convert the sultan, but he failed.

MUSLIM RECONQUEST

Muslim forces did not acquiesce in the loss of their third-holiest city to the detested Franks. The Crusaders had established their independent Christian states of Edessa, Antioch, Tripoli, and Jerusalem because of the disunity of the Muslim peoples, but beginning in the mid twelfth century, Muslim forces crystallized and mounted a huge counteroffensive, aiming to drive the Europeans from Near Eastern soil altogether. Under the attacks of three successive Muslim military leaders—Zengi, Nureddin (Nur ed-Din), and Saladin (Salah ed-Din)—the Crusader states fell one by one, and the Christian church lost its military hold on the Holy Land.

In 1144 the Muslim ruler Zengi conquered the Christian state of Edessa in Armenia. This loss provoked the call for the Second Crusade (1147–1149), which ended in terrible defeat for Christian forces at Damascus. The Crusaders made the mistake of attacking the great Arab capital instead of carrying out their original plan of reclaiming Edessa. The defeat destroyed the Second Crusader army and dispelled the myth of Crusader invincibility forever. Even worse, the Christians ruined their critical buffer zone by attacking the independent Muslim kingdom headquartered in Damascus. Though the Muslims in Damascus repulsed the Crusaders, the city was weakened enough that it was absorbed by the powerful Abbasid caliphate under Zengi in Baghdad.[47]

By 1187 the Latin Kingdom of Jerusalem had been encircled, and Islam's greatest warrior, the Kurdish-born general Saladin, was planning the decisive military blow that would propel his armies to the gates of the Holy City. The borders of the Latin Kingdom were strongly defended by castles, and the Crusaders' mobile, battle-tested force had repulsed Saladin's early forays into the Holy Land. The strike came on 4 July 1187 on a two-pronged hill in the Galilee named the Horns of Hattin. Saladin, respected by both Muslims and Christians as honest and brave, crossed the Jordan with twenty thousand men and met a Crusader force of equal size. Unfortunately, the Crusaders were exhausted after a long forced march through the hot countryside. The results were devastating. The Christian army was destroyed, and all its leaders killed or captured. Jerusalem's king, Guy de Lusignan, was taken prisoner.[48]

Saladin turned south, down the Palestinian coastline, and conquered towns and strongholds with little opposition. Muslim forces reached Jerusalem on 4 September 1187, and by 12 October the Holy City was again in Muslim hands, after eighty-eight years of Christian domination. Before the Muslim siege was over, several of the churches lying on the outskirts of Jerusalem had been destroyed, either by Saladin's troops or by Christians themselves, who followed a scorched-earth policy to keep the infidel from acquiring anything of value.[49]

The general outlines of Crusader Jerusalem have been preserved to the present day. Many Crusader buildings continued to be used in later periods. A wealth of documents describing the Holy City under the Crusaders has survived; in fact, Crusader Jerusalem is probably the best known of all the periods of the City's history.[50] Because of all that has been written about the Crusades, it takes little imagination for Christians familiar with their tradition to see victorious crusading armies marching into Jerusalem singing apocalyptic hymns of joy hailing the millennial day. Such hymns as "Onward, Christian Soldiers" dredge up far different images for Muslims and Jews familiar with the history of the city which they too consider holy and eternal.

NOTES

1. In Idinopulos, *Jerusalem Blessed, Jerusalem Cursed,* 154. For a more colloquial version of the same speech, see Hallam, *Chronicles of the Crusades,* 21.

2. Ben-Arieh and Sapir, *Papers,* 15.

3. Idinopulos, *Jerusalem Blessed, Jerusalem Cursed,* 159.

4. Runciman, *First Crusade,* 74.

5. Hallam, *Chronicles of the Crusades,* 21.

6. Runciman, *First Crusade,* 30.

7. Hallam, *Chronicles of the Crusades,* 25.

8. Runciman, *First Crusade*, 41.

9. Runciman, *First Crusade*, 41.

10. Hallam, *Chronicles of the Crusades*, 34–35.

11. Hallam, *Chronicles of the Crusades*, 35.

12. Runciman, *First Crusade*, 65, 137.

13. Runciman, *First Crusade*, 70–72.

14. Hallam, *Chronicles of the Crusades*, 25.

15. Runciman, *First Crusade*, 90.

16. Hollister, *Medieval Europe*, 154.

17. Prawer, *Latin Kingdom of Jerusalem*, 11.

18. Bahat, *Illustrated Atlas of Jerusalem*, 90.

19. Hallam, *Chronicles of the Crusades*, 68.

20. Hallo et al., *Heritage*, 103–5.

21. Hallo et al., *Heritage*, 103–5.

22. Prawer, *Latin Kingdom of Jerusalem*, 12.

23. Hallam, *Chronicles of the Crusades*, 68–69.

24. This is an excellent example of the tremendous difference between an event that is foreseen and one that has been given God's approval. Some things that God knows will happen he deplores.

25. Why would all these things happen to the Jews? Why would many generations of Jews have to suffer for what one generation of Jews had done in killing their Messiah? And not all "the Jews," to be sure, had opposed Jesus; his friends Peter, James, John, others of the Twelve, Mary, Martha, Lazarus, and many hundreds of other Jews accepted him for what he claimed to be: God's Son and the Savior of the world. When the scriptures, therefore, speak of "the Jews" doing this or "the Jews" doing that, we understand plainly that the intent is certain Jewish leaders and their followers did this or that.

    Given the Latter-day Saint doctrine of personal responsibility for individual sins and not for the sins of others (Article of Faith 2), can anyone rightfully assign direct culpability for the death of Jesus to succeeding generations of Jews long after his mortal life? A specific answer to this provocative question is found in 2 Nephi 25:9: "As one generation hath been destroyed among the Jews because of iniquity, even so have they been destroyed from generation to generation according to their iniquities; and never hath any of them been destroyed save it were foretold them by the prophets of the Lord." In other words, only the Jews who opposed Jesus and killed him are responsible for those actions; later generations are responsible only for their own sins. Human cruelty to others throughout the ages should not, indeed cannot, be equated or confused with divine retribution or punishment. If any people oppose or reject God, that opposition will bring God's punishment.

26. Sachar, *History of the Jews*, 195.

27. Smith, *History of the Church*, 4:376.

28. Prawer, *Latin Kingdom of Jerusalem*, 12.

29. Idinopulos, *Jerusalem Blessed, Jerusalem Cursed*, 165–66.

30. Idinopulos, *Jerusalem Blessed, Jerusalem Cursed,* 166–67.

31. Bahat, *Carta's Historical Atlas of Jerusalem,* 50.

32. Bahat, *Illustrated Atlas of Jerusalem,* 93.

33. Benvenisti, *Crusaders in the Holy Land,* 38.

34. Idinopulos, *Jerusalem Blessed, Jerusalem Cursed,* 168.

35. Bahat, *Illustrated Atlas of Jerusalem,* 90.

36. Bahat, *Carta's Historical Atlas of Jerusalem,* 50.

37. Hyde, *Voice from Jerusalem,* 16.

38. Prawer, *Latin Kingdom of Jerusalem,* 221.

39. Idinopulos, *Jerusalem Blessed, Jerusalem Cursed,* 172.

40. Idinopulos, *Jerusalem Blessed, Jerusalem Cursed,* 174; Bahat, *Illustrated Atlas of Jerusalem,* 97.

41. Nibley, *Mormonism and Early Christianity,* 407–9.

42. Idinopulos, *Jerusalem Blessed, Jerusalem Cursed,* 172–73.

43. Yadin, *Jerusalem Revealed,* 102.

44. Bahat, *Illustrated Atlas of Jerusalem,* 98; Yadin, *Jerusalem Revealed,* 108.

45. Idinopulos, *Jerusalem Blessed, Jerusalem Cursed,* 180.

46. Ben-Arieh and Sapir, *Papers,* 16.

47. Idinopulos, *Jerusalem Blessed, Jerusalem Cursed,* 180–81.

48. Idinopulos, *Jerusalem Blessed, Jerusalem Cursed,* 181–82; Bahat, *Illustrated Atlas of Jerusalem,* 101–2.

49. Bahat, *Illustrated Atlas of Jerusalem,* 101.

50. Bahat, *Illustrated Atlas of Jerusalem,* 90.

17

LATER ISLAMIC JERUSALEM, 1187–1517

As the founder of the new Ayyubid dynasty, Saladin, whose name means "Soundness of the Faith," entered the Holy City on 2 October 1187 at the exact spot where the Crusaders had invaded it in 1099.[1] The date of the Muslim reconquest simply confirmed to the faithful that God had not only approved of but helped with the endeavor: it was the anniversary of the prophet Muhammad's ascent to heaven from the Haram esh-Sharif.[2]

AYYUBID JERUSALEM, 1187–1244

Saladin immediately reestablished Jerusalem as an Islamic city, and it remained so throughout the whole of its Ayyubid period, from 1187 to 1244. First, Saladin expelled the Christians from Jerusalem after forcing them to pay ransom to the new landlords. They left via David's Gate (present-day Jaffa Gate) in three columns, headed by the Templars, the Hospitallers, and the Patriarch, respectively. Those who could not pay were taken prisoner and deported to other Muslim cities.[3] Out of this episode grew stories of Saladin's magnanimity. It was said that he personally offered ransom money for poor but pious nuns and monks.[4]

Though he was a hardened warrior, both friend and foe alike came to view Saladin as an honorable man in dishonorable times. The Crusader chronicles—even in the bitterest hour of defeat—spoke of his tolerance and generosity. It was reported that during the final siege of Jerusalem, an army scout brought to Saladin a distraught woman whose young daughter had been stolen from her the night before. She said to the great Muslim leader: "'Yesterday some Muslim thieves entered my tent and stole my little girl. I cried all night, and our commanders told

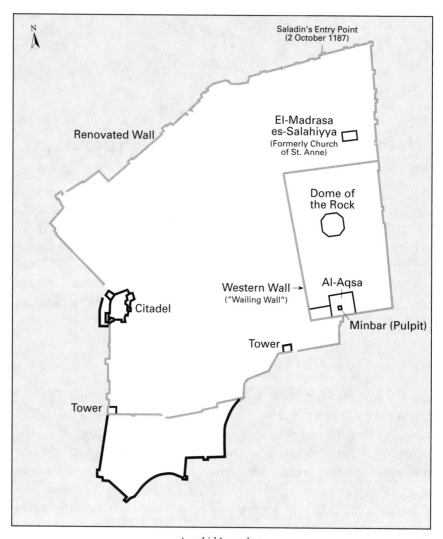

Ayyubid Jerusalem

me: the king of the Muslims is merciful; we will let you go to him and you can ask for your daughter back. Thus have I come, and I place all my hopes in you.' Saladin was touched, and tears came to his eyes. He sent someone to the slave market to look for the girl, and less than an hour later a horseman arrived bearing the child on his shoulders."[5] Such was the compassion reported of the man who now ruled Jerusalem.

Next, Saladin set about restoring the city's mosques by removing

Christian symbols. Crosses and portraits of Christ were removed from the Dome of the Rock. The military barracks at the al-Aqsa Mosque were destroyed, and Solomon's Stables were cleansed of accumulated filth. Crusader mosaics in almost all buildings were either removed or plastered over. All the mosques were purified by sprinkling in them rose water, brought in especially for that purpose from Damascus. As a sign of renewed Muslim pride and worship, a special handcarved *minbar* or pulpit, imported from Aleppo, was placed in the al-Aqsa Mosque. This pulpit had been ordered by Saladin's predecessor, Nureddin, before his death in 1174.[6]

Saladin restored the Dome of the Rock, the oldest existing monument of Muslim architecture in Jerusalem today. He had slabs of marble put on the walls of the shrine in 1189. In 1561 Suleiman the Magnificent added to its beauty by placing blue, white, and green tiles around the windows.[7]

Saladin struck back at Latin Christianity in general by turning churches into Muslim centers of worship and learning. The Church of St. Anne became a college for the study of Islamic law and was named after the conqueror himself, Madrasa Salahiyya. The Church of Mount Zion was transformed into Saladin's own residence. The Tomb of David on Mount Zion, sacred to Muslims as well as to Christians and Jews, was seized for a mosque. And the Church of the Holy Sepulchre had a minaret built above it. The northeast section of the latter church was given to the Dervish community, a mystic Muslim sect.[8] To the dismay of both Christians and Jews, Saladin decreed that the Mount of Olives would henceforth be considered *waqf,* Muslim sacred property. This action meant that Christians were no longer allowed to worship there nor Jews to be buried there.[9]

Later, Saladin became especially generous to non-Latin, Arabic-speaking Greek, Syrian, and Armenian Christians. The Greeks were invited back. The Syrian Jacobites received funds to repair their Church of St. Mark. And the Armenians received a special decree of protection from Saladin himself.

The new ruler was no less beneficent to the Jews, who were allowed to return to the Holy City, owing to the repeal of the ban against them issued by the Crusaders. The Jews resettled in the southeast corner of Jerusalem in 1190, creating a new quarter near the Western Wall, which exists to the present day. They came from many areas to live in the city, though most of the first returnees were former inhabitants of coastal towns destroyed by Saladin's army. Later, Jews immigrated from Morocco and Yemen. In 1211, Jews arrived from England and France, the first of them being three hundred rabbis.[10]

Some Palestinian Muslims were overjoyed at the changes taking place in their beloved city. Others did not care. Some newly returned Muslim inhabitants of Jerusalem had roots in the Holy City stretching back for centuries. They had not forgotten such traditions as those recounted by the tenth-century geographer al-Mukaddasi. He reported the teaching that on Judgment Day, both Mecca and Medina would journey to Jerusalem to pay their respects because it was at Jerusalem, and nowhere else, that the Resurrection would begin. Another tradition extolled the virtues of Jerusalem by indicating the special feeling that Allah himself has for the Holy City: "God looks toward Jerusalem twice a day" and "Judgment Day will not come until Allah leads the best of his bondsmen to live in Jerusalem and the Holy Land."[11]

Of course Jerusalem had its detractors in the twelfth and thirteenth centuries, as any city would. Such attitudes found expression in a famous saying about the absence of any real worth in visiting the city: "If [the whole distance] between me and Jerusalem were two parasangs [seven miles] I would not go there."[12] But Jerusalem's critics made no serious attempt to alter the city's status in the traditional hierarchy of holiness. And it was during this period that reverence for Jerusalem actually increased among some Muslims: "The city's religious ranking in orthodox tradition was virtually formalized in a famous saying which ranks Islamic cities according to the value of prayer in them. As the saying goes: One prayer in Mecca is equal to 100,000 prayers elsewhere; one prayer in Medina is equal to 50,000 prayers elsewhere; one prayer in Jerusalem is equal to 40,000 prayers elsewhere; and one prayer in Damascus is equal to 30,000 prayers elsewhere."[13]

In another Islamic statement of praise for Jerusalem's exalted status, both pilgrim and inhabitant were told that "one day in Jerusalem is like a thousand days, one month like a thousand months, and one year like a thousand years. Dying there is like dying in the first sphere of heaven."[14]

MORE CRUSADES

News of the disasters at Hattin (July 1187) and Jerusalem (October 1187) reached western Europe before the year's end. Pope Urban III is said to have dropped dead of grief over the loss of the Holy City. His successor, Pope Gregory VIII, immediately issued a moving appeal for help. In November, the archbishop of Tyre also called upon western rulers to aid the Latin Kingdom of Jerusalem. By the end of March 1188, Henry II of England, his eldest son Richard, Philip II of France, and the Holy Roman Emperor Frederick I Barbarossa had taken up the cross. The Third Crusade was born.

Meanwhile, the walls of Jerusalem had fallen into such disrepair that Saladin set about to rebuild them. He personally worked on the project to set a good example for his sons and his army commanders as the Third Crusade was bearing down on the Holy City.

Led by the colorful English ruler, Richard the Lionhearted, the Crusade had little effect on Jerusalem. First Richard beseiged Saladin's troops at Acre, north of Haifa, in 1189. The Muslims finally surrendered to Richard after two years of fighting. The Crusaders then marched down the coastline, conquering as they went. Just when it looked as though Richard's army might well reconquer Jerusalem, internal strife back home forced the English ruler to make a truce with Saladin and withdraw to his own realm.[15] By the terms of the treaty the Christians retained control of the coast of Palestine. The interior, including Jerusalem, remained in Muslim hands as long as Christian pilgrims were guaranteed access to the holy places.

Shortly after peace was reestablished, Saladin died (1193), and leadership of the Ayyubid dynasty passed to his descendants who quarreled among themselves. But the imprint Saladin left on Jerusalem remained. In some circles, he was remembered as Jerusalem's greatest Islamic ruler.[16]

Ayyubid control of Jerusalem lasted only until 1229, when the Latin Crusaders saw an opportunity to regain the territory they had lost at the hands of Saladin. In an unexpected turn of events, Saladin's nephew, the Egyptian Sultan Kamil, ceded Jerusalem to a new Crusader leader, King Frederick II of Germany, in return for Frederick's support against Kamil's nephew, Sultan Nasir of Damascus. Frederick entered the city and immediately crowned himself king of Jerusalem in the nearly empty Church of the Holy Sepulchre.

This was a great victory, but the way it had been gained outraged many in the Christian West. For Pope Honorarius III, who had sent the German king on his crusade, the only way Christ's dignity could be regained was by shedding the blood of the infidels who desecrated the Holy City as well as the holy sites by their very presence. To punish Frederick because he had not engaged the Muslims in battle and therefore had not shed enough blood, the pope ordered a local crusade against the king's estates in Italy, excommunicated Frederick, and placed Jerusalem under interdict.[17]

Frederick's difficulties with the pope were just the beginning. The Knights Hospitaller and Templar refused to serve in Frederick's army. The German king soon became fed up with the business of crusading. He left Jerusalem as inauspiciously as he had entered, barely six weeks after his bloodless conquest.

By that time, both Crusader and Ayyubid interest in Jerusalem was waning. Frederick's actions, as well as Sultan Kamil's dealing with the German king, are proof enough of that. Of course the Jews were expelled when Frederick arrived, because Jerusalem was again a Christian city, but it remained in Christian hands for just ten years. In 1239 another Ayyubid prince, al-Nasir Daud, captured it, only to lose it five years later to his Egyptian cousin, who was aided by fierce Khwarazmian Turk warriors from central Asia. They attacked Jerusalem, massacred the Christian inhabitants, destroyed church buildings, including the Holy Sepulchre, and burned Christian relics inside them. Ultimately, the Khwarazmians weakened not only the Ayyubid hold on Jerusalem—which they lost completely in 1244—but also the dynasty itself, which fell in 1250.[18]

For the most part, Saladin's successors did not view Jerusalem as a preeminent treasure to be carefully guarded. They did not share the special feelings toward Jerusalem possessed by rank-and-file Muslims. Though the rulers inherited Saladin's title "Protector of Jerusalem," they hardly lived up to that designation.

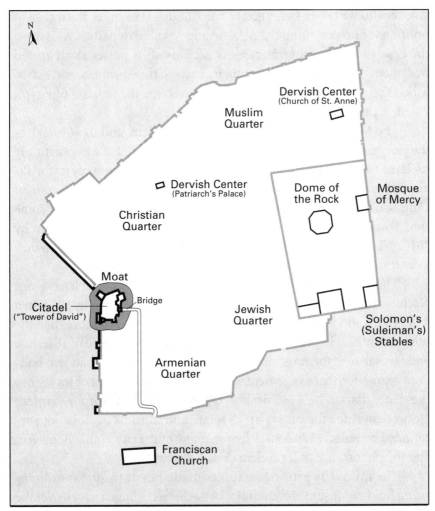

Mamluke Jerusalem

MAMLUKE JERUSALEM, 1244–1517

For nearly three hundred years, from the middle of the thirteenth century until the Turkish conquest of the Near East in 1517, Jerusalem was controlled by powerful, Egyptian-based military rulers. The Mamlukes, as they were called, were descendants of Turkish slaves who had been converted to Islam by the Abbasid caliphs. Indeed, the word *Mamluke* derives from the Arabic root *mulk*, "property," and means "those who had once belonged to the sultan." Mamlukes soon rose to positions of power within the Abbasid and Ayyubid dynasties. As is often the case, once this group became conscious of its power as an armed bodyguard, they turned against their masters, the Ayyubids, and established their own dynasty. The Mamlukes became the masters of Egypt, Palestine, and Syria.[19]

The Mamlukes had little interest in Jerusalem, and their rule over the Holy City was inefficient. The truth is that Jerusalem was practically useless as a political or military headquarters because most of its fortifications had been demolished in 1219 by the Ayyubid governor of Damascus.[20] The government was centered in the Citadel, called by some the "Tower of David" and the only fortification left in Jerusalem by 1310.[21] The city walls themselves remained in ruins until 1539, when they were restored by the Turkish sultan Suleiman the Magnificent.

The neglect of the Holy City was noted by the medieval Jewish sage Nachmanides, who traveled to Palestine for the first time in 1260. In a letter to his son in 1267 he wrote, "Palestine is destroyed more than the other countries, Judaea is the most devastated in the whole of Palestine and Jerusalem is the most destroyed of them all."[22] More than two hundred years later, that assessment was corroborated by another traveler to the Holy Land. In 1488 Rabbi Obadiah of Bertinoro recorded: "Jerusalem is for the most part desolate and in ruins . . . it is not surrounded by walls."[23] Without defenses, many of the city's inhabitants left, and the importance of Jerusalem declined sharply.

The militarily astute Mamlukes made Egypt the great military stronghold of Muslim civilization. They achieved a huge victory over the Mongols in 1260 at Ayn Jalut, near Nazareth. This Mamluke victory was of tremendous significance because it repelled a fierce warrior caste from the Asian steppe and preserved Islamic power in the region. The Mamlukes then turned their attention to the remaining Crusader strongholds in Palestine and systematically wiped them out. The Crusaders were finally expelled from the Holy Land with their loss of Acre in 1291.

Jerusalem was administered by two governors, one for political affairs and one for religious matters. The latter was responsible for the holy sites, including the Haram esh-Sharif and the Cave of the Patriarchs in Hebron, and for the care of pilgrims who still visited the city. He was also responsible for Muslim sacred property and the distribution of income from these holdings.[24]

With most of the Christians gone, Jerusalem became a focal point of Muslim pilgrimage, even though the city itself was neglected politically and economically. The Holy City attracted religious visitors and settlers from countries with large Islamic populations—Afghanistan, Anatolia, Egypt, Morocco, and Spain. In 1492, Muslims living in Spain were forced out of the country by the Christian monarchs, Ferdinand and Isabella, who had undertaken the Reconquista to purge their realm of infidels. The result was an influx of Muslim immigrants to the other countries of the Muslim world, including Palestine. Needy Muslim pilgrims who came to Jerusalem to worship during the Mamluke period found modest hostels in various parts of the city, and increasing numbers of Muslim pilgrims visited the tombs of the Patriarchs in Hebron.

During the fifteenth century, Christian pilgrimage to Jerusalem also increased. Monuments from the Crusader Kingdom still stood in Jerusalem, and travelers were anxious to see the tombs of Godfrey and King Baldwin I as well as the Church of the Holy Sepulchre, though it was in ruin. Many accounts written by pilgrims who went to Jerusalem to sightsee or worship have survived. An important one of these, by Felix Fabri, described Jerusalem as a city of many hills, quite uneven in topography, like Basel, Switzerland. Within the walls of Jerusalem, said Fabri, were areas filled with ruined houses and used by contemporary inhabitants as dumps for garbage and the carcasses of dead animals. In the parts of the city where men actually lived, one saw all kinds of people gathered together from every nation under heaven.[25] The modern reader cannot help but reflect on the contrast between the conditions in Jerusalem of this period and those of an earlier age when strict rules of cleanliness and sanctity were observed within the city.

Interestingly, the Dome of the Rock elicited the most admiration from Christian pilgrims during the Mamluke years. One Christian pilgrim considered it the only beautiful building in Jerusalem. Another wrote that in size and height, it was the most sumptuous work he had ever seen. Still others declared that there was nothing more beautiful or glorious in the Holy City than the Dome of the Rock.

Standing as it did on a pavement of white marble, the Dome of the Rock, from a distance, looked as if it were suspended in a pool of calm,

white water. Visitors thought it was spectacular at night when it was illu-
minated from the interior by numerous lamps, whose number has been
estimated in different sources to range from five hundred to twelve thousand. Felix Fabri described the effect of these lamps on the Dome of the
Rock as a fire of clear flame in a beautiful lantern. Ironically, the roof of
the shrine was destroyed by fire in 1448. But it was effectively restored by
the ruling Mamluke sultan to be even more beautiful than it had been
before.[26]

Christians in Jerusalem were usually tolerated because they were a
source of income and because of the absence of religious fervor among
the Mamlukes. A small Christian community remained in Jerusalem
from the Crusader period throughout the Mamluke years. The most
active members of this community were the Armenians and the Greek
Orthodox. The Franciscans had settled in Jerusalem in the fourteenth
century, mainly on Mount Zion, to guard the holy places of the Christian
faith. The Muslims considered the Franciscans as the official representatives of the country's Christian community. As a result, from time to time
the Franciscans were punished in retaliation for Christian abuse of the
Muslims. In 1365 all of the monks on Mount Zion were arrested and
exiled to Damascus. A similar event occurred in 1422 when Franciscan
monks were arrested and exiled to Cairo.[27]

There appears to have been constant friction between the Jews and
the Christians throughout the entire Mamluke period. In 1428 Jews tried
to purchase the building that housed David's tomb on Mount Zion. This
attempt failed because the site also included the room of the Last Supper
and therefore was of tremendous significance to Christianity. The ensuing dispute was finally settled by the Muslims, who took possession of
the building and turned it into a mosque.[28]

Despite all the difficulties of the period, Christians never quit looking with longing to Jerusalem. Sometimes they even requested burial in
the holy ground of the city. One example is Robert the Bruce, King of
Scotland, who decreed in his will that his heart be entombed in the Holy
City. In compliance with his request, his heart was removed for transport
upon his death in 1328. Unfortunately, the organ did not reach its destination because the vessel carrying it was lost at sea.[29]

Jerusalem was also held in particular reverence by the Dervishes, a
mystic Muslim sect that renounced the world in favor of voluntary

poverty. They adhered to the Qur'anic teaching that declares God to be as close to each person as his own jugular vein. The Dervishes (Persian, *darvish*, "poor") turned to mystical communion with the Divine. Ceremonies evolved in which repetition of words and body movements put the devotee into a trance.[30] The Dervishes had worship and study centers in Jerusalem. Two of the most important were located in the former palace of the Crusader patriarchs and in the former Crusader Church of St. Anne.

SEVERE DECLINE

As time wore on, Mamluke interest in Jerusalem fell even further, until the City was reduced to the status of an insignificant provincial town. The real seat of power was at Cairo, and the governors of Palestine resided at Ramla or at Gaza. Jerusalem was so far removed from any significant political activity that toward the end of the fifteenth century dignitaries who had fallen into disfavor with the Mamluke government were simply exiled to Jerusalem.[31]

Jerusalem's Mamluke rulers took no measures to develop its economy or to improve the material welfare of its citizens. The surrounding countryside could not supply many of Jerusalem's needs. Palestine's agricultural produce was exported to Egypt, and anyone who had any money at all was heavily taxed for the benefit of the Mamluke military leaders. The Mamluke government harassed Jewish craftsmen and small merchants and by 1440 had imposed such heavy taxes on these Jewish businessmen that they were forced to leave the city.[32]

One aspect of life in Jerusalem did flourish under the Mamluke rulers, however. They were great lovers of architecture and lavished the city with *madrasas* and *zawiyas* (schools and monasteries). Most of these buildings, distinguished by their alternate rows of white and red stones, were crowded into the Muslim quarter of the city. The many public buildings erected during this period were simple in design and displayed inscriptions from the Qur'an as well as information about the builder and the date of construction. The dates on buildings reveal that hardly a decade went by without some new structure being erected. Some of those buildings are still standing and may be seen today in the Holy City.

Taken as a whole, however, the two centuries of Mamluke rule were not a period of peace and prosperity for Jerusalem. Economic disaster, natural catastrophes (earthquakes, drought, and plague), and the unstable character of the regime itself caused the population of the Holy City to shrink from forty thousand during the Crusader period to approximately ten thousand at the end of Mamluke rule. Its decline is exemplified in a traditional tale about a pilgrim who had to ask several people for directions to get to the Holy City because no one was quite sure where it was. By the beginning of the sixteenth century, Jerusalem was too big for its inhabitants, and plots of land were actually cultivated within its boundaries.

NOTES

1. Bahat, *Illustrated Atlas of Jerusalem,* 104.

2. Idinopulos, *Jerusalem Blessed, Jerusalem Cursed,* 251.

3. Bahat, *Illustrated Atlas of Jerusalem,* 104.

4. Idinopulos, *Jerusalem Blessed, Jerusalem Cursed,* 250.

5. Hallam, *Chronicles of the Crusades,* 157.

6. Bahat, *Illustrated Atlas of Jerusalem,* 106.

7. Finegan, *Archeology of the New Testament,* 201.

8. Bahat, *Illustrated Atlas of Jerusalem,* 106.

9. Idinopulos, *Jerusalem Blessed, Jerusalem Cursed,* 251.

10. Klein, *Temple beyond Time,* 163; Bahat, *Illustrated Atlas of Jerusalem,* 106.

11. Idinopulos, *Jerusalem Blessed, Jerusalem Cursed,* 252–53.

12. Idinopulos, *Jerusalem Blessed, Jerusalem Cursed,* 254.

13. Idinopulos, *Jerusalem Blessed, Jerusalem Cursed,* 254.

14. Levine, *Jerusalem Cathedra,* 1:180.

15. Hallam, *Chronicles of the Crusades,* 184.

16. Idinopulos, *Jerusalem Blessed, Jerusalem Cursed,* 251–57.

17. Idinopulos, *Jerusalem Blessed, Jerusalem Cursed,* 255.

18. Bahat, *Illustrated Atlas of Jerusalem,* 107.

19. Peters, *Jerusalem,* 379–80.

20. Bahat, *Carta's Historical Atlas of Jerusalem,* 58–60.

21. Bahat, *Illustrated Atlas of Jerusalem,* 108.

22. Holtz, *Holy City,* 127.

23. Cited in Tal, *Whose Jerusalem?* 77.

24. Bahat, *Illustrated Atlas of Jerusalem,* 108.

25. Klein, *Temple beyond Time,* 164–65.

26. Klein, *Temple beyond Time,* 164–65.

27. Bahat, *Illustrated Atlas of Jerusalem,* 117.

28. Bahat, *Illustrated Atlas of Jerusalem,* 117.

29. Tal, *Whose Jerusalem?* 77.

30. Perry, *Middle East,* 72.

31. Bahat, *Illustrated Atlas of Jerusalem,* 113.

32. Avi-Yonah, *Jerusalem,* 75. See also Bahat, *Illustrated Atlas of Jerusalem,* 111.

18

OTTOMAN JERUSALEM, 1517–1917

In 1517 control of Jerusalem was seized from the Mamlukes by the Ottomans. This new Muslim dynasty produced thirty-six sultans who ruled over the Holy City for four hundred years, right into the twentieth century.

The Ottomans were originally a group of nomadic Turks that settled in central Asia to escape the Mongol expansion in the Far East. Having converted to Sunni Islam, they became a warrior dynasty that swiftly carved out an empire for themselves under the leadership of their founder and first sultan, Osman (1259–1326). His name is the Turkish form of the Arabic *Uthman*, the third caliph who succeeded the prophet Muhammad. It is from a distorted form of the founder's name that we derive the name of the dynasty and the empire, *Ottoman*.[1]

In 1326 the Ottomans firmly established their empire when they conquered the city of Bursa in Anatolia. By 1389 they had added the Balkans to their domain, all at Byzantine expense. Then they besieged the Byzantine capital itself, and in 1453 Constantinople fell. The Ottomans appropriated the former Byzantine capital for their own, renaming it *Istanbul* (Turkish, "The City"). The beautiful Church of the Hagia Sophia, built in Constantinople by Justinian in 537, was turned into a mosque (it is now a museum).

Without Christian enemies to fight in the east, the Ottomans trained their cannon and muskets on regions held by their fellow Muslims. They smashed a Mamluke army north of Aleppo, in Syria, in 1516 and became masters of all of Syria-Palestine. In a battle near Cairo, the Ottomans put an end to the Mamluke Empire. With Egypt under his control, Sultan Selim I, "the Grim," (1512–1520) proclaimed himself leader of the entire Muslim world and moved his capital from Cairo to

Istanbul. On 30 December 1516, Selim returned to Palestine and rode into Jerusalem at the head of his cavalry.[2]

The inhabitants of Jerusalem joyously welcomed the new sultan as he rode into the city, scattering coins to the cheering crowds and immediately gaining their approbation. Unfortunately, during the earliest years of Ottoman rule, Jerusalem remained as neglected as it had been under the Mamlukes. Despite the well-established status of Jerusalem as Islam's most important city after Mecca and Medina, Selim I did not designate it a district capital. Jerusalem remained a provincial town under the jurisdiction of the district capital of Damascus. In fact, Selim accorded Jerusalem no greater status than any other town of Palestine. When the sultan received the key to the city of Jerusalem, he did so not when he first took possession of it but later, in Gaza, along with the keys of other towns and cities in the Holy Land.[3]

The sultan appointed a governor, or *pasha*, to administer the day-to-day affairs of Jerusalem. The pasha had his headquarters at the Jawiliyya, the building in the northwest corner of the Haram esh-Sharif where the Antonia Fortress had stood fifteen hundred years earlier. Since 1427 this building had been the residence of the ruler of the city. From there he governed, reinforced by a small garrison and thirty cannon stationed at the Citadel.[4]

SULEIMAN'S REFORMS

Selim was followed by his son, perhaps the greatest of the Ottoman sultans, Suleiman I (1520–1566). In the west he was known as "the Magnificent"; his own people called him Suleiman "the Lawgiver." During his long reign, Suleiman accomplished much. He led armies into Hungary, stormed the walls of Vienna, invaded Persia, and conquered Baghdad. He revised the legal system of the Ottoman Empire and built prolifically in all his domains. He restored many Islamic shrines throughout his empire and guided it to an apex of cultural development.

Suleiman took a personal interest in Jerusalem. His most important accomplishment in the Holy City was the rebuilding of the city's walls, which had been left in ruins since 1219, some three hundred years. According to tradition, Suleiman had a dream in which he saw that he would be devoured by lions unless he rebuilt the wall around the city to

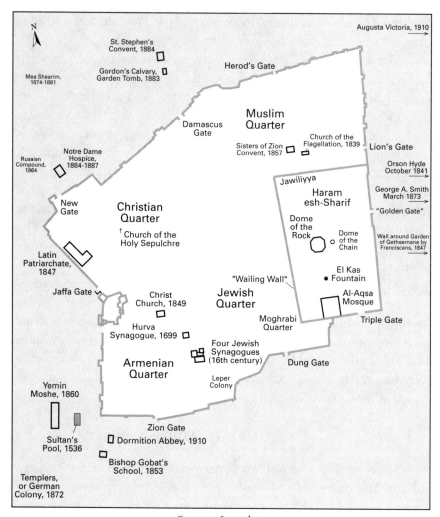

Ottoman Jerusalem

protect its inhabitants. That is why the sultan had images of lions placed in the wall above St. Stephen's Gate (also called Lion's Gate), to perpetuate his name and the story of his dream. In truth, the Turks viewed Jerusalem's reconstructed walls as a strategic necessity. They feared that the Mamlukes might try to reconquer Palestine and the Holy City. The new walls also afforded protection against other marauders.

Suleiman began reconstruction of the walls in 1537. Archaeological studies show that the Turkish builders followed the line of the previous city wall, using whatever building materials they could find—anything from the finely hewn and bevelled stones of the Herodian period to the ordinary building blocks of earlier periods. Suleiman's workers restored two of the city's ancient gates, now called Damascus and Jaffa. Apparently, during this time the Golden Gate and the Triple Gate in the Temple Mount wall were sealed. A traditional tale relates that Suleiman feared a Christian Messiah would try to enter through the Golden Gate, so he had it blocked up.

There were few places in the empire where fortifications were built and embellished on such a grand scale as they were in Jerusalem.[5] Most of the famous gates and the crenelated walls that still surround the Old City date from the reign of Suleiman the Magnificent. The walls themselves are magnificent, and only one mistake was made during their construction. According to legend, the sultan's architects failed to extend the southern wall far enough to bring David's traditional tomb on Mount Zion within the perimeter of the city. Pleased with the reconstructed wall in general but angered over the omission, Suleiman ordered the architects beheaded and then buried with full honors just inside Jaffa Gate.[6]

Suleiman also made improvements to the city's water system. The aqueducts from Solomon's Pools were repaired, and six fountains using water from these aqueducts were built in the city. In 1536 the Sultan's Pool was constructed. The improvement of the city's water system also made possible the creation of public gardens in Jerusalem.[7]

Finally, the great sultan repaired or refurbished important buildings inside Jerusalem. The most celebrated was the Dome of the Rock. To this day, the name of Suleiman and the date of A.H. 935 (A.D. 1528) can be seen inscribed on the lower windows of the shrine.

Suleiman's achievements were applauded by Muslim and Jew alike. The Jewish chronicler Joseph ha-Kohen recorded this approval: "In that year . . . God aroused the spirit of Suleiman king of Greece . . . and Persia and he set out to build the walls of Jerusalem the holy city in the land of Judah. And he sent officials who built its walls and set up its gates as in former times and its towers as in bygone days. And his fame spread throughout the land for he wrought a great deed. And they did also extend the tunnel into the town lest the people thirst for water. May God remember him favorably."[8]

DECLINE SETS IN

It is not hard to believe that God's hand was upon Suleiman, for Jerusalem not only prospered but reached unprecedented heights during his rule. The effects of that prosperity were seen all the way into the twentieth century. But the prosperity itself was short-lived as less able and less interested sultans succeeded Suleiman. During the reign of his son, Selim II (1566–1574), the sewage and water systems were neglected, roads deteriorated, and the number of Jerusalem's inhabitants declined. The Ottoman administration was no longer concerned about the development and maintenance of the city.[9]

Despotic governors of Jerusalem caused further decline by extorting money from the city's citizens. Having obtained their positions by bribery, the governors spent their terms of office recovering their initial outlay and adding as much profit to their personal coffers as they could manage. A reliable method to accomplish that goal was tax farming: anything collected beyond governmental requirements could be kept by the collector or other petty officials. And there was always something to be kept.

This enervating drain on the resources of the citizens resulted in a steady decline of Jerusalem's population. By 1677 there were no more than fifteen thousand inhabitants of Jerusalem. For all intents and purposes we can say that the Holy City ceased to develop from the mid seventeenth century to the mid nineteenth century. The only building that took place during these two centuries was the renovation of structures on the Haram esh-Sharif, which was carried out for religious reasons. The pilgrim literature of the period describes Jerusalem as a ghost town, depressing and filthy, many of its sections lying in ruins or turned into deserted fields, its houses neglected and disintegrating.[10]

The weakness of the Ottoman administration in Jerusalem led to the power and wealth becoming concentrated in the hands of such local families as the Nashashibis, the Husseinis, the Alamis, the Khalidis, and a few others. They held government offices, handed them down from father to son, and got wealthier in the process. By contrast, the lesser ranks of society, both Muslims and Jews, slowly but surely descended deeper and deeper into the mire of poverty.

One modern scholar believes that the Ottoman period was a

profound tragedy in another way for Arabic-speaking peoples of the Near East. From the fifteenth to the twentieth centuries, western Europeans were experiencing the cultural creativity of the Renaissance and the Enlightenment, with new explorations being carried out, scientific discoveries being made, and liberal political movements prompting the formation of modern democratic states. While these revolutionary changes were occurring in the West, the Arab east under the Ottoman sultans "sank more deeply into ignorance and apathy." The author of the foregoing concludes with this stinging rebuke: "Beyond their skill in the military arts, it is difficult to find any political, cultural, or religious achievement that can be credited to the Turks. Through the four hundred years of their rule, the sole preoccupations of the Sublime Porte, as the Turkish government was called, were to maintain peaceful order and to collect taxes. The vast empire was organized for no other purposes, as we can see by the way in which Palestine and Jerusalem were treated."[11]

Though we cannot concur completely with such sweeping criticism, especially considering Suleiman, it does represent the general tenor of the times. Well into the nineteenth century, the streets of Jerusalem were narrow and unpaved and its buildings dilapidated. Much of the Church of the Holy Sepulchre was destroyed by fire in 1808. And in 1825 the city was ravaged by a Bedouin revolt.[12]

Despite the undesirable circumstances, Jews continued to visit Jerusalem and a few settled there, despite the many difficulties. Jews throughout the world looked with longing toward the Holy City, hoping someday to live in the city of their forefathers. They continued to end their prayers and liturgical ceremonies with the words: "Next year in Jerusalem!"

RESTORATION AND REDEMPTION

In 1831 a powerful rebellion rocked the Ottoman Empire, led by the brilliant viceroy of Egypt, Muhammad Ali. He moved his powerful army into Syria-Palestine after being slighted by the government in Istanbul. For nine years (1831–1840), Palestine was ruled by Ali's stepson, Ibrahim Pasha, and Jerusalem's fortunes improved dramatically. Tax farming was abolished, a centralized administrative system supervised material improvements in the city, and Christians as well as Jews were given more freedom. Christians were permitted to run for election to the Jerusalem town council. Jews could pray at the Western Wall without special governmental permission and could repair their synagogues, particularly the four Sephardic synagogues, which had been built in the Jewish Quarter and were known collectively as the Jochanan ben Zakkai Synagogue.[13] For the first time in centuries, the rights to life and property were guaranteed to all inhabitants of the region.[14]

These developments were watched by three groups of people with resentment, fear, or foreboding. The Muslims were incensed that Christians were put on the same level with themselves. The Ottoman government in Istanbul feared that they might be toppled by Muhammad Ali. And the European powers feared that if the Ottomans were replaced, the resulting upset in the balance of power would have dire consequences on world stability. In 1840 a coalition led by Britain forced the Egyptian leaders to withdraw from the region, but it was a very different Palestine and a very different Jerusalem the Egyptians vacated compared to the ones they had conquered in 1831. Economic prosperity and safety, Jewish immigration, Christian missionary activity, travel, pilgrimage, tourism, and political equality were all on the increase. The Ottoman government was forced to take a new look at an old and long-neglected country, especially its holiest city—Jerusalem.[15]

It is not just coincidence that at the same time Jerusalem was being transformed from within, the Lord was moving to transform it from without. After centuries of spiritual decline, his true Church and the fulness of the Priesthood, which includes the keys of the gathering of Israel, were restored through the Prophet Joseph Smith. In the very year that Muhammad Ali and his stepson brought Palestine under their sway and began to restore Jerusalem through political power, God began to teach of and bring about Jerusalem's restoration through divine power. In 1831, the Lord, speaking through the Prophet Joseph Smith, urged: "Let them, therefore, who are among the Gentiles flee unto Zion. And let them who be of Judah flee unto Jerusalem, unto the mountains of the Lord's house" (D&C 133:12–13). Not only was this return of Judah to Jerusalem made possible by the reforms of Muhammad Ali, but it began while Jerusalem was under his control.

The significance of Jerusalem as a starting point for the gathering of Israel was on Joseph Smith's mind from the time the Church was first organized in 1830, just after he had fully encountered the doctrine while translating the Book of Mormon. When twenty-six-year-old Orson Hyde was confirmed a member of The Church of Jesus Christ of Latter-day Saints by the Prophet in 1831, he was given a special blessing: "In due time thou shalt go to Jerusalem, the land of thy fathers, and be a watchman unto the House of Israel; and by thy hands shall the Most High do a great work, which shall prepare the way and greatly facilitate the gathering of that people."[16]

A few years later, in Kirtland, Ohio, Joseph Smith emphasized the importance the Church attached to the doctrine of the gathering of Israel to their lands of inheritance, beginning at Jerusalem. He wrote in 1836: "One of the most important points in the faith of the Church of the Latter-day Saints . . . is the gathering of Israel . . . that happy time when Jacob shall go up to the house of the Lord, to worship Him in spirit and in truth, to live in holiness . . . when it shall . . . be said . . . the Lord lives that brought up the children of Israel from the land of the north, and from all the lands whither He has driven them. That day is one, all important to all men."[17] Later that same year, on March 27, during the dedication of the Kirtland Temple, the Prophet included in his dedicatory prayer the supplication that "Jerusalem, *from this hour,* may begin to be redeemed" (D&C 109:62; emphasis added).

According to Joseph Smith, what he said in that dedicatory prayer was first given to him by revelation (see D&C 109 headnote). In fact, Joseph's petition began to be fulfilled very soon. One week later, on 3 April 1836, the Lord, along with the ancient prophet Moses, appeared to Joseph Smith and Oliver Cowdery and "committed unto [them] the keys of the gathering of Israel from the four parts of the earth" (D&C 110:11). And in 1836 the Jewish population of Jerusalem began to increase significantly, so that by 1837 the Jews had become the largest ethnic group in the Holy City for the first time in eighteen centuries. Latter-day Saint sociologist Spencer J. Condie has shown that a number of interesting occurrences converged to bring this about.[18]

In 1836, while Jerusalem was under the control of Ibrahim Pasha, the property of the Jewish Quarter was finally redeemed from creditors. Once that section of the city was financially secure, its population grew more quickly. Also in 1836 Rabbi Abraham Zoref traveled to Egypt to see Viceroy Muhammad Ali and requested permission to build another synagogue in the Holy City. As an exception to policy, permission was granted. In 1837 an earthquake in the Galilee caused many Jews to flee to Jerusalem. "Although there was far greater absolute growth in the decades following 1840, the Jewish population growth between 1835 and 1840 represents the greatest *proportional growth* rate [in Jerusalem] during any five-year period in modern history."[19] It would appear that in addition to Joseph Smith, Muhammad Ali and Ibrahim Pasha were also partners with God in helping to bring about the fulfillment of prophecy. Their effective governance as well as their benevolence should not be forgotten.

ORSON HYDE AND JERUSALEM'S RESTORATION

In April 1840 the blessing and prophecy pronounced upon Orson Hyde nine years earlier about a pilgrimage to Jerusalem was fulfilled when he, now a member of the Quorum of the Twelve Apostles, left his family and friends in Nauvoo, Illinois, for a "quite peculiar and extraordinary mission" to Jerusalem.[20] During the April 1840 conference of the Church at Nauvoo, Elder Hyde was assigned to go to Jerusalem and dedicate the land of Palestine for the return of Judah and the house of Israel. Credentials were given him, specifically outlining his mission:

> Be it known that we, the constituted authorities of the Church of Jesus Christ of Latter-day Saints, assembled in Conference at Nauvoo, Hancock county, and state of Illinois, on the sixth day of April, in the year of our Lord, one thousand eight hundred and forty, considering an important event at hand, an event involving the interest and fate of the Gentile nations throughout the world—from the signs of the times and from declarations contained in the oracles of God, we are forced to come to this conclusion. The Jewish nations have been scattered abroad among the Gentiles for a long period; and in our estimation, the time of the commencement of their return to the Holy Land has already arrived.... [We] have, by the counsel of the Holy Spirit, appointed Elder Orson Hyde, ... to be our Agent and Representative.[21]

Elder Hyde was not surprised in April 1840 by his new assignment, for while he was contemplating his future labors in the kingdom in early March of that year, a "vision of the Lord, like clouds of light, burst into

[his] view," and he foresaw the details of his mission to the Holy Land.[22] He said:

> The cities of London, Amsterdam, Constantinople, and Jerusalem, all appeared in succession before me, and the Spirit said unto me, "Here are many of the children of Abraham whom I will gather to the land that I gave to their fathers; and here also is the field of your labors. . . . Go ye forth to the cities which have been shown you, and declare these words unto Judah, and say, "blow ye the trumpet in the land; cry, gather together, and say, assemble yourselves, and let us go into the defensed cities. Set up the standard toward Zion—retire, stay not, for I will bring evil from the north and a great destruction. The lion is come up from his thicket, and the destroyer of the Gentiles is on his way—he is gone forth from his place to make thy land desolate, and thy cities shall be laid waste, without an inhabitant. Speak ye comfortably to Jerusalem, and cry unto her, that her warfare is accomplished—that her iniquity is pardoned, for she hath received of the Lord's hand doubly for all her sins. Let your warning voice be heard among the Gentiles as you pass; and call yet upon them in my name for aid and assistance. With you it mattereth not whether it be little or much; but to me it belongeth to show favor unto them who show favor unto you."[23]

Several points are significant. In his vision, Elder Hyde was told to secure the assistance of the Gentiles in aiding his mission to benefit Jerusalem—that is, he was to seek material support from non-Jews for his journey to inaugurate the return of Judah to their ancestral home. That immediately recalls the promise of Gentile help with the gathering of Israel recorded in the Book of Mormon (see 2 Ne. 10:8–10).

Orson Hyde did not set out on a personal pilgrimage to the Holy Land to retrace the footsteps of Jesus, to seek personal fulfillment, or to "find himself," although his odyssey did become an intensely personal experience. Rather, Orson Hyde was sent as the Lord's official advocate for Abraham's posterity. He ministered under the direction of his prophet-leader, knowing his journey was backed by divine authority. He returned again and again in his writings and speeches to his mandate; without divine sanction, his journey to Jerusalem would have been empty of meaning.[24] His was very different from the rationale of other nineteenth-century American and European pilgrims, colonists, travelers, missionaries, and scholars who went to Jerusalem. For example, the American scholar and explorer Edward Robinson went to the Holy Land to uncover the truth of Israel's past and to correct misreadings of scripture. Philip Schaff, eminent German-American theologian and Christian historian, went to the Holy Land seeking comfort in a personal crisis. Others went for spiritual enlightenment or simply to retrace the footsteps of Jesus. Prominent millenarian Horatius Bonar spoke of the magnetic power possessed by the Holy Land. William Jowett, Pliny Fisk, Jonas King, and other Christian missionaries went to Palestine believing in the restoration of a Jewish Holy Land, but their program included proselyting the Jews, who then entered the new Israel by way of Christian baptism. [25]

Orson Hyde was sent to Jerusalem bearing a message of peace, pardon, and concern without insistence on the immediate need for Jews or Muslims to convert to Christianity. That is certainly amazing, if not unique, among Christian religious experiences in the Holy Land of the early nineteenth century. The message he carried from the Lord to Israel, especially the Jews, was to gather to escape destruction from the Gentiles: "Assemble yourselves.... Retire [into your defenced cities] . . . stay not. . . . The lion is come up from his thicket, and the destroyer of the Gentiles is on his way—he is gone forth from his place to make thy land desolate, and thy cities shall be laid waste, without an inhabitant." Yet at the same time he was warning Judah, Elder Hyde was told to comfort her: "Speak ye comfortably to Jerusalem, and cry unto her . . . that her iniquity is pardoned." [26]

Could the destruction to be enacted by the Gentiles include the horrors experienced by the Jews in the twentieth century? Could Orson Hyde, sent to Jerusalem holding keys of gathering, restoration, and redemption, have been saying that the horrors and struggles of the future could be avoided if the Jews heeded the prophetic voice of warning and began immediately to gather to Jerusalem? Could the devastation and atrocities of later decades have been avoided if Israel had listened to a prophet's voice then and there? Given that the Lord has always warned his children of impending destruction (2 Ne. 25:9), such possibilities are not improbable.

The forgotten pilgrim to the Holy Land in early Mormon history was Elder John E. Page, the apostle assigned to accompany Orson Hyde on his mission to Jerusalem. He is less known than Orson Hyde because he failed to complete his assignment, despite encouragement from the

Prophet Joseph Smith. The Prophet reiterated to both of them the significance of their undertaking:

> It is a great and important mission. . . . Although it appears great at present, yet you have but just begun to realize the greatness, the extent and glory of the same. If there is anything calculated to interest the mind of the Saints, to awaken in them the finest sensibilities, and arouse them to enterprise and exertion, surely it is the great and precious promises made by our heavenly Father to the children of Abraham; and those engaged in seeking the outcasts of Israel, and the dispersed of Judah, cannot fail to enjoy the Spirit of the Lord and have the choicest blessings of heaven rest upon them in copious effusions.[27]

Hyde left for Liverpool; Page stayed behind even though he was financially the better off of the two. Another LDS apostle, George A. Smith, attempted to persuade Page not to let Hyde go to Jerusalem alone, but Page rejected the proposal.[28] A young LDS missionary named George J. Adams did accompany Hyde to England, where he became a fervent proponent of the gathering of the Jews and of the downfall of the contemporary political order. After a time, Adams returned to the United States to prepare for the Second Coming. He left the LDS Church and became the leader of the Church of the Messiah and head of the Palestine Emigration Association, hoping to go to the Holy Land to witness firsthand the imminent and glorious events of Christ's return. In 1866 Adams escorted a group to Palestine, but once they settled in Jaffa, he ran off with their money and left them to fend for themselves.[29]

Elder Hyde sought for and received help from Gentile benefactors, just as his vision of March 1841 had instructed. He addressed a group of people at Philadelphia and spoke of the difficult financial circumstances he was in and the nature of the mission he had been sent to perform. As he was shaking hands at the close of his address, a stranger slipped him a purse of money, with only one request: that Elder Hyde remember him in the prayer he offered when he stood upon the Mount of Olives.[30] This the apostle did; in his dedicatory prayer he importuned God, "Do Thou bless the stranger in Philadelphia . . . let blessings come upon him from an unexpected quarter, and let his basket be filled, and his storehouse abound with plenty." In addition to the riches of the earth, Elder Hyde also asked the Lord to bless the stranger with the riches of eternity.[31]

Orson Hyde's journey from Frankfurt to Jerusalem brought him many trials and much suffering. He was exposed to danger, hunger, and disease. While he was in Beirut, a battle was fought within view of the city, and some eight hundred persons were killed. American ministers and missionaries received notice from Ottoman officials that they would have no protection and must leave the country. In a letter to Parley P. Pratt, Elder Hyde closed with, "You will hear from me again at the first opportunity, if the Arabs don't kill me." For days he lived entirely on snails because there was nothing else to eat.[32]

On his way by ship from Beirut to Jaffa, about 1:00 A.M. Elder Hyde and others saw a bright glistening sword with a beautiful hilt etched in the sky, grasped by an extended arm and hand. The sight raised the hair on Orson's head and his flesh tingled; the Arabs on board fell to the deck, crying loudly, "Allah! Allah! Allah!" He took this to be one of the signs in the heavens that had been promised him.[33]

Hyde disembarked at Jaffa, traveled overland to Jerusalem, and entered Jerusalem by the west gate (Jaffa Gate), as did most pilgrims in the early nineteenth century.[34] Once in the Holy City, he visited the sites in and around it, and his meditations upon the scenes of the city's history caused such a welling up of deep emotions that they were "spent only in a profuse shower of tears." His accommodations while in Jerusalem were the "Latin Convent," probably the Franciscan Convent of St. Savior.[35]

One year and six months after he had left Nauvoo, on a Sunday morning, 24 October 1841, before dawn, Orson Hyde walked eastward out of the city of Jerusalem, crossed the Kidron Valley, and ascended the Mount of Olives, where he sat in solemn silence and wrote his dedicatory prayer. Then he offered the prayer vocally. Elder Hyde asked the Lord to remove the barrenness and sterility of the land, to let springs of living water moisten the thirsty soil. He prayed for the return of the Jews and the assistance of kings and queens to help them (again an allusion to Old Testament and Book of Mormon teachings). Finally, the apostle reminded the Lord that he had fulfilled the mission assigned him and closed by ascribing honor and glory to God and the Lamb forever.[36] He erected a pile of stones as a monument and witness to the deed performed that day. (See Appendix 4 for the text of Elder Hyde's prayer.)

While sailing back to England, Orson Hyde wrote to the editor of the Church's British newspaper, *Millennial Star,* describing the details of his journey and predicting the future role of England in helping to bring about the results for which he had worked and prayed those many months. His letters, along with other reflections, were published in a pamphlet by the Church in England entitled, *A Voice from Jerusalem; or, a Sketch of the Travels and Ministry of Elder Orson Hyde.* His predictions proved accurate.

Official British involvement in Jerusalem had already begun in 1838 with the establishment of a consulate there. Other nations followed suit: France, Prussia, and Sardinia-Piedmont set up consulates in 1843, Austria in 1852, Spain in 1854, the United States and Russia in 1858, and Mexico in 1865. In fact, the first building constructed outside the walls of the Old City was the summer house of British consul James Finn, in the early 1850s. Unofficially, the British consulate soon began to perform the role long predicted of them—that of "nursing fathers, and . . . nursing mothers" (Isa. 49:23; 2 Ne. 10:8–9). Being exiles from other countries, Jewish immigrants generally held passports valid only for one year; after twelve months in Palestine, they forfeited citizenship in their homeland, and the Ottoman Empire refused to grant them new citizenship in Palestine. In 1839, British Foreign Secretary Palmerston instructed the consulate in Jerusalem "to protect the Jews generally" and to serve "as their advocate." [37]

Britain's intense interaction with the Jews culminated in the issuance of the Balfour Declaration on 2 November 1917. It stated that "His Majesty's Government view with favour the establishment in Palestine of a national home for the Jewish people." [38] Unfortunately, this declaration created problems because, a year before, Arab leaders had been given the impression that they would be rewarded with the leadership of an independent Arab nation in return for aiding the British war effort. [39]

AFTER ORSON HYDE

Interest in the gathering of Israel, especially the Jews, to their homeland continued among Church leaders after the return of Orson Hyde to America. By 1845 it was not just a tenet of Mormonism; it was a commandment to Jews throughout the world and a warning to Gentile rulers.

The Quorum of the Twelve Apostles issued a special proclamation in 1845 addressed "To all the Kings of the World": "We further testify, that the Jews among all nations are hereby commanded, in the name of the Messiah, to prepare, to return to Jerusalem in Palestine; and to rebuild that city and temple unto the Lord: And also to organize and establish their own political government, under their own rulers, judges, and governors in that country. For be it known unto them that we now hold the keys of the priesthood and kingdom which is soon to be restored unto them."[40]

This bold Proclamation evinced a tone of tremendous anticipation, clearly delineating God's designs for three groups of people: the Gentiles, the remnant of Israel in America, and the Jews in Palestine, particularly Jerusalem: "A great, a glorious, and a mighty work is yet to be achieved, in spreading the truth and kingdom among the Gentiles—in restoring, organizing, instructing and establishing the Jews—in gathering, instructing, relieving, civilizing, educating and administering salvation to the remnant of Israel on this continent; in building Jerusalem in Palestine; . . . that the whole Church of the Saints, both Gentile, Jew and Israel, may be prepared as a bride, for the coming of the Lord."[41]

Between 1845 and 1872, Church leaders focused their energies on solidifying the position of "American Israel," that is, in strengthening the Church after the death of Joseph Smith and the great trek to Utah. Nevertheless, they expressed profound interest in seeing the will of the Great Elohim fulfilled regarding the gathering of the Jews to Jerusalem. Many Jews did emigrate to the Holy City during this period—a development watched with resentment by Jerusalem's Muslims. Their consolation was that even though they were outnumbered, Muslim notables still dominated the town council, which had only token representation from the Jewish and Christian communities.[42]

By 1860 so many newcomers had arrived in Jerusalem that the city had to expand outside its walls. Building activity greatly intensified from the early 1860s until the outbreak of World War I and radically changed the appearance of the city. The first residential quarter built outside the city walls in 1860 was Mishkenot Sha'ananim, also called Yemin Moshe. It was constructed on land purchased by Moses Montefiore. At its center and intended to provide a livelihood for the inhabitants was a windmill, which is still visible today west of the Old City and opposite the

Armenian Quarter. This new residential quarter was a second center of Jewish life in the "New City" of Jerusalem.[43]

As the Spirit of the Lord worked upon Israel's branch of Abraham's posterity, Ishmael's branch was also affected. The Muslim community of Jerusalem tripled from approximately four thousand at the beginning of the nineteenth century to about twelve thousand near the century's end. Muslims also expanded outside Jerusalem's walls, north of Damascus Gate and Herod's Gate. Here one is reminded of the Jewish maxim that all the righteous, not just the Jewish people, have a share in the world to come. Will all the righteous of Abraham's posterity have a share in the Holy Land? One notes the singular condition imposed by Jehovah for any of Abraham's posterity to receive an inheritance of land: "The Lord appeared unto me [Abraham], and said unto me: Arise, and take Lot with thee; for I have purposed to take thee away out of Haran, and to make of thee a minister to bear my name in a strange land which I will give unto thy seed after thee for an everlasting possession, *when they hearken to my voice*" (Abr. 2: 6; emphasis added).

Many other neighborhoods and colonies sprang up during the last four decades of nineteenth-century Jerusalem. The paving of the Jerusalem-Jaffa road, the setting up of the first telegraph between Jerusalem and Beirut (and from there to all of Europe via Constantinople), the opening of the Suez Canal (1869), the improvement of maritime ports—all brought Europeans, both Jews and Christians, to Jerusalem in greater numbers. In 1860 the Palestine Pravoslavic Society started building a complex that included a church, a hospital, and hostels to house religious and consular missions. Today it is known as the Russian Compound. In 1872 the German Colony was established. In 1874 the construction of Mea She'arim, Jerusalem's ultraorthodox, or Hassidic, neighborhood was begun. Planned by architect Conrad Schick, it had attached houses built around the perimeter of a courtyard. It was completed in 1881.[44]

Many foreign Christian powers scrambled to build buildings as symbols of influence and power in the Holy City. Bidding for sites became highly competitive, and the European Christians were the ones able to pay top prices for the most desirable sites. Frequently hilltops were selected to afford wonderful views and make the buildings all the more dominant on the Jerusalem landscape. The Notre Dame Hospice, a massive building, was begun in 1884 across from the New Gate; the Augusta Victoria Sanatorium (now hospital) was constructed in heavy German Romanesque style on the crest of the Mount of Olives (east of the present site of Brigham Young University's Jerusalem Center); the Dormition Abbey and Church was built on Mount Zion. These institutions were a result of the visit of Kaiser Wilhelm II to Jerusalem in 1898 as part of a campaign to encourage German nationalistic sentiment.[45]

To a city lacking some of the most basic facilities, the Europeans brought improvements ranging from medical care to postage stamps. The Ottoman rulers did little to encourage such development. In a book written in 1878, British consul James Finn quoted a local Arab, whose sentiments probably reflected the attitude of other Jerusalem inhabitants: "Now Jerusalem is the Jewel after which all Europeans are greedy; why should we facilitate access to the prize they aim at?"[46]

The presence of certain foreigners in Jerusalem during the last half of the nineteenth century proved a great blessing to scholars interested in the early history and archaeology of the Holy City. Systematic investigation of the remains of ancient Jerusalem dates from the early 1850s and includes some of the greatest names associated with the archaeology of the Holy City. We marvel today at the detailed reports and exact drawings made by such researchers as Charles Wilson, explorer of the Temple Mount/Haram esh-Sharif from 1863 to 1868 and discoverer of Wilson's Arch; Charles Warren, who investigated the Gihon Spring, Hezekiah's Tunnel, and other structures from 1867 to 1870; and Conrad Schick, who is especially known for his documentation of gates and tombs. These are only three of many who have profoundly influenced the physical study of Jerusalem over the decades.[47]

AN APOSTOLIC REDEDICATION

In October 1872 another apostolic mission was organized by the Church to rededicate the Holy Land for Judah's return, to ask the Lord again for blessings upon the land, and to beseech him speedily to gather to it his ancient covenant people. George A. Smith, first counselor to President Brigham Young, headed the delegation. He was assisted by two members of the Quorum of the Twelve Apostles, Lorenzo Snow and

Albert Carrington, as well as Feramorz Little, Paul A. Schettler (a German Jew who had converted to the Church), and Thomas W. Jennings. The group included two women, Eliza R. Snow and Clara Little. The travelers received the following commission from President Brigham Young: "When you go to the land of Palestine, we wish you to dedicate and consecrate that land to the Lord, that it may be blessed with fruitfulness, preparatory to the return of the Jews in fulfillment of prophecy, and the accomplishment of the purposes of our Heavenly Father."[48]

The journey of the group to the Holy Land and back home took eight months. Along the way, they visited sites in Europe and Egypt. Having set sail for England on 6 November 1872, the party finally arrived at Jaffa on 23 February 1873, where they were conducted to the Turkish customs officer, who "examined only one passport, and passed [them through]," according to the account of George A. Smith. At Jaffa the group saw several people connected with the failed scheme of the apostate George J. Adams. On Monday, 24 February, the party started out for Jerusalem on horseback. They pitched camp near Jaffa Gate on the afternoon of 25 February 1873. President Smith noted that it was at Jaffa Gate where "most of the business in Jerusalem is done."[49]

The principal record of the travels of the Smith party contains fascinating details about the culture of Palestine and Jerusalem in the nineteenth century, especially about pilgrimages, and the modern reader may see that some things have not changed appreciably in the more than one hundred years since. Like Orson Hyde before them, the little band of Latter-day Saint pilgrims visited many of the traditional holy places and found swarms of beggars at most of the sites they visited. They also noted that "travelers in Palestine suffer greatly from the sun, but [they] were early in the season—two weeks earlier than travelers generally set out for Jerusalem." President Smith said the hill country around Jerusalem looked like "one immense limestone quarry." At Bethlehem, the group visited the Greek Church of the Nativity to see the spot where Christ was said to have been born, marked by a now-famous silver star. Despite the many beggars and hawkers of goods who had imposed themselves on the holy sites, the Latter-day Saints were thrilled to walk where Jesus had walked nearly nineteen hundred years before.[50]

The climax of the journey for the Smith party came on Sunday,

2 March 1873, while the party was on the Mount of Olives. There President Smith again dedicated the Holy Land for the return of Israel.

> Cloudy, breezy, cool. Our dragoman packed one tent, stools, table etc. on a mule, and we rode to the Mount of Olives, where the tent was pitched and all assembled within it between 9 & 10 A.M., except sister Claire S. Little, who remained in camp. Meeting was opened by prayer by Albert Carrington, in his prayer dedicating the ground, tent, and the land of Israel generally. Thomas W. Jennings then took position as watchman outside, he and bro. Carrington not having robes with them. I, Bros. Lorenzo Snow, Paul A. Schettler, and Feramorz Little, and Sister E. R. Snow being duly prepared, Bro. Snow offered prayer in which the same dedicatory sentiments were contained. After the requisite preliminaries, I was mouth, remembering the general interest of Zion, and dedicating this land, praying that it might become fertile, and the early and latter rains descend upon it, and the prophecies and promises unto Abraham and the prophets be fulfilled here in the own due time of the Lord. After the preliminaries again, Bro. Snow was mouth, remembering the interests of Israel, and again I was mouth, and afterwards dismissed the meeting at 10:34 A.M.[51]

From President Smith's account it appears that the tent which the group was in that day served as a temple or tabernacle, protecting them from "profane eyes." The Holy Land and the Holy City were dedicated by those who wore special robes. For George A. Smith and others, the land of Israel was imbued with a special quality of holiness. To Eliza R. Snow, the dedication of the Holy Land was the profound spiritual experience of the tour, "realizing as I did that we were worshipping on the summit of the sacred Mount."[52]

Bearing a letter of introduction from the rabbi of the Jewish Congregation at San Francisco, George A. Smith called upon Abraham Askenasi, the chief rabbi of Jerusalem. A venerable man, tall, heavy set, and wearing a flowing beard, he was pleased by President Smith's visit and showed him the synagogue. Later he and several Jewish elders visited President Smith, who wrote of the experience to Brigham Young: "March 4, at 10 A.M. We received a visit from Abram Askenasi, Chief Rabbi in Jerusalem; we understand he is selected by the Turkish sultan, and has received some titular orders from him. They [Askenasi and party] express a firm faith in the redemption of Israel and the return of the ten tribes. . . . The interview was very pleasant and interesting, and the Rabbi and three of their principal men who accompanied him appear to be men of intelligence." [53]

After visiting the Garden of Gethsemane and other spots made sacred by the presence of Jesus centuries earlier, the group left for Damascus on 5 March and arrived at Beirut on 21 March. George A. Smith was relieved that so long a journey on horseback had ended without mishap for a man of his age and weight (three hundred pounds). During their month-long sojourn, they were often asked if they were planning to settle in the Holy Land. Smith replied that they were not, but he could take a thousand Mormons, dam up the Jordan River, and make several thousand acres very productive. [54]

Back home in Salt Lake City, President Smith delivered an account of his group's journey to a large crowd assembled in the Tabernacle on 22 June 1873. He expressed sentiments similar to those his predecessor, Orson Hyde, had uttered years before. He, too, was on the Lord's errand, not a personal journey but an "institutional journey" empowered by a special mandate and authority from God. In fact he said that from a personal standpoint very little was, at present, inviting about the country. But the group all believed in their hearts that Zion was moving onward and upward and that no power could stay her progress. When they were on the Mount of Olives, with faces bowed toward Jerusalem, they felt the day was not far distant when Israel would gather and those lands would teem with a people who would worship God and keep his commandments, that the bounties and blessings of eternity would be poured out in abundance upon that desert land, and that all prophecies concerning the restoration of the house of Israel would be fulfilled. [55]

Besides the dedicatory prayers offered by Orson Hyde and George A. Smith (and company), Elders Anthon H. Lund and Ferdinand F. Hintze (first president of the Turkish Mission) dedicated the land on the Mount of Olives, 8 May 1898. Altogether there were ten dedications of the Holy Land by nine latter-day apostles from 1841 through 1933. Always they were for the benefit of Abraham's posterity, the return of the Jews, and the rebuilding of Jerusalem. [56]

ZIONISM

By 1873 almost everything was in place for the Lord's designs to be accomplished. The Holy City and the Holy Land had been dedicated. A proclamation commanding the Jews to return and rebuild Jerusalem had been issued (1845). Jerusalem was being redeemed economically and domestically. Another major occurrence signaled the increase of Jewish interest in Jerusalem. That was the rise of Zionism.

During the last quarter of the nineteenth century, anti-Semitism grew violent. Five million Jews in Russia were restricted to an area known as the Pale of Settlement. After the assassination of Tsar Alexander II in 1881, Russia's rulers used the unpopular Jews as a scapegoat for the country's problems. Local authorities and the Tsar's ministers encouraged savage pogroms, the periodic destruction of Jewish communities. In France in the 1890s, patriots led a popular attack on the French army captain, Alfred Dreyfus, who was a Jew. Other Jews, such as the Viennese journalist Theodor Herzl, reacted forcefully. They asked: If anti-Semitism could occur in the most civilized and sophisticated of countries, how could the Jews thrive in any place except their own country?

In 1896 Herzl published his history-making book, *The Jewish State*. The following year he organized a conference of 206 delegates to form the World Zionist Organization. Zionism was officially born. The Zionists looked back to the model of ancient Israel, when Mount Zion had been the fortress of Jerusalem. They began working toward reestablishing Jerusalem as the capital of their own free and independent nation. In the meantime, the Ottoman Empire limped along as the "sick man of Europe," until it was displaced in Palestine by Great Britain at the end of World War I.

On 9 December 1917 a British force reached the gates of Jerusalem. Two days later the chief of the British Expeditionary Force for the whole Near East, Sir Edmund Allenby, arrived in Jerusalem to take command of the Holy City. As an expression of reverence for the city where Abraham, Jesus, and Muhammad had walked, General Allenby dismounted his horse and walked on foot through Jaffa Gate. On top of the Herodian Citadel, he encouraged "every person [to] pursue his lawful business without fear of interruption."[57] Allenby made good on his promise of physical safety; however, he could not foresee the difficulties that would ensue a few years later as a result of seemingly contradictory promises made by his government to Jews and Arabs.

EARLY MISSIONARIES IN THE HOLY LAND

Before 1886, Church leaders encouraged missionary efforts on the part of those who traveled to Jerusalem to dedicate the Holy Land, but such encouragement was always in connection with the Gentile nations that Church representatives encountered on their way to or from Palestine. Mention of proselyting in the Holy Land itself or among the Jews was either absent or ambiguous.

In the spring of 1886 two Church leaders, Francis M. Lyman and Joseph Tanner, traveled to Palestine from Constantinople. In Haifa they visited the German colonies that had been established about 1870 by devout Templers who had come to Palestine to await the Second Coming of the Lord. Tanner, impressed by the thrift and orderliness of the Germans, wrote to Daniel H. Wells, president of the LDS European Mission, suggesting the possibility of creating a branch of the Church among the German colonists. He believed that would be a stepping-stone to missionary work among the Arabs.[58] He did not discuss the Jews.

President Wells approved the transfer of Elder Jacob Spori to Palestine from Constantinople, where the latter had been proselyting since December 1884. He was chosen because he could speak both German and French, owing to his Swiss background. Joseph Tanner asked him how he felt about the hardships he would surely encounter. Spori happily recounted a dream he had in which he was told to begin his efforts at Haifa. He told of seeing a man in a blacksmith shop who was prepared to receive him and the message he had to deliver. Spori said that if he saw the man again, he would know him.[59]

Elder Spori landed in Haifa not long afterwards and made his way to the street he had seen in his vision. A blacksmith with a short, coal-black beard ran out of his shop and enthusiastically told Spori that he had seen him in a dream the night before and wanted to hear his message. The man's name was Johan Georg Grau. He listened to the gospel message and was baptized on 29 August 1886 in Acre Bay. A month later

Georg baptized his wife, Magdalena, and both became enthusiastic professors of the Latter-day Saint faith to their friends and neighbors.[60]

The conversions of Grau and his wife marked the beginning of a branch of the Church that grew to twenty-five converts over the next six years: nineteen Germans, three Arabs, two Russians, and one Austrian. In the summer of 1888, Church leader Ferdinand F. Hintze visited Haifa and found the branch in good order, ably led by Elder Georg Grau. Grau emigrated to Utah for a few years after his wife's death but returned to Palestine in the late 1890s as a missionary. At one point the idea of a Mormon colony near Jerusalem modeled after the German and American colonies was proposed, but the idea was dropped.[61]

Jacob Spori labored in Palestine, teaching mainly German groups in the Haifa area but also in Jaffa and Jerusalem. The German leaders in Jerusalem listened to his message with patience, and the Templer Society in the Holy City treated him with kindness and spoke of George A. Smith with esteem. Having served the Church well, Spori was finally released as a missionary. He sailed back to Constantinople in 1887 and on to the United States in March 1888.

Elder Joseph Tanner labored about one year in Palestine and was the means of converting fourteen people—nine Germans, four Russians, and one Arab. Three of those converts lived in Jaffa, and the rest in Haifa. Tanner was followed by others who carried on the work of proselyting and strengthening the members of the Church in Jaffa and Haifa during the closing years of the nineteenth century. In 1903, because of political unrest in the area, the Haifa Branch, the only unit of the Church in the Holy Land, was closed; all missionary work in Palestine ceased. Six years later the Turkish Mission was also closed, and for about twelve years no American representatives of the Church labored in the Near East.[62]

The political unrest that kept LDS missionaries out of the Near East at the beginning of the twentieth century also signaled the end of the Ottoman Empire. In 1908 a group of Ottoman military officers called the Young Turks forced Sultan Abdul-Hamid II to restore a constitution that guaranteed parliamentary government throughout the empire. It had been adopted in 1876 but had been suspended after only one year. In 1922 a Turkish military hero named Mustafa Kemal (later called Kemal Ataturk) headed a nationalist movement that led to the abolishment of the Ottoman Empire and the establishment of the Republic of Turkey in

1923. Once the Ottoman government was dissolved, Jerusalem's fate lay in the hands of western powers. But as the events of the nineteenth century demonstrated, the Holy City was always under the watchful eye of her real king, the Lord.

NOTES

1. Peterson, *Abraham Divided,* 245, note.

2. Klein and Klein, *Temple beyond Time,* 167.

3. Bahat, *Illustrated Atlas of Jerusalem,* 118.

4. Bahat, *Illustrated Atlas of Jerusalem,* 118.

5. Bahat, *Carta's Historical Atlas of Jerusalem,* 64.

6. Vilnay, *Legends of Jerusalem,* 208.

7. *Encyclopedia Judaica,* 9:1434.

8. Cited in *Encyclopedia Judaica,* 9:1433.

9. Bahat, *Illustrated Atlas of Jerusalem,* 120.

10. Bahat, *Carta's Historical Atlas of Jerusalem,* 67.

11. Idinopulos, *Jerusalem Blessed, Jerusalem Cursed,* 264.

12. Bahat, *Carta's Historical Atlas of Jerusalem,* 67.

13. Bahat, *Carta's Historical Atlas of Jerusalem,* 66. The complex of four synagogues built in the Jewish Quarter became the center of Spanish-Jewish life in Jerusalem. Those Jews had come to Jerusalem after their expulsion from Spain in 1492.

14. Idinopulos, *Jerusalem Blessed, Jerusalem Cursed,* 267–68.

15. Idinopulos, *Jerusalem Blessed, Jerusalem Cursed,* 271.

16. Barrett, *Joseph Smith and the Restoration,* 469.

17. Smith, *History of the Church,* 2:357.

18. Condie, "Pivotal Year." His thesis is confirmed by Tal, *Whose Jerusalem?* 94.

19. Condie, "Pivotal Year."

20. From Parley P. Pratt's introduction to Hyde, *Voice from Jerusalem,* 2.

21. Smith, *History of the Church,* 4:112–13.

22. Smith, *History of the Church,* 4:375.

23. Smith, *History of the Church,* 4:376.

24. Smith, *History of the Church,* 4:372–79.

25. See the summary in Epperson, *Mormons and Jews,* 158–63.

26. Hyde, *Voice from Jerusalem,* 2–3.

27. Smith, *Teachings of the Prophet Joseph Smith,* 163.

28. Smith, *History of the Church,* 4:372.

29. Holmes, *Forerunners,* 27–36.

30. Barrett, *Joseph Smith and the Restoration,* 471.

31. Smith, *History of the Church,* 4:458.

32. In Barrett, *Joseph Smith and the Restoration,* 472.

33. Hyde, *Sketch,* 24.

34. Hyde, *Voice from Jerusalem,* 7.

35. Epperson, *Mormons and Jews,* 169.

36. For the complete text, see Smith, *History of the Church,* 4:456–59.

37. Blumberg, *Zion Before Zionism,* 113.

38. In Regan, *Israel and the Arabs,* 11.

39. Idinopulos, *Jerusalem Blessed, Jerusalem Cursed,* 273.

40. Clark, *Messages of the First Presidency,* 1:254.

41. Clark, *Messages of the First Presidency,* 1:254.

42. Idinopulos, *Jerusalem Blessed, Jerusalem Cursed,* 270.

43. Bahat, *Illustrated Atlas of Jerusalem,* 122–23.

44. Bahat, *Illustrated Atlas of Jerusalem,* 122–23.

45. Pullam, "Great Building Race," 23.

46. Pullam, "Great Building Race," 21.

47. See Geva, *Ancient Jerusalem Revealed,* 1; and the same author's excellent list and summary in *New Encyclopedia of Archaeological Excavations,* 2:801.

48. Barrett, "Story of the Mormons in the Holy Land," 18.

49. Smith, in *Journal of Discourses,* 16:92.

50. Smith, in *Journal of Discourses,* 16:93–98. See further excerpts from President Smith's discourse in Appendix 5.

51. In Pusey, *Builders of the Kingdom,* 120–21.

52. Barrett, "Story of the Mormons in the Holy Land," 30. See also *Millennial Star,* 35:200–201.

53. Barrett, "Story of the Mormons in the Holy Land," 24. See also "Mormons' Kinship with the Jews," *Jerusalem Post,* 2 July 1975, 5.

54. Smith, in *Journal of Discourses,* 16:100.

55. Smith, in *Journal of Discourses,* 16:101–2. See also Appendix 5.

56. For additional information on these dedications of the land, see Berrett and Ogden, *Discovering the World of the Bible,* 43–44, 159.

57. In Gray, *History of Jerusalem,* 289.

58. Baldridge, *Grafting In,* 5. See also Barrett, "Story of the Mormons in the Holy Land," 36.

59. Barrett, "Story of the Mormons in the Holy Land," 36.

60. Barrett, "Story of the Mormons in the Holy Land," 37.

61. Baldridge, *Grafting In,* 6.

62. Barrett, "Story of the Mormons in the Holy Land," 37; Baldridge, *Grafting In,* 6.

19

JERUSALEM, THE JEWS, AND THE CHURCH

The Jerusalem of the past is linked to the Jerusalem of the present and the future by prophecy. Indeed, the return of the Jews to their ancient homeland in this city and land is in fulfillment of prophecy. Yet the prophecies of a literal, physical gathering are found only in the Old Testament and in uniquely Latter-day Saint scripture, which means that the concept of gathering is known only among Jews and Christians. And even among the Christians there are at least three schools of thought: first, such prophecies were fulfilled in the return of the Jews from Babylonian exile; second, such a gathering belongs in some distant millennial era; and third, the present-day gathering of Judah involves prophecy in the process of being fulfilled (which process will continue into the Millennium).

Elder James E. Talmage of the Quorum of the Twelve Apostles described the "last days," in which we now live, as a "gathering dispensation": "The return of the tribes [of Israel] after their long and wide dispersion is made a preliminary work to the establishment of the predicted reign of righteousness with Christ upon the earth as Lord and King; and its accomplishment is given as a sure precursor of the Millennium. Jerusalem is to be reestablished as the City of the Great King on the eastern hemisphere; and Zion, or the New Jerusalem, is to be built on the western continent; the Lost Tribes are to be brought from their place of exile in the north."[1]

Elder Ezra Taft Benson also taught: "The reestablishment of the Jews in Palestine [is] one of the events to precede the second coming of the Master. Isaiah said they will be gathered together, the dispersed of

Judah, from the four corners of the earth and they will be set in their own land, they will build the old wastes and repair the waste cities (see Isaiah 11:11–12)."[2]

A PRESENT OR YET FUTURE GATHERING?

It is true that the gathering of Israel will continue into the Millennium, but great and glorious are the developments that will precede the fulfillment of the prophecies of gathering. What a shame to look only to the completion of the prophecies and fail to recognize and appreciate the process itself.

This great gathering of Judah is the will of the Lord. Nephi spoke of it as a "marvelous work and a wonder" (2 Ne. 25:17). This gathering is a joyous, marvelous, wonderful thing as it has been revealed and expounded upon by prophets of every dispensation. It is a necessary prelude to great spiritual blessings for those gathering and for the gathered. It is a sign of the times, a sign of the "last days" in which we live, a confirmation of both prophets and prophecy, a signal of the imminency of cataclysmic events in the heavens and upon the earth, and a warning to put our lives and our homes in order, a sign of the Savior's imminent advent to reign personally upon the earth forever and ever.

THE GATHERING: A PART OF THE LATTER-DAY RESTORATION

The Lord first announced the gathering of the Jews in this dispensation through the angel Moroni, who appeared to the Prophet Joseph Smith in 1823. In that visitation Moroni quoted, among other scriptures, the entire chapter of Isaiah 11, which included the verse that "the Lord shall . . . gather together the dispersed of Judah from the four corners of the earth" (Isa. 11:12), and he stated that "the eleventh chapter of Isaiah . . . was about to be fulfilled" (JS-H 1:40). That mention of Judah in such a brief encounter between heaven and earth gives the gathering of the Jews a position of priority in the Restoration.

In 1831, the Lord, speaking through the Prophet Joseph Smith, warned Judah to "flee unto Jerusalem" (D&C 133:13). First, Jerusalem is designated as the ultimate destination for the Jews, a place of refuge, as it were. Second, the formulation "let them . . . flee unto Jerusalem" suggests the need for haste and the probability of peril should they linger.

In March 1832, Joseph Smith inquired of the Lord, "What is to be understood by the two witnesses, in the eleventh chapter of Revelation?" In response, the Lord revealed the following: "They are two prophets that are to be raised up to the Jewish nation in the last days, at the time of the restoration, and to prophesy to the Jews after they are gathered and have built the city of Jerusalem in the land of their fathers" (D&C 77:15). From this revelation, the Prophet Joseph Smith learned a number of details concerning the physical aspects of the gathering of the Jews.

First, the gathering of the Jews would take place in these "last days, at the time of the restoration." This statement confirmed the angel Moroni's message that the gathering was yet future but "about to be fulfilled."

Second, in these last days a Jewish nation would be established after an absence of nearly two thousand years. That the word *nation* in this instance meant a political state with its own territory and government was spelled out in considerable detail in subsequent revelations.

Third, the gathering of the Jews would be to "the land of their fathers," which gathering would allow them to rebuild "the city of Jerusalem."

Fourth, the Church had a role to play in that two prophets would be raised up "to the Jewish nation" and would prophesy to the Jews "after" they had gathered.

Thus, as of March 1832, the Prophet knew that the time for the gathering of Judah had arrived, that their gathering place was in the mountains of Jerusalem, that a nation would be established in the land of their fathers, and, most important, it all was the Lord's will.

On 3 April 1836, a singular event occurred to mark the focal point of all prophecy related to the gathering. Joseph Smith recorded that while he and Oliver Cowdery were engaged in prayer in the Kirtland Temple, they experienced several divine manifestations, including one in which "Moses appeared . . . and committed unto us the keys of the gathering of Israel" (D&C 110:11). Once again the Prophet was instructed from on high about the gathering of Israel in the last days, but this time it was by a prophet who had anciently held the keys of authority through which the Lord would restore the children of Israel, including the Jews, to their promised lands. That was an important part of the divine plan from the beginning.

In a letter written in 1840, Joseph Smith laid to rest the controversy over just when the gathering process of the Jews would begin. The Prophet indicated that the Jews "have been scattered abroad among the Gentiles for a long period; and in our estimation, the time of the commencement of their return to the Holy Land has already arrived."[3] With the restoration of the keys, the great gathering of Judah and the rest of the house of Israel was underway. Never again would it be spoken of by Latter-day Saint leaders as an event yet future.

JUDAH AND JERUSALEM

The Savior, while visiting the lands of the Book of Mormon, explained that the gathering of Israel would take place because of the covenants made with their fathers:

> And I will remember the covenant which I have made with my people; and I have covenanted with them that I would gather them together in mine own due time, that I would give unto them again the land of their fathers for their inheritance, which is the land of Jerusalem, which is the promised land unto them forever, saith the Father. . . .
> . . . Then shall this covenant which the Father hath covenanted with his people be fulfilled; and then shall Jerusalem be inhabited again with my people, and it shall be the land of their inheritance. (3 Ne. 20:29, 46)

Because of the Lord's ancient covenant with them, Judah not only would be gathered in due time but would inherit the land of Jerusalem. Furthermore, the Savior's second coming would be preceded in part by the gathering of the Jews, the building up of Jerusalem, and the construction of a Temple. In 1843, the Prophet Joseph Smith prophesied of the "last days" and the "second coming" in these remarkable words: "Judah must return, Jerusalem must be rebuilt, and the temple. . . . It will take some time to rebuild the walls of the city and the temple, etc., and all this must be done before the Son of Man will make His appearance."[4]

There was no doubt in the Prophet's mind concerning Judah and Jerusalem, although at the time it must have seemed improbable or even impossible, for the words of the Lord were imperative: Judah must return, Jerusalem must be rebuilt, a third Temple must be raised. And then comes an insight into sequence: "All this must be done before the Son of Man will make His appearance"; in other words, it is destined to occur in a premillennial day.

This prophetic utterance captures three central issues—the gathering of the Jews, the restoration of Jerusalem, and the construction of a Temple—and puts them in perspective. The Jews are indeed gathering and Jerusalem is being rebuilt, but what of a premillennial Temple in Jerusalem? Such a prospect raises some serious issues, given the religious and political verities in that part of the world.

The Prophet spoke of the gathering in a discourse on 11 June 1843: "What was the object of gathering the Jews, or the people of God in any age of the world? . . . The main object was to build unto the Lord a house whereby he could reveal unto His people the ordinances of His house and the glories of His kingdom, and teach the people the way of salvation. . . . It was the design of the councils of heaven before the world was, that the principles and laws of the priesthood should be predicated upon the gathering of the people in every age of the world."[5]

Most Jews and, for that matter, most people who are not Latter-day Saints, do not fully comprehend the importance of a future Temple in Jerusalem. But the Prophet made it clear that the gathering in and of itself, which has largely been considered a political movement, often with frightening ramifications, is intended for a more heavenly design, namely, the establishment of a Temple. Indeed, that is the primary way that a people—in this instance, the Jews—can be endowed with spiritual blessings from on high.

It is by no means happenstance that the triad "the gathering of Judah," "Jerusalem," and "the Temple" appear together so often in prophecy. The existence of any one of these appears dependent on the other two. And all three require a physical presence. In other words, the references to gathering, Jerusalem, and Temple are not just metaphorical or spiritual. We are speaking of a temporal, physical, tangible series of developments to be accomplished not by angelic hosts but by mortals. That truth is borne out in the prophecies and is emphasized in the proclamation made by the Quorum of the Twelve Apostles in 1845: "We further testify, that the Jews among all nations are hereby commanded, in the name of the Messiah, to prepare, to return to Jerusalem in

Palestine; and to rebuild that city and temple unto the Lord: And also to organize and establish their own political government, under their own rulers, judges, and governors in that country. For be it known unto them that we now hold the keys of the priesthood and kingdom which is soon to be restored unto them."[6]

If in 1845 there was any doubt in the world at large concerning the gathering of the Jews to the land of their inheritance, there should have been none among the Latter-day Saints. In that proclamation to the world, the Church openly proclaimed that the Jewish people would gather to Jerusalem, rebuild the city, build a Temple, establish their own government, and receive the priesthood and the keys to the kingdom from The Church of Jesus Christ of Latter-day Saints.

The physical gathering of the Jews allows them physically to redeem the land. In other words, the gathering of Judah—and the rest of the house of Israel—is both spiritual and physical, but in the case of Judah, there appears to be a special emphasis on Judah's role in physically redeeming the land. In fact, in all of scripture, no people other than Judah are given the responsibility to redeem the land of Abraham, Isaac, and Jacob.

In the parable of the nobleman and the olive tree, those who are gathering to "redeem the land" are given the charge: "Go ye straightway unto the land of my vineyard, and redeem my vineyard; for it is mine; I have bought it with money. Therefore, get ye straightway unto my land; break down the walls of mine enemies; throw down their tower, and scatter their watchmen. And inasmuch as they gather together against you, avenge me of mine enemies, that by and by I may come with the residue of mine house and possess the land" (D&C 101:56–58).

The Savior speaks in 3 Nephi of a physical redemption of the land: "Then will the Father gather them [his people] together again, and give unto them Jerusalem for the land of their inheritance. Then shall they break forth into joy—Sing together, ye waste places of Jerusalem; for the Father hath comforted his people, he hath redeemed Jerusalem" (3 Ne. 20:33–34).

The evidence seems conclusive: the Lord is in the process of redeeming Jerusalem by gathering the Jews back to it and giving it to them as a land of their inheritance. The Jews are being gathered home, in part, for the following reasons and purposes:

The Lord made solemn covenants, or promises, to gather Israel and Judah in the last days.

In the process of the Jews physically returning, the land would be redeemed for Judah and for all the tribes of Israel, and Jerusalem would be rebuilt to its former glory.

The second coming of the Savior of the world, the Messiah, must be preceded by the rebuilding of Jerusalem and by the construction of a premillennial Temple that can only be built in Jerusalem.

The relevant keys of the priesthood and kingdom held by the Church could be restored to the Jews and others of the house of Israel who have gathered or are gathering back—a divine objective that could not be accomplished in their lost and fallen state.

The long-awaited Messiah would appear to a righteous remnant of His people in keeping with the prophetic word.

Old Jerusalem would serve as one of the two capitals of the Church on earth from which the Messiah would reign personally.

THE MISSION OF ORSON HYDE

The Prophet Joseph Smith commissioned Elder Orson Hyde to travel to Palestine to dedicate that land for the return of the Jewish people. He laid his hands on Elder Hyde's head and promised that through him the Lord would "do a great work, which shall prepare the way and greatly facilitate the gathering together of that people."[7] Thus was Orson Hyde called upon to sacrifice his personal means, the comforts of home and family, and even his health to travel halfway around the earth to dedicate an unfriendly, neglected, and war-torn land not to missionary work but to the gathering of the Jews. That the Prophet Joseph Smith was moved to send an emissary on such a mission in those days is of itself an astounding thing and clearly indicates the place of the Jews in the glorious work of the Restoration.

As we have noted, on 24 October 1841 Elder Hyde climbed the Mount of Olives and there offered an inspiring dedicatory prayer. Elder Hyde explained that this dedicatory prayer came to him by revelation, and thus neither the words nor the prophecies were his but rather reflected the will of heaven.

The purpose of Orson Hyde's mission to the Holy Land, as the

Mount of Olives, showing the Orson Hyde Memorial Park

beginning of the prayer emphasizes, was to dedicate and consecrate that land for three primary objectives: the gathering of Judah, the building up of Jerusalem, and the rearing of a Temple. The remainder of the prayer was for the most part a supplication for blessings to accomplish those three objectives.

THE AWAKENING OF A SLEEPING GIANT

It is no coincidence that the annals of world Jewry point to the 1840s as the period of an awakening among Jews throughout the Diaspora. Out of this new dawn, reaching to the turn of the century, arose such men of influence and stature among the various Jewish communities as Moses Hess, Joseph Salvador, Moses Montefiore, Leo Pinsker, Theodor Herzl, and others. They had been touched by the spirit of gathering, and they in turn instilled in the hearts and minds of Jews worldwide the desire to return to their homeland. This movement of the Jews to return became the rapidly growing religious, political, cultural, and nationalist movement known as Zionism.

In keeping with a divine timetable, the Spirit of the Lord began moving across the world, touching countless lives. Jews numbering in the hundreds began immigrating to what some referred to as Palestine, although the Jews called it "the land of Israel." The number of returnees increased from hundreds to thousands and then to tens of thousands in a torrent of inexplicable fervor and enthusiasm. They came in such numbers that historians have referred to this phenomenon as waves of immigration. Indeed, in several waves—such as the one just before the Gulf War of 1991—Jews came in the hundreds of thousands, primarily out of the former Soviet Union. Never has such a gathering taken place, not even in the return of ancient Judah from the Babylonian captivity.

Many Jews scattered throughout the Diaspora had assimilated over the years and were only vaguely aware of their Jewishness. They had melted into the communities where they had established roots that ran back for centuries. Without being able to articulate a reason, many of these so-called emancipated Jews suddenly began feeling Jewish; they began feeling restless and discontent with their lot. Many were seized with an overwhelming desire to leave the lands of their birth—without really knowing why. A revival of the Zionist ideal of return spread through world Jewry. It was expressed in many different ways, but a common thread was the desire among the Jews to return to their roots in their ancient homeland.

Anti-Semitism, tsarist persecutions and pogroms, Christian religious intolerance, and wars were taking place in the early stages of the gathering of Judah, but in and of themselves these factors were not sufficient to implant in the minds of the Jewish people the idea of return. Persecution and abuse had been their lot for centuries and had served only to further disperse Judah's scattered remnants.

In his own way and for his own reasons, the Lord had preserved Judah through the centuries from complete assimilation. Now the time had come in the divine plan for the Jews to go home. Their two-thousand-year dispersion was not to be reversed overnight, however. The gathering would take decades and would proceed in line with a well-defined, divine timetable, even into the Millennium.

THE ROLE OF THE CHURCH

The restoration of the keys of the gathering could only have been accomplished by divine intercession because the keys had been taken from the earth. With their restoration the gathering truly commenced. In a sense it is a complicated process involving the membership of the Church, but it is in accord with a strict timetable. "Send forth the elders of my church unto the nations which are afar off; . . . call upon all nations, first upon the Gentiles, and then upon the Jews" (D&C 133:8; see also 1 Ne. 13:42).

President Brigham Young said: "It is obligatory upon us to see that the House of Israel have the gospel preached to them; to do all that is in our power to gather them to the land of their fathers, and to gather up the fulness of the Gentiles before the gospel can go with success to the Jews."[8] Eventually the gospel will be taught to the Jews for, according to the Book of Mormon, their relationship to the Church will greatly influence the process of gathering.

Nephi predicted "that the Jews which are scattered also shall begin to believe in Christ; and they shall begin to gather" (2 Ne. 30:7). This scripture, like other Book of Mormon passages, indicates a direct correlation between the Jews' belief in Christ and their gathering.

> The time cometh, when the *fulness of my gospel* shall be preached unto them;
> And *they shall believe* in me, that I am Jesus Christ, the Son of God, and shall pray unto the Father in my name. . . .
> *Then* will the Father gather them together again and give unto them Jerusalem for the land of their inheritance. . . .
> *Then* shall this covenant which the Father hath covenanted with his people be fulfilled; and then shall Jerusalem be inhabited again with my people, and it shall be the land of their inheritance. (3 Ne. 20:30–31, 33, 46; emphasis added)

Although according to Elder Wilford Woodruff a certain number of the Jews will "gather to their own land in unbelief,"[9] the Book of Mormon makes it clear that the greater part will gather only after they have come to believe in Jesus as the Messiah. That places the burden squarely on the shoulders of the Latter-day Saints, who alone are empowered to teach the fulness of the gospel.

The gathering needed a spiritual catalyst in the form of the restoration of the keys of the gathering, and the present process also depends on the Church of Jesus Christ to sustain it. Neither the world at large nor the Jews in particular are aware of the role The Church of Jesus Christ of

Latter-day Saints has played in the return of the Jews to the lands of their inheritance; nonetheless, that gathering depends on the keys, powers, and priesthood of the restored Church of Jesus Christ.

WARS AND RUMORS OF WARS

Prophecy indicates that in these last days we are headed for troubled times—not just in the Holy Land but everywhere. Some are specific prophecies of doom concerning Judah and Jerusalem. But the Lord in his mercy has decreed: "Never hath any of them [the Jews] been destroyed save it were foretold them by the prophets of the Lord" (2 Ne. 25:9).

Zechariah, prophesying of the last days, warned explicitly of catastrophic events preceding the advent of the Messiah:

> For I will gather all nations against Jerusalem to battle; and the city shall be taken, and the houses rifled, and the women ravished; and half of the city shall go forth into captivity, and the residue of the people shall not be cut off from the city. Then shall the Lord go forth, and fight against those nations . . . and his feet shall stand in that day upon the mount of Olives . . . and the mount of Olives shall cleave in the midst thereof. (Zech. 14:2–4)

President Wilford Woodruff corroborated the testimony of Zechariah:

> O house of Judah. . . . It is true that after you return and gather your nation home, and rebuild your City and Temple, that the Gentiles may gather together their armies to go against you to battle . . . ; but when this affliction comes, the living God, that led Moses through the wilderness, will deliver you, and your Shiloh will come and stand in your midst and will fight your battles; and you will know him, and the afflictions of the Jews will be at an end, while the destruction of the Gentiles will be so great that it will take the whole house of Israel who are gathered about Jerusalem, seven months to bury the dead of their enemies, and the weapons of war will last them seven years for fuel, so that they need not go to any forest for wood. These are tremendous sayings—who can bear them? Nevertheless they are true, and will be fulfilled, according to the sayings of Ezekiel, Zechariah, and other prophets. Though the heavens and the earth pass away, not one jot or tittle will fall unfulfilled.[10]

Events in these last days are often confusing, and unless we stay close to the prophets, we will hardly know where to place our allegiances and support. The proclamation issued by the Church in 1845 reads:

> No king, ruler, or subject—no community or individual will stand neutral. All will at length be influenced by one spirit or another, and will take sides either for or against the kingdom of God, and the fulfillment of the Prophets in the great restoration and return of His long-dispersed covenant people. . . .To such an extreme will this great division finally extend, that the nations of the old world will combine to oppose these things by military force. They will send a great army to Palestine against the Jews and they will besiege their city.[11]

The Lord, speaking through the Prophet Joseph Smith concerning this period, warned:

> For then, in those days, shall be great tribulation on the Jews, and upon the inhabitants of Jerusalem, such as was not before sent upon Israel, of God, since the beginning of their kingdom until this time; no, nor ever shall be sent again upon Israel.
>
> All things which have befallen them are only the beginning of the sorrows which shall come upon them.
>
> And except those days should be shortened, there should none of their flesh be saved; but for the elect's sake, according to the covenant, those days shall be shortened.
>
> Behold, these things I have spoken unto you concerning the Jews. (JS—M 1:18–21)

Zechariah further details the terrible destruction:

> Two parts [of the inhabitants of Jerusalem] shall be cut off and die; but the third shall be left therein.
>
> And I will bring the third part through the fire, and will refine them as silver is refined, and will try them as gold is tried: they shall call on my name, and I will hear them: I will say, It is my people: and they shall say, The Lord is my God. (Zech. 13:8–9)

The reason one-third of the people will survive this catastrophic war is that they, having gone through the "refiner's fire," turn to the Lord. Nephi also prophesied of this trying period:

> And behold, according to the words of the prophet, the Messiah will

set himself again the second time to recover them; wherefore, he will manifest himself unto them in power and great glory, unto the destruction of their enemies, when that day cometh when they shall believe in him; and none will he destroy that believe in him.

And they that believe not in him shall be destroyed. . . . And they shall know that the Lord is God, the Holy One of Israel. (2 Ne. 6:14–15)

The Messiah will come just as Judah faces imminent defeat at the hands of her enemies. This time he shall come, as the scriptures record, in power and great glory and save his people from complete annihilation. Zechariah wrote: "Then shall the Lord go forth and fight against those nations, as when he fought in the day of battle" (Zech. 14:3). Then will the people who survive the refiner's fire believe in the true Messiah, even Jesus Christ.

A CHANGE OF HEART

Having examined how the Jews of the Diaspora will, in accord with the divine timetable, be taught the gospel, we turn to those who have gathered to the modern state of Israel in unbelief. We speak of the tens of thousands, possibly millions, that for one reason or another have grown up in a spiritual vacuum and are searching for the truth, "but know not where to find it" (D&C 123:12).

Many Jews are profoundly spiritual and find fulfillment in their interpretation of Judaism. Without calling upon them to discard any truths found in their rich heritage, we would add to this heritage by seeking to convince them, in the words of Nephi, "of the true Messiah, who was rejected by them; and unto the convincing of them that they need not look forward any more for a Messiah to come, for there should not any come, save it should be a false Messiah which should deceive the people; for there is save one Messiah spoken of by the prophets, and that Messiah is he who should be rejected of the Jews. . . . his name shall be Jesus Christ, the Son of God" (2 Ne. 25:18–19).

That the spiritually endowed among the Jews will eventually accept Jesus Christ as their Messiah is clear. What is less clear is the process. Old Testament prophecies describe a major event among the Jews in these last days when the Lord says he "will gather all nations against Jerusalem to battle" (Zech. 14:2). At the moment when the Jews face utter annihilation at the hands of their enemies, their long-awaited Messiah will appear. This time, however, he will appear in power and glory, not as a carpenter's son, and he will "go forth, and fight against those nations . . . and his feet shall stand in that day upon the mount of Olives, which is before Jerusalem on the east" (Zech. 14:3–4).

The Jews of that day will, in the words of the Lord, "look upon me whom they have pierced" (Zech. 12:10) and they shall say, "What are these wounds in thine hands and in thy feet?" (D&C 45:51; see also Zech. 13:6). At that moment a great miracle foreseen by many of the great prophets of old will take place. The Jews that had gathered in unbelief and survived the refiner's fire (see Zech. 13:9) will know that their Messiah, the Savior of the world, stands before them. They will know, if not by the overwhelming majesty of his very being, then certainly by the piercing, penetrating power of his own testimony, for he will declare to all that will hear, the heart-shattering news that "these wounds are the wounds with which I was wounded in the house of my friends" (D&C 45:52).

That statement alone will suffice to convince the honest in heart, but for those who still doubt, he will be more specific: "I am he who was lifted up." This statement will confuse those blinded by the traditions of many centuries and will prompt a further testimony, this time one that cannot be misunderstood, for the Messiah will declare: "I am Jesus that was crucified." The effect this revelation will have on all who hear it is almost impossible to comprehend. For most, it will be all too clear that the Messiah who has just saved them from a terrible destruction is none other than that same Jesus who was crucified.

Then, in one last magnificent announcement: "I am the Son of God" (D&C 45:52), the dark scales accumulated over centuries, blinding whole generations, will suddenly be swept away. A new era will be born. Those solemn words to be uttered from the top of Olivet will penetrate and purge the very souls of all who will believe. Those words will be heard in every corner of the land and will reverberate across the waters and around the world among every kindred, tongue, and people. But those entitled to hear them directly will be his own people, the Jews.

With that soul-rending announcement, the remnant of the Jews that had been especially preserved by the hand of the Almighty to witness the event shall be reduced to unfathomable grief, for "then shall they weep because of their iniquities; then shall they lament because they persecuted their king" (D&C 45:53). Zechariah, speaking of that event, wrote: "In that day there shall be a great mourning in Jerusalem" and in all the land (Zech. 12:11). "The Lord shall utter his voice, and all the ends of the earth shall hear it; and the nations of the earth shall mourn, and they that have laughed shall see their folly" (D&C 45:49). Then shall the cry go out: "O Jerusalem, that bringest good tidings, lift up thy voice with strength; lift it up, be not afraid; say unto the cities of Judah, Behold your God!"[12] Then shall the scripture be fulfilled: "Behold, he cometh with clouds; and every eye shall see him, and they also which pierced him: and all kindreds of the earth shall wail because of him" (Rev. 1:7).

In that instant belief in Jesus Christ as the Son of God, the long-awaited Messiah, the Savior of the world, will become the uniting force rather than the divisive force it had hitherto been, bringing back into the fold his chosen people, and "they shall call on my name, and I will hear them: I will say, It is my people: and they shall say, The Lord is my God" (Zech. 13:9).

The scriptures reveal: "In that day there shall be a fountain opened to the house of David and to the inhabitants of Jerusalem for sin and for uncleanness" (Zech. 13:1). The fountain "for sin and for uncleanness" obviously refers to a baptismal font, and all that believe shall be baptized. And a nation, as it were, shall be born in a day (see Isa. 66:8).

And in that day it will be said of the righteous living in Jerusalem: "And the inhabitants thereof, blessed are they, for they have been washed in the blood of the Lamb; and they are they who were scattered and gathered in from the four quarters of the earth, and from the north countries, and are partakers of the fulfilling of the covenant which God made with their father, Abraham" (Ether 13:3).

So Judah will be gathered physically and spiritually. The physical gathering will be to Jerusalem; the spiritual gathering to the true fold of God. And war and destruction shall come to an end. Wrote Zechariah:

> And many nations shall be joined to the Lord in that day, and shall be my people: and I will dwell in the midst of thee, and thou shalt know that the Lord of hosts hath sent me unto thee.
>
> And the Lord shall inherit Judah his portion in the holy land, and shall choose Jerusalem again. (Zech. 2:11–12)

Thus saith the Lord; I am returned unto Zion, and will dwell in the midst of Jerusalem: and Jerusalem shall be called a city of truth; and the mountain of the Lord of hosts the holy mountain. (Zech. 8:3)

And men shall dwell in it, and there shall be no more utter destruction; but Jerusalem shall be safely inhabited. (Zech. 14:11)

Notes

1. Talmage, *Articles of Faith*, 17.
2. Benson, *Teachings of Ezra Taft Benson*, 91.
3. Smith, *History of the Church*, 4:112–13.
4. Smith, *History of the Church*, 5:337.
5. Smith, *History of the Church*, 5:423.
6. Clark, *Messages of the First Presidency*, 1:254.
7. Smith, *History of the Church*, 4:xxxi.
8. Brigham Young, in *Journal of Discourses*, 12:113.
9. Wilford Woodruff, in *Journal of Discourses*, 15:277–78.
10. Cowley, *Wilford Woodruff*, 509–10. The great blessing to Judah is that they contemplated the coming of Shiloh, who would gather his people to him. The prophecy concerning Shiloh has been subject to several rabbinic and Christian interpretations and the object of considerable controversy. The interpretation given this passage by the Latter-day Saints is one based on revelation to modern prophets, not on scholarly commentary. It was revealed to Joseph Smith that Shiloh is the Messiah. See JST Genesis 50:24; Benson, *This Nation Shall Endure*, 139.
11. Clark, *Messages of the First Presidency*, 1:257.
12. Talmage, *Articles of Faith*, 313; cf. Isa. 40:9.

20

JERUSALEM, THE MUSLIMS, AND THE CHURCH

Jerusalem looms large from a religious perspective, and it seems that the more one religion makes of it, the more sacrosanct it becomes in the minds of others. One cannot negotiate away or compromise spiritual verities. Of course, there is always room for coexistence, cooperation, collaboration, toleration, and even special arrangements, but no conceivable political or religious stratagem will ever make Jerusalem less sacred to Islam. The status of Jerusalem as a spiritual citadel of Islam is not negotiable to Muslims.

Islam does not deny the sanctity of Jerusalem to any faith, but it is concerned that any one political entity would make exclusive claims on the holy city. Says one author: "Islam applauds and commends all those who, like the Muslims, regard Jerusalem as 'blessed' on account of its associations with many of the Prophets of God, from Ibrahim [Abraham] to 'Isa ibn Maryam [Jesus son of Mary]. The problem of Jerusalem is that of finding for it a political and cultural regime which would not violate the relation of the city to any of the religions associated with it."[1]

No city of significance has ever existed for long in political limbo, and Jerusalem is no exception. In theory, the lack of a political sovereign by its very nature creates a vacuum—an open invitation to political processes that will either bless or oppress. The problem is that because Jewish or Christian domination of Jerusalem is unacceptable to Islam, and because internationalization is equally objectionable to Islam (the religion), although from a political perspective it may not be to many Muslims, the alternative appears to be an Islamic Jerusalem.

Islam is willing to govern Jerusalem in such a way that Judaism and Christianity could find full spiritual expression. Islam's adherents point to periods in which Judaism and Christianity flourished under Islamic dominion. Of course, none of the three religions has a perfect record, and history also shows a dark side that none of the three wishes to recall. As each religion makes its case, it accepts for itself what it denies to the others, thereby exacerbating the problem. No one is prepared to allow any one religion a dominant role in what is regarded as its holy city. Neither is it helpful for any one party to denigrate the role Jerusalem has played, historically, culturally, or religiously, in another's past.

Jerusalem's place in Islamic theology is not limited to Muhammad's Night Journey (the *Miraj*) nor to the myriad of events, sacred and profane, that followed, including the construction of the magnificent Islamic shrine, or mosque, the Dome of the Rock. Perhaps more important is Jerusalem's prominence when the world as we know it comes to an end. The Islamic eschatological associations with Jerusalem may be even more important than the historical ones.[2] Thus, in a religion where there is no separation of church and state, there is precious little room for compromise, particularly if there is yet to be an accounting before the judgment bar of God.

In short, the practice of some who attempt to show the diminished role of Jerusalem in Islam over the centuries is naive. Sacred space does not lose its sanctity over time; neither is it diminished by demography, politics, or even neglect.

RELIGIOUS REVIVALISM

The religious revival Islam is experiencing further adds to Jerusalem's sanctity in the minds of believers. Just as Judaism and Christianity have their own revivals, with all their attendant devotion to sacred places and events, so too does Islam. Religious revival is a return to orthodoxy. It can be found or verified through divine revelation or by returning to one's roots embedded in the past. Just as Judaism found redemption in returning to Jerusalem after an absence of two thousand years,[3] so too is Islam certain to lay greater hold, spiritually speaking, on a Jerusalem of the future than it has on a Jerusalem of the past. In other words, Jerusalem's place in Islam will continue to grow, regardless of political exigencies.

Christianity will also seek its place in the sun. Jerusalem figures prominently in Christian theology relating to the last days. Though most Christians for the present are not knocking at Jerusalem's door, neither will they be content to be left out or pushed aside in deliberations over Jerusalem's future. Islam sees an ally in the Christian nations that have taken a stand against a Jerusalem governed by Jews, but many Christians despite the positions their respective governments have taken have typically sided with Judaism on the issue of Jerusalem. This apparent dichotomy is due, in part, to the belief shared by many Christians that the gathering of Judah to Jerusalem in the last days is a sign of the times presaging the advent of the Messiah. In other words, Islam's unyielding position on Jerusalem may be jeopardized by a Christian-Jewish coalition. That raises the question: where do we stand as Latter-day Saints?

MODERN-DAY PROPHETS ON ISLAM

Throughout the eighteenth and into the nineteenth centuries, western knowledge of Islam was limited and largely incorrect. Western scholars contributed to the confusion by promulgating the popular falsehoods of the day, among which was the notion that Muhammad put to the sword all who were unwilling to convert. But many leaders of The Church of Jesus Christ of Latter-day Saints have taken the time to educate themselves about Islam and to share their spiritual insights with the members of the Church.

In 1855, George A. Smith delivered an address in which he provided a remarkably accurate picture of Islam for his time. He taught, among other things, that Muhammad descended from a noble line and that he was a direct descendant of Ishmael, son of Abraham. He pointed out that "there was nothing in his [Muhammad's] religion to license iniquity or corruption; he preached the moral doctrines which the Savior taught." Elder Smith accurately sketched Muhammad's life and basic teachings and concluded his description of Muhammad: "Now this man descended from Abraham and was no doubt raised up by God on purpose to scourge the world for their idolatry."[4]

Another early Church leader, Parley P. Pratt, also spoke to members of the Church about Islam: "I am aware it is not without a great deal of prejudice that we, as Europeans, and Americans, and Christians in religion and in our education . . . have looked upon the history of [Muhammad]." Elder Pratt then undertook to correct some of these prejudices by pointing out several instances in which Islam appeared more correct than traditional forms of Christianity: "Mahometan [Muslim] history and Mahometan doctrine was a standard raised against the most corrupt and abominable idolatry that ever perverted our earth, found in the creeds and worship of Christians, falsely so named." He continued, "I am inclined to think, upon the whole . . . that they [the Muslims] have better morals and institutions than many Christian nations; and in many localities there have been high standards of morals."[5]

Later general authorities have continued to speak about the relationship of the Church to Islam. On 15 February 1978, the First Presidency issued a statement reaffirming the Church's belief that we are all "literal spirit children of an Eternal Father" entitled to the same love and blessings from him "regardless of religious belief, race, or nationality." The statement pointed out the role that "great religious leaders such as Mohammed, Confucius, and the Reformers" have played: "Moral truths were given to them by God to enlighten whole nations and to bring a higher level of understanding to individuals."

Other Church leaders have commented on our responsibility to Muslims in general and Arabs in particular where our interpretation of scripture and our religious beliefs might otherwise seem to favor the Jews. Expressing his heartfelt concern for all the inhabitants of the world—for Jews, Christians, and others—President Spencer W. Kimball asked, "Is anyone learning to speak to the 130 million for whom Arabic is the native tongue?"[6]

It has been observed that "mixing religion and politics often leads to the deepest human emotions and to intense attachments and tenacious devotion to places and symbols."[7] With the various parties unwilling to concede what they regard as matters of principle, how should we as Latter-day Saints view events in Jerusalem? It has rightly been pointed out that "there seems to be a natural human tendency to take sides. We seem to believe that there is a right and a wrong to every situation. But partiality can breed divisiveness and closed-mindedness. It can also create distrust and inhibit an atmosphere of mutual respect and understanding needed for peace. If we take sides in a political context, we compromise our ability to reach out to both sides."[8]

Elder Howard W. Hunter spoke at length on this issue in an address entitled "All Are Alike unto God." He stated: "The Church has an interest in all of Abraham's descendants, and we should remember that the history of the Arabs goes back to Abraham through his son Ishmael." He spoke of his concern that Latter-day Saints not give the impression that the Church favors the goals of the Jews over those of the Arabs: "Both the Jews and the Arabs are children of our Father. They are both children of promise, and *as a church we do not take sides.* We have love for and an interest in each. The purpose of the gospel of Jesus Christ is to bring about love, unity, and brotherhood of the highest order."[9]

THE BRIGHAM YOUNG UNIVERSITY JERUSALEM CENTER

The impressive Brigham Young University Jerusalem Center was purposely located on a site that borders psychologically, if not physically, Arab and Jewish Jerusalem. The intent of its location was symbolically to bridge the gulf between two historical antagonists. Visionaries could foresee the day when the Church and Brigham Young University, acting in concert, could be instrumental in bringing about a lasting peace to this historically troubled city.

During construction of the Center, efforts were made to ensure that work crews and site engineers were a mixture of Arabs and Israelis. Efforts are also being made to see that the faculty represents the Jewish, Muslim, and Christian communities surrounding it. The curriculum, too, is balanced between Jewish and Islamic history, culture, and politics. Required courses include classes on Islam as well as Judaism, and all students are required to take a language course in Hebrew or Arabic. In addition to the informal one-on-one experience students have with their Arab or Palestinian counterparts in Jerusalem, they take study trips to Egypt and Jordan. In keeping with Elder Hunter's mandate, every effort is made to create symmetry and balance in the courses and programs offered to the Latter-day Saint students studying at the Center. For most students it is their first introduction to the world of Islam.

CONCLUSION

Since the early days of the Church, the leaders have looked upon Muhammad and his followers with love and understanding. They have endeavored to correct falsehoods and myths about Islam and have encouraged members of the Church to avoid getting entangled in the emotions surrounding crises in the Near East. Their central message through the years has been one of tolerance for all of God's children.

"We can help prepare the world . . . for a millennium of peace by teaching and living gospel principles. We can also help lay the foundations for peace by learning about and respecting various nations—their peoples, histories, cultures, religious beliefs, and languages. It is hoped that Latter-day Saints can help provide a bridge of understanding between [Muslims] and Jews . . . and that *to the extent that we look with sympathy and understanding at both sides,* we can be an influence to help bring about a just and lasting peace."[10]

Though it is not clear how the issue of Jerusalem will play out politically, it is in the interest of three major world religions to seek a *modus vivendi* that will not compromise religious principle but will allow peaceful coexistence to reign until divine intercession plays a mediating role once and for all.

NOTES

1. Islamic Council of Europe, *Jerusalem, the Key to World Peace,* 103.

2. See Werblowsky, "Jerusalem: Holy City of Three Religions," 428.

3. Historians point out that through the centuries there has always been a Jewish remnant in Jerusalem, however small, a fact that lends credence to the claim that Jerusalem through the ages has retained its central place in Jewish thought and belief.

4. George Albert Smith, in *Journal of Discourses,* 3:31–32.

5. Parley P. Pratt, in *Journal of Discourses,* 3:38, 40–41. It is not uncommon to find many variations of the spelling of Muhammad. Neither is it uncommon to hear people incorrectly refer to Islam as Muhammadanism.

6. Kimball, "Uttermost Parts of the Earth," 8.

7. Ogden and Galbraith, "What are the reasons . . . ?" 52–53.

8. Ogden and Galbraith, "What are the reasons . . . ?" 53.

9. Hunter, *That We Might Have Joy,* 74–75; emphasis added.

10. Ogden and Galbraith, "What are the reasons . . . ?" 53.

21

JERUSALEM FROM WORLD WAR I TO PARTITION, 1917–1947

During the last decades of the Ottoman Empire, Palestine and particularly the *Sanjak* (district) of Jerusalem, which encompassed most of its population and territory, became increasingly significant in the diplomacy of the European powers. Before World War I, France, Russia, and Britain had interests in Palestine. France had long viewed itself as the protector of Latin Christians and their holy places in the Ottoman Empire; Russia considered itself the guardian of all the Orthodox churches; and by the mid nineteenth century, Britain had assumed a similar role for Protestants and Jews in Palestine.

In the years just before World War I, European interests in the Near East expanded beyond missionary concerns. France, Britain, and Russia, each suspicious of the others' designs in the region, secretly planned to divide the Ottoman territories after the war. France sought to increase its influence over Greater Syria, which included Palestine and Lebanon; Britain, desiring a buffer to protect the eastern approaches to the Suez Canal and Egypt, sought to extend its authority over Palestine.[1] France eventually acquiesced to Britain regarding Palestine on condition that the status and protection of the holy places be resolved to its satisfaction. The negotiations culminated in the Sykes-Picot Agreement in 1916, which divided the Near East into two main spheres of influence: the French in Syria and Lebanon, and the British in Palestine and Iraq. After the war, the Bolshevik government in Russia disassociated itself from the secret agreements and relinquished its claim on the former Ottoman territories.[2]

While those talks were proceeding among Britain, France, and Russia, the British negotiated with two other parties: Sherif Hussein of

Mecca and Zionist leaders in Europe. Between July 1915 and March 1916, the British high commissioner in Cairo, Sir Henry McMahon, corresponded with Hussein to incite an Arab revolt against the Ottoman Turks in exchange for assurances of an independent Arab state in the Ottoman territories south of the thirty-seventh parallel. The western boundary of this proposed state was never clarified. Because Palestine was not mentioned specifically in the correspondence of the two leaders, that omission became a means by which Britain attempted to achieve its own ambitions for a British Mandate in Palestine and to honor its pledges to Zionist leaders regarding a Jewish homeland. Colonial Secretary Winston Churchill attempted to lay the question to rest when he declared in 1922 that the Vilayet of Beirut and the Sanjak of Jerusalem were never intended by McMahon to be included in the Arab state, only the territory east of the Jordan.[3]

British negotiations with the Zionists culminated on 2 November 1917 with the Balfour Declaration, which officially affirmed Britain's approval of a national home for the Jewish people in Palestine, declaring: "His Majesty's Government view with favour the establishment in Palestine of a national home for the Jewish people and will use their best endeavours to facilitate the achievement of this object, it being clearly understood that nothing shall be done which may prejudice the civil and religious rights of existing non-Jewish communities in Palestine or the rights and political status enjoyed by Jews in any other country."[4]

Talks between British officials and Zionists had begun early in the war, but not until 1917 did they make significant progress. Indeed, during the decade leading to the Balfour Declaration, the British suspected the Zionists of being too favorably inclined towards German political interests.[5] By 1917, the British controlled much of the Arab Near East, and certain circles in the government looked favorably on the idea of a Jewish homeland in Palestine under British protection. Such a stance, they believed, would guarantee the loyalty of Jews in the Allied countries and legitimize a British protectorate in Palestine.[6]

JERUSALEM UNDER BRITISH OCCUPATION

Jerusalem was captured by British troops under General Edmund Allenby on 9 December 1917 and put under martial law. Allenby made it clear from the start that "every sacred building, monument, holy spot, traditional shrine, endowment, pious bequest, or customary place of prayer, of whatsoever form of the three religions, will be maintained and protected according to the existing customs and beliefs of those to whose faiths they are sacred."[7] The Ottomans attempted to recapture Jerusalem on December 27 but failed. Nevertheless, not until the following summer could Britain claim to control all of Palestine.

The main supply routes to Jerusalem were cut off during the war, and British troops found many in the city suffering from starvation and disease. When Chaim Weizmann visited Jerusalem in 1918 at the head of the Zionist Commission, he noted the "filth and infections, [and] indescribable poverty." He lamented to his wife: "To organize Jerusalem, to bring some order into this hell, will take a long time and need much strength, courage and patience."[8] The military government attempted to alleviate the city's problems by rationing food, improving the city's sanitation system, and creating a working economic and administrative system.[9]

The British military government, which made Jerusalem the administrative capital of Palestine, faced problems stemming from Britain's conflicting commitments to Arabs and Jews. Muslims and Christians feared that Palestine would be handed to the Zionists, who were purchasing large tracts of land from absentee landlords. An intense struggle for control of the municipality of Jerusalem resulted. The Jews, who held an absolute majority in the city, wanted the election rather than the appointment of the mayor, at least half of the municipal council seats, the introduction of Hebrew as the official language of the municipality, and the relaxation of voting requirements. The Muslims, on the other hand, wished to preserve their political advantages, including the centuries-old convention of appointing a Muslim as the city's mayor. The British responded with a system that retained the Muslim mayor but appointed Christian and Jewish deputy mayors and established a council with two members from each of the city's communities.[10]

To foster cooperation between the main communities in Jerusalem, Military Governor Ronald Storrs established the Pro-Jerusalem Society, which was made up of religious and community leaders from the three major faiths. This organization during the 1920s unofficially assumed such responsibilities of the municipality as urban planning, the naming of streets, and renovation and repair of historical and religious sites throughout the city.[11]

Tensions were already high between Muslims and Jews in Jerusalem by 1918. In November, a Jewish procession celebrating the first anniversary of the Balfour Declaration was met by a crowd of Arab demonstrators. A scuffle ensued near Jaffa Gate. The following day the mayor led a procession of Muslims and Christians to the British administrative headquarters, protesting against Palestine being handed over to the Jews. The situation convinced British officials that the Zionist program should be carried out with "great tact and discretion."[12]

In April 1920 the Islamic celebration of the prophet Musa (Moses) in Jerusalem turned into a political demonstration after a Jewish observer allegedly made a derogatory comment and spat towards the procession. The fighting, in which several Arabs and Jews were injured or killed, was ended only after the police called in British troops. The military government reacted harshly towards the Jewish and Muslim leaders it felt were most responsible for the disturbances. Among them was Hajj Amin al-Husseini, who became an important figure in the Palestine nationalist movement. He escaped to Jordan and then to Syria, but he was sentenced in absentia to ten years in prison for inciting violence through his speeches.[13]

In July 1920 the military administration in Palestine was replaced by a civil government. Herbert Samuel, a Jewish Zionist, was appointed, over Arab protest, as the high commissioner in Jerusalem. Samuel proved an able administrator, who achieved some balance between the demands of Arabs and Jews. As a demonstration of conciliation, he pardoned Hajj Amin al-Husseini and recognized him as the *mufti,* or leader, of the Muslim community of Jerusalem. But the goodwill this step earned him was offset by his opening the doors to Jewish immigration.[14]

Muslims and Christian Arabs formed joint associations to organize resistance to Jewish immigration and to work toward establishing an Arab state in Palestine.[15] Arab frustrations burst into riots in Jaffa in May 1921; 27 Jews were killed and about 150 injured. Later that year, on the anniversary of the Balfour Declaration, Jerusalem was the scene of more disturbances that left 4 Jews and 1 Arab dead. The Jews throughout Palestine began to pressure the government to allow them to form their own defense force.[16]

The government investigated. Finding that fear of Jewish immigration lay at the heart of the disturbances, it curtailed Jewish immigration. In June 1922 the British government issued a policy statement denying that Britain was attempting "to create a wholly Jewish Palestine" and insisting that immigration would not be permitted "to exceed whatever may be the economic capacity of the country at the time to absorb new arrivals." This white paper, written by Colonial Secretary Churchill, estimated the number of immigrants since British occupation at approximately 25,000.[17]

THE LEAGUE OF NATIONS AND THE PALESTINE MANDATE

At the Versailles Peace Conference following World War I, the victorious European powers established the League of Nations to promote international cooperation and peace. Its charter gave the League power to assign mandates over the former Ottoman and German territories to prepare them for self-government. Although it was decided in February 1920 that Britain would receive the mandate for Palestine, the terms had yet to be worked out. The draft of the British Mandate was revised under pressure from the French, who objected to its "almost exclusively Zionist complexion and the manner in which the interests and rights of the Arab majority . . . were ignored."[18]

Owing largely to objections raised by other states on the status and accessibility of the holy places in Palestine, Britain drafted a new mandate that left the question of the holy places with the League of Nations. When the League considered the draft mandate in the summer of 1922, it resolved that a special commission would study the rights and claims to the holy places of the religious communities in Palestine. The League then approved the mandate, which went into effect in September 1923.[19]

The preamble of the mandate included the Balfour Declaration, but the status of Jerusalem itself was not mentioned because it was subject to the findings of the special commission on the holy places. The issue was thus destined to resurface.[20]

JERUSALEM UNDER THE BRITISH MANDATE

Because the British Mandate appeared to favor the Jews, the high commissioner hoped to gain Arab support by balancing the political equation in Palestine. A legislative council for Palestine was proposed: nine Muslim and three Christian Arabs, three Jews, and eleven "official" members. The Arabs declined because the question of Jewish immigration and the promise of a Jewish state would not thereby be resolved to their satisfaction. Because the Mandate provided for a Jewish agency to assist in the administration of Palestine, the British offered to establish an Arab agency to fill a similar role. This too was rejected by most Arab leaders, who wanted nothing less than an Arab state. Historian John Gray calls this action a "political blunder, however justified they [the Arabs] might have been on principle." He contends that because of their "lack of foresight beyond the immediate situation . . . they committed themselves to a political limbo and deprived themselves of effective representation."[21] Had they agreed to the offers, they likely would have had a much greater influence on the course of events in Palestine.

The Arabs were by no means united during the early years of the British Mandate. Two rival factions emerged in Jerusalem, led by the two most prominent Arab families in the city: the moderate Nashashibis, from whom the British high commissioner selected the mayor of Jerusalem, and the nationalist Husseinis, led by the city's mufti and president of the Supreme Muslim Council, Hajj Amin al-Husseini. The Nashashibis were willing to work within the system and advance the cause of an Arab government in Palestine through propaganda, protest, and demonstrations. The Husseinis resorted to armed resistance, which led to the introduction of British security forces and the legalization of an armed Jewish defense force, the Haganah.[22]

The years between 1923 and 1928 were relatively calm in Palestine. Political historian Peter Mansfield attributes that to a decline in Zionist immigration, which fell to nearly zero in 1927–28, allaying Arab fears. Nevertheless, the Jewish population of Jerusalem continued to grow, spreading north and west outside the city walls. In 1925, Hebrew University was completed on Mount Scopus, overlooking the Old City. Lord Balfour was greeted by crowds of angry Arab demonstrators when he arrived in the country to preside over the university's inauguration.[23]

In September 1928, a group of Jews set up a screen to divide men from women during the prayers on the Day of Atonement at the Western Wall in Jerusalem. The earlier introduction of chairs by the Wall had already inflamed Muslims, and the mufti saw this new act as yet another step by the Jews toward taking control of their Temple Mount. The screen was removed by police, but tensions erupted in riots and massacres of Jews by Arabs. Disturbances throughout the country over the course of a year resulted in the deaths of 133 Jews and 116 Arabs and the injury of hundreds more on both sides. The Wailing Wall incident was investigated by several commissions, which recommended that all speeches and political demonstrations at the Wall be prohibited.[24]

In October 1930, Colonial Secretary Lord Passfield proposed stricter limitations on Jewish immigration. The resulting outcry by Zionist sympathizers in Britain caused the prime minister to revert to the 1922 policy. Convinced that the British government was indifferent to the Arab cause and hopelessly under Zionist influence, the mufti called a Muslim Congress in Jerusalem to discuss the Zionist threat. In October 1933 he proclaimed a boycott of Jewish and British goods, and demonstrations were held at the government offices in Jerusalem. The demonstration was dispersed by troops; riots broke out later, directed at both the Jews and the British administration.[25]

Throughout the early 1930s, partly as a result of the rise of the Nationalist Socialist Party under Adolf Hitler in Germany and the growth of anti-Semitism in eastern Europe, Jewish immigration to Palestine rose steeply, more than doubling from 30,000 in 1933 to 61,000 in 1935—rising from 18.9 percent of the total population to about 27.7 percent. Arab demands for an end to Jewish immigration went largely unheeded, though the British government attempted to make another concession to the Arabs by proposing a legislative council for Palestine in which Arabs would have fourteen seats and Jews eight. The Arabs were prepared to consider the proposal, but the Zionists rejected it outright.[26]

By the mid 1930s, Britain found it increasingly difficult to keep peace between Arabs and Jews in Palestine. In April 1936, the major Arab political parties and the mayor of Jerusalem established the Arab Higher Committee, chaired by Mufti al-Husseini. The committee called for a general strike and nonpayment of taxes until the administration ended Jewish immigration. Their protest turned into a violent anticolonial uprising that continued until 1939. British troops put down the revolt only after arresting the members of the Arab Higher Committee and after considerable Arab casualties, detentions, and hangings.[27]

A British royal commission under Lord Peel investigated the revolt.

Testimony from Arab political groups and the Jewish Agency led the Commission to conclude in July 1937 that the Mandate was unworkable and that British commitments to Jews and Arabs were irreconcilable. It recommended, therefore, that Palestine be partitioned into Jewish and Arab states. Jerusalem and Bethlehem, with a narrow corridor to Jaffa on the Mediterranean Sea, would constitute the British mandatory enclave.[28]

Most Arabs were opposed to the partition of Palestine, and the Commission's report intensified the anticolonial revolt. Many Zionists were also opposed to partition, feeling that it provided too little for them. Moderates on both sides were willing to consider the proposal, but few were satisfied with the proposed status of Jerusalem. In October 1937, the Jewish Agency proposed boundaries that would have divided Jerusalem between a Jewish state and the British Mandate. The Jewish state would receive Mount Scopus and the western part of the city; the walled city and the area east of it would be administered by the British. The Jewish Agency insisted that "Jewish Palestine without Jerusalem would be a body without a soul"—that the city had been symbolically important throughout Jewish history. Moreover, since the 1880s, Jews had constituted a majority in the city, more than 60 percent of its total population.[29] Naturally, the Arabs would not hear of the proposal, and the British did not take it seriously.

In March 1938, another commission, this one under Sir John Woodhead, advanced three proposals for the boundaries of two new states. All three proposals advocated the same settlement for Jerusalem as had the Peel Commission. Nevertheless, the Woodhead Commission concluded that partition would be disastrous and recommended against it.[30]

In February and March 1939, a conference that hosted a Jewish and an Arab delegation was held in London. Failing to reach a consensus there, the British government produced its own solution in the May 1939 MacDonald White Paper. This white paper represented a shift in British policy towards Palestine. It insisted that the British commitments outlined in the Balfour Declaration had been fulfilled; moreover, Britain was under no obligation to turn the country into a Jewish state against the will of its Arab population nor to permit indefinite Jewish immigration, which it saw as detrimental to peace in Palestine. Jewish immigration was to be limited to an additional 75,000 over the ensuing five years, after which it would be subject to Arab consent; and land sales were to be restricted. The paper envisioned the establishment of an independent Palestinian state within a decade, with Arabs and Jews jointly holding power. Freedom of access to the holy places and protection of religious interests would be assured by treaty between the new state and Great Britain.[31]

The Zionists, who deeply resented the latest white paper, became hostile toward Britain. Some expressed this hostility with violence, turning to such underground Jewish terrorist organizations as the *Irgun Zvai Leumi* and the *Stern Gang,* which resorted to bombings of the British administration and Arabs. The Department of Migration was one of their first targets; it was set on fire in 1939 in protest against the policies outlined in the white paper. World War II saw a lull in their terrorist activities, during which time they stockpiled weapons and ammunition. In 1944 they resumed their violence against the administration, targeting government buildings throughout Jerusalem. Among the Irgun's most notorious acts was the bombing in 1946 of the southern wing of the King David Hotel, where British soldiers were housed. Ninety-one people died. The activities of the terrorist groups played an important role in pressuring the British to leave Palestine.[32]

From 1939 onwards the situation for Jewish immigrants became desperate while Britain attempted to implement its new policies. Illegal immigration, frequently on unseaworthy ships from eastern Europe, grew as Jews sought to escape the horrors of the Nazi concentration camps. The British government was forced to provide shelter for many of them, settling them in refugee camps in Cyprus and elsewhere.[33] In the United States public opinion was rapidly turning to the Zionists' favor with news of German atrocities against Jews in Europe. President Harry S. Truman urged that Jewish refugees be admitted into Palestine immediately. The British government, however, declared that a maximum of fifteen hundred Jewish immigrants could enter Palestine each month.[34]

After the war, the number of Jewish refugees in displaced persons camps in the American zones of Germany and Austria grew rapidly, totaling more than 177,000 people by 1947. A joint British-American committee investigated the resettlement of Jewish refugees and recommended a long-term extension of the Mandate so Arabs and Jews could have time to settle their differences. Called the Morrison-Grady plan, it envisioned a cantonal state, with autonomous Arab and Jewish provinces under a single centralized government in which neither side would dominate the other. In the meantime, the restrictions on land purchases and immigration would be removed, and 100,000 Jewish refugees would be permitted to enter Palestine.[35]

Although the British Cabinet approved the plan, the Arabs rejected it because it permitted additional Jewish immigration and did not provide for an Arab Palestinian state. The Jewish Agency also rejected the plan because it limited the number of future Jewish immigrants. The Jewish Agency produced its own plan, similar to that of 1937, but this time expressing a willingness to consider an Arab Jerusalem. Hoping to salvage the Morrison-Grady plan, the British government refused to consider the new Zionist proposal. The plan foundered when Truman decided it was unworkable and withdrew his support.[36]

Despairing of finding a workable solution for Palestine, Britain decided in April 1947 to turn over the Mandate to the United Nations. A special committee on Palestine recommended two plans to the General Assembly. The first, supported by a majority, proposed that Palestine be partitioned into separate Jewish and Arab states with Jerusalem and Bethlehem to be an international zone administered by the U.N. Trusteeship Council. The second plan, supported by a minority, called for a three-year transition into an independent federal state made up of two autonomous provinces with Jerusalem as its capital. Jerusalem would be administered by two separate municipalities, one with jurisdiction over the Jewish section of the modern city, and the other over the Arab section, including the area within the old city walls. The two municipalities would cooperate in areas of common concern such as public services and utilities.[37]

A committee was established to evaluate the two plans and work out details. The Arab Higher Committee rejected both plans, calling for the immediate establishment of an independent Arab state that incorporated the whole of Palestine. The Jewish Agency rejected federation and only reluctantly consented to partition. With the majority of the U.N. delegates thus in support of partition, the minority plan was discarded. On 29 November 1947, the resolution for partition narrowly passed with the required two-thirds majority: thirty votes in favor and ten against, with ten abstentions.[38]

The situation in Palestine deteriorated. The British colonial secretary announced that the British Mandate in Palestine would end on 15 May 1948. In April, fighting broke out in Jerusalem. The Irgun massacred 250 Arab civilians in the village of Deir Yassin on the outskirts of the city, and the Haganah drove out many Arab inhabitants of West Jerusalem. On 14 May, around midnight, before United Nations proposals to reestablish order in Palestine could be carried out, the Jews declared their independence and created the State of Israel.[39]

On 15 May 1948, Egypt, Jordan, Syria, Iraq, and Lebanon sent forces to crush the newly declared state and assist the Palestinian Arabs, whose "army of deliverance" failed miserably. Only the Arab Legion of Transjordan offered a disciplined challenge to the Jewish armed forces, probably because King Abdullah had the most to gain and committed the largest number of troops. The primary strategy of the Arab Legion was twofold: to capture the eastern approaches to Jerusalem (that is, the West Bank) and to cut off communication between the Jewish section of Jerusalem and the Jewish settlements on the coastal plains. Jewish armed forces eventually lifted the siege by building a road to circumvent the main road blocks. The Arab Legion, now on the defensive, held on to East Jerusalem. Jewish forces, taking control of West Jerusalem, evicted thousands of Arabs from their part of the city and its surrounding villages. The Transjordanians responded in kind. By the time a cease-fire was proclaimed on 11 June 1948, Jerusalem was divided by barbed wire running roughly north and south along the western side of the Old City, a situation that continued until the Six-Day War of 1967, when Israel captured the rest of Jerusalem.[40]

Notes

1. Islamic Council of Europe, *Jerusalem,* 159.

2. Bovis, *Jerusalem Question,* 3–6.

3. Bovis, *Jerusalem Question,* 4; Antonius, *Arab Awakening,* 164–83.

4. Stein, *Balfour Declaration,* 664.

5. Stein, *Balfour Declaration,* 34–41.

6. Bovis, *Jerusalem Question*, 5.

7. Gray, *History of Jerusalem*, 289.

8. Islamic Council of Europe, *Jerusalem*, 161.

9. Asali, *Jerusalem in History*, 252; *Encyclopedia Judaica*, 9:1469, s.v. "Jerusalem."

10. Kraemer, *Jerusalem*, 75–77.

11. Kraemer, *Jerusalem*, 80; Asali, *Jerusalem in History*, 252.

12. Wasserstein, *British in Palestine*, 31–33; Ingrams, *Palestine Papers*, 33–35.

13. Jbara, *Palestinian Leader*, 32–35.

14. Jbara, *Palestinian Leader*, 35, 44–46; Wasserstein, *British in Palestine*, 85–95; Islamic Council of Europe, *Jerusalem*, 162.

15. Islamic Council of Europe, *Jerusalem*, 162; Gray, *History of Jerusalem*, 297.

16. Ingrams, *Palestine Papers*, 121, 153.

17. Ingrams, *Palestine Papers*, 165; Wasserstein, *British in Palestine*, 103–6.

18. Ingrams, *Palestine Papers*, 102.

19. Bovis, *Jerusalem Question*, 9–13; Islamic Council of Europe, *Jerusalem*, 163; Ingrams, *Palestine Papers*, 94–104, 180.

20. Ingrams, *Palestine Papers*, 177.

21. Gray, *History of Jerusalem*, 295.

22. Gray, *History of Jerusalem*, 297; Nashashibi, *Jerusalem's Other Voice*, 32–45; Mattar, *Mufti of Jerusalem*, 31–32, 118–19.

23. Islamic Council of Europe, *Jerusalem*, 164; Gray, *History of Jerusalem*, 299; Asali, *Jerusalem in History*, 252.

24. Wasserstein, *British in Palestine*, 225–37; Mattar, *Mufti of Jerusalem*, 33–49; Jbara, *Palestinian Leader*, 77–96; *Encyclopedia Judaica*, 9:1474, s.v. "Jerusalem"; Asali, *Jerusalem in History*, 255; Tibawi, *Jerusalem*, 33–37.

25. Mattar, *Mufti of Jerusalem*, 65, 120; Jbara, *Palestinian Leader*, 128–29; *Encyclopedia Judaica*, 9:1475, s.v. "Jerusalem."

26. Islamic Council of Europe, *Jerusalem*, 165–66.

27. Bovis, *Jerusalem Question*, 22–23; Islamic Council of Europe, *Jerusalem*, 166–67; Bethell, *Palestine Triangle*, 52–56; Mattar, *Mufti of Jerusalem*, 73–85; Jbara, *Palestinian Leader*, 141–68.

28. Bovis, *Jerusalem Question*, 22–23; Islamic Council of Europe, *Jerusalem*, 166.

29. Bovis, *Jerusalem Question*, 28–29, 128.

30. Bovis, *Jerusalem Question*, 31.

31. Bovis, *Jerusalem Question*, 32–33; Bethel, *Palestine Triangle*, 62–75.

32. In Eckardt, *Jerusalem*, 112; for the activities of the Irgun, see Bethell, *Palestine Triangle*, chaps. 6, 8.

33. On illegal immigration by "death-ships," see Bethell, *Palestine Triangle*, 76–100.

34. Bovis, *Jerusalem Question*, 37.

35. Bovis, *Jerusalem Question*, 37–39.

36. Bovis, *Jerusalem Question,* 40; Gray, *History of Jerusalem,* 303.
37. Bovis, *Jerusalem Question,* 43.
38. Bovis, *Jerusalem Question,* 44–47.
39. Asali, *Jerusalem in History,* 258–59.
40. Gray, *History of Jerusalem,* 306–7; Asali, *Jerusalem in History,* 259–60.

22

JERUSALEM, THE DIVIDED CITY, 1948–1967

The cease-fire arranged by the United Nations on 11 June 1948 left the status of Jerusalem uncertain. The Jews of Jerusalem might have accepted the internationalization of the city before the war, but they became intransigent on the question afterwards. The Israeli provisional government nevertheless approached the issue cautiously, leaving a door open for compromise. When United Nations mediator Count Bernadotte proposed a settlement that would have given Jerusalem to Transjordan, many Jews called for the immediate annexation of West Jerusalem by Israel. The Bernadotte proposal was also opposed by Syria, Egypt, and Saudi Arabia, who felt that Jordan would be receiving too favorable treatment; they wished, rather, to see an independent Arab Palestinian state. King Abdullah of Jordan, on the other hand, welcomed the proposal.[1]

On 2 August 1948, the Israeli provisional government declared that because the United Nations had failed to produce a legal framework for the city, West Jerusalem would be administered as "Israel-occupied territory" under Israeli Military Governor Dov Joseph. Bernadotte then called for the demilitarization of the city, which Israel rejected, fearing that once the city was demilitarized, it would be unable to resist an attempt to hand it over to King Abdullah. Soon after Bernadotte moved his headquarters to Jerusalem in September 1948, he was assassinated by members of the Stern Gang.[2]

Embarrassed, the Israeli provisional government cracked down on the Irgun and Stern Gang and organized all armed forces in Jerusalem under the Israeli Defense Force. Despite the loss of international sympathy because of the assassination, the government notified the United

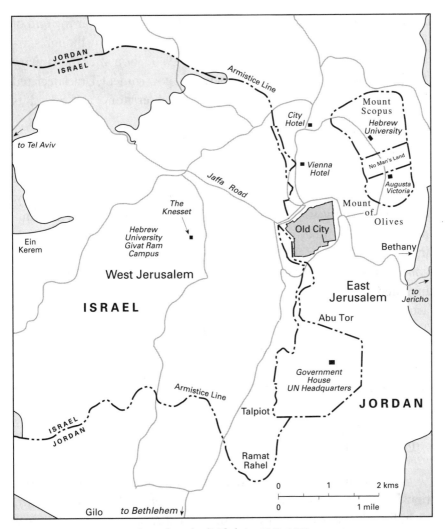

Jerusalem, the divided city, 1948–1967

Nations that no matter what plan it adopted concerning Palestine, Israel would retain West Jerusalem. Moreover, fearing that the United Nations would attempt to implement the Bernadotte proposals, which provided for a smaller Jewish state than that provided by the 1947 partition plan, and knowing from the United Nations armistice negotiations that boundaries would be determined on the basis of territory held at the time of the final armistice agreements, the Israeli army resumed hostilities in October 1948, pushing the Egyptians out of the Negev and the

Lebanese from the Galilee. The Israeli offensive ended at the end of December under United Nations pressure for a cease-fire, though skirmishes continued into the first quarter of 1949. Soon after the January 1949 elections, which ended the provisional government, Israel declared that West Jerusalem was no longer "occupied territory" and ended its military rule there.[3]

On 16 March 1949, Jordan and Israel signed an armistice agreement for Jerusalem and soon afterwards, on 3 April, concluded a general armistice. The agreements established demarcation lines in Jerusalem that divided the city for nineteen years. Israel held most of the New City, outside of the city walls, whereas Jordan held the area east of a line running roughly north to south along the Old City's western walls, including the Old City itself. The armistice also provided for two demilitarized zones: an Israeli enclave on Mount Scopus in Jordanian territory, which included Hebrew University and the Hadassah Hospital, and the area around Government House, the headquarters of the United Nations Truce Supervision Organization.[4] Furthermore, there was to be "free access to the Holy Places and to cultural institutions, and the use of the Jewish cemetery on the Mount of Olives." A special commission of representatives from each side was to work together to resolve other problems.[5]

JERUSALEM AND THE UNITED NATIONS AFTER THE 1948 WAR

The status of Jerusalem remained unresolved so far as the international community was concerned. Most members of the United Nations, including the Vatican and, by this time, most Arab states, insisted on a territorial internationalization of the city as delineated in the 25 November 1947 resolution on partition.[6] Hoping to appeal to both Jordan and Israel, the Palestine Conciliation Commission recommended that immigration to Jerusalem be halted to preserve demographic equilibrium and that the city be demilitarized and divided into two zones corresponding to the sections of the city then occupied by Israel and Jordan. Each zone would have its own municipality, each of which would be headed by a general council of seven representatives from each side. The holy places would be under the protection of a United Nations commissioner, and legal questions would be settled by an international court.[7]

Both the Israelis and the Jordanians denounced the plan as unrealistic and impractical. Now that Jerusalem was in their hands, neither side was interested in relinquishing it. Indeed, the fact that they occupied the city put them in a position of strength when it came to rejecting or accepting proposals made by other United Nations members. During the fourth session of the General Assembly, when the issue of Jerusalem was debated extensively, Israel expressed its willingness to consider a loose arrangement that would give the international body functional power to administer the holy places but was unwilling to give up territory, especially on the scale envisioned by the General Assembly's call for a *corpus separatum* for Jerusalem. Israel argued that with almost all of the Christian, Muslim, and Jewish holy places under Jordanian control, there was no reason why the Jewish section of the New City should be included in the internationalized zone. Nevertheless, Israel was willing to guarantee the security of the holy places that fell within its jurisdiction and assure free access to them; Jordan expressed its willingness to make similar guarantees.[8]

Some members of the United Nations, such as Sweden and the Netherlands, favored United Nations administration of the holy places in the city rather than the creation of a separate, U.N.-governed city-state. They argued that territorial internationalization would be difficult to maintain because the people of Jerusalem and its surrounding states were opposed to the arrangement. Nevertheless, these proponents of a functional solution were outnumbered by those who preferred a territorial one. On 9 December 1949, the General Assembly adopted Resolution 303, which insisted on a *corpus separatum* under international control and called on the trusteeship council, established after the 1947 resolution, to prepare and implement a statute for an internationalized city.[9]

The Israeli stance on territorial internationalization was expressed by Prime Minister David Ben-Gurion, who stated in 1949 that "the Jews will sacrifice themselves for Jerusalem no less than Englishmen for London."[10] In December 1949, in defiance of the United Nations resolution, Israel moved its parliament, the Knesset, from Tel Aviv to West Jerusalem, and in January the following year announced that Jerusalem had always been its capital. Israel immediately moved its government ministries to Jerusalem, except for the ministries of defense, police, and foreign affairs. The latter was left in Tel Aviv because most foreign embassies were located there; however, by 1953 all three had been moved to Jerusalem, despite international protest. This move eventually compelled foreign states to deal with Israel in West Jerusalem, despite their objections to the city's annexation by Israel.[11]

The United Nations immediately called on Israel to retract its decision and proposed a new plan, named after the trusteeship council's president, Roger Garreau of France. It suggested that Jerusalem be divided into three zones: a Jordanian zone under Jordanian sovereignty that would comprise the Muslim quarter of the Old City, the Haram esh-Sharif, and the modern parts of East Jerusalem; an Israeli zone under Israeli sovereignty that would consist of most of West Jerusalem outside the city walls; and an international zone under United Nations sovereignty that would include the city's holy places. The international zone would be administered by a governor appointed by the United Nations and a municipal council elected by the city's inhabitants.[12]

Both Jordan and Israel rejected the plan because it entailed a loss of territory, and most other members of the United Nations supported a Chinese proposal that the trusteeship council implement the statute for Jerusalem as stipulated in Resolution 303. The trusteeship council consequently dropped the Garreau plan and prepared a statute for Jerusalem based on the 1947 plan that called for the entire city and its surrounding areas to become a *corpus separatum* under international control. The statute was once again rejected by Israel and Jordan. In despair, the trusteeship council referred the Jerusalem question back to the General Assembly.[13]

Because of Israel's and Jordan's intransigence on territorial internationalization and the United Nations' inability to implement its decisions, international interest waned. The General Assembly did not seriously consider the problem again until after the 1967 war, although a few proposals were discussed during the early 1950s.[14] In the meantime, Jordan and Israel seemed committed to preserving the status quo in Jerusalem and legitimizing their positions.

EAST JERUSALEM, 1948–1967

In 1950 the Jordanian Assembly merged its occupied territories with Jordan. Thereafter, it worked to integrate East Jerusalem with the rest of the country, fostering economic growth and tourism, arbitrating disputes amongst Christian churches, and dealing with thousands of displaced Arab refugees who had fled from Israel during the 1948 war.

From the early 1950s to 1967, Arab leaders in East Jerusalem frequently complained about the judaization of West Jerusalem and contended that the eastern part of the city was being intentionally discriminated against and neglected by the Jordanian government in Amman. Their main grievances were their lack of power in making decisions on behalf of the city and the government's lack of support for housing, public institutions, and such other needs as reconstruction to repair the damage the city had sustained during the war. Their frustrations with the Jordanian state were doubtlessly enhanced by their awareness of the rebuilding taking place in West Jerusalem. Such services as electricity and running water were lacking in East Jerusalem, and little effort was made towards improvement. The Arabs in East Jerusalem believed Jordan deliberately diverted investments and industries away from Jerusalem to the East Bank and impeded efforts by Arab Palestinians to establish a university and cultural institutions in the city.[15]

While Amman grew from a small town of 20,000 to a city of 300,000, the population of East Jerusalem remained at approximately 60,000 from 1948 to 1967 despite the expansion of its municipal boundaries. The Christian population declined during this period, from approximately 25,000 in 1948 to about 11,000 just before the city's reunification. The Muslim community grew into the void created by departing Christians.[16] Terence Prittie, a noted scholar and an authority on Jerusalem, attributes the Christian exodus to the city's neglect by Jordan and to widespread discrimination. Between 1948 and 1967 the Jordanian government enacted discriminatory laws and regulations against Christians, among which were restrictions on their purchase of land in Jerusalem, government control of Christian education, and stringent regulation of Christian funds.[17]

Jordan's neglect of the city is attributable, in part, to its being on the border with Israel, but more important was the fear of Arab Palestinian nationalism, which was then making a resurgence. The Hashemite rulers of Jordan, who were predominantly from the East Bank, were more interested in the development of the Amman area than that of East Jerusalem with its hostile Arab Palestinian population. Many of Jerusalem's intellectuals, students, business people, and political leaders were attracted to Amman by its political, administrative, economic, cultural, and educational institutions.[18]

The assassination by Arab Palestinians of King Abdullah during his visit to Jerusalem in July 1951 and subsequent attempts on the life of King Hussein hardened the government's attitude toward the city. East Jerusalem became a hotbed of opposition to Jordan and the site of numerous Arab Palestinian demonstrations against the government. To help keep Arab Palestinian aspirations in check and to appease criticism that it was neglecting the city, Jordan proclaimed Jerusalem its second capital in 1959, an action that was little more than symbolic.[19] Only after the creation of the Palestine Liberation Organization by the Arab League (a consortium of Arab states) in Jerusalem in 1964, whose twofold purpose was to unify Arabs and to liberate Palestine, did Jordan show more concern for the city's development. It had little time to demonstrate its new policy, however, before East Jerusalem was taken by Israel in 1967.[20]

THE HOLY PLACES UNDER JORDANIAN CONTROL

Despite the government's neglect of Jerusalem, tourism in the city thrived during the nineteen years of Jordanian control. About 85 percent of Jordan's annual revenue from tourism came from East Jerusalem, which received more than half a million visitors each year.[21] To promote tourism to East Jerusalem, Jordan had agreed to an Israeli proposal that a frontier post be set up through which tourists and pilgrims could cross the demarcation lines in Jerusalem. The crossing point, known as the Mandelbaum Gate, opened on 12 January 1950. Jordan, however, permitted only one-way border crossings from West to East Jerusalem by tourists, pilgrims, and Christian clergymen and denied entrance to Jews and Israeli Muslims. This policy allowed Jordan to virtually monopolize tourism to the city by forcing visitors to lodge in East Jerusalem.[22] The number of hotels in the city grew from one in 1948 to about seventy by 1966. Most of the hotels and services for tourists were local enterprises, though the government participated in a few development and restoration projects to promote pilgrimage and tourism. For example, beginning in 1958 the Haram esh-Sharif underwent a major restoration under the patronage of several Arab states and Islamic organizations, and in 1961 the Church of the Holy Sepulchre received assistance from the Jordanian government for renovations.[23]

The Hashemite rulers of Jordan took their role seriously as protectors of the Muslim and Christian holy places, nearly all of which came under Jordanian control after the 1948 war. In an effort to appease international concern on the matter, King Abdullah affirmed that Jordan would abide by British Mandate orders relating to the holy places. In January 1951, he appointed a guardian of the Haram esh-Sharif and custodian of the holy places to mediate between religious groups in the city. The second part of the title was not recognized by the Christian churches, which felt that the appointment infringed on the status quo of the holy places.[24]

The first person appointed to this position was the former mayor of Jerusalem under the British Mandate, Raghib Pasha al Nashashibi, who died a few months after taking office. Al Nashashibi was replaced by Hussein Fakhri al Khalidi, who arbitrated disputes between Christian churches before he resigned in August 1952 out of frustration with the Jordanian Cabinet for interfering with his decision making. The post of royal custodian was subsequently discontinued, but the duties were transferred to the governor of Jerusalem, whose title was changed in 1955 to the District Head of Jerusalem and the Holy Places. Between 1955 and 1967 the government intervened frequently in the affairs of the Christian churches, enacting legislation to limit their power and twice deporting the Armenian archbishop to influence the outcome of elections.[25]

Although Muslim and Christian holy places were respected and administered reasonably well under Jordanian administration, the Jewish holy places and institutions were unabashedly desecrated and destroyed. Despite the Israeli-Jordanian armistice agreement that there be "free access to the Holy Places," including the Western Wall, the Jordanians refused to allow Jews access to the city. Tourists who were not Muslims were required to produce a baptismal certificate before being issued a visa. The Jewish Quarter in the Old City was ransacked and most of its synagogues demolished, the ruins of which were used as stables, chicken coops, or refuse dumps. Even more insulting to Jews was the desecration of the Jewish cemetery on the Mount of Olives, which by 1948 had more than fifty thousand graves. The municipality of Jerusalem granted concessions to merchants to sell the gravestones, which were used for buildings, fortifications, and, in one case, to pave a path to a latrine of an Arab Legion camp in Bethany. And the Jordanian government built the Jericho-Jerusalem highway right through the middle of the cemetery.[26]

WEST JERUSALEM, 1948–1967

Having declared Jerusalem its eternal capital in 1950, Israel consolidated its hold on the western part of the city. By the end of the 1948 war, the city's Jewish population had declined to about 84,000 from nearly 100,000 in 1946. Many of its aged and infirm residents had fled at the beginning of the war; many business owners and skilled workers left because of the insecurity in the city; and civil servants moved to Tel Aviv, the country's administrative center. To curb the exodus of Jews from Jerusalem, the government instituted a system whereby no one could move away from the city without a permit.[27] The Jewish population began to grow again only after Israel moved its ministries to Jerusalem and enacted the Law of Return, which granted any Jew the right to immigrate to Israel.[28] By 1952 the Jewish population had reached 138,000 and by 1967, when the city was reunited, it stood at approximately 194,000, about 73 percent of its total population.[29]

In 1949, many immigrants to West Jerusalem settled in houses abandoned by Arabs during the war. When these were exhausted, building activities expanded to absorb the city's growing population. New housing projects, government offices, and religious, cultural, and public buildings were erected, including a new Hadassah Hospital and Hebrew University because the older complexes on Mount Scopus were virtually inaccessible. The city also pursued an ambitious policy of tree planting inside and outside the city.[30]

The rapid growth of West Jerusalem outpaced its economic development, which was stunted in part by its geographic isolation, being linked only by a narrow corridor to the rest of the country. Meron Benvenisti, past deputy-mayor of Jerusalem, estimates that "one-third of the city's population occupied substandard housing."[31] Large industry and factories were virtually absent. By 1967, the Israeli government, Hebrew University, Hadassah Hospital, and the Jewish Agency employed one-third of the city's workers. Most people made a living from building or small industry and crafts. Tourism was slow to develop, largely because most of the holy places were located in East Jerusalem. By 1967 there were only about one thousand hotel rooms in West Jerusalem, compared to about twenty-five hundred in East Jerusalem. A lack of jobs and adequate housing forced many young people to seek livelihoods in the coastal towns. The city was only beginning to emerge from economic recession before the 1967 war.[32]

SECURITY IN JERUSALEM DURING PARTITION

The border between Israel and Jordan in Jerusalem, a narrow demilitarized zone, was the scene of constant tension, sporadic skirmishes, and occasional exchanges of sniper fire. During one such occasion in 1954, shooting continued for three days before United Nations observers helped negotiate a cease-fire. To obstruct the view of Jordanian snipers, Israel planted some twenty-two thousand eucalyptus trees along the demarcation lines, though not long afterwards many of them were cut down to make room for housing for immigrants.[33]

According to the armistice agreement between Israel and Jordan after the 1948 war, the Israeli-controlled demilitarized zone on Mount Scopus was to receive a convoy of supplies under United Nations protection every two weeks and to maintain a small garrison of 120 policemen for local security. Suspecting that Israel was smuggling arms and additional men into the area, a charge that Israel denied at the time but admitted to after the 1967 war, the Jordanians now and then held up the convoys. Tensions flared between the two sides. United Nations attempts to resolve the problem were unsuccessful.[34]

The city remained relatively calm during the 1956 Suez Crisis between Egypt and Israel because of Jordan's preoccupation with internal problems, though the following year there were disputes over Israel's planting trees in the demilitarized zone near Government House south of the Old City. Fearing that Israel was attempting to annex the area, Jordan complained to the United Nations, which unanimously called on

Israel to suspend its planting of trees while the issue was investigated. Israel reluctantly complied under pressure from the United States.[35] In 1962 some Israelis were killed and others wounded in a series of incidents. Occasionally, when tensions ran high, the two sides held informal bilateral talks between local military officers.[36]

THE REUNIFICATION OF JERUSALEM

In 1966, with the dedication of the new Knesset (parliament) building in West Jerusalem, international interest in the question of Jerusalem's status was revived. The new multimillion-dollar structure symbolized to the world that Israel was determined to maintain Jerusalem as its capital at all costs. The Arab League states and the Palestine Liberation Organization protested that Israel was once again violating United Nations resolutions and called on Jordan to make Jerusalem its official capital to give a more prominent Arab presence to the city. King Hussein was unwilling to do that, but he declared Jerusalem to be Jordan's "spiritual capital" and encouraged Arab states to contribute to the restoration of Muslim holy places, mosques, and schools and to build Muslim establishments.[37]

Tensions between Israel and its neighboring states erupted on Monday, 5 June 1967. Israel notified King Hussein that unless attacked by Jordan, Israel would "initiate no action" against Jordan. Feeling "obliged to do everything to help . . . [its] allies," Jordan entered the war, and a battle ensued over Jerusalem. By Wednesday morning, Israeli forces had captured East Jerusalem, including the Old City and the Haram esh-Sharif. The war continued in other parts of the country for another three days until the United Nations was able to arrange a cease-fire. Some 840 people died in the battle over Jerusalem—195 Israelis (including 14 civilians) and 645 Arabs (249 of them civilians)—and many more were wounded on both sides. East and West Jerusalem both sustained heavy physical damage.[38]

Israeli troops and reservists combed East Jerusalem for Jordanian soldiers and caches of arms and ammunition. For several days Arab civilians were subjected to humiliating searches and interrogation, charges of theft, vandalism, and mistreatment by Israeli soldiers and civilians. The Jordanian government had been keenly aware of the large hostile population in East Jerusalem and had stringently enforced restrictions on the possession of firearms, with the result that East Jerusalem's civilians had very few weapons during the 1967 war. Most of the arms recovered by Israeli soldiers were found in public buildings and military positions.[39]

The capture of East Jerusalem aroused a tremendous emotional reaction among Israeli Jews. Even before the physical barriers between East and West Jerusalem were removed, many Jews rushed to pray at the Western Wall for the first time since 1948, some even scaling the fences and taking their chances with the mine fields. Standing near the Western Wall, Defense Minister Moshe Dayan declared: "We have reunited divided Jerusalem, . . . returned to our most Holy Places . . . and shall never leave them." Then, in a statement reminiscent of General Allenby's after the capture of the city from the Ottoman Turks in 1917 he said: "To . . . Christians and Muslims, I hereby promise faithfully that their full freedom and all their religious rights will be preserved. We did not come to Jerusalem to conquer the Holy Places of others, nor to hamper the members of other religions, but to ensure its integrity and to live in brotherhood with others."[40]

Desiring to create new faits accomplis to impede any efforts to return Jerusalem to its former partitioned status, Dayan ordered the removal of the barbed-wire fences and mines that had separated Jerusalem for almost two decades. Soon afterwards the city's electricity, telephone system, and water supply were integrated.[41] The Israeli government proceeded cautiously with efforts to unify the city in other ways because some Israeli government officials had not yet ruled out the possibility of internationalization, though most were emphatic that the city remain in Jewish hands.[42] The United States and Britain urged Israel to refrain from annexing the city because it would prejudice Israel's position before the General Assembly. Nevertheless, by the second week of June 1967, Israel's government leaders had decided upon outright annexation in defiance of the United Nations and the international community.[43]

On June 18 the Israeli military government evicted hundreds of Arab residents who had settled in the former Jewish quarter of the Old City after the 1948 war. Many were also removed from the Maghribi quarter and their homes torn down to make room for worshippers at the Western Wall.[44] On June 27, the Knesset passed an ordinance allowing the Minister of the Interior to enlarge municipal boundaries by decree. Simultaneously, it extended Israeli law to any part of Palestine and safeguarded freedom of access to the holy places by people of all religions. The following day the Minister of the Interior formally extended the municipal boundaries of West Jerusalem to include East Jerusalem and many of its suburbs.[45]

Although Israel avoided the term *annexation,* preferring to speak of the city's *reunification,* the act was nevertheless condemned by the international community. The United States declared that it could not recognize Israel's action as anything other than temporary but, convinced that the question of Jerusalem should be considered within a comprehensive peace settlement rather than as a separate issue, it did not pressure Israel to withdraw.[46] France and Britain urged Israel to renounce its claims until the city's status could be determined by a peace agreement. Most Arab states, supported by the Communist bloc, demanded that Israel withdraw from the occupied territories, including East Jerusalem, and urged the Security Council to take disciplinary action.[47]

On 4 July, the General Assembly voted ninety to zero, with twenty abstentions, to call on Israel "to rescind all measures already taken and to desist forthwith from taking any action which would alter the status of Jerusalem."[48] In an attempt to strengthen its deteriorating position in the international community, Israel initiated negotiations with the Vatican, a long-time proponent of internationalization, and several other Christian churches. Israel had some success with its proposition that the holy places be granted a status similar to that of foreign embassies—that is, to be administered by the leaders of the religious communities who would be given quasidiplomatic status—but it was not enough.[49] On 14 July, the General Assembly voted ninety-nine to zero, with eighteen abstentions, to condemn the annexation of Jerusalem and chastise Israel for failing to comply with the 4 July resolution.[50] Israel reiterated its position that it would never give up Jerusalem and, ignoring international public opinion, proceeded to administer the city as a liberator, not an occupier.

Notes

1. Bovis, *Jerusalem Question,* 61–63.
2. Bovis, *Jerusalem Question,* 63–65.

3. Bovis, *Jerusalem Question*, 66–69; Dupuy, *Elusive Victory*, 92–116.

4. Eckardt, *Jerusalem*, 119–20.

5. For partial text of the armistice agreement, see Khouri, *Arab-Israeli Dilemma*, 533.

6. Bovis, *Jerusalem Question*, 72.

7. Bovis, *Jerusalem Question*, 72–73.

8. See *Peace of Jerusalem*, 5–68; Bovis, *Jerusalem Question*, 85–86; Khouri, *Arab-Israeli Dilemma*, 104–7.

9. Bovis, *Jerusalem Question*, 78–79.

10. Khouri, *Arab-Israeli Dilemma*, 107.

11. Khouri, *Arab-Israeli Dilemma*, 110; Bovis, *Jerusalem Question*, 92–93.

12. Bovis, *Jerusalem Question*, 82–84; Kraemer, *Jerusalem*, 66.

13. Khouri, *Arab-Israeli Dilemma*, 107–9; Bovis, *Jerusalem Question*, 84.

14. Khouri, *Arab-Israeli Dilemma*, 109–10.

15. Eckardt, *Jerusalem*, 132; Asali, *Jerusalem in History*, 265–67.

16. Asali, *Jerusalem in History*, 265; Bovis, *Jerusalem Question*, 128–29; Cohen, *Jerusalem*, 69–70; Eckardt, *Jerusalem*, 133; Benvenisti, *Jerusalem*, 43–45, 47–48.

17. Prittie, *Whose Jerusalem?* 69–70; Kraemer, *Jerusalem*, 174; Benvenisti, *Jerusalem*, 54–56.

18. Eckardt, *Jerusalem*, 131.

19. Khouri, *Arab-Israeli Dilemma*, 111; Kraemer, *Jerusalem*, 93.

20. See Cobban, *Palestine Liberation Organisation*, 30–31; Asali, *Jerusalem in History*, 265–67.

21. Cohen, *Jerusalem*, 70; Benvenisti, *Jerusalem*, 59.

22. Bovis, *Jerusalem Question*, 115–16; Eckardt, *Jerusalem*, 137; Prittie, *Whose Jerusalem*, 76.

23. Benvenisti, *Jerusalem*, 59; Eckardt, *Jerusalem*, 134–35; Asali, *Jerusalem in History*, 264; Bovis, *Jerusalem Question*, 96.

24. Kraemer, *Jerusalem*, 173–75.

25. Kraemer, *Jerusalem*, 134–35, 173–75; Benvenisti, *Jerusalem*, 76–77; see also Bovis, *Jerusalem Question*, 96–99.

26. Prittie, *Whose Jerusalem?* 64–68; Eckardt, *Jerusalem*, 135; Benvenisti, *Jerusalem*, 68–70.

27. Cohen, *Jerusalem*, 66.

28. For more on the Law of Return, see Laqueur, *Israel-Arab Reader*, 128.

29. Eckardt, *Jerusalem*, 127; Bovis, *Jerusalem Question*, 128–29.

30. Benvenisti, *Jerusalem*, 31; Eckardt, *Jerusalem*, 127–28; Cattan, *Jerusalem*, 61–63; for Israel's and Jordan's, to a lesser extent, use of tree-planting as a means of gaining control over disputed land, see Cohen, *Politics of Planting*.

31. Benvenisti, *Jerusalem*, 35.

32. Benvenisti, *Jerusalem*, 35–36, 59.

33. Cohen, *Politics of Planting*, 70–71; *Encyclopedia Judaica*, 9:1497, s.v. "Jerusalem."

34. Kraemer, *Jerusalem*, 88–90; Khouri, *Arab-Israeli Dilemma*, 221–22.

35. Khouri, *Arab-Israeli Dilemma*, 222; see also Cohen, *Politics of Planting*, 71.

36. *Encyclopedia Judaica*, 9:1497, s.v. "Jerusalem."

37. Khouri, *Arab-Israeli Dilemma*, 112; Eckardt, *Jerusalem*, 133.

38. Benvenisti, *Jerusalem*, 79–82; Dupuy, *Elusive Victory*, 288–305; see also Medzini, *Israel's Foreign Relations*, 779.

39. Benvenisti, *Jerusalem*, 86–87, 99–100.

40. In Benvenisti, *Jerusalem*, 84.

41. Bovis, *Jerusalem Question*, 103; Benvenisti, *Jerusalem*, 95–96.

42. Bin Talal, *Study of Jerusalem*, 27.

43. Khouri, *Arab-Israeli Dilemma*, 113.

44. Bovis, *Jerusalem Question*, 103.

45. Bovis, *Jerusalem Question*, 103–4; Khouri, *Arab-Israeli Dilemma*, 113; Benvenisti, *Jerusalem*, 109.

46. Boudreault and Salaam, *U.S. Official Statements*, 22, 26–29; Feintuch, *U. S. Policy on Jerusalem*, 127–31.

47. Benvenisti, *Jerusalem*, 123; Bovis, *Jerusalem Question*, 107; Khouri, *Arab-Israeli Dilemma*, 114–16.

48. In bin Talal, *Study on Jerusalem*, 29.

49. Khouri, *Arab-Israeli Dilemma*, 115–16; Bovis, *Jerusalem Question*, 106.

50. In Khouri, *Arab-Israeli Dilemma*, 540.

23

JERUSALEM AND INTERNATIONAL LAW

Jerusalem has been identified as the key to a peaceful solution of the Arab-Israeli conflict. Yet the status of Jerusalem has been so controversial that the practice has been to agree to disagree and to keep it off the agenda lest it ruin what little incentive for agreement might exist on less critical matters. Despite this practice, one day the issue of Jerusalem will have to be addressed in all its complexities. With each passing year the future status of Jerusalem demands consideration with ever greater urgency. The Latter-day Saints may see in this situation a fulfillment of Zechariah's prophecy: "And in that day will I make Jerusalem a burdensome stone for all people" (Zech. 12:3). It is instructive to examine the status of Jerusalem from the perspective of modern international law in light of the ever-present political realities, but in the final analysis, no one seriously believes that the controversy over Jerusalem will be settled in an international court of justice.

INTERNATIONAL LAW AND HISTORICAL RIGHTS

The controversy over Jerusalem did not have its beginning in 1967 nor for that matter in 1947 or 1948. The decisive date in recent history might arguably be 1840. In that year the Egyptian forces under Ibrahim Pasha retreated from Syria and Palestine, and the Turks once again took control of the area.

Before its withdrawal, Egypt had opened Palestine, including Jerusalem, to Western interests; by supporting the Ottomans' return, the West extracted certain far-reaching concessions. For example, every European power was allowed to open a consulate in Jerusalem, and many Christian denominations were allowed to construct churches and monasteries that had heretofore been forbidden to them. This change opened the door to Europeans' acquiring land not only for churches and monasteries but also for hospitals, hospices, and other charitable institutions. These concessions to Western interests placed a certain constraint on the exercise of Ottoman sovereignty over Jerusalem.

In 1855, the outbreak of the Crimean War emphasized the special international status of Jerusalem in the eyes of the West. The war had its roots, in part, in interdenominational strife among Christians over rights to the Church of the Holy Sepulchre in Jerusalem. Russia supported the Russian Orthodox Church, and France took the side of the Roman Catholic Church. The treaty of 1856 that brought the war to a close legitimized the status of the European powers in Jerusalem and established an interdenominational status quo over the Holy Sepulchre. Between the end of the Crimean War and the beginning of World War I, many new churches were constructed in Jerusalem, all under the protection of various foreign consulates.

The end of World War I brought the fall of the Ottoman Empire and with it the special status attained by Jerusalem. The League of Nations appointed Great Britain as the mandatory power over Palestine. The British Mandate was to safeguard the special international status of Jerusalem's churches with their links to the various foreign consulates, preserve existing rights to the holy places, and form a special commission to look into the question of rights with regard to the holy places.[1] In fact, the Commission was never formed, but it is noteworthy that the provision existed.

During the British Mandate the churches in Jerusalem were granted a special tax exemption. By itself that might not seem so extraordinary, but it resulted from international agreements before the Mandate that Britain was bound to honor. It was a reflection of international forces at work, both political and religious, seeking to preserve their respective interests. In 1947, when the League's successor, the United Nations, passed a resolution calling for an international Jerusalem, it was acknowledging an international status that had previously existed.

When the war ended in 1949, and Israel and Jordan divided the spoils in Jerusalem, neither was interested in the internationalization of the city. In what has to be a classic development in international law as it relates to a single city, both Israel and Jordan acknowledged the right of the American, British, French, Belgian, Italian, Turkish, and Spanish consulates in Jerusalem to function without accreditation to any government and with no connection to their respective embassies in Jerusalem, Tel Aviv, or Amman. Furthermore, the tax and customs exemptions continued, as did the special status quo related to the religious sites.

THE LEGAL STATUS OF THE HOLY PLACES: THE STATUS QUO

While law is technically an instrument for resolving conflict, in the case of the holy places in Jerusalem, it appears to be less applicable. Part of the problem is that religious precepts by their very nature reject compromise. An individual may waive personal interests, but no individual may waive rights on behalf of his God. In disputes over holy places, the principal litigant—in this case God—is absent, as it were, and is represented by mortals who, rightly or wrongly, believe that they are not at liberty to yield anything on his behalf. Therein lies the crux of the problem with Jerusalem. Additionally, a secular state with a religiously mixed population must be neutral in religious matters. That requires the state to be both liberal and tolerant—a position that satisfies no one.[2]

The status quo (or prevailing status)[3] seeks to maintain the status of the holy places as they were during the Ottoman period. Authority for maintaining the status quo is found in a British Order in Council from the mandatory period, dated 1924.[4] Although of questionable legal validity, for primarily political reasons this status quo is recognized as binding to this day. This status is particularly useful for those wishing to hide behind it, who can raise their arms in a helpless gesture, suggesting any intervention in a religious dispute is out of their hands.

In fact, it is very difficult to define what legal rights, if any, derive from the status quo. It is simply an outdated edict that countenances no change. The rationale for the Order in Council may have suited the times, but it is a blatantly discriminatory document at the present. It is prejudicial in that it ignores religious equality; it denies to one religious community what it allows to another. Furthermore, it is a nontolerant document in the face of new developments. For example, the Palestine Order in Council of 1931, which bases its decrees on the status quo, severely limits Jewish prayers at the Western Wall and determines that Christians cannot hold services in the Room of the Last Supper.

In 1967, the government of Israel passed the Protection of the Holy Places Law,[5] which guarantees freedom of access to sacred places by all who deem them holy and protects such places from desecration. It raises the question: Does this law contradict the provisions of the status quo, which does limit access to certain sites? For example, to allow Muslims and Christians access to the area around the Dome of the Rock is a form of desecration to religious Jews because of the sanctity of the site to them. Jews themselves will not even set foot on the Mount.

The logical procedure to reverse matters prejudicial to the interests of a given community is to apply to the courts for ruling. In the matter of the holy places, however, the Palestine Order in Council of 1924 determined that the political arm of the governing authority, not the judicial, should decide all such matters. So as things now stand, the government of Israel and not the courts decides all noncriminal disputes connected with the holy places.

The problem of jurisdiction has arisen several times with regard to criminal acts. In each case, the defense has argued that under the Order in Council of 1924 the courts have no jurisdiction to hear the matter. The judges have been divided. In 1977 the Jerusalem District Court determined that the matter before the court affected a holy place and directed that it be brought before the Minister of Religious Affairs.[6] On the other hand, the Beersheba District Court determined by majority vote that it did possess jurisdiction to hear a matter involving a holy place because the dispute involved a criminal act that lay within the purview of the court.[7]

There is such a maze of opinion on this question of jurisdiction that the matter was brought before the Israeli High Court for a ruling.[8] Two of the five judges argued that the Order in Council was no longer in effect and that the courts have full jurisdiction. Two other judges argued that the Order in Council was still in force. A fifth judge found that the Order in Council denying jurisdiction remains in effect subject to the provisions of the Protection of the Holy Places Law. In other words, if the Order in Council conflicts with the Protection Law, the Order in Council is repealed. Thus the courts can hear both civil and criminal disputes affecting free access to the holy places and their desecration because they are matters within the purview of the Protection Law, but the courts may not hear other disputes affecting the holy places—for example, the rights claimed by the various religious communities in relation to these holy sites.

As antiquated as the principle of status quo is, it continues to play an important role in the political and religious complexities of Jerusalem. It allows the government a certain freedom where political realities are concerned that might not be so readily available through the courts. On the other hand, this selective exclusion of jurisdiction remains confusing and bodes ill for the future in dealing with highly sensitive religious matters. This fact is well documented in the case of the single most troublesome issue in Jerusalem: The Temple Mount, or Haram esh-Sharif.

THE TEMPLE MOUNT: A STUDY OF
CONVOLUTED JURISDICTIONS

Anciently the Jews were enjoined to make pilgrimage to Jerusalem and offer sacrifice three times a year—Passover, Shavuot, and Succoth. These spring, summer, and fall festivities are observed even today as holidays in Israel. Although most Israelis relax at home or on the beaches, the observant visit the synagogues and many keep the tradition of going up to Jerusalem. Anyone making a special effort to visit Jerusalem on such occasions would not fail to visit the Western Wall of the ancient Temple Mount, either to worship or to observe others doing so.

In the week of 8 October 1990, during the festivities of Succoth (better known in English as the Feast of Tabernacles), an organization called the Faithful of the Temple Mount, a small group of activists seeking to establish a permanent Jewish presence on the Temple Mount, announced their plans to lay the cornerstone of a future Jewish temple. The Arab Palestinians objected angrily to what they interpreted as a threat to the sacred shrines of Islam.

This dispute has its modern roots in the 1967 Six-Day War, during which the Israeli military overran Arab East Jerusalem and the Old City, including the Temple Mount. Jubilation, if not euphoria, seized Jews worldwide upon learning that for the first time in nearly 2,000 years Judaism's most sacred site, their ancient Temple Mount, was once again in Jewish hands. Both secular and religious leaders among the Israelis vowed that whatever political compromises were made in the future,

Israel would never withdraw from East Jerusalem and the Old City. Shortly afterward, on 28 June 1967, Israel announced the reunification of the city and declared Jerusalem its eternal capital.

The Arab Palestinian communities throughout Israel and the occupied territories, with the backing of Islamic states from Morocco to Indonesia, objected violently, angry that Islam's third most sacred shrine in all the world, next to Mecca and Medina, had fallen under Israeli control. On the site known to Jews and Christians as the Temple Mount but revered by Muslims as the Haram esh-Sharif, "the Noble Sanctuary," Abraham brought Ishmael (not Isaac, as believed by Jews and Christians) to offer as a sacrifice. It was also from here that the Prophet Muhammad ascended into heaven on his mighty steed, al-Buraq. And to venerate the site where these sacred events took place, a magnificent shrine was first built in A.D. 691. Furthermore, Jerusalem had been an Arab and an Islamic city for centuries.

Not only did the Islamic world object to Israel's actions in annexing Arab Jerusalem but so did the United States and Great Britain. The major powers publicly deplored Israel's unilateral move and declared that they would not recognize its validity. The overwhelming international opposition to Israel's edict was reflected in the United Nations when on 4 July 1967, a resolution was passed 99 to 0, condemning Israel's actions with regard to Jerusalem and calling upon Israel to "rescind all measures already taken" and to desist from taking any further action to "alter the status of Jerusalem."[9]

Israel essentially ignored international public opinion and calmly asserted its right to what it regarded as historically a Jewish city. Out of concern for the historical and spiritual traditions of others, however, Israel would assure the universal, pluralistic character of the city and the protection of the holy places. Partly because of international pressure and partly because of interest in community harmony, the government of Israel, while affirming Israel's sovereignty over the whole of Jerusalem, announced that the Temple Mount would be controlled by the Muslims and that access by non-Muslim pilgrims and visitors to the site be allowed only when it did not interfere with Muslim prayers and holy days.

In the meantime, the chief rabbinate in Israel shocked the more secular elements of the Jewish population—the principle was already well known by religious Jews—with the warning: "Entrance to the area of the Temple Mount is forbidden to everyone by Jewish Law owing to the sacredness of the place." This seemingly extreme position reflected an attitude dating back to Maimonides, a great Jewish sage of the twelfth century, who maintained that because of uncertainty about the location of the Holy of Holies, entrance to which was restricted on pain of death (except for the high priest once a year on Yom Kippur), Jews should stay off the Temple Mount altogether. Although it has been challenged from time to time, this belief is held to be correct by most rabbis in Israel and abroad.

At present, the Israeli government cooperates with Muslim authorities to permit nearly everyone to visit the Temple Mount, but because of Muslim sensitivity about this sacred site, the government supports Muslim demands that Jews not be allowed to pray there. These actions are dictated by the quasi-legal status quo. The policy dealing with religious sites seeks to distinguish between religious rights and secular authority—a sort of separation of church and state, as it were, in which all religious communities enjoy a degree of autonomy and equal status. To allow Jews to establish a physical presence on the Temple Mount or even to start a tradition of daily prayers there would be direct contravention of the status quo and would inevitably result in political unrest and worse.

Jewish nationalists, mostly religious adherents of the organization called the Faithful of the Temple Mount, charge that the Temple Mount, Judaism's most sacred site, is desecrated by the Muslim Dome of the Rock and the al-Aqsa Mosque and that the government of Israel is acting illegally in denying Jews the right to worship there. Although the organization has not gone so far as to call for the destruction of the mosques, it does demand the right to establish a permanent Jewish presence there. This fringe group is numerically weak, but it has powerful supporters in the Israeli government and enough outside backing to have established a serious lobby in Israel's parliament, the Knesset.

Unrelenting pressure by the Faithful of the Temple Mount and a curious assortment of their allies (including many Christian fundamentalists), brought the matter to the Israeli High Court in March 1976. The court determined that the matter was not justiciable because it was a political and not a legal matter. It did distinguish between the right of access to a holy place, guaranteed by the Protection of Holy Places Law, and the right to worship there. The High Court noted that the latter comes under the jurisdiction of the government, not the courts; the government could refuse to permit Jewish prayers on the Temple Mount if it suspected they might lead to a disturbance of the peace.

Undaunted, the Faithful of the Temple Mount, in October 1993, again during the festivities of Succoth, attempted to haul a three-and-a-half ton stone up to the Temple Mount. The stone was reportedly quarried to be the cornerstone of the Third Temple. Once again violence erupted, for Muslims interpreted the act as an effort not just to gain a permanent Jewish presence on Haram esh-Sharif but to begin a movement that would ultimately end with the destruction of their sacred mosque and shrine believed to stand on or near the site of the previous two temples. Timely intervention by the Israeli police prevented serious trouble.

The temple activists, nevertheless, remain resolute in their determination to get a foothold on the Temple Mount, even though they are frustrated by the refusal of successive Israeli governments to allow Jews to pray on the Mount; a reluctance of the courts to get involved in what the courts see as a political decision; the Muslim leaders' determination to preserve the site as a Muslim holy place; and the edict of the chief rabbinate forbidding Jews to go onto the Temple Mount.

Members of the Faithful of the Temple Mount, once again hoping to force the issue and demonstrate wide popular support for their cause, on 1 October 1993 called upon the people of Israel to give a Jewish, national, and Zionist answer to Judaism's enemies and above all to Saddam Hussein and Yasser Arafat. The plan was to lay a symbolic cornerstone of the Third Temple at some location on the Temple Mount.

On 4 October, the Arab Palestinian newspaper *Al Fajr* warned on its front page that "Jewish extremists intend to march on Al Aqsa mosque on Monday, October 8th." Arab Palestinians were encouraged to demonstrate to the Israelis that they wouldn't be allowed to violate the areas holy to Islam. Jerusalem municipal authorities, seeing the potential for trouble and in keeping with established policy to prevent desecration of a holy site, denied the temple activists authorization to carry out their plans. Outraged, the leadership of the Temple group appealed to the

Israeli High Court for an injunction that would allow the group to hold their ceremony.

The activists were prohibited from "laying the cornerstone," but they were told they could go up "in pairs with a police escort," which they ultimately did, defiantly waving Israeli flags, according to news reports. Of course, that was a highly provocative act that the Arab Palestinians would not countenance. They were ready with stores of bottles, stones, and other such missiles to deter the Jewish activists. Whatever the catalyst and no matter who did what first, the results were serious casualties to both sides.

Because Israeli nationalist objectives in Jerusalem are mixed with Jewish religious aspirations, to which is added Christian Fundamentalist political, financial, and moral support, some strange alliances are brought to light. Added to that is Muslim unwillingness to countenance even the slightest change to the present status quo with regard to Islam's sacred sites in Jerusalem. The matter of Jerusalem, with its Temple Mount, or Haram esh-Sharif, portends future conflict between Judaism and Islam, between the Arab Palestinians and the Israelis.

THE JURIDICAL STATUS OF EAST JERUSALEM: ISRAEL'S POSITION

With the termination of the British Mandate over Palestine in 1948 and the nonimplementation of the United Nations resolution that would have partitioned the land and internationalized Jerusalem, the newly founded State of Israel claimed to be the "successor state" over certain occupied territories, including West Jerusalem. Theories of internationalizing Jerusalem had been overtaken by facts on the ground. Prime Minister David Ben-Gurion made it clear that "for historical, political and religious reasons, the State of Israel could not accept the establishment of an international regime for the city of Jerusalem."[10] Because Jerusalem was a divided city held by Israel and Jordan respectively until 1967, and because neither was willing to compromise on the matter, internationalization became a moot point.

In the course of the 1967 Six-Day War, Israel occupied the whole of Jerusalem and subsequently extended Israel's law, jurisdiction, and administration to all parts of Jerusalem. Some claim that by this action

Israel in effect illegally annexed East Jerusalem.[11] Israel, however, takes the position that there is no need to annex areas that before 1948 constituted part of British Mandate Palestine. Israel does not regard itself as an occupying power nor does it acknowledge claims by Arab states in the area to exercise any sovereign rights over areas occupied by Israel.

The Israeli government maintains that the Israeli Defense Forces "liberated from foreign yoke" the areas in question, including East Jerusalem. Furthermore, Israel holds that under international law it is entitled to undertake "an open act of sovereignty" in areas under the de facto control of the State.[12] In other words, because no sovereign power could show better title to the land in question than could Israel, the territory occupied by it in the war defaulted to Israel. This position is clarified as follows: "Any law applying to the whole of the State of Israel shall be deemed to apply to the whole of the area including both the area of the State of Israel and any part of Palestine which the Minister of Defence has defined by proclamation as *being held by the Defence Army of Israel.*"[13]

This position is in keeping with the one maintained by Israel that the territory held by the sovereign State of Israel was not delineated by a resolution of the Security Council but in accord with the outcome of the War of Independence. That belief is borne out by a statement made by David Ben-Gurion: "The Government is not bound to the resolution of November 28; the Foreign Minister has explained more than once . . . that the areas under our control (that is, areas beyond the Partition Plan borders) have been liberated from the enemy by the Israel Defence Forces."[14]

This concept has a useful application with regard to Jerusalem, namely, that the government of Israel has never held that the areas of Mandatory Palestine, ceded to Israel, are "occupied territories," which would require "annexation" to become part of the sovereign territory of Israel.[15]

Israel takes the position that with the termination of the British Mandate, the nonimplementation of the United Nations resolutions to internationalize Jerusalem, the de facto occupation and political control of East and West Jerusalem by Israel, and the absence of a stronger claim to Jerusalem by any other state in the area, suggest that Israel can show better title than any other state. According to Yehuda Blum's classical treatise on the juridical status of Jerusalem, this may be sufficient under international law to make Israel's possession of Jerusalem virtually indistinguishable from an absolute title.[16]

Despite Israel's Basic Law[17] of 30 July 1980, which identifies Jerusalem as the "complete and united" capital of Israel and "the seat of the President of the State, the Knesset, the Government, and the Supreme Court," Israel claims that it introduced no change to the status of the city but simply reaffirmed previously passed laws and regulations.

Most states, uncomfortable with Israel's unilateral actions, continue to locate their embassies in Tel Aviv. Israel, incensed by such "political discrimination," maintains that it is her sovereign, fundamental right to choose the location of her capital and the fact that so many states refuse to accord Jerusalem the status of capital has no legal bearing on the issue.

THE JURIDICAL STATUS OF EAST JERUSALEM: THE ARAB PALESTINIAN POSITION

Arab Palestinians believe that first and foremost Jerusalem is an Arab city, a city in which everyone enjoyed "absolute freedom to practice the religion of his choice. From time immemorial, the believer has been able to go there to worship his God in the Temple or Sanctuary which Arab sovereignty has preserved intact for centuries."[18] Embittered by the failure of the international community to intervene, the Arabs describe the modern history of Jerusalem as that of an Arab city torn from its legitimate sovereign, unjustly endowed in 1947 with an international status, cut asunder in 1948 by Zionist aggression, and finally illegally annexed in 1967 by the Zionist entity called Israel. They ask how an international body such as the United Nations could impose on an Arab city, with a clearly defined sovereign (the Arab nation), some form of international status without first having negotiated with them a treaty allowing such action. In fact, they point out, the United Nations partition plan of 1947 that would have internationalized the city was not implemented because of the war launched by the Zionist aggressors. The result of the war was a de facto partition, not a legal partition, of the city by military force, so there could be no derogation of sovereignty over the city and the Arabs remain the legitimate sovereign.

According to the Arabs, a devious plan of deception was suddenly revealed to the world when in 1967 Israel militarily overran the whole of Jerusalem and in a fit of unabashed exhilaration, Israel's chief chaplain divulged: "A people recovers its capital; a capital recovers its people; never shall they be separated again."[19] Clearly the military and political overthrow of Jerusalem had been Israel's intention all along.

Israel then proceeded to cement its ill-gained territory in a declaration proclaiming Jerusalem the undivided, eternal capital of the Jewish state. This blatant act was carried out in the full knowledge that the Arab Palestinian peoples would never, could never, acquiesce in such an unjust usurpation of a great Arab city sacred to all Islam. In flagrant disregard for international public opinion and unmoved by the fact that few nations have recognized Israel's unilateral action by moving their embassies to Jerusalem, the Jewish state surged ahead in its judaization of the whole of the city. One Arab legal authority, Henry Cattan, writes: "In addition to the annexation of Jerusalem, Israel took several other measures in the city which were contrary to international law, to the Geneva Conventions of 1949 and to UN resolutions. These measures included the deportation of persons, the dynamiting and razing of Arab homes, and the confiscation and expropriation of Arab property."[20]

Arab Palestinians charge that Israel has long been involved with the forced replacement of Arab Christians and Muslims in Jerusalem with Jews to change the demography of the city. As a result of these changes, especially since 1948, three-quarters of Jerusalem's population is now Jewish, but because this change has largely come about through illegal means—that is, the forcible dispossession of the Arab inhabitants— Israel cannot be allowed to use the population issue as a factor in determining legal rights.[21]

As for land ownership, Cattan points out, the Jews owned about one-third of the built-up property in Jerusalem before the end of the mandate in 1948, but their ownership of land in greater Jerusalem never exceeded 2 percent. Since 1948, and especially after the annexation of Jerusalem in 1967, the Israelis have systematically expropriated Arab properties in an effort to make it appear to the world that Jerusalem is a Jewish city.[22]

These population and land issues are well documented. The Security Council focused on these very issues, warning Israel to desist from its attempts to change the status of Jerusalem. On 25 September

1971 the Council resolved "in the clearest possible terms that all legislative and administrative actions taken by Israel to change the status of Jerusalem, including the expropriation of land and properties, the transfer of populations and legislation aimed at the incorporation of the occupied section are totally invalid and cannot change that status."[23]

THE UNITED NATIONS AND WORLD PUBLIC
OPINION REGARDING JERUSALEM

After the 1948–49 war that resulted in a divided city, the United Nations, frustrated by Israel's and Jordan's unwillingness to accede to their demands, remained virtually silent over the matter of Jerusalem until the 1967 Six-Day War. Then several resolutions were passed, all critical of Israel's actions with regard to the city.

The following resolution is representative of many resolutions passed by the General Assembly and the Security Council regarding Jerusalem and Israel's attempts to change the status of the city:

> The General Assembly,
> *Deeply concerned* at the situation prevailing in Jerusalem as a result of the measures taken by Israel to change the status of the City,
> 1. *Considers* that these measures are invalid;
> 2. *Calls upon* Israel to rescind all measures already taken and to desist forthwith from taking any action which would alter the status of Jerusalem;
> *Requests* the Secretary-General to report to the General Assembly and the Security Council on the situation and on the implementation of the present resolution not later than one week from its adoption.[24]

Israel felt justified in its position on Jerusalem and ignored the resolution, which prompted another one ten days later. This resolution noted with "deepest regret" Israel's refusal to comply with the earlier resolution and "deplored" Israel's failure to implement its provisions.[25] The Security Council, alarmed by Israel's disregard for international public opinion and, more specifically, for the General Assembly resolutions, passed its own resolution. The pertinent parts of that resolution read:

> The Security Council,
> *Noting* that since the adoption of the above mentioned resolutions,

Israel has taken further measures and actions in contravention of these resolutions . . .

Reaffirming that the acquisition of territory by military conquest is inadmissible,

1. *Deplores* the failure of Israel to comply with the General Assembly resolutions mentioned above;

2. *Considers* that all legislative and administrative measures and actions taken by Israel, including expropriation of land and properties thereon, which tend to change the legal status of Jerusalem are invalid and cannot change that status;

3. *Urgently calls upon* Israel to rescind all such measures already taken and to desist forthwith from taking any further action which tends to change the status of Jerusalem.[26]

Frustrated, if not outraged, by Israel's actions in Jerusalem and determined that such actions would have no bearing on the ultimate status of the city, both the General Assembly and the Security Council passed resolutions representative of international public opinion. Such resolutions are deemed by many legal scholars to bear the weight of international law, and if so, Israel ignores them at her jeopardy. Each year stronger, more forcefully worded resolutions have been passed but seemingly to no avail.

On 21 August 1969, the al-Aqsa mosque in Jerusalem was extensively damaged by arson. The perpetrator, a Christian fundamentalist who claimed to have been called of God to clear the area for a future temple, was quickly tried and imprisoned. The Security Council passed yet another resolution noting that "the execrable act of desecration and profanation of the Holy al-Aqsa Mosque emphasizes the immediate necessity of Israel's desisting from action in violation of [UN] resolutions." It further called upon Israel to "scrupulously observe the provisions of the Geneva Conventions and international law governing military occupation and to refrain from causing any hindrance to the discharge of the established functions of the Supreme Moslem Council of Jerusalem."[27]

It is noteworthy that as of the date of this resolution, 15 September 1969, the Security Council referred to Israel's presence in Jerusalem as one of a military occupant. The reference to the Geneva Conventions and international law governing military occupation also represented a collective opinion that Israel could not act unilaterally to change the status of Jerusalem. In other words, Israel's proclamation that Jerusalem was the united, eternal capital of Israel was regarded by the Muslim world and most nations in the United Nations as null and void.

Israel's presence in the whole of Jerusalem has been accorded de facto recognition by most states pending an ultimate resolution. Some states have elected to give it de jure recognition and, accordingly, have moved their embassies from Tel Aviv to Jerusalem. Still other states, especially those hostile to Israel, refuse to recognize any right at all.

UNANSWERED QUESTIONS

There remain unanswered questions relating to international law and Jerusalem that are difficult to deal with. In some cases the passing of time, political compromise, or mediation or arbitration provide answers; some matters simply go unresolved. What legal rights accrue from "memory"? What weight should be given to conquest? Does long and continuous possession confer title? What weight should be given to ethnic majorities? What is the effect of a United Nations resolution in international law? These and other matters have an important bearing on the future of Jerusalem. Although they have been addressed by legal scholars, there is little international consensus on the findings, particularly among the belligerents involved in the case.

Perhaps more questions have been raised about international law and Jerusalem than have been answered. It is not likely that the issue of Jerusalem will be solved in the courts, but neither will a solution be found in politics. Perhaps a combination of the two will take us a few modest steps forward in the seemingly eternal search for peace.

NOTES

1. *Mandate for Palestine*, Article 13: "All responsibility in connection with the Holy Places and religious buildings or sites in Palestine, including that of preserving existing rights and securing free access to the Holy Places, religious buildings and sites and the free exercise of worship, while ensuring the requirements for public order and decorum, is assumed by the Mandatory, who shall be responsible solely to the League of Nations in all matters connected herewith . . ."

Article 14: "A special Commission shall be appointed by the Mandatory to study, define and determine the rights and claims in connexion with the Holy Places and the rights and claims relating to the different religious communities in Palestine. . . ." Cust, *Status Quo in the Holy Places,* 65.

2. Ahimeir, *Jerusalem, Aspects of Law,* iv–v.

3. See Cust, *Status Quo in the Holy Places,* 65.

4. "Palestine (Holy Places) Order in Council at the Court of Buckingham Palace. The 25th day of July, 1924. . . .

"(1) This Order may be cited as 'The Palestine (Holy Places) Order in Council, 1924.'

"(2) Notwithstanding anything to the contrary in the Palestine Order in Council, 1922, or in any Ordinance or law in Palestine, *no cause or matter in connection with the Holy Places* or religious buildings or sites in Palestine or the rights or claims relating to the different religious communities in Palestine *shall be heard or determined by any Court in Palestine.*" Emphasis added. Cust, *Status Quo in the Holy Places,* 65.

5. *"Protection of the Holy Places Law, 5727–1967"*

"1. The Holy Places shall be protected from desecration and any other violation and from anything likely to violate the freedom of access of the members of the different religions to the places sacred to them or their feelings with regard to those places.

"2. (a) Whosoever desecrates or otherwise violates a Holy Place shall be liable to imprisonment for a term of seven years.

"(b) Whosoever does anything likely to violate the freedom of access of the members of the different religions to the places sacred to them or their feelings with regard to those places shall be liable to imprisonment for a term of five years.

"3. This Law shall add to, and not derogate from, any other law." Ahimeir, *Jerusalem, Aspects of Law,* 50–51.

6. *The State of Israel v. Hanan (1977)* P.M. (1) 392.

7. *The State of Israel v. Freedman* (unpublished). See Ahimeir, *Jerusalem, Aspects of Law,* vii.

8. *HaHugim Ha Leumi'im v. Minister of Police (1970)* 24 P.D. (2) 141.

9. U.N. General Assembly Official Record 2253, 4 July 1967.

10. Kollek, *Washington Institute Policy Papers,* 24.

11. See Islamic Council of Europe, *Jerusalem,* 210–57.

12. *Divrei Ha Knesset* (Parliamentary Records), vol. 49, col. 2420; Ahimeir, *Jerusalem, Aspects of Law,* xxiv.

13. Area of Jurisdiction and Powers ordinance, 5708–1948, Section 1; emphasis added. See Ahimeir, *Jerusalem, Aspects of Law,* 51.

14. Meeting 26 of the Provisional State Council, vol. A, 19 (Hebrew), as cited in Yehuda Zvi Blum, "The Juridical Status of East Jerusalem," xxv. See Ahimeir, *Jerusalem, Aspects of Law.*

15. Ahimeir, *Jerusalem, Aspects of Law.*

16. Ahimeir, *Jerusalem, Aspects of Law,* 153.

17. *"Basic Law: Jerusalem the Capital of Israel, Adopted by the Knesset on July 30, 1980:*

"1. Jerusalem, complete and united, is the capital of Israel.

"2. Jerusalem is the seat of the President of the State, the Knesset, the Government, and the Supreme Court.

"3. The holy places shall be protected from desecration and any other violation, and from anything likely to violate the freedom of access of the members of the different religions to the places sacred to them or their feelings with regard to those places.

"4. (a) The Government will be diligent in the development and the prosperity of Jerusalem and the well-being of its inhabitants by allocating special resources, including a special annual grant to the Jerusalem municipality (the capital grant), with the approval of the Knesset Finance Committee.

"(b) Jerusalem shall be granted special priorities in the activities of state institutions, for the financial, economic and other aspects of development of Jerusalem.

"(c) The Government shall set up a special body or bodies to implement this paragraph."

18. *Palestine Question,* 112.

19. *Palestine Question,* 115.

20. Cattan, *Palestine in International Law,* 139.

21. Cattan, *Palestine in International Law,* 141.

22. Cattan, *Palestine in International Law,* 141.

23. Security Council resolution 298 of 25 September 1971.

24. General Assembly Resolution 2253 (ES-V), 4 July 1967.

25. UN Resolution 2254 (ES-V), 14 July 1967.

26. Security Council resolution 252, 21 May 1968.

27. Security Council resolution 271, 15 Sept. 1969.

24

POLITICAL SOLUTIONS FOR JERUSALEM

It has become axiomatic that Jerusalem is the key to a political solution of the larger Arab-Israeli conflict. It is therefore ironic that every peace discussion leaves out Jerusalem, or at least leaves it until last, lest it spoil the whole process. Leaving Jerusalem out of the negotiations is a general acknowledgment that it is the most intractable element of the process.

Jerusalem raises "chicken or the egg" questions—namely, can the Arab-Israeli conflict be solved in the absence of a resolution of the Jerusalem question, or, conversely, can the Jerusalem question be resolved without a resolution of the Arab-Israeli conflict? In short, is Jerusalem one aspect of the broader picture, or is it central to the conflict, the foremost symbol of the dispute?[1]

Because the United Nations has not altered or repealed its resolutions providing for the internationalization of Jerusalem, these resolutions remain in effect, though there has never been a serious attempt to implement them. Broad-based sentiment favors some form of international status for the city, but no one favors implementing such concepts under force of arms. Both Israel and Jordan oppose the forms of internationalization proposed in the United Nations resolutions, and so the matter remains politically stagnant, yet very much alive. It is obvious that the matter of Jerusalem is not going to be resolved by bringing it before the World Court. That suggests that the only alternative is political compromise, and that too rests on shaky ground.

The Arab world and most other United Nations members remain unreconciled to Israel's unilateral declarations on Jerusalem. If Israel could convince the Christian world that the Christian holy places in Jerusalem are better protected under Israeli sovereignty than under any

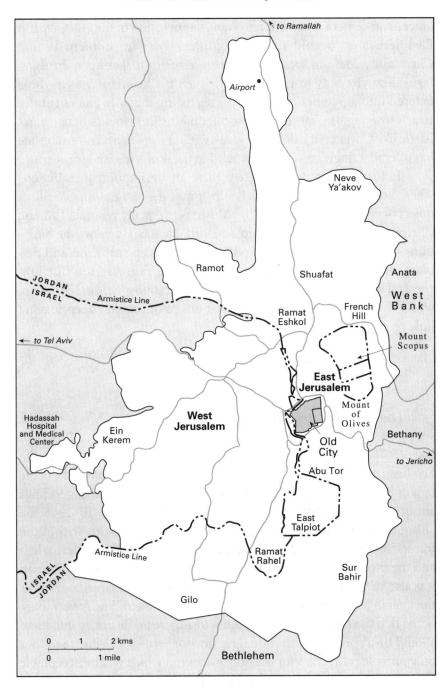

Jerusalem since 1967

other arrangement, opposition to Israel's annexation of the Old City and East Jerusalem would decline significantly. The problem is that Christianity does not speak with one voice, which makes a consensus on Jerusalem virtually impossible.[2] But even if Christianity as a whole entered into agreements with Israel regarding the holy places (under Israeli sovereignty), more than one billion Muslims would not agree. Yet Islam, like Christianity, does not speak with one voice, and no Arab state has offered a single conciliatory sound in favor of a Jewish Jerusalem.

To further complicate matters, there are overlapping jurisdictions where holy sites are concerned. For example, the Haram esh-Sharif, an object of veneration for one billion Muslims, is equally venerated among Christians and Jews as the Temple Mount. Each party views the devotions of the other with regard to the site with deep suspicion and distrust, and occasionally these sentiments are expressed in outright physical violence. In such a religiously charged atmosphere as Jerusalem, where three world religions meet head on, emotions run deep, leaving little or no room for compromise.

POSITIONS OF AMERICAN ADMINISTRATIONS ON JERUSALEM, 1948-1990

The United States, Israel's powerful friend and ally, has taken a strong position on Jerusalem, one not always to Israel's liking. President Harry S Truman (1945–1953), who was very supportive of Israel, was the first head of state to recognize the newly created Jewish State, even in the face of State Department reservations. Still, Truman had strong feelings about Jerusalem that diverged from Israeli interests. In 1948, he announced that the United States continued "to support, within the framework of the United Nations, the internationalization of Jerusalem and the protection of the Holy Places in Palestine."[3] President Truman was also unwilling to consider an official request from Israel to transfer the United States embassy from Tel Aviv to Jerusalem. The government noted that the United States "continues to adhere to the policy that there should be a special international regime for Jerusalem which will not only provide protection for the holy places but which will be acceptable to Israel and Jordan and the world community."[4]

The Eisenhower administration (1953–1961) continued a similar policy. President Dwight D. Eisenhower's Secretary of State, John Foster Dulles, stated that "the world religious community has claims in Jerusalem which take precedence over the political claims of any particular nation."[5] The Department of State announced the following month that "the United States does not plan to transfer its Embassy from Tel Aviv to Jerusalem. It is felt that this would be inconsistent with the U.N. resolutions dealing with the international nature of Jerusalem."[6]

President John F. Kennedy did not express a position on Jerusalem, although Dean Rusk, Secretary of State for both Kennedy and Johnson, publicly favored an international Jerusalem. In an attempt to forestall further unilateral Israeli action with regard to Jerusalem after the Six-Day War, President Lyndon Johnson (1963–1969) spoke of the need for "adequate recognition of the special interest of the three great religions in the holy places of Jerusalem."[7] The White House followed up with an interpretation of President Johnson's remark: "He [President Johnson] assumes that before any unilateral action is taken on the status of Jerusalem there will be appropriate consultation with religious leaders and others who are deeply concerned."[8]

With the announcement of 28 June 1967 that Israel had applied its laws and administration to East Jerusalem, effectively annexing the area in spite of United States urgings, Secretary of State Rusk said: "The United States deeply regrets the administrative actions on Jerusalem which have been taken by the Government of Israel.... These administrative decisions cannot be regarded as determining the future of the holy places or the status of Jerusalem.... We have made this position clear to the Government of Israel both before and after the decisions were taken."[9] Arthur Goldberg, the United States Ambassador to the United Nations, maintained that position a month later while speaking to the General Assembly: "The status of Jerusalem must not be decided unilaterally but in consultation with all concerned and in recognition of the historic interest of three great religions in the holy places."[10] President Johnson called on the parties concerned to "stretch their imaginations" to achieve a settlement in the interest of the whole world. Under the administration of Richard M. Nixon (1969–1974), United States Ambassador to the United Nations Charles W. Yost addressed the Security Council and reiterated the United States position on Jerusalem, which had not changed from the previous administrations: "The United

States considers that the part of Jerusalem that came under the control of Israel in the June War, like other areas occupied by Israel, is occupied territory and hence subject to the provisions of international law governing the rights and obligations of an occupying Power."[11] Noting that under international law Israel as an occupying power had no right to make changes in laws or administration or to confiscate or destroy private property, Yost concluded:

> I regret to say that the actions of Israel in the occupied portion of Jerusalem present a different picture, one which gives rise to understandable concern that the eventual disposition of Jerusalem may be prejudiced, and that the private rights and activities of the population are already being altered and affected.
>
> My Government regrets and deplores this pattern of activity, and it has so informed the Government of Israel on numerous occasions since June 1967. We have consistently refused to recognize those measures as having anything but a provisional character and do not accept them as affecting the ultimate status of Jerusalem.[12]

President Nixon, in an address to Congress outlining United States foreign policy for the 1970s, admitted that "local passions in the Middle East run so deep that the parties in conflict are seldom amenable to outside advice or influence. Each side is convinced that vital interests are at stake which cannot be compromised."[13] Perhaps that was an admission that the United States had little or no influence on Israel when it came to Jerusalem.

President Gerald Ford's administration (1974–1977) did not deviate from the position of its predecessors that the future of Jerusalem would be determined only through negotiation, agreement, and accommodation.[14]

The Carter administration (1977–1981) maintained the same policy. President Jimmy Carter assured President Anwar Sadat of Egypt that the position of the United States on Jerusalem remained unchanged from that of previous administrations.[15]

> When I was at Camp David with Prime Minister Begin . . . and President Sadat, we all three agreed on a paragraph of the Camp David Accords relating to Jerusalem. I know intensely the deep feelings of the Israeli people and Jews all over the world about Jerusalem. Our commitment, agreed to by Prime Minister Begin, is that Jerusalem should forever

stay undivided, that there should be free access to the holy places . . . and that the ultimate status of Jerusalem under international law should be resolved through negotiation, and that the final results of that negotiation would have to be acceptable to Israel. That's my position, and I will maintain it.[16]

President Ronald Reagan (1981–1989) used identical language calling for negotiations and refused to accept any proposal that would divide Jerusalem again. When the Congress called for moving the United States Embassy to Jerusalem, Under-Secretary Eagleburger defended President Reagan's policies on Jerusalem:

> Our policy on this issue has been resolute for more than three decades. In 1949, when the Israelis started moving their government to Jerusalem, we informed them that we could not accept a unilateral claim to the city. Again, in 1960, we informed Jordan of our opposition to its intention to make the eastern part of the city Jordan's second capital. And in 1967, when Israel occupied the eastern sector, we opposed Israel's actions to place all of Jerusalem under Israeli law, jurisdiction and administration. Most recently, President Reagan stated in his September 1, 1982, Middle East Peace Initiative that "we remain convinced that Jerusalem must remain undivided, but that its final status should be decided through negotiations."[17]

Locating the United States Embassy in Jerusalem instead of Tel Aviv would be a way of recognizing Jerusalem as Israel's capital. Under-Secretary Aramacost, speaking to a Congressional committee, addressed this problem: "Our Embassy has remained in Tel Aviv for over three decades. This decision has not been capricious. The rationale has been found persuasive by eight Administrations—both Democratic and Republican. Each has had to deal with the Jerusalem question in one way or another. Each has considered it a mistake for the United States to endorse or acquiesce in the effort of any state to determine the status of the city unilaterally."[18]

Responding to a request from Jerusalem mayor Teddy Kollek that the United States Embassy be moved to Jerusalem, the Department of State pointed out that "moving the Embassy to Jerusalem could be perceived as prejudging the outcome of negotiations and would diminish the ability of the United States to play a useful role in the peace process."[19]

During George Bush's administration (1989–1992), the Congress acknowledged Jerusalem as the capital of the State of Israel[20] in the face of opposition from the White House and the State Department. During an official visit to Washington by Jerusalem's Mayor Kollek, President Bush praised the mayor for his "long and wise stewardship" of the city and for "fostering a climate of reconciliation" in the city but reiterated, along with the eight administrations that preceded his, America's commitment to a negotiated settlement.[21]

The Bush administration, like those before it, saw Jewish settlement in the Arab section of Jerusalem as an obstacle to a peaceful settlement with the Arab Palestinians. When President Bush took a strong stand against new Jewish housing in Arab East Jerusalem, a senior Israeli government official responded that Jewish housing in Jerusalem is one issue that will unite all Israelis against the United States. Prime Minister Yitzhak Shamir rejected the Bush administration's position against settling Soviet Jewish immigrants in Jerusalem, fiercely stating that Jerusalem is not on the agenda of negotiations with the Palestinians. He asserted that Israel does not make any distinction between East and West Jerusalem: "For us there is one *Yerushalayim*, the capital of Israel."[22]

President Bill Clinton is the first American president to publicly consider moving the United States Embassy to Jerusalem, with all the implications that such a move would dictate. During his election campaign, Clinton argued that "Jerusalem must remain Israel's united and permanent capital and that the U.S. embassy will be transferred to the city at the appropriate time."[23] This alarmed Islamic circles, and the President shelved the matter. His initiative on Jerusalem stirred the Palestine National Council to announce that Clinton's statements on Jerusalem contradicted all United Nations resolutions on the issue as well as resolutions approved by the United States itself. The report of the Palestine National Council concluded that Jerusalem represented a "red line" for Palestinians and Arabs that cannot be crossed.

After the Truman administration, American leaders stopped pressing for internationalization, but every administration since 1948 has consistently favored a negotiated settlement—another way of saying that Israel's actions could not unilaterally change the status of the city. For now, that policy allows the United States to walk the diplomatic tightrope among the various parties to the dispute.

SPARRING OVER JERUSALEM: JABS AND UPPERCUTS

Haggling, bargaining, dickering, and negotiating are art forms in which Near Easterners excel. Their reputation as hard bargainers is based on the premise that in the end each party must feel it has won. The following statements help us understand which issues are important to whom, although very little is revealed about where a given party actually stands—otherwise, there would be nothing left to negotiate. Still, such statements help us appreciate at least the outer limits of what is possible as the parties concerned jockey for place in the court of international public opinion.

Israel's Position on Jerusalem

1. Israeli sovereignty over Jerusalem does not conflict with the religious interests of Christianity and Islam.

2. Internationalization of Jerusalem is not a religious imperative of any of the three faiths involved, nor is it the only way of assuring their legitimate needs.

3. The destiny of no city can be divorced from that of its own inhabitants who, in the case of Jerusalem, have constituted a majority for more than a century. To force any so-called solution on such a city, regardless of the will of the majority who live in it, is to disavow the universal principle of self-determination.

4. No city would entrust its welfare to the hands of an ambiguous international body. The policy of such a body would always be bound up with the politics of the member-States, and the welfare of the citizens would become a secondary consideration; nothing is more likely to disrupt the life of a city and its population than imposing upon them a system of government shared by several States, each of which looks to further its own interests.

5. Nowhere in the world has an international body succeeded in administering any territory for any length of time. Such a body acts to suit the political interests of its member-States, and, if they disagree, it is paralyzed.

6. The need to ensure the protection of the holy places cannot justify the internationalization of a whole city and its inhabitants.

7. The best way to protect the holy places is to depoliticize them

and vest administrative authority over each one in the religious body traditionally connected with it, independent of all politics.

Jerusalem, whole and unified, is the capital of Israel. Most of its inhabitants are Israeli Jews. Italy would never agree that Rome be withdrawn from Italian national sovereignty and given over to an international Catholic rule. Saudi Arabia would never agree that Mecca be withdrawn from Saudi Arabian sovereignty and placed under international Islamic rule. And Israel cannot agree to abandon Jerusalem and its inhabitants to a complicated amorphous international rule. Such a rule could only be a source of endless conflict and tension. Jerusalem under such a regime would no longer be the peaceful city of today, where the interests of all faiths are safeguarded. The Government of Israel is ready to undertake international commitments to ensure the totality of those interests.[24]

Israelis Speak Out

Many different voices can be heard on solutions to the conflict over Jerusalem, but perhaps no issue unites world Jewry more than does the question of Jerusalem. Jews are unanimous that Jerusalem must remain the capital of Israel, but some would share the city under certain conditions. There is a profusion of opinions:

Israeli Prime Minister Yitzhak Shamir said: "We shall not be party to any action that brings into question the status of Jerusalem as Israel's capital and the heart and soul of the entire Jewish people. Jerusalem was united and will never be divided again."[25]

Israeli former Deputy Foreign Minister Binyamin Netanyahu called upon the United States to honor Israel's request that the United States embassy be located in Jerusalem. He declared that if the situation were reversed and Israel placed its embassy in New York instead of Washington, United States officials would complain that Israel cannot determine the United States capital. That the United States refuses to place its embassy even in the western part of the city "casts a dark shadow on U.S. policy regarding Jerusalem."[26]

An Israeli newspaper reported that Prime Minister Yitzhak Rabin realized that he would find it difficult to solve the Palestinian problem without finding some solution to the issue of Jerusalem. The newspaper speculated that Rabin would consent to granting extraterritorial status[27] to Jerusalem's holy sites: "We may see a Jordanian or Saudi flag flying over the Temple Mount very soon . . . and a Vatican flag above the Church of the Holy Sepulchre." In the next stage, "Arabs may be given a chance to organize in residential quarters that will manage their own municipal affairs . . . under a joint-roof municipality."[28]

Shmuel Meir, former deputy mayor of Jerusalem, stated in 1994 that discussions were already underway on permanent arrangements for Jerusalem. He claimed that a committee was drawing maps of the areas within the city's current jurisdiction that are indisputably Arab and that those areas will be handed over to the Palestinians. Meir felt that such action would be tantamount to partitioning the city. He also said that an agreement had been reached with the Vatican to grant extraterritorial status to Vatican churches and other Vatican properties in the city. Deputy Foreign Minister Yosi Beilin denied the accusations.[29]

Avraham Kahila, deputy mayor for planning, reported that in 1993 there was "a very small Jewish majority in East Jerusalem." That is the first statistical confirmation of an emerging Jewish majority in the Arab sector of Jerusalem. His report showed that Jews constituted 73.3 percent of the population of Jerusalem and the non-Jews 26.3 percent. Some 64 percent of the Jewish population live in West Jerusalem, and 34 percent live in the areas annexed to the city after 1967.[30]

Prime Minister Rabin insisted that Jerusalem would not be included in the autonomy talks because Israel would not negotiate away its vital interests: "Jerusalem will remain as it is, united under Israel sovereignty and our capital forever, and therefore it will not be included in the interim self-government arrangements for the Palestinians. It's part of Israel, it is so; it will remain so."[31]

Former Israeli Ambassador to Egypt Shimon Shamir warned that "if the peace process leads to total denial of Palestinian rights in Jerusalem, the city may well become the focal point of a holy war."[32]

Former mayor of Jerusalem Teddy Kollek observed that "the status of Jerusalem clearly has to be settled if lasting peace is to be achieved," that a way has to be found to live with the Arabs, and that Jerusalem could accommodate both Arab and Jew. One thing is certain, according to Kollek, "The Arabs will never leave a city they consider holy." He asserted that the only way to keep Jerusalem united under Israeli sovereignty is "to treat minorities as we would like Jews to be treated. You cannot fight anti-Semitism while treating others as second-class citizens." But Mayor Kollek dismissed the idea of two capitals in one united city as "ridiculous."[33] Mayor Kollek wrote: "I do not think you can find any Israeli willing to give up Jerusalem. They cannot and will not. This beautiful golden city is the heart and soul of the Jewish people. You cannot live without a heart and soul. If you want one simple word to symbolize all Jewish history, that word would be 'Jerusalem.'"[34]

Ehud Olmert, who succeeded Teddy Kollek as mayor of Jerusalem, vowed that his "main mission is to keep the city under the integrity of Israel." He has said that his victory over Kollek was a signal to the world that Israel will not compromise with the Palestine Liberation Organization where Jerusalem's sovereignty is concerned.[35]

Arab Palestinians Speak Out

In a statement dated 15 April 1990, Yasser Arafat, head of the Palestine Liberation Organization, noted that "several parties had offered the PLO the establishment of a Palestinian state without Jerusalem." Arafat answered that "there can be flexibility on the time limit for the withdrawal of Israeli occupation troops . . . but there can be no flexibility where the matter concerns Jerusalem."[36]

On the twenty-third anniversary of the burning of the al-Aqsa Mosque, 24 August 1992, a PLO spokesman declared that "Jerusalem will always remain the key for the success or failure of the peace process currently in progress. Without Jerusalem there will be no peace in the region. It is the key to peace, as it has always been down through the ages. We declare that any attempt to leave it out, or exclude it, from any possible settlement will be completely rejected. There will be no forfeiture of Jerusalem, no bargaining over it, and no relinquishing of it or of its Arab nature, despite the intensity of the conspiracies and the magnitude of the sacrifices."[37]

Another PLO spokesman stressed that his organization would not accept any concessions "in form or content in relation to Jerusalem. It will not commit the crime of renouncing the Islamic and Christian holy places or the national rights of the Palestinian people."[38]

Ibrahim al-Sus, the PLO representative in Paris, announced on French public television that Jerusalem could be the capital of two states, an Arab Palestinian state and an Israeli state. The city could be a "spiritual capital of all the heirs of Abraham: Jews, Muslims and Christians."[39]

King Hassan II of Morocco said that the Arabs would be ready to discuss the status of Jerusalem if Israel promised to return control to Muslims of Islamic holy sites in the city. He added, "Hebrew and Christian holy sites do not interest us. We want our own and that is all. If one day they tell us that they will be returned, we will then be willing to openly examine the entire status of Jerusalem."[40]

Egyptian President Hosni Mubarak, in an address on 6 June 1992 marking the twenty-fifth anniversary of the Israeli occupation of Jerusalem, emphasized that Israel's continued occupation of the West Bank can "neither establish a right to the land nor gain legitimacy. What goes for the occupied Palestinian territories goes equally for Arab Jerusalem which constitutes an indivisible part of these occupied territories."[41]

Palestine leader Faysal Al-Husayni said in an interview with the Vienna Kurier: "I love Jerusalem. I suffer under its division. I see two cities, one free and the other one occupied. Our solution: two capital cities in a unified city with open borders and a joint city administration."[42]

A Beirut newspaper, Al-Safir, carried excerpts of a message from Monsignor Jean Louis Tauran, the Vatican's Secretary of State, calling for East Jerusalem to be placed under international supervision in keeping with the Pope's call fifteen years earlier. The Vatican was not interested in deciding the political future of West Jerusalem, "which must be decided at the negotiating table."[43]

Dr. Sari Nusaybah, head of the technical committees of the Palestinian delegation to the peace talks, warned: "Israel, Peres and Kollek are dreaming if they think we will back down on the issue of Jerusalem. We will never do so. Jerusalem will be Arab, Islamic and the capital of Palestine."[44]

King Hussein of Jordan told the Los Angeles Times: "The Holy Places of Jerusalem should be moved out of orbit of attempts of any to impose sovereignty over them. That alone belongs to the Almighty God. ... The Holy City should be separated from any temporal sovereignty." The king spoke of the Christian theologian Hans Kung, who believes that the three religions need a religious symbol, a common holy place, as a great sign that all three worship the one God of Abraham and therefore have something in common that overcomes all divisions and enmity. He noted that such a thing is already in place: a sanctuary of the God of Abraham, which could find its fulfillment in the Dome of the Rock. In this way, Kung says, the "Dome of the Rock would be a Dome of Reconciliation." King Hussein said such a concept expressed the overall spirit of what he had in mind.[45]

Jordanian Prime Minister Abd al-Salam Al-Majali noted in 1993 that Jordan would enter peace talks with the understanding that negotiations would secure the rights of the Arab Palestinians, but, he said: "We will not reach a final solution that does not include Jerusalem. . . . No Arab nor Muslim will accept a solution that does not include the return of Jerusalem."[46]

The Jerusalem *Al-Quds* Arabic newspaper took United States Secretary of State Warren Christopher to task for calling on the parties to postpone discussions on Jerusalem until the final stages of the peace talks. The newspaper argued that the request was "totally biased towards the Israeli position," which seeks to isolate Arab Jerusalem from the rest of the occupied territories. According to the editorial, Christopher's position contradicts United States understandings given to the Palestinians before the Madrid Peace Conference, reserving the right to raise the issue of Jerusalem in any stage of the negotiations.[47]

Faysal Al-Husayni, head of the Palestinian negotiating team to the peace talks, responded to an Israeli claim that Jerusalem must be left to a later stage. He argued that such an approach is problematic: "Everything relating to the negotiating process collides one way or another with the issue of Jerusalem. If we talk about elections, we collide with Jerusalem. If we talk about jurisdiction, we are talking about Jerusalem." Al-Husayni observed: "I am from Jerusalem. Although I do not like to see it, it is very obvious that there are two parts to Jerusalem, one under occupation and the other assuming the tasks of the occupier. We seek an open Jerusalem, but its eastern part should be a Palestinian capital, while its western part can be an Israeli capital."[48]

Dr. Nazmi al-Jubah, advisory committee member to the peace talks, noted that in his opinion Jerusalem should not be divided again, but, he said, "We can accept a united Jerusalem as long as it is under joint Palestinian-Israeli rule. We cannot accept a situation where Jerusalem is the capital of Israel alone. . . . Jerusalem can serve as two capitals for two nations. It is also possible that it will not be the capital of either of the two but nevertheless be jointly ruled by Israelis and Palestinians. The most excellent and ideal solution would be, however, if Jerusalem is the united capital of two nations."[49]

POSSIBLE SOLUTIONS

Short of a messianic solution, which will ultimately resolve the matter once and for all, we are left to mortal devices to accomplish the seemingly impossible. It is doubtful that a solution for Jerusalem could be based on any single formula, be it partition, internationalization, extraterritorial status, boroughs, Vaticanization, cantonization, joint capital, or dual sovereignty. Nevertheless, through the give and take of negotiations, the refining process just might lead to a formula that finally captures the imagination and opens the door to a settlement. For the time being, however, complexity and perplexity remain.

One author suggests "pairing the principles of West Bank autonomy and Jerusalem's unity."[50] That is, Israel should trade autonomy in the West Bank for Palestinian recognition of Israel's sovereignty over a united Jerusalem.

In attempting to apply the wisdom of Solomon in seeking a solution, Jerusalem becomes the baby over which the various mothers contend. One proposal is a return to partition, in which Jews live on the Jewish side of the city and Arabs on the Arab side. This simplified form of a dual capital is, according to the Solomonic model, tantamount to cutting the baby in half—never mind that it will die.

A second proposal is to internationalize the city and place it under some form of United Nations trusteeship. That, according to the Solomonic model, is to render the preposterous judgment that either both women are the child's mother or neither one is and the dispute goes on.

A third possibility is to recognize the sovereignty of one nation over Jerusalem. That presupposes the willingness of one mother to give up her claim in the interest of the child's well-being—but in the analogy with Jerusalem, Solomon's great wisdom breaks down because both sincerely believe that Jerusalem belongs to them.

Another alternative is to recognize Israeli sovereignty over the city but give the Muslims and Christians a special status relative to their respective Holy Places. That is tantamount to recognizing the Jews as the legitimate mother while allowing Muslims and Christians visiting rights. Given that Israel now holds the city and is unwilling to give it up, such an alternative may be worth considering. It might work for a time, but in the end it ignores the rights of the others, and the claim will be made that justice is not served. Alternatively, one might argue for Palestinian sovereignty over the whole of Jerusalem, but given the present political realities and for the foreseeable future, this proposal must be considered nonviable.

Although Israel has not been willing to recognize Arab Palestinian nationalist claims to Jerusalem, it has consistently been ready to recognize religious interests of both Muslims and Christians. This policy was expressed in Israel's willingness to grant extraterritorial status to the holy places. Some proposals put forward by Israel would grant diplomatic status to the various religious representatives in Israel, including political immunity. The Christians, who have no territorial interest in the city apart from the holy places, have been more inclined to seriously consider these proposals than have the Arabs.

The so-called borough system, espoused by Mayor Teddy Kollek and advanced by his deputy mayor, Meron Benvenisti, is based on the London model. It involves the creation of boroughs within the municipal limits of Jerusalem corresponding to the ethnic or geographical divisions in the city—secular Jews, orthodox Jews, Christians, Muslims, Old City, Armenian Quarter, and so forth. The inhabitants of each borough would vote for their own borough council and for representatives to a larger Jerusalem Municipal Council. Such an arrangement would allow each community to look to its own special interests while preserving the city intact, presumably under Israeli sovereignty.

Another suggestion has its antecedents in ancient history. After the division of the tribes, Israel's national capital was at Samaria and the religious capital was at Bethel. Perhaps the political capital of an Arab Palestinian state could be Hebron or Nablus, that of Israel could be Tel Aviv, and both could have their religious capital in Jerusalem.

There is a myriad of possible solutions, but that fact alone suggests that no single proposal presently under consideration will prove acceptable to all parties and that any solution will have to be creative. In other words, if the will exists to solve the problem, there is no end to the creativity that could result in an agreement among all the parties.

The future of the West Bank has been a major stumbling block to progress on the matter of Jerusalem. Without resolution of the West Bank issue, Jerusalem's political status vis-à-vis the Arab Palestinians has remained a moot point. If the lack of political progress since 1948 has made the question of Jerusalem's status irrelevant, then it can be argued that the progress in the peace talks makes Jerusalem's status more weighty than ever and that with each passing year the matter will become more critical.

On the pessimistic side, it may be that the chasm that is Jerusalem will not be bridged. The nationalistic and religious forces at work, imbued with destructive self-interest and emotional and religious frenzy, undermine every effort to reach a compromise. In the end, it may be that such forces will light the flames of Armageddon in the tinderbox of the Near East and out of the smoldering ruins will arise the messianic Jerusalem governed by the Prince of Peace.

NOTES

1. Ahimeir, *Jerusalem, Aspects of Law,* xxii.

2. Certain concentrations of Christians living in the Arab world, such as the Copts, Maronites, Greek Orthodox, and others, would be even less likely to acquiesce to Israel's domination of Jerusalem. Added to them are Christian proselyting faiths that are denied the right to engage in missionary activities in the Jewish state.

3. Truman, *Public Papers of the President,* 844.

4. *U.S. Department of State Bulletin* 27, no. 684 (4 August 1952): 181–82.

5. *U.S. Department of State Bulletin* 28, no. 729 (15 June 1953): 832.

6. *U.S. Department of State Bulletin* 29, no. 734 (20 July 1953): 82.

7. *U.S. Department of State Bulletin* 57, no. 1463 (10 July 1967): 33.

8. *U.S. Department of State Bulletin* 57, no. 1464 (17 July 1967): 60.

9. *U.S. Department of State Bulletin* 57, no. 1466 (31 July 1967): 149.

10. *U.S. Department of State Bulletin* 57, no. 1477 (16 October 1967): 486.

11. *Provisional Verbatim Record of 1483rd Meeting of the Security Council,* S/PV.1483, 56–61.

12. *Provisional Verbatim Record of 1483rd Meeting of the Security Council,* S/PV.1483, 56–61.

13. *U.S. Department of State Bulletin* 62, no. 1602 (9 March 1970): 303.

14. *Provisional Verbatim Record of 1896th Meeting of the Security Council,* S/PV.1896, 7–8.

15. *American Foreign Policy Basic Documents,* 662.

16. Carter, *Public Papers of the President,* 2301–2.

17. *U.S. Department of State Bulletin* 84, no. 2085 (April 1984): 65–66.

18. *Hearings and Markup, 98th Congress,* 2d session, no. 4877, 283–89.

19. *American Foreign Policy Current Documents,* 494.

20. Senate Concurrent Resolution 106, 22 Mar. 1990.

21. *Office of the Press Secretary,* White House, Washington, D.C., 27 May 1992.

22. Foreign Broadcast Information Service NES-90-043, 5 March 1990, 22.

23. Foreign Broadcast Information Service NES-92-219, "PNC Official Criticizes Clinton's Comments on Jerusalem," Cairo, 11 Nov. 1992, 14.

24. *Jerusalem: Issues and Perspectives,* 16–18.

25. *Jerusalem: Issues and Perspectives,* 16–18.

26. Foreign Broadcast Information Service NES-91-123, "U. S. Urged to Move Embassy to Jerusalem," *Qol Yisra'el,* 26 June 1991, 15

27. In this context, "extraterritorial status" means placing the holy sites outside of Israeli sovereignty, as it were. Under such a proposal, the religious leaders connected with such a site might conceivably enjoy diplomatic status.

28. Foreign Broadcast Information Service NES-92-182, "Rabin Urged to Put Jerusalem on Talks Agenda," Tel Aviv, *Al HaMishmar,* 17 Sept. 1992, 9.

29. Foreign Broadcast Information Service NES-94-006, Tel Aviv, *HaAretz,* 10 Jan. 1994, 33–34.

30. Foreign Broadcast Information Service NES-93-155, "Jewish Numbers in East Jerusalem Growing," Tel Aviv, *HaAretz,* 13 Aug. 1993, 26.

31. Foreign Broadcast Information Service NES-93-122, "Rabin Says Jerusalem to Remain United Capital," Jerusalem, *Qol Yisra'el,* 28 June 1993, 47

32. Pinkas, "J'lem may cause Jihad," 5.

33. Kollek, "No One Can Say We Treated Jerusalem's Arabs Badly," 12.

34. Kraemer, *Jerusalem,* 15.

35. *Chicago Tribune,* 3 Dec. 1993, Sec. 1, p. 4.

36. Foreign Broadcast Information Service NES-90-075, "Arafat Says No Flexibility on Jerusalem," 15 Apr. 1990, 1.

37. Foreign Broadcast Information Service NES-92-165, "PLO Reiterates No Peace without Jerusalem," Algiers, *Voice of Palestine,* 24 Aug. 1992, 10.

38. Foreign Broadcast Information Service NES-91-147, "PLO Spokesman—No Concessions Over Jerusalem," Amman, *Al-Ribat,* 30 July 1991, 1.

39. Foreign Broadcast Information Service NES-91-214, "Al-Sus Proposes Jerusalem Capital of 2 States," Paris, *Antenne-2,* 4 Nov. 1991, 15.

40. Foreign Broadcast Information Service NES-91-228, "King Hassan Says Arabs Set to Discuss Jerusalem," Paris, *AFP,* 25 Nov. 1991, 14.

41. Foreign Broadcast Information Service NES-92-110, "Jerusalem 'Indivisible Part' of Territories," Cairo, *Arab Republic of Egypt Radio,* 6 June 1992, 17.

42. Foreign Broadcast Information Service NES-91-077, "Al-Husayni Views Israel, Jerusalem, Intifadah," 19 Apr. 1991, 4.

43. Foreign Broadcast Information Service NES-93-062, "Vatican Proposes International Care of Jerusalem," Beirut, *Al-Safir,* 29 Mar. 1993, 22.

44. Foreign Broadcast Information Service NES-93-118, "Nusaybah: No Peace If Israel Insists on Jerusalem," Jerusalem, *Al-Fajr,* 21 June 1993, 6.

45. Foreign Broadcast Information Service NES-93-207, "King Husayn Discusses Jerusalem," Amman, *Jordan Times,* 28 Oct. 1993, 30.

46. Foreign Broadcast Information Service NES-93-149, "Al-Majali: No Solution Without Return of Jerusalem," Amman, *Al-Ray,* 5 Aug. 1993, 17.

47. Foreign Broadcast Information Service NES-93-141, "Christopher's Position on Jerusalem Called Biased," 26 July 1993, 4.

48. Foreign Broadcast Information Service NES-93-122, "Al-Husayni on Jerusalem Issue," *Jerusalem Israel Television Network,* 28 June 1993, 1–2.

49. Foreign Broadcast Information Service NES-93-122, "Al-Jubah Proposes Jerusalem as United Capital," Jerusalem, *Qol Yisra'el,* 28 June 1993, 8–9.

50. Eckardt, *Jerusalem,* 344–52.

25

JERUSALEM TODAY

Jerusalem today, depending on one's point of view, is a rapidly growing, multifaceted, vibrant city exuding a sense of manifest destiny, or, alternatively, it is a city suffering under the crushing burden of alien occupation, whose citizens are denied their human rights and are subjected to economic and political exploitation. Thomas L. Friedman of the Jerusalem Bureau of the *New York Times* sized up Jerusalem today: "Contrary to all the clichés about it, Jerusalem has not been a city of brotherly love and it is not one today." Friedman gives much credit for what peace does exist to Jerusalem's former mayor Teddy Kollek. Writes Friedman, Jerusalem is a "Noah's Ark of hooded Christian monks, turbaned Moslem sheiks and black-robed Jews.... They pass one another on the white-stoned steps, each one silently contemplating his own grand vision for Jerusalem in which the people walking right next to him have no place." And yet, says Friedman, "[Mayor Kollek] has made Jerusalem work, not by making it something different, but by making it work as it is."[1] Indeed, many would agree that the man who has had greater direct influence on that city than any other person in our time is Mayor Teddy Kollek, who served his city and its mosaic of inhabitants from 1965 to 1993, leaving a legacy that will long be felt.

Mayor Kollek stamped all his outgoing mail, regardless of its intended recipient, with the plea, "Let's be more tolerant." According to him, being more tolerant with respect to the city he loves requires two things: first, everyone, including the Jews, has to accept limits on his vision of Jerusalem; second, people whom fate has thrown together do not have to learn to love each other, merely learn to live together.[2] That might not seem much to ask, but in a city racked by religious and political differences it is not unusual to find, on any given day, an individual or a group invoking God's name and calling down his wrath on a mayor working to accommodate all parties.

Mayor Kollek fought for a pluralistic Jerusalem in which Jews, Arabs, and Christians lived alongside each other and accepted each other for what they were, but he didn't want them just to coexist. He wanted a society in which everyone cooperated, and he worked to create an environment that would foster such a society. Under his leadership, Jerusalem was transformed into a jewel of a city with parks, promenades, street malls, theaters, museums, concert halls, sports arenas, hospitals, and clinics. Yet, despite all Mayor Kollek's accomplishments in both Jewish and Arab Jerusalem, the extent to which he enjoyed the support of the Arab community is questionable. His former deputy mayor, Meron Benvenisti, when asked if Kollek's administration met Arab needs and gained goodwill in the Arab community, replied:

> Some needs, yes, good will, no. . . . Jewish money cannot buy Arab good will. We are no better at playing the colonial administrator than the British were. . . . Kollek deludes himself into thinking that because Arabs will take money for widowed mothers and sing his praises because he opens a day-care center in east Jerusalem—that they feel better about the occupation of Jerusalem. The economic argument [that the Arabs economically have never had it so good] is self-serving. So what if the Arabs have it better under us than under the Jordanians? Does anyone really think that the Arabs of this city . . . prefer our rule to that of the Jordanians merely because they make more money from the jobs that we provide?
>
> Kollek's popularity [among the Arabs] is the popularity of the colonial administrator, the effective, benevolent, and secretly despised colonial administrator. Don't forget that before us the Arabs were ruled by Jordanians, then the British and then the Turks—all colonial administrators.[3]

Integrating Arab and Israeli Jerusalem proved more problematic for the mayor and other municipal authorities than even they had envisioned. Matters of lifestyle and comfort are major issues in any city, but in Jerusalem any oversight may be interpreted as an intentional slight to a whole religious or ethnic community. The mayor was faced with a myriad of delicate situations, some typical to any large city and others more unusual: the removal of barriers and mines, the protection of the holy places, security against terrorist attacks, the legal status of Arab inhabitants of East Jerusalem, and the educational system of East Jerusalem. Even such matters as water, electricity, sewage, and garbage collection—not to mention housing, commercial posters, new streets, Sabbath observance, autopsies, and the selling of pork—could, and did, become enormous issues.

SECURITY CONCERNS IN JERUSALEM

Moshe Dayan, Israel's eye-patched, charismatic Chief of Staff, ordered the removal of the city's cement and barbed wire barriers at the end of the 1967 war, but army officials, police, and civil authorities were concerned about security in the city. Some Israelis feared that clashes between Arabs and Jews could erupt into major disturbances at the holy places and that West Jerusalem would be open to terrorist attacks. Nevertheless, Dayan remained adamant, and the barriers were officially removed on 29 June 1967, the day after Israel's "annexation" of East Jerusalem. As a safeguard against acts of violence by Jews, Israeli soldiers were stationed outside the Muslim holy places, which remained under Muslim administrative control. Jews guarding Muslims was itself an anomaly.

Thousands of Jews poured into East Jerusalem, some to pray at the Western Wall, and others to purchase inexpensive goods in the Old City. Numerous Arabs visited West Jerusalem to view the homes and neighborhoods they had fled during the 1948 war.[4]

When the initial euphoria of victory subsided, responsibility for security was given to the police rather than the army to reduce the visibility of military government. By September 1967 there were bombings in Jerusalem directed at Israelis. The bombs were usually placed in small packages and left in busy areas in West Jerusalem. The first serious blast took place in November 1968 in the Mahane Yehuda market in West Jerusalem. Twelve people were killed, and fifty-four were injured. Bombings increased the following year and even more dramatically over the next five years. Sixty-five people were killed in terrorist attacks in 1974, and seventy-three in 1975. The left-wing Al-Fatah, which had by now taken over the Palestine Liberation Organization, and the Popular Front for the Liberation of Palestine claimed responsibility for most of the "successful" operations.[5] Though such attacks continued in West Jerusalem throughout the 1970s and 1980s, everyday life in the city was surprisingly normal.[6]

UNIFICATION OF THE MUNICIPALITIES

Soon after the 1967 war, the Israeli military government enlisted the cooperation of the Arab municipality of East Jerusalem to restore order. For a time there were two municipalities in the city, and it seemed the situation might continue indefinitely. Then Teddy Kollek, who had been elected mayor of West Jerusalem in 1965, pushed for the unification of the two municipalities under his administration. Largely as a result of Kollek's campaigning, the government dissolved the Arab municipality and placed East Jerusalem under his jurisdiction.[7]

At first, former employees of the Arab municipality were not guaranteed permanent jobs in the new administration, but many were offered temporary positions. Not until the following year, and only after much debate, did the unified municipality offer permanent positions and salaries to those who had held permanent positions in the East Jerusalem municipality. In the meantime disgruntled Arab civic leaders called for the restoration of an Arab municipality. To help alleviate their discontent, Mayor Kollek proposed the creation of an advisory committee of seven employees of the former Arab municipality to work with the unified municipal council. The Arab former municipal employees refused to cooperate. The Jordanian government continued to pay their salaries, and they met regularly in defiance of the unified municipality. Finally the former mayor of East Jerusalem, Rauhi al-Khatib, was deported for encouraging active resistance, and his deputy became acting mayor of East Jerusalem.[8]

MUNICIPAL ELECTIONS

Late in 1967, the Israeli Ministry of the Interior extended the city's municipal franchise to all Arabs in Jerusalem of voting age. The decision was approved by the Knesset, which assumed that most Arabs in Jerusalem would boycott the coming elections. To the surprise of Israeli officials, about seventy-five hundred Arabs voted in the municipal elections of October 1969, helping to give the Labor Party under Kollek an absolute majority in the Municipal Council. After the elections many Arabs were willing to consider positions of public office, but some backed down in the face of Arab public pressure and Fatah Radio broadcasts.[9]

EAST JERUSALEM UNDER ISRAELI LAW

To pacify the international community, Israel had avoided using the term *annexation* when it incorporated East Jerusalem in July 1967; nevertheless, the result was the same: the Israeli law of annexation was applied to East Jerusalem. Accordingly, all residents of the captured part of the city were regarded as enemy aliens and as such were subject to the Absentee Property Law, which stipulated that citizens of Arab states living in Israel were considered absentees and their property assigned to the custodian of absentee property. In other words, Arab Palestinian landowners living in East Jerusalem, which had been occupied by Jordan for nineteen years (1948–1967), were regarded as citizens of an Arab state (enemy aliens) and, according to the Israeli law, were no longer legal owners of their own property.

Further, licenses issued by the Jordanian government to doctors, lawyers, and businesses were no longer valid. Upon instruction by the minister of justice, the law was not enforced against those who remained within the annexed area; however, it gave Israeli authorities a legal means for harassing those who were uncooperative and for expropriating land and property.[10]

In 1968 a law was passed to rectify some of the legal injustices, declaring that residents of East Jerusalem were no longer considered absentees nor enemies and, consequently, had rights to their property. The decree did not apply to other areas of the country or to the occupied territories. In addition, lawyers from East Jerusalem were automatically made members of the Israeli bar and permitted to practice, an act that many resented because it placed them in the awkward position of having to base their cases on Israeli law, parts of which they detested. Most licensed professionals were required to register with the Israeli authorities to await new licenses, which the labor minister was empowered to grant by decree. Because most of those affected did not register, the

Municipality of Jerusalem automatically renewed the licenses of all busi-nesses in the city that had been established before annexation; the national government did the same for many professionals and compa-nies.[11]

The practice of refraining from enforcing in East Jerusalem Israeli laws that were strictly enforced in West Jerusalem was an outgrowth of Mayor Kollek's attempt to make the transition to a united city as easy as possible for the Arab inhabitants. Many Arabs refused to cooperate, but with the passing of time, most saw that it was in their economic best interest to take advantage of such concessions.

EDUCATION IN EAST JERUSALEM

In August 1967, the Israeli government announced it would replace the Jordanian curriculum in Arab schools in East Jerusalem and the West Bank and reopen the schools. The Ministry of Education examined about one hundred textbooks previously in use and rejected about eighty of them because of material critical of Israel. Arab students and teachers angrily charged the government with attempting to Judaize their education. Teachers went on strike and many pupils stayed away from school, refusing to return until the books and curriculum were restored. To encourage the strike, the Jordanian government paid the teachers' salaries.[12]

The military government for the West Bank investigated the con-troversy and found that the Ministry of Education had been excessive in its censorship. The Israeli Cabinet established a committee to reevaluate the textbooks. The committee reinstated all but two of the textbooks and censored twenty of them. It was decided that the Jordanian educational system would continue in the West Bank but the Israeli curriculum for Arabs would be used in the government schools in East Jerusalem.[13]

By the end of 1967, nearly half the teachers and most of the stu-dents in private schools returned to their classes. Teachers who refused to cooperate were dismissed and replaced by new ones. Students dropped out of school or attended private schools, which were not sub-ject to the Israeli curriculum for Arabs. The number of Arab high school students in government schools in Jerusalem dropped from 1,317 in 1967 to 116 in 1970. The Municipality of Jerusalem pressured the national government to change its educational policy in East Jerusalem. The result was the introduction in 1970 of supplemental classes to prepare students for the Jordanian matriculation examinations and, in 1972, a combined Jordanian and Israeli Arab curriculum.[14]

When these measures failed to attract significant numbers of Arab high school students, the government provided two separate curricula beginning with the seventh grade—Jordanian and Israeli Arab. Because most students would not choose the latter, the Ministry of Education designated one school for that purpose and allowed all the other schools in East Jerusalem to follow the Jordanian curriculum. Students in both curricula were required to take classes in Hebrew and in civics. Although this new education program was received more favorably than previous ones, most Arab high school students continued to attend private schools.[15]

COMPENSATION FOR PROPERTY

The government of Israel passed an Absentees Property Law in 1973 to compensate Jerusalem Arabs for properties left within the state of Israel in 1948. Although the law encouraged Arabs to seek the compensation to which they were entitled, in fact few did. Arabs looked upon land sales to Jews as heresy, and compensation was regarded as a form of sale. Such a stigma was attached to land sales that most Arab landholders preferred to suffer the financial loss than face the disgrace and shame. In addition, Jordanian authorities looked upon land sales to Jews as treasonous, and Jordanian law dictated capital punishment for those found guilty of such transactions. Before 1973, the few Arabs who were willing to accept compensation were faced with arbitrary decisions by an Israeli committee headed by the custodian general. There were no set criteria for determining the value of land, and the Arabs felt they were offered a fraction of its actual value. The 1973 law tacitly acknowledged that the old law was unfair, and it laid down specific measures for determining compensation in keeping with policies governing such matters on the Jewish side of the city.

TAX LAWS

Under international law an occupying power cannot raise tax levels beyond those established by the ousted government. Israel argued that East Jerusalem was liberated, not occupied, and therefore came under the same tax laws as West Jerusalem. But because of widespread opposition to attempts to increase taxes in Arab East Jerusalem, or even to collect them at the Jordanian rate, Israeli tax laws were only gradually applied.

LAND OWNERSHIP AND EXPROPRIATIONS

Israel's actions in East Jerusalem could be described for the most part as those of a benevolent occupier, except where land issues were concerned. The national government, anxious to demonstrate that East Jerusalem was an integral part of Israel's capital, started a massive building program in Arab parts of the city. This action meant that considerable tracts of land had to be expropriated from Arab owners for the "common good." To the extent that the land was used for schools, hospitals, clinics, parks, roads, and so forth, it did serve the common good, but the truth is that most of the expropriated land was set aside for new Jewish residential neighborhoods that excluded most Arabs.

It is a well-accepted principle of law that a sovereign power has the right of eminent domain—the right to expropriate land for the common good—but the Arabs, and for that matter, most of the world, refused to attribute to Israel the rights of a sovereign power over East Jerusalem and the Old City. Objections to Israeli construction in East Jerusalem from local, national, and international sources fell on deaf ears.

Giving credence to the Arab claim that Israel was judaizing Arab Jerusalem, Deputy Mayor Avraham Kahila told members of the city's planning committee that "a Jewish majority has recently [1993] been created in East Jerusalem for the first time since the Six-Day War."[16] Kahila, responsible for planning and construction in Jerusalem, identified his sources as data accumulated from the Municipality of Jerusalem, the Jerusalem Institute, and the Construction and Housing Ministry. At the time, according to Kahila, Jerusalem had a combined population of more than 500,000. About 345,000 were Jews, some 160,000 of whom lived among the 152,000 Arabs in East Jerusalem and in the suburbs just north of the city. Those Jewish neighborhoods were built principally on land the Israeli government expropriated in the 1970s.[17]

SECURITY AND CITY PLANNING

With the reunification of Jerusalem in 1967, city planners set about securing the city economically, demographically and strategically.[18] Jerusalem's municipal borders were extended in every direction to encompass vacant Arab lands as well as Arab urban areas.[19]

In June 1967, former Prime Minister David Ben-Gurion urged the Israeli cabinet that "Jews must be brought to Jerusalem at all costs. Tens of thousands must be settled in a very short time. Jews will agree to settle in East Jerusalem even in huts. One shouldn't wait for the building of regular neighborhoods. The importance is that there should be Jews there."[20] This attitude represented the feeling of most Israelis that every effort should be expended to ensure a fait accompli to prevent the international community from redividing the city. Successive Israeli governments expropriated enormous tracts of Arab lands around Jerusalem to encircle the city with Israeli settlements.

The Israelis fortified their capital city with massive fortresslike housing estates to the east, west, north, and south of the city. These housing estates were large enough to provide security for the city.[21]

Tens of thousands of Israelis and new Jewish immigrants have settled in these suburban communities. One is reminded of the prophecy that a future Jerusalem would be built without walls (see Zech. 2:4). The suburbs were designed specifically to surround Jerusalem with a security belt—like the walls of the ancient city.

RESISTANCE TO OCCUPATION

After the 1967 Six-Day War, Israel was faced with an uncooperative and even hostile segment of Jerusalem's population that considered itself under temporary occupation. United Nations resolutions calling upon Israel to rescind all unilateral actions encouraged the belief that the international community would intercede on behalf of the Arabs and restore Arab sovereignty over East Jerusalem and the Old City. Because of their hope that the international community would ultimately prevail, Jerusalem Arabs were unwilling to cooperate with Israeli efforts to unify the city, no matter how magnanimous those efforts were.

The Israeli government, for its part, bent over backwards to accommodate Arab demands in order to make the transition to a united Jewish capital as painless as possible. Administrative regulations were reinterpreted by government and municipal officials (or simply not enforced) in favor of the Arab inhabitants of the city. Certain practices that were illegal on the Jewish side were allowed in East Jerusalem. For example, Arab schools followed Jordanian curriculum, money changers operated independent of most government regulations, taxes were limited and moderate, Arab business licenses were automatically renewed, meetings of Jewish groups were restricted on the Temple Mount, and the Muslim *Shari'a* court system continued to operate, though in certain matters it contradicted Israeli law.

THE INTIFADA: AN UPRISING IN JERUSALEM AND THE WEST BANK

As magnanimous as the Israeli occupation of Jerusalem and the West Bank might have been, the Palestinian Arabs still felt like second-class citizens in their own country—an attitude which gave rise to powerful nationalistic feelings. In December 1987, Palestinians in the occupied territories challenged the Israeli military occupation. The uprising, usually referred to by its Arabic name, *intifada,* has brought the plight of the Arabs in Israel and the occupied territories to the attention of the world, and they have gained considerable international sympathy in the process.

For both Palestinian Arabs and Israelis, the violent confrontations of the *intifada* marked an important turning point. This uprising represented the culmination of years of anger and frustration growing out of the inability of the Palestinian Arabs to create a state of their own, separate from Jordan and from Israel. The self-proclaimed parliament-in-exile of the Palestine Liberation Organization announced on 15 November 1988 the establishment of a Palestinian state in the occupied West Bank and Gaza with Jerusalem as its capital. At the same time the PLO leadership endorsed United Nations Resolutions 242 and 338, implicitly recognizing Israel and acknowledging its right to exist within secure and recognized boundaries, but boundaries that had yet to be negotiated.[22]

Now that the West Bank, Gaza, and Jerusalem have become the central focus for Palestinian Arab national revival and independence, the Jewish settlements in the West Bank and in and around Jerusalem are certain to become major impediments to peace. According to most Palestinians, Israel's settlement policy in the occupied territories, including Jerusalem since 1967, has been nothing less than creeping annexation of Arab lands. They further contend that the settlements have been established in violation of international law.

Perhaps nowhere in the occupied territories has the *intifada* been felt more strongly than in Jerusalem. The beautiful white limestone walls in East Jerusalem have been disfigured by spray-painted protests against the Israeli occupation. Arab shopkeepers were ordered either to open their shops or close them according to the demands of the *intifada* leadership. Accordingly, East Jerusalem was plagued by unannounced commercial strikes that resulted in untold economic dislocation to Arab shopowners and merchants. Some were willing to bear the burden if it meant the eventual end of Israeli domination of their lives; others felt such tactics only harmed Arab unity, and to that extent, benefited the Israelis.

The *intifada* was difficult for everyone. The Israelis were frustrated by their inability to quickly put it down by force and restore a semblance of peace and harmony to the streets of Jerusalem. The Arabs suffered economically, their schools were often closed, and jobs sponsored by the Israelis were unavailable. Arabs lacked strong central leadership, they were being devoured from within by factional fighting, many thousands of their youth languished in Israeli prisons, and, worst of all, there was little hope that their sacrifices would accomplish anything at all.

With the signing of the Israel-PLO Accord on 13 September 1993 and with the real prospect of a brighter political day, the *intifada* faded. Stores in Jerusalem reopened, graffiti was cleaned up, schools reopened, tens of thousands of Arab youth were released from the prisons in a general amnesty, and the prospect of investments from the outside world gave the economy of the West Bank new life.

Although there are several cities of moderate size in the West Bank, Jerusalem was proclaimed by the leaders of the *intifada* the territorial focal point, the capital, the symbol of a free and independent people. The Palestinian Arabs believe that the *intifada* is largely responsible for Israeli concessions on such critical issues as an eventual Palestinian Arab state with Jerusalem as its capital. Never mind that the Israelis espouse quite a different view.

CONTEMPORARY LIFE IN JERUSALEM

In a very real sense, the story of contemporary Jerusalem is a tale of two cities. It is a city that since 1967 has been devoid of physical barriers but is nevertheless about as divided as a city can be. Psychological barriers prevent Arabs and Jews from visiting each other's side of the city. Barriers of distrust, suspicion, intolerance, jealousy, and fear are everywhere. When an Arab visits the west side, he is subject to repeated security checks as he walks along the street. He is given a more thorough body search than his Jewish counterparts upon entering a public building, be it a theater, post office, bus station, or restaurant; if he is driving, he is more likely to be stopped at randomly placed roadblocks. Upon learning he is an Arab from his physical appearance, accent, or identity card, the Israeli police typically subject him to questioning that leaves no doubt that he is regarded by them as an alien, unwelcome in their part of this so-called united city. Few young Arabs participate in the Israeli nightlife of movies, musicals, operas, discotheques, and sidewalk cafes. Constantly on their mind is the danger of being found in the vicinity of a terrorist incident. They know very well they could be physically abused by Israelis who are angry, frustrated, and disheartened by the lack of peace and safety in their own city.

During business hours, the streets of the Arab side of Jerusalem, especially the Old City, are flooded with shoppers and bargain hunters of every nationality and religious persuasion under the sun, many in traditional dress, and speaking a babble of languages. Israeli shoppers, unwilling to entrust their safety to security forces, venture into Arab Jerusalem carrying hidden weapons, belying the confidence and fraternity they exhibit among their fellow Arab citizens.

At nightfall, the scene changes. The shops are closed, the iron shutters are bolted, and the deserted streets are left to a few unwary foreigners, to the incidental but mysteriously ever-present night people, to alley cats, and to security police with their blue flashing lights. A curious onlooker might find East Jerusalem's one poorly attended movie house, a few dimly lit coffee houses whose sole occupants are Arab males, the occasional restaurant, and hotels bursting with tourists who may be oblivious to the political discontent that surrounds them.

In this undivided city with no physical barriers, religion is a barrier with its uncompromising labyrinth of interpretations of God, its false messiahs, and its religious fanatics. Nationalism is a barrier, espousing doctrines of ethnic hatred and flaunting its muscles of armed vigilantes and secret combinations. Darkness is a barrier—the darkness of the unknown, the darkness of contempt and prejudice, the darkness of ignorance and misunderstanding, the darkness of politics and intrigue.

There is also a bright side, a side of Jerusalem that illuminates the hope, the goodwill, and the desire for coexistence that resides in the hearts of many of its citizens: Arabs, Christians, and Jews. There is, for example, the mutual appreciation of sports, especially soccer. Arab soccer stars have been invited to play on Israeli teams, where they have been accepted as equals by players and fans alike. And there is the cooperation in the marketplace as the merchants in the diverse ethnic groups work together to reap a profit from their various enterprises.

Mutual dependency in the labor market has built confidence in interracial relations. The Israelis have depended on relatively inexpensive labor among the Arabs, and the Arabs have sought much-needed jobs in the Israeli sector. The lack of industry in East Jerusalem and the West Bank, together with a healthy, growing economy in Israel, have brought Arabs and Israelis together in a relatively sophisticated symbiotic relationship. This mutual dependency has also affected language; it is now socially acceptable to speak both Hebrew and Arabic. Arabic is taught in the Israeli schools, and Hebrew is taught in the Arab schools. Both societies recognize the value of bilingualism in building trust and understanding between cultures.

Social, academic, and professional groups from both sides interact in a genuine search for mutual accommodation and acceptance. The liberal-minded humanists are at the forefront of this movement, but it is gathering steam and appears destined to build a whole range of confidence-building activities with it, including mixed groups of Israeli and Arab social, academic, and political groups working together for solutions to mutual problems.

A RELIGIOUS MOSAIC

Jerusalem is a religious mosaic made up of adherents of three major world religions, to which must be added a multitude of splinter groups, all intent on seeking their spiritual roots or serving visitors who come for similar reasons. The visitor to Jerusalem is first struck by the profusion of apparel worn by the city's inhabitants. Typically, dress and head coverings identify Jews, Christians, and Muslims, but within these three groups are a plethora of subgroups of people dressing to identify with a certain tradition, religion, or social class. Identifying Jerusalemites as they stroll in the streets in their traditional or religious dress is a most educational pastime.

The main schism in Islam is not reflected in Jerusalem's population. Most Muslims in Jerusalem are Sunnis, in contrast to Shiites, so those who wear traditional Arab garb dress pretty much alike. A religious revival in Islam is well represented in Jerusalem by the girls and young women who are returning to traditional dress (mostly black and occasionally white) that leaves only the face exposed. Many older Arab women can be seen in the streets heavily clothed and veiled, invoking in Westerners a feeling of mystery and desert folklore. There is a broad diversity in the color and patterns of the *Kefiya* worn on the heads of Arab men, but it does not have religious significance.

The Christian community in Jerusalem is made up of Greek Catholics, Greek Orthodox, Roman Catholics, Armenians, Maronites, Copts, Syrians, Chaldeans, Ethiopians (Abyssinians), representatives of many different Protestant faiths, and, of course, a sprinkling of Latter-day Saints. Some religious groups are self-contained communities with their own neighborhoods, schools, court systems, religious facilities, and social organizations. Some such communities go back to the first centuries after Christ; their influence has long been felt in the religious melting-pot that is Jerusalem. The more religious among them dress to identify with their particular religion.

The Druze are a non-Muslim, Arabic-speaking people who are certainly distinctive among Jerusalemites, even if they are not numerous.

Older men often wear gaucholike pants and sport large handle-bar moustaches; the women cover their heads with long, pure white scarves.

Then, of course, there are the modern youth who dress the same as young people do almost anywhere, many of whom are caught up in a variety of fashions that defy description. They too add a colorful dimension to Jerusalem's mosaic.

This profusion of colors and styles of dress—augmented by the native costumes of the many visitors to Jerusalem from other countries around the world—give character and personality to the city. They make Jerusalem unique among the cities of the world and contribute to the city's mystique and charm.

CONCLUSION

Amid the sometimes contradicting and negative forces of religion, nationalism, and politics, there is a glimmer of hope that a solution for Jerusalem is not a zero-sum game in which one group's gain is another's loss. Abba Eban, an Israeli philosopher, politician, and diplomat, once remarked that the real danger to Middle East peace is "one hundred per-centism." That is the fanatic's philosophy of all or nothing. Said Eban, "In diplomatic history, those who ask for all or nothing are more likely to get nothing than to get all."[23]

The alternative to coexistence and compromise is what French author Albert Camus described as the "fatal embrace." Camus wrote, "It is as if two insane people, crazed with wrath, had decided to turn to a fatal embrace, the forced marriage from which they cannot free themselves. Forced to live together and incapable of uniting, they decide at last to die together."[24] It need not come to this with respect to Jerusalem, but with all the favorable evidence in, it still appears that Jerusalem is destined to be a mainstream issue in the foreseeable future, ultimately leading to Armageddon (see Zech. 12:2–3).

NOTES

1. Friedman, "Teddy Kollek's Jerusalem," 16–18.
2. Friedman, "Teddy Kollek's Jerusalem," 22.

3. Idinopulos, *Jerusalem Blessed, Jerusalem Cursed,* 329–30.

4. Idinopulos, *Jerusalem Blessed, Jerusalem Cursed,* 123–25.

5. Prittie, *Whose Jerusalem?* 156–57.

6. See, for example, "Israel and Torture," *Sunday Times* (London), 19 June 1977; *Christian Science Monitor,* 4 Apr. 1979; *Washington Post,* 7 Feb. 1979.

7. Benvenisti, *Jerusalem,* 89–91, 98–100, 102–6.

8. Benvenisti, *Jerusalem,* 129–31, 140–42.

9. Benvenisti, *Jerusalem,* 142–44.

10. Benvenisti, *Jerusalem,* 110–12.

11. In Kraemer, *Jerusalem,* 102.

12. Benvenisti, *Jerusalem,* 196–97; Kraemer, *Jerusalem,* 112–13; Prittie, *Whose Jerusalem?* 149–50.

13. Benvenisti, *Jerusalem,* 196–97.

14. Prittie, *Whose Jerusalem?* 150; Benvenisti, *Jerusalem,* 200; Kraemer, *Jerusalem,* 113.

15. Benvenisti, *Jerusalem,* 201.

16. Foreign Broadcast Information Service NES-93-128, "Official Reports Jewish Majority in East Jerusalem," Tel Aviv, *Ha'aretz,* 7 July 1993, 42.

17. Foreign Broadcast Information Service NES-93-128, "Official Reports Jewish Majority in East Jerusalem," Tel Aviv, *Ha'aretz,* 7 July 1993, 42.

18. See Ogden, "Was City Planning in Modern Jerusalem Foreseen by the Prophets of Judah?" 2.

19. Jerusalem's municipal area was extended to one hundred square kilometers (sixty-two square miles), making it more than three times the size of Jerusalem of 1947. See Ogden, "Was City Planning in Modern Jerusalem Foreseen by the Prophets of Judah?" 2.

20. In Ogden, "Was City Planning in Modern Jerusalem Foreseen by the Prophets of Judah?" 3.

21. Ogden, "Was City Planning in Modern Jerusalem Foreseen by the Prophets of Judah?" 4.

22. This was made possible in part by a Jordanian decision on 31 July 1988 to sever its legal and administrative ties with the West Bank.

23. Eban, "Prospects for Peace in the Middle East," 6–7.

24. Giliomee, "Elusive Search for Peace," 1.

26

THE JERUSALEM CENTER FOR NEAR EASTERN STUDIES

After the State of Israel was created in 1948, efforts to determine whether the Church owned or leased property in Israel proved inconclusive. Latter-day Saints living within the borders of the newly created state had either moved away or become inactive. For the next two decades, Church membership in Israel consisted of only a few semipermanent expatriates, traveling businessmen, diplomats, tourists, and students.

The Swiss-Austrian Mission administered Church affairs in most lands in Europe and the Near East where there was no other official organization of the Church. In 1969, the mission president, M. Elmer Christensen, authorized the few members living in Israel to form an official group of the Church. It was typical for the few Saints living in Israel to congregate at a designated member's home by Friday afternoon before the Israeli bus system shut down for the Sabbath. Church services were held the following day, Saturday, because most members had professional or academic obligations on Sunday, a normal workday in Israel. After sundown Saturday, when the buses started running again, the Saints went their separate ways, spiritually rejuvenated for another week. The Sabbath observances were based in a member's home, but the meetings themselves were often held at sacred sites associated with the Gospel Doctrine lesson for that week, which for years was taken from *Jesus the Christ*, by Elder James E. Talmage.

The number of members in Israel waxed and waned over the years. By 1971, Church services centered more in Jerusalem where, with an average attendance of thirty to forty semipermanent members, including children, they took on more formality.[1] Priesthood and auxiliary meetings were held. The numbers attending sabbath services were bolstered by the many tourists to the Holy Land, including several general authorities. The members looked forward to such visits, always hopeful that the next visit might signal greater Church involvement in the land. At each visit, the Brethren patiently explained that "the time was not yet," suggesting that such a decision had been made in the highest councils of the Church.

Brigham Young University travel study programs became a yearly feature, significantly increasing the number of Latter-day Saints in Israel. The members enjoyed holding church services with faculty members and students at their hotels, but their course of study often took the BYU participants out of Jerusalem, leaving the church auxiliary programs with no place to meet. This situation led to the lease of a facility in East Jerusalem that could accommodate everyone and help Church members who were not students be less dependent on the university program. This meeting place became known as Mormon House.

PRESIDENT HAROLD B. LEE'S VISIT TO THE HOLY LAND

In September 1972, President Harold B. Lee visited Israel, accompanied by Elder Gordon B. Hinckley and President Edwin Q. Cannon of the Switzerland Mission. This was the first visit by the earthly leader of the Church in nearly two millennia. He formally organized the resident group of Saints into the first Jerusalem branch of the Church, possibly the first since the days of Peter. President Lee took other steps that had far-reaching implications for the Church in the land of Israel. Branch leaders asked President Lee for permission to hold regular church services on Saturday, the Jewish Sabbath, instead of Sunday. President Lee asked that a formal request be addressed to the First Presidency. A couple of months later the request was officially authorized.[2] At the same time, the Church authorized the translation of the Book of Mormon and various tracts into Hebrew.[3] This action was in keeping with a statement President Lee repeated several times during his visit that the Church had entered a preparatory period in its relationship to the Jews.

While he was in Jerusalem, in keeping with protocol, President Lee met with Israel's chief rabbis. The matter of proselyting was raised in the course of a cordial discussion. The rabbis expressed their hope that President Lee's visit did not signal the Church's intention to begin missionary work in Israel. President Lee, knowing the strong antiproselyting stance of most Israelis, religious or otherwise, responded that the Church does not come into a country through the back door, but through the front door, invited.

Also during his visit, President Lee suggested to local Church leaders that they search for a parcel of land on the Mount of Olives on which a memorial could be built to commemorate the visit of Orson Hyde to Jerusalem in 1841. Although the proposal did not originate with President Lee, his suggestion began the seven-year endeavor that culminated in 1979 in a five-acre memorial in Orson Hyde's name in the middle of the Mount of Olives. The park, developed on the steep slopes of the Mount, has pleasant walks that lead down through the park and out to Gethsemane and a small amphitheater set back into the hill, with a beautiful panoramic view over Jerusalem. Within the amphitheater was set a large bronze plaque containing portions of the text of Orson Hyde's dedicatory prayer.[4] The park is not owned by the Church; it simply honors the name of Orson Hyde and recognizes his efforts to bless the city. The Orson Hyde Foundation was established to raise one million dollars for the beautification of the city.

President Lee authorized local Church leaders to search for land on which a church building could be constructed. That was unusual, because the number of members living in Israel at the time, mostly expatriates, did not warrant such an edifice, according to the Church building criteria of the time. President Lee, with the mantle of a prophet, foresaw the need for a building in Jerusalem that far exceeded the expectations of the Saints.

President Lee's visit to Jerusalem is a landmark in Church history there. Most developments related to the Church in the Holy Land have their foundation in his visit.

THE CHURCH IN ISRAEL, 1972–1980

The Brigham Young University travel study program in Jerusalem grew rapidly. The students were an asset to the branch, and the resident Saints enjoyed meeting with them, but their academic schedule often took them out of Jerusalem for weeks at a time. This situation eventually led to the creation of two branches in Jerusalem: a student branch and a regular branch.

In 1975, the Church in the Holy Land was put under the jurisdiction of the International Mission, headquartered in Salt Lake City, which had been organized to see to the spiritual needs of members of the Church not covered by missions. The number of expatriate Church members going to live in Israel continued to grow. Their influence was felt not only in Jerusalem but also in Tel Aviv and in the Galilee, where small branches of the Church were created in 1976.

In 1977, in an important step toward creating a permanent presence in the Holy Land, the Church was officially recognized by the state of Israel as a legal entity with the right, among other things, to "acquire, retain and dispose of real and personal property" and to "carry, through peaceful means, the Church's message throughout Israel, sharing its ideals with all interested people."[5] In the same year the Israel District was organized. It was responsible for two branches in Jerusalem and branches in Tel Aviv, Haifa, and Tiberias. The district functioned as if it were a stake, but it answered to the International Mission in Salt Lake City.

A distinguishing characteristic of the Church in Israel was the rapid turnover of members. The students came and went within a few months, but even the semipermanent members averaged only one or two years. Apart from the BYU students, Church members were typically professionals representing many different international, commercial interests or were attached to a country's diplomatic service. A few professionals came to Israel on humanitarian programs; others worked on postgraduate degrees at one of Israel's institutions of higher learning. Among all these transitory expatriates were a few pioneers who had moved to Israel to make it their home. They became the real backbone of the Church in Israel, giving continuity to branch programs and helping to establish a permanent presence of the Church in the land.

Many general authorities visited the Holy Land over the years. Often their schedules allowed them to attend regular church services with the Saints; when that was not possible, special firesides were arranged midweek so Church members could hear from them. The members felt isolated from the rest of the Church, so these visits were especially welcome.

In 1979, President Spencer W. Kimball, accompanied by five other general authorities, arrived in Israel to dedicate the Orson Hyde Memorial Garden. The service conducted on the slopes of the Mount of Olives was attended by more than two thousand Church members (mostly visitors), as well as Israeli government officials, Mayor Teddy Kollek and other municipal officials, Arab community leaders and dignitaries, and leaders of the various Christian denominations. During this visit President Kimball announced Church plans to build a center in Jerusalem that would have a chapel to accommodate local branches as well as visiting Church members and facilities to house the Jerusalem BYU Travel Study program. Under the direction of the First Presidency, Brigham Young University would take the lead in the project.

BRIGHAM YOUNG UNIVERSITY IN THE LANDS OF THE BIBLE

Brigham Young University has sponsored travel study programs in the Holy Land since 1968, when a group of students went to Israel under the direction of Robert C. Taylor, chair of the BYU Department of Travel Study, and Daniel H. Ludlow, a member of the BYU religion faculty. The group studied in Israel for only a few months, but the success of that first venture laid the foundation for study-abroad programs in Israel that far exceeded everyone's expectations. Interest in the program soon required two programs a year, which coincided with the fall and winter semesters at BYU. As the popularity of the programs grew, spring and summer programs were added, along with special interest programs designed for older couples and singles.

The travel study program in Jerusalem was developed to offer courses in the Old and New Testament and ancient and modern Near Eastern history and more specialized classes in the archaeology, geography, and cultures of the Near East, including Hebrew and Arabic languages. The program serves students who are Church members with a variety of educational backgrounds as it promotes understanding of other peoples, cultures, and religious faiths that trace their roots to the Holy Land. Public lectures, conferences, symposia, and concerts are available to Jerusalem residents and visitors alike.[6]

Brigham Young University's Jerusalem Center

PHYSICAL FACILITIES IN JERUSALEM

Growing participation in the travel study program required ever larger facilities. Because hotels were not adequate for the classroom, library, and study room requirements of an academic program, a search was made for more appropriate facilities. That search led to Kibbutz Ramat Rahel on the southern edge of the city. Its modest, youth-hostel-like living quarters were modified to provide additional classroom and library space. Here the study program settled down for seven years while the search for land continued. In the course of time, Church leaders and Brigham Young University leaders decided to build a facility that would meet the present and future requirements of both Church and academic program. The Center would include a chapel, a visitors center, and a classroom and dormitory complex for the study-abroad program.

THE FORMATIVE YEARS

The development of the Jerusalem Center was a First Presidency project[7] that included Brigham Young University. The logic of the joint building effort was obvious: first, it satisfied the requirements of the BYU-sponsored educational programs operating in the Holy Land, which were becoming increasingly attractive to Latter-day Saint students and tourists alike; and second, it met the ecclesiastical imperatives of the Church, which included a physical presence of the Church in the Holy Land after an absence of nearly two thousand years. Additionally, there was the significance of Jerusalem in Church theology and the necessity of a place of worship for Saints residing or visiting in Israel.

Local Church members were pleased with the prospect of a visitors center as part of the Jerusalem Center complex. They hoped that a visitors center could serve as a base for passive, and therefore acceptable, missionary work in a land where Christian proselyting was anathema to the greater part of the population. The well-known missionary reputation of the Church, together with uninformed statements by a few about the so-called real reasons for the proposed building in Israel, fed the fears of opponents, and the proposal for a visitors center was not approved. This combination of concerns resulted in an often bitter, four-year campaign by Jewish nationalists and the more religious elements of Israeli society to end the project.

The visit to Jerusalem in 1979 by President Spencer W. Kimball eliminated all the proposed sites except the one on the northern end of the Mount of Olives, also called Mount Scopus. Hindsight makes it apparent that the other sites, which had been so painstakingly considered, were not in keeping with what the Lord had in mind. First, many miracles occurred, readily acknowledged by member and nonmember alike, that eventually led to the Church's obtaining the most prominent and prestigious building site in all Jerusalem on the Mount of Olives. Second, there have been incredible attempts on the part of the adversary to obstruct, frustrate, and thwart the whole undertaking.

PREPARATIONS ARE BEGUN

Between 1980 and 1984, tedious and lengthy negotiations took place for the land and the building permits. The First Presidency had appointed Elder Howard W. Hunter, Elder James E. Faust, and BYU president Jeffrey R. Holland as an executive committee responsible for overseeing the development of the Jerusalem Center. They were assisted by

BYU administrators Fred A. Schwendiman, vice president of support services; Robert C. Taylor, chair of the department of travel study; and David B. Galbraith, resident director in Jerusalem. Robert J. Smith, BYU vice president of finance, and Wayne Nelson, Church budget officer, were added to the committee later. Robert P. Thorn was called by the Brethren in 1980 to assist in negotiating with the Israeli government, the Lands Authority, and Jerusalem municipal officials in obtaining the land. Joseph Kokia, an Israeli lawyer, Fuad Shehade, an Arab Palestinian lawyer, and the Israeli architectural firm of David Reznick and Associates were retained to assist in the process.[8] The contributions of each of the many participants in the Jerusalem project, named or unnamed, member or nonmember, were so extraordinary that it became apparent that they had been raised up by the Lord for this singular task.

There was a great deal of support for a so-called "Mormon Center" in Jerusalem among Israelis, but nowhere was more support forthcoming than from Mayor Teddy Kollek. The mayor had had positive experiences in his past contacts with Church leaders, and the million-dollar contribution to the city of Jerusalem from the Orson Hyde Foundation for the beautification of the city had cemented this relationship. Mayor Kollek and other municipal leaders were convinced that the Church was a genuine friend of the City and the Jewish people. The mayor took a personal interest and a leading role in finding a suitable location to build a center. Once the opposition started, he took a forceful, influential, and very public position in support of the Center, for which he was severely maligned by fellow Jews who questioned the permanent establishment of a Christian institution in the heart of the Jewish capital. Mayor Kollek never wavered in his support, and on at least one occasion, in the heat of the opposition, he expressed concern that the Church and university might withdraw from the project. He stood firm for a pluralistic society with tolerance for all religious faiths, with the proviso that they be sensitive to the opposition felt by most Jews towards Christian proselyting among the Jewish people.

Resident leaders of the BYU study program in Jerusalem imbued the academic offerings with a spiritual quality that changed lives. The years of dedicated service by those resident leaders and by the religion instructors who joined them had a positive influence on the youth who came to learn. In the final analysis, it was the success of the Jerusalem study program, through the combined efforts of administrators, faculty, and students, that served as a catalyst in the decision to build a center in Jerusalem.

THE NEGOTIATING STAGE, 1980–1984

Although Church leaders had selected their first choice of a site in 1979 from among several attractive alternatives, most of 1980 was taken up with intense negotiations to persuade the Israeli authorities to lease that particular piece of real estate.[9] Once an agreement in principle had been reached, the next three years (1981 to 1984) were involved with efforts to have the land in question rezoned for public use and the complicated and time-consuming process of obtaining the required building permits, determining lease and construction costs, defining and refining the architectural plans for the multifaceted center, satisfying the zoning laws, officially announcing and publicizing the project, testing the soil, retaining a construction manager, and putting the construction project out to bid.

In August 1984, construction began. As large, earth-moving machines started to tear into the hillside, this "Mormon project" came under visible public scrutiny. Although all the appropriate government and city officials had signed off on the project, and although every legal detail had been carefully scrutinized and attended to, a cry went up, primarily from the Jewish orthodox community, that an alien, non-Jewish, Christian proselyting sect had surreptitiously, if not illegally, obtained one of the finest building sites in all of Jerusalem.

OPPOSITION TO THE CENTER, 1984–1988

In the first few months of 1985, the negative press about the presence of the Church and Brigham Young University in Jerusalem increased significantly. In most cases, the issues dealt with the missionary reputation of the Church and the fear that the Jerusalem Center represented a missionary headquarters to proselyte Jews. Allegations included the following:

The Mormon organization is one of the most dangerous, and in

America they have already struck down many Jews. At the present the Mormons are cautious because of the tremendous opposition their missionary activities would engender, but the moment their new Center is completed, we won't be able to stop them.[10]

What has the city actually done to evaluate the true intentions of such a notorious proselyting group establishing a branch in the Jewish capital?[11]

How would the Mormons actually be controlled against missionary activities? What could we do once they have established themselves in Jerusalem? What would throwing them out do to our international "open-minded" image?[12]

At the heart of the "emotional" and "bitter" controversy brewing in Jerusalem is whether Christian Zionism, based on Christian eschatological expectations, should function in Israel with the help and active aid of government and municipal authorities, such as the assistance being rendered to the Brigham Young University.[13]

Zionism means that Jews were acquiring land from non-Jews, and now we find that Christians are building their institutions by acquiring land from Jews. What a reversal . . . and if we must give land to Christians, why must it be one of the most prestigious and beautiful locations overlooking the ancient Jewish holy city?[14]

The Mormons seek international legitimization through the university center they are building in Israel so as to acquire for themselves a respectable status with the ultimate objective to proselyte Jews. They plan to operate under the camouflage of "education" and "culture."[15]

According to internal publications of the Mormons, the university will become a world center for the spread of Mormon Christianity, or in other words, a vast missionary center that will dwarf all other churches and missions that are operating in the country.[16]

The Mormons are conducting vast missionary work throughout the world. Are we to believe that in the Holy Land, which is central in their thinking, they will sit with their arms folded?[17]

One member of the Knesset stated that he had evidence that "dirty" things have taken place in the Mormon acquisition of this land, and "I mean dirty."[18] Other critics charged that Jerusalem Mayor Teddy Kollek's acquiescence to the plan was on account of the Mormons' contribution of one million dollars to the Jerusalem Foundation.[19]

Early efforts to stop construction of the Center took the form of organized letter writing to Mayor Teddy Kollek, articles in the newspapers both in Israel and abroad, and lobbying in the Israeli Knesset. Mayor Kollek was unfairly singled out as the sole Israeli official who allowed a Christian proselyting faith to establish a permanent presence in Jerusalem. Thousands of letters were sent to him by those opposing the Center, urging him to stop its construction. In a typical response, Mayor Kollek wrote:

> I am . . . disappointed that you should lend yourself to the influence of certain Jewish sectors who are motivated by a hysterical attitude as far as the threat of Christian missions in Jerusalem is concerned, and particularly that of Mormonism.
>
> Firstly let me assure you that Christian missionary activity in Jerusalem is almost nonexistent. None of the churches engage in missionary work and the few isolated cases of "missionary talk" that occur from time to time are individual initiatives, mostly attempted by temporary residents or tourists who have no organization behind them and therefore, no possibility of followup.
>
> The Mormon presence in Jerusalem is of 15 years duration. They bring students from Brigham Young University for courses which include the study of modern and ancient Israel. So do other Christian institutes who engage lecturers from the Hebrew University for this purpose, ie., the Jesuits' Priests' Seminary, the Evangelicals at the American Institute of Holy Land Studies and the German Benedictine Fathers of the Dormition Abbey.
>
> There has not been one instance of Jewish conversion as a result of this academic activity. On the contrary, many Christian students who may have had a certain bias before coming here, have become good-will ambassadors of Jerusalem and Israel among their own communities abroad.
>
> As to the Mormons themselves—their record in Jerusalem for 15 years shows *no* proselyting attempts. Their leaders, who come here frequently, have time and time again assured me that they do not intend to use the university for any missionary activities, and they understand that, after the tragedy of the holocaust no such activity is, or will be tolerated by Israelis in their own land.
>
> Jerusalem prides itself on being a city with a pluralistic society where each community, creed or ethnic group can pursue its own way of life without hinderance. This can only be done if we continue to put tolerance at the head of our concerns and convictions.[20]

Not all Jews were opposed to the Center. The mayor received considerable outside support for the public position he took. For example, Rudy Boschwitz, a United States senator from Minnesota and a Jew, wrote:

> As you may know, Mormons are among Israel's most ardent supporters in this country. I must tell you I go to these [Mormon] Senators asking them for support for Israel and I find this whole matter embarrassing—indeed outrageous. If God had provided more Mormon neighbors for Israel, we would all be better off. I recognize Israelis—as we Americans—have rights of assembly and protest, but I sincerely request that you educate these Hasidim and others who protest. If my friends the Lubavitchers are involved, let me know and I will take it up with the Rebbe. Life is too short for Jews and Mormons to antagonize one another.[21]

To address the misunderstanding that was building up because of the propaganda campaign undertaken by the opposition, Dr. David B. Galbraith, the resident director of the BYU study-abroad program in Jerusalem, released the following letter to the press:

> After 17 years of a Mormon presence in Israel, elements within Israeli society are suddenly making this presence a major issue. Concern has been expressed that the Mormons will proselyte among the Jews in Israel once construction of the Brigham Young University's Jerusalem Center for Near Eastern Studies is completed.
>
> Leaders of the Mormon faith have given assurances verbally and in writing to responsible authorities in Israel to the effect that there are no plans to carry out missionary work in Israel. The Mormon missionary program is not found in a country in the world where we do not have the authorization of the host government or in other words where we have not been invited through the "front door." Likewise in Israel without such authorization the Church would not engage in proselyting nor seek to send missionaries through the "back door" in the guise of university students.
>
> Mormon leaders are very sensitive to the point raised in a letter a number of years ago by Mayor Kollek in which he stated that "at this point in our history having lost six million Jews in the holocaust it is inconceivable that the Jewish nation tolerate any religious missionary activity...." We have voluntarily complied with both the letter and the spirit of that request.
>
> It needs to be emphasized that the Center being built on Mt. Scopus in Jerusalem is a legitimate extension of the Brigham Young University, USA.

We clearly distinguish between academic endeavors and missionary work. The student regulations of the Jerusalem Center prohibit proselyting activities of any kind.

As we proceed with the construction of the Jerusalem Center for Near Eastern Studies we will continue to bring hundreds of Mormon university students and thousands of tourists to Israel as we have been doing for years. These visitors return home as "ambassadors of goodwill" for Israel. Many Israeli friends in government, business and educational circles have encouraged us to continue these efforts.[22]

ACTION BY THE ISRAELI GOVERNMENT

Despite efforts to counter the propaganda campaign, opposition to the Center gathered so much momentum that by December 1985 the government of Israel faced a vote of nonconfidence. The question was put to Prime Minister Shimon Peres: What will it be, the Mormons or another Israeli war? The belief was that only Peres' Labor government could move Israel towards peace and if the government should fall over the Mormon issue or if Mr. Peres were unable to persuade the religious parties into joining a narrow coalition because he sided with the Mormons, the party in opposition (the Likud party) would form the next government and return Israel to a war footing with its Arab neighbors. In short, the religious orthodox parties were essential to the survival of the coalition government; that, in turn, gave them a great deal of political leverage. In this instance, they threatened to topple the government if that government did not halt the construction of the Mormon center.[23]

In December 1985, Prime Minister Peres responded by establishing a committee of four Cabinet ministers generally supportive of the Center and four Cabinet ministers opposed. The committee was to hold hearings and recommend for or against the continued construction of the Center.[24] This action effectively neutralized the religious parties' efforts to bring down the government. At about the same time, the Israeli Attorney General launched an investigation into the allegations of misconduct made by the opposition. Meanwhile, a subcommittee of the Israeli Knesset, the Interior Committee, had called upon the Center to give an official undertaking (promise) not to proselyte Jews.

BRIGHAM YOUNG UNIVERSITY GIVES A LEGAL UNDERTAKING

Church and university leaders decided to comply with the demands of the Knesset subcommittee. It was not an easy decision because the request was clearly discriminatory. It singled out the Mormons from all other Christian denominations in Israel and, furthermore, it constituted a political call to renounce a basic tenet of all Christendom—to take the gospel to all the world.[25] Nevertheless, in August 1985, President Jeffrey R. Holland presented a formally signed document, which reads:

> Brigham Young University, one of the largest private universities in the United States of America, is a fully accredited academic institution of higher education widely recognized and honored for the strength of its educational and research programs.
>
> For many years the University has operated study abroad programs in a number of international locations including Jerusalem, London, Vienna, Madrid, Salzburg, Paris, and Hawaii. The programs are designed to give students and faculty the opportunity to learn of and appreciate the history and cultures of the people among whom they are established. They have not been designed nor used for proselytizing activities.
>
> Since 1968 some 2,000 students have participated in our academic programs in Jerusalem. In addition, 13,000 BYU alumni and other adults in our continuing education programs have visited Israel for short-term travel study tours organized through this university department. These thousands who have participated, including many young men and women who will become future leaders of business, industry, and government, have come to understand and appreciate Israel and the peoples of the Near East in a manner not otherwise possible.
>
> Because of the increasing popularity of these programs, and because the study of both ancient and modern civilizations in the region is so vital to the academic curriculum of Brigham Young University, better accommodations were required and an extension of the University was proposed. It has been in the planning stage for years, has received all legal approvals, and has been a matter of common knowledge. Nothing has been done secretly or covertly. This annex is an integral part of the university's academic offering and is *not* in any way a missionary center. During the seventeen years that this program has been operating in Israel, we know of no Jew who has been converted to Mormonism through the activities of the students or faculty in this program.
>
> Now, out of an acute awareness of the public sensitivity surrounding the construction of this BYU annex and at the request of the Interior

Committee of the Knesset, this undertaking is hereby given to reaffirm that the Jerusalem Center for Near Eastern Studies (hereinafter referred to as the Institution), an extension program of Brigham Young University (USA) is being constructed and will be used for the academic programs and other activities commonly associated with universities, including religious services, as provided in the following declaration and undertaking.

We Declare and Undertake:

1. In harmony with the law and consistent with our own past policy and practice, students, faculty, and staff connected with the Institution will not be permitted to engage in proselytizing activities in Israel.

2. To assist in enforcing this policy the Institution will continue, as it has in the past, to require all students, faculty, and staff involved in the study programs of the Institution to sign an undertaking not to engage in proselytizing activity in Israel.[26] Violators will be subject to dismissal from the program and returned home.

3. The academic programs of the Institution are especially designed for participants from the worldwide Latter-day Saint (Mormon) community coming through Brigham Young University (USA). As long as required by the Israel Council of Higher Education, students from Israel shall not be, in any way, enrolled by the Institution for academic coursework (i.e. classes for which university credit is available or any student program leading to a degree).

4. Some educational and cultural programs and exhibits may be open to the general public in keeping with a university's public role but will not be designed nor used for proselytizing.[27]

This document had a calming effect on those who had yet to take a position for or against the Center but who were confused by the allegations that swirled through the media.

A PUBLIC RELATIONS OFFENSIVE

Early in January 1986, BYU went on a public relations offensive. Too much was at stake, and millions of dollars had been committed to the project, yet opposition to the Center continued to build. An Israeli public relations firm, Gitam, was retained and a strategy devised to communicate to the public what the presence of the Center in Jerusalem was all about. The editors of the various English, Hebrew, and Arabic newspapers were contacted and given an explanation of the LDS position, appearances were made by Jerusalem Center personnel on local television talk shows, and full-page advertisements were purchased.

In May 1986, Israel's prime minister and all 120 members of the Knesset received a letter from 154 members of the United States Congress supporting the establishment of the Center. It was unusual that members of the United States Congress would in a sense appeal to fellow lawmakers of another country; it was also unusual that members of both parties signed the letter. The letter read:

> Members of the Knesset
> Dear Colleagues:
>
> We have become increasingly concerned by reports here in the United States concerning certain groups in Israel who have undertaken a campaign to halt the construction and use of the Brigham Young University Center for Near Eastern Studies currently under construction in Jerusalem. We commend Israel for its admirable record of keeping Jerusalem open and we hope that this record will not be blemished in any way by this situation.
>
> One of the main motivations for our longstanding support for Israel has been its commitment to democracy and plurality. Recent events in the region, and increased terrorist activities by numerous states, stand in sharp contrast to Israel's dedication to democratic ideals and respect for human life. Of course, an important facet of Israel's democracy has been its commitment to basic freedoms, including freedom of religion. These factors, as well as many others, have formed the basis for the long and healthy relationship we enjoy.
>
> While we are aware of the sensitivity which many Jews feel regarding proselytizing, it is our understanding the officials of Brigham Young University have signed an undertaking in which it pledges that the Center will not be used for missionary activities. We also understand that it has been the longstanding policy of Brigham Young University that none of its students or faculty engage in proselytizing in Israel. We have been assured that this policy will continue. Many of us know the sponsoring organization and the reputation of its members, and they are known as a trustworthy and moral people who live up to their promises. We therefore believe this promise will be strictly abided by.
>
> By allowing this center to be built and used as intended, Israel will be reaffirming its commitment to pluralism and to the special nature of Jerusalem. We believe that rather than hinder U.S.-Israeli ties, the BYU Center will be a further source of understanding and cooperation between our two countries. Those students who study there will be uniquely able to teach the rest of us about your society, your culture and

your rich and fascinating history. We therefore request, gentlemen, that you do all that is necessary to see that this project is allowed to be completed and occupied without undue impediments or delays.[28]

About the time this letter was sent, Israel's Attorney General's office issued a lengthy report of a nearly nine-month investigation. They found BYU and the LDS Church not guilty of all charges. The many spurious allegations devised by the opposition were answered in one official document, thereby making it unnecessary for BYU's public relations firm to dignify the charges by answering them directly.

In August 1986, the ministerial committee of eight recommended that the government allow the construction of the Center to continue. It did, however, call for a reaffirmation that the Center would not be used for missionary work. The congressional letter, the Israeli Attorney General's report, the ministerial committee's recommendation combined with the many other public relations efforts to good effect, and it soon appeared that the vast majority of Israelis (something on the order of 80 percent) supported the Center. Of the remaining 20 percent, approximately half were religious elements unwilling to countenance an alien Christian presence in their midst on any grounds, and the remainder was made up of nationalists and others who were still unconvinced of the Center's declared purpose and wanted to wait and see.

The Israeli Cabinet, responding to the recommendation of the ministerial committee, gave final authorization to the Lands Authority to lease the property on which the Center was built for forty-nine years with an option to renew for another forty-nine. The Cabinet requested that a public review committee be formed to oversee the nonacademic operations of the Center to ensure that no proselyting took place. This was obviously a conciliatory gesture to the powerful orthodox parties whose constituents, for the most part, remained convinced that the Center would find a way around its commitments not to proselyte Jews.[29] As it turned out, the review committee reduced concerns from certain elements of society while cooperating with the Center in accomplishing its stated goals.

On 18 May 1988, Elder Howard W. Hunter, Elder James E. Faust, and President Jeffrey R. Holland arrived in Jerusalem to sign the official lease documents. It was an historic day, just three months short of four years from the time when the first spade of earth was turned. The following year, in May 1989, Elder Hunter offered a beautiful dedicatory prayer in a quiet, private ceremony.

The students had moved into the partially completed Center in March 1987. Once fully operational, it would house about two hundred individuals, including students, faculty, administrators, and their families. The Center comprises living quarters, classrooms, library, offices, laundry, recreation spaces, study rooms, underground parking, kitchen and dining facilities, bomb shelters, two large auditoriums, audiovisual theaters, learning resource center, and a magnificent pipe organ, one of the finest in the Near East. The view from the huge plate-glass windows is of the ancient walled city of Jerusalem. Luxurious gardens are everywhere, including a large biblical garden with indigenous flowers, plants, shrubs, and trees that will grow at that elevation. Ancient and operable grinding mills and grape and olive presses adorn the grounds—a constant reminder of the land's rich and ancient history. The architects used open spaces, limestone arches, panoramic views, and the gardens to ensure that visitors who walked through the building, lounged on the terraces, studied in the classrooms, or meditated in the gardens would never forget that they stood on sacred ground, hallowed by peoples and events of the past.

THE CHURCH IN ISRAEL IN THE 1980s AND 1990s

President N. Eldon Tanner was fond of saying that the Church discovered Israel in the 1970s and Israel discovered the Church in the 1980s. Latter-day Saint tours had started visiting Israel in earnest in the early seventies, and publicity about the Center made *Mormons* a household word throughout Israel in the eighties. Most Israelis had never heard of the Church before all the publicity put the Church in headlines and kept it there for more than four years. Of course, many American Jews had heard of the Church and BYU, but most Israelis had come from Europe, Africa, or the Near East.

For their part, as Church members in Israel endured the years of opposition to the Center, they suffered disappointment in the misunderstanding of the Church exhibited by so many Jews. The Church members had developed a great love and appreciation for both Muslims and

Jews, and to see so much enmity was painful—never mind that only a small portion of Israeli society was actively opposed to a Christian presence, in any form, in the land. It was disappointing that the orthodox Jews, the group most opposed to the presence of the Church in Israel, was the very group with which the Church had most in common, especially with regard to many religious and moral issues of the day.

The members of the Church in Israel, including the transitory students, became a force for good among both Jews and Muslims. Their actions, their lives, their example, their faith and prayers helped convince people that the Church was no threat; on the contrary, it was a genuine friend. Often, while the Center was being built, the fasting and prayers of the members resulted in miracles at critical junctures in obtaining building permits, contracts, and various other governmental and municipal approvals.

In the end, the opposition to the Center seems to have created many more friends for the Church than it did enemies. Many bonds of friendship were forged in the heat of the opposition. Many, though not all, of those who most vigorously opposed the Center were eventually won over. One Israeli official, after quietly observing the many Jews who attended one of the performances of the Mormon Tabernacle Choir in Israel, wrote:

> As satisfactory as was this musical event in Jerusalem's cultural calendar, there are dividends . . . that will be even more durable. As a social scientist trained to observe group behavior and [its] meaning, I was quite struck by the audience. . . . Not only how many, but also, who . . . I recognized the many members of the cultural and power elite of the nation's diplomats, government officials, industrialists, academicians, clergymen, mayors and solons. Some of them noticed each other at the gracious reception that followed the concert, and one could almost hear this one or that one saying to himself, "H-mm! Look who's here." . . . It was as if this assembly was validating the presence of BYU in our midst.
>
> Most of all, was the religious crowd in your audience. I recall the source of the fiercest reaction to the idea of your school on the mountain. . . . To see these religious Jews of all stripes, including some wearing *kipot,* and then to note that they were ready to enjoy your hospitality and to be seen there, tells me that we are witnessing a turning point.
>
> While many extremists are still at large, as I think of the "Mormon" concert . . . I feel comfortable in saying—perhaps for the first time—that

View of Jerusalem and Temple Mount from BYU's Jerusalem Center

the war is being won. We have met the enemy and they have become our friends.[30]

Could there be a greater tribute to Latter-day Saints, whether in Israel or abroad, who had anything to do with the Center? Through their example and their desire to see a permanent Latter-day Saint presence in Jerusalem, BYU and the Church have not only a magnificent building in Jerusalem but, even more important, friends who have made them feel that Jerusalem is their home, too.

A VISION OF THE JERUSALEM CENTER

The view from the Center allows an unparalleled panoramic view of such rich historical sites as the Old City, the Temple Mount, Mount Zion, Gethsemane, and Golgotha. In fact, one can, without moving one's head, take in the entire area of Jerusalem known to the Savior in his ministry. The whole inspirational setting can only cause one to pause and ponder the purpose, the mission, the ultimate destiny, of this Center.

The Latter-day Saints' multidecade presence with a study program in Jerusalem has suggested to most people (Israelis, Arabs, and even Mormons) a continuing institutional need. Of course, that could have been accomplished with a much less beautiful building at a much less controversial location, with much less visibility, and at a much lower cost. The location and beauty of the Center suggest not that the original premise is wrong but rather that the Latter-day Saint presence in this land portends something far greater. Is it possible, for example, that this Center is destined to become a great center of spiritual learning for the worldwide Church—a great pedagogical center, not unlike the Temples of old, where the faithful gathered by the thousands to be instructed in spiritual matters? The scriptures bear eloquent witness that Jerusalem is to become a great seat of learning in the last days. Isaiah saw our day and prophesied: "For out of Zion shall go forth the law, and the word of the Lord from Jerusalem" (Isa. 2:3).

David Galbraith, a former director of the Center, wrote:

> As I think on the grand panorama that is Jerusalem, from our Center located on the Mount of Olives before old Jerusalem on the east, I am compelled to believe that there is not a more historically majestic, exalted view in all the world. Meditation comes easily with such a view, and as the great historic landmarks pass before my vision, I am reminded that this city, because of its messianic ties, has had and will continue to have a greater impact on man, past, present and future, than any other city on earth; a city with a divine destiny that has determined that it shall be one of the two great capitals of the world in the "last days."[31]

The Lord has said through his prophets that Jerusalem is to become one of the two centers of the Church on earth. Not by chance has a great facility been built here, but it is up to the Latter-day Saints to ensure that the Center realizes the full purpose of its creation.

David Galbraith wrote further:

> With the "stones and mortar" in place, perhaps we can afford a moment to reminisce and reflect on what has been accomplished and where we go from here. It is often said by visitors that it is the most beautiful building in all of Jerusalem, while still others laud it in glowing terms as an inspiring work of art that will inevitably attract international recognition as a masterpiece of architecture and landscaping. But to us, it is much more than that; it is a sacred edifice—a "worthy offering to the Lord."
> If it is true that in the final analysis the Center is still an inanimate shell,

then let us, at the same time, acknowledge that what happens within its walls is the sanctifying force that gives it a life and meaning, perhaps not even confined to this dispensation. Indeed, everything that has transpired to date bears testimony of its grand destiny. The fact that it has the unique status of being a First Presidency project, coupled with the reality that Jerusalem is destined to become one of the two centers of the Church on earth, all bear eloquent witness to a future millennial role.

To our Jewish friends, some of whom are watching with distrust and even fear that the programs of the Center embody a form of spiritual threat which could lead to the conversion of many Jews, and to those who are uncomfortable with our references to millennial roles and world-wide centers, we say, peace! We will abide by our commitments to the letter. In keeping with the verbal and written assurances of our Church and university leaders, we will seek the spiritual development and well-being of our own. As President Harold B. Lee once promised, we will not enter Israel with our missionaries through the "back door." If the Church were to ever send missionaries, it would be through the "front door," invited. And if, as our opponents believe, such an invitation will never be extended, so be it. In some future millennial day when all that distinguishes and separates men will be dropped and when there will be no such designations as Mormon, Muslim or Jew, we will all choose from the best each has to offer and we will be "one."

Likewise, Latter-day Saints can rest assured that every official commitment related to our presence in Jerusalem is doctrinally sound and in keeping with the original intent to provide an educational center—a great spiritual hub of learning, for the world-wide Latter-day Saint community. And if for some, a millennial role is too distant, beyond our physical ability to reach or comprehend, who can doubt the present role of the Center as an institutional "forerunner," preparing the way for the advent of the Messiah. If such statements seem pretentious, even among our own, we would do well to consider the sobering fact that the prophet Isaiah prophesied of our day. One of the references to that prophecy is found in 2 Nephi 25:15–19, where it becomes readily apparent that Isaiah was portraying future developments that included Jerusalem when he so eloquently described what he saw—even "a marvelous work and a wonder" among the children of men.[32]

NOTES

1. For a more comprehensive history with names, dates and details, see Baldridge, *Grafting In.*

2. In a letter dated 20 November 1972, President Lee authorized the Saints in Israel to meet on Saturdays and the Saints in Muslim lands to meet on Fridays.

3. The translation of an abridged version of the Book of Mormon in Hebrew was completed in 1977, although the entire book has yet to be published.

4. For the text of Elder Orson Hyde's prayer, see Appendix 4.

5. From the Articles of Association of The Church of Jesus Christ of Latter-day Saints in Israel.

6. *Jerusalem Center Policy and Procedures Manual*, 1.

7. That the Jerusalem Center was a First Presidency project meant that the Brethren gave direction not only to the "shape and form" during construction but also to what would happen within the walls once the Center was completed. This is particularly significant in light of developments in Jackson County, Missouri, which are also under the direction of the First Presidency. In other words, both the Old and the New Jerusalem projects remain under the watchful eye of the First Presidency outside the regular channels for development projects.

8. The Utah architectural firm of Fowler, Ferguson and Associates was retained for the project with Frank Ferguson taking the lead. Ferguson and his Israeli counterpart, David Resnick, worked together to give the building its unique shape, form, and architectural beauty.

9. The land in question had been expropriated by the Israeli government from Arab owners after the 1967 Six-Day War. Israeli law prohibited the sale of such land, but this suited the Church's purposes because as a lease-holder, the Church would not be caught up in the political question of ownership. In other words, if rights of ownership were to revert to the original Arab owners, the Church, as lease-holder, would simply negotiate a new lease.

10. *Kol Ha'Ir* [an Israeli newspaper], 8 June 1984.

11. *Boston Jewish Times*, 6 Dec. 1984.

12. *Boston Jewish Times*, 6 Dec. 1984.

13. *Inter Mountain Jewish News*, 4 Jan. 1985.

14. Adler to *Yad L'Achim*, 27 Jan. 1985.

15. *Yad L'Achim* [a small group of Jewish religious activists opposed to Christian proselyting] to Knesset, Feb. 1985.

16. Gil, in *Erev Shabbat* [a Hebrew weekly], 8 Feb. 1985.

17. Binder, "Time Bomb on Mt. Scopus."

18. *Kol Israel* [Hebrew radio station], 1 June 1985.

19. *Jerusalem Post*, 4 June 1985.

20. Kollek to "Emunah Women of America," 7 Feb. 1985.

21. Letter to Peres with copy to Kollek, 2 Jan. 1985.

22. Letter to the editor, *Jerusalem Post*, 25 Feb. 1985.

23. The orthodox Jewish parties had several items on their political agenda along with the "Mormon Center," including a definition of who is a Jew, raising and selling pork in the Jewish state, and the desecration of bodies through autopsies. The refusal of the government to deal with any one of these issues was sufficient cause for the orthodox parties to call for a vote of nonconfidence in an effort to bring the government down.

24. Presumably, had the committee ruled against the Center, the government would have been compelled to reimburse the Church for all expenditures incurred to that date.

25. The commission by the Savior to "go ye therefore, and teach all nations, baptizing them in the name of the Father, and of the Son, and of the Holy Ghost" (Matt. 28:19) is understood by most Christians as a divine injunction to take the gospel to all the world.

26. All students applying to the Jerusalem program sign a form which includes the following paragraph: "Since some students may have served proselyting missions for The Church of Jesus Christ of Latter-day Saints, or have plans to do so, attention is drawn to instructions from the president of the International Mission of the Church *requiring that participants in BYU Travel Study programs refrain from any form of proselyting activity in any country where the Church is not officially recognized or where proselyting is not sanctioned by the host government.* . . . A student's signature on this application form constitutes acceptance of this restriction and infractions will be considered a violation of the honor code. Violators will be subject to dismissal from the program and immediate return home."

27. This document appeared on university letterhead and was signed and notarized 1 August 1985.

28. Letter from the Congress of the United States, 8 May 1986.

29. The review committee was made up of five members: one appointed by the government of Israel; one appointed by the attorney general; one appointed by the Mayor of Jerusalem; and two appointed by the Center. The committee was to serve for ten years (until 1998), after which its term might be extended by mutual consent. According to the lease addendum: "Should the Lessee [Center] wish to undertake any activity or event not designed solely for the students of the Center, the Lessee shall be bound to submit such activity or event to the Committee to consider whether the same is in conflict with Jewish educational or cultural values."

30. Dr. M. Bernard Resnikoff, director emeritus of the American Jewish Committee, to Truman Madsen, director of the Jerusalem Center, 13 Jan. 1993.

31. Galbraith journal, 19 May 1988.

32. Baldridge, *Grafting In,* 131–34.

27

THE TEMPLE MOUNT IN JERUSALEM

For Jews, Christians, and Muslims, the Temple Mount, or Haram esh-Sharif, has always been venerated as a place of holiness. It is not just the magnificent buildings that adorn the site, nor the walls that bespeak such great antiquity, but rather it seems to be the spirit of the place that beckons religious and nonreligious alike, bestowing on them a sense of solemnity and awe. Here their forefathers communed with the heavens, and here a feeling of reverence envelops those who come to worship or to visit. Whatever the site is called today, it is the place for a future sanctuary that will spiritually serve all of God's children who will come unto him.

THE THIRD TEMPLE IN JEWISH THOUGHT

Ever since the Roman destruction in A.D. 70, the Jews have prayed for the day when they might return and rebuild Jerusalem and the Temple. That dream of nearly two millennia saw partial fulfillment in the restoration of the site of the Holy Temple to the jurisdiction of a sovereign Jewish state as a result of the Six-Day War in 1967. Once again the question was raised: When will the Third Temple be built?

In addition to its legal and political ramifications, the question of a Third Temple must be looked at in light of Jewish traditions as well as Jewish halakhah, or religious law. First and foremost, the Temple Mount in Jerusalem is Jewry's most sacred site. Although the Western Wall, sometimes called the Wailing Wall, was long regarded as perhaps the most sacred site on earth to the Jewish people, it was sacred only because of its proximity to an even more sacred—but inaccessible—site: the Temple Mount itself.

A view of the Temple Mount

That the Temple site in Jerusalem was divinely selected makes it a sacred place. Many Jewish sages taught that once Solomon built his Temple on Mount Moriah in Jerusalem, it became the permanent and solely acceptable site for the future Temple.

In its day, the Temple was the hub of all spiritual activity. Twice each day the *cohanim* (priests) brought sacrifices to offer up on the altar of the Temple. Three times a year—on the festivals of Passover, Pentecost, and Tabernacles—Jews were enjoined to make pilgrimage to the Temple to be spiritually rejuvenated. The Sanhedrin was in permanent session in the Temple Court interpreting the law for all Israelites. From the Temple precincts many biblical prophets and even the Savior of the world taught the people, telling them of the blessings that awaited the obedient and the destruction that would be the lot of the wicked if they did not repent. Indeed, at certain times tens of thousands converged on the Temple Mount to worship there. All this came to an end with the destruction of the Second Temple and the subsequent dispersion of the House of Judah.

Nevertheless, the Jews of the Diaspora never abandoned hope for their eventual return from exile to participate in the reconstruction of Jerusalem and the Temple. This hope is visible in many aspects of Jewish life. To this day, certain prayers of observant Jews are formulated as a spiritual reenactment of the Temple sacrifices. The wording of many established prayers reflects the individual's longing for the restoration of the Temple.

Further manifestations of this desire for a Temple are seen at the so-called Wailing Wall, where many Jews gather to wail and bemoan the destruction of their Temple and pray for its imminent reconstruction. Jews throughout the world pray facing Jerusalem and the Temple. Parts of every synagogue are designated by the names of corresponding parts of the Temple. Even certain furnishings in a synagogue resemble those used in the Temple, such as the Holy Ark, or the receptacle of the Torah Scroll; the *Paroket,* or decorative cover that hangs over the Ark; the *Ner Tamid,* or perpetual light placed near the Ark; and the menorah, a replica of the seven-armed candlestick in the Temple.

Even small customs serve as reminders of the Temple's destruction, for example, leaving a small corner of the house unpainted, and a bride-groom's breaking a glass at a wedding as a gesture of mourning for the loss of the Temple.

Four days of Temple remembrance are observed each year, the most important being Tisha b'Av. On this day thousands of Jews converge on the Western Wall to mourn the destruction of the Temple and the ravages of the exile. It is a day of fasting in which the large crowds dressed in their Sabbath best approach the Wall—the more observant wear rubber, plastic, or wooden shoes instead of leather, as a sign of mourning. The devout hang close to the Wall weeping or silently praying, pressing little bits of folded paper with petitions to their Maker into the crevices of the Herodian-carved blocks of stone forming the Wall. On such occasions as this one sees the place of the Temple in the hearts of the Jewish people.

Against this background, one can imagine the emotion, even the euphoria, in 1967, that seized many Jews upon learning that the Temple Mount was once again in Jewish hands. The jubilation was soon dampened, however, by the announcement by the chief rabbinate that the Mount was out of bounds. This action was taken out of extreme veneration for the site and out of fear that one might inadvertently step on the very site of the Holy of Holies. Until such time as the chief rabbinate reconsiders their action in closing the Mount, there is little hope among

Jews for the reconstruction of the Temple, including the resumption of animal sacrifice.

JEWISH SCHOOLS OF THOUGHT
CONCERNING A FUTURE TEMPLE

Over the centuries the Jews have given a great deal of consideration to the matter of a Temple. Although there are many opinions and teachings on the matter, six schools of thought represent the better-known concepts.

The first school of thought, derived from a popular notion among religious Jews and followers of the Jewish sage Rashi, holds that God will send down a perfect "Temple of Fire" from heaven. This concept has grown out of the belief that the First and Second Temples were destroyed because they were man made and thus not eternal. This school holds that the Third Temple will be built by God himself and will endure forever.[1]

A second approach maintains that the Messiah will miraculously build the Temple at his coming. The matter of the Third Temple is out of mortal hands, and there is nothing mankind can do to hasten or delay the divine initiative. According to halakhah, the Temple will be built when the Messiah has come. It is therefore inconceivable that mankind should make any plans for the rebuilding of the Temple.[2]

A third school of thought also looks to a messiah to build the Temple, but in this case, it won't be a miraculous event. Maimonides wrote of a Messiah as a man who will prove himself by his competence in the Law and his devotion to it. Maimonides saw nothing miraculous in the Temple's construction but emphasized the inevitability of its construction by the Messiah at a time when the "dispersed of Israel" are being gathered home.

The fourth school of thought holds that a prophet of God will build the Temple. Its advocates maintain that Jewish law does not permit the rebuilding of the Temple or the resumption of sacrifices unless explicit prophetic requests are issued and obeyed. As for the actual construction of the much-yearned-for Third Temple, adequate floor plans and building dimensions for it and its altars and other contents are to be found in the Scriptures and Talmud. But digging the first spade of earth for the building must await approval of a bona fide prophet.[3] Former Chief

Rabbi Kook was of the opinion that arrangements pertaining to the building of the Temple and the Altar depend upon prophecy and divine inspiration.

The distinct minority who make up the fifth school urge reconstruction of the Temple and the resumption of sacrifices in the near future before the coming of the Messiah. This teaching is based, in part, on Rabbi Acha in the Jerusalem Talmud, who proved from the Mishnah that the Temple "will be built *before* the re-establishment of the Kingdom of David."[4] The followers of this school believe that a careful study of halakhic and historical materials will disclose how to achieve this monumental enterprise. Their call to resume animal sacrifice is based on the halakhic statement that "they may offer sacrifices although there is no Temple." Although the study of sacrifice is underway at Yeshivat Torat Hacohanim, for example, no animal sacrifice has yet been conducted.[5]

The sixth school of thought is a curious combination that calls for the construction of a Temple by mortals in order that the Almighty might encompass it with a celestial Temple of Fire. This approach seems to be an attempt to reconcile the two longstanding differences of opinion between the great Jewish sages Rambam and Rashi. Rambam believed that the Third Temple would be built by human hands, whereas Rashi took the view that it would be made of fire and come down miraculously from heaven. Both opinions can be justified on the basis of Talmudic and Midrashic sources.

CURRENT TEMPLE-RELATED ACTIVITIES IN JERUSALEM

A yeshiva (school) in Jerusalem called Ateret Cohanim concentrates on studies pertaining to Temple service and ritual to "enable their students to step in the moment a Temple is erected." The dean of the yeshiva, Matityahu Hacohen, maintained that "we are ready to begin building the Temple the minute we get the go-ahead from the Chief Rabbinate and the Israeli government." His enthusiasm was tempered by former Chief Rabbi Shlomo Goren, one of the country's foremost experts on the Temple and its religious meaning to Jews. Goren warned that "one of the greatest Jews who ever lived, King David, lost the privilege of building the First Temple simply because he did not enjoy the proper guidance by a prophet."[6] According to Goren, the Temple Mount to this day retains holiness because it has been sanctified "for eternity." Thus, when the Third Temple goes up, said Goren, it will have to be in the Old City of Jerusalem, just beyond the Western Wall and "nowhere else."[7]

Not only yeshivot but also individuals have been preparing for the Temple. One is Menahem Bar-Shalom, a Jerusalemite, who sells a twenty-eight-page pamphlet written in Hebrew that describes down to the last detail the Temple sacraments performed by the High Priest. Another is David Elbaum of Jerusalem, who for the last few years has been weaving at his own expense pure linen that will be needed to dress the priests of the Temple once it is built. According to scripture, the temple clothing can be made only from flax spun by hand into six-stranded threads. Elbaum's small workshop is one of several in Jerusalem where religious artisans make artifacts for the Temple, strictly following instructions they have interpreted from the scriptures and such traditional sources as the Mishnah and Talmud.[8]

Researchers have also been at work. Jewish groups have traced family lines to identify priests who could officiate in the Temple, and Rabbi Shlomo Goren believes he has located the exact site of the Holy of Holies. That is important to many Jews because it would allow them to visit the Temple Mount without desecrating the Temple by inadvertently walking over the actual site.

An organization called the Temple Institute has reconstructed thirty-eight ritual implements required for temple service. The Institute hopes to finish the remaining sixty-five items as funds become available.[9] Small shops, such as Beged Ivri, create clothing; Harrari Harps make musical instruments. The Institute spokesman, Zev Golan, said, "If we do not prepare and show God that we want a temple, then God won't give it to us." Accordingly, the Institute is using a computer to draw up blueprints for rebuilding the Temple.[10]

The objective of those physically preparing for a future Temple is to be ready when the time comes. Without exception, those preoccupied with studying or actually preparing for the Temple concede that they do not know when it will come about, but they all share a common goal: to be ready when the time does come.

LEGAL AND POLITICAL IMPLICATIONS OF A TEMPLE

Since the Six-Day War in 1967, when the Israelis extended their sovereignty to East Jerusalem and the Old City—and thus over the Temple Mount—there has arisen what one newspaper described as a messianic impulse, prompting various Jewish and Christian movements towards building a Third Temple. "This movement," says one reporter, is "gaining momentum."[11] Whatever this momentum might be, it has been frustrated by the refusal of successive Israeli governments to allow Jews to pray on the Temple Mount; a reluctance on the part of the courts to step into what they see as a political decision; a Muslim Waqf (council) determined to preserve the site as a Muslim holy place; and the edict of the chief rabbinate forbidding Jews to enter the Temple Mount.

On 21 March 1976, the Israeli High Court confirmed a 1968 decision[12] reiterated in 1970, in which a petition for Jews to be allowed to pray on the Temple Mount was denied. The court decided by majority vote that the matter was not justiciable because a Palestine Order in Council—which provided that "no matter in connection with the Holy Places shall be determined by any court"—was still in force. The courts also distinguished between the right of access to holy places, which is guaranteed by the Protection of Holy Places Law of 1967, and the right to worship at them. The latter right comes within the jurisdiction of the government and not the courts.

A five-judge panel of the High Court ruled in September 1970 that though Jews had the inherent right to pray on the Temple Mount, the government could refuse to permit such prayers if they might lead to disturbances of the peace. The sanctity of the Temple Mount to the Jewish people and the right of Jews to pray at the Mount have never been disputed by the courts. Nevertheless, the country's finest legal minds have dealt with the question four times since 1967. They have been unanimous in their decision that the road to implementing Jewish rights regarding the Temple Mount is long and full of pitfalls, and that because of the circumstances, the issue of Jewish rights to pray on the Temple Mount must be left to the executive arm of the state and not to the courts. The Israeli government has held that the Temple Mount is sacred to the Jews, but though it permits anyone to visit there, it refuses to allow Jews to pray on the site, primarily for political reasons.

On 30 January 1976, Ruth Or, a judge in the lowest court in Israel, ruled that the Jews had a right to pray on the Temple Mount. She argued that the government of Israel had no authority to deny Jews their inherent right to pray on Judaism's most sacred site. The judge asked the Minister of Religious Affairs to fix a time and place for Jews to engage in prayers on the Mount. This ruling caused a political furor among Muslims, some of whom rioted and demonstrated against the government of Israel and its policies in the occupied territories. Many Israelis were also alarmed by the ruling. Jerusalem's mayor, Teddy Kollek, was very critical of the government of Israel for failing to respond quickly to the magistrate court's decision. Mayor Kollek reiterated his belief that there was no question about Jewish sovereignty over "united Jerusalem" including the Temple Mount, but what was needed, he said, "was to strengthen this sovereignty with a large Jewish population which knew how to behave with tolerance and generosity and not with irresponsible action."[13]

The Jerusalem District Court overturned Magistrate Or's ruling. Noting that "the Jews have an unquestionable historical and legal right" to pray on the Temple Mount, the Court determined that these rights could not be exercised if they would lead to a breach of the peace. "Public order overrides the right to pray."[14] On 15 September 1981, the Israeli High Court ruled that the right of Jews to pray on the Temple Mount is a political issue, not a legal one, and it is incumbent upon the government to decide.[15]

ADMITTANCE TO THE TEMPLE MOUNT

Immediately following the Six-Day War and the rabbinical council's ban on anyone entering the Temple Mount, Israel's Sephardic Chief Rabbi Mordecai Eliahu said that as far as he was concerned, everyone— Jew and non-Jew alike—is forbidden to tread on the Temple Mount, but, he added, "I wouldn't throw non-Jews off it." His Ashkenazi counterpart, Chief Rabbi Avraham Shapiro, concurs that until the Messiah comes, ascent to the Holy Mount is forbidden.[16] Their position reflects an attitude dating from Maimonides, the great Jewish rabbi of the twelfth century. He maintained that because of uncertainty about the location of the Holy of Holies—entry to which was restricted to the high priest on Yom

Kippur—Jews should stay off the Mount altogether. The ban has been strongly upheld in recent generations by the rabbis of Jerusalem and is by far the dominant attitude today, but it has been challenged from time to time over the centuries, recently by former Chief Rabbi Shlomo Goren. He maintains publicly that there are places on the Temple Mount clearly outside the area occupied by the Temple and therefore open to Jews and Jewish prayer. Other rabbis have argued that no one is halakhically authorized to delineate where the Temple stood on Mount Moriah or to encourage Jews to tread anywhere in the area until the Messiah comes. Says one, "No Jew may trespass on the holy site; the punishment is 'karet' or the cutting off of a Jew from his people."[17]

For orthodox Jews, access to the Temple Mount can wait, but in principle, for them, the Jewish nation is incomplete without the Temple. Says Rabbi Shabtai Rappoport, head of the Shvut Yisrael Yeshiva, "it is the very foundation of the Jewish people's existence in Eretz Yisrael [the land of Israel]. It is the very backbone of our history."[18] Chaim Richman of the Temple Institute noted that "in terms of our mission as a people, we cannot in any way reach our spiritual status without the Temple."[19]

ARCHAEOLOGICAL PROBING

On 28 August 1981, an archaeological storm struck Jerusalem when it was discovered that workmen from the Ministry of Religious Affairs had penetrated under the Temple Mount. Muslim authorities had strongly warned of their opposition to any attempt by archaeologists to dig in the mount, and Israeli authorities had restricted such work. Whether responsible parties were aware of it or not, work had been going on unnoticed underground.

A tunnel had been dug over a ten-year period in an attempt to expose the entire length of the Western Wall of the mount. At one point, earth and stones were moved away from the Wall to expose an ancient, filled-in gate. In the vicinity of the gate, water was suddenly noticed leaking through from the Wall from inside the mount. At that point, Religious Affairs Minister Aharon Abuhatzeira gave permission to break through the sealed gate to deal with the problem. A large cistern was discovered on the other side.

Chief Rabbi Goren hurried to inspect the site and ordered the gate to be sealed again because of the area's sensitivity. In an Israeli Television program of 3 September 1981, Goren said, "The cistern was a tunnel from the Second Temple period that could lead to the treasures of the Temple including the Holy Ark." Tradition holds that the Ark of the Covenant was buried in a chamber under the Court of the Women.

Israeli archaeologist Yigael Yadin protested to the government over the "quasi archaeological activities of the Ministry of Religious Affairs." Yadin pointed out the political dangers of the Ministry's probing under the Temple Mount. He also objected to archaeological activities being undertaken by unqualified persons.[20] Yadin's political observations were soon borne out, as Jews and Arabs clashed with stones and fists in the area of the excavations. The Supreme Muslim Council called for a strike of all Arab shops and schools to protest excavations under the Haram esh-Sharif. The Muslim Waqf sealed their side of the wall at the underground cistern to prevent "Jewish penetration." Only the intervention of the police prevented even more serious incidents from taking place.

EFFORTS TO PREPARE FOR A TEMPLE

Since 1967, the pressure on successive governments to create a Jewish presence on the Temple Mount has been unrelenting—yet until recently, relatively unsuccessful. In 1981, when the Israeli government's settlement program began to accelerate, certain Jewish nationalist groups began concentrating their energies on the Temple Mount. According to the *Jerusalem Post,* in recent years a lobby supported by a wide range of the more conservative members of the Knesset has been set up to press for Jewish access to the Temple Mount. Supporters of the Temple Mount lobby have two extremely difficult obstacles to overcome: the government's firm decision not to change the status quo on the Temple Mount, and the orthodox ban against entering the Mount.

The secular authorities largely ignored the religious edict not to enter the Temple Mount. Defense Minister Moshe Dayan ordered security forces in 1967 to take control of the Mograbi Gate, a southwestern entrance to the Mount, to ensure free access to visitors, Jewish and non-Jewish alike. The only restriction was that such visits not take place during such hours as would interfere with Muslim prayers or holy days.

Nevertheless, these same authorities have consistently refused to permit Jews to pray on the Mount lest that provoke the Muslims.

An indication that perhaps the Temple Mount activists were achieving some of their goals was the decision by the Israeli High Court on 11 May 1983 to allow the Faithful of the Temple Mount to hold prayers at the Mograbi Gate on Jerusalem Day. Permission was later granted to Jews to pray at the gate on the Jewish holidays of Tisha b'Av and Yom Kippur as well.

Some Jewish activists have demonstrated that they would take the Temple Mount by force if given a chance. In 1984, an attempt to blow up the Dome of the Rock was foiled at the last minute when an Arab guard discovered men working their way towards the Dome of the Rock with more than forty pounds of explosives, after having scaled the outside wall of the Temple Mount with grappling hooks. Their purpose was "to purify the Temple Mount from Muslim possession in order to bring about the redemption of Israel and the establishment of the promised Kingdom of Israel."[21]

In 1989, activists from the Faithful of the Temple Mount announced plans to lay a three-ton "cornerstone of the Third Temple" near the Western Wall. This proposal was viewed by the Muslims as an aggressive act designed to ultimately deprive Islam of one of its most sacred sites. The Israeli authorities intervened in time to prevent a serious conflict from erupting.[22]

Despite the lobby and the activists, most secular Jews have little interest in a Third Temple. They feel Judaism has outgrown the need for such an edifice and, in any case, it is not clear to them how it would differ from a synagogue. What is clear to them is that the construction of a Temple on the site of the previous Temples would disturb the delicate status quo and would, in the process, incur the wrath of a billion Muslims worldwide. Hebrew University professor Rabbi Pesach Schindler remarked, "We have respect for the past, but it has no operational significance. With the establishment of the State of Israel, we have all our spiritual centers within us. That is where the temples should be built."[23]

MUSLIM FEARS OF JEWISH DESIGNS ON THE TEMPLE MOUNT

Muslims believe that an attempt by the Jews to pray on the Mount would represent the beginning of a Jewish takeover of sacred Muslim shrines. The head of the Supreme Muslim Council in Jerusalem, Sheikh Sa'ad e-Din el-Alami, was quoted as saying, "The Moslems will never permit any Jew to pray on Haram al-Sharif or any council to establish a synagogue in the area. The Moslems are prepared to die for this."[24]

Muslims are particularly nervous about activists, whether Jew or Christian, who speak openly about a Third Temple. In Muslim eyes there is no room for a Temple alongside the mosques, prompting Adnan Husseini, senior Waqf official in Jerusalem, to warn, "The mosques on the Temple Mount were built by the order of God.... Our sovereignty is not subject to compromise."[25]

CHRISTIAN INTERESTS IN A THIRD TEMPLE

Interest in a Third Temple seems to be growing among Christians as well. The Faithful of the Temple Mount have established a fund-raising organization called the Temple Foundation to work with Christian fundamentalists, primarily in America, that see in Israel the fulfillment of prophecy. Many of these Christian groups feel that Israel is moving toward a critical period in history, and they want to help the Jews fulfill prophecy and hasten the second coming of the Messiah. These Christians long to see the Temple rebuilt, so an organization was established to accept their funds. Although there is a clear divergence in theology, pro-Temple elements within Judaism and Christianity have found a common objective, and they are willingly, even enthusiastically, cooperating.

As Israeli nationalist objectives are mixed with Jewish religious aspirations—along with Christian political, financial, and moral support—some provocative combinations are brought to light. Added to all that is the Arab Muslim unwillingness to countenance even the slightest change in the status quo with regard to the Temple Mount. The whole concoction strongly suggests that the question of the Temple Mount and an eventual Third Temple is moving inexorably toward becoming the heart and substance of future conflict.

SUMMARY

A small but clearly identifiable minority among the more religious elements in Jewish society is actively working, studying, and preparing for a Third Temple in Jerusalem. There are also nationalist, nonreligious movements that seek to restore to the Jewish people possession and control of the Temple Mount. The objectives of the nationalist movements with regard to a Third Temple are difficult to determine. Perhaps because their immediate objectives are more political than religious and because they represent a broad cross-section of Israeli society, they have yet to formulate a clear position on the question of a future Temple.

Both the religious and the nationalist movements that concern themselves with the question of the Temple Mount desire to reestablish a Jewish presence there. Some are content simply to demand the right of Jews to pray on the Mount. Others press for the construction of a synagogue on the Mount in some noncontroversial corner where they are certain not to violate the sanctity of the site. No serious group is publicly calling for the construction of a Temple in the place of the present Dome of the Rock.

Although there is, beyond a doubt, a growing interest in a future Temple in Jerusalem, it would be an exaggeration to suggest that it is a movement that is politically powerful or nationally relevant. Most Israelis are simply not religious and have no opinion on the matter. Only when pressed do secular individuals express an opinion in favor of a future Temple, but even that guarded sentiment is based on the condition that the delicate status quo of the Temple Mount remain undisturbed.

NOTES

1. Goren, *Jerusalem Post*, 10.

2. In Comay, *Temple of Jerusalem*, 263.

3. Sittner, "Chores for Cohen," 5.

4. Goren, *Jerusalem Post*, 10; emphasis added.

5. Siegel-Itzkovich, "Temple Mount," 4.

6. Sittner, "Chores for Cohen," 5.

7. Sittner, "Chores for Cohen," 5.

8. Sittner, "Chores for Cohen," 5.

9. Ostling, "Time for a New Temple?" 64–65.

10. *Jerusalem Post,* 5 Nov. 1989, 19.

11. Rosenberg, "Target: Temple Mount," 1.

12. High Court, 99/76, 1976 and High Court, 222/68, 1968.

13. *Jerusalem Post,* 19 Mar. 1976.

14. "Chronology of Events," *Jerusalem Post,* 30 Sept. 1983, 8.

15. "Chronology of Events," *Jerusalem Post,* 30 Sept. 1983, 9.

16. Siegel-Itzkovich, "Temple Mount," 4.

17. *Jerusalem Post,* 13 Oct. 1977.

18. Kohn, "Speedily in Our Time?" 13.

19. Ice and Price, *Ready to Rebuild,* 85.

20. *Jerusalem Post,* 30 Aug. 1981.

21. *Jerusalem Post,* 5 June 1984.

22. *Jerusalem Post,* 11 Oct. 1989.

23. Ostling, "Time for a New Temple?" 65.

24. Shalev, "Rabbis to Press for Prayers on Mount," 1.

25. Ice and Price, *Ready to Rebuild,* 85.

28

The Meaning of Jerusalem

We have walked down the long corridors of time—forty centuries—and glanced at scenes, listened to conversations, and watched characters play out their brief parts in the grand drama that is Jerusalem. Certain stars appeared on the stage, displayed their momentary brilliance, and then faded. From one act to the next, some themes and motifs consistently recur. To a world heavy with history, Jerusalem has many meanings.

Jerusalem is not just a city but a symbol, a principle as well as a place. Throughout history she has stood for holiness, for ascendancy, for centrality. Jerusalem is the connection—the umbilical cord—between heaven and earth.

Jerusalem is not only the holy place; she is the holy of holies. Not only does she have a rock but she is the rock—the *Even ha-Shetiyyah*, the Stone of Foundation, the Foundation of Zion. The foundation for the Jew is a city; for the Muslim, a site; for the Christian, a Savior.

As there was a chosen people and a chosen doctrine, so there is a chosen place—a City and a House. The *Har ha-Bayit*, the "Mountain of the House," towered over Jerusalem, a place where the Lord could sanctify his people. Jerusalem means sanctuary: a Temple to the Most High God, to Jehovah. Later a temple to Jupiter, Minerva, and Juno was erected; later still, a shrine to Muhammad. Jerusalem is the Gate of Heaven.

Besides the Mountain of the House, there have been other holy places in the City where God chose to put his name. The Gihon Spring imparted the temporal waters of life to a thirsty populace; to the north, in the Temple on Moriah, he was worshipped who was the Living Water. Pools such as Siloam and Bethesda stored precious water as security in time of famine, but the Source of Living Water promised to be a fountain, not a stagnant pool, "springing up into everlasting life" (John 4:14). In a garden called Gethsemane, the consequences of transgression in a garden called Eden were overcome. The burden of human sin was paid for as justice met mercy. The Lord gave up his life at the "place of a skull," and a tomb was emptied when God raised his body into living immortality. From the Mount of Olives, the Savior ascended to heaven, leading the way; through him, his people could ascend to heaven also.

Jerusalem means sacrifice: a beloved son, countless animals, a Beloved Son, the wealth of a lifetime to make a pilgrimage, tens of thousands of lives to protect a sanctuary or penetrate a wall. Blood and life have rejoined their native clay for the cause of Jerusalem, for her inhabitants and her holy places.

Jerusalem means direction. For ages people have turned to the Holy City to pray. The supreme answers would not come from a city, however, but from God in heaven. Although most of historical Jerusalem does not exist today, it lives on in stories and traditions, in the word of man and the word of God. Great words from great people living in Jerusalem have been preserved in the world's greatest book; through his servants the word of the Lord has come forth from Jerusalem (see Isa. 2:3). Because of the Book of books, Jerusalem is sacred to millions of people who have never seen her. Jerusalem is a dream, and a memory.

Jerusalem, *Uru Shalem,* means city, or foundation, of peace. Peace is not a political condition but a manner of living. Jerusalemites always sought protection within walls, but walls could never keep out evil, destruction, and death. Their way of living was their ultimate protection. Only righteousness could assure them that their Holy City would remain invulnerable, invincible, and inviolable.

One whole city—the original Salem—established peace and was eventually taken up, lifted out of this world of war. Later, because of a righteous king, a righteous prophet, and enough righteous inhabitants, Jerusalem was protected from destruction at imperial hands by the intervention of God himself. And later still, a prophet's family was ushered out of the city to avoid destruction.

Though in name Jerusalem is the City of Peace, in reality she has been the city of war—the quintessential object of conquest. Her inhabitants usually desired peace, but outsiders wanted to fight. People fought fiercely to establish peace. Whereas the vision of Jerusalem is unity, history generally shows her wallowing in divisiveness and dissension.

Jerusalem has always meant glory. For the Jew, Jerusalem bespeaks David; for the Muslim, Muhammad; for the Christian, Jesus.

Jerusalem means patriarchs, prophets, priests, princes, praefects, procurators, pashas, presidents, and prime ministers—some leading in the ways of life, others in the ways of death. He who was Prophet, Priest, and King—the Anointed One—came to provide the Way, the Truth, and the Life. He came "that they might have life, and that they might have it more abundantly" (John 10:10).

Jerusalem means royalty. One of her earliest kings was titled "king of righteousness"; two millennia later, a long line of Davidic kings culminated in One whose kingdom was "not of this world" (John 18:36). He claimed to be *the* King of Righteousness and promised to return to Jerusalem again to reign in righteousness.

Jerusalem means finality—end of time, end of the world, final battle, final judgment, final resurrection. But Jerusalem also means anticipation, reinstatement, restoration, and redemption. Jerusalem is the power of reviving, the hope of regaining and retaining the City of God.

The ultimate meaning of Jerusalem is the doctrine of the ideal, the heavenly Jerusalem. Four thousand years ago Abraham "looked for a city which hath foundations, whose builder and maker is God" (Heb. 11:10). Abraham, Sarah, and their son "all died in faith, not having received the promises, but having seen them afar off, and were persuaded of them, and embraced them, and confessed that they were strangers and pilgrims on the earth. . . . But now they desire a better country, that is, an heavenly: wherefore God is not ashamed to be called their God: for he hath prepared for them a city" (Heb. 11:13, 16).

Abraham's descendants for generations have looked for the promised city, the City of God, and the ascendancy entailed by that heavenly objective. Latter-day Saints know that the earthly Jerusalem is transient. There is yet a terrestrial Jerusalem coming—in fact, two terrestrial Jerusalems, Old and New. Afterward, the celestial Jerusalem will be established: the abode of God Almighty, the Eternal City.

It is essential to know the past to understand the present, and it is essential to know the past and present to appreciate the future.

Jerusalem's past exudes consequence and relevance. Jerusalem's future, however, goes beyond the fascination and signification of the past; the future holds triumph and glory.

We turn now to a prophetic glimpse of future Jerusalems announced and anticipated. Latter-day Saints rely on the scriptures and on the words of modern-day prophets and apostles for information concerning the Old and the New Jerusalem (see also Appendix 6).

JERUSALEMS OF PROPHECY

Two separate cities are spoken of in the scriptures: Zion and Jerusalem. "The New Jerusalem to be built in Jackson County, Missouri, is also called the City of Zion or Zion. Dozens of revelations in the Doctrine and Covenants speak about this Zion. . . . Isaiah and others of the ancient prophets have much to say both about it and about the Jerusalem of old which shall be restored in grandeur and beauty in the last days. These two great cities, dual world capitals, are needed to fulfill the great millennial promise: 'Out of Zion shall go forth the law, and the word of the Lord from Jerusalem' (Isa. 2:3)."[1]

Old Jerusalem is to be rebuilt and inhabited by the seed of Judah; a new Temple will also be built. The Prophet Joseph Smith said, "Judah must return, Jerusalem must be rebuilt, and the temple and water come out from under the temple, and the waters of the Dead Sea be healed. It will take some time to rebuild the walls of the city and the temple, etc.; and all this must be done before the Son of Man will make his appearance."[2]

In a future day the nations of the world will gather to fight against the Jews at Jerusalem: "For I will gather all nations against Jerusalem to battle; and the city shall be taken, and the houses rifled, and the women ravished; and half of the city shall go forth into captivity, and the residue of the people shall not be cut off from the city. . . . Then shall the Lord go forth, and fight against those nations, as when he fought in the day of battle. . . . And Judah also shall fight at Jerusalem" (Zech. 14:2–5, 12, 14).

In that day two prophets or witnesses will prophesy in Jerusalem. "They are two prophets that are to be raised up to the Jewish nation in the last days, at the time of the restoration, and to prophesy to the Jews after they are gathered and have built the city of Jerusalem in the land of their fathers" (D&C 77:15). Following their ministry they will be killed, and a great earthquake will shake the Mount of Olives and Jerusalem. The Savior will then appear and rescue the righteous, and his own people will recognize him. The siege of Jerusalem will end the final war in this world. Then, "the Lord, whom ye seek, shall suddenly come to his temple" (Mal. 3:1).

Meanwhile, another Zion will flourish on the other side of the world. As the tenth Article of Faith states, "We believe in the literal gathering of Israel and in the restoration of the Ten Tribes; that Zion (the New Jerusalem) will be built upon the American continent; that Christ will reign personally upon the earth; and, that the earth will be renewed and receive its paradisiacal glory." Zion will be located at Independence, Missouri, in the United States of America, on the former site of the Garden of Eden.[3]

This New Jerusalem will be built up and inhabited by the seed of Joseph. "Hearken, O ye elders of my church, saith the Lord your God, who have assembled yourselves together, according to my commandments, in this land, which is the land of Missouri, which is the land which I have appointed and consecrated for the gathering of the saints. Wherefore, this is the land of promise, and the place for the city of Zion. . . . Behold, the place which is now called Independence is the center place; and a spot for the temple is lying westward, upon a lot which is not far from the court-house" (D&C 57:1–3). Establishing Zion, we are told, must be our greatest object.[4] Said Elder Marion G. Romney: "I hope we are all familiar with these words of the Lord [D&C 45] and with his predictions concerning other coming events, such as the building of the New Jerusalem and the redemption of the old, the return of Enoch's Zion, and Christ's millennial reign. . . . Not only do I hope that we are familiar with these coming events; I hope also that we keep the vision of them continually before our minds."[5]

A unique and extraordinary Temple will occupy the dedicated grounds of Zion, the New Jerusalem. The ten tribes and the city of Enoch will return. Land masses will become one as the earth returns to its paradisiacal condition, that is, as it obtains a terrestrial glory. After the Lord's millennial reign, the earth will be purified even further, this time to a celestial glory. John recorded in his great vision, "I saw no temple therein: for the Lord God Almighty and the Lamb are the temple of it. And the city had no need of the sun, neither of the moon, to shine in it: for the glory of God did lighten it, and the Lamb is the light thereof" (Rev. 21:22–23).

President Joseph Fielding Smith taught: "That temples and temple ordinances are essential to the Christian faith is well established in the Bible. Malachi predicted the coming of the Lord suddenly to his temple, in the day of vengeance, in the latter times, as a refiner and purifier. . . . John the Revelator saw the day when, after the earth is sanctified and celestialized, the presence of the Father and the Son in the New Jerusalem would take the place of the temple, for the whole city, due to their presence, would become a temple."[6]

Elder Bruce R. McConkie further explained: "John the Revelator saw in vision the holy city come down from God in Heaven twice. First he saw the City of Enoch, a Holy City called New Jerusalem, come down after the Second Coming to remain with men on earth a thousand years. Then with seeric eyes he beheld the celestial Jerusalem, the Holy City where God and angels dwell, come down from heaven to be with men forever in that day when this earth becomes a celestial sphere."[7]

There are, therefore, actually *four* Jerusalems—or at least four stages of the two Jerusalems: one in the past and three in the future: (1) Old Jerusalem in the Holy Land, (2) Zion, the New Jerusalem, built by the Saints in Independence, Missouri, joined by (3) Zion, the New Jerusalem, Enoch's city, coming down from heaven, and finally, (4) the celestial City of Jerusalem, the Eternal City of God.

Notes

1. McConkie, *Mormon Doctrine*, 855.

2. Smith, *History of the Church*, 5:337.

3. See quotations and references in Appendix 6.

4. Smith, *Teachings of the Prophet Joseph Smith*, 160.

5. Romney, in Conference Report, Oct. 1966, 52.

6. Smith, *Doctrines of Salvation*, 2:244.

7. McConkie, *New Witness*, 588. For a more detailed collection of quotations from the prophets concerning the future Jerusalems, see Appendix 6.

APPENDIX 1

Josephus' Description of Jerusalem

1. The city of Jerusalem was fortified with three walls, on such parts as were not encompassed with unpassable valleys; for in such places it had but one wall. The city was built upon two hills which are opposite to one another, and have a valley to divide them asunder; at which valley the corresponding rows of houses on both hills end. Of these hills, that which contains the upper city is much higher, and in length more direct. Accordingly, it was called the "Citadel," by king David; he was the father of that Solomon who built this temple at the first; but it is by us called the "Upper Marketplace." But the other hill, which was called "Acra," and sustains the lower city, is of the shape of a moon when she is horned; over-against this was a third hill, but naturally lower than Acra, and parted formerly from the other by a broad valley. However, in those times when the Asamoneans reigned, they filled up that valley with earth, and had a mind to join the city to the temple. They then took off part of the height of Acra, and reduced it to be of less elevation than it was before, that the temple might be superior to it. Now the Valley of the Cheesemongers, as it was called, and was that which we told you before, distinguished the hill of the upper city from that of the lower, extended as far as Siloam; for that is the name of a fountain which hath sweet waters in it, and this in great plenty also. But on the outsides, these hills are surrounded by deep valleys, and by reason of the precipices to them belonging on both sides, they are everywhere unpassable.

2. Now, of these three walls, the old one was hard to be taken, both by reason of the valleys, and of that hill on which it was built, and which was above them. But besides that great advantage, as to the place where they were situated, it was also built very strong; because David and Solomon, and the following kings, were very zealous about this work. Now that wall began on the north, at the tower called "Hippicus," and

extended as far as the "Xistus," a place so called, and then joining at the council-house, ended at the west cloister of the temple. But if we go the other way westward, it began at the same place, and extended through a place called "Bethso," to the gate of the Essens; and after that it went southward, having its bending above the fountain Siloam, where it also bends again towards the east at Solomon's pool, and reaches as far as a certain place which they called "Ophlas," where it was joined to the eastern cloister of the temple. The second wall took its beginning from that gate which they called "Gennath," which belonged to the first wall; it only encompassed the northern quarter of the city, and reached as far as the tower Antonia. The beginning of the third wall was at the tower Hippicus, whence it reached as far as the north quarter of the city, and the tower Psephinus, and then was so far extended till it came over against the monuments of Helena, which Helena was queen of Adiabene, the daughter of Izates; it then extended further to a great length, and passed by the sepulchral caverns of the kings, and bent again at the tower of the corner, at the monument which is called the "Monument of the Fuller," and joined to the old wall at the valley called the "Valley of Cedron." It was Agrippa who encompassed the parts added to the old city with this wall, which had been all naked before; for as the city grew more populous, it gradually crept beyond its old limits, and those parts of it that stood northward of the temple, and joined that hill to the city, made it considerably larger, and occasioned that hill, which is in number the fourth, and is called "Bezetha," to be inhabited also. It lies over against the tower Antonia, but is divided from it by a deep valley, which was dug on purpose, and that in order to hinder the foundations of the tower of Antonia from joining to this hill, and thereby affording an opportunity for getting to it with ease, and hindering the security that arose from its superior elevation; for which reason also that depth of the ditch made the elevation of the towers more remarkable. This new-built part of the city was called "Bezetha" in our language, which, if interpreted in the Grecian language, may be called the "New City." Since, therefore, its inhabitants stood in need of a covering, the father of the present king, and of the same name with him, Agrippa, began that wall we spoke of; but he left off building it when he had only laid the foundation, out of the fear he was in of Claudius Caesar, lest he should suspect that so strong a wall was built in order to make some innovation in public affairs; for the city could no way have been taken if that wall had been finished in the manner it was begun; as its parts were connected together by stones twenty cubits long, and ten cubits broad, which could never have been easily undermined by any iron tools, or shaken by any engines. The wall was, however, ten cubits wide, and it would probably have had a height greater than that, had not his zeal who began it been hindered from exerting itself. After this it was erected with great diligence by the Jews, as high as twenty cubits, above which it had battlements of two cubits, and turrets of three cubits altitude, insomuch that the entire altitude extended as far as twenty-five cubits.

3. Now the towers that were upon it were twenty cubits in breadth and twenty cubits in height; they were square and solid, as was the wall itself, wherein the niceness of the joints and the beauty of the stones were no way inferior to those of the holy house itself. Above this solid altitude of the towers, which was twenty cubits, there were rooms of great magnificence, and over them upper rooms, and cisterns to receive rainwater. They were many in number, and the steps by which you ascended up to them were every one broad; of these towers then the third wall had ninety, and the spaces between them were each two hundred cubits; but in the middle wall were forty towers, and the old wall was parted into sixty, while the whole compass of the city was thirty-three furlongs. Now the third wall was all of it wonderful; yet was the tower Psephinus elevated above it at the northwest corner, and there Titus pitched his own tent; for being seventy cubits high, it both afforded a prospect of Arabia at sun-rising, as well as it did of the utmost limits of the Hebrew possessions at the sea westward. Moreover, it was an octagon, and over against it was the tower Hippicus; and hard by two others were erected by king Herod, in the old wall. These were for largeness, beauty, and strength, beyond all that were in the habitable earth: for besides the magnanimity of his nature, and his munificence towards the city on other occasions, he built these after such an extraordinary manner, to gratify his own private affections, and dedicated these towers to the memory of those three persons who had been the dearest to him, and from whom he named them. They were his brother, his friend, and his wife. This wife he had slain out of his love [and jealousy,] as we have already related; the other two he lost in war, as they were courageously fighting. Hippicus, so named from his friend, was square; its length and breadth each

twenty-five cubits, and its height thirty, and it had no vacuity in it. Over this solid building, which was composed of great stones united together, there was a reservoir twenty cubits deep, over which there was a house of two stories, whose height was twenty-five cubits, and divided into several parts; over which were battlements of two cubits, and turrets all around of three cubits high, insomuch that the entire height added together amounted to fourscore cubits. The second tower which he named from his brother Phasaelus, had its breadth and its height equal, each of them forty cubits; over which a cloister went round about, whose height was ten cubits, and it was covered from enemies by breast-works and bulwarks. There was also built over that cloister another tower, parted into magnificent rooms and a place for bathing; so that this tower wanted nothing that might make it appear to be a royal palace. It was also adorned with battlements and turrets, more than was the foregoing, and the entire altitude was about ninety cubits; the appearance of it resembled the tower of Pharus, which exhibited a fire to such as sailed to Alexandria, but was much larger than it in compass. This was now converted to a house, wherein Simon exercised his tyrannical authority. The third tower was Mariamne, for that was his queen's name; it was solid as high as twenty cubits; its breadth and its length were twenty cubits, and were equal to each other; its upper buildings were more magnificent, and had greater variety than the other towers had; for the king thought it most proper for him to adorn that which was denominated from his wife, better than those denominated from men, as those were built stronger than this that bore his wife's name. The entire height of this tower was fifty cubits.

4. Now as these towers were so very tall, they appeared much taller by the place on which they stood; for that very old wall wherein they were was built on a high hill, and was itself a kind of elevation that was still thirty cubits taller; over which were the towers situated, and thereby were made much higher to appearance. The largeness also of the stones was wonderful, for they were not made of common small stones, nor of such large ones only as men could carry, but they were of white marble, cut out of the rock; each stone was twenty cubits in length, and ten in breadth, and five in depth. They were so exactly united to one another, that each tower looked like one entire rock of stone, so growing naturally, and afterwards cut by the hands of the artificers into present shape and

corners; so little or not at all, did their joints or connexion appear. Now as these towers were themselves on the north side of the wall, the king had a palace inwardly thereto adjoined, which exceeds all my ability to describe it; for it was so very curious as to want no cost or skill in its construction, but was entirely walled about to the height of thirty cubits, and was adorned with towers at equal distances, and with large bed-chambers, that would contain beds for a hundred guests a-piece, in which the variety of the stones is not to be expressed; for a large quantity of those that were rare of that kind was collected together. Their roofs were also wonderful, both for the length of the beams and the splendour of their ornaments. The number of the rooms was also very great, and the variety of the figures that were about them was prodigious; their furniture was complete, and the greatest part of the vessels that were put in them was of silver and gold. There were besides many porticoes, one beyond another, round about, and in each of those porticoes curious pillars; yet were all the courts that were exposed to the air everywhere green. There were moreover several groves of trees, and long walks through them, with deep canals, and cisterns, that in several parts were filled with brazen statues, through which the water ran out. There were withal many dove-courts of tame pigeons about the canals; but, indeed, it is not possible to give a complete description of these palaces; and the very remembrance of them is a torment to one, as putting one in mind what vastly rich buildings that fire which was kindled by the robbers hath consumed; for these were not burnt by the Romans, but by these internal plotters, as we have already related, in the beginning of their rebellion. That fire began at the tower of Antonia, and went on to the palaces, and consumed the upper parts of the three towers themselves. (*Wars* 5.4. 1–4.)

STATEMENTS BY LDS CHURCH LEADERS ABOUT SITES IN JERUSALEM

BETHANY

Lorenzo Snow (1873)

Mounting our horses, we soon reached Bethany, situated about two miles from Jerusalem. Its location is pleasant and romantic, being built on the eastern slope of Mount Olivet . . . a place of sacred interest. Here dwelt the sisters, Mary and Martha, with Lazarus their brother. Here Christ raised Lazarus from the tomb and presented him alive to his weeping sisters. The tomb of Lazarus . . . is a deep vault, partly excavated to rock, and partly lined with masonry. We stopped our horses at the front of the entrance. This opens on a winding staircase leading to a small chamber, whence a few steps more lead to a small vault in which the body is said to have been placed. *(Correspondence of Palestine Tourists, 240–41)*

Harold B. Lee (1958)

For three miles out of the walled city of Jerusalem we traversed the road with the Master . . . [to Bethany, the home of Martha, Mary, and Lazarus] where he found more congenial company than within the gates of Jerusalem among many of the self-sufficient of the Jews. Only a block away from the homesite of Martha and Mary is the rock-built tomb of Lazarus. As we stood there at the mouth, we remembered the drama that took place as he declared just prior to the raising of Lazarus, the significance of his great mission. . . .

In our mind's eye we fancied we had witnessed the miracle of raising Lazarus as He peered into the mouth of that tomb on the whited figure of Lazarus who had been buried for several days and he said in a commanding voice, "Lazarus come forth." ("I Walked Today Where Jesus Walked," 6–7)

THE MOUNT OF OLIVES

Lorenzo Snow (1873)

Off to our left, that lofty eminence, with an aspect so barren, is the Mount of Olives, once the favorite resort of our Saviour, and the spot last pressed by His sacred feet before He ascended into the presence of His Father. (*Correspondence of Palestine Tourists*, 240–41)

Spencer W. Kimball (1961)

We stand upon Mt. Olivet, the mile-long mountain above Jerusalem. It is a long, rugged way to its top, but the Lord must have climbed it numerous times. . . .

We climb this lofty Mount of Olives to its rounded top and stand on sacred ground. Here Christ's earthly ministry was completed; here the apostles gathered about him, saw the overshadowing cloud receive him out of their sight, and breathless, stood in awe and wonder as the angels said, "Ye men of Galilee, why stand ye gazing up into heaven?" ("Unforgettable Holy Land," 425)

Hugh B. Brown (1971)

The Mount of Olives was made famous and sacred by the frequent visits of the Christ; and when he comes again, this mount will be cleft in twain as he descends. (In Conference Report, Oct. 1971, 174)

Spencer W. Kimball (1979)

My heart leaps and then is subdued as I think of some of the momentous events that have occurred on this historical mount. . . .

In New Testament times, Jesus Christ traversed this mount on several occasions while traveling between Jerusalem and Bethany. . . .

On this mount the Savior gave some of the greatest teachings ever recorded in holy writ. (*Deseret News*, 3 Nov. 1979, Church Section, 3)

THE TEMPLE MOUNT

Mount Moriah is the site of the First and the Second Temples.

Lorenzo Snow (1873)

I ascended this mountain [the Mount of Olives], and obtained a favorable position upon the highest point on its summit, spent a happy hour surveying the "Holy City." . . . Through the olive trees . . . could be discerned . . . the Mosque of Omar [Dome of the Rock], with its magnificent dome in the centre, occupying the site of Araunah's threshing floor, and Solomon's temple. (Smith, *Biography and Family Record of Lorenzo Snow*, 543)

David O. McKay (1921)

We had now reached Mt. Moriah and were standing on the site of the outer court of Solomon's temple. The altar of sacrifice was supposed to be on the spot where Abraham was ready to offer Isaac. . . . We left the Mosque of Omar [Dome of the Rock], which stands on the old temple site. (*Cherished Experiences*, 124–25)

Spencer W. Kimball (1979)

Before us, across the Kidron Valley, is the famed Mount Moriah, the traditional place where Father Abraham went to offer his son as a sacrifice and the location of the temples of Solomon and Herod. (*Deseret News*, 3 Nov. 1979, Church Section, 3)

THE GARDEN OF GETHSEMANE

Lorenzo Snow (1873)

We visited the reputed Garden of Gethsemane which belongs to the Latin Church. An opposition one has recently been established by the Greek Church. As soon as the trees have sufficiently grown, and other fixtures remained long enough to impart an ancient and venerable appearance, it will then be exhibited to devout pilgrims as the real genuine Garden of Gethsemane. (*Correspondence of Palestine Tourists*, 252)

David O. McKay (1921)

We visited the Garden of Gethsemane, now the property of Franciscan Fathers. As at every other sacred spot in Jerusalem there are too many modern things around here to realize at first that this is the garden to which Jesus and his disciples repaired so frequently for prayer. (*Cherished Experiences,* 120)

Harold B. Lee (1958)

We walked on the sacred ground in these places and again in Gethsemane. As the sweet singer has put it: "I walked today where Jesus walked, and felt His presence there."

I, too, in company with my lovely companion, walked where Jesus walked, and we felt him close to us.

Here in the Garden of Gethsemane, one of the deeply spiritual places, there are eight old gnarled olive trees showing the evidences of great antiquity, which could have been some sprouts from trees that could have been there hundreds of years ago. It was here where He knelt, in the vicinity of the very spot where we were standing. ("I Walked Today Where Jesus Walked," 7–8)

Spencer W. Kimball (1961)

At the foot of this mount [of Olives] is Gethsemane where his sufferings were beyond all mortal comprehension. ("Unforgettable Holy Land," 425)

Hugh B. Brown (1971)

It was a glorious trip, and upon returning to Jerusalem we took it upon ourselves to go again into the Garden of Gethsemane. Here it was that Jesus suffered his greatest anguish. Here it was that he sweat drops of blood . . . as he knelt there in the garden alone. (In Conference Report, Oct. 1971, 174–75)

Gordon B. Hinckley (1972)

Reverently, we visited the Garden of Gethsemane and looked upon an olive tree, gnarled and shaggy, which botanists say is probably 3,000 years old. If this be so, it was witness to the Savior's agony. . . .

There we read together the account of the sorrowful events which occurred here. It was a time for meditation and sober thought. (*Deseret News,* 16 Dec. 1972, Church Section, 5, 12)

Bruce R. McConkie (1985)

Two thousand years ago, outside Jerusalem's walls, there was a pleasant garden spot, Gethsemane by name, where Jesus and his intimate friends were wont to retire for pondering and prayer. . . .

This sacred spot . . . is where the Sinless Son of the Everlasting Father took upon himself the sins of all men on condition of repentance.

We do not know, we cannot tell, no mortal mind can conceive, the full import of what Christ did in Gethsemane. . . .

As near as we can judge these infinite agonies—this suffering beyond compare—continued for some three or four hours. ("Purifying Power of Gethsemane," 9)

GOLGOTHA

Golgotha, or Calvary, is also called "the Place of a Skull."

Spencer W. Kimball (1961)

Beyond [the Temple Mount] is Golgotha, the place of the skull, the hill of crucifixion. There he suffered and bled and died. ("Unforgettable Holy Land," 425)

Hugh B. Brown (1971)

We went up through the Via Dolorosa Road, where he carried his cross up to Golgotha. We are told of that struggle. While there is a great deal of disputation and disagreement as to just where this event happened, something seems to be quite sure, and that is, that he was crucified on this Hill of Skulls, as it is called. (In Conference Report, Oct. 1971, 175)

Bruce R. McConkie (1985)

Finally, on a hill called Calvary—again it was outside Jerusalem's walls . . . the Roman soldiers laid him upon the cross.

With great mallets they drove spikes of iron through his feet and hands and wrists. . . .

Then the cross was raised that all might see and gape and curse and deride. This they did, with evil venom, for three hours from 9 A.M. to noon. . . . There was a mighty storm, as though the very God of Nature was in agony.

And truly he was, for while he was hanging on the cross for another three hours, from noon to 3 P.M. all the infinite agonies and merciless pains of Gethsemane recurred. ("Purifying Power of Gethsemane," 10)

CHURCH OF THE HOLY SEPULCHRE

David O. McKay (1921)

[We] made our way to the Church of the Holy Sepulchre. Here gold in great profusion, diamonds, and other precious stones adorn the sacred spot and pictures of Christ and Mary, to the value of millions of dollars. . . . We came out from this church sensing the significance of the following expressions by Count Eberhardt of Wurttemberg: "There are three acts in a man's life which no one ought either to advise another to do or not to do. The first is to contract matrimony, the second is to go to the wars, the third is to visit the Holy Sepulchre. I say that these three acts are good in themselves, but they may easily turn out ill; and when this is so, he who gave the advice comes to be blamed as if he were the cause of its turning out ill." (*Cherished Experiences,* 125)

Harold B. Lee (1958)

We followed the way of the cross supposedly to the place of crucifixion and the place of the holy sepulchre. But all of this, according to tradition, we felt, is in the wrong place. We felt none of the spiritual significance which we had felt at other places. ("I Walked Today Where Jesus Walked," 8)

THE GARDEN TOMB

Harold B. Lee (1958)

There was yet another place we had to visit and feel ourselves on holy ground. It was called the Garden Tomb. It is owned by the Church of the United Brethren. Here our guide took us . . . and as the woman guide with her little son led us through the garden there was the hill outside the "gate" of the walled city of Jerusalem. It was just a short way from where the hall of judgment had been inside the city walls. The garden was right close by or "in the hill" as John had said, and in it was a sepulchre hewn out of a rock evidently done by someone who could afford the expense of excellent workmanship. There was something that seemed to impress us as we stood there that this was the holiest place of all, and we fancied we could have witnessed the dramatic scene which took place there. That tomb has a mouth which could be sealed by a rolling stone and there is the stone track they built to guide the stone as it was rolled across the mouth of the tomb. The stone has now been removed but the stone track is still there. ("I Walked Today Where Jesus Walked," 9)

Harold B. Lee (1970)

My wife and I were in the Holy Land. We have spent some glorious days visiting those places. . . .

But a strange thing happened after we had gone to the garden tomb, and there we felt it was definitely the place. It was in the hill, it was a garden, and here was a tomb. . . . But the strange thing was that when we moved it seemed as though we had seen all this before. We had seen it before somewhere. ("Qualities of Leadership," 7)

Harold B. Lee (1971)

The most thrilling of all places where we knew, was out at the garden tomb. Here according to the description of John, there was a hill and into the hill was a garden, and in the garden was a cave in which never had man laid. Here they hurriedly buried Jesus because the preparation of the Jews was nigh at hand. That is how John described it. And as the Apostle Paul explained, they didn't bury him inside the walls but outside the walls. And when they took us up the road to the Church of the Holy Sepulchre, it didn't have any meaning at all, and we even wondered what in the world this place was. But, out there as we stood at that spot—the most sacred spot on earth, for here was the way by which the resurrected Lord had opened the doors of resurrection and was going shortly to open the doors of salvation to those who were in the spirit world—with all our souls we knew. (Fireside address, 10)

Gordon B. Hinckley (1972)

Moonlight filtered through the olive trees. We stood, as we believe, at the place where the body of the Lord was laid in a new tomb hewn from rock.

It was easy to believe that this was indeed the place, and that it was here that the tomb was emptied that first Easter morning, and the stone was rolled away. We felt that we were standing where the risen Lord had talked with Mary.

Here, where occurred the greatest event in human history, we sang hymns of praise, and bore testimony to one another and organized the Jerusalem branch of The Church of Jesus Christ of Latter-day Saints with Elder Galbraith as president. (*Deseret News,* 3 Nov. 1979, Church Section, 12)

Spencer W. Kimball (1979)

We accept this as the burial place of the Savior. We realize people have different ideas about these places, but this seems to be the logical place.

I feel quite sure that this is the place where His body was laid. It gives me such a sacred feeling just to be here.

I've preached quite a few sermons about this spot. (*Deseret News,* 3 Nov. 1979, Church Section, 5)

THE TRAVELS AND MINISTRY OF ORSON HYDE

Elder Orson Hyde wrote an account of his travels in the Holy Land in a letter to his fellow members of the Quorum of the Twelve Apostles.

Trieste, January 1, 1842
Dear Brethren of the Twelve,

As a member . . . of your honorable quorum, bearing, in common with you, the responsibility under which HEAVEN has laid us, to spread the word of life among the perishing nations of the earth, allow me to say, that, on the 21st of October last, "my natural eyes, for the first time beheld" Jerusalem; and as I gazed upon it and its environs, the mountains and hills by which it is surrounded, and considered, that this is the stage upon which so many scenes of wonders have been acted, where prophets were stoned, and the Saviour of sinners slain, a storm of commingled emotions suddenly arose in my breast, the force of which was only spent in a profuse shower of tears. . . .

Jerusalem at this time contains about twenty thousand inhabitants; about seven thousand are Jews, and the remainder mostly Turks and Arabs. It is enclosed by a strong wall from five to ten feet thick. On those sides which are most accessible, and consequently most exposed to attack, the wall is thickest, and well mounted with cannon; it is from twelve to thirty feet in height. The city is situated at the south-eastern extremity of an inclined plane, with the valley of Kedron on the east, and the vallies of Hinnom and Gihon on the south and west, all converging to a point in the valley of Jehosaphat, south-east of the city: from the eastern gate of the city to the top of Mount Olivet, as you pass through the valley of Kedron, is just about one English mile. On the top of this mount you have a fair view of the Dead Sea and river Jordan, which are about fifteen miles in the distance. As I stood upon this almost sacred spot and gazed upon the surrounding scenery, and contemplated the history of the past in connection with the prophetic future, I was lost in wonder and admiration, and felt almost ready to ask myself—Is it a reality that I am here gazing upon this scene of wonders? or am I carried away in the fanciful reveries of a night vision? Is that city which I now look down upon really Jerusalem, whose sins and iniquity swelled the Saviour's heart with grief, and drew so many tears from his pitying eye? Is that small enclosure in the valley of Kedron, where the boughs of those lonely olives are waving their green foliage so gracefully in the soft and gentle breeze, really the garden of Gethsemane, where powers infernal poured the flood of hells dark gloom around the princely head of the immortal Redeemer? Oh, yes! The fact that I entered the garden and plucked a branch from an olive, and now have that branch to look upon, demonstrates that all was real. There, there is the place where the Son of the Virgin bore our sins and carried our sorrows—there the angels gazed and shuddered at the sight, waiting for the order to fly to his rescue; but no such order was given. The decree had passed in heaven, and could not be revoked, that he must suffer, that he must bleed, and that he must die. What bosom so cold, what feelings so languid, or what heart so unmoved that can withhold the humble tribute of a tear over this forlorn condition of the Man of sorrows?

From this place I went to the tombs of the prophets in the valley of Jehosaphat, and on my way around the city, I entered the pool of Siloam and freely washed in its soft and healing fountain. I found plenty of water there for baptizing, besides a surplus quantity sent off in a limpid stream as a grateful tribute to the thirsty plants of the gardens in the valley. The pool of Bethsada, which had five porches, yet remains in the city, but in a dilapidated state, there being plenty of water to meet the demands of the city of a better quality, and more convenient this vast reservoir is consequently neglected. This pool was unquestionably as free and accessible to all the people of Jerusalem as the Thames is to the Cockneys, or the Mississippi to the people of Nauvoo; and from its vast dimensions, it would certainly contain water enough to immerse all Jerusalem in, in a day: so the argument against immersion, on the ground that there was not water enough in Jerusalem to immerse three thousand persons in, in one day, is founded in an over anxiety to establish the traditions of men to the subversion of a gospel ordinance; and it will be borne in mind also, that the day of Pentecost was in the month of May, just at the close of the rainy season, when all the pools and fountains in and about the city were flush with water.

What were anciently called Mount Zion and Mount Calvary, are both within the present walls of the city. We should not call them mountains in America, or hardly hills; but gentle elevations or rises of land. The area of what was called Mount Zion, I should not think contained more than one acre of ground; at least as I stood upon it and contemplated what the prophets had said of Zion in the last days, and what should be done in her, I could no more bring my mind to believe that the magnet of truth in them which guided their words, pointed to this place, any more than I could believe that a camel can go through the eye of a needle, or a rich man enter into the kingdom of God. But on the land of Joseph, far in the west, where the spread eagle of America floats in the breeze and shadows the land; where those broad rivers and streams roll the waters of the western world to the fathomless abyss of the ocean: where those wide-spreading prairies (fields of the wood) and extensive forests adorn the land with such an agreeable variety, shall Zion rear her stately temples and stretch forth the curtains of her habitation. The record of Mormon chimes in so beautifully with the scriptures to establish this position, that an honest and faithful examination of the subject is all that is required to expel every doubt from the heart.

The customs and manners of the people of the east are so similar to what they were in the days of our Saviour, that almost everything which the traveller beholds is a standing illustration of some portion of scripture: for example, I saw two women grinding wheat at a little hand mill, consisting of two small stones with a little rude tackling about it, the whole of which one man might take in his arms and carry almost any where at pleasure. One would turn the top stone until her strength was exhausted, and then the other would take her place, and so alternately keep the little grinder in operation. It appears that our Lord foresaw the perpetuity of this custom, even to the time of his second coming; for he said, "Two women shall be grinding at the mill; one shall be taken and the other left"; and for ought I know, these two I saw were the identical ones. I also saw the people take a kind of coarse grass and mix it with some kind of earth or peat that had been wet and reduced to the consistency of common mortar, and then lay it out in flattened cakes to dry for fuel. I then, for the first time in my life, saw the propriety of our Saviour's allusion. "If God so clothe the grass of the field, which to-day is, and to-morrow is cast into the oven, &c." I might swell this letter to a volume upon these subjects, but I forbear for the present. One may read of the customs of the east, but it is not like seeing them. To read of a good dinner may brighten up a man's ideas about eating, especially if he be a little hungry; but to sit down at the luxurious board and eat is far more satisfactory. The two cases are not exactly parallel, yet the latter serves to illustrate the former.

As I walked about the environs of the town, my spirit struggled within me in earnest prayer to the God of Abraham, Isaac, and Jacob, that he would not only revolutionize this country, but renovate and make it glorious. My heart would lavish its blessings upon it in the greatest prodigality in view of what is to come hereafter. After returning to the city, I found my feet and legs completely coated with dust; for the whole face of the country was like an ash bed in consequence of the great length of the dry season. I then thought how very convenient it must have been for the ancient disciples to fulfil one injunction of the Saviour, "shake off the dust of your feet."

Syria at present is in a very unsettled state. The Drewzes and Catholics are fighting almost constantly. They sometimes kill hundreds and hundreds of a day. In some sections it is not unfrequent that the traveller meets some dozen or twenty men by the way side without heads, in a day. In a letter from Bavaria, I stated that hostilities had re-commenced between the Turks and Egyptians; I took the statement from a German paper, but it was a mistake. The hostilities were between the lesser tribes in Syria. The American missionaries at Beyrout and Mount Lebanon have received official notice through Commodore Porter, our minister to Constantinople, from the Grand Sultan, that hereafter they can have no redress by law for any violence, outrage, or cruelty, that may be practiced upon them by the people; and advises them to leave the country. This course is approved of by Commodore Porter. I read the correspondence between him and Mr. Chassan, our consul at Beyrout; but all is going on in the Providence of God. Syria and Palestine must ferment and ferment, work and work, until they work into the hands of Abraham's children to whom they rightly belong; and may the God of their fathers bless the hand that aids their cause. (*Times and Seasons* 3 [15 July 1842]: 847, 850–53)

Orson Hyde's Prayer of Dedication

Elder Orson Hyde's prayer of dedication was given on the Mount of Olives in Jerusalem in 1841. He included the text of it in a letter he wrote to the Prophet Joseph Smith.

I have only time to say that I have seen Jerusalem precisely according to the vision which I had. I saw no one with me in the vision; and although Elder Page was appointed to accompany me there, yet I found myself there alone.

The Lord knows that I have had a hard time, and suffered much, but I have great reason to thank Him that I enjoy good health at present, and have a prospect before me of soon going to a civilized country, where I shall see no more turbans or camels. The heat is most oppressive, and has been all through Syria.

I have not time to tell you how many days I have been at sea, without food, or how many snails I have eaten; but if I had had plenty of them, I should have done very well. All this is contained in a former letter to you written from Jaffa.

I have been at Cairo, on the Nile, because I could not get a passage direct. Syria is in a dreadful state—a war of extermination is going on between the Druses and Catholics. At the time I was at Beyroot, a battle was fought in the mountains of Lebanon, near that place, and about 800 killed. Robberies, thefts and murders are daily being committed. It is no uncommon thing to find persons in the streets without heads. An English officer, in going from St. Jean D'Acre to Beyroot, found ten persons murdered in the street, and was himself taken prisoner, but was rescued by the timely interference of the pasha. The particulars of all these things are contained in a former letter. . . .

On Sunday morning, October 24, a good while before day, I arose from sleep, and went out of the city as soon as the gates were opened, crossed the brook Kedron, and went upon the Mount of Olives, and there, in solemn silence, with pen, ink, and paper, just as I saw in the vision, offered up the following prayer to Him who lives forever and ever—

"O Thou! who art from everlasting to everlasting, eternally and unchangeably the same, even the God who rules in the heavens above, and controls the destinies of men on the earth, wilt Thou not condescend, through thine infinite goodness and royal favor, to listen to the prayer of Thy servant which he this day offers up unto Thee in the name of Thy holy child Jesus, upon this land, where the Sun of Righteousness set in blood, and thine Anointed One expired. . . .

"Now, O Lord! Thy servant has been obedient to the heavenly vision which Thou gavest him in his native land; and under the shadow of Thine outstretched arm, he has safely arrived in this place to dedicate and consecrate this land unto Thee, for the gathering together of Judah's scattered remnants, according to the predictions of the holy Prophets— for the building up of Jerusalem again after it has been trodden down by the Gentiles so long, and for rearing a Temple in honor of Thy name. Everlasting thanks be ascribed unto Thee, O Father, Lord of heaven and earth, that Thou hast preserved Thy servant from the dangers of the seas, and from the plague and pestilence which have caused the land to mourn. The violence of man has also been restrained, and Thy providential care by night and by day has been exercised over Thine unworthy servant. Accept, therefore, O Lord, the tribute of a grateful heart for all past favors, and be pleased to continue Thy kindness and mercy towards a needy worm of the dust.

"O Thou, Who didst covenant with Abraham, Thy friend, and Who didst renew that covenant with Isaac, and confirm the same with Jacob with an oath, that Thou wouldst not only give them this land for an everlasting inheritance, but that Thou wouldst also remember their seed forever. Abraham, Isaac, and Jacob have long since closed their eyes in death, and made the grave their mansion. Their children are scattered and dispersed abroad among the nations of the Gentiles like sheep that have no shepherd, and are still looking forward for the fulfillment of those promises which Thou didst make concerning them; and even this land, which once poured forth nature's richest bounty, and flowed, as it were, with milk and honey, has, to a certain extent, been smitten with barrenness and sterility since it drank from murderous hands the blood of Him who never sinned.

"Grant, therefore, O Lord, in the name of Thy well-beloved Son, Jesus Christ, to remove the barrenness and sterility of this land, and let springs of living water break forth to water its thirsty soil. Let the vine and olive produce in their strength, and the fig-tree bloom and flourish. Let the land become abundantly fruitful when possessed by its rightful heirs; let it again flow with plenty to feed the returning prodigals who come home with a spirit of grace and supplication; upon it let the clouds distil virtue and richness, and let the fields smile with plenty. Let the flocks and the herds greatly increase and multiply upon the mountains and the hills; and let Thy great kindness conquer and subdue the unbelief of Thy people. Do Thou take from them their stony heart, and give them a heart of flesh; and may the Sun of Thy favor dispel the cold mists of darkness which have beclouded their atmosphere. Incline them to gather in upon this land according to Thy word. Let them come like clouds and like doves to their windows. Let the large ships of the nations bring them from the distant isles; and let kings become their nursing fathers, and queens with motherly fondness wipe the tear of sorrow from their eye.

"Thou, O Lord, did once move upon the heart of Cyrus to show favor unto Jerusalem and her children. Do Thou now also be pleased to inspire the hearts of kings and the powers of the earth to look with a friendly eye towards this place, and with a desire to see Thy righteous purposes executed in relation thereto. Let them know that it is Thy good pleasure to restore the kingdom unto Israel—raise up Jerusalem as its capital, and constitute her people a distinct nation and government, with David Thy servant, even a descendant from the loins of ancient David to be their king.

"Let that nation or that people who shall take an active part in behalf of Abraham's children, and in the raising up of Jerusalem, find favor in Thy sight. Let not their enemies prevail against them, neither let pestilence or famine overcome them, but let the glory of Israel overshadow them, and the power of the Highest protect them; while that nation or kingdom that will not serve Thee in this glorious work must perish, according to Thy word—'Yea, those nations shall be utterly wasted.'" (Smith, *History of the Church*, 4:455–57)

On the top of Mount Olives I erected a pile of stones as a witness according to ancient custom. On what was anciently called Mount Zion, where the Temple stood, I erected another. (Smith, *History of the Church,* 4:459)

George A. Smith's Journey to Palestine

President George A. Smith reported on the remarkable journey he and his party made to the Holy Land in 1873.

Having obtained our horses and saddles, Monday morning, Feb. 24th, we started for Jerusalem. I could not obtain a Syrian saddle large enough for me to ride on, and I was compelled to ride on an English saddle. This made a great difference in my comfort. If I had carried a Spanish saddle from home, I should have been much more comfortable on my journey. . . . I am pretty heavy, and had not been on horseback for fifteen years. . . .

Miss E. R. Snow and Miss Clara Little had a tent; Elder Paul A. Schettler and myself occupied another, over which floated the "Stars and Stripes." Elders Lorenzo Snow, Albert Carrington, Feramorz Little and Thos. Jennings occupied another. My tent was used as our dining-room. Our dragoman and cook had each his tent, and we had another for convenience sake. We were supplied with good camp stools; we had iron-framed bedsteads, with good mattresses, and good, clean nice blankets and sheets. All the difficulty about it with me was that my bedstead was too small for me. . .

. . . [As] we crossed over and got a view of Jerusalem, a feeling of disappointment was evident on the countenances of every one of the party, or else I was disappointed and they were not, one or the other. But the whole thing presented itself to us in a different light from what we had anticipated, and I then understood why Dr. Burns, in his "Guide," recommends people to pass round Jerusalem by another route, and come in from the east and get a first view from the eastern side. It is because the view from the Mount of Olives—on the eastern side—is a very great deal better than when you go from the west. It is said that there is a great deal in first impressions.

The Russians have built some monasteries in and about Jerusalem, and the Latins have got some, and within the last few years there have been a number of good new buildings put up. Sir Moses Montefiore has built a block outside, and not far from the wall. The venerable Abraham Askenasi, the chief rabbi of Jerusalem, with the contributions of his friends throughout the world, has erected a considerable number of rooms as a home for widows and orphans. At first view we could pick out the mosque of Omar—the place where Solomon's temple stood; we could also see the church of the Holy Sepulchre—the place where the Savior was crucified. We pitched our tent in the valley of Hinnom, near the Jaffa gate—the gate at which most of the business in Jerusalem is done. While our tents were pitching we passed in at the gate, and saw a good many beggars, some of them lepers, also quite a number of women dressed in white, some of whom were hired mourners and were wailing. . . .

It is not easy to describe that city, nor, so far as I have seen, any of those Asiatic cities. The streets, if they can be called streets, are very narrow, and many of them are so crowded with camels, donkeys and packhorses, that they can only pass each other at certain places. The houses are rudely built, of a kind of concrete, or of rock and mortar. They are low and small and the roof flat, generally covered with cement. There are many buildings in Jerusalem that go to show it off—mosques and churches, with their minarets, towers and rotundas. The principal business street in Jerusalem is Christian street, which is fifteen feet wide. It leads up from the street that we enter from Jaffa's gate, and has an avenue that leads off to the entrance of the church of the Holy Sepulchre. In front of that church is a little open space filled with beggars, and men with articles for sale—beads, photographs, jewelry of different kinds, and relics of all kinds. We could get almost anything in the way of relics we wanted there, and be assured that they were genuine.

President Carrington remained at Jerusalem while we went to the Dead Sea. He wanted to do some business connected with the Liverpool office; and he is not very fond of horseback riding. As you are aware he has been afflicted with rheumatism considerably, so he remained in the Mediterranean Hotel while we went to the Dead Sea and the Jordan. That gave him more time to pass around, and through and over Jerusalem, than any of us. He had several days, and he declared that he could never make up his mind as to what induced King David to locate his capital there. The chief rabbi told me that, anciently, Jerusalem was well supplied with water; but at the present time there was really no living water there. The pool of Hezekiah, and other pools were filled in the rainy season, but in a month from the time we were there a quart bottle of water would cost a farthing, and sometimes pretty hard to get. If the aqueducts from the pools of Solomon were repaired, they would not bring in sufficient water to supply the city, but in the days of Israel's prosperity, there was abundance of water there, and we believed there would be again.

I had a letter of introduction, procured by Mr. James Linforth, from the Rabbi of the Jewish congregation at San Francisco, to Rabbi Askenasi. He is a very venerable-looking man—tall, heavy set and a good supply of beard, like the Apostles in the picture. He seemed very much pleased with my visit, treated me with courtesy, showed me their synagogue and the building they were erecting, and returned the visit, accompanied by several of the Jewish elders, at my tent, where we had a very pleasant interview. . . . This gentleman told me that no Jew had been inside the enclosure of the Mosque of Omar, although he believed it stands on the sight of Solomon's temple, though not in the centre of it.

In looking around Jerusalem, I did not regard it in the same light as President Carrington did. Kingdoms, in those days, were small and densely populated, and it was necessary for a ruler, in locating a capital, to have it so that it could be easily defended; and until the time when modern arms were invented, Jerusalem could be easily defended. Its siege and capture by the Romans proved, to all intents and purposes, that it was a very difficult city to take, for though it was surrounded by several walls, fortified with strong towers, and naturally defended by its mountainous position and the ravines around it, each one of these walls was occupied by rival parties, for it will be remembered by readers of the destruction of Jerusalem, that there were three separate leaders, and that when the Jews were not fighting the Romans, they were fighting each other; and it is even doubtful to this day that, if either John or Simon had had absolute command in their city and the confidence of the people, whether the Romans could have taken the place at all or not. An old proverb says that whom the Gods would destroy they first make mad. It was so with these Jews. They had slain the Savior, they had violated the commands of God, and they had brought upon their heads the curses pronounced upon them in the 27th chapter of Deuteronomy and in a great many other places, if they did not abide in the law of the Lord; and notwithstanding their strong city and their numbers, they were so divided among themselves that they could not make a successful defence. Speaking of this destruction of Jerusalem carries me back to Rome and the Arch of Titus, erected to commemorate his victories, on which is engraved a representation of the seven branched candlesticks, and a great variety of the treasures brought by him from Jerusalem.

King David had learned the strength of Jerusalem by the difficulty he encountered in taking it from the Jebusites; and it is more than probable that God commanded him to locate the city there.

Rabbi Askenasi, speaking of the ten tribes, said he had no idea where they were, but he believed they were preserved, and that their posterity would return, and the time would come when God would bless Israel, and when water would be abundant in Jerusalem. We read in the 47th chap. of Ezekiel, that living waters were to come out from Jerusalem, and that they should run toward the east; and that the Prophet saw a man with a measuring line in his hand. He measured a thousand cubits, and the water was to his ankles; he measured another thousand, and it was to his knees; another thousand, and it was to his loins; another thousand, and it was a river with waters to swim in, that could not be passed over. He goes on and describes this as something that should take place at Jerusalem. I could but reflect, when standing on the Mount of Olives, on the saying concerning it in the last chapter of Zechariah, where, in speaking of the coming of the Savior, it says his feet shall stand on the Mount of Olives, which is before Jerusalem to the east, and the mount shall cleave in the midst thereof, half going toward the north, and half toward the south. There shall be a very great valley, and the land shall be turned into a plain from Geba to Rimmon, south of Jerusalem, and shall be lifted up, and men shall dwell on it. The same Prophet tells us that living waters shall come out of Jerusalem, half toward the former sea, and half toward the hinder sea, and that in summer and in winter shall it be. . . .

I made two careful visits to the Church of the Holy Sepulchre, and one to the Mosque of Omar and the grounds connected with it. I also visited many other places of interest about Jerusalem, but in giving you a detailed account of what we saw and passed through, in such a scattering way, I cannot communicate to so large an audience, to any extent, the impressions I felt at the time. I had no doubt that I passed over the grounds where the Savior and his Apostles, and the Prophets, kings and nobles of Israel had lived, although I did not believe a great deal about the identical spots set down by the monks, yet I was satisfied that I was in the localities in which the great events recorded in Scripture took place. But now little remains on the top of the ground that can be identified beyond the period of the occupation of the Crusaders or the Romans. We certainly saw the top of Mount Moriah, on which stands the Mosque of Omar. There are the rocks and the caves in them. The rocks have not been made by men. The Valley of Jehosophat is there. Learned men have dug deeply under Jerusalem in search of evidence to determine its original site, but an alarm was created that the monkery of the place might be spoiled by determining that certain localities were not where they are now represented, and the Turkish government was moved, so I was informed by some gentlemen, to stop the investigations and to close up the excavations, and we were not permitted to enter them.

President Lorenzo Snow's correspondence to the *Deseret News,* Elder Paul A. Schettler's correspondence to the *Salt Lake Herald,* and Miss E. R. Snow's communications and poems to the *Woman's Exponent,* with other published letters, all composed under circumstances of great labor and fatigue, give a very correct idea of our visit to Jerusalem and journeyings generally. Elder Paul A. Schettler speaks six languages, and in attending to the financial business of the party, he had to make exchanges and was compelled to keep accounts in the currency of a dozen different nations, and even among the Arabs he could generally find some one who could speak in some one of the languages with which he was acquainted.

God has preserved me. Our party of eight went though the entire journey without an accident. We never missed a connection that amounted to any difficulty. We were in no matter injured; we had no sickness, except, peradventure, a little cold or a pinch of rheumatism now and again for a day or two. Our minds were clear, we saw more, I believe, in the eight months, than ordinary travelers see in two years. . . .

My time is exhausted. I thank God for the privilege of seeing you. When on the Mount of Olives, with our faces bowed toward Jerusalem, we lifted our prayers to God that he would preserve you and confound your enemies. We felt in our hearts that Zion was onward and upward, and that no power could stay her progress; that the day was not far distant when Israel would gather, and those lands would begin to teem with a people who would worship God and keep his commandments; that plenty and the blessings of eternity would be poured out bounteously upon that desert land, and that all the prophecies concerning the restoration of the house of Israel would be fulfilled. God has commenced his work by revealing the everlasting Gospel to the Latter-day Saints, and may we all be faithful and fulfill our part is my prayer in the name of Jesus. Amen. (In *Journal of Discourses,* 16:93–102)

A Prophetic Glimpse of Future Jerusalems

TWO JERUSALEMS: OLD AND NEW

"And it shall come to pass in the last days, that the mountain of the Lord's house shall be established in the top of the mountains, and shall be exalted above the hills; and all nations shall flow unto it. And many people shall go and say, Come ye, and let us go up to the mountain of the Lord, to the house of the God of Jacob; and he will teach us of his ways, and we will walk in his paths: for *out of Zion shall go forth the law, and the word of the Lord from Jerusalem*" (Isa. 2:2–3; emphasis added).

"Then the moon shall be confounded, and the sun ashamed, when the Lord of hosts shall reign in mount Zion, and in Jerusalem, and before his ancients gloriously" (Isa. 24:23; see also Isa. 64:10; Joel 3:16; Zech. 1:16–17; 3 Ne. 20:29, 33, 46; 3 Ne. 21:23–24; Ether 13:10–11; D&C 133:21).

"The City of Zion spoken of by David, in the one hundred and second psalm, will be built upon the land of America.... And then they will be delivered from the overflowing scourge that shall pass through the land. But Judah shall obtain deliverance at Jerusalem. (See Joel 2:32; Isa. 26:20– 21; Jer. 31:12; Ps. 1:5; Ezek. 34:11–13)" (Smith, *History of the Church,* 1:315).

"I shall say with brevity, that there is a New Jerusalem to be established on this continent, and also Jerusalem shall be rebuilt on the eastern continent (see *Book of Mormon,* Ether xiii:1–12). 'Behold, Ether saw the days of Christ, and he spake also concerning the house of Israel, and the Jerusalem from which Lehi should come; after it should be destroyed, it should be built up again, a holy city unto the Lord, wherefore it could not be a New Jerusalem, for it had been in a time of old'" (Smith, *Teachings of the Prophet Joseph Smith*, 86).

"The Lord has said by the ancient prophets, in the last days there should be deliverance in Jerusalem and in Mount Zion... And pointed out the location of Zion and commanded the saints among the Gentiles to gather thereunto and build it up, while the Jews gather to Jerusalem" (Woodruff, "A Word to the Wise," 3).

"In 1831, the Prophet Joseph Smith received a revelation designating the place called Independence, Jackson County, Missouri, as the center place of the kingdom of God on the western hemisphere. A city called Zion or the New Jerusalem would there be built. There also, the foremost temple to the Lord should be erected. From the temple in Zion the law of the Lord would issue, as the word of the Lord would come from Jerusalem (D. &C. 57:1–3; Isa. 2:3; Mic. 4:2; *[History of the Church,]* 1:188.)" (Widtsoe, *Evidences and Reconciliations*, 395).

"In each land a holy city shall be built which shall be the capital from whence the law and the word of the Lord shall go forth to all peoples.

"Jerusalem of old, after the Jews have been cleansed and sanctified from all their sins, shall become a holy city where the Lord shall dwell and from whence he shall send forth his word unto all people. Likewise, on this continent the city of Zion, New Jerusalem, shall be built, and from it the law of God shall also go forth. There will be no conflict, for each city shall be headquarters for the Redeemer of the world, and from each he shall send forth his proclamations as occasion may require. Jerusalem shall be the gathering place of Judah and his fellows of the house of Israel, and Zion shall be the gathering place of Ephraim and his fellows, upon whose head shall be conferred 'the richer blessings ...'

"... These two cities, one in the land of Zion and one in Palestine, are to become capitals of the kingdom of God during the millennium" (Smith, *Doctrines of Salvation*, 3:68–71).

"Both church and state, as the world knows them, will soon cease to be. When the Lord comes again, he will set up anew the political kingdom of God on earth. It will be joined with the ecclesiastical kingdom;

church and state will unite; and God will govern in all things. But even then, as we suppose, administrative affairs will be departmentalized, for the law will go forth from Zion [in Jackson County, Missouri], and the word of the Lord from Jerusalem [in the Holy Land]. But, nonetheless, once again the government of the earth will be theocratic. God will govern. This time he will do it personally as he reigns over all the earth. And all of this presupposes the fall of Babylon, and the death of false religions, and the fall of all earthly governments and nations." (McConkie, *Millennial Messiah*, 596).

"And so it shall yet be in a future day when, during the Millennial era there are two great world capitals—one in the Zion of America, the New Jerusalem, whence the law should proceed, and the other in the Zion of old, the Old Jerusalem, whence the word of the Lord shall go forth. Truly the great marvels of the gathering of Israel lie ahead, marvels that shall come to pass during the Millennium" (McConkie, *New Witness*, 540).

OLD JERUSALEM: ISRAEL

Jerusalem to Be Rebuilt and Inhabited by the Seed of Judah

"At that time they shall call Jerusalem the throne of the Lord; and all the nations shall be gathered unto it, to the name of the Lord, to Jerusalem: neither shall they walk any more after the imagination of their evil heart. In those days the house of Judah shall walk with the house of Israel, and they shall come together out of the land of the north to the land that I have given for an inheritance unto your fathers" (Jer. 3:17–18).

"Therefore thus saith the Lord; I am returned to Jerusalem with mercies: my house shall be built in it, saith the Lord of hosts, and a line shall be stretched forth upon Jerusalem. Cry yet, saying, Thus saith the Lord of hosts; My cities through prosperity shall yet be spread abroad; and the Lord shall yet comfort Zion, and shall yet choose Jerusalem" (Zech. 1:16–17).

"And the Lord shall inherit Judah his portion in the holy land, and shall choose Jerusalem again" (Zech. 2:12).

"Behold, I will make Jerusalem a cup of trembling unto all the people round about, when they shall be in the siege both against Judah and against Jerusalem. And in that day will I make Jerusalem a burdensome stone for all people: all that burden themselves with it shall be cut in pieces, though all the people of the earth be gathered together against it. . . . In that day will I make the governors of Judah like an hearth of fire among the wood, and like a torch of fire in a sheaf; and they shall devour all the people round about, on the right hand and on the left: and Jerusalem shall be inhabited again in her own place, even in Jerusalem" (Zech. 12:2–6).

"And I will remember the covenant which I have made with my people; and I have covenanted with them that I would gather them together in mine own due time, that I would give unto them again the land of their fathers for their inheritance, which is the land of Jerusalem, which is the promised land unto them forever, saith the Father. . . .

"Then shall their watchmen lift up their voice, and with the voice together shall they sing; for they shall see eye to eye.

"Then will the Father gather them together again, and give unto them Jerusalem for the land of their inheritance.

"Then shall they break forth into joy—Sing together, ye waste places of Jerusalem; for the Father hath comforted his people, he hath redeemed Jerusalem.

"The Father hath made bare his holy arm in the eyes of all the nations; and all the ends of the earth shall see the salvation of the Father; and the Father and I are one.

"And then shall be brought to pass that which is written: Awake, awake again, and put on thy strength, O Zion; put on thy beautiful garments, O Jerusalem, the holy city, for henceforth there shall no more come into thee the uncircumcised and the unclean. . . .

"Verily, verily, I say unto you, all these things shall surely come, even as the Father hath commanded me. Then shall this covenant which the Father hath covenanted with his people be fulfilled; and then shall Jerusalem be inhabited again with my people, and it shall be the land of their inheritance" (3 Ne. 20:29–46).

"And he spake also concerning the house of Israel, and the

Jerusalem from whence Lehi should come—after it should be destroyed it should be built up again, a holy city unto the Lord; wherefore, it could not be a new Jerusalem for it had been in a time of old; but it should be built up again, and become a holy city of the Lord; and it should be built unto the house of Israel....

"And then also cometh the Jerusalem of old; and the inhabitants thereof, blessed are they, for they have been washed in the blood of the Lamb; and they are they who were scattered and gathered in from the four quarters of the earth, and from the north countries, and are partakers of the fulfilling of the covenant which God made with their father, Abraham" (Ether 13:5, 11).

"We therefore ask thee to have mercy upon the children of Jacob, that Jerusalem, from this hour, may begin to be redeemed; and the yoke of bondage may begin to be broken off from the house of David; and the children of Judah may begin to return to the lands which thou didst give to Abraham, their father" (D&C 109:62–64, Kirtland Temple Dedicatory Prayer).

The City and the Temple

Elder Orson Hyde arrived in Jerusalem on 24 October 1841, to dedicate and consecrate the Holy Land "for the building up of Jerusalem again after it has been trodden down by the Gentiles so long, and for rearing a Temple in honor of Thy name.... Let that nation or that people who shall take an active part in behalf of Abraham's children, and in the raising up of Jerusalem, find favor in Thy sight" (Smith, *History of the Church*, 4:456–59).

Means by Which Jerusalem and the Temple Will Be Rebuilt

"The time is not far distant when the rich men among the Jews may be called upon to use their abundant wealth to gather the dispersed of Judah and purchase the ancient dwelling places of their fathers in and about Jerusalem and rebuild the holy city and temple" (Woodruff, "Epistle," 244; see also Zech. 14:14; Isa. 60:9, 14).

A New Temple

See Ezekiel 40 through 44 for partial blueprints and description of services in the temple.

"I am returned to Jerusalem with mercies: my house shall be built in it, saith the Lord of hosts" (Zech. 1:16).

"Thus speaketh the Lord of hosts, saying, Behold the man whose name is The BRANCH; and he shall grow up out of his place, and he shall build the temple of the Lord" (Zech. 6:12–15).

"For it is ordained that in Zion, and in her stakes, and in Jerusalem, those places which I have appointed for refuge, shall be the places for your baptisms for your dead. And again, verily I say unto you, how shall your washings be acceptable unto me, except ye perform them in a house which you have built to my name?" (D&C 124:36–37).

"What was the object of gathering the Jews, or the people of God in any age of the world? The main object was to build unto the Lord a house whereby He could reveal unto His people the ordinances of His house and the glories of His kingdom, and teach the people the way of salvation; for there are certain ordinances and principles that, when they are taught and practiced, must be done in a place or house built for that purpose" (Smith, *History of the Church*, 5:423).

"I remember, some time ago, having a conversation with Baron Rothschild, a Jew. I was showing him the temple here [Salt Lake City], and said he,—'Elder Taylor, what do you mean by this temple? What is the object of it? Why are you building it?' Said I 'Your fathers had among them prophets, who revealed to them the mind and will of God; we have among us prophets who reveal to us the mind and will of God, as they did. One of your prophets said—'The Lord whom ye seek shall suddenly come to his temple; but who may abide the day of his coming? . . . ' 'Now . . . will you point me out a place on the face of the earth where God has a Temple?' Said he, 'I do not know of any. . . . Do you consider that this is that temple?' 'No, sir, it is not.' 'Well, what is this temple for?' Said I, 'The Lord has told us to build this temple so that we may administer therein baptisms for our dead . . . and also to perform some of the sacred matrimonial alliances and covenants that we believe in, that are rejected by the world generally, but which are among the purest, most exalting and ennobling principles that God ever revealed to man.' 'Well, then this is not our temple?' 'No, but . . . you will build a Temple, for the Lord has shown us, among other things, that you Jews have quite a role to perform in the latter days, and that all the things spoken by your old prophets will be fulfilled, that you will be gathered to old Jerusalem, and that you will build a temple there; and when you build that temple, and the time has arrived, "the Lord whom you seek will suddenly come to his temple"'" (John Taylor, in *Journal of Discourses,* 18:199–200).

Nations Battle against the Jews

See Ezekiel 38–39. Though called by Ezekiel the battle of Gog and Magog, the usual title for this conflict is the battle of Armageddon. This name originated with the site of *Har Megiddo,* the mount or tel of Megiddo, a fortress city at the western end of the Jezreel Valley where many famous battles were fought in antiquity and which gives its name to the future battle to end this world's history.

"I will also gather all nations, and will bring them down into the valley of Jehoshaphat, and will plead with them there for my people and for my heritage Israel, whom they have scattered among the nations, and parted my land. . . . Multitudes, multitudes in the valley of decision: for the day of the Lord is near in the valley of decision" (Joel 3:2, 14).

"In that day shall there be a great mourning in Jerusalem, as the mourning of Hadadrimmon in the valley of Megiddon" (Zech. 12:11).

"For I will gather all nations against Jerusalem to battle; and the city shall be taken, and the houses rifled, and the women ravished; and half of the city shall go forth into captivity, and the residue of the people shall not be cut off from the city.

"Then shall the Lord go forth, and fight against those nations, as when he fought in the day of battle.

"And his feet shall stand in that day upon the mount of Olives, which is before Jerusalem on the east, and the mount of Olives shall cleave in the midst thereof toward the east and toward the west, and there shall be a very great valley; and half of the mountain shall remove toward the north, and half of it toward the south.

"And ye shall flee to the valley of the mountains; for the valley of the mountains shall reach unto Azal: yea, ye shall flee, like as ye fled from before the earthquake in the days of Uzziah king of Judah: and the Lord my God shall come, and all the saints with thee.…

"And this shall be the plague wherewith the Lord will smite all the people that have fought against Jerusalem; Their flesh shall consume away while they stand upon their feet, and their eyes shall consume away in their holes, and their tongue shall consume away in their mouth.…

"And Judah also shall fight at Jerusalem; and the wealth of all the heathen round about shall be gathered together, gold, and silver, and apparel, in great abundance" (Zech. 14:2–14).

"And he gathered them together into a place called in the Hebrew tongue Armageddon" (Rev. 16:16).

"For then, in those days, shall be great tribulation on the Jews, and upon the inhabitants of Jerusalem, such as was not before sent upon Israel, of God, since the beginning of their kingdom until this time; no, nor ever shall be sent again upon Israel. All things which have befallen them are only the beginning of the sorrows which shall come upon them. And except those days should be shortened, there should none of their flesh be saved; but for the elect's sake, according to the covenant, those days shall be shortened. Behold, these things I have spoken unto you concerning the Jews" (JS–M 1:18–21).

"He will gather up millions upon millions of people into the valleys around about Jerusalem in order to destroy the Jews after they have gathered. How will the Devil do this? He will perform miracles to do it. The Bible says the kings of the earth and the great ones will be deceived by these false miracles.… What will they do? Gather them up to battle unto the great day of God Almighty. Where? Into the valley of Armageddon" (Orson Pratt, in *Journal of Discourses,* 7:188–89).

The Causes and Description of Armageddon

"Armageddon is a holy war. In it men will blaspheme God. They will be in rebellion against Jehovah. The armies that face each other will have opposing philosophies of life. It will be religious instincts that cause them to assemble to the battle." (McConkie, *Millennial Messiah*, 398).

"There will be political overtones, of course. Wars are fought by nations, which are political entities. But the underlying causes and the moving power in the hearts of men will be their views of religious issues" (McConkie, *Millennial Messiah*, 478).

"Armageddon is the hill of the valley of Megiddo west of Jordan on the plain Jezreel. And Armageddon is the place where the final war will be fought, meaning, as we suppose, that it will be the focal point of a worldwide conflict, and also that as a place of ancient warfare, it will be a symbol of the conflict that will be raging in many nations and on many battlefronts....

"...All nations are at war; some are attacking Jerusalem and others are defending the once holy city. She is the political prize. Three world religions claim her—Christianity, Islam, and Judaism. Emotion and fanaticism run high....

"'And it shall come to pass, that in all the land, saith the Lord, two parts therein shall be cut off and die; but the third shall be left therein.' This is Israel of whom he speaks. These are the armies who are defending Jerusalem and whose cause, in the eternal sense, is just. Two-thirds of them shall die.

"'And I will bring the third part through the fire, and will refine them as silver is refined, and will try them as gold is tried: they shall call on my name, and I will hear them: I will say, it is my people: and they shall say, the Lord is my God.' (Zech. 13:8–9.) We repeat: It is a religious war. The forces of antichrist are seeking to destroy freedom and liberty and right; they seek to deny men the right to worship the Lord; they are the enemies of God. The one-third who remain in the land of Israel are the Lord's people" (McConkie, *Millennial Messiah*, 464–66).

"'And again shall the abomination of desolation, spoken of by Daniel the prophet be fulfilled.' That which once happened to Jerusalem and its inhabitants shall happen again....

"'And when ye shall see Jerusalem compassed with armies, then know that the desolation thereof is nigh . . .'

"'Then let them which are in Judah flee to the mountains; and let them that are in the midst of it depart out; and let not them that are in the countries enter thereinto.' Is this the way the saints shall be saved in the last days when two-thirds of the inhabitants shall be cut off and die and only one-third be left: If more than a million were put to the sword in A.D. 70, how great shall be the slaughter when atomic bombs are used?" (McConkie, *Millennial Messiah*, 473).

"The kings of the earth and of the whole world will gather to fight the battle of that great day of God Almighty. Their command center will be at Armageddon, overlooking the valley of Megiddo. All nations will be gathered against Jerusalem. Two hundred thousand thousand warriors and more—two hundred million men of arms and more—shall come forth to conquer or die on the plains of Esdraelon and in all the nations of the earth.

" . . . This war will be a religious war. . . .

" . . . We do not speculate as to what nations are involved in these wars. It is well known that the United States and Great Britain and the Anglo-Saxon peoples have traditionally been linked together in causes designed to promote freedom and guarantee the rights of man. It is also well known that there are other nations, ruled by a godless communistic power, that have traditionally fought to enslave rather than to free men. It is fruitless to try and name nations and set forth alliances that are to be" (McConkie, *Millennial Messiah*, 476–77).

Two Witnesses, or Prophets, in Jerusalem

"Q. What is to be understood by the two witnesses, in the eleventh chapter of Revelation?

"A. They are two prophets that are to be raised up to the Jewish nation in the last days, at the time of the restoration, and to prophesy to the Jews after they are gathered and have built the city of Jerusalem in the land of their fathers" (D&C 77:15; see also Isa. 51:19–20; Zech. 4:3, 11–14; Rev. 11:3–12; 2 Ne. 8:19).

"We might bring up, also, the declaration of John in relation to the two witnesses who are to prophesy about that period. They are to prophesy three and a half years, and their field of labor will be Jerusalem, after it shall have been rebuilt by the Jews. By means of their prophecies and the power of God attending them, the nations who are gathered against Jerusalem will be kept at bay, these Prophets will hold them in check by their faith and power. By and by these nations overcome the two witnesses and, having finished their mission, they are slain, and their bodies will lie three days and a half in the streets of the city. Then a great earthquake will take place, and these two witnesses will be caught up into heaven" (Orson Pratt, in *Journal of Discourses*, 16:329).

The Great Earthquake Affecting the Mount of Olives and Jerusalem

"And his feet shall stand in that day upon the mount of Olives, which is before Jerusalem on the east, and the mount of Olives shall cleave in the midst thereof toward the east and toward the west, and there shall be a very great valley; and half of the mountain shall remove toward the north, and half of it toward the south. And ye shall flee to the valley of the mountains; for the valley of the mountains shall reach unto Azal: yea, ye shall flee, like as ye fled from before the earthquake in the days of Uzziah king of Judah: and the Lord my God shall come, and all the saints with thee" (Zech. 14:4–5).

"And the same hour was there a great earthquake, and the tenth part of the city fell, and in the earthquake were slain of men seven thousand: and the remnant were affrighted, and gave glory to the God of heaven" (Rev. 11:13).

"And then shall the Lord set his foot upon this mount, and it shall cleave in twain, and the earth shall tremble, and reel to and fro, and the heavens also shall shake" (D&C 45:48).

"For behold, he shall stand upon the mount of Olivet, and upon the mighty ocean, even the great deep, and upon the islands of the sea, and upon the land of Zion.

"And he shall utter his voice out of Zion, and he shall speak from Jerusalem, and his voice shall be heard among all people;

"And it shall be a voice as the voice of many waters, and as the voice of a great thunder, which shall break down the mountains, and the valleys shall not be found.

"He shall command the great deep, and it shall be driven back into the north countries, and the islands shall become one land;

"And the land of Jerusalem and the land of Zion shall be turned back into their own place, and the earth shall be like as it was in the days before it was divided" (D&C 133:20–24).

"'And his feet shall stand in that day upon the mount of Olives, which is before Jerusalem on the east, and the mount of Olives shall cleave in the midst thereof toward the east and toward the west, and there shall be a very great valley; and half of the mountain shall remove toward the north, and half of it toward the south . . .' This shall be the immeasurably great earthquake foreseen by John and spoken of by the prophets" (McConkie, *Millennial Messiah,* 468).

"'And it shall come to pass at the same time when Gog shall come against the land of Israel, saith the Lord God, that my fury shall come in my face. For in my jealousy and in the fire of my wrath have I spoken, Surely in that day there shall be a great shaking in the land of Israel'—this is the mighty earthquake when the Mount of Olives cleaves and mountains and valleys and continents change their shapes.

"The earthquakes and the tremblings and the distortions of the landmasses of our planet shall all take place when and as he comes to dwell again among men" (McConkie, *Millennial Messiah,* 484).

The Siege of Jerusalem to End the Final War

"Ezekiel has given us in the 38th and 39th chapters much detail in relation to the great battle which shall precede the coming of the Son of Man to reign. Joel and Daniel also prophesied of these great events.

"One thing we are given by these prophets definitely to understand is that the great last conflict before Christ shall come will end at the siege of Jerusalem. So said Ezekiel and Daniel, and the Lord declared to Joel: 'For behold, in those days, in that time, when I shall bring again the captivity of Judah and Jerusalem. . . .'

"When the armies gather in Palestine will be the time when the Lord shall come in judgment. . . .

"Zechariah is another prophet who has plainly spoken of these great events. According to his predictions the nations will gather and lay siege to Jerusalem. Part of the city will fall, with dire consequences to its inhabitants, when a great earthquake will come, the Mount of Olives will cleave in twain, and the persecuted people will flee into this valley for safety. At that particular time will the Savior come as their Deliverer and show them his hands and his feet. They will look upon him and ask him where he received his wounds, and he will tell them they were received in the house of his friends—he is Jesus Christ, their Redeemer.

"At that time shall come the redemption of the Jews. Jerusalem shall then be rebuilt and the promises that it shall become a holy city will be fulfilled" (Smith, *Doctrines of Salvation,* 3:46–47).

The Savior Appears and Rescues the Jews; They Recognize Him

"In that day shall the Lord defend the inhabitants of Jerusalem; and he that is feeble among them at that day shall be as David; and the house of David shall be as God, as the angel of the Lord before them.

"And it shall come to pass in that day, that I will seek to destroy all the nations that come against Jerusalem.

"And I will pour upon the house of David, and upon the inhabitants of Jerusalem, the spirit of grace and of supplications: and they shall look upon me whom they have pierced, and they shall mourn for him, as one mourneth for his only son, and shall be in bitterness for him, as one that is in bitterness for his firstborn" (Zech. 12:8–10).

"And one shall say unto him, What are these wounds in thine hands? Then he shall answer, Those with which I was wounded in the house of my friends" (Zech. 13:6).

"And behold, according to the words of the prophet, the Messiah will set himself again the second time to recover them; wherefore, he will manifest himself unto them in power and great glory, unto the destruction of their enemies, when that day cometh when they shall believe in him; and none will he destroy that believe in him" (2 Ne. 6:14).

"And then shall the Jews look upon me and say: What are these wounds in thine hands and in thy feet? Then shall they know that I am the Lord; for I will say unto them: These wounds are the wounds with which I was wounded in the house of my friends. I am he who was lifted up. I am Jesus that was crucified. I am the Son of God. And then shall they weep because of their iniquities; then shall they lament because they persecuted their king" (D&C 45:51–53).

"It is true that after you (the house of Judah) return and gather your nation home and rebuild your city and temple, that the Gentiles may gather together their armies to go against you to battle, to take you a prey and to take you a spoil, which they will do, for the words of your prophets must be fulfilled; but when this affliction comes, the living God . . . will deliver you, and your Shiloh will come and stand in your midst and will fight your battles; and you will know him, and the afflictions of the Jews will be at an end, while the destruction of the Gentiles will be so great that it will take the whole house of Israel who are gathered about Jerusalem seven months to bury the dead of their armies, and the weapons of war will last them seven years for fuel, so that they need not go to any forest for wood" (Cowley, *Wilford Woodruff*, 509–10).

The Second Coming to Old and New Jerusalem Temples

"Behold, I will send my messenger, and he shall prepare the way before me: and the Lord, whom ye seek, shall suddenly come to his temple, even the messenger of the covenant, whom ye delight in: behold, he shall come, saith the Lord of hosts" (Mal. 3:1; see also D&C 36:8; 42:36; 133:2).

Summary of Events During the Last Days of Old Jerusalem

"Suffice it to say, the Jews gather home, and rebuild Jerusalem. The nations gather against them in battle. Their armies encompass the city, and have more or less power over it for three years and a half. A couple of Jewish prophets, by their mighty miracles, keep them from utterly overcoming the Jews, until at length they are slain, and the city is left in a great measure to the mercy of their enemies for three days and a half, the two prophets rise from the dead and ascend up into heaven. The Messiah comes, convulses the earth, overthrows the army of the Gentiles, delivers the Jews, cleanses Jerusalem, cuts off all wickedness from the earth, raises the saints from the dead, brings them with him, and commences his reign of a thousand years, during which time his Spirit will be poured out upon all flesh, men and beasts, birds and serpents, will be perfectly harmless and peace and the knowledge and glory of God shall cover the earth" (Pratt, *Voice of Warning*, 42).

NEW JERUSALEM: MISSOURI

The Nature and Name of the New Jerusalem

"And it shall be called the New Jerusalem, a land of peace, a city of refuge, a place of safety for the saints of the Most High God; and the glory of the Lord shall be there, and the terror of the Lord also shall be there, insomuch that the wicked will not come unto it, and it shall be called Zion" (D&C 45:66–67).

"Yea, and blessed are the dead that die in the Lord, from henceforth, when the Lord shall come, and old things shall pass away, and all things become new, they shall rise from the dead and shall not die after, and shall receive an inheritance before the Lord, in the holy city" (D&C 63:49).

"And the Lord called his people ZION, because they were of one heart and one mind, and dwelt in righteousness; and there was no poor among them.

"And Enoch continued his preaching in righteousness unto the people of God. And it came to pass in his days, that he built a city that was called the City of Holiness, even ZION.

"And it came to pass that Enoch talked with the Lord; and he said unto the Lord: Surely Zion shall dwell in safety forever. But the Lord said unto Enoch: Zion have I blessed, but the residue of the people have I cursed.

"And it came to pass that the Lord showed unto Enoch all the inhabitants of the earth; and he beheld, and lo, Zion, in process of time, was taken up into heaven. And the Lord said unto Enoch: Behold mine abode forever" (Moses 7:18–21).

A Temple City with Outlying Stakes

"Let me take the liberty to say to this congregation that the City of

Zion, when it is built in Jackson County, will not be called a Stake. We can find no mention in all the revelations that God has given, that the City of Zion is to be the Centre Stake of Zion; the Lord never called it a Stake in any revelation that has been given. It is to be the head quarters, it is to be the place where the Son of Man will come and dwell, where He will have a Temple, in which Temple there will be a throne prepared where Jesus will dwell in the midst of His people; it will be the great central city, and the outward branches will be called Stakes wherever they shall be organized as such" (Orson Pratt, in *Journal of Discourses*, 22:35).

"Jackson County, Missouri, is the chosen site for the City of Zion. No other place has been or will be appointed for that purpose. All other gathering places of God's people are only Stakes of Zion, holding the outside cords and curtains of the spiritual Tabernacle of the Lord.

"Zion's first Stake was at Kirtland, Ohio; and other stakes were organized in Missouri, Illinois, and Iowa. All these have been abandoned; but many others, since established, now flourish. . . . Zion is greater than any of her stakes" (Whitney, *Saturday Night Thoughts*, 183).

New Jerusalem Is Also Called Zion

"The teachings of the Book of Mormon, and the truths made known through revelation in the present dispensation, regarding the Zion of the last days, while agreeing with the Biblical record as to the general description of the situation and the glories of the city, are more explicit in regard to location. In these scriptures, the names Zion and New Jerusalem are used synonymously, the latter designation being given in honor of the Jerusalem of the east" (Talmage, *Articles of Faith*, 316).

"At the Second Coming, 'the Lamb shall stand upon Mount Zion, and with him a hundred and forty four thousand, having his Father's name written on their foreheads.' (D. & C. 133:18; Rev. 14:1–5.) The Mount Zion spoken of is identified by latter-day revelation as the New Jerusalem to be built in Jackson County, Missouri. (D.&C. 84:1–4.)" (McConkie, *Mormon Doctrine*, 855).

The Location of New Jerusalem

"[America] is the cradle of humanity, where life on this earth began in the Garden of Eden. This is the place of the new Jerusalem. This is the place that the Lord said is favored above all other nations in the world. This is the place where the Savior will come to His temple. This is the favored land in all the world. Yes, I repeat, men may fail, but this nation won't fail. I have faith in America; you and I must have faith in America" (Lee, *Ye Are the Light of the World*, 351).

Jackson County Was the Site of the Garden of Eden

"It is a pleasant thing to think of and to know where the garden of Eden was . . . In Jackson County was the garden of Eden. Joseph has declared this, and I am as much bound to believe that Joseph was a prophet of God" (Brigham Young, in Journal History of the Church, 15 March 1857, 1).

"The spot chosen for the garden of Eden was Jackson county, in the state of Missouri, where Independence now stands; it was occupied in the morn of creation by Adam and his associates who came with him for the express purpose of peopling this earth" (Heber C. Kimball, in *Journal of Discourses*, 10:235).

"In accord with the revelations given to the Prophet Joseph Smith, we teach that the Garden of Eden was on the American continent located where the City Zion, or the New Jerusalem, will be built. . . . When Adam and Eve were driven out of the Garden, they eventually dwelt at a place called Adam-ondi-Ahman, situated in what is now Daviess County, Missouri" (Smith, *Doctrines of Salvation*, 3:74).

Adam-ondi-Ahman Priesthood Conference/Sacrament Meeting

As Daniel the prophet foresaw, there will one day be a large gathering of high priests and righteous souls in the valley of Adam-ondi-Ahman, the greatest congregation of faithful Saints ever assembled in the history of the world. It will be a sacrament meeting. The Ancient of Days (Adam) will come, and those who have held keys in all dispensations will report on their stewardships. The Lord Jesus Christ will come and assume the reins of government. The world will not know of this conference, and members of the Church in general will not know of it. Some of those attending will be Adam, Abraham, Isaac, Jacob, Joseph, Elijah, John the Baptist, Peter, James, John, Moroni, and "all those whom my Father hath given me out of the world" (D&C 27:14; see also 27:4–13; 116; Dan. 7:9–14; Matt. 26:29; Smith, *History of the Church*, 3:386–87; Smith, *Way to Perfection*, 289–91; *Doctrines of Salvation*, 3:13–14; McConkie, *Millennial Messiah*, 578–79, 587).

"Yes, there will be wrenching polarization on this planet, but also the remarkable reunion with our colleagues in Christ from the City of Enoch. Yes, nation after nation will become a house divided, but more and more unifying Houses of the Lord will grace this planet. Yes, Armageddon lies ahead. But so does Adam-ondi-Ahman!" (Maxwell, "O, Divine Redeemer," 10).

Conditions for the Building Up of Zion

Those who help build up Zion, the New Jerusalem, will be prepared and worthy; they will be obedient and united (see Brigham Young, in *Journal of Discourses*, 9:137; McConkie, *New Witness*, 586, 596).

Zion will be built only by conforming to the law of consecration (see the following in *Journal of Discourses:* Orson Pratt, 2:261; Brigham Young, 2:299; George Q. Cannon, 13:97; Orson Pratt, 15:361; Lorenzo Snow, 16:276; George A. Smith, 17:59; Wilford Woodruff, 17:250. See also Snow, *Teachings of Lorenzo Snow*, 168; McConkie, *New Witness*, 618).

Men and Angels Will Work Together, and Jesus Will Manifest Himself

"Men and angels are to be coworkers in bringing to pass this great work, and Zion is to be prepared, even a New Jerusalem, for the elect that are to be gathered from the four corners of the earth and to be established an holy city, for the tabernacle of the Lord shall be with them" (Smith, *History of the Church*, 2:260).

"We look forward to the day when the Lord will prepare for the building of the New Jerusalem, preparatory to the city of Enoch's going to be joined with it when it is built upon this earth. We are anticipating to enjoy that day, whether we sleep in death previous to that, or not. We look forward, with all the anticipation and confidence that children can possess in a parent, that we shall be there when Jesus comes; and if we are not there, we will come with him: in either case we shall be there when he comes" (Brigham Young, in *Journal of Discourses*, 8:342).

"[The Lord] will return them to Jackson county, and in the western part of the State of Missouri they will build up a city which shall be called Zion, which will be the head-quarters of this Latter-day Saint Church; and that will be the place where the prophets, apostles and inspired men of God will have their head-quarters. It will be the place where the Lord God will manifest Himself to His people, as He has promised in the Scriptures, as well as in modern revelation" (Orson Pratt, in *Journal of Discourses*, 13:138).

"We talk of returning to Jackson County to build the most magnificent temple that ever was formed on the earth and the most splendid that was ever erected; yea, cities, if you please. The architectural designs of those splendid edifices, cities, walls, gardens, bowers, streets, etc., will be under the direction of the Lord, who will control and manage all these matters; and the people, from the president down, will all be under the guidance and direction of the Lord in all the pursuits of human life; until eventually they will be enabled to erect cities that will be fit to be caught up—that when Zion descends from above, Zion will also ascend from beneath, and be prepared to associate with those from above" (John Taylor, in *Journal of Discourses*, 10:147).

The Redemption of Zion Is Not Understood

"The Lord acts with us as we act with our children, to some extent. He does not tell us everything. I suppose that if the early Elders of this Church could have seen all that we had to pass through and the length of time that would elapse before the redemption of Zion was achieved, they would have fainted by the wayside and have felt that human nature could not endure such trials.

"I know, in my early recollections of the teachings of the Elders, they imagined, judging from their remarks, that it would be only a few years before Zion would be redeemed. When we were coming to these valleys, I happened to be present when some of the Twelve Apostles were talking concerning the future, and the recollection of that conversation is in my mind now; and I know that, though they were inspired men and filled with revelation, they did not conceive, as we now can conceive, of the events that would take place before Zion would be redeemed. It was necessary, seemingly, according to the mind of the Lord, that they should be encouraged with the hope that their efforts would result in complete triumph" (Cannon, *Gospel Truth,* 1:41).

Construction of the New Jerusalem

For the manner of construction and durability of Zion, and the moderate size of the expanding cities of Zion, see Brigham Young, in *Journal of Discourses,* 13:313; also Orson Pratt, 15:365; 21:152–53; *History of the Church,* 4:453; Roberts, *Comprehensive History of the Church,* 3:282–83 note.

New Jerusalem Built and Inhabited by the Seed of Joseph

"And behold, this people will I establish in this land, unto the fulfilling of the covenant which I made with your father Jacob; and it shall be a New Jerusalem. And the powers of heaven shall be in the midst of this people; yea, even I will be in the midst of you" (3 Ne. 20:22).

"But if they will repent and hearken unto my words, and harden not their hearts, I will establish my church among them, and they shall come in unto the covenant and be numbered among this the remnant of Jacob, unto whom I have given this land for their inheritance;

"And they shall assist my people, the remnant of Jacob, and also as many of the house of Israel as shall come, that they may build a city, which shall be called the New Jerusalem.

"And then shall they assist my people that they may be gathered in, who are scattered upon all the face of the land, in unto the New Jerusalem.

"And then shall the power of heaven come down among them; and I also will be in the midst" (3 Ne. 21:22–25).

"Behold, Ether saw the days of Christ, and he spake concerning a New Jerusalem upon this land.

"And he spake also concerning the house of Israel, and the

Jerusalem from whence Lehi should come—after it should be destroyed it should be built up again, a holy city unto the Lord; wherefore, it could not be a new Jerusalem for it had been in a time of old; but it should be built up again, and become a holy city of the Lord; and it should be built unto the house of Israel.

"And that a New Jerusalem should be built upon this land, unto the remnant of the seed of Joseph, for which things there has been a type.

"For as Joseph brought his father down into the land of Egypt, even so he died there; wherefore, the Lord brought a remnant of the seed of Joseph out of the land of Jerusalem, that he might be merciful unto the seed of Joseph that they should perish not, even as he was merciful unto the father of Joseph that he should perish not.

"Wherefore, the remnant of the house of Joseph shall be built upon this land; and it shall be a land of their inheritance; and they shall build up a holy city unto the Lord, like unto the Jerusalem of old; and they shall no more be confounded, until the end come when the earth shall pass away. . . .

"And then cometh the New Jerusalem; and blessed are they who dwell therein, for it is they whose garments are white through the blood of the Lamb; and they are they who are numbered among the remnant of the seed of Joseph, who were of the house of Israel" (Ether 13:4–10).

"And there shall they fall down and be crowned with glory, even in Zion, by the hands of the servants of the Lord, even the children of Ephraim. And they shall be filled with songs of everlasting joy. Behold, this is the blessing of the everlasting God upon the tribes of Israel, and the richer blessing upon the head of Ephraim and his fellows" (D&C 133:32–34).

"And the graves of the saints shall be opened; and they shall come forth and stand on the right hand of the Lamb, when he shall stand upon Mount Zion, and upon the holy city, the New Jerusalem; and they shall sing the song of the Lamb, day and night forever and ever" (D&C 133:56; see also D&C 42:9, 62, 69; 103:16–18).

"If we are not Jews we are not required to go to old Jerusalem, but we are required to build up a Zion; that is spoken of as well as the building of Jerusalem" (Orson Pratt, in *Journal of Discourses,* 18:67).

"First, a remnant will be converted; second, Zion will be redeemed, and all among the Gentiles who believe will assist this remnant of Jacob in building the New Jerusalem; third, a vast number of missionaries will be sent throughout the length and breadth of this great continent, to gather all the dispersed of his people in unto the New Jerusalem; fourth, the power of heaven will be made manifest in the midst of this people, and the Lord also will be in their midst, in the character of a shepherd, and he will lead Joseph as a flock, and he will instruct and counsel them personally as he did their ancient fathers in the days of their righteousness" (Orson Pratt, in *Journal of Discourses*, 17:302).

"In addition to the rebuilding of the Jerusalem of old, the latterdays are to see the initial building of a New Jerusalem on the American continent, a city which like its ancient counterpart will be a holy city, a Zion, a city of God. (3 Ne. 20:22.) This New Jerusalem is to be built by the Church of Jesus Christ of Latter-day Saints; Jackson County, Missouri, is the spot designated by revelation for its construction. (D. & C. 28; 42:8–9, 30–42; 45:66–67; 52:2, 42–43; 57:7, 44–58; 84:2–5.) It shall be built when the Lord directs. (*Doctrines of Salvation* 3:66–79; D. & C. 124:49–54.)" (McConkie, *Mormon Doctrine*, 532; Smith, *Doctrines of Salvation*, 2:247–51).

Zion Established throughout America

"You know there has been great discussion in relation to Zion— where it is, and where the gathering of the dispensation is, and which I am now going to tell you. The prophets have spoken and written it; but I will make a proclamation that will cover a broader ground. The whole of America is Zion itself from north to south, and is described by the Prophets, who declare that it is the Zion where the mountain of the Lord should be, and that it should be in the center of the land. When Elders shall take up and examine the old prophecies in the Bible, they will see it" (Smith, *History of the Church*, 6:318–19; Brigham Young, in *Journal of Discourses*, 9:138; 12:229).

The Unique Temple in New Jerusalem

"There . . . we expect to build a temple different from all other temples in some respect. It will be much larger, cover a larger area of ground. . . . Will it be built in one large room, like this tabernacle? No; there will be 24 different compartments in the Temple that will be built in Jackson County. The names of these compartments were given to us 45 or 46 years ago" (Orson Pratt, in *Journal of Discourses*, 24:24).

"The Latter-day Saints are building temples and believe that the time will come when they will be called on to build the great temple which shall grace the New Jerusalem, or City of Zion, the capital city of God on this continent" (Smith, *Doctrines of Salvation*, 2:246).

"This great prophecy [Isaiah 2:2–4], as is often the case, is subject to the law of multiple fulfillment. 1. In Salt Lake City and other mountain locations temples, in the full and true sense of the word, have been erected, and representatives of all nations are flowing unto them to learn of God and his ways. In this connection and as part of the general fulfillment of Isaiah's prophecy, is the fact that one of the world's greatest genealogical societies has been established in Salt Lake City—a society to which people of all nations come to do the ancestral research which must precede the performance of vicarious temple ordinances. 2. But the day is yet future when the Lord's house is to be built on the 'Mount Zion' which is 'the city of New Jerusalem' in Jackson County, Missouri. (D. & C. 84:2–4) Mount Zion, itself, will be the mountain of the Lord's house in the day when that glorious temple is erected. 3. When the Jews flee unto Jerusalem, it will be 'unto the mountains of the Lord's house' (D. & C. 133:13), for a holy temple to be built there also as part of the work of the great era of restoration. (Ezek. 34:24–28.)" (McConkie, *Mormon Doctrine*, 518).

Purposes of Millennial Temples

"What are we going to do in these temples? . . . In these temples we will officiate in the ordinances of the gospel of Jesus Christ for our friends , for no man can enter the kingdom of God without being born of the water and of the Spirit. We will officiate for those who are in the spirit world, where Jesus went to preach to the spirits as Peter has written [1 Pet. 3:18–20]" (Brigham Young, in *Journal of Discourses*, 13:329).

"In the Millennium, when the kingdom of God is established on the earth in power, glory and perfection, and the reign of wickedness that has so long prevailed is subdued, the Saints of God will have the privilege of building their temples and of entering into them, becoming, as it were, pillars in the temples of God, and they will officiate for their dead. Then we will see our friends come up and perhaps some that we have been acquainted with here. . . . And we will have revelations to know our forefathers clear back to Father Adam and Mother Eve, and we will enter into the temples of God and officiate for them. Then man will be sealed to man until the chain is made perfect back to Adam, so that there will be a perfect chain of priesthood from Adam to the winding-up scene. This will be the work of the Latter-day Saints in the Millennium" (Brigham Young, in *Journal of Discourses*, 15:138–39).

"When the Savior comes, a thousand years will be devoted to this work of redemption; and temples will appear all over this land of Joseph,—North and South America—and also in Europe and elsewhere; and all the descendants of Shem, Ham, Japheth, who received not the gospel in the flesh, must be officiated for in the temples of God, before the Savior can present the kingdom to the Father, saying, 'It is finished'" (Wilford Woodruff, in *Journal of Discourses*, 19:230).

The Ten Tribes Will Return

See Doctrine and Covenants 133:26–34; Orson Pratt, in *Journal of Discourses*, 18:67–68; McConkie, *Millennial Messiah*, 320, 324; *New Witness*, 520.

The City of Enoch Will Return

"And that it was the place of the New Jerusalem, which should come down out of heaven, and the holy sanctuary of the Lord" (Ether 13:3).

"And the bow shall be in the cloud; and I will look upon it, that I may remember the everlasting covenant, which I made unto thy father Enoch; that, when men should keep all my commandments, Zion should again come on the earth, the city of Enoch which I have caught up unto myself.

"And this is mine everlasting covenant, that when thy posterity shall embrace the truth, and look upward, then shall Zion look downward, and all the heavens shall shake with gladness, and the earth shall tremble with joy;

"And the general assembly of the church of the first-born shall come down out of heaven, and possess the earth, and shall have place until the end come. And this is mine everlasting covenant, which I made with thy father Enoch" (JST Gen. 9:21–23).

"Him that overcometh will I make a pillar in the temple of my God, and he shall go no more out: and I will write upon him the name of my God, and the name of the city of my God, which is new Jerusalem, which cometh down out of heaven from my God: and I will write upon him my new name" (Rev. 3:12).

"And I John saw the holy city, new Jerusalem, coming down from God out of heaven, prepared as a bride adorned for her husband. . . . And he carried me away in the spirit to a great and high mountain, and shewed me that great city, the holy Jerusalem, descending out of heaven from God" (Rev. 21:2–10).

"Now many will feel disposed to say, that this New Jerusalem spoken of, is the Jerusalem that was built by the Jews on the eastern continent. But you will see, from Revelation xxi:2, there was a New Jerusalem coming down from God out of heaven, adorned as a bride for her husband; that after this, the Revelator was caught away in the Spirit, to a great and high mountain, and saw the great and holy city descending out of heaven from God. Now there are two cities spoken of here" (Smith, *Teachings of the Prophet Joseph Smith*, 86).

"We have no business here other than to build up and establish the Zion of God. It must be done according to the will and law of God, after that pattern and order by which Enoch built up and perfected the former-day Zion, which was taken away to heaven, hence the saying went abroad that Zion had fled. By and by it will come back again, and as Enoch prepared his people to be worthy of translation, so we through our faithfulness must prepare ourselves to meet Zion from above when it shall return to the earth, and to abide the brightness and glory of its coming" (Brigham Young, in *Journal of Discourses,* 18:356).

"When Zion descends from above, Zion will also ascend from beneath and be prepared to associate with those from above. The people will be so perfected and purified, ennobled, exalted, and dignified in their feelings and so truly humble and most worthy, virtuous and intelligent that they will be fit, when caught up, to associate with that Zion that shall come down from God out of heaven" (John Taylor, in *Journal of Discourses*, 10:147).

"Ether the Jaredite, and John the Revelator, separated by more than six centuries of time and prophesying on opposite hemispheres, each saw the New Jerusalem come down from heaven, 'prepared' says the Jewish apostle, 'as a bride adorned for her husband'" (Talmage, *Articles of Faith*, 317).

"The Church in this day teaches that the New Jerusalem seen by John and by the prophet Ether, as descending from the heavens in glory, is the return of exalted Enoch and his righteous people; and that the people or Zion of Enoch, and the modern Zion, or the gathered saints on the western continent, will become one people" (Talmage, *Articles of Faith*, 318).

"What is the interpretation of Revelation 21:1,2 with reference to the New Jerusalem coming down from God out of Heaven? . . . The prevailing notion in the world is that this is the city of Jerusalem, the ancient city of the Jews which in the day of regeneration will be renewed, but this is not the case. We read in the Book of Ether that the Lord revealed to him many of the same things which were seen by John. . . . In his vision, in many respects similar to that given to John, Enoch saw the old city of Jerusalem and also the new city which has not yet been built, and he wrote them as follows: [see Ether 13:2–11].

"In the day of regeneration, when all things are made new, there will be three great cities that will be holy. One will be the Jerusalem of old which shall be rebuilt according to the prophecy of Ezekiel. One will be the city of Zion, or of Enoch, which was taken from the earth when Enoch was translated and which will be restored; and the city Zion, or New Jerusalem, which is to be built by the seed of Joseph on this the American continent.

" 'And righteousness will I send down out of heaven; and truth will I send forth out of the earth, to bear testimony of mine Only Begotten; his resurrection from the dead; yea, and also the resurrection of all men; and righteousness and truth will I cause to sweep the earth as with a flood, to gather out mine elect from the four quarters of the earth, unto a place which I shall prepare, an Holy City, that my people may gird up their loins, and be looking forth for the time of my coming; for there shall be my tabernacle, and it shall be called Zion, a New Jerusalem.

" 'And the Lord said unto Enoch: Then shalt thou and all thy city meet them there, and we will receive them into our bosom, and they shall see us; and we will fall upon their necks, and they shall fall upon our necks, and we will kiss each other;

" 'And there shall be mine abode, and it shall be Zion, which shall come forth out of all the creations which I have made; and for the space of a thousand years the earth shall rest' " [Moses 7:62–64] (Smith, *Answers to Gospel Questions,* 2:103–6).

"This New Jerusalem on the American continent will have a dual origin. It will be built by the saints on earth and it will also come down from heaven, and the cities so originating will be united into one holy city" (McConkie, *Mormon Doctrine,* 532).

"Enoch and his people, being translated, were taken away from the carnal and evil society of the world. But they went with the promise that when the earth was cleansed and made new, they would return again. Speaking of the latter days, after the restoration of the gospel, the Lord said to Enoch: 'Righteousness and truth will I cause to sweep the earth as with a flood, to gather out mine elect from the four quarters of the earth, unto a place which I shall prepare, an Holy City, that my people may gird up their loins, and be looking forth for the time of my coming; for there shall be my tabernacle, and it shall be called Zion, a New Jerusalem.' The New Jerusalem in Jackson County will be built before the Second Coming" (McConkie, *New Witness,* 590).

Land Masses Become One and Earth Returns to Paradisiacal Glory

"And the land of Jerusalem and the land of Zion shall be turned back into their own place, and the earth shall be like as it was in the days before it was divided" (D&C 133:24).

"When the Millennium is ushered in, there will be a new heaven and a new earth. It will be renewed and will receive again its paradisiacal glory. The islands and continents will come together again, and there will be one land mass, as it was in the days before it was divided. It will become a terrestrial sphere. As it was baptized in water in the days of Noah, so it shall be baptized by fire in the day of the Lord Jesus Christ. The entire vineyard will be burned and the wicked will be as stubble" (McConkie, *Millennial Messiah*, 356–57).

"'And the heaven departed as a scroll when it is rolled together; and every mountain and island were moved out of their places.' Surely this has reference to the continents becoming one land again" (McConkie, *Millennial Messiah*, 381).

"This is the time when the earth's land masses shall unite; when islands and continents shall become one land; when every valley shall be exalted and every mountain shall be made low; when the rugged terrain of today shall level out into a millennial garden; when the great deep shall be driven back into its own place in the north. It is no wonder that the earthquake shall exceed all others in the entire history of the world" (McConkie, *Millennial Messiah*, 397).

"In this day of burning there will be the new heavens and the new earth of which the revelations speak. The earth will become again a paradisiacal or terrestrial sphere. It will be renewed and be as it originally was in the day of the Garden of Eden" (McConkie, *Millennial Messiah*, 536; see also 413, 623).

The Celestial Jerusalem

"For Christ is not entered into the holy places made with hands, which are the figures of the true; but into heaven itself, now to appear in the presence of God for us" (Heb. 9:24).

"And I saw no temple therein: for the Lord God Almighty and the Lamb are the temple of it.

"And the city had no need of the sun, neither of the moon, to shine in it: for the glory of God did lighten it, and the Lamb is the light thereof.

"And the nations of them which are saved shall walk in the light of it: and the kings of the earth do bring their glory and honour into it.

"And the gates of it shall not be shut at all by day: for there shall be no night there.

"And they shall bring the glory and honour of the nations into it.

"And there shall in no wise enter into it any thing that defileth, neither whatsoever worketh abomination, or maketh a lie: but they which are written in the Lamb's book of life" (Rev. 21:22–27).

"And there shall be no night there; and they need no candle, neither light of the sun; for the Lord God giveth them light: and they shall reign for ever and ever" (Rev. 22:5).

"After the close of the millennial reign we are informed that Satan, who was bound during the millennium, shall be loosed and go forth to deceive the nations. Then will come the end. The earth will die and be purified and receive its resurrection. During this cleansing period the City Zion, or New Jerusalem, will be taken from the earth; and when the earth is prepared for the celestial glory, the city will come down according to the prediction in the Book of Revelation" (Smith, *Answers to Gospel Questions*, 2:105).

GLOSSARY

A.D. Latin, *anno domini*, "the year of our Lord"; used for dates after the birth of Christ.

Abbasids. Muslim rulers of the Near East from A.D. 750 to 969; capital at Baghdad.

Abyssinians. Christians in northeast Africa, especially Ethiopia; founders of the oldest Christian church in Jerusalem.

Acropolis. Greek. Usually a high, fortified hill of a city. *See also* **Citadel.**

Aggadah. Hebrew, "legend." The body of traditions giving extrabiblical information about biblical stories and people. *See also* **Midrash.**

Agora. Greek, "to gather." The main marketplace or square of a city. *See also* **Forum.**

Agudat Israel. "Union" or "Association" of Israel; political movement of Jews founded in Poland in 1912.

Akkad. A city and a region in northern Babylon, now Iraq.

Al-Aqsa. Arabic, "the farthest point." The place in distant Jerusalem to which Muhammad journeyed from Mecca in the Night Vision; the traditional place from which he ascended into heaven; now the mosque at the southern end of Haram esh-Sharif.

Al-Fatah. The guerrilla group that is the power base of Yasser Arafat's Palestine Liberation Organization (PLO).

Al-Quds. Arabic, "the Holy." Jerusalem.

Aliyah. Hebrew, "going up"; immigration to the Holy Land and to Jerusalem.

Allah. Arabic, "God." *See also* **Elohim.**

Alluvium. Earth, sand, gravel, and other matter that has been washed away and redeposited by flowing water.

Amphora. Plural, *amphorae.* Latin. A jar or vase with a large oval body, narrow neck, and two handles; if flat-bottomed, usually for grains; if pointed, for liquids (oil, wine).

Amulet. A charm or a piece of jewelry often worn around the neck as a remedy or protection against evils.

Amurru. Akkadian, "West land." The name for the Holy Land in Akkadian and Assyrian texts of the Middle Bronze Age. The people of Amurru were the Amorites of the Bible.

Anatolia/Hittites. Indo-European kingdom in east-central Asia Minor between 1900 and 1200 B.C.

Annals. Written accounts of events in chronological order by year; historical records; chronicles.

Apis. The bull worshipped anciently at Memphis; identified originally with Ptah and later assimilated with Osiris as the Hellenistic Serapis.

Apocrypha. Greek, "hidden." Old Testament and intertestamental books written in Greek rather than Hebrew; generally rejected as scripture by Jews and some Christians, though they are included in Catholic Bibles (see D&C 91).

Appurtenances. Accessories or implements; objects used in the services of the Temple.

Apse. A semicircular recess in a church, generally at the east end, with a domed or vaulted roof.

Aqueduct. A conduit or canal for transporting water.

Aquifer. Porous rock stratum capable of carrying a usable supply of water.

Aram/Syria. The land northeast of Canaan and eastward to the Euphrates; Damascus was the capital.

Aramaic. Northwest Semitic language and a close relative of Hebrew and Arabic; the lingua franca of the ancient Near East for many centuries; one of the languages spoken by Jesus and his apostles.

Archaeology. Greek, *archae*, "ancient." The scientific study of material remains of past peoples and cultures.

Arcosolium. Plural, *arcosolia*. Latin. An arched recess for burial. *See also* **Loculus.**

Armenians. People of a kingdom once located in the eastern part of what is now Turkey and eastward; the first nation to officially accept Christianity.

Armistice. Temporary cessation of warfare by mutual agreement preliminary to the signing of a peace treaty; a truce.

Asherah. Plural, *asheroth.* Ancient Canaanite fertility goddess.

Ashkenazim. Jews from western or European background.

Ashlar. Masonry of square or rectangular stones.

Ashur. An ancient Assyrian city on the west bank of the Tigris River. One of the capitals of the Assyrian Empire.

Autonomy. Self-government; independent and self-contained rule of a people over themselves.

B.C. "Before Christ."

B.C.E. "Before the Common Era." Used by those disposed not to make reference to Christ in calculating time. *See also* C.E.

Babylon. Capital city of ancient Babylonia in Mesopotamia, now Iraq.

Bailey. Outer wall of a castle or a wall surrounding the keep.

Baksheesh. Gratuity, present, payment for services.

Barbican. Outer defensive tower at a gate or bridge.

Basilica. Latin, from Greek *basilikos*, "royal." In Roman times, a royal palace; a building with one or more colonnaded aisles, used anciently as a courtroom or public assembly hall. Later adopted as the shape of early Christian church buildings, having a nave, two to four aisles, and one or more semicircular vaulted apses.

Berbers. People living in North Africa who adopted Islam during the seventh century after Christ; now concentrated in northwest Africa.

Brith. Hebrew, "covenant."

British Mandate. Government of Palestine by the British, as authorized by the League of Nations in 1922.

Bronze Age. Period of time characterized by bronze tools and weapons, dating from 3100 to 1200 B.C.

Bulla. Plural, *bullae.* Latin. Clay seal or stamp used to seal documents.

Byzantines. People who created the Eastern Roman Empire, ruling from Byzantium, or Constantinople, from A.D. 324 to 638.

C.E. "Of the Common Era." Used by those disposed not to make reference to Christ in calculating time. *See* B.C.E.

Caliph. Arabic, *khalifa,* "successor." The title of successors to Muhammad as leader of the *ummah,* or community of Islam.

Canaan/Palestine/Holy Land. The land between the Mediterranean Sea on the west and the Syrian-Arabian deserts or the Rift Valley on the east, with Lebanon to the north and Sinai to the south.

Cardo. Latin, "heart." The designation of the main street of a Roman city, running north and south, was cardo maximus. *See also* **Decumanus maximus.**

Cartography. The science of studying and drawing maps.

Casemate. A double fortification wall, often with partitioned rooms for storage or habitation.

Cenotaph. Greek, *kenos,* "empty," combined with *taphos,* "tomb." A monument or memorial honoring a dead person buried elsewhere.

Chalcolithic. Copper Age; characterized by tools and weapons made of copper or brass; 4000 to 3100 B.C.

Chaldea. The region in southern Mesopotamia from which came the Chaldeans, builders of ancient Babylon.

Circumvallation. A wall surrounding a city or place.

Cisjordan. Latin, *cis,* "on this side," or "on the nearer side," combined with *Jordan.* Inhabited land between the Jordan River and the Mediterranean Sea. *See also* **Transjordan.**

Cistern. A large, man-made receptacle for storing water; often excavated from stone and covered with plaster.

Citadel. Latin. Fortress on a commanding height for defense of a city. *See also* **Acropolis.**

Coalition. A temporary alliance of parties with the purpose, for example, of acquiring enough votes to control a government.

Cohen. Hebrew, "priest." A priest of the tribe of Levi.

Colonia. A Roman colony established outside the immediate jurisdiction of Rome and granted special privileges.

Column. In architecture, a pillar designed to support some weight; composed of three parts: the base, the shaft, and the capital. The three Greek orders are Doric, which is the oldest, simplest type, without elaborate carving of the capital; Ionic, in which the capital has two scrolls connected by a horizontal band; and Corinthian, often a slender, fluted shaft with a highly ornamented capital, frequently carvings of acanthus leaves.

Copts. From the Greek *Aigyptios.* Native Egyptians descended from the ancient Egyptians and members of the Coptic (Christian) Church. Coptic, the nearly extinct language of Egypt that developed from ancient Egyptian, is still used in liturgy.

Corvee. Enforced and unpaid labor extracted by a government.

Crenellation. An indented battlement, alternating solid parts and open spaces, atop a wall.

Crusades. Christian military expeditions from the eleventh through the thirteenth centuries to recover the Holy Land from the Muslims.

Cuneiform. Wedge-shaped writing used by Akkadians, Assyrians, and Babylonians.

Cylinder seal. A small, barrel-shaped stone or clay object bearing a cuneiform inscription or design, worn by Assyrians and Babylonians as an amulet; rolled in wet clay as a seal or signature in a document.

Decumanus maximus. The paved and colonnaded street running east and west which intersects with the main street. *See also* **Cardo maximus.**

Demography. Study of human populations with reference to size, density, distribution, birthrate, and other vital statistics.

Diadochi. The three generals who divided the empire of Alexander the Great after his death.

Diaspora. Greek, "dispersion." Designates the Jews scattered after the Babylonian captivity and especially after A.D. 70 to all parts of the earth; now also all Jews outside Israel.

Donjon. The strongest, most secure part of a castle, often a lower room of the keep.

Dynasty. A succession of rulers belonging to one family.

Ebla. A previously unknown city in Syria in which thousands of texts were discovered in recent decades illuminating aspects of life in the third millennium before Christ.

Egypt, Upper and Lower. "Upper" and "Lower" refer to the south-to-north flow of the Nile River. Upper Egypt, or southern Egypt, is the Nile River region from the first cataract to modern Cairo; Lower Egypt is the Delta.

Elam. A mountainous country east of Babylonia with the Persian Gulf on the south and southwest.

Elohim. Hebrew, "God." *See also* Arabic **Allah.**

Eretz Israel. Hebrew, "the land of Israel." The present state of Israel plus its territories; often used in a political sense.

Essenes. A Jewish sect that practiced self-denial. Members lived in Qumran near the Dead Sea and on Mount Zion in Jerusalem, flourishing from 200 B.C. to A.D. 70. They wrote some of the Dead Sea Scrolls.

Euphrates. The western of the two rivers that flow from Asia Minor to the Persian Gulf. The area between the two rivers is Mesopotamia, the place where powerful empires arose anciently.

Expropriation. Transfer of another's property to one's own possession, usually by a government.

Fatimids. Shiite Muslims ruling the Near East and North Africa from A.D. 969 to 1071. Their capital was at Cairo.

Fault. A geological fracture in the earth's crust with displacement of sides relative to each other.

Felafel. Near Eastern sandwich: balls of fried garbanzo beans (chick peas) and salad greens in pita (pocket) bread.

Fertile Crescent. The semicircular region of fertile land in the Near East extending from the southeastern coast of the Mediterranean around the Syrian Desert north of Arabia to the Persian Gulf; comprised the Levant and Mesopotamia.

First Revolt. The revolt of the Jews against the Romans from A.D. 66 to 70 resulting in the destruction of Jerusalem and the Temple.

First Temple period. From the building of the Temple in Jerusalem by Solomon in the tenth century before Christ to its destruction by Babylon in 586 B.C.

Forum. Latin. The main marketplace or square of a city. *See also* **Agora.**

Fosse. Fortification ditch or trench; a moat.

Fresco. Decorative painting or mural executed on fresh, moist, lime plaster.

Galut. Hebrew, "exile." Refers to the condition of the Jews in the Diaspora.

Gemarah. Hebrew, "the finishing off" or "completion." Many volumes of commentary on the commentaries, mainly on the Mishnah.

Glacis. (Glah-see.) French. The sloping bank erected against the lower portion of a city wall to protect it from battering rams or erosion.

Goyim. Hebrew, "Gentiles." People who are not Jews.

Graben. German, "grave." Depressed segment of the earth's crust bounded on two sides by faults and longer than it is wide. The Rift Valley is a graben.

Grove. A small stand of trees in an open-air sanctuary, especially on high hills, or what the Bible calls "high places." Often the site of the worship of fertility goddesses. *See also* **Asherah.**

Habiru/Apiru. Nomadic people who moved into the land of Canaan during the reign of Amenhotep IV. Some associate them with the Hebrews.

Hadith. A saying or teaching of Muhammad that was written down.

Haganah. Clandestine Jewish organization for armed self-defense in early twentieth-century Palestine during the British Mandate; later the basis for the Israel Defense Forces (IDF).

Hagiographa. Greek, "sacred writings."

Hajj. The pilgrimage to Mecca; one of the basic tenets, or pillars, of Islam.

Halakhah. From the Hebrew verb meaning "to walk." The way a Jew should walk, or conduct himself, in life. The oral law based on authoritative interpretations of the Torah by the rabbis, which forms the larger part of the Talmud.

Haram esh-Sharif. Arabic, "the Noble Sanctuary." The same place as the Temple Mount of the Jews.

Haran. City of northern Mesopotamia on the Euphrates River where Abram resided after leaving Ur.

Hashemite. Pertaining to descent from the clan that included Muhammad's family; also the ruling dynasty in Jordan.

Hassidism. Religious movement established by the Ba'al Shem Tov in early eighteenth century.

Hasmonaeans. A priestly family who fought the Seleucids for control of the Holy Land to end religious suppression. They liberated and expanded the Jewish domain and ruled from 167 to 63 B.C. Popularly called "Maccabees" after one of Mattathias' sons, Judah haMaccabi ("the hammerer").

Hellenism. The character, thought, culture, and ethics of ancient Greece, spread by Alexander the Great.

Hierocentrality. The concept of a place being a holy center.

Hieroglyphics. From the Greek, *hiero,* "holy, sacred" combined with *glyphein,* "to carve." A system of writing using pictorial characters.

Hijrah. The flight of Muhammad and his companions from Mecca to Yathrib (Medina) in A.D. 622, marking the beginning of the Muslim calendar (abbreviated A.H., "after hijrah"). Also spelled *hegira.*

Hippodrome. An oval-shaped course for horse and chariot races.

Holocaust. Organized mass persecution and extermination of Jews and others by the Nazis from 1933 to 1945.

Hospitaller knights. A crusader religious-military order established in Jerusalem in the eleventh century. Also known as Knights of St. John, the members helped the poor and the sick and fought the Muslims. *See also* **Templar knights.**

Hydrology. The study of water on the surface of the land, in soils, in underlying rock, and in the atmosphere.

Hyksos. Egyptian, *Hequ khoswe,* "rulers of foreign lands." Nomadic Amorite tribes who invaded Egypt from the north about 1750 B.C. and ruled for a century and a half.

Hypocaust system. Greek, *hypo,* "under, beneath," combined with *kauston,* "to burn." Heat from a fire blown by bellows under a tile floor supported by stone pillars (*hypocaustae*) to produce a sauna effect.

Hypostyle. Greek, *hypo,* "under, beneath" combined with *stylos,* "pillar." A roof resting on rows of columns.

Icon. A representation or image of Mary, Christ, or a saint in a painting or statuary; common in the Eastern Orthodox Church.

Imam. Shiite Muslim religious leader.

Insula. Latin. A complex of rooms or buildings.

Intifada. Arabic, "uprising." The revolt of young Palestinians in Gaza and the West Bank, beginning in late 1987.

Irgun. An underground military organization similar to the Haganah but more radical. Led by Menahem Begin, it fought the British and the Arabs to establish the state of Israel.

Iron Age. The period of time from 1200 to 586 B.C. which is characterized by the development of iron tools and weapons.

Islam. Arabic, "submission," that is, submission to the will of Allah. The religion originating with Muhammad in the Arabian peninsula in the seventh century after Christ; now encompasses many countries of the world and has approximately one billion adherents.

Jewish Agency. Organization that facilitates Jewish immigration and absorption into Israel.

Jewish National Fund. Zionist land-purchasing and development organization in Palestine founded in 1901.

Jihad. Arabic, "struggle." A holy war undertaken as a sacred duty by Muslims.

Josephus. Commander of Jewish forces in Galilee at the time of the First Revolt (A.D. 66). He defected to the Romans and wrote *Antiquities* and *Wars of the Jews.*

Judaea. Graeco-Roman form of *Judah.* The area, mostly south of Jerusalem, which later included most of the Holy Land.

Ka'bah. Arabic, "cube," that is, a square building. The main Islamic sanctuary housed in the Grand Mosque in Mecca and believed by Muslims to have been built by Abraham and Ishmael.

Kabbalah. Hebrew, "receipt." Orally transmitted mysticism written down in the medieval period. Comprises many books, especially commentaries called the *Zohar* ("splendor") and *Gematria* (devising meanings from the numerical value of words).

Kafiyeh. Arabic. Headdress worn by Arab men.

Karaites. Jewish sect of the Near East beginning in the eighth century after Christ who accepted the Tanakh (the Bible) but rejected the oral interpretations (the Talmud).

Kasher, kosher. Ritually acceptable food.

Kashrut. Jewish dietary laws.

Keep. The strongest, most secure part of a castle. The dungeon was often in a lower room of the keep.

Kibbutz. Plural, *kibbutzim.* Collective farming settlement in Israel emphasizing mainly agriculture but also including industry.

Knesset. Hebrew, "assembly." Israel's parliament.

Kokh. Plural, *kokhim.* Hebrew. Roman-period rock-cut burial niche. *See also* **Loculus.**

Legate. Governor of a Roman province administered directly by the emperor.

Levant. Eastern Mediterranean lands; modern Lebanon, Syria, Israel, and Jordan.

Lingua franca. Language adopted for communication over an area in which several languages are spoken.

Loculus. Plural, *loculi.* Latin. Long burial recess or niche cut into the interior wall of a tomb.

Loophole. A narrow aperture in a thick wall that gradually widens toward the inside; used for shooting arrows through.

Maccabees. *See* **Hasmonaeans.**

Madrasa. A Muslim school or college developed by the Mamlukes.

Maimonides. One of the greatest of the medieval Jewish rabbis.

Mamlukes. Military class of mostly Turkish and Circassian former slaves who ruled Egypt and influenced all the Near East from A.D. 1250 to 1517.

Mandate. Administration or government of Palestine by the British under authority of the League of Nations.

Mari. Ancient city of Mesopotamia on the eastern bank of the Euphrates and an important intersection of caravan roads: one leading to the Mediterranean and another to Babylon and other countries. A library of cuneiform documents was discovered there and called the Mari Texts.

Maronites. A Christian community from Syria but living in Lebanon; one of the largest religious bodies in Lebanon, having a Syriac liturgy and married clergy.

Massorah. Hebrew, "tradition." The text received by tradition from the Ben Asher family in Tiberias between the fifth and tenth centuries after Christ; the basis of printed Hebrew Bibles.

Mausoleum. A large, often ornate burial house. Named after Mausolus of Caria, whose magnificent tomb at Halicarnassus in the fourth century before Christ was one of the seven wonders of the ancient world.

Mecca. Birthplace of Muhammad and the spiritual center of Islam. All Muslims face Mecca when they pray.

Medes. Inhabitants of ancient Media, now northwest Iran. They united with the Persians to destroy Babylon in 539 B.C.

Menorah. A seven-branched candlestick or lampstand used in the Tabernacle and the Temple and later in Jewish ceremonies.

Mesopotamia/Aram-naharaim. The region between the Tigris and the Euphrates rivers.

Midrash. Hebrew, "investigation," "searching out." Rabbinic commentary on sacred writings; for example, Torah and Talmud.

Mihrab. Arabic. Niche in a mosque signaling the direction of Mecca.

Mikveh. Jewish ritual purification bath.

Minaret. Tower of a mosque from which the call to prayer is made five times a day by a muezzin, a trained caller, or by a recording.

Minyan. The minimum of ten Hebrew males over thirteen years of age required for communal prayers.

Mishnah. Hebrew, "the repetition." The initial writing of oral law compiled by Rabbi Judah the Prince about A.D. 200. The basis of the Talmud, it contains six books: Agriculture, Women, Justice, Purity, Temple, and Sabbath.

Mitanni/Hurrians. A kingdom in northern Mesopotamia in the late Bronze Age mentioned in the El Amarna texts.

Monasticism. The lifestyle of monks and nuns, who dedicate their lives to prayer, meditation, study, and self-denial, along with strict adherence to vows of silence, celibacy, solitude, and so forth.

Monophysite. Greek, "one nature." One who holds the belief that the human and the divine in Christ constitute only one nature.

Monotheism. The belief in and worship of one god.

Muezzin. The Muslim man who announces from the minaret the time to pray.

Mufti. A leader of Muslim scholars and jurists.

Muhammad. The prophet of Islam who lived in the Arabian peninsula during the seventh century after Christ.

Muslim. A follower of Islam; literally, "one who submits" to the will of Allah.

Nationalism. Devotion to the interests of a particular nation, government, or culture.

Nave. The central hall of a basilica or church.

Near East/Middle East. Geographically, "Near East" is the more correct designation, though "Middle East" is the more popular term. Originally coined by the Portuguese in reference to the countries of the eastern Mediterranean and the Arabian peninsula: Turkey, Syria, Lebanon, Israel, Jordan, Saudi Arabia, Iraq, and Egypt.

Necropolis. Greek, "city of the dead." The cemetery of an ancient city.

Nicaean Creed. The Christian creed established by Emperor Constantine in A.D. 325 at the council of Nicaea which stated that the Godhead is one God but three separate entities.

Nineveh. Capital of the Assyrian Empire on the banks of the Tigris. It was the site of Jonah's preaching and Ashurbanipal's library.

Nubia. Region in Africa south of Egypt extending from the Nile to the Red Sea.

Occupied territory. Lands of disputed claim occupied by outside forces. In the Holy Land, these lands have been the West Bank, Gaza, and the Golan.

Omayyads (or Umayyads). Muslim rulers of the Near East from A.D. 640 to 750. Their capital was Damascus.

Omphalos. Greek, "navel." Jerusalem is considered the navel or center of the earth.

Orient. The East or an eastward direction.

Orthostat. Greek, "standing upright." A monumental structure guarding the entrance to ancient temples.

Ossuary. Greek, "bone box." About a year after interment, when a body was sufficiently decomposed, the bones were removed from the sarcophagus and placed in an ossuary; secondary burial.

Ostracon. Plural, *ostraca*. Greek. A piece of pottery (potsherd) with writing on it.

Ottoman. Muslim Turks who ruled Asia Minor, Syria, Palestine, and North Africa from Istanbul from the 1500s to 1917.

Palestine Liberation Organization (PLO). A group formed to fight for the rights of Arab Palestinians displaced by the nation of Israel. *See also* **Al-Fatah.**

Palestinian. A person who lived in the geographical area of Palestine before 1948. Many non-Jewish residents of Israel describe their nationality as Palestinian; as of the early 1990s, a citizen of the declared nation of Palestine.

Papyrus. An aquatic plant of the Nile Valley that was cut into strips, pressed, and made into writing material; ancient paper.

Parchment. Animal skin prepared for writing.

Partition. Separation or division, as in the 1917 League of Nations' division of Palestine and surrounding lands between England and France, or the later division of Palestine by the United Nations into separate enclaves for Arabs and Jews.

Patriarchate. The office, jurisdiction, province, or residence of an ecclesiastical patriarch.

Pax Romana. Latin, "Roman peace." The period of relative peace in the Roman era.

Pentateuch. Greek. The five books of Moses, or the Torah; the first five books of the Bible.

Philology. The study of written records and the determination of their meaning.

Phoenicia. Ancient kingdom on the eastern Mediterranean coast; modern Lebanon. *See* **Sea Peoples.**

Pilaster. Upright pier or column attached to a wall.

Polis. Greek city-state.

Portico. A colonnade or porch.

Praefect/procurator. Roman official who managed the financial and military affairs of a conquered province or acted as governor there.

Pseudepigrapha. Greek, "false writings." Works attributed to certain biblical characters. They were not included in the Bible when it was canonized.

Ptolemies. The dynasty founded by Ptolemy I, a general of Alexander's army, which ruled in Egypt until the Roman period.

Publican. A Jew who collected taxes for the Romans and was therefore quite despised. Matthew and Zacchaeus were two New Testament publicans.

Pylon. Greek, "gate." A massive gateway building in a truncated pyramidal shape.

Qibla. Arabic. The direction a Muslim faces for prayer. *See also* **Mihrab.**

Qur'an. Arabic, "recitation." The holy book of Islam, believed by Muslims to contain the word of Allah revealed by the angel Gabriel to Muhammad. Also spelled *Koran.*

Rain shadow. The area of less rainfall on the lee of a mountainous area, caused by rising air dropping most of its moisture on the windward side.

Ramadan. Ninth month of the Islamic calendar. This month is a time of rededication and purification, including rigid fasting from dawn to dusk; one of the pillars, or basic rules, of Islam.

Rampart. Fortification wall of a city or castle.

Refectory. Dining hall in a castle or monastery.

Resolution 242. Security Council Resolution of November 1967 stating principles for achieving peace between Arabs and Israelis. It has been accepted by both sides but with differing interpretations.

Revetment. Fortified embankment or retaining wall.

Rift Valley. The region from Syria to Mozambique (approximately four thousand miles long), which is the deepest crack in the earth's surface. Caused by the collision of tectonic plates of the earth's crust, it averages ten miles in width.

Robinson, Edward. Often called the father of exploration of Israel. He and Eli Smith spent months in 1838 and again in 1852 investigating and identifying ancient sites in the Holy Land.

Samaritans. People who inhabited Samaria after the exile of Israelites by Sargon of Assyria; also descendants of the foreign people transferred there by Sargon; they intermarried with the native Israelites who remained in the land. Being "half-breeds," they were despised by the Jews.

Sanhedrin. Jewish supreme court of justice from the first century before Christ to the sixth century after Christ.

Sarcophagus. Plural, *sarcophagi.* Greek, "flesh-eating stone." A stone coffin so called because in it the flesh gradually decayed, dried, and essentially vanished.

Satrapy. A Persian province ruled by a governor.

Sea Peoples. Philistines, Phoenicians, and other Indo-Europeans from Crete and the Aegean who, upon failing to invade Egypt, settled on the eastern Mediterranean coast.

Second Temple period. From the rebuilding of the Temple by Jews returned from Babylon, about 515 B.C. to the destruction of Jerusalem and the Temple in A.D. 70.

See. The center of authority or jurisdiction of a bishop; for example, the Holy See of the Pope.

Seleucids. The dynasty founded by Seleucus I, a general of Alexander's army, who ruled in Asia Minor, Syria, Persia, and Bactria from 332 to 167 B.C.

Sephardim. Jews from the Iberian peninsula, North Africa, the Near East, and south-central Asia.

Septuagint. Greek, Latin, "seventy." The Greek Old Testament dating from the first centuries before Christ. The name is derived from the supposed seventy translators who traditionally worked seventy days in rendering the Hebrew scriptures into Greek.

Sharia. Arabic. The traditional Muslim religious and social code of law based on the Qur'an and Hadith.

Sheikh. Arabic, "elder." The head of a tribe; clan leader.

Shema. Hebrew, "hear." Deuteronomy 6:4 begins "Hear, O Israel: the Lord our God is one Lord."

Shephelah. The region of low hills west and southwest of Jerusalem.

Shewarma. Arabic. Pita bread filled with spiced lamb or beef, sauces, and vegetables.

Shia/Shiites. Muslim sect that follows Ali, son-in-law of Muhammad.

Simhat Torah. Hebrew, "rejoicing in the Law." A Jewish holiday celebrating the close of the Feast of Tabernacles (Succot) and recommencing the annual cycle of Torah reading.

Sirocco. Italian. Hebrew, *sharav;* Arabic, *khamsin.* Strong, dry winds with high temperatures and dust storms usually originating in the eastern or southeastern deserts.

Stele, stela. Plural, *stelae.* Greek, Latin. An upright stone slab or pillar with an inscription, often boasting of victory over enemies.

Sumer. The region of southern Babylon in which recorded history begins, according to the world's belief.

Sunni. Orthodox Muslims who acknowledge the first four caliphs as successors to Muhammad.

Supersessionism. The idea that Christianity as "the new Israel" superseded or replaced the old covenant made with ancient Israel.

Sura. Arabic. A chapter of the Qur'an.

Talmud. Hebrew, "learning." The Mishnah and the Gemarah make up the Talmud, which is claimed to be the oral law passed on from Moses to Joshua to the elders to the prophets to the rabbis. Compiled in Babylon and in Galilee, A.D. 200 through 500.

Tanakh. Hebrew acronym formed from the letters *T* of *Torah* (five books of Moses), *N* of *Neviim* ("Prophets"), and *K* of *Ktuvim* ("Writings")—the three parts of the Hebrew Bible; what Christians call the Old Testament.

Targum. Aramaic translation of the Hebrew Bible.

Tel. Hebrew, *tel;* Arabic, *tell.* An artificial mound created by layers of civilizations built one on top of another.

Temenos. Greek. A sacred precinct.

Templar knights. A religious-military order established in twelfth-century Jerusalem to provide security for pilgrims and the Church of the Holy Sepulchre.

Templers. A group of German Christians who considered themselves the spiritual temple of Christ. Beginning in the late 1860s, the Templers established nine settlements in the Holy Land.

Temple Mount. The esplanade whereon were built ancient Temples of the covenant peoples. *See* **Haram esh-Sharif.**

Thermae. Latin, "baths." A complex including *apodyterium,* a disrobing or changing room; *frigidarium,* a cold pool; *tepidarium,* a tepid (lukewarm) pool; *caldarium,* a hot bath.

Tigris. The eastern of the two rivers that flow from Asia Minor to the Persian Gulf. The area between these rivers is known as Mesopotamia, the place where powerful empires arose anciently.

Topography. The science of drawing and studying land surface, especially of relative positions and elevations.

Toponymy. Study of place names.

Torah. Hebrew. The five books of Moses. *See also* **Pentateuch.**

Tosafot/Tosefta. Hebrew, "additions." Explanatory and critical supplementary notes to parts of the Talmud.

Transjordan. Latin, *trans*, "across, beyond," combined with *Jordan.* Inhabited land between the Jordan River and the Syrian-Arabian deserts. *See also* **Cisjordan.**

Transpopulation. The Assyrian practice of moving conquered peoples from their own country to another area and repopulating the vacated area with other conquered peoples.

Triclinium. Couches around a three-sided, U-shaped table; also a dining room furnished with a *triclinium.*

Tumulus. Plural, *tumuli.* Latin. Artificial mound over a burial.

Turris, Tour. Tower.

Ugarit. A coastal city on the Mediterranean in northern Syria directly east of Cyprus where Ugaritic tablets were found. Ugaritic is a language similar to biblical Hebrew.

Ulpan. Hebrew. A course or school in modern Israel for teaching Hebrew to immigrants.

Ur. An ancient Sumerian city on the Euphrates River in Chaldea.

Via Dolorosa. Latin, "the way of sorrow." The traditional path from Pilate's judgment hall to Calvary.

Via Maris. Latin, "Way of the Sea." The coastal highway between Mesopotamia and Egypt; the most important international highway of the ancient Near East.

Vulgate. The Latin version of the Bible which was translated by Jerome in Bethlehem; authorized by the Roman Catholic Church.

Wadi. Arabic. A valley or ravine containing a river bed that is usually dry but flows with water during the rainy season.

Waqf. Arabic. Muslim religious trust or endowment fund and its supervisory council.

West Bank. Ancient Judaea and Samaria; territory taken from Jordan by the Israelis in the 1967 War.

Yehud. *See* **Judaea.**

Yeshiva. A school or academy for the study of rabbinic literature and training for prospective rabbis.

Yom Kippur. Hebrew, "Day of Atonement," the most sacred holy day of the Jews.

Zealot. A fanatical Jew who openly fought against Roman rule of Judaea.

Ziggurat. A terraced, pyramidlike structure used as a temple by ancient Babylonians.

Zionism. The Jewish nationalistic movement to first secure and then maintain a territorial homeland for Jews.

Zoroaster/Zarathustra. Founder of a Persian religion about the sixth century before Christ.

Bibliography

Adams, Roger J. "The Iconography of Early Christian Initiation: Evidence for Baptism for the Dead." Unpublished manuscript. Brigham Young University, 1977.

Ad-Din, Mujir. *The Great Familiarization with the History of Jerusalem and Hebron.* Cairo, 1886.

Aharoni, Yohanan. *The Land of the Bible: A Historical Geography.* 2d ed. Philadelphia: Westminster Press, 1979.

———. "Arad: Its Inscriptions and Temple." *Biblical Archaeologist* 31 (1968): 18–27.

Aharoni, Yohanan, and Michael Avi-Yonah. *Macmillan Bible Atlas.* New York: Macmillan, 1974.

Ahimeir, Ora, ed. *Jerusalem, Aspects of Law.* Jerusalem: The Jerusalem Institute for Israel Studies, 1983.

American Foreign Policy Basic Documents, 1977–1980. Document no. 294. Washington, D.C.: Government Printing Office, 1983.

American Foreign Policy Current Documents. 1985. Document no. 205. Washington, D.C.: Government Printing Office, 1986.

Amiran, David H. K., et al., eds. *Atlas of Israel.* Published by the Survey of Israel and Ministry of Labor, Jerusalem. Amsterdam: Elsevier Publishing, 1970.

———. *Atlas of Jerusalem.* Berlin and New York: Walter de Gruyter, 1973.

———. *Urban Geography of Jerusalem: A Companion Volume to the Atlas of Jerusalem.* Berlin and New York: Walter de Gruyter, 1973.

Anchor Bible Dictionary. 6 vols. Ed. David Noel Freedman. New York: Doubleday, 1992.

Antonius, George. *The Arab Awakening: The Story of the Arab National Movement.* London: Hamish Hamilton, 1938.

Arden-Close, C. F. "The Rainfall of Palestine." *Palestine Exploration Quarterly* (January 1941): 122–28.

Asali, K. J., ed. *Jerusalem in History.* Essex, England: Scorpion, 1989.

Atiyeh, George N. *Jerusalem, Past and Present: An Annotated Bibliography.* New York: Americans for Middle East Understanding, Inc., 1975.

Avigad, Nahman. *Discovering Jerusalem.* Nashville: Thomas Nelson, 1983.

———. "Baruch the Scribe and Jerahmeel the King's Son." *Israel Exploration Journal* 28 (1978): 52–56.

Avi-Yonah, Michael. *Our Living Bible*. Jerusalem and Ramat Gan: International Publishing, 1962.

————. *The Holy Land from the Persian to the Arab Conquests: A Historical Geography*. Grand Rapids, Mich.: Baker Book House, 1977.

————, ed. *Jerusalem*. Jerusalem: Keter Books, 1973.

————, ed. *Sefer Yerushalayim [The Book of Jerusalem]: Jerusalem, Its Natural Conditions, History and Development from the Origins to the Present Day*. Jerusalem: Bialik Institute / Tel Aviv: Dvir Publishing, 1956.

————, ed. *The Herodian Period*. Vol. 7 of *World History of the Jewish People*. New Brunswick: Rutgers University Press, 1975.

Bahat, Dan. *Carta's Historical Atlas of Jerusalem*. Jerusalem: Carta, 1989.

————. *The Illustrated Atlas of Jerusalem*. New York: Simon and Schuster, 1990.

————. "Jerusalem Down Under: Tunneling along Herod's Temple Mount Wall." *Biblical Archaeology Review* 21, no. 6 (November-December 1995): 30–47.

Baldridge, Steven W. *Grafting In: A History of the Latter-day Saints in the Holy Land*. Murray, Utah: Roylance Publishing, 1989.

Baly, Denis. *The Geography of the Bible*. Rev. ed. New York: Harper & Row, 1974.

————, and A. D. Tushingham. *Atlas of the Biblical World*. New York: World Publishing, 1971.

Baring-Gould, S. *Legends of the Patriarchs and Prophets and other Old Testament Characters*. New York: Holt and Williams, 1872.

Barkay, Gabriel. "Divine Name Found in Jerusalem." *Biblical Archaeology Review* 9, no. 2 (March-April 1983): 14–19.

Barrett, Ivan J. *Joseph Smith and the Restoration*. Provo, Utah: Brigham Young University Press, 1973.

————. "The Story of the Mormons in the Holy Land." Unpublished manuscript, n.p., n.d.

Beitzel, Barry J. *The Moody Atlas of Bible Lands*. Chicago: Moody Press, 1985.

Ben-Arieh, Yehoshua. *Jerusalem in the Nineteenth Century: The Old City*. Jerusalem: Yad Izhaq Ben-Zvi; New York: St. Martin's Press, 1984.

Ben-Arieh, Yehoshua, and S. Sapir, comps. *A Collection of Papers Complementary to the Course: Jerusalem through the Ages*. Jerusalem: Hebrew University, 1989.

Ben-Dov, Meir. *In the Shadow of the Temple: The Discovery of Ancient Jerusalem*. Jerusalem: Keter Publishing House, 1985.

————. *The Ophel Archaeological Garden*. Jerusalem: East Jerusalem Development, Ltd., 1987.

Benson, Ezra Taft. *The Teachings of Ezra Taft Benson*. Salt Lake City: Bookcraft, 1988.

————. *This Nation Shall Endure*. Salt Lake City: Deseret Book, 1979.

Benvenisti, Meron. *The Crusaders in the Holy Land*. New York: Macmillan, 1970.

————. *Jerusalem, the Torn City*. Minneapolis: University of Minnesota Press, 1976.

Berrett, LaMar C., and D. Kelly Ogden. *Discovering the World of the Bible*, 3d ed. Provo, Utah: Grandin Book, 1996.

Berrett, LaMar C. "The So-called Lehi Cave." Unpublished manuscript circulated by the Foundation for Ancient Research and Mormon Studies (F.A.R.M.S.), Provo, Utah.

Bethell, Nicholas. *The Palestine Triangle: The Struggle between the British, the Jews, and the Arabs, 1935-1948.* London: Andre Deutsch, 1979.

Bin Talal, Hassan. *A Study of Jerusalem.* London: Longman, 1979.

Biran, Avraham. "'David' Found at Dan." *Biblical Archaeology Review* 20, no. 2 (March-April 1994): 26-39.

Birnbaum, Philip, trans. *Daily Prayer Book.* New York: Hebrew Publishing, 1977.

Blumberg, Arnold. *Zion Before Zionism, 1838-1880.* Syracuse: Syracuse University Press, 1985.

Boudreault, Jody, and Yasser Salaam, eds. *U. S. Official Statements: The Status of Jerusalem.* Washington, D. C.: Institute for Palestine Studies, 1992.

Bovis, Eugene H. *The Jerusalem Question, 1917-1968.* Stanford: Hoover Institution Press, 1971.

Bright, John. *A History of Israel.* Philadelphia: Westminster Press, 1981.

Broshi, M. "The Expansion of Jerusalem in the Reigns of Hezekiah and Manasseh." *Israel Exploration Journal* 24 (1974): 21-26.

———. "The Role of the Temple in the Herodian Economy." *Journal of Jewish Studies* 38 (Spring 1987): 31-37.

Brown, Hugh B. In Conference Report, Oct. 1971, 174-75.

Bruce, F. F. *New Testament History.* London: Oliphants, 1977.

Cannon, George Q. *Gospel Truth.* 2 vols. Sel. Jerreld L. Newquist. Salt Lake City: Deseret Book, 1974.

Carter, Jimmy. *Public Papers of the President.* Government Printing Office, 1980.

Cary, M., and H. H. Scullard. *A History of Rome.* 3d ed. London: Macmillan, 1975.

Cattan, Henry. *Jerusalem.* London: Croom Helm, 1981.

———. *Palestine in International Law.* London: Longman Group Ltd., 1973.

Chapman, Colin. *Whose Promised Land?* Oxford: Lion Publishing Corporation, 1992.

"A Chronology of Events Affecting the Temple Mount Since the Six Day War," *Jerusalem Post,* 30 Sept. 1983, 8-9.

Clark, James R., ed. *Messages of the First Presidency of The Church of Jesus Christ of Latter-day Saints.* 5 vols. Salt Lake City: Bookcraft, 1971.

Clark, J. Reuben, Jr. *Behold the Lamb of God.* Salt Lake City: Deseret Book, 1991.

Clarke, K. W. "Worship in the Jerusalem Temple after A.D. 70." In *New Testament Studies* 6 (1959-1960): 269-80.

Clay, A. T. "The Amorite Name Jerusalem." *Journal of the Palestine Oriental Society* (October 1920): 28-32.

Cobban, Helen. *The Palestine Liberation Organisation: People, Power, and Politics.* Cambridge: Cambridge University Press, 1984.

Cohen, Ephraim. *The Politics of Planting: Israeli-Palestinian Competition for Control of the Land in the Jerusalem Periphery.* Chicago: University of Chicago Press, 1993.

Cohen, Saul B. *Jerusalem: Bridging the Four Walls.* New York: Herzl Press, 1977.

Comay, Joan. *The Temple of Jerusalem.* New York: Holt, Rhinehart, and Winston, 1975.

Conder, Claude R. *The City of Jerusalem.* London: John Murray, 1909.

Condie, Spencer J. "A Pivotal Year in the Redemption of Jerusalem: 1836." Unpublished manuscript, 1989.

Connolly, Peter. *Living in the Time of Jesus of Nazareth.* Oxford: Oxford University Press, 1983; Tel Aviv: Steimatsky, Ltd., 1988.

Correspondence of Palestine Tourists. Salt Lake City, Utah Territory: Deseret News Steam Printing Establishment, 1875.

Cowan, Richard O. *Temples to Dot the Earth.* Salt Lake City: Bookcraft, 1989.

Cowley, Matthias F. *Wilford Woodruff: History of His Life and Labors.* Salt Lake City: Bookcraft, 1964.

Cust, L. G. A. *The Status Quo in the Holy Places.* Jerusalem: Ariel Publishing House, 1980.

Danby, Herbert, trans. *The Mishnah.* London: Oxford University Press, 1933.

Davies, Philip R. "'House of David' Built on Sand." *Biblical Archaeology Review* 20, no. 4 (July-August 1994): 54–55.

Delcor, M. "Melchizedek from Genesis to the Qumran Texts and the Epistle to the Hebrews." *Journal for the Study of Judaism* 2 (1971): 115–35.

Derrick, Royden G. *Temples in the Last Days.* Salt Lake City: Bookcraft, 1988.

DeYoung, James Calvin. *Jerusalem in the New Testament: The Significance of the City in the History of Redemption and in Eschatology.* Amsterdam: J. H. Kok N. V. Kampen, 1960.

Dio Cassius. *History of Rome.* 9 vols. Loeb Classical Library. Trans. E. W. Cary. Cambridge, Mass.: Harvard University Press.

Dupuy, Trevor. *Elusive Victory: The Arab-Israeli Wars, 1947–1974.* London: MacDonald and Jane's, 1978.

Eban, Abba. *Heritage: Civilization and the Jews.* New York: Summit Books, 1984.

———. "Prospects for Peace in the Middle East." Annual memorial lecture of the David Davies Memorial Institute of International Studies. London, 26 October 1988.

Eckardt, Alice L., ed. *Jerusalem: City of the Ages.* New York: American Academic Association for Peace in the Middle East and Lanham, Md.: University Press of America, 1987.

Edersheim, Alfred. *The Life and Times of Jesus the Messiah.* 1883. Reprint. McLean, Va.: MacDonald Publishing, n.d.

———. *The Temple: Its Ministry and Services As They Were At the Time of Jesus Christ.* 1874. Reprint. Grand Rapids, Mich.: William B. Eerdmans Publishing, 1990.

Emerton, J. A., ed. *Congress Volume: Jerusalem.* Leiden: E. J. Brill, 1988.

———. "The Riddle of Genesis XIV." *Vetus Testamentum* 21 (1971): 412–13.

Encyclopedia Judaica. Ed. Geoffrey Wigoder. 16 vols. Jerusalem: Keter, 1972.

Encyclopedia of Freemasonry. Ed. Albert G. Mackey. 2 vols. Chicago: Masonic History Co., 1921.

Epperson, Steven. *Mormons and Jews: Early Mormon Theologies of Israel.* Salt Lake City: Signature Books, 1992.

Epstein, Isidore. *Judaism.* New York: Penguin Books, 1975.

Eusebius. *History of the Church.* Trans. G. A. Williamson. New York: Penguin Books, 1965.

————. *Life of Constantine.* Trans. Ernest C. Richardson. In *A Select Library of Nicene and Post-Nicene Fathers of the Christian Church.* Ed. Philip Schaff and Henry Wace. Vol. 1, 2d series, 1890; reprint, 1986.

Feintuch, Yossie. *U. S. Policy on Jerusalem.* New York: Greenwood Press, 1987.

Finegan, Jack. *The Archeology of the New Testament: The Life of Jesus and the Beginning of the Early Church.* Rev. ed. Princeton: Princeton University Press, 1992.

Fisher, Sydney Nettlefon, and William Ochsenwald. *The Middle East: A History.* 4th ed. New York: McGraw-Hill, 1990.

Foschini, Bernard M. "Those Who Are Baptized for the Dead." *Catholic Biblical Quarterly* 13 (1951): 328–44.

Friedman, Thomas L. "Teddy Kollek's Jerusalem." *New York Times Magazine,* 4 August 1985.

Galbraith, David B. Personal journal. 19 May 1988.

"Gethsemane's Ancient Olive Trees." *Biblical Archaeologist* 40, no. 2 (May 1977): 50.

Geva, Hillel, ed. *Ancient Jerusalem Revealed.* Jerusalem: Israel Exploration Society, 1994.

Gilbert, Martin. *Jerusalem: Illustrated History Atlas.* 2d rev. ed. Jerusalem: Steimatsky's, 1978.

Giliomee, Hermann. *The Elusive Search for Peace.* Cape Town, South Africa: Oxford University Press, 1990.

Gill, D. "How They Met—Geology Solves Long-Standing Mystery of Hezekiah's Tunnelers." *Biblical Archaeology Review* 20, no. 4 (July-August 1994): 20–38, 64.

Ginzberg, Louis. *The Legends of the Jews.* Philadelphia: Jewish Publication Society of America, 1909.

Goldschmidt, Arthur. *A Concise History of the Middle East.* Boulder, Colo.: Westview Press, 1991.

Goren, Shlomo. *Jerusalem Post,* 2 June 1989, 10.

Grant, Michael. *The Jews in the Roman World.* London: Weidenfeld and Nicolson, 1973.

Gray, John. *A History of Jerusalem.* New York: Frederick A. Praeger, 1969.

Greenhut, Zvi. "Burial Cave of the Caiaphas Family." *Biblical Archaeology Review* 18, no. 5 (September-October 1992): 29–44, 76.

Hallam, Elizabeth. *Chronicles of the Crusades.* New York: Weidenfeld and Nicolson, 1989.

Hallo, William W., David B. Ruderman, and Michael Stanislawski. *Heritage: Civilization and the Jews.* New York: Praeger Publishers, 1984.

Har-El, Menashe. *This Is Jerusalem.* Jerusalem: Canaan Publishing House, 1977.

Harker, Ronald. *Digging Up the Bible Lands.* New York: Henry Z. Walck, 1972.

The Harper Atlas of the Bible. Ed. J. B. Pritchard. New York: Harper and Row, 1987.

Harper's Bible Dictionary. Ed. Paul J. Achtemeier. New York: Harper and Row, 1985.

Hayes, John H., and J. Maxwell Miller. *Israelite and Judaean History.* Philadelphia: Westminster Press, 1977.

Herodotus. *History.* Trans. A. D. Godley. Loeb Classical Library. Cambridge, Mass.: Harvard University Press, 1926.

Heschel, Abraham Joshua. *Israel: An Echo of Eternity.* New York: Farrar, Straus, and Giroux, 1969.

Hilton, Lynn, and Hope Hilton. *In Search of Lehi's Trail.* Salt Lake City: Deseret Book, 1976.

Hollister, Warren C. *Medieval Europe: A Short History.* New York: John Wiley & Sons, 1968.

Holmes, Reed. *The Forerunners.* Independence, Mo.: Herald Publishing House, 1981.

Holtz, Avraham. *The Holy City: Jews on Jerusalem.* New York: Norton, 1971.

Holy Quran: English Translation of the Meanings and Commentary. Edited by the Presidency of Islamic Researches, IFTA, Call and Guidance. Riyadh, Saudi Arabia: King Fahd Holy Quran Printing Complex, n.d.

Holzapfel, Richard Neitzel, and David Rolph Seely. *My Father's House: Temple Worship and Symbolism in the New Testament.* Salt Lake City: Bookcraft, 1994.

Horn, S. "When Was the Babylonian Destruction of Jerusalem?" *Biblical Archaeology Review* 20, no. 4 (July-August 1994): 63.

Hunt, E. D. *Holy Land Pilgrimage in the Later Roman Empire, A.D. 312–460.* Oxford: Oxford University Press, 1982.

Hunter, Howard W. *That We Might Have Joy.* Salt Lake City: Deseret Book, 1994.

Hyde, Orson. *A Voice from Jerusalem; or, A Sketch of the Travels and Ministry of Elder Orson Hyde.* Liverpool: P. P. Pratt, 1842.

———. *Sketch of the Travels and Ministry of Elder Orson Hyde.* Salt Lake City: Deseret News Office, 1869.

Hymns of The Church of Jesus Christ of Latter-day Saints. Salt Lake City: The Church of Jesus Christ of Latter-day Saints, 1985.

Ice, Thomas, and Randall Price. *Ready to Rebuild: The Imminent Plan to Rebuild the Last Days Temple.* Eugene, Oreg.: Harvest House Publishers, 1992.

Idinopulos, Thomas A. *Jerusalem Blessed, Jerusalem Cursed.* Chicago: Ivan R. Dee, 1991.

Ingrams, Doreen. *Palestine Papers, 1917–1922: Seeds of Conflict.* New York: George Braziller, 1973.

The Interpreter's Dictionary of the Bible. Ed. George Arthur Buttrick. Nashville: Abingdon Press, 1962.

Israel Pocket Library: Jerusalem. Jerusalem: Keter, 1973.

Islamic Council of Europe. *Jerusalem, the Key to World Peace.* London: Islamic Council of Europe, 1980.

Jackson, Kent P., ed. *1 Kings to Malachi.* Vol. 4 of *Studies in Scripture.* Salt Lake City: Deseret Book, 1993.

———, ed. *1 Nephi to Alma 29.* Vol. 7 of *Studies in Scripture.* Salt Lake City: Deseret Book, 1987.

Jacobs, Louis. *The Book of Jewish Practice.* West Orange, N.J.: Behrman House, 1987.

Jbara, Taysir. *Palestinian Leader Hajj Amin al-Husaynia: Mufti of Jerusalem.* Princeton: Kingston Press, 1985.

Jenson, Andrew. "History and Genealogy," *Salt Lake Herald,* 9 February 1895, in *Collected Discourses,* vol. 5. From *LDS Collectors Edition [CD-ROM].* Provo, Utah: Infobases International, 1994.

Jerusalem Center Policy and Procedures Manual. Provo, Utah: Brigham Young University, May 1994.

Jerusalem: Issues and Perspectives. Jerusalem: Ministry for Foreign Affairs, Division of Information, 1977.

The Jewish Encyclopedia. Ed. Isidore Singer. 12 vols. New York: Funk and Wagnalls, 1901–1905.

Jones, A. H. M. *Constantine and the Conversion of Europe.* New York: Collier Books, 1962.

———. *The Herods of Judea.* Oxford: Clarendon Press, 1938.

Josephus. *The Complete Works.* Trans. William Whiston. Grand Rapids, Mich.: Kregel Publications, 1960.

Journal of Discourses. 26 vols. London: Latter-day Saints' Book Depot, 1854–86.

Kaufman, Asher. "Where the Ancient Temple of Jerusalem Stood." *Biblical Archaeology Review* 9, no. 2 (March-April 1983): 40–59.

Kenyon, Kathleen M. *Digging Up Jerusalem.* New York: Praeger, 1974.

———. *Jerusalem: Excavating 3000 Years of History.* London: Thames and Hudson, 1967.

———. *Royal Cities of the Old Testament.* London: Barrie and Jenkins, 1971.

Khouri, Fred. *The Arab-Israeli Dilemma.* Syracuse: Syracuse University Press, 1985.

Kimball, Spencer W. "The Unforgettable Holy Land." *Improvement Era* 64, no. 6 (June 1961): 422–25.

———. "The Uttermost Parts of the Earth." *Ensign* 9, no. 7 (July 1979): 2–9.

Klein, Mina C., and H. Arthur Klein. *Temple beyond Time: The Story of the Site of Solomon's Temple at Jerusalem.* New York: Van Nostrand Reinhold, 1970.

Kleven, T. "Up the Waterspout: How David's General Joab Got Inside Jerusalem." *Biblical Archaeology Review* 20, no. 4 (July-August 1994): 34–35.

Kohn, Moshe. "Speedily in Our Time?" *Jerusalem Post Magazine,* 22 Dec. 1989, 13.

Kollek, Teddy. *Jerusalem: A History of Forty Centuries.* New York: Random House, 1968.

———. *The Washington Institute Policy Papers: Jerusalem.* No. 22. 1990.

———. "No One Can Say We Treated Jerusalem's Arabs Badly," *Jerusalem Post International,* 11 June 1994, 12.

———. To the "Emunah Women of America." 7 February 1985.

Kotker, Norman. *The Earthly Jerusalem.* New York: Charles Scribner's Sons, 1969.

Kraeling, Carl H. "The Episode of the Roman Standard at Jerusalem." *Harvard Theological Review* 35 (1942).

Kraemer, Joel L., ed. *Jerusalem: Problems and Prospects.* New York: Praeger, 1980.

Kufield, F., to Teddy Kollek. 12 February 1985.

Laqueur, Walter, ed. *The Israeli-Arab Reader: A Documentary History of the Middle East Conflict.* New York: Bantam, 1969.

Lee, Harold B. *Ye Are the Light of the World.* Salt Lake City: Deseret Book, 1974.

———. Fireside address given at Utah State University, Logan, Utah, 10 Oct. 1971.

———. "I Walked Today Where Jesus Walked," address delivered at Brigham Young University, Provo, Utah, 10 Dec. 1958.

————. "Qualities of Leadership," address to the Latter-day Saint Student Association (LDSSA) Convention, Aug. 1970.

Lemaire, Andre. "'House of David' Restored in Moabite Inscription." *Biblical Archaeology Review* 20, no. 3 (May-June 1994): 30–37.

Levine, L. I., ed. *The Jerusalem Cathedra: Studies in the History, Archaeology, Geography and Ethnography of the Land of Israel.* 3 vols. Jerusalem: Yad Izhak Ben-Zvi Institute, 1981–83.

Lundquist, John M. "Life in Ancient Biblical Lands." *Ensign* 11, no. 12 (December 1981): 31–43.

Lundquist, John M., and Stephen D. Ricks, eds. *By Study and Also by Faith.* 2 vols. Salt Lake City: Deseret Book and Foundation for Ancient Research and Mormon Studies (F.A.R.M.S.), 1990.

McConkie, Bruce R. *Doctrinal New Testament Commentary.* 3 vols. Salt Lake City: Bookcraft, 1976.

————. *The Millennial Messiah.* Salt Lake City: Deseret Book, 1982.

————. *Mormon Doctrine.* 2d ed. Salt Lake City: Bookcraft, 1966.

————. *The Mortal Messiah.* 4 vols. Salt Lake City: Deseret Book, 1979–81.

————. *A New Witness for the Articles of Faith.* Salt Lake City: Deseret Book, 1985.

————. "The Purifying Power of Gethsemane." *Ensign* 15, no. 5 (May 1985): 9–11.

McKay, David O. *Cherished Experiences.* Comp. Clare Middlemiss. Salt Lake City: Deseret Book, 1967.

Mackowski, Richard M. *Jerusalem, City of Jesus: An Exploration of the Traditions, Writings, and Remains of the Holy City from the Time of Christ.* Grand Rapids, Mich.: William B. Eerdmans Publishing, 1980.

Madsen, Truman G., ed. *The Temple in Antiquity: Ancient Records and Modern Perspectives.* Provo, Utah: Brigham Young University, Religious Studies Center, 1984.

Malachi. In *Soncino Books of the Bible.* Edited by A. Cohen. London: Soncino Press, 1956.

Mare, W. Harold. *The Archaeology of the Jerusalem Area.* Grand Rapids, Mich.: Baker Book House, 1987.

Mattar, Philip. *The Mufti of Jerusalem: Al-Hajj Amin al-Husayni and the Palestinian National Movement.* New York: Columbia University Press, 1988.

Maxwell, Neal A. "O, Divine Redeemer." *Ensign* 11, no. 11 (November 1981): 8–10.

Mazar, Amihai. *Archaeology of the Land of the Bible.* New York: Doubleday, 1990.

Mazar, Benjamin. *The Mountain of the Lord.* Garden City, N.Y.: Doubleday, 1975.

————. "Herodian Jerusalem in the Light of the Excavations South and South-West of the Temple Mount." *Israel Exploration Journal* 28, no. 4 (1978): 230–37.

Medzini, Meron, ed. *Israel's Foreign Relations: Selected Documents, 1947–1974.* Jerusalem: Ministry for Foreign Affairs, 1976.

Meyers, J. M. *Ezra-Nehemiah.* Vol. 14 of *Anchor Bible Commentaries.* Garden City, N.Y.: Doubleday, 1965.

Mommsen, Theodor. *Provinces of the Roman Empire.* New York: Charles Scribner's Sons, 1899.

Morgenstern, Julian. "Jerusalem 485 B.C." *Hebrew Union College Annual* 27 (1956): 101–79.

Murphy-O'Connor, Jerome. *The Holy Land: An Archaeological Guide from Earliest Times to 1700.* 3d ed. Oxford: Oxford University Press, 1992.

Nashashibi, Nasser. *Jerusalem's Other Voice: Ragheb Nashashibi and Moderation in Palestinian Politics, 1920–1948.* Reading, England: Ithaca Press, 1990.

The New Encyclopedia of Archaeological Excavations in the Holy Land. Ed. Ephraim Stern. 4 vols. New York: Simon and Schuster, 1993.

Nibley, Hugh. *Mormonism and Early Christianity.* Vol. 4 of *The Collected Works of Hugh Nibley.* Salt Lake City: Deseret Book and Foundation for Ancient Research and Mormon Studies (F.A.R.M.S.), 1986–.

————. *When the Lights Went Out: Three Studies on the Ancient Apostasy.* Salt Lake City: Deseret Book, 1976.

————. "Baptism for the Dead in Ancient Times." *Improvement Era* 51–52 (December 1948–April 1949).

————. "The Lachish Letters: Documents from Lehi's Day." *Ensign* 11, no. 12 (December 1981): 48–54.

Ogden, D. Kelly. *Illustrated Guide to the Model City and to New Testament Jerusalem.* 2d ed. Jerusalem: The Jerusalem Center for Near Eastern Studies, 1990.

————. *Where Jesus Walked: The Land and Culture of New Testament Times.* Salt Lake City: Deseret Book, 1991.

————. "Was City Planning in Modern Jerusalem Foreseen by the Prophets of Judah?" Address delivered at the Annual Meeting of the Association of American Geographers, Washington, D. C., 1984.

Ogden, D. Kelly, and Jeffrey R. Chadwick. *The Holy Land: A Geographical, Historical, and Archaeological Guide to the Land of the Bible.* Jerusalem: The Jerusalem Center for Near Eastern Studies, 1990.

Ogden, D. Kelly, and David B. Galbraith. "What are the reasons behind the long-standing conflicts in the Holy Land, and how should Latter-day Saints view such conflicts?" *Ensign* 23, no. 9 (September 1993): 52–53.

Orni, Efraim, and Elisha Efrat. *Geography of Israel.* 3d rev. ed. Jerusalem: Keter, 1971.

Ostling, Richard N. "Time for a New Temple?" *Time Magazine,* 16 Oct. 1989, 64–65.

The Palestine Question. Seminar of Arab Jurists on Palestine. Beirut: Institute for Palestine Studies, 1968.

Palmer, Spencer J. *The Expanding Church.* Salt Lake City: Deseret Book, 1978.

Parrot, Andre. *The Temple of Jerusalem.* New York: Philosophical Library, 1955; London: SCM Press, 1957.

Parry, Donald W., ed. *Temples of the Ancient World.* Salt Lake City: Deseret Book, 1994.

Paton, Lewis Bayles. *Jerusalem in Bible Times.* Chicago: University of Chicago Press, 1908.

Paul, Shalom M., and William G. Dever, eds. *Biblical Archaeology.* Jerusalem: Keter, 1973.

Payne, David F. *Kingdoms of the Lord: A History of the Hebrew Kingdoms from Saul to the Fall of Jerusalem.* Grand Rapids, Mich.: W. B. Eerdmans Publishing, 1981.

The Peace of Jerusalem. New York: Israel Office of Information, [1949].

Perrin, Norman. *The New Testament: An Introduction.* New York: Harcourt Brace Jovanovich, 1974.

Perry, Glenn E. *The Middle East: Fourteen Islamic Centuries.* Englewood Cliffs, N.J.: Prentice-Hall, 1992.

Peters, F. E. *Jerusalem: The Holy City in the Eyes of Chroniclers, Visitors, Pilgrims, and Prophets from the Days of Abraham to the Beginning of the Modern Period.* Princeton: Princeton University Press, 1985.

Peterson, H. Donl, and Charles D. Tate, eds. *The Pearl of Great Price: Revelations from God.* Provo, Utah: Brigham Young University, Religious Studies Center, 1989.

Peterson, Daniel C. *Abraham Divided.* Salt Lake City: Aspen Books, 1992.

Philo. *The Embassy to Gaius.* Vol. 10 of Loeb Classical Library. Trans. F. H. Colson. Cambridge, Mass.: Harvard University Press.

———. *Every Good Man Is Free.* Vol. 9 of Loeb Classical Library. Trans. F. H. Colson. Cambridge, Mass.: Harvard University Press.

———. *Hypothetica.* Vol. 9 of Loeb Classical Library. Trans. F. H. Colson. Cambridge, Mass.: Harvard University Press.

Pinkas, Alon. "J'lem may cause Jihad," *Jerusalem Post,* 28 May 1994.

Pixner, B. "Church of the Apostles Found on Mt. Zion." *Biblical Archaeology Review* 16, no. 3 (May-June 1990): 16–35, 60.

Pliny. *Natural History.* Vol. 2 of Loeb Classical Library. Trans. H. Rackham. Cambridge, Mass.: Harvard University Press.

Porten, Bezalel. *Archives from Elephantine: The Life of an Ancient Jewish Military Colony.* Berkeley: University of California, 1968.

Pratt, Parley P. *Key to the Science of Theology and A Voice of Warning.* Classics in Mormon Literature. Salt Lake City: Deseret Book, 1978.

Prawer, Joshua. *The Latin Kingdom of Jerusalem.* London: Weidenfeld & Nicolson, 1972.

Pritchard, James B., ed. *Ancient Near Eastern Texts Relating to the Old Testament.* Princeton: Princeton University Press, 1955.

———. *The Ancient Near East in Pictures Relating to the Old Testament.* Princeton: Princeton University Press, 1954.

Prittie, Terrence. *Whose Jerusalem?* London: Frederick Muller, 1981.

Pullam, Wendy. "The Great Building Race: Foreign Architecture in Nineteenth-Century Jerusalem." *Eretz Magazine,* Autumn 1987.

Purvis, James D. *Jerusalem, the Holy City: A Bibliography.* 2 vols. Metuchen, N. J., and London: The American Theological Library Association and The Scarecrow Press, 1988 and 1991.

Pusey, Merlo J. *Builders of the Kingdom, George A. Smith, John Henry Smith, George Albert Smith.* Provo, Utah: Brigham Young University Press, 1981.

Qimron, Elisha, and John Strugnell. *Qumran Cave 4.V, Miqsat Ma'ase HaTorah.* Vol. 10 of *Discoveries in the Judaean Desert.* Oxford: Oxford University Press, 1994.

———. "For This You Waited 35 Years: MMT as Reconstructed by Elisha Qimron and John Strugnell." *Biblical Archaeological Review* 20, no. 6 (November-December 1994): 56–61.

Rabinovich, Abraham. "Word for Word." *Jerusalem Post Magazine,* 18 July 1986, 11.

Rasmussen, Carl G. *Zondervan NIV Atlas of the Bible.* Grand Rapids, Mich.: Zondervan Publishing House, 1989.

Rasmussen, Ellis T., and D. Kelly Ogden. *The Old Testament.* 2 vols. Provo, Utah: Brigham Young University, Department of Independent Study, 1992.

Regan, Geoffrey. *Israel and the Arabs.* Cambridge: Cambridge University Press, 1987.

Reznick, Leibel. *The Holy Temple Revisited.* Northvale, N.J.: Jason Aronson, 1990.

Rhoads, David M. *Israel in Revolution 6–74 C.E.* Philadelphia: Fortress Press, 1976.

Ritmeyer, L. "Locating the Original Temple Mount." *Biblical Archaeology Review* 18, no. 2 (March-April 1992): 24–45, 64–65.

Ritmeyer, L., and K. Ritmeyer. "Akeldama—Potter's Field or High Priest's Tomb?" *Biblical Archaeology Review* 20, no. 6 (November-December 1994): 22–46.

Ritmeyer Archaeological Design. *A Model of Herod's Temple* (slide set). York, England.

Roberts, B. H. *A Comprehensive History of The Church of Jesus Christ of Latter-day Saints, Century One.* 6 vols. Salt Lake City: The Church of Jesus Christ of Latter-day Saints, 1930.

Robinson, Edward. *Biblical Researches in Palestine.* 3 vols. Boston: Crocker and Brewster, 1841.

Romney, Marion G. In Conference Report, Oct. 1948, 72–77; Oct. 1966, 52.

Rosenberg, Robert. "Target: Temple Mount," *Jerusalem Post,* 30 Sept. 1983, 1.

Rosovsky, Nitza. "A Thousand Years of History in Jerusalem's Jewish Quarter." *Biblical Archaeology Review* 18, no. 3 (May-June 1992): 22–40, 78.

Rubenstein, Aryeh. *Jerusalem Post,* 21 July 1982.

Runciman, Steven. *The First Crusade and the Foundation of the Kingdom of Jerusalem.* Vol. 1 of *A History of the Crusades.* London: Folio Society, 1951, 1994.

Russell, D. S. *Between the Testaments.* Philadelphia: Fortress Press, 1977.

Sachar, Abram Leon. *A History of the Jews.* New York: Alfred A. Knopf, 1974.

Schneider, T. "Six Biblical Signatures." *Biblical Archaeology Review* 17, no. 4 (July-August 1991): 26–33.

Shalev, Menachem. "Rabbis to Press for Prayers on Mount." *Jerusalem Post,* 5 Aug. 1986, 1.

Shanks, Hershel. *Jerusalem: An Archaeological Biography.* New York: Random House, 1995.

———. "Sprucing Up for Jerusalem's 3,000th Anniversary." *Biblical Archaeology Review* 21, no. 1 (January-February 1995): 59–61.

———. "The Tombs of Silwan." *Biblical Archaeology Review* 20, no. 3 (May-June 1994): 38–51.

———. "Yigal Shiloh." *Biblical Archaeology Review* 14, no. 2 (March-April 1988): 14–27.

———, ed. *Ancient Israel: A Short History from Abraham to the Roman Destruction of the Temple.* Englewood Cliffs, N.J.: Prentice-Hall, 1988.

———, ed. *Christianity and Rabbinic Judaism.* Washington, D. C.: Biblical Archaeology Society, 1991.

———, ed. *Understanding the Dead Sea Scrolls.* New York: Random House, 1992.

Sherman, Nosson, and Meir Zlotowitz, eds. *Yechezkel.* Translation and Commentary by Moshe Eisemann. Vol. 3 of *The ArtScroll Tanach Series: A New Translation with a*

Commentary Anthologized from Talmudic, Midrashic, and Rabbinic Sources. Brooklyn, New York: Mesorah Publications, Ltd., 1980.

Shiloh, Yigal. *Qedem 19, City of David I.* Jerusalem: Hebrew University of Jerusalem, Institute of Archaeology, 1984.

———. "A Group of Hebrew Bullae." *Israel Exploration Journal* 36, nos. 1–2 (1986): 27–38.

———. "Jerusalem's Water Supply During Siege—The Rediscovery of Warren's Shaft." *Biblical Archaeology Review* 7, no. 4 (July-August 1981): 24–39.

———. "Yigal Shiloh." *Biblical Archaeology Review* 14, no. 2 (March-April 1988): 22.

Siegel-Itzkovich, Judy. "The Temple Mount." *Jerusalem Post,* 30 Sept. 1983, 4.

Simons, Jan. *Jerusalem in the Old Testament: Researches and Theories.* Leiden: E. J. Brill, 1952.

———. *The Geographical and Topographical Texts of the Old Testament.* 2 vols. Leiden: E. J. Brill, 1959.

Sittner, Aaron. "Chores for Cohen." *Jerusalem Post,* 30 Sept. 1983, 5.

Smith, Eliza R. Snow. *Biography and Family Record of Lorenzo Snow.* Salt Lake City: Deseret News Company Printers, 1884.

Smith, George Adam. *Jerusalem: The Topography, Economics and History from the Earliest Times to A.D. 70.* 2 vols. London: Hodder and Stoughton, 1907.

Smith, Joseph. *History of The Church of Jesus Christ of Latter-day Saints.* 7 vols. 2d ed. rev. Edited by B. H. Roberts. Salt Lake City: The Church of Jesus Christ of Latter-day Saints, 1932–51.

———. *Teachings of the Prophet Joseph Smith.* Sel. Joseph Fielding Smith. Salt Lake City: Deseret Book, 1938.

Smith, Joseph Fielding. *Doctrines of Salvation.* Comp. Bruce R. McConkie. 3 vols. Salt Lake City: Bookcraft, 1954–56.

———. *The Way to Perfection.* Salt Lake City: Deseret Book, 1975.

———. "Was Temple Work Done in the Days of the Old Prophets?" *Improvement Era* 58, no. 11 (November 1955): 794.

Sperry, Sidney B. "Some Thoughts Concerning Ancient Temples and Their Functions." *Improvement Era* 58, no. 11 (November 1955): 814–16, 826–27.

Spiegel, Shalom. *The Last Trial: The Akedah.* New York: Pantheon Books, 1967.

Stein, Leonard. *The Balfour Declaration.* London: Vallentine and Mitchell, 1961.

Sukenik, E. L. "The Account of David's Capture of Jerusalem." *Journal of the Palestine Oriental Society* 8 (1928): 12–16.

Tacitus. *Histories.* Trans. Kenneth Wellesley. New York: Viking Penguin, 1988.

Tal, Eliyahu. *Whose Jerusalem?* Jerusalem: The International Forum for a United Jerusalem. 1994.

Talmage, James E. *The Articles of Faith.* Classics in Mormon Literature Series. Salt Lake City: Deseret Book, 1984.

———. *The House of the Lord: A Study of Holy Sanctuaries, Ancient and Modern.* Rev. ed. Salt Lake City: Deseret Book, 1976.

The Talmud of Babylonia: An American Trans. Trans. Jacob Neusner. Chico, Calif.: Scholars' Press, 1984.

Taylor, John. "Ancient Ruins." *Times and Seasons* 5 (15 December 1844): 746.

Terrien, S. "The Omphalos Myth and Hebrew Religion." *Vetus Testamentum* 20 (1970): 317.

Thomas, D. Winton, ed. *Documents from Old Testament Times*. New York: Harper & Row, 1961.

Thompson, J. A. *The Bible and Archaeology*. 3d ed. Grand Rapids, Mich.: William B. Eerdmans Publishing, 1982.

Thy People Shall Be My People: 22d Annual Sidney B. Sperry Symposium on the Old Testament. Salt Lake City: Deseret Book, 1994.

Tibawi, A. L. *Jerusalem: Its Place in Islam and Arab History*. Beirut: Institute for Palestine Studies, 1969.

Torczyner, Harry. *Lachish I: Lachish Letters*. London: Oxford University Press, 1938.

Truman, Harry S. *Public Papers of the President*. Washington, D.C.: Government Printing Office, 1964.

United States. *Department of State Bulletins*. Washington, D.C.: Government Printing Office, 1952–1967.

Ussishkin, David. *The Conquest of Lachish by Sennacherib*. Tel Aviv: Tel Aviv University Institute of Archaeology, 1982.

Vermes, Geza. *Scripture and Tradition in Judaism*. Leiden: E. J. Brill, 1973.

———. *The Dead Sea Scrolls: Qumran in Perspective*. Cleveland, Ohio: William Collins and World Publishing, 1978.

Vilnay, Zev. *Legends of Jerusalem*. Philadelphia: The Jewish Publication Society, 1973.

Wasserstein, Bernard. *The British in Palestine: The Mandatory Government and the Arab-Jewish Conflict, 1917–1929*. Oxford: Basil Blackwell, 1991.

Werblowsky, R. J. Zwi. "Jerusalem: Holy City of Three Religions." *Jaarbericht Ex Orient Lux*, 23 (1973–74): 423–39.

The Westminster Historical Atlas to the Bible. Rev. ed. Ed. George Ernest Wright and Floyd Vivian Filson. Philadelphia: Westminster Press, 1956.

Whitney, Orson F. *Saturday Night Thoughts: A Series of Dissertations on Spiritual, Historical and Philosophic Themes*. Rev. ed. Salt Lake City: Deseret Book, 1927.

Widtsoe, John A. *Evidences and Reconciliations*. 3 vols. in 1. Arr. G. Homer Durham. Salt Lake City: Bookcraft, 1960.

Wilken, Robert L. *The Land Called Holy: Palestine in Christian History and Thought*. New Haven: Yale University Press, 1992.

Wilkinson, John. *Jerusalem As Jesus Knew It: Archaeology as Evidence*. London: Thames and Hudson, 1978.

Williamson, H. G. M. "Nehemiah's Walls Revisited." *Palestine Exploration Quarterly* 116 (July-December 1984): 81–88.

Wilson, Charles, and Charles Warren. *The Recovery of Jerusalem*. London: Richard Bentley and Son, 1871.

Woodruff, Wilford. "A Word to the Wise Is Sufficient." *Millennial Star* 6, no. 1 (15 June 1845): 3.

————. "Epistle of Elder Wilford Woodruff." *Millennial Star* 41, no. 16 (21 April 1879): 241–46.

Wright, G. Ernest. *Biblical Archeology.* Philadelphia: Westminster Press, 1960.

Yadin, Yigael. *Hazor, the Head of All Those Kingdoms.* London: Oxford University Press, 1972.

————. *The Temple Scroll: The Hidden Law of the Sect.* New York: Random House, 1985.

————, ed. *Jerusalem Revealed: Archaeology in the Holy City, 1968–1974.* New Haven and London: Yale University Press and the Israel Exploration Society, 1975.

Young, Brigham. *Discourses of Brigham Young.* Sel. John A. Widtsoe. Salt Lake City: Deseret Book, 1971.

INDEX

About the Authors

Professors David B. Galbraith, D. Kelly Ogden, and Andrew C. Skinner are all highly respected Latter-day Saint scholars who collectively have lived for nearly four decades in Jerusalem.

Dr. Galbraith, who holds a Ph.D. in international relations from Hebrew University in Jerusalem and is an emeritus professor of political science at Brigham Young University, was the first resident director of the Brigham Young University Jerusalem Center for Near Eastern Studies. He served as president of the Jerusalem Branch in Israel and later as president of the Bulgaria Sofia Mission, which included Serbia, Macedonia, and Turkey. He and his wife, Frieda Kruger Galbraith, are the parents of five children.

Dr. Ogden earned a master's degree in Hebrew language and historical geography of the Bible at the Institute of Holy Land Studies in Jerusalem and a Ph.D. in Middle East Studies from the University of Utah. The first associate director of the BYU Jerusalem Center, he is a professor of ancient scripture at BYU and the author of numerous works on the Holy Land. After serving twice as president of the Jerusalem Branch, he served as a mission president in Santiago, Chile, and later as president of the Missionary Training Center in Guatemala. He and his wife, Marcia Hammond Ogden, are the parents of four children.

Dr. Skinner, who pursued graduate studies at Hebrew University in Jerusalem and taught at the BYU Jerusalem Center, holds a master's degree from the Iliff School of Theology and Harvard University and a Ph.D. in history from the University of Colorado. A professor of ancient scripture and former dean of Religious Education at BYU, he has served as a member of the international team of translators working on the

Dead Sea Scrolls and as the first executive director of BYU's Neal A. Maxwell Institute for Religious Scholarship. He was a Scoutmaster in the Jerusalem Branch and has since served in the Church as a bishop. He and his wife, Janet Corbridge Skinner, are the parents of six children.